Choices in Relationships:

AN INTRODUCTION TO MARRIAGE AND THE FAMILY

⅋

FOURTH EDITION

Choices in Relationships:

AN INTRODUCTION TO MARRIAGE AND THE FAMILY

ℬ

FOURTH EDITION

David Knox
East Carolina University

Caroline Schacht
East Carolina University

WEST PUBLISHING COMPANY
Minneapolis/St. Paul   New York   Los Angeles   San Francisco

WEST'S COMMITMENT TO THE ENVIRONMENT

In 1906, West Publishing Company began recycling materials left over from the production of books. This began a tradition of efficient and responsible use of resources. Today, up to 95 percent of our legal books and 70 percent of our college and school texts are printed on recycled, acid-free stock. West also recycles nearly 22 million pounds of scrap paper annually—the equivalent of 181,717 trees. Since the 1960s, West has devised ways to capture and recycle waste inks, solvents, oils, and vapors created in the printing process. We also recycle plastics of all kinds, wood, glass, corrugated cardboard, and batteries, and have eliminated the use of Styrofoam book packaging. We at West are proud of the longevity and the scope of our commitment to the environment.

PRODUCTION, PREPRESS, PRINTING AND BINDING BY WEST PUBLISHING COMPANY.

COPYRIGHT © 1985, 1988, 1991   By WEST PUBLISHING COMPANY
COPYRIGHT © 1994   By WEST PUBLISHING COMPANY
610 Opperman Drive
P.O. Box 64526
St. Paul, MN 55164-0526

LIBRARY OF CONGRESS CATALOGING-IN-PUBLICATION DATA

Knox, David, 1943-
    Choices in relationships : an introduction to marriage and the family / David Knox, Caroline Schacht.—4th ed.
        p.   cm.
    Includes index.
    ISBN 0-314-02605-3
    1. Family life education.   2. Marriage—United States.
    I.   Schacht, Caroline.   II.   Title.
    HQ10.K57   1994
    306.8—dc20   93-30592
                                                  CIP

Text Design: Janet Bollow
Copy Editor: Cheryl Wilms
Compositor: Carlisle Communications
Index: Northwind Editorial
Artwork: Rolin Graphics
Cover Design: Roslyn Stendahl, Dapper Design
Cover Image: Pablo Picasso, Spanish, 1881–1973. *The Lovers*, canvas, 1923, 51¼ × 38¼ in.; National Gallery of Art, Washington, Chester Dale Collection. © 1993 ARS, New York/SPADEM, Paris. All rights reserved.

PHOTO CREDITS

Contents

XIII © Bill Bachman/PhotoEdit. **XIV** (Top) © Tony Freeman/PhotoEdit; (Bottom) © Myrleen Ferguson/PhotoEdit. **XV** (Top) © Bob Daemmrich/Stock Boston; (Bottom) © Tony Freeman/PhotoEdit. **XVI** (Top) © Ellis Herwig/Stock Boston; (Bottom) © Jeff Greenberg/PhotoEdit. **XVII** © Tony Freeman/PhotoEdit. **XVIII** (Top) © InFocus International/The Image Bank; (Bottom) © Michael Newman/PhotoEdit. **XIX** © Elena Rooraid/PhotoEdit. **XX** © Elena Rooraid/PhotoEdit. **XXI** (Top) © Michael Newman/PhotoEdit; (Bottom) © Ulrike Welsch/PhotoEdit. **XXII** © Bob Daemmrich/Stock Boston. **XXIII** © Amy Etra/PhotoEdit. **XXIV** (Top) © Michael Newman/PhotoEdit; (Bottom) © Myrleen Ferguson/PhotoEdit. **XXV** (Top) © Robert Brenner/PhotoEdit; (Bottom) © Myrleen Ferguson/PhotoEdit. **XXVI** © Robert Brenner/PhotoEdit. **XXVII** © Robert Brenner/PhotoEdit. **XXVIII** (Top) © Alan Oddie/PhotoEdit; (Bottom) © Eliane Sulle/The Image Bank. **XXIX** © Robert Brenner/PhotoEdit.

Main Text

1 © Peter Menzel/Stock Boston. **16** © Robert Brenner/PhotoEdit. **21** © Bill Bachman/PhotoEdit. **45** © Tony Freeman/PhotoEdit. **54** © Rick Smolan/Stock Boston. **57** © Dave Schaefer/PhotoEdit. **59** © Myrleen Ferguson/PhotoEdit. **60** © Tony Freeman/PhotoEdit. **68** © Amy Etra/PhotoEdit. **84** © Bob Daemmrich/stock Boston. **86** © Tony Freeman/PhotoEdit. **89** Universitatsbibliothek, Heidelberg (Manesse Codex, Cod. Pal. Germ. 848, f. 249v). **102** © Kent Reno/Jeroboam. **104** © Micheal Newman/PhotoEdit. **117** © Ellis Herwig/Stock Boston. **118** Cartoon © Stephanie Smith. **121** © Jeff Greenberg/PhotoEdit. **126** © Culver Pictures. **129** © Alan Oddie/PhotoEdit. **142** © Myrleen Ferguson/PhotoEdit.

(continued on p. I-13)

To Herb and Emily
who have always encouraged
others
to make their own choices.

↶ **Preface** ↷

This fourth edition of *Choices in Relationships: An Introduction to Marriage and the Family* continues the theme of the earlier editions—encouraging you to take control of your life by making deliberate choices in your personal relationships, especially marriage and the family. Rather than passively reacting to events in your life so that choices are made for you, the text encourages you to identify alternative courses of action and actively make choices based upon knowledge of potential outcomes. By doing so, you increase the control over your happiness and the happiness of those you care about.

The text also continues to reflect the ideas and perspectives of its new co-author, Caroline Schacht, who brings to each chapter a more balanced perspective of choices in relationships than is possible when only one gender view is represented. While her influence is evident throughout the text, specific areas that benefit from a more balanced perspective are reflected in the chapters on Gender Roles, Sexuality in Relationships, Work, Leisure, and Relationships, Communication and Conflict, and Becoming a Parent.

The revised text also features a reordering of the chapters so that the content is presented more in line with what a person often experiences across the life span. Chapters that have been extensively rewritten include Gender Roles, Sexual Values and Behavior, Sexuality in Relationships, Violence and Abuse in Relationships, and Work, Leisure and Relationships. In addition, a great deal of new information has been added including:

- the future of the family
- the effects of the aging of family members
- HIV and safer sex issues
- the new familism
- family values
- the gay lifestyle
- the age wave
- programs to help ensure marital success
- dishonesty in relationships
- gender differences in communication

- single black women
- Strategies for balancing work and family
- divorce mediation
- unrealistic expectations of marriage
- feminist views of research in marriage and the family
- unemployment effects on marriage
- social constructionist's view of "deviant" family forms
- "office" relationships
- enhancing emotional intimacy through effective communication
- theories of love
- cross-cultural views of love
- the "feminization of love"
- date rape
- single-parent families
- selecting the "best" partner for marriage
- getting married at the "best" time
- Asian and Pacific Islander marriages
- unhappy but stable marriages
- new methods of birth control
- abortion
- fatherhood fears during pregnancy
- relationship/sexual changes during pregnancy
- psychological adjustment to genital herpes
- new partners as co-parents
- systems theory and therapy
- terminating an abusive relationship

New features added to this edition include the following:

Expanded Cross-Cultural Coverage

We have attempted to emphasize that the choices we make are often not the same choices people in other cultures and societies may make. Rather, choices are culturally determined, which suggests that few choices are "universally correct." At various places in the text, we have placed a marker *Across Cultures* in the margin to note how other societies handle the issue we are discussing. For example, such *Across Culture* markers occur in our discussion of marriage types (Chapter 1), gender roles (Chapter 2), love relationships (Chapter 3), sexual values (Chapter 4), and dating and mate selection (Chapter 5). Other markers occur throughout the text. Although this is not a text on cross-cultural patterns of marriage and the family, we do want to note how culture influences the choices we make and the potential outcome of those choices.

National Data

Nationwide studies on a variety of topics related to marriage and the family are available. Whenever we discuss a topic for which nationwide data are available, we present such data and offset it from the rest of the text. Data from smaller studies are integrated into the body of the text.

New Self-Assessment Scales

Each chapter continues to provide a self-assessment scale for the topic being discussed. These are designed to supplement the student's understanding and provoke insight. Several new scales to this edition include those in reference to relationship commitment status (Chapter 1), the sexual double standard (Chapter 2), abusive behavior (Chapter 12), level of sexual satisfaction (Chapter 10), and motivation for parenthood (Chapter 13).

In Focus Inserts

Sections previously entitled "Exhibits" have been retitled, In Focus. These provide more detailed information relevant to the content being discussed. New In Focus inserts in this edition include "Twelve Ways Gender Role Socialization Affects Life and Relationship Choices of Women and Men" (Chapter 2), "University Students' Motivations to Have Intercourse" (Chapter 4), "A Palestinian's Experience in Mate Selection" (Chapter 5), and "A College Student's Experience with Date Rape" (Chapter 12).

Relationship Choices Autobiography Outline

Consistent with the applied focus of the text, we provide a "Relationship Choices Autobiography Outline" in Appendix A for students who wish to review their relationship history. Some instructors may wish to assign extra credit for students who write an autobiographical paper.

Because of success in the earlier editions, several unique features of the text have been continued. The goal of these features is to provide a basis for making the best possible interpersonal choices.

Choices

Before the summary in each chapter, a special section emphasizes the choices relevant to the content of that chapter. New choices added to this edition include "Who is the Best Person to Marry?" (Chapter 5), "Should One Disclose Attractions to Others to One's Partner?" (Chapter 9), and "Which Method of Contraception to Use?" (Chapter 13).

Age, Racial, Ethnic, and Cultural Diversity of Choices

This edition also provides a continued emphasis on choices in relationships made by individuals representing a variety of ages, racial, ethnic, and cultural backgrounds. Although individuals from 18 to 24 years of age still comprise the majority of college students, 41 percent are over the age of 25 (*Statistical Abstract of the United States: 1993*, Table 272).

Nonwhite racial and ethnic groups are also increasing and currently represent over 16 percent of all students in U.S. colleges and universities (*Statistical Abstract of the United States: 1993*, Table 272). Eighteen percent of the 1992 freshmen class in American colleges and universities were nonwhite (American Council on Education and University of California, 1992). Below is the breakdown on the various racial groups in the freshman class:

White	82.3%
Black	9.1%
Mexican American	3.3%
Asian American	3.1%
American Indian	1.7%
Puerto Rican American	0.7%
Other	2.6%

Given our society's racial diversity, "a multi-cultural perspective that emphasizes diversity and plurality among contemporary families in ethnicity, economic and social context, gender roles, marital status and regional location" is critical (Smith & Ingoldsby, 1992, 25). For example, blacks, when compared to whites, are much less likely to consult an elderly family member about the elderly family member's care. "Perhaps black families perceive a care-related decision as a burden to be carried for the older person while white families perceive the older person's decision-making involvement as a right" (Deimling & Smerglia, 1992, 90).

Considerations

Throughout the text are short paragraphs that suggest a new way of looking at something or a unique insight. These encourage you to relate what you have been reading to your life and interpersonal relationships. An example follows from Chapter 3, Love Relationships.

> **CONSIDERATION**
>
> Acker and Davis (1992) analyzed questionnaires from 204 adults about their love relationships (both married and unmarried). They found that the most powerful and consistent predictor of relationship satisfaction was commitment. The longer the relationship, the more important commitment was to the satisfaction of the relationship. Not all partners want committed relationships, many enjoy them at whatever level of commitment exists. However, the most satisfying relationships seem to be those in which the partners are mutually committed.

Acknowledgments

The fourth edition of *Choices in Relationships: An Introduction to Marriage and the Family* is a result of the work of many people. Peter Marshall, as executive editor, provided cutting-edge information in regard to the critical issues in marriage and the family and how faculty and students want these issues addressed. Jane Bass provided quick turnaround on the first round of reviews. Becky Tollerson obtained subsequent reviews and kept the project on schedule. Judy Holt conducted research and "cleaned" bibliographies. Cheryl Wilms copyedited the manuscript. Angela Musey secured permissions and Kara ZumBahlen served as production editor at West Publishing; all were superb in their respective roles.

We would also like to thank Susan McCammon for her insights on sexuality, Jack Turner for his information about communication skills, and Charles Snow for his knowledge of day care issues. A number of professors who teach the course for which this text is written read the manuscript and provided valuable insights and suggestions which have been incorporated into the final manuscript:

Rosemary Bahr
Eastern New Mexico University

Craig Campbell
Weber State University

Jean Cobbs
Virginia State University

Richard Jolliff
El Camino College

Diane Keithly
Southern State University

Carol May
Illinois Central College

Terry Smith Hatkoff
California State University—Northridge

Tommy Smith
Auburn University

Janice Weber-Breaux
University of Southwestern Louisiana

David Knox

Caroline Schacht

⌁ Contents in brief ⌁

☙ **Contents** ☙

CHAPTER 2

Gender Roles 45

CHAPTER 3

Love Relationships   84

IN FOCUS 2.2
Twelve Ways Gender Role
Socialization Affects Life and
Relationship Choices of
Women and Men   73

SELF-ASSESSMENT
The Love Attitudes Scale   92

IN FOCUS 3.1
Love: A Natural Euphoric
Feeling?   99

IN FOCUS 3.2
Love and the Broken
Heart   106

IN FOCUS 6.1
Living Together as Preparation
For Marriage?   218

SELF-ASSESSMENT
Living Together Consequences
Scale   221

CHAPTER 8

Marriage Relationships 271

CHAPTER 9

Communication and Conflict   308

CHAPTER 10

Sexuality in Relationships   351

CHAPTER 11

Work, Leisure, and Relationships   399

CHAPTER 12

Violence and Abuse in Relationships   442

CHAPTER 13

Planning Children and Birth Control 483

CHAPTER 14

Becoming a Parent   533

CHAPTER 15

Rearing Children   567

CHAPTER 16

Divorce and Widowhood   604

CHAPTER 17

Remarriage and Stepfamilies 648

IN FOCUS 17.1
From Outsider to Intimate:
Stages in Becoming a
Stepfamily 659

SPECIAL TOPIC 1

HIV Infection and Other STDs   679

Contents

❧ 1 ❧
CHAPTER

Choices in Marriage and the Family: A First View

Is It True?

1. Making deliberate choices and exercising control over one's life is one of the strongest predictors of happiness.

2. College freshmen rarely socialize with someone from a different racial or ethnic group.

3. As baby boomers become parents they are more likely to value familism over individualism.

4. Although polygyny is permitted in most societies, monogamy is the most prevalent form of marriage.

5. Increasingly, families are being defined by function (emotional and economic interdependence) rather than by structure (one man and one woman).

1 = T; 2 = F; 3 = T; 4 = T; 5 = T

When did the choices get so hard with so much more at stake?
Life gets mighty precious when there's less of it to waste.

BONNIE RAIT

G arth Brooks, winner of the country entertainer of the year award in 1993, announced to Jane Pauley on an evening news special that he was retiring from the music business. He lamented that too much of his life was being consumed by concert tours, dealing with agents, and cutting new CDs. Since the birth of his daughter, he noted that the way he chooses to spend his time had changed. (Subsequent to the Pauley interview, Brooks noted that he was not retiring but was taking an eight-month parental leave from the music/touring business.)

Brooks' dilemma of choosing between competing alternatives is common to all of us. Making choices in your relationships—particularly in regard to marriage and the family—is the most important set of decisions you will make in your life, and will result in your greatest joys and sorrows. In no other area of life will choices be so important.

Although you will make an array of relationship choices throughout your life, five basic choices, which will dramatically affect your life and relationships, are emphasized in this text.

1. Whether to remain single or get married. By age 75, 95 percent of women and 96 percent of men in the United States have married (*Statistical Abstract of the United States: 1993,* Table 60).

2. Whether to have children. About 90 percent of women 18 to 34 expect to have children (*Statistical Abstract of the United States: 1993,* Table 108).

3. Whether to have a one- or two-earner marriage. Over 75 percent of couples with children ages 6 to 17 are in two-earner marriages. (*Statistical Abstract of the United States: 1993,* Table 634).

4. Whether to be sexually faithful to your partner. Although 98 percent of married adults report being sexually faithful to their partner the last 12 months (Smith, 1991), a review of studies on extramarital sexual behavior suggests that half of both husbands and wives have intercourse at least once with someone other than their partner at some time during the marriage (Thompson, 1983). This percentage includes extramarital sexual behavior that occurs during the period of time that couples are separated prior to divorce.

5. Whether to engage in behavior so as to reduce your risk of HIV and STD infection (i.e., select partner carefully, restrict number of partners, use condoms). Despite public education and media attention regarding the spread of HIV, many individuals deny or underestimate their risk of becoming infected (Jurich et al., 1992).

Destiny is not determined by chance but by choice.

WILLIAM JENNINGS BRYAN

Each of these choices is discussed in detail in Chapters 7, 13, 11, 10, and 4 respectively. Numerous other choices discussed throughout the text are presented in the In Focus insert 1.1

⚡ Some Facts About Choices

When you make choices, it is important to keep several issues in mind. Myers (1992) noted that making deliberate choices and exercising control over one's life is one of the strongest predictors of happiness.

Relationship choices are continuous and require a great deal of careful thought.

Not to Decide Is to Decide

It is important to recognize that not making a decision is a decision by default. For example, if you are sexually active and do not decide to use birth control, you have inadvertently decided to increase the chance of pregnancy. As a childfree career woman, if you don't decide to have a baby, you may be inadvertently deciding not to have one forever. Choosing—through action or through inaction—means taking responsibility for the consequences of your decisions. Such responsibility also implies making informed decisions. The maxim, "If you don't know your choices, you don't really have any choices," emphasizes the importance of looking carefully at alternative courses of action.

Outcomes of Choices Are Only Probabilities

The outcome of any choice is at best a probability, because it is difficult, if not impossible, to know exactly what the best choice is for all time. We can only make decisions based on the information available to us at the time of the decision. Later we may become aware of new information which, had we known it initially, may have influenced us to have made a different decision. Even though outcomes of choices are only probabilities, choices based on knowledge are certainly better than choices based on default. For example, the knowledge that teen marriages are three times as likely to end in divorce as marriages begun in one's twenties suggests that teen couples consider delaying their marriage.

Chance favors only the mind that is prepared.

LOUIS PASTEUR

Choices Are Continual

Making choices is a continual process. Life is not one or two BIG decisions. It is a series of some big decisions and a constant stream of smaller ones. For example, if you choose to be single, you can live alone, with another partner in a heterosexual or homosexual relationship, or with a roommate. You can live in a one-room apartment or on a communal farm with 300 others. If you choose to marry, you can select from a variety of marital styles (traditional, open,

---

One Hundred and One Choices in Relationships

LIFESTYLE

Marriage?

Singlehood?

Live together?

Communal living?

MARRIAGE

Age to marry?

Partner to marry?

Bicultural marriage?

Marry while in college?

Reasons to marry?

Know partner how long before marriage?

Live together first?

Consider parents' approval?

Premarital counseling?

Prenuptial agreement?

Traditional or egalitarian relationship?

One or two checking accounts?

Live with parents?

Partner's night out?

Separate or joint vacations?

Who has what roles in relationship?

COMMUNICATION

How much about past to disclose?

Talk about issues or avoid them?

Consult a marriage therapist?

Attend marriage encounter weekend?

How honest to be?

Secrets?

Emotionally open/closed?

Discuss previous sexual abuse?

SEX

How much sex how soon in a relationship?

Number of sexual partners?

Require condom for intercourse or oral sex?

Require HIV test before sexual behavior with new partner?

Monogamy in relationship?

Open marriage?

Homosexual? Heterosexual? Bisexual? (may not be "choices")

Consult sex therapist with problems?

Masturbate with one's partner?

Disclose sexual fantasies?

LOVE

Prerequisite for marriage?

Prerequisite for sex?

Romantic or realistic?

Several loves at one time?

Tolerance of partner loving others?

EMPLOYMENT

Job or career?

Part-time or full-time career?

One or two earners in marriage?

Move if one career requires?

Chores after both workers return home?

Commuter marriage?

Hire outside help?

⌁ IN FOCUS 1.1 ⌁

Age of child when return to employment?

Age to retire?

BIRTH CONTROL

Use of contraceptive?

Which contraceptive?

How often use contraceptive?

Partner responsible for contraceptive?

Sterilization?

If pregnant, keep child, abort, place for adoption?

CHILDREN

Whether to have children?

How many children?

Age when having first and subsequent children?

Adopt children?

Single parent by choice?

Artificial insemination by husband?

Artificial insemination by donor?

Ovum transfer?

Test-tube fertilization?

Amniocentesis?

Chorion biopsy?

Home or hospital birth?

Daycare for child?

Public or private school?

Method of childbirth?

Method of discipline?

DIVORCE

Stay married or divorce if unhappy?

Tolerate violence and abuse?

Tolerate sexual abuse of one's child by partner?

When to divorce?

Divorce mediation?

Shared parenting with ex-partner after divorce?

Shared parenting with ex-partner's new partner after divorce?

When and how to tell parents?

Take responsibility or blame partner?

When and what to tell children?

Relationship with ex-spouse?

Amount of child support?

Seek an annulment?

REMARRY

Whether to remarry?

How soon after divorce?

Remarry a person with or without children?

Remarry against children's wishes?

Have baby with new partner?

Live in one of partner's houses or get another house?

Type of relationship to establish with partner's child?

WIDOWHOOD

Power of attorney?

Living will?

Develop a regular will?

Amount of life insurance?

Remarry after death of spouse? How soon?

Live with one's children?

Live with a companion?

dual-career, childfree). If you decide to separate and eventually to divorce (as most of us visualize "somebody else" doing), you will be making an additional choice to remain single or to remarry. Remarriage will involve still other choices, including whether to marry a person with children or to be childfree.

You will continually be faced with choices; in fact, you may be faced with the same choice more than once. Choices to continue or end a relationship, to have children, or to be disclosing to your partner are often made more than once.

Choices Involve Trade-offs

> But I think the simple reality that we all have to face is that you can't do everything in life. There really are forks in the road, where in order to do one thing, you give up something else.
>
> PETE DAWKINS

Any choice you make involves gains and losses. Barbara Streisand once considered having her nose altered by a plastic surgeon, but she was told that to do so might also alter the nasal sound and timbre of her voice. The trade-off was not worth the risk for her.

Interpersonal choices also involve trade-offs. For example, one spouse said:

> Everything is a trade-off. If you get married, you are less free; if you don't get married, you may be more lonely. If you have kids, they cost money, make noise, and tear up the house; if you don't have kids, you may miss them. If you have an affair, you feel guilty and may lose your marriage; if you don't have sex with others, you wonder what it would be like. So what's the answer?

Trade-offs occur in the choice of lifestyle and family life. Spouses with large homes, expensive cars, and a vacation cottage may (unless they are of the elite social class) need to spend time away from each other earning the money to pay for the lifestyle. "Generally, such success can be achieved only at some sacrifice of family life" (John, 1988, 355).

CONSIDERATION

Making choices also involves relinquishing the options that are not chosen. "For every yes there must be a no, each decision eliminating or killing other options" (Yalom, 1989, 10). The root of the word *decide* means "slay" as in homicide or suicide. Making decisions, or choices, involves the "slaying" of options not chosen.

Choices Produce Ambivalence and Uncertainty

> If you marry, you will regret it; if you do not marry, you will regret it.
>
> SOREN KIERKEGARD

Choosing among options and trade-offs often creates ambivalence—conflicting feelings that produce uncertainty or indecisiveness as to what course of action to take. There are two forms of ambivalence: sequential and simultaneous. In sequential ambivalence, the individual experiences one wish and then another. For example, a person may vacillate between wanting to stay together and break up. In simultaneous ambivalence, the person experiences two conflicting wishes at the same time. For example, the individual may, at the same time, feel both the desire to stay together and the desire to break up. The latter dilemma is reflected in the saying, "You can't live with 'em and you can't live without 'em."

Choice is one of the hallmarks of living in the United States. You have been socialized to relish your freedom and encouraged to choose wisely in regard to your sexual values and mate. But uncertainty is the price. When will you have sex, with how many, and which person will you choose to marry? In contrast, if you were socialized in Palestine, you would have little uncertainty and ambivalence over your choices in regard to sexual values and marriage partner. You would be expected to remain a virgin until marriage, and your father would approve of the person you would be expected to marry.

Most Choices Are Revocable, Some Are Not

Most choices are revocable, that is, they can be changed. For example, a person who has chosen to be sexually active with multiple partners can later decide to be monogamous or to abstain from sexual relations. Or, individuals who, in the past have chosen to emphasize career over marriage and family can choose to emphasize marriage and family over career.

The emotional or financial price for altering certain choices is higher for some choices than for others. For example, backing out of the role of spouse is somewhat less difficult than backing out of the role of parent. While the law permits disengagement from the role of spouse (formal divorce decree), the law ties parents to dependent offspring (e.g., child support).

> The two biggest mistakes in life are failing to recognize bad choices and failing to correct those choices (if possible) once they have been recognized.
> MARTY ZUSMAN

> Once a parent, always a parent.
> LOUISE SAMMONS

Some Choices Involve Selecting a Positive or a Negative View

A basic choice in life and relationships concerns how you choose to view things. Life has positive and negative aspects. Your choice of whether to focus on the positives or on the negatives is critically important to your personal and interpersonal happiness.

For example, when you look at your partner, you can focus on his or her loving eyes or on facial pimples. Similarly, you can focus on the times your partner did something you liked or on the times he or she did something that offended or hurt you. You can focus on your partner preparing a meal rather than forgetting to put the ketchup on the table. In dissolving a relationship, you can view it as the end of a life or as the beginning of a life.

In other words, how you choose to view a situation will often have more to do with your personal and marital happiness than the situation itself. Indeed, in a study of couples *married* from 50 to 69 years, personality and attitude (a positive view) were more significant in marital success than socioeconomic factors (Field & Weishaus, 1992).

> Life goes by so quickly . . . It's important to focus on what you have rather than on what you don't have.
> JEAN–PIERRE TROADEC

> Most people are about as happy as they have made up their minds to be.
> UNKNOWN

CONSIDERATION

Our society also makes a decision about how it evaluates (positively or negatively) a particular marriage or lifestyle. Some politically conservative critics have argued that there is only one true family, a husband and wife with children born after the marriage. Yet this view is sometimes "constructed from the belief systems of influential elites: political, religious, economic, even academic" (Gross, 1992, 7). Alternatively, we might choose the view that there is nothing inherently wrong with an array of alternative family forms (childfree, single parent families, stepfamilies, cohabiting couples).

Choices Are Influenced by Social Context and Social Forces

Children's experiences in the home shape the families they later form.

FRANCES GOLDSCHEIDER
LINDA WAITE

Just as a sailor's fate depends on knowing about the iceberg under the water, so a family's fate depends on understanding the feelings and needs and patterns that lie beneath everyday family events.

VIRGINIA SATIR

Although the theme of this book focuses on the importance of taking active control of your life, we must also be aware of the social forces that influence and limit our choices. For example, the choice of a marital partner may be influenced by the approval of parents/peers and by social norms. Interracial marriages represent less than one percent of all marriages because approval from parents/peers may be lacking, and social norms dictate that persons from different races should not marry each other.

In essence, you do not make choices in a vacuum. Your choices are influenced by the social context in which they occur. For example, in a study on the coital frequency of single women, the researchers noted that "ready availability and accessibility of a partner are two of the strongest determinants of coital frequency, as are the types of living arrangements that provide privacy and anonymity" (Tanfer & Cubbins, 1992, 245). Individuals involved in a love relationship are in one of the strongest social contexts for intercourse to occur.

CONSIDERATION

"I am a part of all that I have met" wrote the famous poet, Tennyson, in *Ulysees*. His statement suggests that who we are and the choices we make are influenced by other people and previous interactions. For example, the person who has been date raped may be hesitant about sexual contact and choose to date only in groups. The person who has had a sexually transmitted disease may insist on abstinence as a sexual value or insist on knowing the sexual history of new partners and using a condom.

We can also use social context to our advantage. If we value making certain choices, we can create social contexts to influence those choices. For example, if we value commitment and fidelity to an absent partner, placing ourselves in contexts that foster that commitment (dinner with the absent partner's parents) is a choice. On the contrary, choosing to go drinking with friends who are unfaithful to their respective partners (and who are bar hopping to pick up a sex partner) may be incompatible with the goal to be faithful.

Beyond your personal social context, which influences your choices, larger social changes and social forces influence your relationship choices. (See In Focus 1.2.) One example of how social context influences choices and behavior is the social context of Navy wives who are expected to "go along."

> "Going along" implies that wives accept both heavy Navy demands on their husbands and on themselves. The Navy secures the wife's involvement by making the Navy an all-encompassing community where her family can reside (in Navy housing), shop, receive medical care and legal advice, plus attend to leisure-time activities (movies, dances, restaurants and clubs, sports facilities, and activities). Even friendships are largely determined by the Navy—the husband's duty station provides wives with a ready-made circle of friends with whom she is encouraged to interact. . . . (Mederer & Weinstein, 1992, 338).

Just as the Navy can influence the choices of its Navy husbands and wives, the larger economy also impacts choices. For example, when the economy is in a recession and unemployment is high, men are less likely to marry and more likely to divorce (South & Lloyd, 1992).

To a large degree, the well-being of individuals and families is influenced by choices made by politicians and other powerful officials in government and business. Gottlieb (1992) observed:

> The poor, single mother who thinks she is "crazy" and deficient because she cannot handle a full-time, poorly paid job along with the care of her children and her home, cannot find decent housing, and worries constantly about good medical care for her family has a right to know the political origins of her problems. Personal, therapeutic benefit can result from her knowing that those real hardships result, in large part, from political and economic decisions (p. 6).

CONSIDERATION

A basic assumption of this text is that humans have free will—the capacity to make our own choices. Although heredity and social factors may influence our choices, they do not determine them. However, the influence of heredity and environment is so significant so that whether one is truly "free" to make choices continues to be fiercely debated. Charles Spezzano (1992) articulated the respective positions of this dilemma.

> All of us experience ourselves as both active and reactive. We act with will and a sense of purpose, but we also react to what the world presents to us. The critical question is whether we believe that the scale is tipped in the direction of our being in control of our behavior or on the side of external forces determining what we do (p. 55).

Both the social variables of your immediate social context and in the larger society influence your choices in relationships. Other social influences include your family of origin, unconscious motivations, habit patterns, individual personality, and previous experiences. The family in which you were reared is a major influence on your attitudes, perceptions, and choices (Toman, 1993). For instance, individuals reared in homes in which their parents had a high quality marital relationship are more optimistic about their own marriage than individuals reared in homes in which their parents divorced (Carnelley & Janoff-Bulman, 1992).

NATIONAL DATA ℀ Almost one-fourth (24.2 percent) of the freshman class throughout all U.S. colleges and universities have divorced parents (American Council on Education and University of California, 1992).

On the other hand, an adverse family background may also turn into a strength. Bill Clinton grew up in an alcoholic stepfamily and is said to have learned how to persevere in the face of adversity.

Unconscious motivations may also be operative in making choices. A person reared in a lower class home without adequate food and shelter may become overly concerned about the accumulation of money and make all decisions in reference to gaining higher income. An adult who, as a child, was sexually abused by a parent may reject subsequent sexual advances from a partner with whom he or she is emotionally involved.

Habit patterns also influence choices. A person who is accustomed to and enjoys spending a great deal of time alone may find it difficult to choose to become involved with a person who begins to make demands on his or her time.

Personalities (e.g., introvert, extrovert; passive, assertive) also influence choices. For example, a person who is a risk taker is more likely to have an affair than someone who is comforted by stability and security.

Previous relationship experiences also influence one's perceptions and choices. Individuals who have had a number of positive love experiences are more likely to feel optimistic about future love relationships than those who have had unhappy, frustrated love experiences (Carnelley & Janoff-Bulman, 1992).

At the end of each chapter we will review several choices relevant to the topic of each chapter. When making your own choices, you might consider the degree to which social forces, family of origin, unconscious motivations, habit patterns, personality patterns, and previous relationship experiences influence you.

℀ What Is Marriage?

Choices in marriage and the family are the focus of this text. We now define marriage and look at various types of marriage.

Definition of Marriage

Marriage in the United States is a legal contract with the state that regulates the format for economic and sexual interaction between two heterosexual adults.

🖋 **IN FOCUS 1.2** 〜

Factors Influencing Your Choices: Recent Changes in Marriage and the Family

Our changing society provides the social backdrop against which choices in marriage and the family are made. Some of these changes follow.

DIVERSITY

There is no one model for individuals, relationships, marriages, or families (Ahlburg & De Vita, 1992). All are characterized by an incredible array of diversity. Individuals may be described as existing on a continuum from heterosexuality to homosexuality, from rural to city dwellers, and from being single and living alone to being married and living in communes. Relationships range from cohabiting to marriage to group marriage and from being intimate and satisfying to being distant and conflictual. Family diversity includes two parents, single parent family, same sex parents, opposite sex parents, stepfamilies, families with adopted children, and multigenerational families.

Diversity in marriage and the family exists between as well as within various societies. Even among industrialized societies such as Japan and Sweden, there are dramatic domestic relationship differences. "In Japan we find traditional family and gender norms persisting; in Sweden, a high rate of cohabitation, divorce, and women working for pay" (Tepperman & Wilson, 1993, 27).

Regarding multicultural diversity, "The contemporary ideal is not assimilation but ethnicity. We used to say *e pluribus unum*. Now we glorify *pluribus* and belittle *unum*. The melting pot yields to the Tower of Babel" (Arthur Schlesinger, Jr. as quoted in Njeri, 1991).

FAMILISM

There is professional disagreement (Tepperman & Wilson, 1993; Fine, 1992) about whether our society is drifting toward individualism (choices based more strongly on what is best for the individual and less on what is best for the family) or familism (choices made in reference to family considerations). However, Whitehead (1992) observed that "there is a shift away from an ethos of expressive individualism and toward an ethos of family obligation and commitment" (p. 1). Cox (1992) similarly noted, "There are

many signs that families and institutions have returned to a more solid foundation of traditional values compared with the departures of the 'me first' 80s" (p. 1). One explanation for this renewed emphasis on family values is the aging of the baby boomers. During the seventies and eighties, they were self-absorbed in pursuit of singlehood, career development, and getting their own credit card; during the nineties they are at a new stage of the family life cycle. "They've married. They are becoming parents. And they are discovering that the values that served them in singlehood no longer serve them in parenthood" (Whitehead, 1992, 1).

The reemergence of familism may have positive benefits for spouses and their marital satisfaction. Based on a national sample of over 13,000 adults, the greater the emphasis on personal gratification, the lower the level of reported marital satisfaction (Lye & Biblarz, 1993).

HOT MONOGAMY

Related to familism is *hot monogamy,* a term coined by sex therapist Helen Kaplan. She emphasized that "nineties couples want the marriages their grandparents and parents had. The emphasis is stability, children, family togetherness—plus something more: great sex" (Cutross, 1992, 63).

HIV INFECTION

Contracting HIV is a possibility all sexually active individuals are encouraged to take seriously. Debates on the value of abstinence, safer sex, and the regular use of latex condoms with non-oxynol 9 reflect the fact that we are now in a new sexual era. Due to the spread of HIV and AIDS, individuals may consider the possibility that each new sexual encounter could result in disease and death. In spite of this risk, between 15 and 31 percent of a national sample of adults in the United States reported having two or more sexual partners per year (Catania et al., 1992). In a national sample of never married and formerly married men, twenty percent had had four or more sexual partners in the last 18 months (Billy et al., 1993).

(continued on next page)

✄ IN FOCUS 1.2 ✄

ABORTION

A woman's right to have an abortion may become less restricted. With the Clinton administration, the Supreme Court is likely to reverse restrictive rulings made during the Bush administration. Almost two-thirds (64.1 percent) of the freshman class throughout all U.S. colleges and universities "strongly or somewhat agree" that abortion should be legal (American Council on Education and University of California, 1992).

SINGLEHOOD

Although most people eventually marry, increasing numbers are delaying marriage to pursue education and to establish economic independence (Ahlburg & DeVita, 1992). Only seven percent of the freshman class throughout all U.S. colleges and universities estimate that their "chances are very good that they will marry while in college" (American Council on Education and University of California, 1992).

LIVING TOGETHER

Living together is regarded by some as an extension of courtship. Over three million households today are composed of cohabiting couples in contrast to only 500,000 in 1970. This represents a 500% increase. An increase in age at marriage, women delaying having their first child, a high divorce rate, and an increasing acceptance of cohabitation have all contributed to the rise in the frequency of living together among unmarrieds. Once considered a lower-class practice, living together has become more acceptable in the middle class. As we will discuss in Chapter 6, living together is found more often among older, childfree, less educated individuals.

TWO-EARNER MARRIAGES

Two-earner marriages have become more common in recent decades. About 60 percent of all wives and 75 percent of those between the ages of 35–44 are employed outside the home (*Statistical Abstract of the U.S.: 1993*, Table 631). Although most couples need two incomes to survive, others who have two incomes can afford expensive homes, cars, vacations, and greater opportunities for their children. When children come, about sixty percent of mothers continue their employment. The stereotypical family consisting of the husband who earns the income and the wife who stays at home with two or more children describes only 20 percent of all married couples (Ahlburg & De Vita, 1992). The implication for two-earner families is an increased need for more childcare services and flexible family leave policies (Wisensale, 1992).

EGALITARIAN RELATIONSHIPS

Egalitarian relationships between women and men are becoming more common, particularly in the middle class. Choices about each partner's education, number and timing of children, and who does what chores at home are more frequently being made by partners who regard each other as equals. Such egalitarian relationships based on mutual intimacy, caring, and cooperation are thought to be the most rewarding (Allen & Baber, 1992).

DIVORCE

Compared with the 1960s, both the number of divorces (now about 1.2 million per year) and the divorce rate (now about 4.7 per 1000 population) have more than doubled (National Center for Health Statistics, 1993). One way of regarding the increase in divorce is that "Americans today place a higher value on forming a successful marriage than did earlier generations. People may now expect more of marriage and be less tolerant of marital problems. If irreconcilable problems arise, divorce is seen as an acceptable alternative to an unhappy marriage" (Ahlburg & DeVita, 1992, 15). Alternatively, divorce often means emotional stress for the spouses and children and an increased likelihood of poverty for divorced women and their children (Wisensale, 1992). Indeed, some family scholars believe that the decline of the two parent family will result in "the first generation of children and youths in our history who are less

---

---

well off—psychologically, socially, economically, and morally—than their parents were at the same age" (Pope-noe, 1993, A 48). Although some conservatives have promoted the idea that divorce between parents of minor children should be outlawed (Schrof, 1992), divorce is likely to continue to affect the lives of many children and adults.

TECHNOLOGY

The use of technology to find a partner has become more common. Ahuvia and Adelman (1992) observed, "Historically, matching has long claimed a commercial niche in the marriage market. Today, a modem, phone line, or advertisement might bring potential partners together" (p. 452). Video dating services have also become more widespread with over 600 firms using this technology (p. 457).

Technology has also affected choices regarding childbearing. Infertile couples, single women who want a child,

and lesbian couples may now have children through technological means, such as artificial insemination, in-vitro fertilization, microinjection, and ovum transfer. These reproductive technologies involve new choices in relationships. For example, if a single woman decides to become artificially inseminated with an unknown donor's sperm, how does she respond when her child later asks, "Where's my daddy?" And will society come to regard the family of the future as "one socialized adult and an offspring"? (Edwards, 1991, 359).

RECESSION

As a recession continues, families suffer. Unemployment, underemployment, and uncertain job stability creates strain on families. Worrying about financial matters affects both husbands and wives but tends to affect the psychological well-being of husbands more profoundly (Mills et al., 1992).

The marriage between the partners is usually emotional, monogamous, protective of future children, and formal. These various elements are discussed in the following pages.

NATIONAL DATA ॐ Between 2 and 2.5 million marriage licenses are issued each year (National Center for Health Statistics, 1993).

Legal Contract Marriage in our society is a legal contract that may be entered into only by two people of the opposite sex and of legal age (usually 18 or older), who are not already married to someone else. The marriage license certifies that the individuals were married by a legally empowered representative of the state often with two witnesses present. While common law marriages do exist, they are the exception.

The license, as regarded by the laws of the state, means that all future property acquired by the spouses will be jointly owned and that each will share in the estate of the other. In most states, whatever the deceased spouse owns is legally transferred to the surviving spouse at the time of death. In the event of divorce, the property is usually divided equally regardless of the contribution

> Long-term personal relationships are making a comeback.
>
> ED COX

of each partner. The license also implies the expectation of sexual fidelity in the marriage. In some states, infidelity is grounds for alimony. State law regulating marriage varies. Check with an attorney in your state to find out about the laws operating where you live.

C O N S I D E R A T I O N

The marriage license entitles the spouses to file a joint income tax return, to receive payment by health insurance companies for medical bills if the partner is insured, and to collect social security benefits at the death of the spouse. While the definition of what constitutes a "family" is being reconsidered by the courts, the law is currently designed to protect spouses, not lovers and live-ins. An exception is common law marriage (recognized in some states) which means that if a couple cohabit and present themselves as married, they will be regarded as legally married.

Help! I've fallen in love and I can't get up.

ANONYMOUS

Emotional Relationship   Most people in the United States regard being in love with the person they marry as important. In a study of 1000 undergraduate students at Bowling Green State University, 87 percent of the men and 91 percent of the women said that they would not marry someone unless they were in love with that person. They insisted on being in love as a prerequisite to marriage regardless of whether the person had all the other qualities that they desired in a mate (Allgeier & Wiederman, 1991).

Your movement toward an emotionally committed relationship may be measured by the following Relationship Events Scale. The scale suggests that a developing relationship can be measured on a continuum characterized by increasing intimacy, emotional involvement, interdependence, and commitment by identifying the occurrence of specific events that have happened in a couple's relationship. Each individual of a couple might take the scale separately.

Sexual Monogamy   Marital partners are expected to be sexually faithful to each other. Indeed, most partners are faithful most of the time. However, in Chapter 10, Sexuality in Relationships, we will examine the frequency and causes of extradyadic (external to the couple or dyad) sexuality.

Legal Responsibility for Children   Although individuals marry for love, fun, and companionship, the *real* reason (from the viewpoint of the state) for marriage is the legal obligation of a woman and man to nurture and support any children they may have. In our society, childrearing is the primary responsibility of the family, not of the state.

Marriage is a relatively stable unit that helps to ensure children will have adequate care and protection, will be socialized for productive roles in society, and will not become the burden of those who did not conceive them. Thus,

---

SELF-ASSESSMENT ∼

Relationship Events Scale by Christensen and King

DIRECTIONS: Read each item under Level 1. The term *pass* after each level on the scale denotes the number of events that must have occurred for the individual or couple to be designated as being at this level, or proceed to the next level. If two or more events at Level 1 have occurred in your relationship, proceed to Level 2. If one or more events at Level 2 have occurred, proceed to Level 3, and so on. The highest level at which you pass the designated number of required events is the level at which you may describe your relationship. The various levels (from 1 to 6) represent a continuum of intimacy, emotional involvement, interdependence, and commitment. Level 6, the highest level on this scale, means that the couple is engaged to be married, have lived together, or are currently living together. The average levels of 222 undergraduate women and 136 undergraduate men who regarded themselves as "currently involved in a dating or romantic relationship" were 4.51 and 4.84 respectively (King & Christensen, 1983).

LEVEL 1 (PASS 2)

My partner has called me an affectionate name (sweetheart, darling, etc.).

I have called my partner an affectionate name (sweetheart, darling, etc.)

We have spent a whole day with just each other.

We have arranged to spend time together without planning any activity.

We have felt comfortable enough with each other so that we could be together without talking or doing an activity together.

LEVEL 2 (PASS 1)

We have received an invitation for the two of us as a couple.

My partner has referred to me as his/her girlfriend/boyfriend.

I have referred to my partner as my girlfriend/boyfriend.

LEVEL 3 (PASS 2)

My partner has said "I love you" to me.

I have said "I love you" to my partner.

My partner does not date anyone other than myself.

I do not date anyone other than my partner.

LEVEL 4 (PASS 1)

We have discussed the possibility of getting married.

We have discussed living together.

LEVEL 5 (PASS 2)

I have lent my partner more than $20 for more than a week.

My partner has lent me more than $20 for more than a week.

We have spent a vacation together that lasted longer than three days.

LEVEL 6 (PASS 1)

We are or have been engaged to be married.

We have lived together or we live together now.

SOURCE: Charles E. King and Andrew Christensen, "The Relationship Events Scale: A Guttman Scaling of Progress in Courtship," *Journal of Marriage and the Family*, 45 no. 3 1983, 671–678. Using Appendix Copyright 1983 by the National Council on Family Relations, 3989 Central Ave. NE, Suite 550, Minneapolis, MN 55421. Reprinted by permission.

---

there is tremendous social pressure for individuals to be married at the time they have children. Even at divorce, the legal obligation of the father and mother to the child is theoretically maintained through child-support payments.

Although love is private, marriage is a public/social event.

We changed our wedding ceremony from "For better or worse" to "For better or forget it."

RITA RUDNER

Formal Ceremony   The legal bonding of a couple is often preceded by an announcement in the local newspaper and a formal ceremony in a church or synagogue. Of their announcement one groom-to-be said, "The fact that Barbara and I were actually getting married was not real to me until I saw her picture in the paper and read the sentence that we were to be married on June third." The newspaper is not the only means of publicly announcing the private commitment. Telling parents, siblings, and friends about wedding plans helps to verify the commitment of the partners and also helps to marshal the social and economic support to launch the couple into marital orbit.

Marriage in Cross-Cultural Perspective

ACROSS CULTURES

While we think of marriage in the United States as involving one man and one woman, other societies view marriage differently. *Polygamy* is a form of marriage in which there are more than two spouses. Polygamy occurs in societies or subcultures whose norms sanction multiple partners. One form of polygamy is *polygyny,* in which one husband has two or more wives. "Societies allowing polygyny are by far the commonest" (Brown & Hotra, 1988, 154). However, monogamy is the most prevalent form of marriage in all societies.

NATIONAL DATA   Polygyny is permitted in 83 percent of 862 societies studied by Murdock (1967). Polygyny is particularly prevalent in Nigeria. Based on nationwide data from the Nigeria Fertility Survey, 44 percent of marriages are polygynous (Gage-Brandon, 1992).

The Yolngu tribe of the Aborigines in Northern Australia also practice polygyny. Among the Yolngu, a girl between the ages of 12 and 16 is married to a man in his forties. She is usually the fifth or sixth wife, many of whom are her sisters. The wives receive the sexual affection of their husband as he chooses (Money & Musaph, 1977).

CONSIDERATION

Most people in the United States assume that polygyny exists to satisfy the sexual desires of the man, that the women are treated like slaves, and that jealousy among the wives is common. In most polygynous societies, however, polygyny has a political and economic rather than a sexual function. Polygyny is a means of providing many male heirs to continue the family line. In addition, by having many wives, a greater number of children for domestic/farm labor can be produced. Wives are not treated like slaves (although women have less status than men in general) as all household work is evenly distributed among the wives and each wife is given her own house or own sleeping quarters. Jealousy is minimal because the husband often has a rotational system for conjugal visits which ensures that each wife has equal access to sexual encounters (Smith, 1990).

Gage-Brandon (1992) studied polygynous marriages in Nigeria. She found that first wives often selected second wives to assist them with childcare, housework, and economic activities. However, the husband often selected the third and fourth wife for "romantic love" or other considerations which the first wives may not have liked. Such marriages with three or more wives were much more prone to divorce than those polygynous marriages with just two wives. Hence, it may not be the number of wives but who selects them and why that influences marital stability.

Polygyny is illegally practiced in the United States by some religious fundamentalist groups in Arizona, New Mexico, and Utah which have splintered off from the Church of Jesus Christ of LatterDay Saints (commonly known as the Mormon Church). Among these small sects, polygyny serves a religious function in that large earthly families are believed to result in large heavenly families. Notice that polygynous sex is only a means to accomplish another goal—large families (Embry, 1987).

The Buddhist Tibetans foster yet another brand of polygamy, referred to as *polyandry* in which one wife has two or more (up to five) husbands. These husbands, who may be brothers, pool their resources to support one wife. Polyandry is a much rarer form of polygamy than polygyny and is sometimes motivated by the need to keep the population rate down (Crook & Crook, 1988). Several men marrying one wife will have fewer children than one man marrying several women since each woman can have only a limited number of children but several women, can, collectively have numerous children.

However, the major reason for polyandry is economic. A family that cannot afford wives or marriages for each of its sons may find a wife for the eldest son only. Polyandry allows the younger brothers to also have sexual access to the one wife or marriage the family is able to afford. When a Tibetan woman marries a man, it is understood that she becomes the wife of his brothers as well.

Sexual access by Tibetan brothers who are polyandrously linked to one wife is handled by age and maturity with the eldest brother having the greatest access. This necessarily implies that younger brothers will have less access and are less likely to be the biological fathers of the children born to the wife (Crook & Crook, 1988).

Finally, just as other societies permit more than one spouse to a marriage, some permit same–sex marriages. Among the Nuer tribe in the Sudan an older wealthy sterile woman could marry a younger woman who was fertile and select a man to impregnate her. The older woman would be known as the husband and the children born to the marriage would call her "father" (Evans-Pritchard, 1951).

The Cheyenne Indians permitted married men to take on *berdaches,* or male transvestites, as second wives. In the African Sudan, Azande warriors who could not afford wives were allowed to marry "boy-wives" to satisfy their sexual needs and perform household chores.

❦ What Is Family?

As with marriage, the term *family* may be defined and categorized.

Definition of Family

The United States Bureau of the Census defines family as a group of two or more persons related by blood, marriage, or adoption. According to this definition, married couples and their biological or adopted children, a parent and child, and two or more siblings or cousins who live together are the only groups that constitute a family. Figure 1.1 shows the projection percentages of various types of families in the United States for 1995.

CONSIDERATION

There is considerable confusion about what constitutes a family. For example, excluded from the U.S. Census definition of family are couples who live together (heterosexual and homosexual) and foster families. Also, when a person moves out of the household in a divorce, has the person left the "family?" Finally, some adults and some children include animals as being in their family (Levin & Trost, 1992, Trost, 1993).

As family scholars we know that there is no unity whatsoever in our definitions of family.

IRENE LEVIN
JAN TROST

More recently, the definition of what constitutes a family has been changing to include two emotionally bonded and economically interdependent homosexuals. In 1991, an Ohio appellate court ruled that lesbian and gay domestic partners must be included in the interpretation of the state's domestic violence laws which protect those "who live as spouses or otherwise cohabit." Previously the New York Court of Appeals (*Braschi v. Stahl Associates*) had ruled that a gay couple who had lived together for 10 years could be considered a family. At issue was whether a partner in a ten-year homosexual relationship

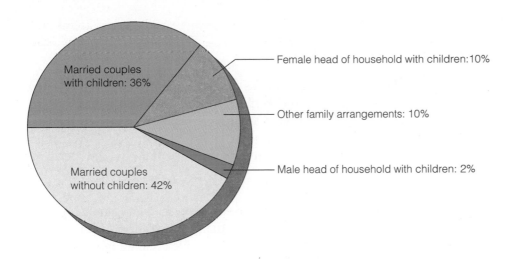

FIGURE 1.1
FAMILY COMPOSITION IN THE UNITED STATES FOR 1995 (TOTAL NUMBER OF FAMILIES = 68 MILLION)
Source: Dennis A. Ahlburg and Carol J. DeVita, "New Realities of the American Family" *Population Bulletin* 47, no. 2 (1992). Used by permission of Population Reference Bureau.

could take over the couple's rent-controlled apartment when the lease-holding member dies. Since state law limited such takeovers to family members, the partner would have been evicted without the court ruling.

In effect, the court ruled that the definition of a family may include two adult partners whose relationship is long term and characterized by an emotional and financial commitment and interdependence. Rather than view family members as partners related by blood, marriage, or adoption, increasingly the courts are looking at the nature of the relationship between the partners: How long have they lived together? What is the level of emotional and financial commitment and interdependence? Do the partners view themselves as a family? Increasingly, families are being defined by function rather than by structure. Scanzoni and Marsiglio (1993) reemphasized this perspective when they stated that contemporary families are more often defined by interdependencies including extrinsic (economic and instrumental), intrinsic (companionship and intimacy) and sexual (bonded physical access) characteristics.

At the present time over 24 cities and counties recognize some form of domestic partnership (National Gay and Lesbian Task Force, 1992). Although gay marriages are not legally recognized in any of the 50 states, the state Supreme Court in Hawaii ruled that not allowing gay marriages may be a violation of sex discrimination laws (*Newsweek*, 1993).

Such recognition of gay relationships has implications for other types of dyadic units that might be considered family on the basis of the nature of the relationships. According to Levin and Trost (1992):

> There could be niece–aunt dyads, friend dyads, cousin dyads, grandmother–grandson dyads, and so forth. Almost any sort of household or family could be defined in this way (p. 350).

In effect, marriages and families will more often be defined in terms of closeness (Zimmerman, 1992).

> The basic social unit of almost all human populations is the family.
>
> JOHN H. CROOK
> STAMATI J. CROOK

Types of Family

There are various types of families.

Family of Orientation   Also referred to as the *family of origin,* this is the family into which you were born or the family in which you were reared. This represents you, your parents, and your siblings. When you go to your parents' home for the holidays, you return to your family of orientation. We earlier emphasized the importance of your family of orientation on the interpersonal choices you make.

Family of Procreation   The *family of procreation* represents the family you will begin if you marry and have children. More than 90 percent of us marry and establish our own family of procreation. Across the life cycle we move from the family of orientation to the family of procreation.

Nuclear Family   The *nuclear family* may refer to either your family of orientation or procreation (if you decide to have children). Your nuclear family consists of you, your parents (or parent), and siblings, or of you, your spouse, and your children (or just of you and your children).

> The idealized image of the family is an ahistorical amalgam of structures, values, and behaviors that never coexisted in the same time and place.
>
> STEPHANIE COONTZ

> Talk about family values is a shorthand way of appealing to prejudices against minority groups, working-class people, single mothers, and homosexuals.
>
> ELAINE TYLER MAY

CONSIDERATION

During the 1992 presidential campaign , both parties touted the theme of family values. Implied in the rhetoric was the implication that somehow the nuclear family of yesteryear with its working father, homemaking mother, and two children in suburbia was self-sufficient, patriotic, and God-fearing. Stephanie Coontz (1992), a historian, argued that this is an inaccurate, nostalgic view of the family that never was. The title of her book reflects her thesis—*The Way We Never Were: American Families and the Nostalgia Trap.* She emphasized that there has always been family diversity (single parent homes, high teen birthrates, out-of-wedlock babies placed for adoption) that is never given visibility with the nostalgic view.

Extended Family   The *extended family* includes not only your nuclear family but other relatives as well. These relatives include your parents, grandparents, aunts, uncles, and siblings. An example of an extended family living together would be a husband and wife, their children, and the children's grandparents. African Americans, Hispanics, Asian Americans, Native Americans, and Native Alaskan Innuits are more likely to live with their extended families than Anglo-Americans. Such extended families are sometimes the result of historical and religious influences.

∿ **ACROSS CULTURES**

For example, the extended family model of Native Americans is related to the historical place of elders in the family. Not only are elderly men accorded respect because they provide spiritual guidance and maintenance of cultural heritage, elderly women (now grandmothers) provide needed childcare and help with household chores. In exchange, they are taken care of when they are too frail to care for themselves (Yee, 1992).

Among Asians, the status of the elderly in the extended family derives from religion. Confucian philosophy prescribes that all relationships are of the subordinate-superordinate type—husband-wife, parent-child, and teacher-pupil. "This implies that elders have more authority than younger members of the family" (Yee, 1992, 6). Abandoning the elderly rather than including them in larger family units would be unthinkable, although this may be changing due to the Westernization of China.

In addition to their concern for the elderly, Asian Americans are socialized to subordinate themselves to the group. Familism and group identity are valued over individualism and independence (Walters & Chapman, 1991). Divorce is not prevalent because Asians are discouraged from bringing negative social attention to the family. In addition, the relationship that is emphasized in Asian families (particularly among the Japanese) is the mother-child relationship, not the husband-wife relationship (Tamura & Lau, 1992).

Black families are also characterized by their extended nature, multiple parenting and informal adoption practices, and child-centeredness. The family is regarded as the greatest source of life satisfaction for Blacks in America (Walters & Chapman, 1991).

The child living in an extended family may be connected to both parents and grandparents.

Blacks and Hispanics are more likely to have extended families for both economic and cultural reasons. As incomes are lower among these groups (due to racism, discrimination), extended family living is a way of pooling resources. In addition, many Blacks and Hispanics have grown up in extended families, which results in this type of family being perceived as culturally normative.

> **CONSIDERATION**
>
> There are numerous types of families that we discuss later in the text. Single-parent families headed by either a woman or a man, childfree families, communal families, and stepfamilies are examples. Awareness of these alternative family types expands the range of choices.

Although the concepts of marriage and family are closely related, they are distinct concepts. Differences between U.S. concepts of legal marriage and family are listed in Table 1.1.

TABLE 1.1

Differences Between Marriage and the Family in the United States

MARRIAGE	FAMILY
Usually initiated by a formal ceremony.	Formal ceremony not essential.
Involves two people.	Can be as few as two.
Ages of the individuals tend to be similar.	Individuals represent more than one generation.
Individuals usually choose each other.	Members are born or adopted into the family.
Ends when spouse dies or is divorced.	Continues beyond the life of the individual.
Sex between spouses is expected and approved.	Sex between near kin is neither expected nor approved.
Requires a license.	No license needed to become a parent.
Procreation expected.	Consequence of procreation.
Spouses are focused on each other.	Focus is diluted with the addition of children.
Spouses can voluntarily withdraw from marriage with approval from the state.	Spouses/parents cannot easily voluntarily withdraw from obligations to children.
Money in unit is spent on the couple.	Money is diverted from the couple to the children.
Recreation revolves around adults.	Recreation revolves around children.

Source: Axelson, 1993.

Marriages and Families in the Year 2000

As the year 2000 approaches, demographic and lifestyle trends permit an accurate forecast of what is ahead for marriages and families. Dr. Ken Dychtwald (1990) emphasized that the "new 'matrix' family will be adult centered, will span three, four, even five generations, and will be bound together as much by friendship and choice as by blood and obligation" (p. 232).

Adult-Centered By 1995, the median age of an individual in the United States will be close to the mid-thirties. The older median age is a result of individuals having a longer life expectancy, with an average life expectancy of 75.4 years (National Center for Health Statistics, 1993b). No longer will families predominately be two young adults looking after several children but two adults relating as peers to their adult offspring. And, as parents age, the adult children will increasingly be in the role of caring for them.

Transgenerational Extended life will further redefine the focus of adults in the family from their small nuclear unit, to adult friends and relatives across two or three generations. An increasing number of adults, particularly women, will become a part of the "sandwich generation" in which they are taking care of their elderly parents as well as their own children (Brubaker, 1991).

Bondings by Choice In the past, relationships in the family have been according to bloodline, genes, and economics. Increasingly, relationships will be influenced by choice. Individuals will supplement their family relationships with other adult relationships. For example, many elderly people have large homes with empty bedrooms as a result of their children moving away and establishing their own families. New programs such as roommate matching and shared housing result in people sharing their resources and companionship.

Older couples will increasingly characterize marriages in the 21st century.

❧ Perspectives Other Than Choices in Viewing Marriage and the Family

Although we will focus on choices in relationships as the framework for viewing marriage and the family, there are other conceptual frameworks. Various theoretical marriage and family frameworks are examined in the following sections.

Structure–Function Perspective

The *structure-function view* of marriage and the family emphasizes the functions these institutions serve for the rest of our society. Just as the religious institution helps to explain the unknown, the economic institution ensures the production and distribution of goods and services, and the legal institution provides social control, so the institutions of marriage and the family have specific major functions.

First, marriage and the family serve to replenish society with socialized members. Our society cannot continue to exist without new members, so we must have some way of ensuring a continuing supply. But just having new members is not enough. We need socialized members—those who can speak our language and know the norms and roles of our society. The legal bond of marriage and the obligation to nurture and socialize offspring help to assure that this socialization will occur.

Second, marriage and the family promote the emotional stability of the adult partners and give children a place to belong. Society cannot afford enough counselors to help us whenever we have problems. Marriage provides an in-residence counselor who is, theoretically, a loving and caring partner with whom we share our most difficult experiences. For example, Smart (1992) emphasized the degree to which married couples were emotionally supportive of each other when they experienced a pregnancy loss (miscarriage) or infant death.

Children also need people to love them and to give them a sense of belonging. This need can be fulfilled in a variety of family contexts (two-parent family, single-parent family, extended family). The affective function of the family is one of its major offerings. No other institutions focus so completely on fulfilling the emotional needs of its members as do marriage and the family.

While replacement of societal members and the provision of emotional stability are the primary functions of marriage and the family for society, other functions include:

- Physical care—Families provide the primary care for their infants, children, and aging parents. Other agencies (daycare, school, and nursing homes) may help but the family remains the primary caretaker.
- Regulation of sexual behavior—Spouses are expected to confine their sexual behavior to each other, which reduces the risk of having children who do not have socially and legally bonded parents and of spreading AIDS or other sexually transmitted diseases.
- Status placement—Being born in a family provides social placement of the individual in society. One's social class, religious affiliation, and future occupation are largely determined by one's family of origin.

Family Life Cycle Perspective

The *family life cycle view* of marriage and the family emphasizes the stages and transitions in families over time. Examples of family life cycles reveal what is happening to us at various ages. (See Table 1.2.) Cycle (A) is for people who marry only once and have two children. Cycle (B) is for people who get divorced and who remarry. Income, education, and age at marriage affect the

TABLE 1.2
Alternative Family Life Cycles*

(A) FAMILY LIFE CYCLE OF THOSE WHO MARRY ONLY ONCE*

LIFE STAGE	APPROXIMATE AGE
Marriage	Males: 26
	Females: 24
First child born	Males: 29
	Females: 27
Last child born	Males: 35
	Females: 33
Last child leaves	Males: 53
	Females: 51
Grandparent	Males: 55
	Females: 53
Widowhood	Females: 72
Death	Males: 72
	Females: 79

(B) FAMILY LIFE CYCLE OF THOSE WHO MARRY AND DIVORCE*

LIFE STAGE	APPROXIMATE AGE
First Marriage	Males: 26
	Females: 24
Divorce	Males: 35
	Females: 33
Remarry if divorced	Males: 37
	Females: 34
Remarriage if widowed	Males: 63
	Females: 54
Widowhood	Females: 72
Death	Males: 72
	Females: 79

*Data are taken from 1993 *Statistical Abstract of the United States.* Timing of death taken from National Center for Health Statistics, 1993b.

chance of moving through the respective family life cycles. For example, having a low income, having completed fewer than 12 years of education, and having married during the teen-age years increases a person's chance of divorce. Other factors associated with divorce are discussed in Chapter 16.

The family life cycle is a useful concept because it helps to identify the choices with which individuals are confronted. For example, the never married are choosing partners, the newly married are making choices about careers and when to begin their family, the soon to be divorced are making decisions about custody/child support/division of property, and the remarried are making choices in regard to stepchildren and ex-spouses. Grandparents are making choices about their grandchildren and widows/widowers are concerned with where to live (children, retirement home, with a friend, alone).

Social-Psychological Perspective

As individuals progress throughout the family life cycle, they experience various social-psychological variables that affect them. Examples of two of these variables are the self-concept and the self-fulfilling prophecy.

The *self-concept* is affected by family members who are social mirrors into which we look for information about who we are and how others feel about us. If we see approval from our parents and spouses, we develop and maintain a positive feeling about ourselves. Such a feeling allows us to believe that we are worthy of love and provides a positive basis for us to both love and be loved by others. Individuals who grow up feeling unloved by their parents find it more difficult to establish loving relationships with others.

The *self-fulfilling prophecy* implies that we behave according to the expectations of others. If our spouses expect us to be on time, faithful, and productive, we are likely to behave to make those expectations come true. On the other hand, if they expect us to be late, unfaithful, and lazy, we are likely to behave accordingly.

I acted like someone I wanted to become and finally I became that person.

CARY GRANT

CONSIDERATION

What expectations do you have of your partner and what expectations does your partner have of you in regard to punctuality, faithfulness, and productivity? If these expectations are positive, then the behavior is also likely to be positive. In a sense, you find what you look for in your partner and your partner finds what he or she looks for in you.

It is particularly important for parents (and other child caregivers) to be aware of the self-fulfilling prophecy. Parents give children powerful messages that may become self-fulfilling prophecies. For example, parents who tell their children that they are "bad" are providing a negative label ("bad") that the children then internalize or accept as true. The children then begin to view themselves as "bad" and act in a manner consistent with this view. In other words, children may act "bad" because they have been labeled "bad" by parents, teachers, or other child caregivers. Similarly, children may act "good" if they are labeled as such.

Social Exchange Perspective

Social exchange theorists view relationships in marriage and the family as individuals making choices on the basis of perceived profit (the greatest rewards at the least cost). For example, a social exchange view of mate selection suggests that we select the partner who offers the most desirable characteristics and the fewest undesirable characteristics of those potential partners available to us. A social exchange view of marital roles suggests that spouses negotiate the division of labor on the basis of exchange (he helps with childcare in exchange for her earning an income, which relieves him of total financial responsibility). Indeed, employed wives who do not feel that their husbands are fair in terms of sharing housework and child care feel exploited and the level of marital satisfaction drops (Blair, 1993).

Social exchange theorists also emphasize that power in a relationship is the ability to influence, and avoid being influenced by, the partner. The various bases of power, such as money, need for partner, and brute force may be expressed in various ways, including withholding resources, decreasing investment in relationship, and violence (Brehm, 1992). We discuss power in greater detail in Chapter 9 on Communication and Conflict.

Social Class and Race Perspective

Stratification refers to the ranking of people into layers or strata according to their socio-economic status, which includes income, occupation, and educational attainment. Individuals who occupy a similar socio-economic status are said to be in the same *social class*.

Marriages and families are also stratified into different social classes, such as the upper, middle, working, or lower social class. Families in these various social classes reflect dramatic differences in their attitudes, values, and behavior. For example, individuals from the lower class are more likely to divorce than individuals from the higher social classes.

I was born rich because of my parents.

H. ROSS PEROT

I'm from the project—I became a movie star.

WHOOPI GOLDBERG

CONSIDERATION

Since white middle class individuals are more likely to attend college and since most of the studies on marriage and the family are based on college students, the majority of research is biased in terms of the white middle class. Other groups, less convenient to researchers, are less often represented in the marriage and family literature.

Social class is also associated with race. Table 1.3 reflects the racial minority population of the United States.

TABLE 1.3

Racial Minorities in the United States

Group	Total Number	% of U.S. Population	Examples
African-American	30 million	12%	African-Caribbean
Hispanics	22 million	8	Mexican, Puerto Rican, Cuban, Central and South Americans
Asian/Pacific Americans	7 million	3	Chinese, Japanese, Korean, Vietnamese, Cambodian, Thai, Filipino, Laotian, Lao-Hmong, Somoan, Guamanian
American Indian Alaskan Native	2 million	1	Cherokee, Navajo, Sioux, Cippeawai, Aleut, Innuits

Source: Statistical Abstract of the United States: 1993, Table 33, 113th ed., Washington, D.C.: U.S. Bureau of the Census, 1993.

CONSIDERATION

A person's membership in a particular racial and/or ethnic group is sometimes not as clear cut as might be expected. For example, all black people are not African Americans. Black immigrants from the Caribbean have a strong ethnic identity that is not African American (Coughlin, 1993).

The term race is a social construct the meaning of which has less to do with biological differences than social, cultural, political, economic, behavioral, and health differences (Hummer, in press). In regard to the latter, Hummer (in press) observed that the infant mortality rate of African-Americans is 2.2 times higher than for non-Hispanic whites (18.6 versus 8.1 per 1000 births). He postulated that the reasons for such differences are sociodemographic and include less maternal education, less adequate prenatal nutrition, and lower age at childbirth.

Indeed, many of the differences between blacks and whites reflect differences in social class, rather than race. Individuals in the lower class (whether white or black) have higher rates of unemployment, premarital pregnancies, divorce, and crime. In looking at the comparisons between blacks and whites throughout this text, it is important to keep in mind that many presumed "racial" differences are really those of social class. However, racism still exists in the form of discrimination against minorities in education, employment, and housing.

> The L. A. riots shouldn't have been a surprise to anyone, except maybe whites whose only contact with blacks is through Bill Cosby or Michael Jackson.
>
> **SPIKE LEE**

Role Perspective

Marriage and family relationships may also be viewed from a role perspective. *Roles* are behaviors in which individuals in various statuses, such as wife, husband, parent, and child are expected to engage. *Role theory* emphasizes that one role does not exist without another (there is no wife without a husband), that roles are interactive (parents make rules and children comply), and that roles influence behavior (The expectant mother will drink less alcohol than the non pregnant adult fiancée).

A role perspective of marriage and family relationships also emphasizes instrumental and expressive roles (Kaplan & Hennon, 1992). *Instrumental roles* are necessary for the basic maintenance of a household and/or family and include provider, housekeeper, and child rearer. *Expressive roles* are those involving human emotion and feeling and include recreation, sex, therapeutic, child socializer, self-maintenance, and kinship. Marital satisfaction and stability are influenced by the degree to which partners agree on who is to perform which roles in the relationship. Partners tend to differ in their role expectations depending on whether it is the first or subsequent marriage. For example, traditional gender-role expectations are more common among spouses in first marriages (Smith, Goslen, Byrd, & Reece, 1991).

> The probabilities of two people holding perfectly congruent expectations on every dimension for every role is minute.
>
> LORI KAPLAN
> CHARLES HENNON

CONSIDERATION

Most of the changes that occur in marriage and the family are role changes. Two researchers (Goldscheider & Waite, 1991) noted:

> What is at the heart of these changes is a restructuring of male-female relationships, both at work and at home, in which men are increasingly expecting their wives to share in economic responsibilities and women are increasingly expecting help with domestic tasks (p. 1).

Crisis Perspective

> No one gets out of life without tremendous pain.
>
> MARY TYLER MOORE

Marriage and the family may also be viewed from a crisis perspective. A *crisis* may be defined as an event for which old patterns of adaptation are no longer helpful. Most individuals, spouses, and parents experience one or more crisis events in their lifetimes. Examples of crisis events include planned and unplanned pregnancy, divorce, widowhood, alcoholism, extramarital intercourse, incest, infertility, the birth of a child, unemployment, military separation, imprisonment of spouse, and spouse abuse. A crisis event may stem from an external source (for example, a recession may cause unemployment) or from an internal source (discovery of a spouse's affair may encourage alcoholism). The death of a newborn is one of the most devastating internal crisis events that happens to a couple (Callan & Murray, 1989). Couples who successfully respond to crisis events have high degrees of *cohesion*, or emotional bonding, and adaptability—which is the ability of the marital system to change its power structure, role relationships, and rules in response to new situations.

> **CONSIDERATION**
>
> Family members may be particularly helpful to each other during crisis events. One researcher observed that virtually all of the 52 parents (age 54 to 87) studied were helpful to their children who were going through a divorce. Expressions of assistance included financial support for basic needs, attorney fees, and mortgage payments as well as housing, child care, and emotional support (Hamon & Elliott, 1992).

Systems Perspective

Recent theorists have emphasized that marriage and the family may be understood as a system that is comprised of interdependent parts (Emery & Tuer, 1993). Family members (spouses, parents, children) are viewed as influencing each other in reciprocal fashion. Just as children influence the marriage of their parents, the marriage to which the children are constantly exposed will influence the children. Family systems theory also suggests that families exhibit a tendency to maintain a steady state. "Changes occur, but the principle of homeostasis suggests that they will be resisted in order to maintain equilibrium" (p. 123). For example, the drug abuse of a family member may be denied by other family members because to acknowledge such behavior is to risk significant family change. Finally, within a family system there are subsystems. The marital relationship, sibling relationship, and parent—child relationship (both with one's young children and one's aging parents) are all subsystems within the same system.

The nine major perspectives on marriage and the family are summarized in Table 1.4.

These two sisters represent a subsystem of a larger family system.

℘ Information Sources for Marriage and the Family

This text is based primarily on studies in marriage and the family that have been reported in professional journals. Some of the more than 50 journals in which this research is published include the following:

Family Relations	*Journal of Family History*
Family Process	*Journal of Family Therapy*
Journal of Family Issues	*Sex Roles*
Journal of Marriage and the Family	*American Journal of Family Therapy*
American Sociological Review	*American Journal of Sociology*

TABLE 1.4

Nine Major Perspectives of Viewing Marriage and the Family

1. Choice perspective	Emphasizes choices individuals make in regard to relationships, lifestyles, and parenthood.
2. Structure-function perspective	Examines the ways in which marriage and the family help our society survive.
3. Family life cycle perspective	Identifies stages and transitions in families over time.
4. Social psychological perspective	Examines how family members influence our self concept and create self–fulfilling prophecies.
5. Social exchange perspective	Emphasizes that choices in relationships are based on perceived profit.
6. Social class and race perspective	Examines how social class variables (education, income, occupation) and race influence marriages and families.
7. Role perspective	Examines the nature and interaction of roles (expectations of behavior) that are associated with various positions (e.g., spouse, parent, child).
8. Crisis perspective	Examines how individuals and families respond to crisis events.
9. Systems perspective	Emphasizes that family members are interconnected and strive to maintain homeostasis.

Marriage and Family Review
Journal of Comparative Family Studies
Child Development
Child Study Journal
Archives of Sexual Behavior
Journal of Divorce and Remarriage
Journal of Family Law
Family Planning Perspectives
Adolescence
Journal of Sex and Marital Therapy
Journal of Sex Research
Journal of Family Welfare
Journal of Marital and Family Therapy

Family Law Quarterly
Journal of Adolescence
Journal of Home Economics
Child Development
Journal of Gerontology
Studies in Family Planning
Family Perspective
Journal of Social Issues
American Journal of Orthopsychiatry
SIECUS Report
Gerontologist
Home Economics Research Journal

ℬ Some Cautions About Research

The findings of the various studies presented in professional journals furnish a basis for making choices in marriage and the family; however, it is wise to be cautious about research. Some research limitations are discussed in the following sections.

Sampling

Some of the research on marriage and the family is based on random samples. In a *random sample,* each individual in the population has an equal chance of being included in the sample. Random sampling involves selecting individuals at random from an identified population. Studies that use random samples are based on the assumption that the individuals studied are similar to, and therefore representative of, the population that the researcher is interested in. For example, suppose you want to know the percentage of unmarried seniors (US) on your campus who are living together. Although the most accurate way to get this information is to secure an anonymous "yes" or "no" response from every US, doing so is not practical. To save yourself time, you could ask a few USs to complete your questionnaire and assume that the rest of the USs would say "yes" or "no" in the same proportion as those who did. To decide who those few USs would be, you could put the names of every US on campus on separate note cards, stir these cards in your empty bathtub, put on a blindfold, and draw 100 cards. Because each US would have an equal chance of having his or her card drawn from the tub, you would obtain a random sample. After administering the questionnaire to this sample and adding the "yes" and "no" answers, you would have a fairly accurate idea of the percentage of USs on your campus who are living together.

> My latest survey shows that people don't believe in surveys.
>
> LAURENCE PETER

CONSIDERATION

Two researchers observed that random samples are often not "random samples" in that "randomly targeting a sample does not ensure that the sample that is obtained remains random" (Braver & Bay, 1992, 925). For example, in conducting the previously mentioned study of unmarried seniors who are living together, you may find it difficult to actually find and get everyone in your sample to complete a questionnaire. Hence, your sample would not reflect those who had changed addresses or who were unwilling to participate.

Due to the trouble and expense of obtaining random samples, most researchers study subjects to whom they have convenient access. This often means students in the researchers' classes. The result is an overabundance of research on "convenience" samples consisting of white, Protestant, middle class college students. Because college students cannot be assumed to be similar to their noncollege peers or older adults in their attitudes, feelings, and behaviors, research based on college student samples is biased. Although the data presented in this text include those obtained from young unmarried college students, they also refer to people of different ages, marital statuses, racial backgrounds, lifestyles, religions, and social classes.

Control Groups

Experimental research involves randomly assigning research participants to two groups—the *experimental group,* which is exposed to the experimental treatment, and the *control group,* which is not exposed to the treatment and thus serves as a comparison group. Experimental research allows researchers to conclude that any differences between the two groups (experimental and control) are due to the experimental treatment.

In most marriage and family research, the experimental design cannot be used because researchers cannot randomly assign subjects to be in either the experimental or control group. For example, a researcher interested in studying the effects of divorce cannot select a sample and then randomly assign one-half of the subjects to the experimental group that gets divorced and the other half of the subjects to the group that stays married. Rather than select a sample and then randomly assign subjects to different groups, researchers must sometimes choose samples that are already grouped. For example, a researcher interested in the effects of divorce on children chooses subjects that are already in the category of "children of divorced parents." This type of research in which subjects cannot be randomly assigned to groups is known as *quasi-experimental research.*

In quasi-experimental research, it is difficult to determine if any differences between two groups are due to the research variable of interest or some other factor. For example, if children of divorced parents are being compared to children of parents who stayed married, any differences between the two groups may not necessarily be due to the fact that the parents are divorced. Perhaps the differences between the two groups are due to the fact that children of divorced parents are more likely to have fewer siblings than children of parents who stayed married (couples who stay married tend to have more children than couples who divorce).

Although we should be cautious in interpreting the results of quasi-experimental research in which the experimental and control groups are not based on random assignment, we should be even more cautious when research involves no control group at all. In a study of adult children of divorced parents, Wallerstein and Blakeslee (1989) found that many of these children reported entering adulthood as worried, underachieving, and self-deprecating. Forty percent between the ages of 19 and 29 were "drifting." These findings are of questionable value because no control group was used. Children from intact families may also be worried, underachieving, self-deprecating, and drifting. Hence, if we are to have any level of confidence in the interpretation of our research findings, we need to include a control group, even if the control group is not formed on the basis of random assignment.

Age and Cohort Effects

In some research designs, different cohorts or age groups are observed and/or tested at one point in time. One problem that plagues such research is the difficulty—even impossibility—of discerning if observed differences between the subjects studied are due to the research variable of interest, cohort differences, or to some variable associated with the passage of time (e.g., biological aging). A good illustration of this problem is found in research on changes in marital satisfaction over the course of the family life cycle. In such studies, researchers may compare the level of marital happiness reported by couples who have been married for different lengths of time. For example, a researcher may compare the marital happiness of two groups of people—those who have been married for fifty years and those who have been married for five years. But differences between these two groups may be due to either 1) differences in age (age effect), 2) the different historical time period that the two groups have lived through (cohort effect), or 3) being married different lengths of time (research variable). It may be helpful to keep these issues in mind when we report studies on marital satisfaction over time. .

Terminology

In addition to being alert to potential shortcomings in sampling and control groups, you should consider how the phenomenon being researched is defined. For example, in a preceding illustration of unmarried seniors (US) living together, how would you define *living together*? How many people, of what sex, spending what amount of time, in what place, engaging in what behaviors will constitute your definition? Indeed, researchers have used more than 20 definitions of what constitutes "living together."

What about other terms? What is meant by marital satisfaction, commitment, interpersonal violence, and sexual fulfillment? Before accepting that most people report a high degree of marital satisfaction or sexual fulfillment, be alert to the definition used by the researcher. Exactly what is the researcher trying to measure?

Researcher Bias

Although one of the goals of scientific studies is to gather data objectively, it may be impossible for researchers to be totally objective. Researchers are human and have values, attitudes, and beliefs that may influence their research methods and findings. It may be important to know what the researcher's bias is in order to evaluate that researcher's findings. For example, a researcher who does not support abortion rights may conduct research that focuses only on the negative effects of abortion.

The research topics selected by researchers may also reflect the researchers' values and attitudes. For example, due to the male bias in the scientific

Childbirth, motherwork, and housework were not studied until feminist researchers raised the questions.

LORNE TEPPERMAN
SUSANNAH WILSON

community, research has not focused adequately on women's issues (Thompson, 1992). In recent years, feminist approaches to marriage and family research have developed to overcome the traditional male bias in research.

In Focus 1.3 provides a more detailed view of feminist views of research in marriage and the family.

Time Lag

There is typically a two-year lag between the time a research study is completed and its appearance in a professional journal. Because textbooks are based on these journals and take from three to five years from writing to publication, by the time you read the results of a study, other studies may have been conducted that reveal different findings. Be aware that the research you read in this or any text may not reflect current reality. Many of the journals listed earlier will be in your library; you might compare the findings of recent studies with the studies reported in this text.

Distortion and Deception

Researchers in all fields may encounter problems of sampling, terminology, lack of a control group, researcher bias, and time lag, but other problems specific to social science research—particularly to marriage research—are distortion and deception. Marriage is a very private relationship that happens behind closed doors, and we have been socialized not to reveal to strangers the intimate details of our marriages. Therefore, we are prone to distort, omit, or exaggerate information, perhaps unconsciously, to cover up what we may feel is no one else's business. Thus, the researcher sometimes obtains inaccurate information. Marriage and family researchers know more about what people say they do, than what they actually do.

When I was younger I could remember anything, whether it happened or not.

MARK TWAIN

An unintentional and probably more frequent form of distortion is inaccurate recall. Sometimes researchers ask respondents to recall details of their relationships that occurred years ago. Time tends to blur some memories, and respondents may not relate what actually happened but only what they remember to have happened.

In addition to distortion on the part of the person being surveyed, researchers have been known to intentionally distort or fabricate research (Schacht, 1990; Kohn, 1987). In response to pressures to publish or a desire for prestige and recognition, some researchers have doctored their data. For example, the late British psychologist Cyril Burt was renowned for his research designed to test the relative importance of heredity and environment on a person's development. Burt studied identical twins who had been reared in separate environments since birth and presented data that seemed to indicate clearly that heredity was more important. Five years after Burt's death, evidence came to light that he had altered his data, that his coauthors had never existed, and that the investigations had never been conducted. More recently, Dr. Barry

---

↙ IN FOCUS 1.3 ↘

Feminist Approaches to Marriage and Family Research

"Feminism is fundamentally a political movement and a political analysis that aims to understand and change the subordinate situation of women throughout the world" (Tiefer, 1988, 16). Marriage and the family are a primary interest and concern of feminist thinkers because these domains of intimate interpersonal experience have been the locus of oppression for some women.

Feminist researchers agree that traditional research is incompatible with the principles of feminism. One major feminist criticism of traditional research is that much of it is sexist (Eichler, 1987). For example, it has been noted that many studies generalize to both sexes even though only one sex was studied (McHugh, Koeske, & Frieze, 1986). In studies based on samples composed of only one sex, it is more often men rather than women who are studied. The overrepresentation of male single-gender studies has resulted in basing many behavioral, attitudinal, and personality norms on the male experience (Ward & Grant, 1985). Women, who may deviate from such male-based norms, are often viewed as "subnormal." For example, in regard to sexual dysfunctions of women, the focus is more often on the fact that women have difficulty achieving an orgasm during intercourse rather than emphasizing the importance of the partner providing adequate stimulation to encourage such an experience.

Feminist research may be characterized by the following features (McHugh et al., 1986; Harding, 1987; Tiefer, 1988; Pollis, 1988):

1. An emphasis on qualitative research that is based on women's experiences
2. The recognition that the researcher's beliefs and biases affect the research question and findings
3. The commitment to design research with the aim of eliminating bias and improving the lives of women
4. An emphasis on the heterogeneity of human experience and behavior
5. The recognition that race, class, community, culture, and language play central roles in shaping our sexual attitudes and behaviors
6. An acknowledgment of the pervasive influence of gender in all aspects of social life, including the practice of science
7. The conceptualization of gender as a socially created category
8. The conceptualization of sexuality as a social construction, rather than as a biological imperative

McHugh, Koeske, and Frieze (1986) distinguish between nonsexist research (also called *sex-fair* research), which does not discriminate against women, and feminist research, which actively works toward the advancement of women. They view sex-fair research as one aspect of feminist research.

Garfinkel, a psychiatry professor at the University of Minnesota, was indicted in 1992 on federal charges that he faked research on a drug used to treat obsessive compulsive patients.

Table 1.5 summarizes some potential weaknesses of any research study.

Other Research Problems

Nonresponse on surveys and the discrepancy between attitudes and behaviors are other research problems. In regard to nonresponse, not all individuals who complete questionnaires or agree to participate in an interview are willing to

T A B L E 1.5
Potential Weaknesses of Research Studies

WEAKNESS	CONSEQUENCES	EXAMPLE
Sample is biased	Inaccurate conclusions	Opinions of students in your marriage class do not reflect opinions of all college students.
No control group	Inaccurate conclusions	Wallerstein study on the effects of divorce on children did not have a control group. Kids from intact families may also report having problems.
Unclear terms	Cannot measure what is not clearly defined	What is marital happiness? What is good communication?
Bias of researcher	Slanted conclusions	Male researcher may assume that since men usually ejaculate each time they have intercourse, women should experience orgasm each time they have intercourse.
Time lag	Outdated conclusions	Often quoted Kinsey research on sexuality is 45 years old.
Distortion	Invalid conclusions	Research subjects exaggerate, omit information, and/or recall facts or events inaccurately.
Deception	Invalid conclusions	British psychologist Cyril Burt altered his data on twins.

provide information about such personal issues as money, spouse abuse, family violence, rape, sex, and alcohol abuse. They leave the questionnaire blank or tell the interviewer they would rather not respond. Others respond but give only socially desirable answers. The implications for research are that data gatherers do not know the nature or extent to which something may be a problem because people are reluctant to provide accurate information.

The discrepancy between the attitudes people have and their behavior is another cause for concern about the validity of research data. It is sometimes assumed that if a person has a certain attitude (for example, extramarital sex is wrong), then his or her behavior will be consistent with that attitude (avoid extramarital sex). However, this assumption is not always accurate. People do indeed say one thing and do another. This potential discrepancy should be kept in mind when reading research on various attitudes.

Finally, most research reflects information provided by volunteers. The question we must ask is, "Do volunteers represent nonvolunteers in terms of answering questions similarly?" We do not know the answer, which suggests that our research may be flawed.

C O N S I D E R A T I O N

In view of the research problems outlined here, you might ask, "Why bother to report the findings?" The research picture is not as bleak as it may seem at first. A number of studies have been conducted that have none of these research drawbacks. The articles in *Journal of Marriage and the Family*, for example, illustrate the high level of methodologically sound articles that are being published. Even less sophisticated journals provide us with useful information about what is currently happening. The alternative to gathering data is relying on personal experience alone, and this is unacceptable to social scientists who study marriage and the family.

❧ Trends

Being married and having children will continue to be goals for most people due to the interpersonal satisfaction that these relationships provide. Seventy-one percent of the freshman class throughout all U.S. colleges and universities identified raising a family as an "essential or very important objective" (American Council on Education and University of California, 1992). Indeed, based on a sample of 300 adults, a team of researchers concluded, "There is no question that the family remains one of the most significant contributions to individuals' feelings about the quality of their lives" (Mills et al., 1992).

Marriage and family relationships involve primary groups of intimate individuals. In contrast, we more easily tire of impersonal, secondary group relationships with those with whom we interact during the business day (e.g., the person who serves you a burger at McDonald's) and look forward to more personal interaction with primary group members at the end of the day. Although a marriage relationship may no longer be considered essential for well-being (Allen & Baber, 1992), marriage will continue as the dominant lifestyle.

In spite of the goal of having a happy durable marriage, fewer people will expect that marriage will result in a lifetime of happiness. Glenn (1993) observed that only about a third (35.7%) of the first marriages entered into the mid-1970s were successful a decade later. In addition, the ideal of marital permanence will decline (Glenn, 1991). Serial monogamy will become more common. Because of increased life expectancy and a high divorce rate, more people will experience a series of bonded relationships rather than one till-death-do-us-part relationship.

Traditional definitions of what is considered a family will continue to change and the issue of family diversity will assume even greater importance in the decade ahead. As noted earlier, more than 90 percent of citizens in the United States live outside the definition of the "traditional" family. Whether in single-parent or extended families, intergenerational families, blended, adopted, or foster families, same-sex or dual-earner families, individuals today are experiencing a wide array of families. Traditional homogamous matings will more often be accompanied by interracial interaction, dating, and marriage. Although interracial marriages are rare (less than one percent of marriages),

Lifetime monogamy is becoming the rare exception.

KEN DYCHTWALD

Rather than traditional marriage vows such as "as long as we both shall live," more honest vows would more often be "as long as we both shall love" or "as long as no one better comes along."

NORVAL GLENN

What the coming multicultural, polyethnic, pluralistic—unarguably diverse—America will be no one knows for certain. There are no models anywhere for what is happening here.

ITABARI NJERI

they have tripled since 1970, and an increasing number of individuals are socializing across racial and ethnic lines. Over half of all college freshmen in the United States said that they had socialized "frequently" with someone from a different racial or ethnic group in the past year (American Council on Education and University of California, 1992).

Researchers of marriage and the family will less often focus on the traditional family but become more open to studying the diversity of intimate lifestyles.

> Using this approach, no family form is privileged as normal or given priority. It is just as possible to explore the committed relationship between a lesbian couple with a child conceived through artificial insemination, or a cohabiting couple in which one partner has joint custody of a child by a previous relationship, as it is to research a married couple and their two children (Allen & Baber, 1992, 380).

❧ CHOICES ❧

---

*A*s you begin your course of study in marriage and family, you may want to consider the following three basic choices: whether you will read this text from an academic, personal, or career view; whether you will make your relationship choices deliberately or by default; and whether you will be tolerant of the choices of others. We now examine each of these.

Marriage and Family: An Academic, Personal, or Career Search?

Until your final grade for this course is posted, you will be involved in the systematic study of marriage and the family. One way to regard this course and the content of this text is as an academic exercise in which you come to class, take notes, skim the book, take tests, and go to the next course without ever becoming involved with the content. This is a legitimate choice. People take marriage and family courses for a variety of reasons and may do so to complete a social science requirement, to fill a transcript, or out of intellectual curiosity.

An alternative reason for studying marriage and the family is to explore the intimate relationship between you and your lover, spouse, parents, or children with the goal of making better decisions in your own life about marriage and family issues. While the outcome of taking a course in marriage and the family has not been adequately researched (Sollie & Kaetz, 1992), one student said:

> A lot of people I know, including my parents and brother, are divorced or running around on their partners. I want to know all I can about why people do these things so I can help avoid similar things happening to me. My partner and I are taking this course together in hopes that we can beat the odds.

You may choose to regard the study of marriage and the family as an

---

CHOICES

---

academic or personal search, or as both. Some people have mixed feelings:

> Somehow I feel that some things should remain a mystery and maybe marriage, love, and sex are things you shouldn't "study"—it might take the spontaneity out of them if you do. On the other hand, I think of marriage the same way I do a garden. Some things make it flourish, and some things make it wither. Knowing what those things are could make the differences in being happily married and being divorced three times.

You may also study marriage and the family in preparation for a career as a marriage and family therapist and/or a family life educator. As the latter, your goal may be to "strengthen and enrich individuals and family well-being" by exposing your students to such topic areas as human development, interpersonal relationships, sexuality, and parenthood (Thomas & Arcus, 1992, 5). A career that focuses on these aspects of life can be richly rewarding.

Choosing Carefully or Choosing by Default?

Some of us believe we can avoid making decisions about marriage and the family. We cannot, because not to decide is to decide by default. Some examples follow:

- If we don't make a decision to pursue a relationship with a particular person, then we have made a decision (by default) to let that person drift out of our lives.
- If we don't decide to do the things that are necessary to keep or improve the relationships we have, then we have made a decision to let them slowly disintegrate.
- If we don't make a decision to be faithful to our dating partner or spouse, then we have made a decision to be open to situations and relationships in which we are likely to be unfaithful.
- If we don't make a decision to avoid having intercourse with a new partner early in the relationship, then we have made a decision to let intercourse occur.
- If we are sexually active and don't make a decision to use birth control or a condom, we have made a decision for pregnancy or an STD.
- If we don't make a decision to break up with our dating partner or spouse, then we have made a decision to continue the relationship with him or her.

Throughout the text, we consider various choices with which we are confronted in the area of marriage and the family. It will be helpful for us to keep in mind that we cannot avoid making choices—that not to make a choice is to make one.

Tolerance or Condemnation for the Choices of Others?

Regardless of the choices we make about our own behavior and lifestyles, we must also make a choice about the rights of others to make choices that are different from ours. Most people are relatively tolerant of the choices others make. According to one woman:

> One of my closest friends has started living with her partner. While I wouldn't want to do this myself, I feel it is okay for her to do what she wants.

Some people find it more difficult to be tolerant about homosexuality. The same woman remarked of another friend:

> I couldn't believe she was gay when she told me. I can't handle her being gay and told her so. My tolerance stops when my friends want to be or do something that is unnatural. I guess I'd feel the same way if my boyfriend said he wanted to tie me up to have sex.

While you may not choose or agree with any number of specific behaviors and lifestyles, you might consider choosing to be tolerant of others who choose these behaviors or lifestyles. Such a perspective of tolerance recognizes that "there is, in sum, no one right way to be" (Tavris, 1992, 333).

❧ Summary

Choices in relationships are among the most important you will ever make. Deciding whether to engage in safer sexual behavior, whether to marry, whether to have children, whether to have one or two earners in one marriage, and whether to be monogamous are significant life and relationship choices. This text examines the nature and consequences of these and other choices relating to marriage and the family.

Although we tend to think of choosing as an act, if you decide not to choose, you have already made a decision by default. For example, if you do not make a conscious deliberate choice to engage in safer sexual behavior, you have made a decision by default to leave yourself open to engaging in high risk sexual behavior.

The choices that we make do not occur in a vacuum. Rather, they are influenced by the choices we see others make and the degree to which they approve of our choices (e.g., interracial dating/marriage). Societal events such as the recession, unemployment, and legislation also influence our choices. Finally, our choices are influenced by the families in which we were reared, by unconscious motivations, and by individual personality patterns.

Perspectives for viewing marriage and the family other than "choices" include structure-function, family life cycle, social-psychological, social class and race, exchange, role, crisis, and systems. The structure-function perspective emphasizes the benfits the institution of marriage and the family provide for the society. Not only does the family replenish society with new socialized members, it provides for the emotional needs of its members.

The definitions of what constitutes a family are changing. Increasingly, same-sex, single-parent, emotionally and economically interdependent individuals are being defined as family. Other changes include increases in bicultural diversity, hot monogamy, and two-earner relationships.

Marriage and family research should be viewed cautiously due to potential methodological problems such as the use of small unrepresentative convenience samples, lack of control groups, and vague terminology. A feminist perspective has also been noticeably absent from much of the marriage and family research.

Questions for Reflection

1. What are the most significant choices you have made in reference to your interpersonal relationships?
2. If you knew that studying marriage and the family as a personal search would contribute to the break up of your relationship with your partner, would you still choose to study the subject from this perspective?
3. Describe several decisions you have made by deciding not to decide.

References

Acker, M. and M. H. Davis. Intimacy, passion and commitment in adult romantic relationships: A test of the triangular theory of love. *Journal of Social and Personal Relationships,* 1992, *9,* 21–50.

Ahlburg, D. A. and C. J. De Vita. New realities of the American family. *Population Bulletin,* 1992, *47,* no. 2, 2–44.

Ahuvia, A. C. and M. B. Adelman. Formal intermediaries in the marriage market: A typology and review. *Journal of Marriage and the Family,* 1992, *54,* 452–463.

Allen, K. R. and K. M. Baber. Starting a revolution in family life education: A feminist vision. *Family Relations,* 1992, *41,* 378–384.

Allgeier, E. R. and M. W. Wiederman. Love and mate selection in the 1990s. *Free Inquiry,* 1991, *11,* 25–27.

American Council on Education and University of California. The American freshman: National norms for fall, 1992. Los Angeles, Calif. Los Angeles Higher Education Research Institute, 1992.

Axelson, L. Professor Emeritus Department of Child Development. Virginia Polytechnic Institute and State University, Blacksburg, Va. Personal communication. 1993. Used by permission.

Billy, J. O. G., K. Tanfer, W. R. Grady, and D. H. Klepinger. The sexual behavior of men in the United States. *Family Planning Perspectives;* 1993, *25,* 52–60.

Blair, S. L. Employment, family, and perceptions of marital quality among husbands and wives. *Journal of Family Issues,* 1993, *14,* 189–212.

Braver, S. L. and R. Curtis Bay. Assessing and compensating for self-selection bias (non-representativeness) of the family research sample. *Journal of Marriage and the Family,* 1992, *54,* 925–939.

Brehm, S. S. *Intimate relationships,* 2d ed. New York: McGraw-Hill, Inc., 1992.

Brown, D. E. and D. Hotra. Are prescriptively monogamous societies effectively monogamous? In Laura Betzig, Monique B. Mulder, and Paul Turke, eds., *Human Reproductive Behavior: A Darwinian Perspective.* Cambridge, Mass.: Cambridge University Press, 1988, 153–160.

Brubaker, T. H. Families in later life: A burgeoning research area. *Contemporary Families,* Alan Booth, ed. Minneapolis, Minn.: National Council on Family Relations, 1991, 226–226.

Burr, W. R. and C. Christensen. Undesirable side effects of enhancing self-esteem. *Family Relations,* 1992, *41,* 460–464.

Callan, Victor J. and Judith Murray. The role of therapists in helping couples cope with stillbirth and newborn death. *Family Relations,* 1989, *38,* 248–253.

Carnelley, K. B. and R. Janoff-Bulman. Optimism about love relationships: General vs. specific lessons from one's personal experiences. *Journal of Social and Personal Relationships,* 1992, *9,* 5–20.

Catania, J. A., T. J. Coates, R. Stall, H. Turner, J. Peterson, N. Hearst, M. M. Dolcini, E. Hudes, J. Gagnon, J. Wiley, and R. Groves. Prevalence of AIDS-related risk factors and condom use in the United States. *Science,* 1992, *258,* 1101–1106.

Coontz, S. *The way we never were: American families and the nostalgia trap.* New York: Basic Books, 1992.

Coughlin, E. K. Sociologists examine the complexities of racial and ethnic identity in America. *The Chronicle of Higher Education,* March 24, 1993, A7-A8

Cox, E. Strengthening our values. *CalFam,* Fall 1992, 1–19.

Crook, J. H. and S. J. Crook. Tibetan polyandry: Problems of adaptation and fitness. In Laura Betzig, Monique B. Mulder, and Paul Turke, eds., *Human Reproductive Behavior: A Darwinian Perspective.* Cambridge, Mass.: Cambridge University Press, 1988, 97–114.

Cutross, T. Hot monogamy. *Redbook,* February 1992, 62–67.

Deimling, G. T. and V. L. Smerglia. Involvement of elders in care-related decisions: A black/white comparison. *Family Relations,* 1992, *41,* 86–90.

Dychtwald, Ken *Age wave*. New York: Bantam Books, 1990.

Edwards, J. N. New conceptions: Biosocial innovations and the family. *Journal of Marriage and the Family*, 1991, *53,* 349–360.

Eichler, M. The relationship between sexist, nonsexist, woman-centered, and feminist research in the social sciences. In Greta Hofmann Nemiroff, ed., *Women and men: Interdisciplinary readings on gender*. Markham, Ontario: Fitzhenry & Whiteside, 1987, 21–53.

Embry, J. L. *Mormon polygamous families*. Salt Lake City: University of Utah Press, 1987.

Emery, Robert E. and Michele Tuer. Parenting and the marital relationship. *Parenting: An Ecological Perspective*. Edited by Tom Luster and Lynn Okagaki. Hillsdale, New Jersey: Lawrence Erlbaum Associates, Publishers, 1993, 121–148.

Evans-Pritchard, E. E. *Kinship and marriage among the Nuer*. London: Oxford University Press, 1951.

Fine, M. A. Families in the United States: Their current status and future prospects. *Family Relations*, 1992, *41,* 430–435.

Gage-Brandon, Anastasia J. The polygyny-divorce relationship: A case study of Nigeria. *Journal of Marriage and the Family*, 1992, *54,* 285–292.

Glenn, N. D. The news is bad, but not quite as bad as first reported: A correction. *Journal of Marriage and the Family*, 1993, 55, 242–243.

Glenn, N. D. The recent trend in marital success in the United States. *Journal of Marriage and the Family*, 1991, *53,* 261–270.

Goldscheider, F. K. and L. J. Waite. *New families, no families?* Berkeley, Calif.: University of California Press, 1991.

Gottlieb, N. Challenges and strengths. *Affilia: Journal of Women and Social Work*, 1992, *7,* 5–6.

Gross, E. R. Are families deteriorating or changing? *Affilia: Journal of Women and Social Work,* 1992, *7,* 7–22.

Hamon, R. R. & J. Elliott. Parents as resources when adult children divorce. Paper, 54th annual conference, National Council on Family Relations, Orlando, 1992. Used by permission.

Harding, S. Introduction: Is there a feminist method? In Sandra Harding, ed., *Feminism and methodology: Social science issues*. Bloomington, Ind.: Indiana University Press, 1987, 1–12.

Heiss, J. Women's values regarding marriage and the family. *Black Families,* 2d ed. Harriette Pipes McAdoo, ed. 1988, 201–214.

Hummer, R. A. Racial Differentials in infant mortality in the U.S.: An examination of social and health determinants. *Social Forces,* in press.

John, Robert. The Native American family. *Ethnic families in America: Patterns and variations,* C. H. Mindel, R. W. Habenstein, and R. Wright, Jr., eds. New York: Elsevier, 1988, 325–363.

Jurich, J. A., R. A. Adams, and J. E. Schulenberg. Factors related to behavior change in response to AIDS. *Family Relations*, 1992, *41,* 97–103.

Kaplan, L. and C. B. Hennon. Remarriage education: The personal reflections program. *Family Relations*, 1992, *41,* 127–134.

King, Charles E. and A. Christensen. The Relationship Events Scale: A Guttman scaling of progress in courtship. *Journal of Marriage and the Family*, August 1983, 671–687.

Kohn, A. *False prophets*. New York: Basil Blackwell, 1987.

Levin I. and J. Trost. Understanding the concept of family. *Family Relations*, 1992, *41,* 348–351.

Lye, D. N. and T. J. Biblarz. The effects of attitudes toward family life and gender roles on marital satisfaction. *Journal of Family Issues*, 1993, *14,* 157–188.

McHugh, M. C., Randi Daimon Koeske, and I. Hanson. Issues to consider in conducting nonsexist psychological research. *American Psychologist*, 1986, *41,* 879–890.

MacDermid, S. M., J. A. Jurich, J. A. Myers-Walls, and A. Pelo. Feminist teaching: Effective education. *Family Relations*, 1992, *41,* 31–38.

Mancini, J. A. and R. Blieszner. Aging parents and adult children. *Contemporary Families,* Alan Booth, ed. Minneapolis, Minn.: National Council on Family Relations, 1991, 249–264.

Mederer, H. J. and L. Weinstein. Choices and constraints in a two-person career. *Journal of Family Issues*, 1992, *13,* 334–350.

Mills, R. J., H. G. Grasmick, C. S. Morgan, and D. Wenk. The effects of gender, family satisfaction, and economic strain on psychological well-being. *Family Relations,* 1992, *41,* 440–445.

Money, J. and H. Musaph, eds. *Handbook of Sexology.* North Holland: Excerpta Medica, 1977, 519–540.

Murdock, G. P. *Ethnographic atlas.* Pittsburgh: University of Pittsburgh Press, 1967.

Myers, D. G. How to be happy! *Psychology Today,* July/August 1992, *25,* 38–45.

National Center for Health Statistics. Annual summary of births, marriages, divorces, and deaths: United States, 1991. Monthly vital statistics report; vol. 40, no. 13. Hyattsville, Md.: Public Health Service, 1992.

National Center for Health Statistics. Births, marriages, divorces, and deaths for August 1992. Monthly vital statistics report; vol. 41, no. 8. Hyattsville, Md.: Public Health Service, 1993.

National Center for Health Statistics. Advance report of final mortality, 1990. Monthly vital statistics report; vol. 41, no. 7, supp. Hyattsville, Md.: Public Health Service, 1993b.

National Gay and Lesbian Task Force Policy Institute. Domestic partner recognitions: Families project. 1734 Fourteenth Street NW, Washington, D.C. 20009-4309. January, 1992.

Newsweek. For gays, wedding bells may soon ring. May 17, 1992, p. 62.

Njeri, Itabari. The American melting pot has lent itself to diversity. *Austin American Statesman,* February 1991, D1, D4.

Pollis, C. A. An assessment of the impacts of feminism on sexual science. *The Journal of Sex Research,* 1988, *25,* 85–105.

Popenoe, D. Point of view: Scholars should worry about the disintegration of the American family. *The Chronicle of Higher Education,* 1993, April 14, p. A48.

Scanzoni, J. and W. Marsiglio. New action theory and contemporary families. *Journal of Family Issues,* 1993, *14,* 105–132.

Schacht, C. Fraud in science: An autobiographical case analysis. Paper, Eighteenth Annual Sociological Research Symposium, February 23, 1990. Greenville, N.C.

Schrof, J. M. Wedding bands made of steel. *U.S. News and World Report,* April 6, 1992, 62–63.

Smart, L. S. The marital helping relationship following pregnancy loss and infant death. *Journal of Family Issues,* 1992, *13,* 81–98.

Smith, L. S. Human sexuality from a cultural perspective. In C. I. Foegel and D. Lauver, eds. *Sexual Health Promotion,* Philadelphia: W. B. Saunders. 1990, 87–96.

Smith, R. M., M. A. Goslen, A. J. Byrd, and L. Reece. Self-other orientation and sex-role orientation of men and women who remarry. *Journal of Divorce and Remarriage,* 1991, *14,* 3–32.

Smith, S. and B. Ingoldsby. Multicultural family studies: Educating students for diversity. *Family Relations,* 1992, *41,* 25–30.

Smith, T. W. Adult sexual behavior in 1989: Number of partners, frequency of intercourse, and risk of AIDS. *Family Planning Perspectives,* 1991, *23,* 102–107.

Sollie, D. L. and J. F. Kaetz. Teaching university-level family studies courses: Techniques and outcomes. *Family Relations,* 1992, *41,* 18–24.

South, S. J. and K. M. Lloyd. Marriage opportunities and family formation: Further implications of imbalanced sex ratios. *Journal of Marriage and the Family,* 1992, *54,* 440–451.

Sparrow, K. H. Factors in mate selection for single black professional women. *Free Inquiry in Creative Sociology,* 1991, *19,* 103–109.

Spezzano, C. What to do between birth and death: The art of growing up. *Psychology Today,* January/February 1992, *54-55,* 86–87.

Statistical Abstract of the United States: 1993. 113th ed. Washington, D.C.: U.S. Bureau of the Census, 1993.

Tamura, T. and A. Lau. Connectedness versus separateness: Applicability of family therapy to Japanese families. *Family Process,* 1992, *31,* 319–340.

Tanfer, K. and L. A. Cubbins. Coital frequency among single women: Normative constraints and situational opportunities. *The Journal of Sex Research,* 1992, *29,* 221–250.

Tavris, C. *The mismeasure of woman.* New York: Simon & Schuster, 1992.

Tepperman, L. and S. J. Wilson. *Next of kin: An international reader on changing families.* Englewood Cliffs, N.J.: Prentice-Hall, Inc., 1993.

Thomas, J. and M. Arcus. Family life education: An analysis of the concept. *Family Relations,* 1992, *41,* 3–8.

Thompson, A. P. Extramarital sex: A review of the research. *Journal of Sex Research,* 1983, *19,* 1–22.

Thompson, Linda. Feminist methodology for family studies. *Journal of Marriage and the Family,* 1992, *54,* 3–18.

Tiefer, L. 1988. A feminist perspective on sexology and sexuality. In M. McCanney Gergen, Ed., *Feminist Thought and the Structure of Knowledge.* New York: New York University Press, 1988, 16–26.

Toman, W. *Family constellation: Its effects on personality and social behavior* 1993 New York: Springer Publishing Company

Trost, J. Family from a dyadic perspective. *Journal of Family Issues* 1993, *14,* 92–104.

Wallerstein, Judith S. and Sandra Blakeslee. *Second chances: Men, women and children a decade after divorce.* New York: Tichnor and Fields, 1989.

Walters, L. H. and S. F. Chapman. Changes in legal views of parenthood: Implications for fathers in minority cultures. In F. W. Bozett and S. M. H. Hanson, eds., *Fatherhood and Families in Cultural Context.* New York: Springer Publishing Co., 1991, 83–113.

Ward, K. B. and L. Grant. The feminist critique and a decade of published research in sociology journals. *Sociological Quarterly,* 1985, *26,* 139–157.

Whitehead, B. D. A new familism? *Family Affairs,* 1992, *5,* 1–2.

Wisensale, S. K. Toward the 21st century: Family change and public policy. *Family Relations,* 1992, *41,* 417–422.

Yalom, I. D. *Love's executioner and other tales of psychotherapy.* New York: Basic Books, 1989.

Yee, B. W. K. Gender and family issues in minority groups. *Cultural Diversity and Families.* K. G. Arms, J. K. Davidson, Sr., and N. B. Moore, eds. Dubuque, Iowa: Brown and Benchmark, 1992, 5–10.

Zimmerman, S. L. Family trends: What implications for family policy? *Family Relations,* 1992, *41,* 423–429.

Contents

2
CHAPTER
Gender Roles

Is It True?

1. In the United States, women earn more than half of all bachelor's and master's degrees.

2. Heterosexual men tend to value women who are youthful and physically attractive, while heterosexual women tend to value men who are economically stable.

3. Unlike the United States, sexist attitudes are virtually nonexistent in the former Soviet Union.

4. Women in high-status occupations (medicine) earn salaries similar to men.

5. Women tend to be less satisfied with their marriages than men.

1 = T; 2 = T; 3 = F; 4 = F; 5 = T

There isn't any clear consensus about how we are defining ourselves, the changing roles between men and women.

HILLARY CLINTON

"*I*t's Pat" is the title of a skit featured on *Saturday Night Live* during the 1992–1993 NBC television season. Pat, the central character, is an androgynous person, and Pat's friends are continually trying to determine Pat's gender. Pat frustrates them by providing ambiguous cues. For example, when speaking of her or his own birth, Pat notes that the doctor announced to her or his parents on delivery, "It's a . . . baby!" (rather than "it's a girl" or "it's a boy"). The skit emphasizes the important role gender plays in defining a person and the traditional scripts projected on people whose gender is known. If Pat were a woman, her friends would be more likely to expect her to date men, want to marry, and to have children. Alternatively, if Pat were a man, his friends would be more likely to expect him to date women, be somewhat reluctant to marry, and be less interested in children.

In this chapter we are concerned with the development of gender roles and the consequences of gender role expectations for the relationship choices of women and men. We end the chapter with some specific gender choices with which individuals are confronted. First, we define some terms related to the study of gender.

ॐ Terminology

Home economists, sociologists, social workers, and other family life specialists often have different definitions and connotations for the terms *sex, gender, gender identity, gender role,* and *gender role ideology.* We use these terms in the following ways.

Sex refers to the biological distinction of being female or male. The primary sex characteristics that differentiate women and men include external genitalia (vulva and penis), gonads (ovaries and testes), sex chromosomes (XX and XY), and hormones (estrogen, progesterone and testosterone). Secondary sex characteristics include the larger breasts of women and the deeper voice and presence of a beard in men.

I was never so bethumpe'd with words.

SHAKESPEARE

CONSIDERATION

Even though we commonly think of biological sex as consisting of two dichotomous categories (female and male), current views suggest that biological sex exists on a continuum. This view is supported by the existence of individuals

---

with mixed or ambiguous genitals (hermaphrodites and pseudohermaphrodites, or intersexed individuals). Evidence of overlap between the sexes is also found in the fact that some normal males produce fewer male hormones (androgens) than some females, just as some females produce fewer female hormones (estrogens) than some males (Morrow, 1991).

Gender refers to the social and psychological characteristics associated with being female (e.g., being gentle and cooperative) and male (e.g., being forceful and competitive). In popular usage, gender (like the term *sex*) is dichotomized as an either/or concept (male or female). However, gender may also be viewed as existing along a continuum of femininity and masculinity (Freimuth & Hornstein, 1982).

Gender identity is the psychological state of viewing one's self as a girl or a boy, and later as a woman or a man. Such identity is largely learned and is a reflection of the society's conceptions of femininity and masculinity.

Transsexuals have the gender identity that is opposite of their biological sex. A transsexual person may have the self concept of a woman but have the biological makeup of a man (or vice versa).

Gender roles are the behaviors assigned to women and men in a society. For example, traditionally in American culture, the role of men is to be strong, aggressive, and decisive. They are also expected to take financial responsibility for their families (England, 1992). Traditionally, the role of women has been to be weak, passive, and indecisive. Women have also traditionally been expected to be the primary caregiver in marital and family relationships.

Gender identity is the private experience of gender role, and gender role is the public experience of gender identity.

JOHN MONEY
ANKE EHRHARDT

CONSIDERATION

The term *sex roles* is often confused with and used interchangeably with the term *gender roles*. However, while gender roles are socially defined and can be enacted by either sex, sex roles are defined by biological constraints and can be enacted by members of only one biological sex. Examples of true sex roles (as opposed to gender roles) include wet nurse, sperm donor, and childbearer (Schur, 1984).

Traditional gender role stereotypes are changing. Women, who have traditionally been expected to give top priority to domestic life, are now expected to be more ambitious in seeking a career outside the home. Men, who have traditionally been expected to be aggressive and task-oriented, are now expected to be more caring and nurturing. However, while 84 percent of 600 adult women said that the ideal man is caring and nurturing, only 52 percent of 601 men said that the ideal woman is ambitious (Rubenstein, 1990).

Gender roles also carry sexual expectations. The Self-Assessment on the Sexual Double Standard is designed to help you identify the gender role expectations you have in regard to the sexual behaviors of women and men.

Sexual Double Standard Scale

Rank each statement according to the following scale:

	Agree Strongly A	Agree Mildly B	Disagree Mildly C	Disagree Strongly D
1. It's worse for a woman to sleep around than it is for a man.	____	____	____	____
2. It's best for a guy to lose his virginity before he's out of his teens.	____	____	____	____
3. It's okay for a woman to have more than one sexual relationship at the same time.	____	____	____	____
4. It is just as important for a man to be a virgin when he marries as it is for a woman.	____	____	____	____
5. I approve of a 16-year-old girl having sex just as much as a 16-year-old boy having sex.	____	____	____	____
6. I kind of admire a girl who has had sex with a lot of guys.	____	____	____	____
7. I kind of feel sorry for a 21-year-old woman who is still a virgin.	____	____	____	____
8. A woman having casual sex is just as acceptable to me as a man having casual sex.	____	____	____	____
9. It's okay for a man to have sex with a woman with whom he is not in love.	____	____	____	____
10. I kind of admire a guy who has had sex with a lot of girls.	____	____	____	____
11. A woman who initiates sex is too aggressive.	____	____	____	____
12. It's okay for a man to have more than one sexual relationship at the same time.	____	____	____	____
13. I question the character of a woman who has had a lot of sexual partners.	____	____	____	____
14. I admire a man who is a virgin when he gets married.	____	____	____	____
15. A man should be more sexually experienced than his wife.	____	____	____	____
16. A girl who has sex on the first date is "easy."	____	____	____	____
17. I kind of feel sorry for a 21-year-old man who is still a virgin.	____	____	____	____
18. I question the character of a guy who has had a lot of sexual partners.	____	____	____	____
19. Women are naturally more monogamous (inclined to stick with one partner) than are men.	____	____	____	____
20. A man should be sexually experienced when he gets married.	____	____	____	____
21. A guy who has sex on the first date is "easy."	____	____	____	____
22. It's okay for a woman to have sex with a man she is not in love with.	____	____	____	____
23. A woman should be sexually experienced when she gets married.	____	____	____	____
24. It's best for a girl to lose her virginity before she's out of her teens.	____	____	____	____
25. I admire a woman who is a virgin when she gets married.	____	____	____	____
26. A man who initiates sex is too aggressive.	____	____	____	____

Sexual Double Standard Scale *continued*

SOURCE: Muehlenhard, Charlene L., and Debra M. Quackenbush, (1988, November). *Can the sexual double standard put women at risk for sexually transmitted disease? The role of the double standard in condom use among women.* Paper presented at the annual meeting of the Society for the Scientific Study of Sex, San Francisco. Used by permission.

SCORING   Convert A's to 0's, B's to 1's, C's to 2's, and D's to 3's. Compute the total = #4 + #5 + #8 + (3 − #1) + (3 − #15) + (3 − #19) + (#24 − #2) + (#3 − #12) + (#6 − #10) + (#7 − #17) + (#22 − #9) + (#26 − #11) + (#18 − #13) + (#14 − #25) + (#21 − #16) + (#23 − #20)

INTERPRETING YOUR SCORE   A score of 0 indicates identical sexual standards for women and men. Scores greater than 0 reflect more restrictive standards for women than for men; the highest possible score is 48. Scores less than 0 reflect more restrictive standards for men than for women; the lowest possible score is −30.

In a study of students at Texas A & M University, the men's average score was 13.15 (n = 255) and the women's average score was 11.99 (n = 461) (Muehlenhard & Quackenbush, 1988). Hence, both men and women have more restrictive standards for women than men. Women tend to believe that men adhere more to the sexual double standard than they actually do (Muehlenhard & McCoy, 1991).

Gender role ideology refers to what is regarded as the proper role relationships between women and men in any given society.

> All human societies consist of men and women who must interact with one another, usually on a daily basis, and who have developed customs embracing prescriptive beliefs about the manner in which men and women are to relate to one another (Williams & Best, 1990a, 87).

Traditional American gender role ideology has perpetuated and reflected male dominance and male bias in almost every sphere of life. Even our language reflects this male bias; for example, the words *man* and *mankind* have traditionally been used to refer to all humans. There has been a growing trend away from using male biased language. A recent version of *Random House Webster's College Dictionary* has adopted terms that reflect the growing trend away from male biased or sexist language (Hopkins, 1991). Examples include replacing chairman with chairperson and mankind with humankind.

What we are going through is generational and social and global, and a large part of it has to do with the role and responsibilities of women.

HILLARY CLINTON

CONSIDERATION

Whether gender roles are primarily a function of biological or social influences is a continuing controversy. In response to this "nature versus nurture" debate, most researchers acknowledge that biological and social factors interact to produce an individual's personality. According to Basow (1992):

> It seems likely that some biological predisposition, possibly due to prenatal hormones, interacts with the environment to determine whether the ability itself will be actualized. The environment can either reinforce or discourage such actualization, depending on the behavior's gender-appropriateness in that society (p. 52).

(continued)

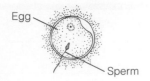

FIGURE 2.1

FERTILIZATION

Fertilization occurs when a sperm penetrates an egg (normally occurs in a Fallopian tube).

> In essence, although most children are born either female or male, they learn culturally defined feminine or masculine characteristics. In the following sections, we will review the biological beginnings of women and men and examine the ways in which the sexes are socialized.

ℬ Biological Beginnings

Although all human life begins with a *zygote*—a fertilized egg (see Figure 2.1)—all zygotes are not alike. They carry different *chromosomes* that result in women and men being housed in different bodies.

Chromosomes

Women and men have different genetic makeups. Every normal human *ovum* (egg) contains 22 "regular" chromosomes or *autosomes* (see Figure 2.2) and one sex chromosome. Every normal human sperm contains 22 "regular" chromosomes and one X *or* Y chromosome. The autosomes contain various genes that determine such characteristics as individual's eye color, hair color and body type. Because the sex chromosome in the ovum is *always* X (the female

FIGURE 2.2

CHROMOSOME PAIRS

Within each cell of a person's body are 23 chromosome pairs.

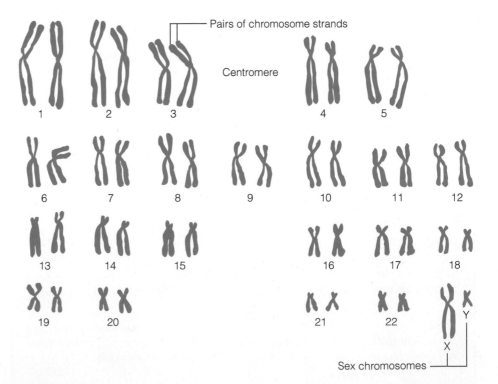

chromosome), the sex chromosome in the male sperm determines the biological sex of the child. If the sperm contains an X chromosome, the match with the female chromosome will be XX, and a female person will result. If the sperm contains a Y chromosome, the male chromosome, the match with the female chromosome will be XY, and a male person will result. Hence, the normal woman has 44 regular chromosomes (22 from each parent) plus an X chromosome from her mother and an X chromosome from her father. The normal man also has 44 regular chromosomes and an X chromosome from his mother but a Y chromosome from his father.

Hormones

Although the same hormones are in each sex, the release of various hormones into the bloodstream in varying amounts causes the development of a female or a male *embryo* (the human organism from conception until the end of the eighth week). Male and female embryos are indistinguishable from one another during the first several weeks of intrauterine life. In both, two primitive gonads and two paired duct systems form during the fifth or sixth week of development (see Figures 2.3 and 2.4). The male reproductive system develops from the Wolffian ducts, and the female reproductive system develops from the Müllerian ducts. However, both are present in the developing embryo at this stage.

FIGURE 2.3

EMBRYO BEFORE SIX WEEKS WITH UNDIFFERENTIATED SEXUAL STRUCTURES

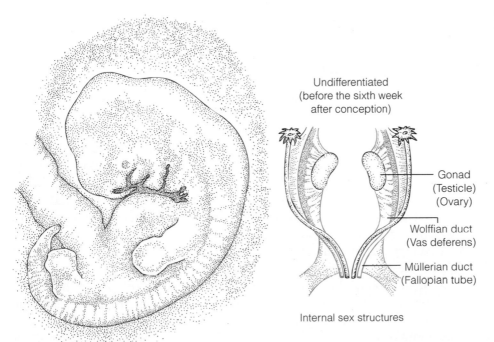

Undifferentiated
(before the sixth week
after conception)

Gonad
(Testicle)
(Ovary)

Wolffian duct
(Vas deferens)

Müllerian duct
(Fallopian tube)

Internal sex structures

Fetus at six weeks

FIGURE 2.4

EMBRYO AT 12 WEEKS, SHOWING DIFFERENTIATED SEXUAL STRUCTURES

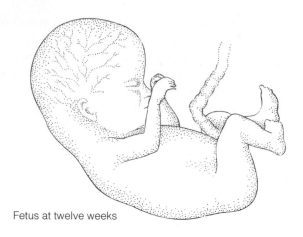

Fetus at twelve weeks

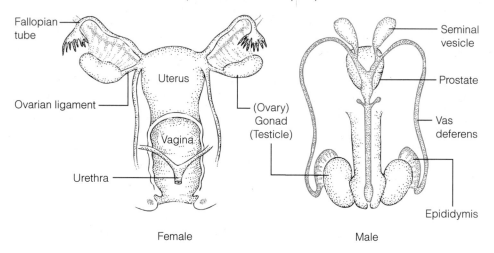

Differentiated internal sex structures
(12 weeks after conception)

Fallopian tube

Ovarian ligament

Uterus

Vagina

Urethra

(Ovary) Gonad (Testicle)

Female

Seminal vesicle

Prostate

Vas deferens

Epididymis

Male

Nature does sometimes overcome nurture.

C. H. SPURGEON

If the embryo is genetically a male (XY), a chemical substance controlled by the Y chromosome stimulates the primitive gonads to develop into testes. The testes, in turn, begin secreting the male hormone testosterone, which stimulates the development of the male reproductive and external sexual organs. The testes also secrete a Müllerian duct-inhibiting substance, which causes the potential female ducts to degenerate or become blind tubules. Thus, the development of male anatomical structures depends on the presence of male hormones at a critical stage of development.

The development of a female embryo requires that no (or very little) male hormone be present. Without the controlling substance from the Y chromosome, the primitive gonads will develop into ovaries and the Müllerian duct system into the Fallopian tubes, uterus, and vagina. Also without testosterone, the Wolffian duct system (epididymis, vas deferens, and ejaculatory duct) will degenerate or become blind tubules.

The impact of hormones becomes even more evident at puberty. The testes and ovaries release hormones that are necessary for the development of secondary sex characteristics. Higher levels of testosterone account for the growth of facial hair in men and pubic and underarm hair in both men and women. Breast development, on the other hand, results from increasing levels of estrogen.

In addition to chromosomal and hormonal differences, a number of physical characteristics differentiate women from men. These differences begin before birth; the male *fetus* (the human organism from the eighth week of pregnancy until birth) is more likely than the female fetus to be miscarried during the early months of pregnancy. Male infants (under 1 year), neonates (under 28 days), and postneonates (28 days-11 months) are also more likely to die than female infants, neonates, and postneonates (National Center for Health Statistics, 1993).

Money (1987) summarized the following eight biological and social variables that are related to one's sex and gender.

1. Chromosomal gender: XX in the female; XY in the male.
2. Gonadal gender: Ovaries in the female; testes in the male.
3. Prenatal hormonal gender: Estrogen and progesterone in the female; testosterone in the male before birth.
4. Internal accessory organs: Uterus and vagina in the female; prostate and seminal vesicles in the male.
5. External genital appearance: Clitoris and vaginal opening in the female; penis and scrotum in the male.
6. Pubertal hormonal gender: At puberty, estrogen and progesterone in the female; testosterone in the male.
7. Assigned gender: The announcement at birth, "It's a girl" or "It's a boy," based on the appearance of the external genitals; the gender the parents and the rest of society believe the child to be; the gender in which the child is reared.
8. Gender identity: The person's private, internal sense of maleness or femaleness—which is expressed in personality and behavior—and the integration of this sense with the rest of the personality and with the gender roles prescribed by society.

People do not always fit neatly into the category of "male" or "female." In some cases, the gender indicated by one of the eight variables may disagree with the gender indicated by the other variables. For example, a person may have the external genital appearance of one gender but the chromosomes or hormones of another gender. Persons with these mixed characteristics are referred to as hermaphrodites or pseudohermaphrodites. Specifically, a *her-*

> Leave a little to Nature: she understands her business better than we do.
>
> MONTAIGNE

maphrodite is an individual who has genitalia, gonads, and internal reproductive organs of both sexes. The term *pseudohermaphrodite* refers to a condition in which an individual is born with gonads matching the sex chromosomes but genitals resembling those of the other sex.

This little girl is learning that women must keep their bodies covered while in public.

ACROSS CULTURES

Male and female personalities are socially produced.

MARGARET MEAD

§ Gender Roles in Other Societies

While women and men are biologically different, it is important to emphasize that gender roles are largely a product of culture. What it means to be a woman or a man depends on the culture in which the individual is reared. Some examples of gender role patterns in different societies are described in the following paragraphs.

Gender Roles in New Guinea

When Margaret Mead visited three New Guinea tribes in the early 1930s, she observed that the Arapesh socialized both sexes to be feminine by Western standards. The Arapesh person was taught to be cooperative and responsive to the needs of others. In contrast, the Tchambuli where known for their dominant women and submissive men- just the opposite of traditional gender roles in our society.

Both the Arapesh and Tchambuli societies were unlike the Mundugumor, which socialized only dominant, ruthless, aggressive personalities. The Mundugumor tribesman or tribeswoman was typically incapable of experiencing or expressing emotion that was not grounded in hostility. While some researchers disagreed with Mead's observations (Fortune, 1939), her inescapable conclusion is that individuals learn gender roles from the society in which they live.

Gender Roles in the Middle East

In most cultures of the world, men dominate and control women. In India, male domination exists to an extreme. A Hindu code reads, "In childhood a woman must be subject to her father; in youth, to her husband; when her husband is dead, to her sons. A woman must never be free of subjugation" (quoted in Doyle & Paludi, 1991, 159).

Hindu and Muslim women are expected to cover their heads with veils, which is "but one feature of the mandatory code for a woman's conduct which requires that she behave modestly, restrained in speech, restricted in movement" (Mandelbaum, 1988). Within the household, men and women often sleep in separate rooms, and they sit apart at all social or religious occasions. In the presence of others, a young wife must not speak to her husband or stare at him. At meals, a woman eats only after the men have been served. A wife walking with her husband is expected to follow a few steps behind him.

Gender Roles in Sweden

The Swedish government has been making efforts toward establishing equality of the sexes since before American women won the right to vote (Scriven, 1984). The government has instituted a family policy that provides benefits to either the mother or the father who stays home with children. By encouraging fathers to participate more in child rearing, the government aims to provide more opportunities for women to pursue other roles. Women hold about a quarter of the seats in the Swedish Parliament. However, few Swedish women are in high status positions in business; governmental efforts to reduce gender inequality are weak compared to the power of tradition.

Gender Roles in Japan

Based on a comparison of 728 Japanese and 608 American families, Japanese husbands were more likely (than American husbands) to want wives to be responsible for housework, child discipline, and financial management. Japanese wives were more likely (than American wives) to want husbands to be responsible for recreation planning, employment outside the home, and maintaining relationships with relatives. Indeed, Japanese, compared with Americans, have or prefer more traditional or sex-typed divisions of labor and are less prone to idealize sharing of family tasks and responsibilities (Engel & Kimmons, 1992).

ꙮ Theories of Gender Role Development

A number of theories attempt to explain why women and men exhibit different characteristics and behaviors. The four main theories about how female and male roles develop include sociobiological, identification, social learning, and cognitive-developmental.

Sociobiological Theory

Sociobiological explanations of gender roles emphasize that the biological differences between males and females account for differences in male and female gender roles. Sociobiologists do not view gender role behaviors as acquired, but rather as innate. Consider the following differences between patterns of female and male sexual behavior.

- In a national sample of adult sexual behavior in the United States, men reported an average of 12 sexual partners; women reported an average of three sexual partners since age 18 (Smith, 1991).
- Men are more likely to engage in casual sex—defined as sex that does not involve an emotional relationship component. As evidence, 232 women and

Nature is no spendthrift, but takes the shortest way to her ends.

EMERSON

183 men enrolled in introductory-level general education courses were asked the following question:

> If the opportunity presented itself of having sexual intercourse with an anonymous member of the opposite sex who was as competent a lover as your partner but no more so, and who was as physically attractive as your partner but no more so, and there was no risk of pregnancy, discovery, or disease, and no chance of forming a more durable relationship, do you think you would do so?

Half of the men and 17 percent of the women in one study reported that they "certainly would" or "probably would" (Symons & Ellis, 1989, 136).

- Most acts of sexual aggression (e.g., rape and sexual harassment) are perpetrated by men.

Sociobiologists have attempted to explain these differences in the patterns of sexual behavior of women and men on the basis of the different hormonal makeups of women and men. For example, the hormone testosterone, which is usually found in higher levels in males, has been associated with male aggressive behavior. Before puberty, male and female testosterone levels are about the same. At maturity, these levels have increased by a factor of ten or twenty in males, but they only double in females (Udry, Talbert, & Morris, 1986). Progesterone, a hormone usually found in higher levels in women, has been associated with female nurturing behavior. When female rats are given large doses of testosterone they become aggressive; similarly, when male rats are given large doses of progesterone, they become nurturers (Arnold, 1980). The same hormonal reversal findings have been found in monkeys (Goy & McEwen, 1980).

In mate selection, heterosexual men tend to value women who are youthful and physically attractive, while heterosexual women tend to value men who are economically stable. The pattern of men seeking physically attractive young women and women seeking economically ambitious men was observed in 37 groups of women and men in 33 different societies (Buss, 1989). This pattern is also evident in courtship patterns in the United States (Davis, 1990). An evolutionary explanation for this pattern argues that men and women have different biological agendas in terms of reproducing and caring for offspring (Symons & Ellis, 1989; Symons, 1987).

The term *parental investment* refers to any investment by a parent that increases the offspring's chance of surviving and hence, increases reproductive success. Parental investments require time and energy. Women have a great deal of parental investment in their offspring (nine months gestation, taking care of dependent offspring) and tend to mate with men who have high status, economic resources, and a willingness "to invest their resources in a given female and her offspring" (Ellis & Symons, 1990, 533). Men on the other hand, focus on the importance of "health and youth" in their selection of a mate because young healthy women are more likely to produce healthy

It matters not if you were born in a duck pond, provided that you were born from a swan egg.

HANS CHRISTIAN ANDERSON

offspring (Ellis & Symons, 1990, 534). Men also "have an aversion to invest in relationships with females who are sexually promiscuous" since men want to ensure that the offspring is their own (Grammer, 1989, 149).

The sociobiological explanation for mate selection is extremely controversial. Critics argue that women may show concern for the earning capacity of a potential mate because women have been systematically denied access to similar economic resources, and selecting a mate with these resources is one of their remaining options. In addition, it is argued that both women and men, when selecting a mate, think more about their partners as companions than as future parents of their offspring. Finally, the sociobiological perspective fails to acknowledge the degree to which social and psychological factors influence our behavior.

CONSIDERATION

The view that at least some gender role behaviors are biologically based is deeply ingrained in our culture. For example, we tend to think of mothers as naturally equipped and inclined to perform the role of primary child caregiver. Chodorow (1978) argued that the role of child caregiver has been assigned to women, although there is no biological reason why fathers cannot be the primary caregiver or participate in child rearing activities.

Identification Theory

Freud was one of the first researchers to study gender role development. Freud suggested that children acquire the characteristics and behaviors of their same-sex parent through a process of identification. Boys identify with their fathers, girls identify with their mothers.

In *The Reproduction of Mothering,* Nancy Chodorow (1978) uses Freudian identification theory as a basis for her theory that gender role specialization occurs in the family because of the "asymmetrical organization of parenting" (p. 49).

Children often learn by identifying with their same sex parent.

> Women, as mothers, produce daughters with mothering capacities and the desire to mother. These capacities and needs are built into and grow out of the mother-daughter relationship itself. By contrast, women as mothers (and men as not-mothers) produce sons whose nurturant capacities and needs have been systematically curtailed and repressed (p. 7).

In other words, all activities associated with nurturing and childcare are identified as female activities because women are the primary caregivers of young children. This one-sidedness (or asymmetry) of nurturing by women increases the likelihood that females, because they identify with their mother, will see their own primary identities and roles as mothers.

Nature without learning is a blind thing . . .

PLUTARCH

Social Learning Theory

Derived from the school of behavioral psychology, social learning theory emphasizes the roles of reward and punishment in explaining how a child learns gender role behavior. For example, two young brothers enjoyed playing "lady." Each of them would put on a dress, wear high-heeled shoes, and carry a pocketbook. Their father came home early one day and angrily demanded that they "take those clothes off and never put them on again. Those things are for women," he said. The boys were punished for playing "lady" but rewarded with their father's approval for playing "cowboys," with plastic guns and "Bang! You're dead!" dialogue.

Reward and punishment alone are not sufficient to account for the way in which children learn gender roles. Direct instruction ("girls wear dresses," "a man walks on the outside when walking with a woman") is another way children learn—through social interaction with others. In addition, many of society's gender rules are learned through modeling. In modeling, the child observes another's behavior and imitates that behavior. Gender role models include parents, peers, siblings, and characters portrayed in the media.

The impact of modeling on the development of gender-role behavior is controversial. For example, a modeling perspective implies that children will tend to imitate the parent of the same gender, but children in all cultures are usually reared mainly by women. Yet this persistent female model does not seem to interfere with the male's development of the behavior that is considered appropriate for his gender. One explanation suggests that boys learn early that our society generally grants boys and men more status and privileges than girls and women; therefore boys devalue the feminine and emphasize the masculine aspects of themselves.

Cognitive-Developmental Theory

The cognitive-developmental theory of gender role development reflects a blend of biological and social learning views. According to this theory, the biological readiness, in terms of cognitive development, of the child influences how the child responds to gender cues in the environment (Kohlberg, 1966; Kohlberg, 1976).

For example, gender discrimination (the ability to identify social and psychological characteristics associated with being female or male) begins at about age 30 months. At that age, toddlers are able to assign a "boy's toy" to a boy and a "girl's toy" to a girl (Etaugh & Duits, 1990). However, at this age, children do not view gender as a permanent characteristic. Thus, while young children may define people who wear long hair as girls, and those who never wear dresses as boys, they also believe they can change their gender by altering their hair or changing clothes.

Not until age six or seven does the child view gender as permanent (Kohlberg, 1966; Kohlberg, 1969). In Kohlberg's view, this cognitive under-standing involves the development of a specific mental ability to grasp the idea that certain basic characteristics of people do not change. Once children learn the concept of gender permanence, they seek to become competent and proper members of their gender group. For example, a child standing on the edge of a school playground may observe one group of children jumping rope while another group is playing football. That child's gender identity as either a girl or a boy connects with the observed gender-typed behavior, and she or he joins one of the two groups. Once in the group, the child seeks to develop the behaviors that are socially defined as appropriate for her or his gender.

Agents of Socialization

Three of the four theories discussed in the previous section emphasize that gender roles are learned through interaction in the environment. The environment influences the development of gender roles through various agents of socialization including parents, peers, teachers, religion, and media. We now discuss each of these agents.

Parents

Parents are usually the first and most durable influence in a child's life. Although parents generally report that they treat their daughters and sons similarly, some research suggests they have different expectations of their daughters and sons, that they tend to give their children gender-typed toys, and that they assign them gender-typed chores. For example, researchers have found that:

What the mother sings to the cradle goes all the way down to the grave.

HENRY WARD BEECHER

- Regarding expectations, most middle-class parents expect their daughters to be more emotional than their sons, and expect their sons to be more aggressive and noisy than their daughters (Antill, 1987).
- Regarding toys, a study of the rooms of 120 girls and boys ages two and younger found that girls were provided with more dolls, children's furniture, fictional characters, manipulative toys, and the color pink; boys were provided with more sport equipment, toy vehicles, tools, and the colors blue, red, and white (Pomerleau, Bolduc, Malcuit, & Cossette, 1990).
- Regarding chores, of 2,238 fathers and mothers, 45 percent reported that they socialize their children to adopt traditional roles in family settings (Lackey, 1989).

Parents are an important source of gender role socialization.

CONSIDERATION

What are the effects of assigning gender-typed chores to girls and boys? First, girls learn how to do domestic chores better than boys, and boys learn how to do maintenance work better than girls. In addition, children learn to associate certain types of work with gender, which may influence their future educational

(continued)

and occupational choices. Children who are assigned gender-typed chores may also develop different personal qualities. For example, girls may develop nurturing behaviors because domestic chores (taking care of siblings) may be associated with caring for others. Boys may fail to develop nurturing behaviors because they are assigned chores that focus on caring for things, rather than people.

Peers

Same sex peer socialization is powerful.

While parents are usually the first socializing agents that influence a child's gender role development, peers become increasingly important during the school years.

The gender role messages from adolescent peers are primarily traditional.

For adolescent boys, such traits include being tough (through body build or athletic achievement), being cool (not showing emotions, not fearful of danger, staying reasonable under stress), being interested in girls and sex, being good at something, being physically attractive and having an absence of any trait or characteristic that is female or feminine (Harrison & Pennell, 1989, 32).

Female adolescents are under tremendous pressure to be physically attractive, popular, and achievement-oriented. The latter may be traditional (cheerleading) or nontraditional (sports or academics). Adolescent females are sometimes in great conflict in that high academic success may be viewed as being less than feminine. (Andrea in the weekly television drama *Beverly Hills 90210* must constantly struggle against being too bright and being accepted as being feminine).

CONSIDERATION

Peer disapproval for failure to conform to traditional gender stereotypes is reflected in the terms *sissy* and *tomboy*. These terms are used pejoratively to refer to children who exhibit behaviors that are stereotypically associated with the other gender.

Teachers and Educational Materials

Although parents have the earliest influence and adolescent peers the most significant influence during the teen years, teachers are another important socialization influence. Research suggests that teachers provide differential treatment to boys and girls (Sadker & Sadker, 1990):

. . . elementary and secondary teachers give far more active teaching attention to boys than girls. They talk to boys more, ask them more lower- and higher-order questions, listen to them more, counsel them more, give them more extended directions, and criticize and reward them more frequently.

This pattern of more active teacher attention directed at male students continues at the post-secondary level . . . In general, women are rarely called on; when female students do participate, their comments are more likely to be interrupted and less likely to be accepted or rewarded (p. 177).

The pattern of sex bias in teacher-student interaction that is prevalent at all levels (elementary, secondary, and post-secondary) of the educational process "may result in lower levels of achievement, career aspiration, and self-esteem for women. Although girls start out ahead of boys in most academic areas, as they progress through school their achievement as measured by standardized tests declines" (Sadker & Sadker, 1990, 180).

Gender role stereotypes are also conveyed through educational materials. In a study of 1,883 stories used in schools, Purcell and Stewart (1990) found that males were more often presented as clever, brave, adventurous, and income-producing, while females were more often presented as passive and as victims. Females were also more likely to be in need of rescue and were depicted in fewer occupational roles compared to males. Gender stereotyping also occurs in textbooks at the college level. Ferree and Hall (1990) found that women were underrepresented in sociology textbooks in terms of their participation in American society and their contributions to sociological theory and research.

Religion

Whether inadvertently or intentionally, some of the more traditional and conservative churches use the *Bible* to perpetuate the idea that the sexes are not to be regarded as equal. Basow (1992) claimed that "to the extent that a child has any religious instruction, he or she receives further training in the gender stereotypes" (p. 156). For example, the *Bible* emphasizes the patriarchal nature of the family:

> But I want you to understand that the head of every man is Christ, the head of every woman is her husband, and the head of Christ is God (I Corinthians 11:3).

> You shall be eager for your husband, and he shall be your master (Genesis 3:16).

It has also been argued that the *Bible* does not promote inequality of the sexes. For example, Elizabeth Achtemeier commented, " . . . the Scriptures are a clear proclamation of our freedom and equality in Jesus Christ and our sure guide to abundant and joyful life" (1991, 11). While the *Bible* identifies different roles for women and men, these roles are to be carried out with mutual love, respect, and honor encouraged for both. In regard to the role relationship between women and men:

> Wives be subject to your husband, as to the Lord. . . . Husbands, love your wives, even as Christ also loved the church. (Ephesians 5: 22–25). (See Colossians 3: 18–19)

In Islam, the most male-oriented of the modern religions, a woman is nothing but a vehicle for producing sons.

JOSEPH CAMPBELL

. . . that both male and female are created in the image of God (Genesis 1:27).

While the *Bible* has been interpreted in both sexist and nonsexist terms, male dominance is indisputable in the hierarchy of religious organizations, where power and status have been accorded mostly to men. Until recently, only men could be priests, ministers, and rabbis. Basow (1992) noted that the Catholic church does not have female clergy and men dominate the 19 top positions in the U.S. dioceses.

Male-bias is also reflected in terminology used to refer to God in Jewish, Christian, and Islamic religions. For example, although God (according to the Christian religion) is not a person and therefore has no gender, God is traditionally referred to as "He," "Father," "Lord," and "King."

Media

The media—film, magazines, television, newspapers, books, music, and art—both reflect and shape gender roles. Media images of women and men typically conform to traditional gender stereotypes and media portrayals depicting the exploitation, victimization, and sexual objectification of women are common. For example:

- In the 1991 fall television season, all dominant characters on Saturday morning children's programs were male, with females playing secondary roles, if any (Carter, 1991). This was a marketing decision by television executives based on the finding that boys will only watch shows that feature male characters, while girls will watch shows that feature either female or male characters.
- Most women on prime-time television are young, attractive, and sexy (Davis, 1990).

> The portrait developed here is of the young, attractive, and sexy female who is more ornamental in many shows than functional. For example, in one episode of *Miami Vice,* there were 14 speaking characters, all male. There were two female characters with more than three minutes of screen time, but neither spoke. Both were ornamental girlfriends of male episodic characters (p. 331).

CONSIDERATION

Media images of women may be changing, however. In a study of prime-time television programming, researchers (Atkin, Moorman, & Lin, 1991) found that the number of series featuring female leads increased through the 1980s. The portrayal of women working in professional or blue-color roles also increased during the 1980s. One explanation for the changes in television portrayals of women is that more women have entered management positions, such as television producer. For example, female producers were behind such assertive or competent female roles illustrated in *Murphy Brown, Designing Women,* and *Roseanne.*

- Top 40 radio stations typically have male disc jockeys, sportscasters, newscasters, and weathercasters (Lont, 1990).
- Music videos (MTV) typically portray women in sexually provocative ways, emphasizing female sexuality and male aggression.
- Christian family magazines emphasize the traditional role of mother for the woman. Little support is given for a woman's career (Sorenson & Sorenson, 1992).

In sum, all forms of mass media reflect gender stereotypes. Given that gender role stereotypes are perpetuated by family, peers, education, religion, and mass media, it is no wonder that such stereotypes have continued. Each agent of socialization reinforces gender roles that are learned from other agents of socialization, thereby creating a gender role system that is deeply embedded in our society.

> I am a tramp.
>
> MADONNA

🙰 Consequences of Traditional Gender Role Socialization

Given that women and men are exposed to different socialization experiences as they grow up in our society, there are different consequences for women and men. Next we examine both negative and positive consequences of traditional female and male socialization.

> While woman's intellect is confined, her morale crushed, her health ruined, her weaknesses encouraged, and her strength punished, she is told that her lot is cast in the paradise of women.
>
> HARRIET MARTINEAU, 1837

Consequences of Traditional Female Socialization

Table 2.1 summarizes some of the negative and positive consequences of being socialized as a woman in our society. Each consequence may or may not be true for a specific woman. For example, a particular woman may not live longer than a particular man, and a particular woman may have a very positive self-concept, as well as a happy marriage.

The potential negative consequences for being socialized as a woman include less income and education, a negative self-concept with women's value defined in terms of appearance and age, less marital satisfaction, and no "wife" at home.

Less Education/Income   Women earn fewer advanced degrees beyond the masters than men.

ADVANTAGES	DISADVANTAGES
Live longer?	Less education/income? (more dependent)
Closer mother-child bond?	Greater HIV infection risk?
Greater emotionality?	Negative self-concept?
Identity not tied to job?	Value defined by youthfulness and beauty?
Greater relationship focus?	Less marital satisfaction? No "wife" at home?

TABLE 2.1

Consequences of Traditional Female Role Socialization

TABLE 2.2
Effect of Education and Sex on Income

DEGREE	MEDIAN INCOME	
	WOMEN	MEN
High school diploma	$19,338	$28,230
Some college, no degree	22,833	33,758
Bachelor's degree or more	33,144	50,747

Source: Statistical Abstract of the United States: 1993, 113th ed. (Washington, D. C.: U.S. Bureau of the Census, 1993. Table 731).

I go up in arms against the silly old–fashioned prejudice that woman's place is in the home.

AGATHA CHRISTIE

NATIONAL DATA ❧ Women earn more than half of all bachelor's (53.1 percent) and masters's (52.4 percent) degrees. However, women earn only 36.8 percent of the Ph.D. degrees, and a lower percentage of M.D. and dental degrees (*Statistical Abstract of the United States: 1993,* Table 291).

The strongest explanation for why women earn fewer advanced degrees than men is that women are socialized to choose marriage and motherhood over long-term career preparation (Olson, Frieze, & Detlefsen, 1990). From an early age, women are exposed to images and models of femininity that stress the importance of domestic family life. When 821 undergraduate women were asked to identify their lifestyle preference, less than 1 percent selected being unmarried and working full time. In contrast, 53 percent selected "graduation, full-time work, marriage, children, stop working at least until youngest child is in school, then pursue a full-time job" as their preferred lifestyle sequence (Schroeder et al., 1993, 243). Only six percent of 535 undergraduate men selected this same pattern. This lack of career priority on the part of women influences the lack of priority given to education to prepare for a career.

Less education is associated with lower income. However, women still tend to earn about two thirds of what men earn, even when the level of educational achievement is identical (see Table 2.2).

One factor that contributes to both the educational and salary differentials of women and men is occupational segregation. Most workers are employed in gender-segregated occupations, that is, occupations in which workers are either primarily male or primarily female. Compared to male-dominated occupations, female-dominated occupations tend to require less education, have lower status, and pay lower salaries. However, this is not always true. The job of childcare attendent requires more education than the job of dog pound attendant. However, dog pound attendents, who are more likely to be male, earn more than childcare attendants, who are more likely to be female.

CONSIDERATION

Women who do not pursue higher levels of education or do not pursue higher paying occupations may find themselves economically dependent on their

The Feminization of Poverty

The term *feminization of poverty* refers to the disproportionate percentage of poverty experienced by women living alone or with their children. Compared to men, twice as many women (27 percent versus 12 percent) have incomes less than $5,000 (*Statistical Abstract of the United States: 1993*, Table 729). Of the more than 18 million families with children living below poverty level, there are six times as many single mothers as married mothers (*Statistical Abstract of the United States: 1993*, Table 745). The reason for such poverty being specific to women is that they tend to be employed fewer hours than men, and even when they work full time, they earn less money. Not only is discrimination in the labor force operating against women, women usually prioritize their families over their employment, which translates into less income.

One of the reasons women earn less income in full-time positions is that they tend to work in occupations that generate relatively low incomes. For example, when women move into certain occupations such as teaching and nursing, a tendency toward increased segregation of women develops in the marketplace (women in one occupation, men in another), and the salaries of women in these occupational roles increase at slower rates. The salaries of the teaching and nursing professions, which are predominantly female occupations, have not kept pace with infla-

tion, resulting in a concentration of segregated women in lower-paid occupations. Poverty is primarily a feminine issue became more women than men have inadequate incomes. One of the consequences of being a woman is to have an increased chance of feeling economic strain throughout life.

Divorce has also increased the proportion of women in poverty. According to Goldscheider and Waite (1991), "The rise in divorce has created a new class of poor. These 'displaced homemakers' have few marketable skills and have been forced to find some means of support after their marriages have ended" (p. 62). Even women who have worked outside the home but have held low-income jobs are vulnerable to poverty after they are detached from their husband's income. Unless women attend to the fact that they cannot depend on the income of a mate, they become economically vulnerable. Women in professional careers (and men in such careers) feel much less economic impact after divorce or widowhood.

Single black women are particularly vulnerable to being economically disadvantaged. When black head-of-household women are compared with white head-of-household women, the former have about 57 percent of the income of the latter (*Statistical Abstract of the United States: 1993*, Table 715).

partners or spouses. By choosing to pursue advanced education and well-paying occupations, women create more interpersonal choices and will not be pressured to stay in unsatisfying relationships because they are economically dependent.

With a more than 50 percent chance of divorce for marriages begun in the nineties, the likelihood of being a widow for seven or more years, and the almost certain loss of her parenting role midway through her life, a woman without education and employment skills is often left high and dry. As one widowed mother of four said, "The shock of realizing you have children to support and no skills to do it is a worse shock than learning that your husband is dead." In the words of a divorced, 40-year-old mother of three, "If young women think it can't happen to them, they are foolish."

Higher HIV Infection Risk   Since men are the primary sexual partners of women and since men are at greater risk for HIV infection and other STDs due to a higher number of sexual partners, women are more likely to contract HIV from men than men are from women. Women's greater vulnerability to HIV infection is due to the fact that semen, which may carry HIV, is deposited in the woman's body. Women also report that their partners are less likely to use a condom and women feel relatively powerless to influence them to do so (Catania et al., 1992).

> For the first time, women are starting to be able to think of themselves as entitled to pleasure and nut just responsible for pleasing others.
>
> DELMA HEYN

Negative Self-Concept   Some researchers have found that women are likely to feel more negatively about themselves than men do about themselves. In a national study of more than 3,000 students in grades 4 through 10, self-esteem levels of boys decreased only slightly after elementary school; for girls, the drop in self-esteem was more dramatic (American Association of University Women, 1991). For example, the percentage of girls who agreed with the statement "I'm happy the way I am" went from 60 percent during elementary school to only 37 percent during middle school and 29 percent during high school. A negative perception of females begins as early as the second grade where elementary school pupils regard girls in their classes as inferior to boys (Safir et al., 1992). These negative perceptions continue into college where undergraduate women report significantly higher self-dislike, sense of failure, and self-accusations than undergraduate men (Oliver & Toner, 1990). The "ideal person" according to university females at the University of Colorado in Denver is one who is more "masculine than feminine" (Grimmell & Stern, 1992).

Women in the United States live in a society that devalues them. "Women's natures, lives and experiences are not taken as seriously, are not valued as much as those of men" (Walker, Martin, & Thomson, 1988, 18). *Sexism* is defined as an attitude, action, or institutional structure that subordinates or discriminates against an individual or group because of his or her sex. Sexism against women reflects the tradition of male dominance and presumed male superiority in our society. Sexist attitudes exist not only in the United States, but in the former Soviet Union, China, India, Japan, and Latin America (Lindsey, 1990).

Not all research demonstrates that women have a more negative self-concept than men. Summarizing their research on the self-concepts of women and men in the United States, Williams and Best (1990a) noted "no evidence of an appreciable difference" (p. 153). They also found no consistency in the self-concepts of women and men in 14 different countries. "In some of the countries the men's perceived self was noticeably more favorable than the women's, whereas in others the reverse was found" (p. 152). In another study by Porter and Beuf (1991), there were no significant differences in the self-esteem ratings between women and men.

Women's Value Defined in Terms of Appearance and Youthfulness   The value of a woman is often defined by men in terms of her body and appearance. One hundred males rated various body types and showed a decided preference for women with large breasts and hourglass shapes (Furnham, Hester, & Weir, 1990). Men also tend to emphasize that physical appearance is an important factor in deciding who to date. In one study, 67 percent of 143 men in contrast to 44 percent of 50 women emphasized that physical appearance is an important factor in deciding who to date (Davis, 1990).

Rubin (1991) commented on society's preoccupation with youth and beauty:

> A woman who's 40 is already over the hill. Like a fine wine, he gets better with age, but she deteriorates, wilting like a flower left too long in the sun (p. 152).

Some women feel particularly burdened by the notion that they are valuable only insofar as they are young and pretty. In our youth-oriented society where it is good to be young and bad to be old, women are more victimized by this looks-value connection. In a study of 600 adult women, 97 percent said that they feel feminine when they are happy about their appearance. Those most happy with their physical appearance were between the ages of 18–24; women least happy with their physical appearance were between the ages of 35–44 (Rubenstein, 1990). Being trim is also regarded as important. A study of 195 female undergraduates revealed that women who were trim, had higher self-esteem than those who were heavier than the "normative ideal" (Gray, 1993, 108).

Less Marital Satisfaction   In general, wives are less satisfied in their marriages than husbands (Basow, 1992). A major contributing factor is that women experience role overload; they are expected to keep their husbands, children, parents, and employers happy, and to be a good homemaker (cook, clean, wash dishes/laundry). The result of coping with these unrealistic expectations internalized or imposed on women is, when compared to men, more frequent nervous breakdowns, greater psychological anxiety, increased self-blame for not living up to these expectations and poorer physical health (Bird & Fremont, 1991). Many women develop resentment toward their husbands.

> Dammit, it makes me furious, because when it gets down to the brass tacks of real life, what they (men) really want is a woman who can pay her share of the bills, then turn into some sweet little thing who looks up at them adoringly, cooks wonderful meals, takes care of the kids, and after all that, turns into a sexpot at midnight (Rubin, 1991, 147).

When we are taught that our worth and identity are to be found in loving and being loved, it is indeed devastating to have our attractiveness and womanliness questioned.

HARRIET G. LEARNER

Age is strictly a case of mind over matter—If you don't mind, it doesn't matter.

JACK BENNY

We can't seem to live with the men who want to sit at home with us, and the men we want to live with can't sit at home with us, and there's no peace to be found either way.

MABEL LUHAN

CONSIDERATION

To decrease their frustration, wives might reject the expectation that they be all things to all people, alert their partners to the need for help with housework and childcare, and choose to stop doing things that create more frustration than joy (e.g., sending Christmas cards to both sets of relatives).

Husbands tend to do less housework than wives unless prompted to do so.

No "Wife" at Home   As we will discuss in Chapter 11 on Work and Leisure in Relationships, both spouses may need a "wife" at home to take care of the house and children to free them to pursue their job and career. Since wives typically do more housework and childcare, they have no help ("wife") as do husbands. One exception is Sally Jessy Raphael whose husband (Karl Soderlund) has adopted the role of the "wife." Of their relationship Karl said, "If either of us is going to be rich, it'll probably be Sally. Therefore, I'm going to take jobs and give them up, and she'll have the career. . . ." (Rader, 1993, 5).

Successful professional career women are more likely to be single than their male counterparts. In her book, *The Third Sex: The New Professional Woman,* anthropologist Pat McBroom (1992) notes that 60 percent of top female executives live single lives versus five percent of top male executives.

We have been discussing the negative consequences of being socialized as a female. There are also advantages, which include the following.

Benefits of Traditional Female Socialization   Three primary benefits of being born female and being socialized as a woman include the potential to live longer, a stronger relationship focus, and a closer emotional bond with children.

NATIONAL DATA ❦ Life expectancy for women in 1995 is expected to be 79.5; for men, 72.6 (*Statistical Abstract of the United States: 1993, Table 115*).

Being embedded in a network of relationships may be related to longevity. Women are more involved in such relationships than men. Two primary sets are with their parents and same sex peers. This pattern occurs worldwide. Williams and Best (1990b) collected data from university students in 28 countries (including England, Australia, Nigeria, Japan, and Brazil) and observed that women were more likely to be associated with having certain relationship characteristics than men:

1. Succorance—soliciting sympathy, affection, or emotional support from others
2. Nurturance—engaging in behavior that extends material or emotional benefits to others
3. Affiliation—seeking and sustaining numerous personal relationships.

Other research supports the idea that women place more importance on relationships (Hammersla & Frease-McMahan, 1990), have more close friends (Jones, Bloys, & Wood, 1990), and are more cooperative than men (Garza & Borchert, 1990).

In contrast, men were viewed as being more dominant, autonomous, aggressive (Williams & Best, 1990b), and competitive (Garza & Borchert, 1990). These qualities are counter to developing close relationships with others.

Just looking at Gene made me want to give up my career, made me want to cook, made me want to start a garden, to have a family and settle down.

GILDA RADNER, ON HER RELATIONSHIP WITH GENE WILDER

CONSIDERATION

Close emotional relationships may provide enormous life satisfaction outcomes for both women and men. Personal interviews with 2,374 adults revealed that satisfaction with family life (rather than work life) is the most important determinant of overall life satisfaction (Carlson & Videka-Sherman, 1990). In addition, the result of such relationships on health and mortality is that they provide a sense of meaning and facilitate health promoting behaviors such as proper sleep, diet and exercise, and adherence to medical regimens (House, Landis, & Umberson, 1990).

Another advantage of being socialized as a woman is the potential to have a closer bond with children. In general, women tend to be more emotionally bonded with their children than men. Although the new cultural image of the father is one who engages emotionally with his children, most fathers continue to be content for their wives to take care of their children with the result that mothers, not fathers, become more bonded with their children. The mother-child bond is particularly strong in Black, Asian American, and Hispanic families (Mindel, Habenstein, & Wright, 1988).

CONSIDERATION

In an effort to eliminate the potential negative consequences of being socialized as a woman, parents might be alert to the societal bias against their daughters and attempt to minimize it. For example, parents might teach their daughters to view every occupation as an option for them, and to supplement marital and family roles with a meaningful job/career that will provide an independent source of income and identity. In addition, should a daughter not evidence an interest in getting married or in having children, the parents might consider providing complete support for her choices.

Consequences of Traditional Male Socialization

Male role socialization in our society is associated with its own set of consequences. The women's movement has given widespread visibility to the restrictions imposed upon women by the traditional female role. However, there is a growing recognition that the traditional male gender role is also restrictive. Sociologist Edwin Schur stated that:

> There is no denying that the gender system controls men too. Unquestion ably, men are limited and restricted through narrow definitions of "masculinity." . . . They too face negative sanctions when they violate gender prescriptions. There is little value in debating which sex suffers or loses more through this kind of control; it is apparent that both do (Schur, 1984, 12).

TABLE 2.3
Consequences of Traditional Male Role Socialization

ADVANTAGES	DISADVANTAGES
Higher occupational status?	Identity tied to work role?
More positive self-concept?	Masculinity tied to income?
Less job discrimination?	Limited emotional expression?
Higher income?	Shorter life?
Less marital stress?	Less time with children?

In the following sections we discuss some of the potential negative and positive consequences of being socialized as a male. These are summarized in Table 2.3.

I learned from my father how to work. I learned from him that work is life and life is work, and work is hard.

PHILIP ROTH

Identity Synonymous with Occupation   Ask men who they are, and many will tell you what they do. Society tends to equate a man's identity with his occupational role. Male socialization toward greater involvement in the labor force is evident in adolescence. Based on data from 1481 rural high school students, males were more likely to be employed, to begin work earlier, to receive higher pay, and to work longer hours than females (Clifford & Shoffner, 1992).

Work is the principal means by which men confirm their masculinity and success. Black men and Mexican American men, due primarily to racism and discrimination, are more likely to be unemployed than white men. Hence, they may suffer more emasculation because of the connection between identity and occupation.

Women feel that they are sex objects. Men feel that they are success objects (their value is in reference to how much money they make or what things they bring home).

MARVIN ALLEN

Our society not only expects men to have a job, but also equates masculinity with the income a man generates. In a study of 601 adult men, those who reported feeling "more masculine" than other men earned an average of $35,800. In contrast, men who felt "less masculine" than other men earned an average of $28,300 annually (Rubenstein, 1990).   .

CONSIDERATION

The identification men have with their work is changing. Some men are becoming less competitive and more family-oriented. Some corporations are aware that today, in contrast to the past, men are less willing to move because of family considerations and more interested in time off to be with their families than in making more money. The quality of family life is important for the psychological health of men. Based on data from 300 employed husbands, aged 25 to 40, a team of researchers concluded that "the quality of men's work roles and the quality of their family roles contribute equally to their psychological health" (Barnett et al., 1992, 366).

Expression of Emotions Is Limited   Some men feel caught between society's expectations that they be competitive, aggressive, independent, and unemotional and their own desire to be more cooperative, passive, dependent, and emotional. Not only are men less likely to cry than women, they are also less able to express their feelings of depression, anger, fear, and sadness. According to Derlega et. al. (1993):

> Men raised in North American culture (emphasis on white, Protestant, northern European background) are more likely to believe that task accomplishment is an important goal and that emotional control is one general strategy for facilitating that goal. Women, however, are more likely to believe that social-emotional closeness is an important goal and that emotional expression is one general strategy for facilitating that goal (p. 45).

Men also tend to be less tolerant of or interested in the emotional expression of others. One study found that male English teachers are also less tolerant of emotional writing than female English teachers (Barnes, 1990).

CONSIDERATION

Men who are more emotional, nurturing, and sensitive report positive benefits for their marriages. In a study of 452 married couples, the researchers concluded, "The factor which most strongly affects the marital quality experienced by both spouses appears to be the ability to give and receive support. Husbands with sensitive personalities experience higher quality marriages and produce higher quality marriages for their wives" (Vannoy & Philliber, 1992, 397).

Shorter Life   Men die about seven years earlier than women. Black men are the most vulnerable in that they die about 12 years earlier than white women (*Statistical Abstract of the United States: 1993*, Table 115). Although biological factors may play a role in greater longevity for women than men, traditional gender roles play a major role (Rodin & Ickovics, 1990; Strickland, 1988). For example, the traditional male role emphasizes achievement, competition, and suppression of feelings, all of which may produce stress. Not only is stress, itself, harmful to physical health, it also may lead to compensatory behaviors, such as smoking, alcohol and drug abuse, and dangerous risk-taking behavior. Phillips (1992) observed in her study of a random sample of 820 first-year students at a mid-sized southeastern university that the men (compared to the women) were more likely to ride motorcycles, drink and drive, carry a weapon, and use illegal drugs. Furthermore, the jobs of men tend to be more hazardous than women's jobs (Waldron, 1990). For example, men are more likely to be miners than women, and this occupation has the highest rate of mortality.

The degree to which males are socialized to be violent and aggressive is another factor in their shorter life expectancy. For example, in 1989, homicide was the leading cause of death among black males between the ages of 15 and

Men kinda have to choose between marriage and death. I guess they figure at least with marriage they get meals. Then they get married and find out we don't cook anymore.

RITA RUDNER

24. Luckenbill and Doyle (1989) suggested that the high rate of homocide among young, lower-income males is related to the culturally transmitted willingness to settle disputes, especially those perceived as a threat to their masculinity, by using physical force.

The poorer health and shorter life expectancy of minority men compared to white men may also be explained by the stress experienced by minority men that results from racism, prejudice, discrimination, and poverty. The frustration and anger that may result from the social and economic disadvantages of minority status may lead to hazardous compensatory behaviors, such as those described earlier.

In sum, the traditional male gender role is hazardous to men's physical health. However, as women have begun to experience many of the same stresses and behaviors as men, their susceptibility to stress-related diseases has increased (Rodin & Ickovics, 1990). For example, since the 1950s, male smoking has declined, while female smoking has increased, resulting in an increased incidence of lung cancer in women.

> I want to find someone with a strong sense of self, someone who's ready to be an equal partner.
>
> JOAN LUNDEN

> As women became more independent, they leave a lot of men struggling with confusion over how to define themselves.
>
> SUSAN FALUDI

Adapt to New Expectations from the Modern Woman   Men can no longer dictate the role relationships between men and women. Equality is emerging in relationships between women and men (Schroeder et al., 1993). Today's modern heterosexual woman (according to 600 adult women) expects her male partner to be caring and nurturing and open with his thoughts/feelings. He is also expected to be ambitious and to participate in domestic chores (Rubenstein, 1990). Husbands in dual earner marriages who do not share the workload of house and children are deemed "unfair" by their employed wives and marital satisfaction drops (Blair, 1993). In another study, women described the romantic partner they were looking for as "kind, considerate and honest with a keen sense of humor" (Goodwin, 1990, 501).

Benefits of Traditional Male Socialization   While men may have a limited identity independent of occupational success, have a limited range of emotional expression, die earlier, and have to cope with learning how to be sensitive without being called a wimp, men also have a number of benefits. As compared to women, men tend to have a more positive self-concept, have greater confidence in themselves, and enjoy higher incomes and occupational status than women. They also experience less job discrimination and sexual harassment than women.

We have been discussing the respective ways in which women and men are socialized in our society. The In Focus 2.2 insert summarizes 12 implications that traditional gender role socialization has for the life and relationship choices of women and men.

There is a growing recognition that traditional gender stereotypes are restrictive and oppressive to both women and men. The Women's Movement

---

 IN FOCUS

Twelve Ways Gender Role Socialization Affects Life and Relationship Choices of Women and Men

---

WOMEN

1. A woman who is not socialized to pursue advanced education (which often translates into less income) may feel pressure to stay in an unhappy relationship with someone on whom she is economically dependent.
2. Women who are socialized to play a passive role and not initiate relationships are limiting interactions that could develop into valued relationships.
3. Women who are socialized to accept that they are less valuable and important than men are less likely to seek or achieve egalitarian relationships with men.
4. Women who internalize society's standards of beauty and view their worth in terms of their age and appearance are likely to feel bad about themselves as they age. Their negative self-concept, more than their age or appearance, may interfere with their relationships.
5. Women who are socialized to accept that they are solely responsible for taking care of their parents, children, and husband are likely to experience role overload. Potentially, this could result in feelings of resentment in their relationships.
6. Women who are socialized to emphasize the importance of relationships in their lives will continue to seek relationships that are emotionally satisfying.

MEN

1. Men who are socialized to define themselves in terms of their occupational success and income and less in terms of positive individual qualities leave their self-esteem and masculinity vulnerable should they become unemployed or work in a low-status job.
2. Men who are socialized to restrict their experience and expression of emotions are denied the opportunity to discover the rewards of emotional interpersonal sharing.
3. Men who are socialized to believe it is not their role to participate in domestic activities (child-rearing, food preparation, housecleaning) will not develop competencies in these life skills. Domestic skills are often viewed as desirable qualities to potential partners.
4. Heterosexual men who focus on cultural definitions of female beauty overlook potential partners who might not fit the cultural beauty ideal, but who would nevertheless be a good life companion.
5. Men who are socialized to view women who initiate relationships in negative ways are restricted in their relationship opportunities.
6. Men who are socialized to be in control of relationship encounters may alienate their partners, who may desire equal influence in relationships.

---

and the Men's Movement have contributed to the development of new conceptions of gender roles. Yet, reconstructing gender can only be achieved through massive changes in society. Basow (1992) expressed support and optimism for the movement toward changing traditional conceptions of gender:

> Eliminating gender stereotypes and redefining gender in terms of equality does not mean simply liberating women, but liberating men and our society as well. What we have been talking about is allowing people to be more fully human and creating a society that will reflect that humanity. Surely that is a goal worth striving for (p. 359).

ℽ Beyond Gender Roles: Androgyny and Gender Role Transcendence

Imagine a society in which women and men each develop characteristics, lifestyles, and values that are independent of gender role stereotypes. Characteristics such as strength, independence, logical thinking, and aggressiveness are no longer associated with maleness, just as passivity, dependence, showing emotions, intuitiveness, and nurturing are no longer associated with femaleness. Both sexes are considered equal and women and men may pursue the same occupational, political, and domestic roles. Some gender scholars have suggested that persons in such a society would be neither feminine nor masculine, but would be described as androgynous, or a blend of feminine and masculine. Next, we discuss androgyny and the related concept of gender role transcendence.

Androgyny

I'm very much in touch with my feminine side.

LUKE PERRY

Androgyny refers to a blend of traits that are stereotypically associated with masculinity and femininity. Androgyny also implies flexibility of traits; for example, an androgynous individual may be emotional in one situation, logical in another, assertive in another, and so forth.

> Thus, each androgynous individual has the opportunity to develop his or her potential to its fullest, without the restriction that only gender-appropriate behaviors are allowed (Basow, 1992, 326).

While some studies have found that androgyny is associated with high self-esteem, social competence, flexibility, and fewer psychological problems, others have found androgyny to be associated with increased work stress, difficulty in directing behavior effectively, and less overall emotional adjustment (Harrison & Pennell, 1989).

Sandra Bem (1974) devised a classification system based on individuals' scores on a scale that measures nurturant-expressive and active-instrumental traits. According to Bem's classification system, individuals who score high on nurturant-expressive traits (such as passivity, compassion, and affection) and low on active-instrumental traits (such as assertiveness, self-reliance, and independence) are considered feminine sex-typed. Individuals who score high on active-instrumental traits and low on nurturant-expressive traits are considered masculine sex-typed. Individuals who score high on both active-instrumental and nurturant-expressive traits are considered androgynous and those who score low on both sets of traits are considered "undifferentiated." In a longitudinal study of androgyny across the life span, researchers found that both men and women tend to score higher on nurturant-expressive traits as they age (Hyde, Krajnik, & Skuldt–Niederberger, 1991).

Androgyny may be viewed as an alternative to traditional gender roles, but gender scholars have noted several problems concerning the concept of androgyny. One problem is that "androgyny has come to be seen as a combination of the traits of the two sexes rather than as a transcendence of gender categorization itself" (Unger, 1990, 112).

> The androgyny model continues to acknowledge and even depend on the conventional concepts of femininity and masculinity. Thus, in spite of its emancipatory promise, the model retains the classic dualism and, hence, the assumption of some real gender difference (Morawski, 1990, 154).

In other words, while androgyny represents a broadening of gender role norms, it still implies two differing sets of gender-related characteristics (i.e., masculine = active-instrumental; feminine = expressive-nurturant). One solution to this problem is to simply describe characteristics such as active-instrumental and expressive-nurturant without labeling these traits as masculine or feminine. Another solution is to go beyond the concept of androgyny and focus on gender role transcendence.

Gender Role Transcendence

As noted earlier, we tend to impose a gender-based classification system on the world. Thus, we associate many aspects of our world, including colors, foods, social/occupational roles, and personality traits, with either masculinity or femininity. The concept of *gender role transcendence* involves abandoning gender schema (i.e., becoming "gender aschematic," Bem, 1983), so that personality traits, social/occupational roles, and other aspects of our life become divorced from gender categories.

One way to transcend gender roles (or become gender aschematic) is to be reared that way, since gender schema develops at an early age. For example, parents can foster non-sex-typed functioning in their children by encouraging emotional expression and independence in both boys and girls. Parents can also deemphasize the importance of gender in children's lives with respect to choosing clothes, toys, colors, and activities.

Even though many individuals may move toward gender role transcendence as they reach and pass middle age, few if any individuals completely reach this stage. As long as gender stereotypes and gender inequalities are ingrained in our social and cultural ideologies and institutions, gender role transcendence will remain unrealized.

❦ Trends

Relationships are becoming more egalitarian and the trend toward "egalitarianism in education and employment is irreversible" (Brehm, 1992, 403). The result is changed relationships between women and men and more opportunities for women.

Inequality distorts the character and vision of both the oppressors and the oppressed.

SUSAN BASOW

The men's movement (Robert Bly and Marvin Allen are important influences) is becoming more visible, and men's issues are becoming more prominent. One such issue is that men sometimes feel their perceptions of relationships are not given equal weight. Stein (1992) noted in his article, "Pigs 'R Us," a trend toward greater acrimony between the sexes, as men begin to lash back in kind.

> The attitude is already increasingly apparent between the lines in men's talk, expressed in casual asides and new twists on old annoyances. The complaints involve wives or girlfriends who automatically assume the right to the high moral ground in any argument. Or reflexively give less weight to their mates' emotional insights than their own (p. 27).

Men are going to have to try to develop a bimodal personality—tough on the outside and soft on the inside.

DAVID GILMORE

The media is continuing to reflect the changing role of women. Three researchers (Buckland, Garrison, & Witt, 1992) analyzed the comic strip "Blondie" from 1942 until 1991 and observed dramatic differences in the way she was portrayed. In the forties, she was a domestic lady in a frilly dress and an apron. By the nineties she was a working woman in a tailored suit fixing quick meals.

❧ CHOICES ❧

---

*T*he result of our society becoming less rigid in its gender role expectations for women and men is a new array of choices in gender role behavior. Such choices are becoming increasingly apparent in initiating relationships, seeking egalitarian relationships, and pursuing nontraditional occupational roles.

New Relationships: Women Asking Men?

Traditionally, men have been socialized to be assertive and women to be passive in initiating new relationships. In a study of 418 undergraduate students, 60 percent of the women versus 33 percent of the men agreed that on the first few dates, before a couple has really gotten to know each other, the man should be the one to ask the woman out (Asmussen & Shehan, 1992). However, some women decide that traditional female passivity in regard to initiating relationships is a disadvantage and choose to become more assertive. One woman said:

> I was taught never to call men or to initiate anything with men. "A real lady," my mom said, "waits till the man makes his move." But I've learned that some men are too shy to risk speaking and if the woman doesn't, nothing happens. I also know that some of my female friends think nothing of calling up a guy to go out with him and these are the women that end up with the guys.

The following are examples of what men in the authors' classes said when they were asked, "How would you feel about a woman asking you to a movie if you had never been with her to an event before?"

> I'd love it. It makes me feel wanted, and I like for a woman to be aggressive.

> I prefer that the woman ask me out. I get tired of having to be the aggressor all the time.

> I'm the traditional type. I'll do the asking.

CHOICES

Three girls called me up for date last year. I went out with two of them and had a terrific time. I'm now engaged to one of them.

Women who have questioned their socialization and asked men out often feel very good about their choice.

The boyfriend I have now I asked out over a year ago (he's shy). Things have been going great ever since. He told me about a month ago that if I had never asked him out, he would never have asked me out first because he thought I wasn't interested. I'm glad I let him know that I was.

I don't have much of a problem asking a guy out. Of course, I wait a little in hopes that he will ask me out first. But if he doesn't, I figure he needs a little push in the right direction—my direction.

Men might evaluate the consequences of behaving in traditional gender roles and consider allowing women to be assertive without regarding their initiation of interaction in negative ways. By doing so they increase the chance of more frequent encounters (because women will be reinforced for assertiveness). As noted above, men often express positive feelings about women who initiate interaction.

Seek Egalitarian Relationships?

Egalitarian relationships are those in which the partners have mutual respect for each other, share the power,

and share the work of the relationship. Mutual respect translates into each acknowledging the credibility of the other's thoughts, feelings, and perspectives. Relationships with mutual respect are those in which the power is also shared. Neither partner is dominant but discusses the options and collaborates on a mutual decision with the other.

Partners in egalitarian relationships also share the work of their relationship. Either may cook, clean the house, or change the oil in the car. For pair-bonded couples, egalitarian relationships provide an opportunity for empathy unknown in traditional relationships. When only the man was employed outside the home and the woman stayed home to take care of the house and children, each partner had a set of experiences that was unknown to the other partner. He might be tired at the end of the day from working at the office; she might be tired from cleaning the house, preparing the food, and taking care of two young children. Each was sure that he or she was more tired than the other and regarded his or her own role as the more difficult role and the partner's role as "nothing to complain about." Alternatively, when couples decide to share the income getting, food preparation, housecleaning, and childcare, each has an experiential understanding of what the other feels.

Research findings suggest that being in a relationship of mutual respect, power, and work sharing is associated

with high relationship satisfaction. In one study, of the wives who reported that they had "excellent marriages," 88 percent reported that they shared the decision making equally with their husbands (Schwartz & Jackson, 1989, 72). In another study based on 349 college students, those involved in equitable dating relationships reported more contentment and commitment than those in inequitable dating relationships (Winn et al., 1991).

Pursue Nontraditional Occupational Roles?

The general trend toward gender role flexibility has implications for occupational role choices. Jobs traditionally occupied by one gender are now open to the other. Men may become nurses and librarians and women may become construction workers and lawyers. Since the 1960s, occupations have become slightly less segregated on the basis of gender and social acceptance of nontraditional career choices has increased slightly, especially among younger cohorts (Raymond, 1989; Reskin & Roos, 1990). The trend continues; in 1993 women began to fly jet aircraft on military combat missions.

Choosing nontraditional occupational roles may have benefits for both the individual and for society. On the individual level, women and men can make career choices on the basis of

(continued)

∿ CHOICES ∿

---

their personal talents and interests, rather than on the basis of arbitrary social restrictions regarding who can and cannot have a particular job or career. Because traditionally male occuaptions are generally higher paying than traditionally female occupations, women who make nontraditional career choices can gain access to higher paying and higher status jobs.

On the societal level, an increase in nontraditional career choices reduces gender-based occupational segregation, thereby contributing to social equality among women and men. In addition, women and men who enter nontraditional occupations may contribute greatly to the field that they enter. For example, such traditionally male-dominated occupations as politics, science and technology, and medicine may benefit greatly from increased involvement of women in these fields. Similarly, the field of public school teaching, which is currently a female-dominated occupation, has not provided male role models for children in school.

⅌ Summary

Sex refers to the biological distinction of being female or male based on biological differences in chromosomal and hormonal makeup. The term *gender* refers to the social and psychological characteristics associated with being female (i.e., being gentle and cooperative) and male (i.e., being competitive and aggressive).

A person's gender identity is the psychological state of viewing one's self as a girl or a boy and later as a woman or a man. Gender roles are the expectations societies have of how women and men "should" behave (e.g., women are expected to be more family and less career-oriented than men). Gender role ideology refers to the socially expected role relationships between women and men.

Four explanations of how children develop gender role behaviors are provided by sociobiology, identification, social learning, and cognitive-developmental theories. Sociobiological theory emphasizes biological differences between males and females as the basis for differences in gender roles. Identification theory suggests that children take on the role of the same-gender parent due to identifying with that parent. Social learning theory states that children learn their roles through direct instruction, modeling, and reward and punishment. Cognitive-developmental theory emphasizes that children first reach the stage at which they understand that their gender is permanent and then actively seek to acquire masculine or feminine characteristics. Whereas biological differences may predispose people to behave in certain ways, society (represented by parents, peers, teachers, religion, and media) and culture influence what people learn. The "nature versus nurture" debate recognizes the interaction of biological and environmental influences.

Traditional female socialization may result in less education, less income, greater dependence, lower marital satisfaction, a longer life, a closer emotional bond with children, and a larger number of quality relationships for women. Traditional male socialization may result in the fusion of self and occupation, a more limited expression of emotion, a shorter life, higher income, and higher status.

Androgyny refers to the blend of traits stereotypically associated with masculinity and femininity. Gender role transcendence involves abandoning gender schema so that the world is not divided into feminine and masculine categories.

Trends include greater equality in relationships and greater visibility of the men's movement.

Questions for Reflection

1. How are your gender role ideologies different from those of your parents?
2. To what degree do you feel free to exhibit gender role behaviors typically associated with the opposite sex?
3. To what degree do you feel that men will participate equally in childcare? Why or why not?

References

Achtemeier, E. A critique of the report of the special committee on human sexuality *News: A Publication of Presbyterians for Renewal,* March 1991, 1–12.

American Association of University Women. *Shortchanging girls, shortchanging America.* Washington, D.C.: Greenberg-Lake Analysis Group, 1991.

Antill, J. K. Parents' beliefs and values about sex roles, sex differences, and sexuality: Their sources and implications. *Sex and Gender,* P. Shaver and C. Hendrick, eds. Newbury Park, Calif.: Sage, 1987, 294–328.

Arnold, A. P. Sexual differences in the brain. *American Scientist,* March–April 1980, 165–173.

Asmussen, Linda and Constance L. Shehan. Gendered expectations and behaviors in dating relationships. *Proceedings: Family and Work* 54th Annual Conference of National Council on Family Relations, 1992, Vol 2, #1, p. 32.

Atkin, David J., Jay Moorman, and Carolyn A. Lin. Ready for prime time: Network series devoted to working women in the 1980s. *Sex Roles,* 1991. *25,* 677–685.

Barnes, Linda Laube. Gender bias in teachers' written comments. *Gender in the Classroom: Power and Pedagogy* Susan L. Gabriel and Isaiah Smithson, eds. Chicago: University of Illinois Press, 1990, 140–154.

Barnett, R. C., N. L. Marshall, and J. H. Pleck. Men's multiple roles and their relationship to men's psychological distress. *Journal of Marriage and the Family,* 1992, *54,* 358–367.

Basow, Susan A. *Gender: Stereotypes and roles, 3d ed.* Pacific Grove, Calif.: Brooks/Cole Publishing Co., 1992.

Bem, Sandra Lipsitz. Gender schema theory and its implications for child development: Raising gender-aschematic children in a gender schematic society. *Signs,* Summer *8,* 1983, 596–616.

Bem, S. L. The measurement of psychological androgyny. *Journal of Consulting and Clinical Psychology,* 1974, *42,* 155–162.

Bird, C. E. and A. M. Fremont. Gender, time use, and health, *Journal of Health and Social Behavior,* 1991, *32,* 114–129.

Blair, S. L. Employment, family, and perceptions of marital quality among husbands and wives. *Journal of Family Issues,* 1993, *14,* 189–212.

Brehm, S. S. *Intimate relationships,* 2d ed. New York: McGraw-Hill, Inc., 1992.

Buckland, S. K., M. E. Garrison, and D. D. Witt. The life and times of "Blondie": A longitudinal content analysis. *Proceedings: Families and Work,* 54th Annual Conference of the National Council on Family Relations, Orlando, Florida, 1992, vol 2, #1, p. 22.

Buss, D. M. Sex differences in human mate preferences: Evolutionary hypotheses tested in 37 cultures. *Behavioral and Brain Sciences,* 1989, *12,* 1–13.

Carslon, B. E. and Lynne Videka-Sherman. An empirical test of androgyny in the middle years: Evidence from a national survey *Sex Roles,* 1990, *23,* 305–324.

Carter, B. Children's TV, where boys are king. *New York Times,* May 1, 1991, A1, C18.

Catania, J. A., T. J. Coates, R. Stall, H. Turner, J. Peterson, N. Hearst, M. M. Dolcini, E. Hudes, J. Gagnon, J. Wiley, and R. Groves. Prevalence of AIDS-related risk factors and condom use in the United States. *Science* 1992, *258,* 1101–1106.

Chodorow, N. *The reproduction of mothering.* Berkeley, Calif.: University of California Press, 1978.

Clifford, D. M. and S. M. Shoffner. Gender-based differences in high school employment: Is there differential socialization for work? *Proceedings: Family and Work.* 54th Annual Conference of the National Council on Family Relations 1992, Vol 2, #1, p. 30.

Davis, Donald M. Portrayals of women in prime-time network television: Some demographic characteristics. *Sex Roles,* 1990, *23,* 325–332.

Davis, Simon. Men as success objects and women as sex objects: A study of personal advertisements. *Sex Roles,* 1990, *23,* 43–50.

Derlega, V. J. S., S. Metts, S. Petronio, and S. T. Margulis. *Self-disclosure.* Newbury Park, Calif.: Sage Publications, 1993.

Doyle, James A. and Michele A. Paludi. *Sex and gender,* 2d ed. Dubuque, Iowa: W. C. Brown Publishers, 1991.

Ellis, Bruce J. and Donald Symons. Sex differences in sexual fantasy: An evolutionary psychological approach. *The Journal of Sex Research,* 1990, *27,* 527–556.

Engel, J. and L. Kimmons. Division of labor in Japanese and American families. Paper, 54th Annual Conference of National Council on Family Relations, Orlando, Florida, 1992. Used by permission.

England, E. M. College student gender stereotypes: Expectations about the behavior of male subcategory members. *Sex Roles,* 1992, *27,* 699–716.

Etaugh, Claire and Terri Duits. Development of gender discrimination: Role of stereotypic and counterstereotypic gender cues. *Sex Roles,* 1990, *23,* 215–222.

Ferree, M. M. and E. J. Hall. Visual images of American society: Gender and race in introductory sociology textbooks. *Gender and Society,* 1990, *4,* 500–533.

Fortune, W. F. Arapesh warfare. *American Anthropologist,* 1939, 41, 22–41.

Freimuth, M. and G. Hornstein. A critical examination of the concept of gender. *Sex Roles,* 1982, 8, 515–532.

Furnham, Adrian, Catherine Hester, and Catherine Weir. Sex differences in the preferences for specific female body shapes. *Sex Roles,* 1990, *22,* 743–754.

Garza, Raymond T. and Jill E. Borchert. Maintaining social identity in a mixed-gender setting: Minority/majority status and cooperative/competitive feedback. *Sex Roles,* 1990, *22,* 679–691.

Goldscheider, F. K. and L. J. Waite. *New families, no Families?: The transformation of the American home.* Berkeley, Calif.: University of California Press, 1991.

Goodwin, Robin. Sex differences among partner preferences: Are the sexes really very similar? *Sex Roles,* 1990, *23,* 501–514.

Goy, R. W. and B. S. McEwen. *Sexual differentiation of the brain.* Cambridge, Mass.: MIT Press, 1980.

Grammer, Karl. Human courtship behavior: Biological basis and cognitive processes. *Sociobiology of Sexual and Reproductive Strategies,* A. E. Rasa, C. Vogel, and E. Voland, London: Chapman and Hall, 1989, 147–169.

Gray, Elizabeth A. Women's body image: A multivariate study. *Free Inquiry in Creative Sociology,* 1993, *21,* 103–110.

Grimmell, D. and G. S. Stern. The relationship between gender role ideals and psychological well-being. *Sex Roles,* 1992, *27,* 487–497.

Hammersla, Joy Fisher and Lynne Frease-McMahan. University students' priorities: Life goals vs. relationships. *Sex Roles,* 1990, *23,* 1–14.

Hare-Mustin, Rachel T. and Jeanne Marecek. The meaning of difference: Gender theory, postmodernism, and psychology. *American Psychologist,* 1988, *43,* 455–464.

Harrison, D. F. and R. C. Pennell. Contemporary sex roles for adolescents: New options or confusion? *Journal of Social Work and Human Sexuality,* 1989, *8,* 27–45.

Hopkins, Anne. Defining womyn (and others). *Time,* June 24, 1991, 51.

House, James S., Karl R. Landis, and Debra Umberson. Social relationships and health. *The Sociology of Health and Illness: Critical Perspectives,* 3d ed. Peter Conrad and Rochelle Kern, eds. New York: St. Martin's Press, 1990, 85–94.

Hyde, J. S., M. Krajnik, and K. Skuldt–Niederberger. Androgyny across the lifespan: A replication and longitudinal followup. *Developmental Psychology,* 1991, *27,* 516–519.

Jones, Diane Carlson, Nancy Bloys, and Marie Wood. Sex roles and friendship patterns. *Sex Roles,* 1990, *23,* 133–145.

Kohlberg, L. A cognitive-developmental analysis of children's sex-role concepts and attitudes. *The Development of Sex Differences,* E. E. Macoby, ed. Stanford, Calif.: Stanford University Press, 1966.

Kohlberg, L. State and sequence: The cognitive-developmental approach to socialization. *Handbook of Socialization Theory and Research,* D. A. Goslin, ed. Chicago: Rand-McNally, 1969, 347–480.

Kohlberg, L. Moral stages and moralization: The cognitive-dvelopmental approach. *Moral Development and Behavior,* T. Lickona, ed. New York: Holt, Rinehart, and Winston, 1976.

Lackey, P. N. Adults' attitudes about assignments of household chores to male and female children. *Sex Roles,* 1989, *20,* 271–281.

Lindsey, L. L. *Gender roles: A sociological perspective.* Englewood Cliffs, N.J.: Prentice-Hall, Inc., 1990.

Lont, C. M. The roles assigned to females and males in non-music radio programming. *Sex Roles,* 1990, *22,* 661–668.

Luckenbill, D. F. and D. P. Doyle. Structural position and violence: Developing a cultural explanation. *Criminology,* 1989, *27,* 419–433.

Mandelbaum, D. G. *Women's seclusion and men's honor: Sex roles in North India, Bangladesh, and Pakistan.* Tuscon, Ariz.: University of Arizona Press. 1988.

McBroom, P. A. *The third sex: The new professional woman.* New York: Paragon House Publishers, 1992.

Mead, M. *Sex and temperament in three primitive societies.* New York: William Morrow, 1935.

Mindel, C. H., R. W. Habenstein, and R. Wright, Jr., eds. *Ethnic families in America: Patterns and variations,* 3d ed. New York: Elsevier, 1988.

Money, J. Sin, sickness, or status? Homosexual gender identity and psychoneuroendocrinology. *American Psychologist,* 1987, *42,* 384–399.

Morawski, J. G. The troubled quest for masculinity, femininity, and androgyny. *Sex and Gender,* P. Shaver and C. Hendrick, eds. Newbury Park, Calif.: Sage, 1987.

Morrow, Frances. *Unleashing our unknown selves: An inquiry into the future of femininity and masculinity.* New York: Praeger, 1991.

Muehlendard, C. L. and M. McCoy. Double standard/double bind: The sexual double standard and women's communication about sex. *Psychology of Women Quarterly,* 1991, *15,* 447– 461.

Muse, Corey J. Women in Western Samoa. *Women in Cross-Cultural Perspective,* L. L. Adler, ed. New York: Praeger, 1991, 221–241.

National Center for Health Statistics. Advance report of final mortality statistics, 1990. Monthly vital statistics report; Vol. 41, no. 7, supplement. Hyattsville, Maryland: Public Health Service, 1993.

Oliver, Sarah J. and Brenda B. Toner. The influence of gender role typing on expression of depressive symptoms. *Sex Roles,* 1990, *22,* 775–790.

Olson, Josephine E., Irene H. Frieze, and Ellen G. Detlefsen. Having it all? Combining work and family in a male and a female profession. *Sex Roles,* 1990, *23,* 515–534.

Phillips, Jennifer C. Self-reported health behaviors of college freshmen. Unpublished thesis, Department of Health, Physical Education, Recreation and Safety, May 1992. Used by permission of Jennifer C. Phillips, Health Educator, Student Health Service, East Carolina University, Greenville, North Carolina 27858.

Pomerleau, A., D. Bolduc, G. Malcuit, and L. Cossette. Pink or blue: Environmental stereotypes in the first two years of life. *Sex Roles,* 1990, *22,* 359–367.

Porter, J. R. and A. H. Beuf. Racial variation in reaction to physical stigma: A study of degree of disturbance by Vitiligo among black and white patients. *The Journal of Health and Social Behavior,* 1991, *32,* 101–113.

Purcell, P. and L. Stewart. Dick and Jane in 1989. *Sex Roles,* 1990, *22,* 177–185.

Rader, D. How to live without answers. *Parade Magazine,* April 25, 1993, 4–5.

Raymond, C. Shift of many traditionally male jobs to women. *Chronicle of Higher Education,* October 11, 1989, A4, A6.

Reskin, B. F. and P. A. Roos. *Job queues, gender queues: explaining women's inroads into male occupations.* Philadelphia: Temple University Press, 1990.

Rodin, J. and J. R. Ickovics. Women's health: Review and research agenda as we approach the 21st century. *American Psychologist,* 1990, *45,* 1018–1034.

Rosenzweig, J. M. and D. M. Dailey. Women's sex roles in their public and private lives. *Journal of Sex Education and Therapy,* 1991, *17,* 75–85.

Rubenstein, C. A brave new world. *New Woman,* October 1990, 158–164.

Rubin, Lillian B. *Erotic wars: What happened to the sexual revolution.* New York: Harper Perennial, 1991.

Sadker, Myra and David Sadker. Confronting sexism in the college classroom. *Gender in the Classroom: Power and Pedagogy,* Susan L. Gabriel and Isaiah Smithson, eds. Chicago, Ill: University of Illinois Press, 1990, 176–187.

Safir, M. P., R. Hertz-Lazarowitz, S. BenTsvi-Mayer, and H. Kuppermintz. Prominence of girls and boys in the classroom: Schoolchildren's perceptions. *Sex Roles,* 1992, *27,* 439–453.

Schroeder, K. A., L. L. Blood, and D. Maluso. Gender differences and similarities between male and female undergraduate students regarding expectations for career and family roles. *College Student Journal,* 1993, *27,* 237–249.

Schur, Edwin. *Labeling women deviant: Gender, stigma, and social control.* New York: Random House, 1984.

Schwartz, Pepper and Donna Jackson. How to have a model marriage. *New Woman,* February 1989, 66–74.

Scriven, J. Women at work in Sweden. *Working Women: An International Survey,* M. J. Davidson and C. L. Cooper, eds. New York: Wiley, 1984, 153–182.

Smith, T. W. Adult sexual behavior in 1989: Number of partners, frequency of intercourse and risk of AIDS. *Family Planning Perspectives,* 1991, 23, 102–107.

Sorenson, R. S. and J. D. Sorenson. Content analysis of Christian family magazines. *Proceedings: Families and Work* 54th Annual conference, National Council on Family Relations, Orlando, Florida 1992, Vol 2, #2 p. 96.

Statistical Abstract of the United States: 1993, 113th ed. Washington, D.C.: U. S. Bureau of the Census, 1993.

Stein, H. Pigs 'R us. *Psychology Today,* July-August 1992, 25, 24–et passim.

Strickland, B. R. Sex-related differences in health and illness. *Psychology of Women Quarterly,* 1988, 12, 381–399.

Symons, D. Can Darwin's view of life shed light on human sexuality? *Theories of Human Sexuality,* J. H. Greer and W. T. O'Donohue, eds. New York: Plenum, 1987.

Symonds, D. and B. Ellis. Human male-female differences in sexual desire. *Sociobiology of Sexual and Reproductive Strategies,* A. E. Rasa, C. Vogel, and E. Voland, eds. London: Chapman and Hall, 1989, 131–146.

Udry, R. J., L. M. Talbert, and N. M. Morris. Biosocial foundations for adolescent female sexuality. *Demography,* 1986, 23, 217–227.

Unger, Rhoda K. Imperfect reflections of reality: Psychology constructs gender. *Making a Difference: Psychology and the Construction of Gender,* R. T. Hare-Mustin and J. Marecek, eds. New Haven, Conn.: Yale University Press, 1990, 102–149.

Waldron, Ingrid. What do we know about the causes of sex differences in mortality? A review of the literature. *The Sociology of Health and Illness: Critical Perspectives,* 3d ed. Peter Conrad and Rochelle Kern, eds. New York: St. Martin's Press, 1990, 45–57.

Walker, Alexis J., Sally S. Kees Martin, and Linda Thomson. Feminist programs for families. *Family Relations,* 1988, 37, 17–22.

Williams, John E. and Deborah L. Best. *Measuring sex stereotypes: A multination study.* London: Sage Publications, 1990b.

Williams, John E. and Deborah L. Best. *Sex and psyche: Gender and self viewed cross-culturally.* London: Sage, 1990a.

Winn, K. I., D. W. Crawford, and J. L. Fischer. Equity and commitment in romance versus friendship. *Journal of Social Behavior & Personality,* 1991, 6, 301–314.

Contents

3
CHAPTER

Love Relationships

Is It True?

1. North America is one of the few societies in the world that values passionate love.

2. In general, being in love is good for your physical and mental health.

3. Most U.S. college students report that they would marry even though they were not in love.

4. Some research suggests that men are likely to fall in love more quickly than women.

5. Idealizing a love partner is not necessarily bad.

1 = F; 2 = T; 3 = F; 4 = T; 5 = T

Choose your love and then love your choice.

H. G. BOHN

𝒱 alentines' Day emphasizes the value we place on love relationships in our society. Soon after the beginning of each new year, stores begin to stock heart-shaped cards and candy to be given to one's love partner. On Valentine's Day, individuals are encouraged to be particularly expressive of their love to their partner.

Ain't no doubt in no one's mind, love's the finest thing around.

JAMES TAYLOR

College students in the United States are among the most romantic in the world. Over 96 percent say that they would not marry a person they did not love and over 35 percent say they would divorce if love died (Levine, 1993). Due to the importance of love in our decision to marry and divorce, it is crucial that we try to understand love.

In this chapter we examine the nature of love (both ancient and modern views), various theories about the origins of love, how love develops, and its dilemmas. We also discuss the causes and consequences of jealousy in relationships. We end with a discussion of whether to listen to one's heart or head in making relationship choices and the issues to consider in regard to having sex in the context of varying degrees of love. We begin with the nature of love.

🕉 The Nature of Love: Ancient and Modern Views

There is no single definition of love. When students in the authors' classes were asked to define the meaning of love, some listed various qualities like caring, compassion, respect, sharing, and commitment. One student said that "love is sacrificing because you want to"; another said "love is being in a crowded room full of attractive people and wishing you were alone with your partner."

What is love? 'tis nature's treasure, 'Tis the storehouse of her joys.

CHATTERTON

> **CONSIDERATION**
>
> One reason that no single definition of love is possible is because love has emotional, physical, social, intellectual, and spiritual elements. Different definitions of love arise from placing varying degrees of emphasis on these elements. Pedersen (1991) noted that, oftentimes,
>
> > Two people who proclaim that they love each other have not considered that even though they use the same word, each of them attaches very different meanings to it. They may be "in love" and have entirely different behavioral expectations of what that means (p. 187).
>
> (continued)

In the discussion to follow it may be insightful to try and assess the degree to which you and your partner have a common view of love. It is also important to keep in mind that one's own view of love, and that of one's partner, is likely to change over time.

Philosophers, theologians, and social scientists have speculated on love throughout human history. Some ancient and modern views of love follow:

Ancient Views on Love

Many of our present-day notions of love stem from early Buddhist, Greek, and Hebrew writings.

In the cuisine of love there are flavors for all tastes.

JAMES HUNEKER

Buddhist Conception of Love The Buddhists conceived of two types of love–an "unfortunate" kind of love (self-love), and a "good" kind of love (creative spiritual attainment). Love that represents creative spiritual attainment was described as "love of detachment," not in the sense of withdrawal from the emotional concerns of others but in the sense of accepting people as they are and not requiring them to be different from their present selves as the price of friendly affection. To a Buddhist, the best love was one in which you accept others as they are without requiring them to be like you (Burtt, 1957).

Greek and Hebrew Conceptions of Love Three concepts of love introduced by the Greeks and reflected in the New Testament are: phileo, agape, and eros. *Phileo* refers to love based on friendship and can exist between family members, friends, and lovers. The city of Philadelphia was named after this phileo type of love. Another variation of phileo love is *philanthropia,* which is the Greek word meaning "love of humankind."

Agape refers to a love based on a concern for the well-being of others. Agape is spiritual, not sexual, in nature. This type of love is altruistic and requires nothing in return. "Whatever I can do to make your life happy" is the motif of the agapic lover, even if this means giving up the beloved to someone else. Such love is not always reciprocal.

Family love (similar to Agape love) is voluntary, unconditional, and enduring.

CONSIDERATION

Bahr (1992) noted that the "family love" parents have for their children is the love of altruism—a selfless concern for the welfare of one's offspring (similar to *Agape*). Family love is also voluntary, unconditional, and enduring. Such love in families is one of the reasons families, in all societies, are regarded as important for individuals.

Eros refers to sexual love. This type of love seeks self-gratification and sexual expression. In Greek mythology, Eros was the god of love and the son of Aphrodite. Plato described "true" eros as sexual love that existed between two men. According to Plato's conception of eros, homosexual sex was the highest form of love because it existed independent of the procreative instinct and free from the bonds of matrimony. Also, the women had low status and were uneducated and were, therefore, not considered ideal partners for the men. By implication, love and marriage were separate (Brehm, 1992).

Modern Views on Love

While love has been pondered for centuries, it may be no less mysterious today than it was a thousand years ago. Among the modern-day thinkers who have speculated on the nature of love are Abraham Maslow, John Lee, Zick Rubin, and Robert Sternberg.

Maslow: B-Love and D-Love   Abraham Maslow believed love was a basic psychological need. The need to love and be loved must be satisfied, according to Maslow, in order for individuals to realize their innate potential for maturity and self-actualization.

Maslow identified two types of love: B-love (love for the *being* of another person) and D-love (love based on *deficiencies*) (1968). *B-love* is unneeding love, or unselfish love. B-love is not possessive, and B-lovers are more independent of each other, more autonomous, and less jealous or threatened. B-lovers encourage each other to pursue their goals and grow as individuals.

D-love is selfish love. D-lovers have deficiencies in their nurturing and have been deprived of love and thus hunger for it desperately. D-love seeks gratification rather than growth. D-lovers are dependent on each other and tend to be jealous and possessive. Love partners are valued for their ability to satisfy an intense hunger for love.

Love is merely the exchange of two fantasies.

NICHOLAS CHAMFORT

Lee: Love Styles   Lee (1973, 1988) identified six styles of love: Eros (romantic, passionate love), Ludus (game-playing love), Storge (friendship love), Pragma (logical, pragmatic love), Mania (possessive, dependent love), and Agape (altruistic, selfless love). Two of the major styles that emerged from Lee's studies were those of romantic, passionate love and of game-playing (ludus) love in which the partners avoided emotional intimacy with each other.

The ludic lover views love as a game, refuses to become dependent on any one person, and does not encourage another's intimacy. Two essential skills of the ludic lover are to juggle several people at the same time and to manage each relationship so that no one is seen too often. These strategies help to ensure that the relationship does not deepen into an all-consuming love. Don Juan represented the classic ludic lover.

Sternberg: Intimacy, Passion, and Commitment Robert Sternberg (1986) identified several states of love on the basis of the presence or absence of three elements: intimacy, passion, and commitment (see Figure 3.1 below). Sternberg defined these three elements of his "triangular theory of love" as follows:

Intimacy:	Emotional connectedness or bondedness
Passion:	Romantic feelings and physical sexual desire
Commitment:	Desire to maintain the relationship

The commitment aspect of love may be particularly important.

> **CONSIDERATION**
>
> Acker and Davis (1992) analyzed questionnaires from 204 adults about their love relationships (both married and unmarried). They found that the most powerful and consistent predictor of relationship satisfaction was commitment. The longer the relationship, the more important commitment was to the satisfaction of the relationship. While not all partners want committed relationships, the most satisfying relationships seem to be those in which the partners are mutually committed.

According to Sternberg (1986), various types of love can be described on the basis of the three elements he identified:

1. Nonlove: Absence of all three components of love
2. Liking: Intimacy without passion or commitment

Love well who will, love wise who can,
But love, be loved.

JOAQUIN MILLER

FIGURE 3.1
TRIANGULAR THEORY OF LOVE

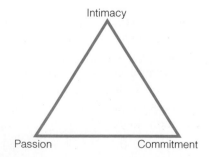

Intimacy

Passion   Commitment

3. Infatuation: Passion without intimacy or commitment
4. Romantic love: Intimacy and passion without commitment
5. Companionate love: Intimacy and commitment without passion
6. Fatuous love: Passion and commitment without intimacy
7. Empty love: Commitment without passion or intimacy
8. Consummate love: Combination of intimacy, passion, and commitment

Romantic Versus Realistic Love

Love may also be described as being on a continuum from romanticism to realism. For some people, love is romantic; for others, it is realistic. Romantic love is characterized by such beliefs as "love at first sight," "there is only one true love," "love conquers all," and "the beloved will meet one's highest ideals." The symptoms of romantic love include drastic mood swings, palpitations of the heart, and intrusive thoughts about the partner.

Romantic love is valued in our society. Notice that the bulk of popular and country songs played on the radio are either about becoming involved in a romantic relationship ("Love Changes Everything") or getting over a broken one ("Achey Breakey Heart"). Movies also celebrate the beginning (*Bodyguard*, with Whitney Houston/Kevin Costner) and ending of love (*Husbands and Wives*, with Woody Allen and Mia Farrow). Television series such as *Beverly Hills 90210* and *Melrose Place* and the "soaps" regularly feature romantic love themes each episode.

This obsession with love, and particularly with romantic love, has its roots among the aristocracy during the 12th century in the south of France. Knights pledged loyalty and love for their beloved who was both idealized and inaccessible. The high-status woman of their affection was married to someone she did not love (she had married for political and economic reasons). "Courtly love was a peak experience; marriage, in contrast, was a deadly serious matter of politics and property" (Brehm, 1992, 95).

One of the most famous romances during this era was that between Tristan and Iseult. Sir Tristan was commissioned by his king to bring the neighboring princess, Iseult, to be his queen. But Tristan and Iseult fell in love. The inaccessibility and forbidden nature of their illicit love served to enhance their romantic feelings for each other. This separation of love and marriage continued until the seventeenth and eighteenth centuries when the English began to connect love with marriage and it was believed that there could be a happy ending to such a relationship.

We have already noted the importance of love in the United States. But what about other societies? Jankowiak and Fischer (1992) found evidence of passionate love in 147 out of 166 (88.5%) of the societies they studied. Passionate love was evidenced by the presence of at least one of the following: accounts depicting personal anguish and longing; love songs; elopement due to mutual affection; native accounts affirming the existence of passionate love;

Twelfth century love relationships in Western Europe featured the romantic love of a knight for a lady who was usually married.

Love looks through spectacles which make copper appear gold.

CERVANTES

In that strange unsettlement of love, we are always crazy.

SUSAN RICHARDS SHREVE

Love is a gross exaggeration of the difference between one person and everybody else.

GEORGE BERNARD SHAW

ACROSS CULTURES 🙰

FIGURE 3.2

CROSS-CULTURAL IMPORTANCE OF LOVE

Source: Robert V. Levine. Is love a luxury? *American Demographics* 1993, *15*, 27–29. Title of chart has been changed; data for chart is based on author's research in 1990–1991. Reprinted with permission, ©*American Demographics* (February, 1993, #2). For subscription information, please call 1-800-828-1133.

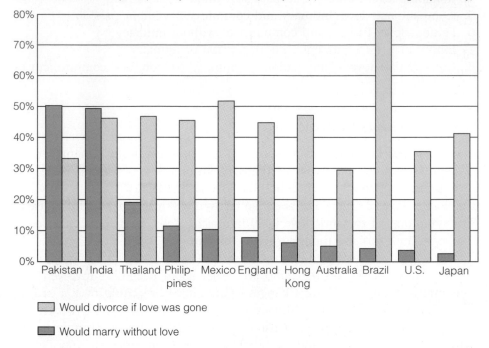

(Percent of college students who say they would marry someone they did not love, and percent who say that it is best for the couple to part ways if love has completely disappeared from a marriage, by country)

Would divorce if love was gone

Would marry without love

or the researchers' affirmation that romantic love was present. Their study stands "in direct contradiction to the popular idea that romantic love is essentially limited to or the product of Western culture. Moreover, it suggests that romantic love constitutes a human universal, or at the least a near-universal" (p. 154).

The degree to which love is important for marriage does vary by society. Figure 3.2 reflects the percent of college students in various countries who would be willing to marry someone they did not love and the percent who would divorce if love was absent. The chart shows that college students in Pakistan are the most willing to marry without love and that Brazilians are the quickest to divorce if love dies (Levine, 1993).

For a moment, I was in a very sweet place.

LENA OLIN

CONSIDERATION

Is romantic love a sound basis for marriage? If the love you have for your partner (as Bobbie in *Havanna*) is based primarily on physical attraction, little time together, and few shared experiences, marrying on this basis may be taking an unnecessary risk. To marry someone without spending a great deal of time with him or her (at least one year) in a variety of situations (your home, your partner's home, four- or five-day trips, and so on) is making a lifetime choice with very limited information.

Infatuation is sometimes regarded as synonymous with romantic love. *Infatuation* comes from the same root word as fatuous, meaning "silly" or "foolish," and refers to a state of passion or attraction that is not based on reason. Infatuation is characterized by the tendency to idealize the love partner. People who are infatuated magnify their lover's positive qualities ("My partner is always happy") and overlook or minimize their negative qualities ("My partner doesn't have a problem with alcohol but just likes to have a good time").

There's nothing half so sweet in life as love's young dream.

THOMAS MOORE

Do I love you because you're beautiful? Or are you beautiful because I love you?

OSCAR HAMMERSTEIN II (from *Cinderella*)

CONSIDERATION

Walsh (1991) suggested that some level of idealization is normal and healthy. He pointed out that people often idealize their parents, children, and even countries to varying degrees and that such idealization reflects enthusiasm and optimism toward a love object. Furthermore, Walsh asserted that "the idealization of the loved one may in fact result in his or her conforming more to the idealized image . . ." (p. 191). Projecting an idealized image of a loved one may create a self-fulfilling prophecy whereby the loved one internalizes the idealized image and acts according to this image. (Of course, idealization may have negative implications, such as those identified above this paragraph.)

In contrast to romantic love, realistic love, or conjugal love, tends to be characteristic of married people. Conjugal love is less emotional, passionate, and exciting than romantic love; it is characterized by calmness, depth, and endurance. The Love Attitudes Scale provides a way to assess the degree to which you are romantic or realistic about love.

Conjugal love involves calmness, depth, and endurance.

CONSIDERATION

When you determine your score on the Love Attitudes Scale, be aware that you are merely assessing the degree to which you are a romantic or a realist. Your tendency to be one or the other is not good or bad. Both romantics and realists may be happy, mature people. However, being ultra-romantic may be associated with a more difficult adjustment to having children since children involve a great deal of unselfish, nonreciprocal love (Belsky & Rovine, 1990).

Are men or women more romantic in their attitudes toward love? Two researchers examined the love attitudes of 110 university students and found that men were more romantic and women more pragmatic (i.e. realistic) about love (Dion & Dion, 1991). The researchers found that the men in their sample tended to play at love and were less serious and less committed than women. Similarly, in a study of 68 unmarried Caucasians in South Africa, the women scored higher on "conjugal love" than men. Conjugal love was defined as "the belief that love demands serious thought and careful consideration" (Stones & Philbrick, 1991, 220). Conjugal love is similar to realistic love described earlier. Hendrick et al. (1984) also found in their study of 800 university

---

This scale is designed to assess the degree to which you are romantic or realistic in your attitudes toward love. There are no right or wrong answers.

Directions: After reading each sentence carefully, circle the number that best represents the degree to which you agree or disagree with the sentence.

1 Strongly agree   4 Mildly disagree
2 Mildly agree   5 Strongly disagree
3 Undecided

SA MA U MD SD

1. Love doesn't make sense. It just is.   1   2   3   4   5
2. When you fall "head over heels" in love, it's sure to be the real thing.   1   2   3   4   5
3. To be in love with someone you would like to marry but can't is a tragedy.   1   2   3   4   5
4. When love hits, you know it.   1   2   3   4   5
5. Common interests are really unimportant; as long as each of you is truly in love, you will adjust.   1   2   3   4   5
6. It doesn't matter if you marry after you have known your partner for only a short time as long as you know you are in love.   1   2   3   4   5
7. If you are going to love a person, you will "know" after a short time.   1   2   3   4   5
8. As long as two people love each other, the educational differences they have really do not matter.   1   2   3   4   5
9. You can love someone even though you do not like any of that person's friends.   1   2   3   4   5
10. When you are in love, you are usually in a daze.   1   2   3   4   5
11. Love "at first sight" is often the deepest and most enduring type of love.   1   2   3   4   5
12. When you are in love, it really does not matter what your partner does because you will love him or her anyway.   1   2   3   4   5
13. As long as you really love a person, you will be able to solve the problems you have with the person.   1   2   3   4   5
14. Usually you can really love and be happy with only one or two people in the world.   1   2   3   4   5
15. Regardless of other factors, if you truly love another person, that is a good enough reason to marry that person.   1   2   3   4   5

---

students that women were more pragmatic than men in their view of love. Hendrick and Hendrick (1991) suggested that women are more practical in their attitudes toward love than men because of their future parental interest with the men they encounter. In effect, the woman must delay her romantic investment until she is sure that the man has an interest in providing for and protecting her offspring.

The Love Attitudes Scale *continued*

	SA	MA	U	MD	SD
16. It is necessary to be in love with the one you marry to be happy.	1	2	3	4	5
17. Love is more of a feeling than a relationship.	1	2	3	4	5
18. People should not get married unless they are in love.	1	2	3	4	5
19. Most people truly love only once during their lives.	1	2	3	4	5
20. Somewhere there is an ideal mate for most people.	1	2	3	4	5
21. In most cases, you will "know it" when you meet the right partner.	1	2	3	4	5
22. Jealousy usually varies directly with love; that is, the more you are in love, the greater your tendency to become jealous will be.	1	2	3	4	5
23. When you are in love, you are motivated by what you feel rather than by what you think.	1	2	3	4	5
24. Love is best described as an exciting rather than a calm thing.	1	2	3	4	5
25. Most divorces probably result from falling out of love rather than failing to adjust.	1	2	3	4	5

26. When you are in love, your judgment is usually not too clear.	1	2	3	4	5
27. Love often comes only once in a lifetime.	1	2	3	4	5
28. Love is often a violent and uncontrollable emotion.	1	2	3	4	5
29. When selecting a marriage partner, differences in social class and religion are of small importance compared with love.	1	2	3	4	5
30. No matter what anyone says, love cannot be understood.	1	2	3	4	5

SCORING: Add the numbers you circled. 1 (strongly agree) is the most romantic response and 5 (strongly disagree) is the most realistic response. The lower your total score (30 is the lowest possible score), the more romantic your attitudes toward love. The higher your total score (150 is the highest possible score) the more realistic your attitudes toward love. A score of 90 places you at the midpoint between being an extreme romantic and an extreme realist.

NOTE: This Self-Assessment is designed to be fun and thought provoking; it is *not* intended to be used by students as a clinical evaluation device.

*From D. Knox, *The love attitudes inventory,* rev. ed. (Saluda, N.C.: Family Life Publications, 1983). Reprinted by permission.

However, after analyzing the results of a romance survey of slightly less than 12,000 *Psychology Today* readers, the researcher concluded that "more women than men say that romance is important, and men rate their partners as being more romantic" (Rubenstein, 1983, 49). In this context, when women say romance is important, they mean it is important to be attentive to the relationship.

I have learned that love, sincere and total, can overcome any problem. Love will always win.

PIERRE TROADEC

> **CONSIDERATION**
>
> The answer to the question: Who is more romantic, men or women? depends on how one defines and measures romanticism. If one conceptualizes romanticism as a tendency to fall in love quickly, men are more romantic as they tend to fall in love more quickly than women. But if one conceptualizes romanticism as a tendency to form intense and lasting bonds, women are more romantic (Walsh, 1991).

ᐟ⌒⸴ **A C R O S S   C U L T U R E S**

From a cross-cultural perspective, Japanese students view love differently than U.S. students. Japanese students are more realistic than white American students in their attitudes toward love. Japanese students are more likely to have been taught that love may follow rather than precede marriage. In addition, their parents are more involved in the selection and approval of the people they date than the parents of American students (Simmons, Kolke, & Shimizu, 1986).

The Feminization of Love

When we think of love, we commonly think of expressive qualities—those that are associated with our cultural definitions of femininity. For example, "we identify love with emotional expressions in talking about feelings, aspects of love that women prefer and in which women tend to be more skilled than men" (Cancian, 1987, 69). Love then, has become "feminized" (Cancian, 1987; Tavris, 1992). Indeed, Tavris (1992) suggested that "love is the one domain in which women are thought to excel and to represent the healthy model of normalcy . . ."(p. 248).

One consequence of the feminization of love is that men are not given credit or validation for their instrumental style of loving. "Men tend to have a distinctive style of love that focuses on practical help, shared physical activities, spending time together, and sex" (Cancian, 1987, 75). But these qualities and behaviors are not always recognized as expressions of love—hence men are viewed as inferior to women in their ability to love and many heterosexual women feel unsatisfied in their love relationships. Therapist Loren Pedersen (1991) observed

> A man's expectations of himself as a loving partner may strongly rest on the traditional idea of "providing for," so that he feels he is being loving by fulfilling those expectations. He is surprised, as well as hurt, when his partner expresses disappointment in his providence as well as his performance. A man typically counters his wife's accusations that he doesn't love her with reference to all the things he's done to make her happy . . . he bought her a new car . . . he makes a good salary . . . he sends the kids to private school, and so on, but none of these satisfies his wife's sense of what it means to feel loved by him (p. 188).

In a study of the determinants of marital satisfaction (cited in Cancian,

1987), researchers told a husband to increase his affectionate behavior toward his wife. The husband decided to wash his wife's car "and was surprised when neither his wife nor the researchers accepted that as an " 'affectionate act' " (Cancian, 1987, 76).

> From a wife's point of view,
> It is not enough that he supports us and takes care of us. I appreciate that, but I want him to share things with me. I need for him to tell me his feelings (Cancian, 1987).

As an alternative to a feminized conception of love, Cancian suggested that love be viewed as a combination of expressive (feminine) and instrumental (masculine) qualities. Her definition of enduring love between adults is:

> A relationship where a small number of people both (1) express affection, acceptance, and other positive feelings to each other, and (2) provide each other with care and practical assistance. Love also includes (3) commitment—an intention to maintain the affection and the assistance for a long time, despite difficulties and (4) specialness—giving the loved person priority over others . . . (1987, 70).

Some Theories on the Origins of Love

Different ways have been used to describe the nature of love, but where does love come from? What are its various origins? Various theories have been suggested to answer these questions.

Evolutionary Theory

According to the evolutionary view of the origin of love, love is part of nature's design to achieve reproductive success and to ensure the survival of the human species (Buss, 1988). The love of a mother for her child is basic to the survival of the child. As Walsh (1991) explained:

> If no one feeds a human infant it will starve; . . . if no one shelters and protects it, it will die. The human infant is at the mercy of the adults of its species far longer than any other newborn. Only a strong biologically based tendency on the part of the mother to care for the infant unconditionally will see it successfully through its period of dependency. The human adult's willingness to invest time and energy in someone else's goals, even at the expense of one's own, is called love—an active concern for the well-being of another (p. 42).

Walsh (1991) also explained the evolutionary basis of love between men and women:

> Men and women fall in love today because ancient couples with the propensity to do so stayed bonded together long enough to allow for their offspring to survive and pass on that propensity. Couples who simply copulated

and parted were less likely to have any [offspring] of that union survive. Evolution selected love as a way of insuring that men would stick around long enough to assist women to care for the children (p. 189).

Learning Theory

Unlike evolutionary theory, which views the human experience of love as innate, learning theory views love as a set of feelings and cognitions that are learned. These feelings may be learned in infancy. Erikson (1963) suggested that infants must experience love and trust with a parent or parent surrogate and that failure to have initial developmental bonding experiences makes it difficult for the individual to form attachments.

Hazen and Shaver (1987) further noted the various attachment styles that people may develop as a result of early learning experiences: secure lovers, avoidant lovers, and anxious-ambivalent lovers.

"I love you" means "you please me or make me feel good."

B. F. SKINNER

1. Secure lovers are those who find it easy to become emotionally close, to depend on others, and to allow others to depend on them.
2. Avoidant lovers become uncomfortable as the relationship becomes closer. They find it difficult to trust others or to depend on them. They panic when someone evidences an interest in getting them more committed to the relationship.
3. Anxious-ambivalent lovers fear that no one will want to become emotionally involved with them. They want to merge completely with another person, which sometimes scares the other person away.

A learning model of love also emphasizes that emotional feelings are sometimes based on the behavior of one's partner. Partners who look at each other, smile at each other, compliment each other, touch each other endearingly, do things for each other, and do things together find it easier to experience love feelings with each other than partners who avoid, criticize, and reject each other.

You can trust love only when there is nothing to be gained by it.

CHINESE PROVERB

During a developing relationship, couples also have a high frequency of reinforcing each other for behaviors they enjoy in each other. The continuation of love feelings depends on each partner continuing to reinforce the desirable behaviors of the other so these behaviors (and the love feelings they elicit) continue.

CONSIDERATION

The "death" of love may result from failure on the part of both partners to reinforce appropriate behavior in each other. For example, smiling, caressing, complimenting, spending time together, and sharing childcare are behaviors in long-term relationships that may not be reinforced. When these behaviors are no longer reinforced, they will stop. If your partner stops doing things that you like, your love feelings may disappear. It is important that you reinforce your for desired behavior (so that the behavior will continue) to ensure a continued basis for your love feelings.

Love also dies when partners spend little time together and stop sharing activities that are mutually enjoyable. Love can be created or destroyed by pairing or failing to pair the partner with pleasurable activities over time. While not spending time together or sharing enjoyable activities may cause love feelings to dissipate, it is also true that lack of love feelings may cause couples to stop engaging in activities together.

Love is also learned in a context. Sternberg and Beall (1991) noted that "one can become attracted to someone else not because of who he or she is, but because one just happens to experience positive reinforcement in the presence of the person—reinforcement that may have nothing to do with the person to whom one is attracted" (p. 264). For example, doing a lot of fun things with a partner can positively influence the development of love feelings, but it may be the enjoyable events not the person that elicit or facilitate the development of the love feelings.

> People wonder why I ride with a smile—it's because my baby loves me Cadillac style.
> **SAMMY KERSHAW**

Psychosexual Theory

According to psychosexual theory, love results from blocked biological sexual desires. In the sexually repressive mood of his time, Sigmund Freud (1905–1938) referred to love as "aim-inhibited sex." Love was viewed as a function of the sexual desire a person was not allowed to express because of social restraints. In Freud's era, people would meet, fall in love, get married, and have sex. He felt that the socially required delay from first meeting to having sex resulted in the development of "love feelings." By extrapolation, Freud's theory of love suggests that love dies with marriage (access to the sex partner).

> Hot love is soon cold.
> **RICHARD WHITFORD**

Ego-ideal Theory

Theodore Reik (1949) suggested that love sprang from a state of dissatisfaction with one's self and that love represented a vain urge to reach one's "ego-ideal." He believed that love was a projection of one's ideal image of himself/herself on another person. For example, suppose you are a shy, passive, dependent person but wished that you were assertive, out-going, and independent. According to Reik's theory, you would probably fall in love with a person who had the qualities you admired but lacked in yourself.

Researcher David Lewis (1985) invites his readers to make a list of their qualities, both favorable and unfavorable. Such a list describes one's "real self." Then he asks the readers to make another list of the qualities that they don't possess, but would like to. This list describes the "ideal self." Lewis suggested that many people seek mates who possess the qualities they put on their ideal

> I love you not only for what you are, but for what I am when I am with you.
> **ROY CROFF**

> Tell me whom you love and I will tell you who you are, and, more especially, who you want to be.
> **THEODORE REIK**

self list. He noted that by attaching ourselves to and loving a person who possesses the qualities of our ideal self we compensate for our inadequacies. We vicariously love our ideal self through loving someone who is a reflection of that ideal self.

Ontological Theory

Love is basically not an emotion but an ontological power, it is the essence of life itself, namely, the dynamic reunion of that which is separated.

MAHATMA GANDHI

Ontology is a branch of philosophy that is concerned with being. Love, from an ontological perspective, arises from a lack of wholeness in our being. Such lack of wholeness is implied by the division of humans into males and females. From an ontological perspective, love represents women's desire to be united with their other half (i.e., men) and men's desire to be united with their other half (i.e., women). Eric Fromm (1963) viewed love as a means of overcoming the "separateness" of an individual and of quelling the anxiety associated with being lonely. When men and women love each other, they become whole.

Biochemical Theory

Being in love is the closest most of us will come to a true addiction.

JOHN MONEY

In *The Chemistry of Love,* (1983), Michael Liebowitz suggested that the experience of romantic love is associated with a natural amphetamine-like substance called phenylethylamine (PEA). When we are in love, our brain produces increased amounts of PEA. One food that contains PEA is chocolate, which may explain why some love-deprived individuals crave chocolate. However, the Chocolate Manufacturer's Association disagrees with Liebowitz's theory:

> The PEA content of chocolate is extremely small, especially in comparison with that of some other commonly consumed foods. The standard serving size of three and a half ounces of smoked salami contains 6.7 mg. of phenylethylamine; the same size serving of cheddar cheese contains 5.8 mg. of phenylethylamine. The standard 1.5-ounce serving of chocolate (the size of the average chocolate bar) contains much less than 1 mg (.21 mg.). Obviously, if Dr. Liebowitz's theory were true, people would be eating salami and cheese in far greater amounts than they are today (quoted in Ackerman, 1990, 155).

Although we don't fully understand the role that biochemical factors play in the experience of love, we can be fairly certain that they do play an important role in producing physiological arousal that is associated with love. However, physiological arousal alone is not experienced as love unless cognitive processes define such arousal as love. Thus, in order to experience romantic love, the individual must be physiologically aroused and interpret this stirred-up state as love (Schacter, 1964; Walster & Walster, 1978).

The biochemical perspective on love suggests that love may be viewed as a natural euphoric feeling. The In Focus 3.1 insert suggests that love is a natural euphoric feeling which may be addictive.

Table 3.1 presents criticisms of each of the theories of love discussed in this chapter.

↳ IN FOCUS 3.1 ↲

Love: A Natural Euphoric Feeling?

In the previous section, we noted that biochemical processes are associated with a sense of euphoria and well-being: love makes us feel energized and feel less need for food and sleep. These euphoric feelings are also characteristic of some drug induced highs. Walsh (1991) said:

> Stimulant drugs such as cocaine and amphetamine have much the same effect as love—love is a natural high (p. 188).

Walsh suggested that some people may be driven to take drugs because their lives are lacking in love. Without love, and the natural chemical high associated with love, some people seek to artificially induce euphoria through the use of drugs.

> It is precisely because some people experience so little joy mediated by the brain's own internal chemicals that they resort to artificial chemicals that briefly mimic pleasure, and soon become physically addicted (Walsh, 1991, 188).

The natural chemical high associated with love may also explain why the intensity of passionate love decreases over time. Individuals who regularly use amphetamines or cocaine must take increasing amounts of the drug in order to experience the same effects. This is because the drug user's body develops a tolerance for the drug, which means that the drug no longer produces its former effects. Similarly, lovers who are high on the "love drug" develop a tolerance for each other over a period of time.

Indeed, love may be addictive (Peele & Brodsky, 1976). It produces a feeling of euphoria that a person learns to enjoy and depend on. Once the person becomes accustomed to the euphoria of love, the person needs to be with the partner to feel the heightened sense of contentment and happiness. Withdrawal symptoms—depression, unhappiness, even somatic complaints—may begin when the love relationship is broken. According to Peele and Brodsky, the person suffering from a broken love relationship goes through withdrawal in much the same way as an alcoholic who has given up alcohol.

THEORY	CRITICISM
Evolutionary	Assumption that women and children need men for survival is not necessarily true today. Women can have and rear children without male partners.
Learning	Does not account for (1) why some people will share positive experiences yet will not fall in love, and (2) why some people stay in love despite negative behavior.
Psychosexual	Does not account for people who report intense love feelings yet are having sex regularly.
Ego-Ideal	Does not account for the fact that people of similar characteristics fall in love.
Ontological	The focus of an ontological view of love is the separation of women and men from each other as love objects. Homosexual love is unaccounted for.
Biochemical	Does not specify how much of what chemicals result in the feeling of love. Chemicals alone cannot create the state of love; cognitions are also important.

TABLE 3.1

Love Theories and Criticisms

Love Relationships

Some of the theories just discussed regard love as an experience or force that exists independent of any particular interpersonal relationship. However, when most people think of love, they think of love in the context of intimate relationships. Next we focus on the social, psychological, physiological, and cognitive conditions under which love relationships develop. We also discuss two dilemmas of love: having simultaneous love relationships and being involved in an unfulfilling love relationship. Lastly, we look at the relationship between health and love and discuss love and the "broken heart."

Conditions Under Which Love Relationships Develop

The development of love relationships is affected by various social, psychological, physiological, and cognitive conditions.

ACROSS CULTURES

Social Conditions   The society in which an individual lives influences the development of one's love relationships. In India and other countries (e.g., Palestine), which practice arranged marriages, the development of romantic love relationships is tightly controlled. For example, parents select the mate for their children in an effort to prevent any potential love relationship from forming with the "wrong person" and to ensure that the child marries the "right person." Such a person must belong to the desired social class and have the economic resources desired by the parents. Marriage in these traditional child marriages are regarded as the linking of two families; the love feelings of the respective partners is insignificant. Love is expected to follow marriage, not precede it.

CONSIDERATION

Our society gives us mixed messages about the importance of love. On the one hand, our capitalistic system encourages us to prioritize career success, work long hours, and accumulate material and economic wealth. But other social influences, such as the media and our peers, emphasize the importance of love relationships. Popular music, movies, television, and novels, convey the message that love is an experience to enjoy and to pursue and that you are missing something if you are not in love.

Psychological Conditions   Two psychological conditions associated with the development of healthy love relationships are a positive self-concept and the ability of self-disclosure.

A positive self-concept is important for developing healthy love relationships because it enables an individual to feel worthy of being loved. Feeling good about yourself allows you to believe that others are capable of loving you, too. Indeed, there is a direct positive relationship between self-esteem by either or both partners and relationship stability (Christensen & Busby, 1992).

In contrast, a negative self-concept has devastating consequences for individuals and the relationships in which they become involved. Individuals who cannot accept themselves tend to reject others. "My daddy always told me I was no good and would never amount to anything," said one individual. "I guess I have always believed him, have never liked myself, and can't think of why someone else would either" (Authors' files).

People with negative self-concepts may require constant affirmation from their partner as to their worth and/or cling desperately to that person so as to not feel alone. Such dependence (the modern term is *codependency*) may encourage unhealthy relationships.

One characteristic of individuals with a negative self-concept is that they may "love too much" and be addicted to "unhealthy love relationships." Petrie et al. (1992) studied 52 women who reported that they were involved in unhealthy love relationships in which they had selected men with problems (e.g., alcohol/drug addiction) they attempted to solve at the expense of neglecting themselves. "Their preoccupation with correcting the problems of others may be an attempt to achieve self-esteem" (Petrie et al., 1992, 17).

Negative self-concepts often have their origin in the family in which one was reared. The 52 women in unhealthy relationships with low self-concepts reported that they grew up "in nonsupportive, nonaffectionate childhood homes in which their emotional needs were not met" (Petrie et al., 1992, 16).

> Criticism slides off my back. It's always been part of my makeup, a certain confidence in myself.
> SPIKE LEE

> I look good from the neck up
> CARNIE WILSON (of wilson-phillips)

CONSIDERATION

Although it helps to have a positive self-concept at the beginning of a love relationship, sometimes this develops after becoming involved in a love relationship. "I've always felt like an ugly duckling," said one woman. "But once I fell in love with him and he with me, I felt very different. I felt very good about myself then because I knew that I was somebody that someone else loved." A positive self-concept then is not a prerequisite for falling in love. People who have a very negative self-concept may fall in love with someone else as a result of feeling deficient (ego-ideal theory of love). The love they perceive the other person having for them may compensate for the deficiency and improve their self-esteem.

While our focus here has been how self-concept affects adult love relationships, it is important to note that love also affects self-esteem. The role that love plays in determining one's self-concept is especially important during the formative years. The degree that love is expressed to children strongly affects their feelings of self-worth in later years. One study found that early parental nurturance was the strongest predictor of a positive self-concept among college students (Buri, Kirchner, & Wash, 1987).

The effect that love has on one's self-concept may be different for men and women. Two researchers found that love is approximately 2.8 times more important in influencing a positive self-concept for women than it is for men

A positive self concept and self-disclosure are related to the development of love feelings.

(Walsh & Balazs, 1990). The researchers found that women who felt they received little love had a much more negative self-concept than men who received little love. However, women who felt deeply loved had significantly more positive self-concepts than men who also felt deeply loved.

In addition to feeling good about yourself, it is helpful to disclose your thoughts and feelings to others if you want to love and be loved. Disclosing yourself is a way of investing yourself in another. Once the other person knows some of the intimate details of your life, you will tend to feel more positively about that person because a part of you is now a part of him or her. Open communication in this sense tends to foster the development of an intense love relationship.

It is not easy for some people to let others know who they are, what they feel, or what they think. They may fear that if others really know them, they will be rejected as a friend or lover. To guard against this possibility, they may protect themselves and their relationships by allowing only limited access to their past behaviors and present thoughts/feelings.

Trust is the condition under which people are most willing to disclose themselves. When people trust someone, they tend to feel that whatever feelings or information they share will not be judged and will be kept safe with that person. If trust is betrayed, a person may become bitterly resentful and vow never to disclose herself or himself again. One woman said, "After I told my partner that I had had an abortion, he told me that I was a murderer and he never wanted to see me again. I was devastated and felt I had made a mistake telling him about my past intimate life. You can bet I'll be careful before I disclose myself to someone else" (Authors' files).

Physiological and Cognitive Conditions   In addition to social and psychological conditions of love, physiological and cognitive conditions of love are also important. The individual must be physiologically aroused and interpret this stirred-up state as love (Walster & Walster, 1978).

> Suppose, for example, that Dan is afraid of flying, but his fear is not particularly extreme and he doesn't like to admit it to himself. This fear, however, does cause him to be physiologically aroused. Suppose further that Dan takes a flight and finds himself sitting next to Judy on the plane. With heart racing, palms sweating, and breathing labored, Dan chats with Judy as the plane takes off. Suddenly, Dan discovers that he finds Judy terribly attractive, and he begins to try to figure out ways that he can continue seeing her after the flight is over. What accounts for Dan's sudden surge of interest in Judy? Is she really that appealing to him, or has he taken the physiological arousal of fear and mislabeled it as attraction? (Brehm, 1992, 44).

Since most people are not aroused in this way, yet develop love feelings, they may be aroused or anxious about other issues (being excited at a party, feeling apprehensive about meeting new people) and mislabel these feelings as those of attraction when they meet someone. Gold and Wegner (1991) demonstrated that physiological arousal occurs in response to thoughts about one's romantic obsession. They found that thinking about an "old flame" was significantly more physiologically arousing (as measured by higher skin conductance levels) than thinking about a "cold flame."

CONSIDERATION

The social, psychological, physiological, and cognitive conditions are not the only factors important for the development of love feelings. The timing must also be right. There are only certain times in your life when you are seeking a love relationship. When those times occur, you are likely to fall in love with the person who is there and is also seeking a love relationship. Hence, many love pairings exist because each of the individuals is available to the other at the right time—not because they are particularly suited for each other.

Dilemmas of Love Relationships

Being in love may create dilemmas. Two such dilemmas include being in love with two people at the same time or being involved in an abusive or unfulfilling love relationship.

Love is a sour delight, a sugar'd grief, a living death, an ever-dying life.

THOMAS WATSON

Simultaneous Loves   The lyrics of Mary McGregor's "Torn Between Two Lovers" reflect the dilemma of being in love with two people at the same time:

> Torn between two lovers, feeling like a fool,
> loving both of you is breaking all the rules.

It is better to love two too many than one too few.

SIR JOHN HARRINGTON

"I know that I love my spouse," said one individual, "but I also love the person I work with." Such a dilemma is not unusual. It is possible to be involved in several relationships at the same time and to have love feelings for each person.

Although it is possible to love two or more people at the same time, it is not possible to love them to the same degree (or in exactly the same way) at any particular moment because an individual must make a choice in terms of how to spend his or her time. If you choose to spend time with person X, then you value that person more than others—at least for that moment in time.

CONSIDERATION

Some people do not like the feeling of being in love with two people at once and try to reduce their feelings for one of them. This may be accomplished by deciding to see only one of the persons and by thinking negative thoughts about the other. For example, Jan, who was in love with both her husband and her colleague, decided to stop seeing her colleague socially. When she did think of him, she made herself think only of what she perceived to be the negative aspects of being involved with him: he was married, he drank heavily, he smoked, he was 12 years older than she, he had little ambition, and he had three teenage children he would bring to live with them if they eventually married.

Love is a sweet tyranny because the lover endureth his/her torments willingly.

H. G. BOHN

It is possible to be in love with someone with whom there is perpetual conflict.

Abusive or Unfulfilling Love Relationship   Another dilemma of love is being in love with someone who may be emotionally or physically abusive (we will discuss abusive relationships in detail in Chapter 12). Someone who is an alcoholic and beats you, who criticizes you continually ("you're ugly, stupid, pitiful"), or who is dishonest with you (sexually unfaithful) may create a great deal of pain, stress, and disappointment. Nevertheless, you might love that person and feel emotionally drawn to him or her. Most marriage therapists would suggest that you examine why you love and continue to stay with this person. Do you feel that you deserve this treatment because you are "no good"? Do you feel pity for the person and feel responsible for rescuing him or her? Do you feel you would not be able to find a better alternative? Do you feel you would rather be with a person who treats you bad than to be alone? These questions imply that your love relationship may be based on motivations that you might want to examine carefully with a therapist or counselor.

Love relationships that do not involve emotional or physical abuse may be unfulfilling for other reasons. Partners in love relationships may experience lack of fulfillment if they have radically different values, religious beliefs, role expectations, recreational or occupational interests, sexual needs, or desires concerning family size. One woman said,

> I want to have a child, but my partner doesn't. He already has two children from a previous marriage and doesn't want any more. I love him and want to marry him, but I don't know how difficult it will be for me to accept having no children of my own. (Author's files)

CONSIDERATION

Some students in the authors' classes have asked, "Is there a difference between loving and being in love?" A possible answer to this question is as follows: Loving involves loving a person; being in love involves loving the relationship as well as the person. This implies that we may love a person but not love the relationship we have with that person because of the way that person treats us. Some people going through divorce have indicated that they wanted to divorce not because they did not love their spouse, but because the partner had hurt them so many times that they needed to stop being in the relationship with that person. In other words, they still loved their spouse, but they were not in love (with the relationship).

Love and Health

When children scrape their knees, bang their elbows, or bump their heads, their parents often respond by kissing the knee or whatever to make it feel better. While not all people believe the adage that "Love heals all wounds," many believe that love has healing properties. This belief also implies that lack of love may be injurious to our health. Indeed, Freud wrote that ". . . in the last resort we must begin to love in order that we may not fall ill . . ." (1924, 42).

Considerable research supports the idea that love promotes physical well-being. In *Love, Medicine, and Miracles,* Dr. Bernie Siegel (1986) describes some of this research:

- At the Menninger Foundation in Topeka, Kansas, people who are in love, in the romantic sense, have been found to have reduced levels of lactic acid in their blood, making them less tired, and higher levels of endorphins, making them euphoric and less subject to pain. Their white blood cells also responded better when faced with infections, and thus they got fewer colds (p. 182–183).
- In 1982, Harvard psychologists David McClelland and Carol Kirshnit found that even movies about love increase levels of immunoglobulin-A in the saliva, the first line of defense against colds and other viral diseases (p. 183).

While love may enhance physical well-being, love deprivation may jeopardize it. Rene Spitz (1945) conducted a classic study on early love deprivation with institutionalized infants. Spitz was concerned about the unexplained high infant death rates among infants in foundling homes, despite adequate nutrition, medical care, and hygiene. In contrast, Spitz found that there was less illness and death among infants in a nursery in a penal institution for delinquent girls, even though the level of medical care, hygiene, and nutrition was below that of the foundling home.

Within two years after the start of his study, Spitz observed that 37 percent of the foundling home children had died while all of the children in the penal nursery were alive five years later. He concluded that the high death

> It is not the threat of death, illness, hardship, or poverty that crushes the human spirit; it is the fear of being alone and unloved in the universe.
>
> ANTHONY WALSH

❧ **IN FOCUS 3.2** ❧

Love and the Broken Heart

Poets and songwriters have often written about "broken hearts" resulting from the loss of love or a loved one. But physicians and medical researchers have also explored the effect of terminated love relationships on the heart. In *The Broken Heart: The Medical Consequences of Loneliness* (1977), James Lynch stated that: "Growing numbers of physicians now recognize that the health of the human heart depends not only on such factors as genetics, diet, and exercise, but also to a large extent on the social and emotional health of the individual" (p. 13).

Some research suggests that love, or more accurately the absence of it, can "break your heart." Research also suggests that love may help to heal a heart that is "already broken."

Heart disease is often related to high blood pressure. Research by Sisca, Walsh, and Walsh (1985) suggests that high blood pressure is associated with love deprivation. The researchers measured love deprivation in college students by administering two questionnaires that tapped respondents' subjective perceptions of the degree to which they felt loved or unloved. Love deprivation was found to be significantly and positively related to elevated blood pressure levels, i.e., the higher the love deprivation, the higher the blood pressure. This effect was independent of age and weight variables.

In addition to research, there is anecdotal evidence that supports the folk belief that love can mend a "broken" heart. Joy Lynn Shumante, a nurse at the Leesburg Regional Medical Center in Florida, describes an incident which reveals such a belief: An eighty-year-old man, who arrived at a hospital with chest pains, went into cardiac arrest at the hospital. He was in very serious condition and the doctors and nurses thought there was no hope for this man to survive. The man's wife of 60 years approached her unconscious husband on the hospital bed. Nurse Shumante describes:

> Mrs. Carroll touched her husband's face and leaned close to his ear . . . as she whispered, "I'm going to miss you, darling. I love you." Suddenly, Mr. Carroll's heart rate increased to a normal sinus rhythm. . . . Mrs. Carroll just kept whispering loving words to her husband. And as she talked to him, his vital signs stabilized (Shumante, 1990, 112).

Thus, research and anecdotal reports give credence to the comments of James Lynch (1977) who observed, "If lack of human love . . . can disturb the heart, then just as clearly the presence of human love may serve as a powerful therapeutic force, helping the heart to restore itself" (p. 113).

---

rate among the foundling home infants was due to lack of love. The penal children were cared for by their own mothers, who kissed, held, talked to, played with, and showed affection toward their children. In other words, the penal children were loved. While nurses in the foundling home provided adequate medical and nutritional care to the infants, they did not have the time nor the inclination to develop affectionate bonds with all the babies in their care.

In the In Focus 3.2 insert, we discuss the effects of love and love deprivation on one's heart. While love may not literally break your heart, the absence of it may be deleterious to your coronary health.

❧ Jealousy in Relationships

Jealousy may be defined as an emotional response to a perceived or real threat to a valued relationship (Bringle & Buunk, 1991). One researcher defined jealousy as "a protective reaction to a perceived threat to a valued relationship or to its quality" (Clanton, 1990, 180). Although jealousy does not occur in all cultures (polyandrous societies value cooperation, not sexual exclusivity; Cassidy & Lee, 1989), it is common in our society.

NATIONAL DATA ॐ A nationwide survey of marriage therapists reported that jealousy is a problem in one-third of all couples coming for marital therapy (Pines, 1992).

Over 2000 college students from seven industrialized countries (Hungary, Ireland, Mexico, the Netherlands, the former Soviet Union, the former Yugoslavia, and the United States) were asked about what makes them jealous. Jealousy existed in all countries, with flirting and sexual involvement eliciting the most negative reactions. Students from the Netherlands and the former Soviet Union tended to be the least and most jealous respectively. Students from the United States were mid–range (Buunk & Hupka, 1987).

Causes of Jealousy

Jealousy may be caused by external or internal factors.

External Causes   External factors refer to behaviors of the partner that suggest:

1. an emotional and/or sexual interest in someone (or something) else; or
2. a lack of emotional and/or sexual interest in the primary partner.

Examples of external causes of jealousy include flirting or spending a lot of time with or expressing interest in someone else. External causes may also result from spending little time with and expressing little interest in the primary partner.

Internal Causes   Jealousy may also exist even when there is no external behavior that indicates the partner is involved or interested in an extradyadic relationship. Internal causes of jealousy refer to characteristics of individuals that predispose them to jealous feelings, independent of their partner's behavior. Examples of internal causes of jealousy include being mistrustful, having low self-esteem, being highly involved in and dependent on the relationship, and having no perceived alternative partners available (Pines, 1992). These internal causes of jealousy are explained below.

1. Mistrust: If an individual has been deceived or "cheated on" in a previous relationship, that individual may learn to be mistrustful in subsequent relationships. Such mistrust may manifest itself in jealousy.
2. Low self-esteem: Individuals who have low self-esteem tend to be jealous because they lack a sense of self-worth and, hence, find it difficult to believe anyone can value and love them. Feelings of worthlessness may contribute to suspicions that someone else is valued more.
3. High degree of relative involvement or dependency: In general, individuals

To demand of love that it be without jealousy is to ask of light that it cast no shadows.

OSCAR HAMILTON

ACROSS CULTURES ॐ

The jealous are troublesome to others but a torment to themselves.

WILLIAM PENN

who are more involved in the relationship than their partner, or who are more dependent on the relationship than their partner, are prone to jealousy (Radecki et al., 1988).

CONSIDERATION

The person who is more involved or dependent on the relationship is not only more likely to experience jealousy, but may also intentionally induce jealousy in the partner. Such attempts to induce jealousy may involve flirting, exaggerating or discussing an attraction to someone else, and spending time with others. According to White (1980), individuals may try to make their partner jealous in order to test the relationship (e.g., see if the partner still cares) and/or to increase specific rewards (e.g., get more attention or affection). White found that women, especially those who thought they were more involved in the relationship than their partners, were more likely to induce jealousy in a relationship than men.

---

4. Lack of perceived alternatives: In a study of jealousy among spouses, the most jealous were those who felt they could not find another partner if their partner became attracted to someone else (Hansen, 1985).

Consequences of Jealousy

Jealousy may have both desirable consequences (reinforce one's sense of value, confirm unacceptability of outside relationship, reevaluation of relationship, increase communication) and undesirable consequences (increase stress, ignite self-fulfilling prophecy, homicide, suicide).

Desirable Outcomes   Low levels of jealousy may be functional for a couple's relationship. Not only may jealousy keep the partner aware that he or she is cared for (the implied message is "I love you and don't want to lose you to someone else"), but also the partner may learn that the development of romantic and sexual relationships "on the side" is unacceptable. One wife said:

> When I started spending extra time with this guy at the office my husband got jealous and told me he thought I was getting in over my head and asked me to cut back on the relationship because it was "tearing him up" and he couldn't stay married to me with these feelings. I felt he really loved me when he told me this and I chose to stop spending time with the guy at work (Authors' files).

Jealousy may improve a couple's relationship in yet another way. When the partners begin to take each other for granted, involvement of one or both partners outside the relationship can encourage them to reevaluate how important the relationship is and can help recharge it. Bringle & Buunk (1991) summarized the potential desirable outcomes of jealousy:

> Suspicious jealousy is not necessarily unhealthy jealousy. When there is a pattern of minor incidents suggesting that the partner might be involved with

We need to admit that jealousy is okay, even helpful at times.

AYALA PINES

someone else, vigilance to determine what is happening may be a prudent response that reflects reasonable concern and good strategies to cope with the situation. Furthermore, emotional reactions to these events may forewarn the partner of what will happen if there are serious transgressions and thereby serve the role of *preventing* extradyadic involvements (p. 137).

CONSIDERATION

Sometimes the reaction to one's partner's jealousy encourages further jealous behavior. Suppose John accuses Mary of being interested in someone else, and Mary denies the accusation and responds by saying "I love you" and by being very affectionate. From a behavioral or social learning perspective, if this pattern continues, Mary will teach John to continue being jealous. When John acts jealous, good things happen to him—Mary showers him with love and physical affection. Inadvertently, Mary may be reinforcing John for exhibiting jealous behavior.

To break the cycle, Mary should tell John of her love for him and be affectionate when he is *not* exhibiting jealous behavior. When he does act jealous, she might say she feels badly when he accuses her of something she isn't doing and to please stop. If he does not stop, she might terminate the interaction until John can be around her and not act jealous.

> **Jealousy is nourished by doubt.**
> LA ROCHEFOUCAULD

Undesirable Outcomes   Shakespeare referred to jealousy as the "green-eyed monster," suggesting that jealousy is a frightening emotion with undesirable outcomes for individuals and for relationships. Jealousy that stems from low self-esteem may result in the partner withdrawing from the relationship. Walsh (1991) explained:

> An individual with feelings of negative self-worth . . . is continually imagining that no one could really be faithful to such an undeserving soul. If a person feels this way about him or herself, that atmosphere of insecurity, possessiveness, and accusations. . . . makes it more probable that the mate will eventually come to share the self-evaluation and go forth to seek someone more deserving of his or her love. If such an event does occur, it merely seems to vindicate what we've known all along—we're no good.

> **'Tis well to be off with the old love,**
> **Before you are on with the new.**
> C. R. MATURIN

CONSIDERATION

Jealousy may also create a self-fulfilling prophecy whereby the partner who is accused of having an interest in or being involved with someone else reacts by engaging in the behavior of which they are accused. The self-fulfilling prophecy is illustrated by the partner who says "If I'm going to get accused all the time for something I'm not guilty of, I might as well go ahead and sleep with other women. After all, I get accused of it whether I do or I don't so I might as well enjoy what I'm being accused of."

In its extreme form, jealousy may have devastating consequences, including murder, suicide, spouse beating, and severe depression. Makepeace (1989) found that violence in steady dating relationships is likely to be precipitated by arguments over jealousy. Violence in cohabiting and marital relationships is also frequently precipitated by jealousy.

Jealousy is not an easy emotion with which to cope. A beginning might be for individuals experiencing jealousy to make their partners aware of such feelings and to ask for their help. By doing so, the feelings become visible and permit the couple to work on them as a unit (thus helping to improve their solidarity as a couple).

> **Jealousy is always born with love, but does not always die with it.**
>
> LA ROCHEFOUCAULD

CONSIDERATION

Two researchers suggested four basic options individuals might consider in coping with a problem of jealousy in their relationship (Clanton & Smith, 1986):

1. Terminate the relationship.
2. Ignore and/or tolerate the external behaviors that cause the jealousy.
3. Influence the partner who engages in various behaviors that elicit jealousy to stop or modify those behaviors.
4. Work on the internal causes of the jealousy (p. 161).

℅ Trends

The most predictable trend in love relationships is that romantic love will, in this society, continue to characterize each new love relationship. Although a person may have been disappointed in previous relationships, love feelings help to create the illusion that the current love relationship will be different. One person cannot convince another that love is something more than illusion, deception, and idealization; such a perception is grounded in experience. Even those with extensive interpersonal experience are not immune to falling in love.

While love will continue to be a reason to get married, it is losing its value as a reason to stay married. Increasingly, college students are less willing to end a marriage if love dies. "In 1979, 59 percent of college students said that a marriage without love should end. That figure dropped to 45 percent in 1986 and to 35 percent in 1988–1989" (Levine, 1993, 29). Reasons for the decline are that individuals are becoming more accepting of the fact that infatuation doesn't last forever, no matter whom you're with, and that staying in a monogamous relationship is smart in an age of HIV infection.

CHOICES

*C*hoosing to listen to one's heart or head when making decisions and choosing to have sex with or without love are two important decisions individuals make about their love relationships. We now examine each of these choices.

Heart or Head: Which Should You Listen To?

Lovers are frequently confronted with the need to make decisions about their relationships, but they are divided on whether to let their heart or head rule in such decisions. In a marriage and family class, 120 students were asked whether they used their hearts or their heads in making such decisions. Some of their answers follow.

Heart

Those who relied on their heart (women more likely) for making decisions felt that emotions were more important than logic and that listening to your heart made you happier. One woman said:

> In deciding on a mate, my heart should rule because my heart has reasons to cry and my head doesn't. My heart knows what I want, what would make me most happy. My head tells me what is best for me. But I would rather have something that makes me happy than something that is good for me.

Some men also agreed that your heart should rule. One said:

> I went with my heart in a situation, and I'm glad I did. I had been dating a girl for two years when I decided she was not the one I wanted and that my present girlfriend was. My heart was saying to go for the one I loved, but my head was telling me not to because if I broke up with the first girl, it would hurt her, her parents, and my parents. But I decided I had to make myself happy and went with the feelings in my heart and started dating the girl who is now my fiancée.

Relying on one's emotions does not always have a positive outcome, as the following experience illustrates:

> Last semester, I was dating a guy I felt more for than he did for me. Despite that, I wanted to spend any opportunity I could with him when he asked me to go somewhere with him. One day he had no classes, and he asked me to go to the park by the river for a picnic. I had four classes that day and exams in two of them. I let my heart rule and went with him. Nothing ever came of the relationship and I didn't do well in those classes.

Head

Most of the respondents (men more likely) felt that it was better to be rational than emotional.

> In deciding on a mate, I feel my head should rule because you have to choose someone that you can get along with after the new wears off. If you follow your heart solely, you may not look deep enough into a person to see what it is that you really like. Is it just a pretty face or a nice body? Or is it deeper than that, such as common interests and attitudes? After the new wears off, it's the person inside the body that you're going to have to live with. The "heart" sometimes can fog up this picture of the true person and distort reality into a fairy tale.

> Love is blind and can play tricks on you. Two years ago, I fell in love with a man whom I later found out was married. Although my heart had learned to love this man, my mind knew the consequences and told me to stop seeing him. My heart said, "Maybe he'll leave her for me," but my mind said, "If he cheated on her, he'll cheat on you." I got out and am glad that I listened to my head.

Some feel that both the head and the heart should rule when making relationship decisions.

> When you really love someone, your heart rules in most of the situations. But if you don't keep your head in some matters, then you risk losing the love that you feel in your heart. I think that we should find a

(continued on the next page)

way to let our heads and hearts rule together.

There is an old saying from an unknown source, "Don't wait until you can find the person you can live with; wait and find the person that you can't live without!" One individual hearing this quote said, "I think both are important. I want my head to find the right person to live with but my heart to tell me that now is the time to do it!" (Authors' files).

Sex With or Without Love?

Most college students are likely to approve of sex in the context of a love relationship. In one study, love and intimacy were the most frequently stated motives for their last intercourse experience reported by a sample of university students (Brigman & Knox, 1992).

The following is an example of what a female student said about the importance of an emotional relationship as a context for sexual expression:

> Sex is good and beautiful when both parties want it, but when one person wants sex only, that's bad. I love sex, but I like to feel that the man cares about me. I can't handle the type of sexual relationship where one night I spend the night with him and the next night he spends the

night with someone else. I feel like I am being used. There are still a few women around like me who *need* the commitment before sex. (Authors' files)

Other people feel that love is not necessary for sexual expression. "Some of the best sex I've had," remarked one person, "was with people I was not in love with." The idea that sex with love is wholesome and sex without love is exploitative may be an untenable position. For example, two strangers can meet, share each other sexually, have a deep mutual admiration for each other's sensuous qualities, and go their separate ways in the morning. Such an encounter is not necessarily an example of sexual exploitation. Rather, it may be an example of two individuals who have a preference for independence and singlehood rather than emotional involvement, commitment, and marriage.

Each person in a sexual encounter will undoubtedly experience different degrees of love feelings; and the experience of each may differ across time. One woman reported that the first time she had intercourse with her future husband was shortly after they had met in a bar. She described their first sexual encounter as "raw naked sex" with no emotional feelings. But they continued to see each other over a

period of months, an emotional relationship developed, and "sex took on a love meaning for us."

Sex with love can also drift into sex without love. One man said he had been deeply in love with his wife but that they had gradually drifted apart. Sex between them was no longer sex with love. Similarly, some women report being in relationships with men who feign love but actually use them for sex. Bepko and Krestan (1991) emphasized the importance of women breaking from these codependent relationships and establishing their own self-love as a secure base for making choices in relationships with others.

Both love and sex can be viewed on a continuum. Love feelings may range from being nonexistent to being intense, and relationships can range from limited sexual interaction to intense interaction. Hence, rarely are sexual encounters completely with or without love; rather, they will include varying degrees of emotional involvement. Also, rarely are romantic love relationships completely with or without sex. Rather, they display varying degrees of sexual expression. Where on the continuum one chooses to be—at what degree of emotional and sexual involvement—will vary from person to person and from time to time.

𝒮 Summary

Love is a central feature in North American relationships and is considered a prerequisite for marriage. While most people agree on the importance of love, they do not always agree on its definition. Buddhists, Greeks, and Hebrews had different conceptions of love. Love may best be described as being composed of various elements—emotional, physical, social, intellectual, and spiritual.

One way of conceptualizing love is on a romantic versus realistic continuum. Romantics believe in love at first sight, only one true love, and love conquers all. Romantic love has its roots in 12th century France when knights professed love to unavailable (married) ladies of the aristocracy. Love and marriage were kept separate in that the former was for reasons of money and social position, not love. The connection of love and marriage began in the 18th and 19th century among the English and imported to the Americas. Today an individual would be embarrassed not to be in love with a potential marriage partner.

Theories of love include evolutionary (love provided the social glue needed to bond parents and dependent children and spouses to care for their dependent offspring), social learning (positive experiences create love feelings), psychosexual (love is a feeling that results from a blocked biological drive), ego-ideal (love springs from a dissatisfaction with one's self), ontological (love is the urge to reunite the separated), and biochemical (love involves feelings produced by biochemical events).

Love occurs under certain conditions. Social conditions include a society that promotes the pursuit of love, peers who enjoy it, and a set of norms that link love and marriage. Psychological conditions involve a positive self-concept and a willingness to disclose one's self to others. Physiological and cognitive conditions imply that the individual experiences a stirred-up state and labels it "love." All of these conditions are important but not essential. What is essential is a high frequency of positive verbal and nonverbal behavior from the partner to furnish the basis on which love feelings may develop. It is easy for us to fall in love with someone who compliments us, is affectionate, and shares our value system. We are less likely to develop love feelings for those who criticize us, do not enjoy touching us, and do not respect our values.

Dilemmas of love include being in love with two people at the same time and being in love with someone who is abusive, an alcoholic, or who is unfulfilling. It is not unusual for someone to be in love with a person he or she finds difficult to live with.

Jealousy is an emotional response to a perceived or real threat to a valued relationship. Jealous feelings may have both internal and external causes and may have both positive and negative consequences for a couple's relationship.

Love relationships in the future will be the same as those in the past—exciting. Each new love relationship often involves the same sense of exhilaration. In Western societies, love is the most sought after feeling in the human experience. In time, romantic love feelings change to a more comfortable though less intense set of feelings.

Questions for Reflection

1. To what degree are you romantic or realistic in your view of love. How has your view affected your various relationships?
2. Why do you think people stay in relationships that others can "see" are not good for them?
3. To what degree are you comfortable disclosing yourself to others? How did you develop this level of comfort or discomfort?

References

Acker, M. and M. H. Davis. Intimacy, passion and commitment in adult romantic relationships: A test of the triangular theory of love. *Journal of Social and Personal Relationships*, 1992, *9*, 21–50.

Ackerman, Diane. *A natural history of the senses.* New York: Random House, 1990.

Bahr, K. S. Family love as a paradigmatic alternative to family studies. *Family Perspective*, 1992, *26*, 281–304.

Belsky, J. and M. Rovine. Patterns of marital change across the transition to parenthood: Pregnancy to three years postpartum. *Journal of Marriage and the Family*, 1990, *52*, 5–19.

Bepko, Claudia and Jo-Ann Krestan. *Too good for her own good: Searching for self and intimacy in important relationships.* New York: Harper-Collins Publishers, 1991.

Brehm, S. S. *Intimate relationships*, 2d ed. New York: McGraw-Hill, 1992.

Brigman, B. and D. Knox. University students' motivations to have intercourse. *College Student Journal*, 1992, *26*, 406–408.

Bringle, R. G. and B. P. Buunk. Extradyadic relationships and sexual jealousy. *Sexuality in Close Relationships*, K. McKinney and S. Sprecher, eds. Hillsdale, N.J.: Lawrence Erlbaum Associates, 1991, 135–154.

Buri, John, Peggy Kirchner, and Jane Wash. Familial correlates of self-esteem in young American adults. *The Journal of Social Psychology*, 1987, *127*, 583–588.

Burtt, E. A. *A man seeks the divine.* New York: Harper and Brothers, 1957.

Buss, D. M. The evolutionary biology of love. *The Psychology of Love*, R. J. Sternberg and M. L. Barnes, eds. New Haven, Conn.: Yale University Press, 1988, 100–118.

Buunk, B. and R. B. Hupka. Cross–cultural differences in the elicitation of sexual jealousy. *Journal of Sex Research*, 1987, *23*, 12–22.

Campbell, Joseph. *Myths to live by.* New York: Bantum, 1972.

Cancian, F. M. *Love in America: Gender and self-development.* New York: Cambridge University Press, 1987.

Carnelley, K. B. and R. Janoff-Bulman. Optimism about love relationships: General vs. specific lessons from one's personal experiences. *Journal of Social and Personal Relationships*, 1992, *9*, 5–20.

Cassidy, M. L. and G. Lee. The study of polyandry: A critique and synthesis. *Journal of Comparative Family Studies*, 1989, *20*, 1–11.

Christensen, C. D. and D. M. Busby. Homogamy of personality variables and relationship stability. *Proceedings: Families and work* 54th Annual Conference of the National Council on Family Relations, Orlando, Florida, 1992, vol 2, #1, p. 35.

Clanton, G. Jealousy in American culture, 1945–1985: Reflections from popular culture. *The Sociology of Emotions: Original Essays and Research,* D. D. Franks & E. D. McCarthy, eds. Greenwich, Conn.: JAI Press, 1990, 179–193.

Clanton, G. and L. G. Smith. Managing jealousy. *Jealousy* G. Clanton and L. G. Smith, eds. Lanham, Md.: University Press of America, 1986, 161–165.

Delamater, John. Emotions and sexuality. *Sexuality in Close Relationships,* K. McKinney and S. Sprecher, eds. Hillsdale, N.J.: Lawrence Erlbaum Associates, 1991, 49–70.

Dion, K. K. and K. L. Dion. Psychological individualism and romantic love. *Journal of Social Behavior and Personality,* 1991, *6,* 17–33.

Erickson, E. H. *Childhood and society.* New York: Norton, 1963.

Freud, Sigmund. On narcissism. *Collected Papers of Sigmund Freud,* vol. 4, New York: International Psychoanalytic Press, 1924.

Freud, Sigmund. Three contributions to the theory of sex. *The Basic Writings of Sigmund Freud,* A. A. Brill, ed. New York: Random House, 1938 (originally published in 1905).

Fromm, E. *The art of loving.* New York: Bantam Books, 1963.

Gold, D. and D. M. Wegner. Fanning old flames: Arousing romantic obsession through thought suppression. Paper, American Psychological Association, August, 1991, San Francisco, California. Used by permission of Daniel M. Wegner.

Hansen, G. L. Perceived threats and marital jealousy. *Social Psychology Quarterly,* 1985, *48,* 262–268.

Hazen, C. and P. Shaver. Romantic love conceptualized as an attachment process. *Journal of Personality and Social Psychology,* 1987, *52,* 511–524.

Hendrick, C. and S. S. Hendrick. Dimensions of love: A sociobiological interpretation. *Journal of Social and Clinical Psychology,* 1991, *10,* 206–230.

Hendrick, C., S. Hendrick, F. H. Foote, and M. J. Slapion-Foote. Do men and women love differently? *Journal of Social and Personal Relationships,* 1984, *1,* 177–195.

Hendrick, S. S., C. Hendrick, and N. L. Adler. Romantic relationships: Love, satisfaction, and staying together. *Journal of Personality and Social Psychology,* 1988, *54,* 980–988.

Jankowiak, W. R. and E. F. Fischer. A cross-cultural perspective on romantic love. *Ethnology* 1992, *31,* 149–155.

Lee, J. A. *The colors of love: An exploration of the ways of loving.* Don Mills, Ontario: New Press, 1973.

Lee, J. A. Love-styles. *The Psychology of Love,* R. Sternberg and M. Barnes, eds. New Haven, Conn.: Yale University Press, 1988, 38–67.

Levine, R. V. Is love a luxury? *American Demographics,* February 15, 1993, 27–29.

Lewis, David. *In and out of love: The mystery of personal attraction.* London: Methuen, 1985.

Liebowitz, M. *The chemistry of love.* Boston: Little, Brown, 1983.

Lynch, James. *The broken heart: The medical consequences of loneliness.* New York: Basic Books, 1977.

Makepeace, James. Dating, living together, and courtship violence. *Violence in dating relationships,* M. Aa. Pirog-Good and Jan E. Stets, eds. New York: Greenwood Press, 1989, 94–107.

Maslow, Abraham. *Toward a psychology of being.* New York: D. Van Nostrand, 1968.

Pedersen, L. E. *Dark hearts: The unconscious forces that shape men's lives.* Boston: Shambhala, 1991.

Peele, S. and A. Brodsky. *Love and addiction.* New York: New American Library, 1976.

Petrie, J., J. A. Giordano, and C. S. Roberts. Characteristics of women who love too much. *Affilia: Journal of Women and Social Work,* 1992, *7,* 7–20.

Pines, A. M. *Romantic jealousy: Understanding and conquering the shadow of love.* New York: St. Martins Press, 1992.

Radecki Bush, C. R., J. P. Bush, and J. Jennings. Effects of jealousy threats on relationship perceptions and emotions. *Journal of Social and Personal Relationships,* 1988, *5,* 285–303.

Reik, T. *Of love and lust.* New York: Farrar, Straus, and Cudahy, 1949.

Rubenstein, C. The modern art of courtly love. *Psychology Today.* July 1983, 40–49.

Rubin, Z. Measurement of romantic love. *Journal of Personality and Social Psychology,* 1970, *16,* 265–273.

Schacter, S. The interaction of cognitive and physiological determinants of emotional state. *Advances in Experimental Social Psychology.* L. Berkowitz, ed. New York: Academic Press, 1964, 49–80.

Shumante, Lynn. What nurses can't cure, love can. *Nursing,* July 1990, 112.

Siegel, B. S. *Love, medicine and miracles.* New York: Harper & Row, 1986.

Simmons, C. H., A. V. Kolke, and H. Shimizu. Attitudes toward romantic love among American, German, and Japanese students. *The Journal of Social Psychology,* 1986, *126,* 327–336.

Sisca, Sam; Anthony Walsh, and Patricia Walsh. Love deprivation and blood pressure levels among a college population: A preliminary investigation. *Psychology,* 1985, *22,* 63–70.

Spitz, T. S. Hospitalism. *The Psychoanalytic Study of the Child,* Anna Freud et al., eds. 1945, *1,* 52–57.

Sternberg, R. J. A triangular theory of love. *Psychological Review,* 1986, *93,* 119–135.

Sternberg, R. J. and A. E. Beall. How can we know what love is? An epistemological analysis. *Cognition in Close Relationships,* Garth J. O. Fletcher and F. D. Fincham, eds. Hillsdale, N.J.: Lawrence Erlbaum Associates, 1991, 257–278.

Stone, C. R. and J. L. Philbrick. Attitudes toward love among members of a small fundamentalist community in South Africa. *The Journal of Social Psychology,* 1991, 131, 219–233.

Tavris, C. *The mismeasure of women.* New York: Simon & Schuster, 1992.

Walsh, Anthony. *The science of love: Understanding love and its effects on mind and body.* Buffalo, New York: Prometheus Books, 1991.

Walsh, Anthony and Grace Balazs. Love, sex, and self-esteem. *Free Inquiry in Creative Sociology,* 1990, *18,* 37–42.

Walster, E. and G. W. Walster. *A new look at love.* Reading, Mass.: Addison-Wesley, 1978.

White, G. L. Inducing jealousy: A power perspective. *Personality and Social Psychology Bulletin,* 1980, *6,* 222–227.

Contents

ೱ **4** ೱ

CHAPTER

Sexual Values and Behaviors

Is It True?

1. Most adults in the United States approve of premarital intercourse and disapprove of extramarital intercourse.

2. One's sexual values and behaviors affect one's risk of contracting HIV and other STDs.

3. Women in the United States tend to have intercourse at an earlier age than men.

4. One study found that the most frequently reported lie told to potential sexual partners was in regard to the number of previous sexual partners they had had.

5. Women are as likely as men to have intercourse for reasons of sexual release.

1 = T; 2 = T; 3 = F; 4 = T; 5 = F

For the first time in history, sex is more dangerous than the cigarette afterward.

JAY LENO

*I*n the 1993 movie *Indecent Proposal* with Robert Redford and Demi Moore, a wealthy man offers a married couple one million dollars to sleep with the wife. This offer forced the couple to examine their sexual values: Is extramarital sex always wrong? Even for a million dollars? The roles of the various characters emphasize the complexity of sexual values in relationships. This chapter explores sexual values and behaviors.

Consider the following situations, which elicit one's values:

- Two people are talking at a party. Although they met only two hours ago, they feel a strong attraction to each other. Each is wondering how much sex how soon is appropriate in a new relationship?
- A woman has a career that involves being away from home for extended periods of time. While she loves her spouse, she is lonely, bored, and sexually frustrated when she is traveling. She has been asked to dinner by an unmarried colleague (whom she finds attractive) while she is in another city. Should she go to dinner with him?
- While Mary was away for a weekend visiting her parents, her partner with whom she has lived for two years had intercourse with a previous lover. Mary's partner "confessed" and apologized, promising never to be unfaithful again. What should Mary do?

The individuals in these situations will make a decision based on their personal value system. Although we may not have experienced these particular encounters, we have confronted others that have required us to examine our own sexual values. In this chapter, we examine various value perspectives and their behavioral expression in masturbation, petting, and sexual intercourse.

Moral indignation is jealousy with a halo.

H. G. WELLS

Definition and Functions of Sexual Values

Values are moral guidelines for behavior. Sexual values are moral guidelines for sexual behavior. For example, choices about premarital and extramarital intercourse are made on the basis of sexual values. Of 188 university students in the United States, 91 percent of the men and 87 percent of the women approved of premarital intercourse; only three percent of the men and three percent of the women approved of extramarital intercourse (Rubinson & De Rubertis, 1991). Before looking at how sexual values function in our self-identity, in the selection of a mate, and in the avoidance of contracting various sexually transmissible diseases, we emphasize that sexual values are influenced by the society in which one lives.

Sexual Values in Cross-Cultural Perspective

There are wide variations in sexual values in different societies in regard to premarital and extramarital intercourse.

Premarital Sex   Premarital sexual behavior may be punished in one society, tolerated in a second, and rewarded in a third (see Table 4.1). In the Gilbert Islands, virginity until marriage is an exalted sexual value and violations are not tolerated. Premarital couples who are discovered to have had intercourse before the wedding are put to death. Our society tolerates premarital intercourse, particularly if the partners are "in love." In contrast, the Marquesans on Nuku Hiva Island in Eastern Polynesia encourage premarital sexual explorations (homosexual and heterosexual) in both men and women at an early age (ten). To ensure proper sexual instruction, young men have their first intercourse with a woman in her thirties or forties; young women have intercourse with elder tribal leaders.

As the woman reaches adolescence her parents will encourage nocturnal meetings between her and a high-status, financially well off male with the hope of establishing ties with him and his family. Marquesan mothers develop a sense of pride that their daughters have a number of lovers.

In contrast to group approval for premarital intercourse among the Marquesan, the Kenuzi Nubians (a group located along the Nile River in Egypt) strongly impress upon a girl the importance of being a virgin when she marries. In addition to removing the clitoris and sewing up the vagina by age four, the penalty for premarital intercourse is to be killed by her nearest relative.

> Where punishment is severe, the woman's actions seem to be regarded as an offense to the men in her family or to her prospective husband. For example, the friends of a young Fijian girl strangled her because of a premarital transgression. They then apologized to her fiancé for her disloyalty to him. The fact that male relatives or friends slay the woman attest to their interest in the maintenance of her sexual integrity (Frayser, 1985, 205).

Short of death, most societies communicate disapproval to the woman who has premarital intercourse by shunning her, making it difficult for her to marry (her reputation is ruined), and divorce if it is discovered after marriage that she is not a virgin. A Wolof man (of Gambia) has the right to demand an immediate divorce if his wife is not a virgin when he marries her.

Extramarital Sexuality   Most societies are less tolerant of extramarital than premarital sexuality. Frayser (1985) observed that three-quarters of 58 societies forbade extramarital intercourse for one or both sexes. Extramarital intercourse involves not only the couple and their children but also the larger kinship system. In some cases, the entire community is affected. Among the Suku of the southwest Congo, intercourse between the wife of a chief and a man of

---

ACROSS CULTURES

TABLE 4.1

Premarital Sex in Four Cultures

CULTURE	NORM REGARDING PREMARITAL SEX
United States	Tolerated
China	Prohibited
India	Prohibited
Pokomo (Kenya, East Africa)	Expected

Source: Bunger, Robert. Department of Anthropology, East Carolina University, Greenville, North Carolina. 1993. Prepared specifically for this chapter. Used by permission of Dr. Robert L. Bunger.

another tribe could result in the chief going to war against the lover's village (Frayser, 1985).

Even when extramarital intercourse is permitted, there are limitations involved. For example, the wife of an Aleut male may have intercourse with a house guest as a symbol of hospitality extended by the husband. Such wife-lending illustrates how tightly extramarital intercourse may be controlled.

Other examples of restricted but approved extramarital intercourse include the following:

- The Marshallese of Jaluit Atoll allow a woman to have sexual access to her sister's husband.
- The Comanche male may have intercourse with his brother's wife (but only with the express consent of the brother).
- The Hidatsa allow a man to have intercourse with his wife's sister but only when his own wife is in the advanced stages of pregnancy. "The woman's parents think it is preferable to offer him another daughter than to risk having him get involved with an unrelated woman" (Frayser, 1985, 209).
- The Fijians allow extramarital intercourse after the men have returned to the village with war captives.

Cross-culturally, the double standard seems evident in regard to who is allowed to have extramarital intercourse with whom. In her study of 58 societies, Frayser (1985) reported that she found no society that gave the option to women to have affairs while denying them to men (p. 210).

Sociologists operating from a structure-function perspective emphasize that most norms that exist in a society provide some benefits for the society. For example, permitting extramarital intercourse may have political benefits for a group as illustrated by the Aleut who lend their wives to guests. Such wife lending may solidify the friendships of the males.

Individuals who ignore the rules under which extramarital intercourse is to occur are often severely punished. Such severe punishment was observed in 85 percent of 54 societies studied (Frayser, 1985). Forms of punishment include: lover pays a fine to the woman's husband and brother, lover submits to a public beating by the husband, wife submits to a private beating by the husband, temporary public ostracism, and death. A Kenuzi husband (in Egypt) can kill his wife if he even suspects her of infidelity.

Self-Identity and Sexual Values

One of the functions of sexual values is that they help to establish and maintain one's self-identity. Our self-identity refers to who we are, that is, how we perceive that others view us and how we view ourselves. Our sexual values are a reflection of how we view ourselves. Persons who value sex without love, sex with casual partners, extramarital sex, and sex with children, may have a different view of themselves than those who value sex with love, sex in long-term committed, monogamous relationships, and sex with consenting

Adultery may or may not be sinful, but it is never cheap.

RAYMOND POSTGATE

Respect yourself.

SUIDAS

adults. The sexual behaviors individuals engage in influence how others view them. Sixty-four percent of 256 university women reported that a woman who has sexual intercourse with "a great many men" is immoral. Thirty-eight percent of 205 university men reported that a man who has intercourse with "a great many women" is immoral (Rubinson & De Rubertis, 1991, 219).

Mate Selection and Sexual Values

Sexual values are also an important factor in selecting dating partners and mates. The value theory of mate selection suggests that individuals with radically dissimilar sexual values are unlikely to consider each other as potential dating or marriage partners (Williams & Jacoby, 1989). Those who value monogamous sexual relationships tend not to select mates who approve of extradyadic sexual relationships. For another example, one women from a conservative religious background stated (in the authors' marriage and family class) that she valued virginity. While she felt that this value was not predominant on the university campus, she felt that it was right for her. A man in the class also spoke up in support of virginity. The two of them emphasized their disgust in the casual sex norms that permeate the university. Before the semester was over, they began to date.

In contrast, other individuals in the same class felt that intercourse before marriage was essential and provided important information about the person. One woman said, "I wouldn't want to become involved with anyone who wouldn't have intercourse . . . it would mean that they were too uptight about sex." It is likely that this student will attract and be attracted to others who share her value. It is also true that there are cases in which couples with opposite values date and marry.

> If I were the man that you wanted, I would not be the man that I am.
>
> LYLE LOVETT

CONSIDERATION

Compatible sexual values are an important consideration in mate selection. However, some couples develop and maintain a relationship in spite of differences between their sexual values. For example, a person who values sexual monogamy may become involved with a person who values sex with multiple partners. Couples with conflicting sexual values may consider the following options: changing their values, changing their behavior (while retaining their values), accepting their differences, or ending the relationship.

Individuals tend to select partners who share their sexual values.

STD Avoidance and Sexual Values

One's sexual values (and behavior which reflects these values) also have implications for the degree to which one is at risk of acquiring or transmitting sexually transmissible diseases. Persons who have sexual values that dictate having few sexual partners and using a condom have a lower risk of

> Today, partners can no longer remain silent about their sexual pasts, nor can they fear to voice their concerns about a mutual sexual future.
>
> MARA ADELMAN

contracting sexually transmissible diseases than those whose sexual values permit numerous sexual partners without using a condom (see Figure 4.1). In the Choices section at the end of the chapter, we emphasize that the risk of contracting a sexually transmissible disease is one of the important issues to consider in making a decision to have intercourse in a new relationship. More importantly, we emphasize the need to initiate talking about sex to increase the chance of a safer sex experience.

If you're smart, you will assume that everybody is infected with HIV.

SCOTT WALKER

CONSIDERATION

Some people who have tested positive for HIV limit their dating/relationships to others who have also tested positive for HIV. Kevin Dimmick, a 35-year-old heterosexual who has AIDS, organized numerous parties for "Infected and Affected Straight Folks" and noted that ". . . people feel safe at these gatherings. Everybody understands without a word spoken" (Seligmann et al., 1992, 57).

FIGURE 4.1

Sexual Values and Risk of Contracting a STD

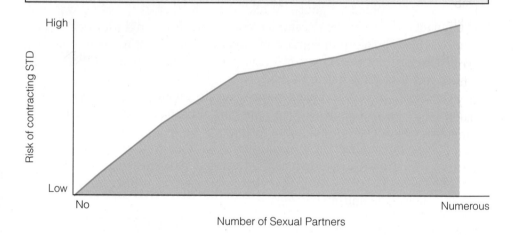

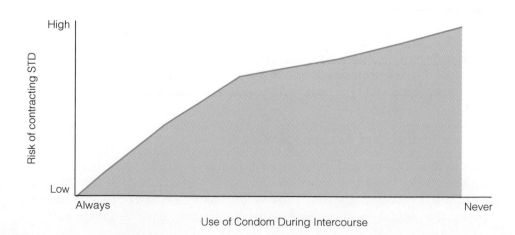

Historical Roots of Sexual Values

Although we live in a pluralistic society in which people have different values, many of the roots of our sexual values are religious. The Jewish and Christian influences have been the most prominent.

Jewish Heritage

Many of our values concerning sexuality can be traced to the laws and customs of Mosaic Judaism. The Old Testament, written between 800 and 200 B.C., reflects the society of the Jewish people at that time and should be viewed in its historical context. The Jews were a small, persecuted group. While they believed in God and that their sexual values were God-given, from a sociological perspective, their goal was to increase their numbers as rapidly as possible and to minimize defections. From this need to solidify their position as a group and a nation, they developed the following sexual norms.

Marriage is Good   Marriage (to a person of one's faith) was a way to encourage the birthing of new members into the Jewish faith. Males were permitted to marry at 15; females even younger. Eighteen was considered the maximum age a male could remain single before he would have to explain to the elders of the community why he was still unmarried. Hence, singlehood was regarded as unnatural and immoral. Even widows and widowers were encouraged to remarry as soon as possible.

Children Are Expected   Once married, the couple were expected to "be fruitful and multiply." Sexual intercourse was encouraged. During the first year of marriage, the husband was exempt from military service so he could be with his wife. "When a man hath taken a new wife, he shall not go out to war, neither shall he be charged with any business: but he shall be free at home one year, and shall cheer up his wife which he hath taken" (Deuteronomy 24:5).

Adultery Is Wrong   The couple was restricted to having intercourse with each other. The Jewish society did not tolerate adultery. "And the man that committeth adultery with another man's wife, even he that committeth adultery with his neighbor's wife, the adulterer and the adulteress shall surely be put to death" (Leviticus 20:10).

Other Sexual Admonitions   Homosexuality, bestiality (sex with animals), and masturbation were forbidden as they did not involve marriage or procreation. As in many other societies, incest was prohibited. Indeed, any form of genital expression outside of heterosexual marriage was regarded as immoral.

History is particularly important in throwing light on the source of our attitudes about sex because many of the assumptions we make are not necessarily scientific or rational but holdovers of past belief systems that are no longer held by modern society.

VERN BULLOUGH

There is no wealth where there are no children.

GEORGE HERZOG

> **CONSIDERATION**
>
> Judaism has had a major impact on our view of sexual values. Our feelings about marriage (more than 90 percent of us marry), children (more than 90 percent of us express a desire to have children), and monogamy (most Americans disapprove of extramarital intercourse) have been significantly influenced by the ancient Hebrews.

Christian Heritage

Just as Judaism was based on the teachings of Moses in the Old Testament, Christianity was based on the teachings of Jesus in the New Testament. Since early Christian congregations were geographically scattered, interpretations differed; "there were hundreds of competing groups with different and contradictory doctrines" (Bullough, 1987, 52).

Teachings of Jesus   Most of Jesus' teachings were about salvation and living positively. He said very little about sex, although in one instance, he equated thoughts about having intercourse with the act itself. "But I say unto you that whosoever looketh on a woman to lust after her hath committed adultery with her already in his heart" (Matthew 5:28).

Teachings of St. Paul   After the death of Jesus, his followers continued to preach the message of Christianity. Among these was St. Paul, who added his own interpretations of sexuality. He approved of marriage and believed that it was the most desirable context for sex. He felt that premarital intercourse was to be avoided.

    The writings of St. Paul should be viewed in their historical context. He and others of his day believed that the return of Christ (the "second coming") was imminent. Sex was seen as unnecessary uses of a person's time when there was so much to do in preparation for Christ's return (such as recruit new members) and so little time.

> **CONSIDERATION**
>
> St. Paul's ideas about sex reflected the impact of Greco-Roman culture and its Hellenist philosophy—spiritualistic dualism. The body and spirit or mind were seen as being at odds with each other. The body was temporal, material, and corruptible while the spirit was pure and responsible for delivering the body from sin. "Sex was particularly bad because it was not only pleasurable but because it might lead to procreation and the imprisonment of other souls" (Bullough, 1987, 50).
>
>   This preoccupation with the body-spirit dichotomy continues today. "Much sex-negativity in this culture displays this spiritualistic distortion, which generates both fear of and, simultaneously, fixation with sex and the body" (Special Committee on Human Sexuality, 1991, 29).

Teachings of St. Augustine   Around 386 A.D., at the age of 32, Augustine read the writings of St. Paul. Before this time he had lived a promiscuous life, which included fathering a son outside of marriage, cohabitating with his son's mother while becoming engaged to another woman, and being unfaithful to his fiancée. Frustrated with his inability to control his sexual desires, he converted to Christianity, broke off his engagement, stopped his affairs, and never married.

His own writings, particularly *The City of God*, reflect a very negative view of sex and sexuality. He felt that sexual desires, emotions and passions, expressed through sexual intercourse, were sinful. While the only justification or purpose for intercourse was procreation, even in marriage, the act itself was tainted with shame. This shame, according to St. Augustine, was a result of the lust Adam and Eve felt for each other, their disobedience to God by engaging in sexual intercourse, and their expulsion from the Garden of Eden.

St. Augustine became a bishop in the Roman Catholic Church and his views became widespread. The ritual for infant baptism grew out of the belief that children were conceived in an impure act (original sin) and must be cleansed of this sin. This sacrament is still practiced and recognized by many Christian faiths.

> Lord give me chastity—but not yet.
>
> SAINT AUGUSTINE

CONSIDERATION

Early Christian interpretations of sexuality as evil led to the adoption of a reward-punishment model to control believers. People who controlled their sexual appetites were rewarded by the knowledge that they were like Christ who was essentially asexual. Those who gave in to their lusts believed that they would be punished in Hell's fires after death. However, a way to avoid such threats was to confess one's sins to members of the clergy. Such confession helped the church to monitor the sexual behavior of its members and to help ensure compliance (Bullough, 1987).

Other Influential Religious Leaders   Martin Luther and John Calvin, in their break from the Roman Catholic Church, adopted a more positive view of sexuality. According to Luther (who married and had ten or more children), marriage was a good and positive relationship and not second to singlehood. He also regarded sexual desires as normal appetites much like hunger and thirst. Calvin, too, viewed sex, at least in marriage, as holy, honorable, and desirable. Hence, marital sex was for more than procreation (Carswell, 1969).

The Puritans

The Puritans who settled along the coast of New England in the seventeenth century were radical Protestants who had seceded from the Church of England. We can trace many of our sexual values to their beliefs and social norms. Tannahill (1982) noted that the forcefulness and power of the Puritans in

> The hostile attitude of the church toward sex was so extreme that it actually had little effect on most members of society.
>
> RANDALL COLLINS
> SCOTT COLTRANE

imposing their ways on others and the fact that new immigrants were predominantly Protestant explain why the Puritans influenced several generations of later colonists. In fact, the Puritan ethic has had a disproportionate influence in the history of the United States. "Senators and Congressmen today, struggling (whatever the state of their faith and/or marital relationships) to project an image of dedicated family men, at work, at rest, at church, at play, owe this particular electoral hazard to the early New England settlers who wove the public demonstration of family solidarity into the American ethos" (p. 330).

The Puritans wanted their members to get married and stay married. The Puritan woman had little choice of an adult position other than wife and mother. Only in marriage could she achieve the status accorded to an adult woman. Men and women were taught that their best chance for survival was to find a spouse to satisfy their needs for clothing, food, companionship, and sex.

The Puritans approved of sex but only within marriage. Like Augustine, they viewed sex as a passion to conquer or control and marriage as the only safe place for its expression. Rigid codes of dress helped to discourage sexual thoughts.

Any discussion of sex among the Puritans would not be complete without reference to *bundling*, also called tarrying. Not unique to the Puritans, bundling was a courtship custom in which the would-be groom slept in the girl's bed in her parents' home. But there were rules to restrict sexual contact. Both partners had to be fully clothed, and a board was placed between them. In addition, the young girl might be encased in a type of long laundry bag up to her armpits, her clothes might be sewn together at strategic points, and her parents might be sleeping in the same room.

It is better to marry than to burn.

NEW TESTAMENT (1 Corinthians 9)

Puritan courtship couples (mid 18th century) were allowed to sleep together only if they were fully clothed ("bundled up") and if there was a board between them.

The justifications for bundling were convenience and economics. Aside from meeting at church, bundling was one of the few opportunities a couple had to get together to talk and learn about each other. Since daylight hours were consumed by heavy work demands, night became the time for courtship. But how did bed become the courtship arena? New England winters were cold. Firewood, oil for lamps, and candles were in short supply. By talking in bed, the young couple could come to know each other without wasting valuable sources of energy. Although bundling flourished in the middle of the eighteenth century, it provoked a great deal of controversy. By about 1800 the custom had virtually disappeared.

The Victorians

Another influence that lingers in our society is the Victorian. The Victorian era, which took its name from the English queen Alexandria Victoria, who reigned from 1837 to 1901, is popularly viewed as a time of prudery and propriety in sexual behavior. However, there was a great disparity between expressed middle-class morality and actual practices. In his study of this era, Wendell Johnson (1979) wrote:

> What were the Victorians actually doing? One might reply "Just about everything." Free love, adultery, male homosexuality and (in spite of the Queen's disbelief) lesbianism, nymphetism, sadism, and masochism, exhibitionism—the Victorians practiced them all . . . the number of whores per acre in mid-Victorian London and the consumption of pornography . . . would put today's Times Square to shame (p. 11).

But the official view of sexuality during the Victorian era was that sexual behavior and the discussion of it should be suppressed. The Victorian influence continues today as parents still find it difficult to talk with their children about sex. Some specific Victorian notions of sexuality are discussed in the following paragraphs.

Marital Sexuality   According to the Victorians, sex was a passion that should be channeled into marriage. Uncontrollable sexual desires were believed to be characteristic only of men. Women were thought to be asexual and nonorgasmic. William Hammond, the surgeon general of the United States Army during the 1860s, wrote that it was doubtful that women experienced the slightest degree of pleasure in even one-tenth of the occasions of sexual intercourse. (Of course, such lack of female sexual pleasure may have been due to insensitive husbands who were not concerned about creating pleasure for their partners during intercourse.)

Prudishness   Examples of Victorian prudishness include skirts to the ankle, and discreet references to anything sexual. Woman were not pregnant, they were "in an interesting way." Ladies delicately nibbled their "bosom of chicken" and librarians shelved books by male and female authors separately.

Female Types There were "good" women and "bad" women in Victorian society. The latter were whores or women who practiced no social graces in expressing their sexuality. Women who were not whores but who did enjoy sexual feelings were in conflict. Some felt degraded, even insane. "If I love sex I must be like a whore" was an inescapable conclusion. Some women even had clitoridectomies (surgical removal of the clitoris) performed to eliminate the "cause" of their sexual feelings.

〰 Alternative Sexual Value Perspectives

In the United States today, there are at least three sexual value perspectives in regard to choices in sexual behavior. These include absolutism, relativism, and hedonism. Sometimes people change their sexual values as they get older.

Absolutism

Absolutism refers to a belief system based on the unconditional allegiance to the authority of the principles of science, codes of law, tradition, or religion. A religious absolutist makes sexual choices on the basis of moral considerations. To make the correct moral choice is to comply with God's will and not to comply is a sin. A legalistic absolutist makes sexual decisions on the basis of a set of laws. People who are guided by absolutism in their sexual choices have a clear notion of what is right and wrong.

The official creeds of most Christian and Jewish religions reflect an absolutist's view of sexual values. According to these creeds, intercourse between a man and a woman has a spiritual meaning and is to be expressed only in marriage; violations (premarital sex, masturbation, homosexuality, and extramarital sex) are sins against God, self, and community.

Many people in the United States are absolutist in their sexual values in that they are certain of what they consider acceptable and unacceptable sexual behavior.

NATIONAL DATA 〰 Based on interviews with over 3,000 adult respondents throughout the United States, researchers at the Kinsey Institute concluded the following (Klassen, Williams, and Levitt, 1989):

> With regard to many forms of sexual expression, our respondents were extremely conservative. A majority disapproved of homosexuality, prostitution, extramarital sex, and most forms of premarital sex. Even masturbation, a near universal behavior among males, was disapproved by 48 percent of our respondents. Furthermore, except for masturbation and for premarital sex between people who are in love, our data suggest that a majority of Americans are "moral absolutists" in that they see these behaviors as *always* wrong (p. 17).

Researchers at the Kinsey Institute also noted that the moral standards of these respondents were reported to be stable over time. "A large majority of our respondents reported that they have always held the same standards" (p. 19).

You've got to stand for something or you'll fall for anything.

AARON TIPPIN

There are a lot of advantages to a clear allegiance to traditional morality, including the protection it often offers against sexually transmitted disease, and every discussion of safer sex needs to emphasize the strengths of traditional values and the resilience and depth sometimes achieved in relationships whose exclusivity is unquestioned.

MARY CATHERINE BATESON
RICHARD GOLDSBY

God reserved sex for marriage. So I'm waiting.

A. C. GREEN

Idealism increases in direct proportion to one's distance from the problem.

JOHN GALSWORTHY

Some demographic characteristics of absolutists include:

1. The older a person, the more likely that person is to disapprove of various sexual behaviors.
2. Women are more likely to disapprove of various sexual behaviors than men. Whether the behavior is premarital sex, homosexuality, or extramarital sex, women are more disapproving.
3. Blacks, when compared with whites, are more absolutist in regard to viewing masturbation as wrong.
4. The married are more likely to disapprove of premarital and extramarital sexual behaviors than the unmarried.

   A subcategory of absolutism is asceticism. The ascetic believes that giving into carnal lust is unnecessary and attempts to rise above the pursuit of sensual pleasure into a life of self-discipline and self-denial. Accordingly, the spiritual life is viewed as the highest good, and self-denial helps us to achieve it. Catholic priests, monks, nuns, and some other celibates have adopted the sexual value of asceticism.

Catholic priests have adopted the sexual value of asceticism which demands rejecting the experience of sexual pleasure.

Relativism

In contrast to absolutism is relativism—a value system emphasizing that sexual decisions be made in the context of a particular situation (hence, values are relative). Figure 4.2 reflects that one's willingness to engage in petting, sexual

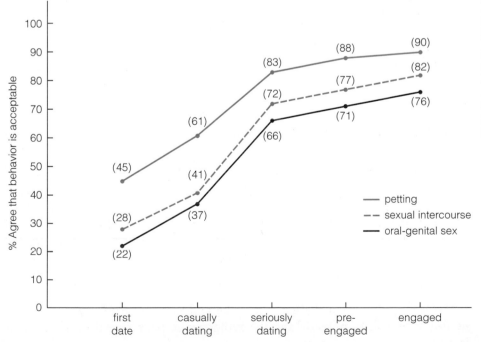

FIGURE 4.2

ACCEPTANCE OF SEXUAL ACTIVITY BY RELATIONSHIP STAGE

Source: Sprecher, S., K. McKinney, R. Walsh, and C. Anderson. A revision of the Reiss Premarital Sexual Permissiveness Scale. *Journal of Marriage and the Family,* 1988, *50,* 821–828, Using Figure #1, p. 825. © Copyrighted 1988 by the National Council on Family Relations, 3989 Central Ave., NE., Suite 550, Minneapolis, MN 55421. Reprinted by permission.

intercourse, and oral-genital sex depends on the stage of a couple's relationship (from first date to being engaged).

The relativist, also known as the situationist (i.e., situation ethics), believes that to make all decisions on the basis of rules is to miss the point of human love. King Edward VIII of England was acting as a relativist when he gave up his throne to marry Wallis Simpson, a divorcee. He did so in the name of love and, at least publicly, said he never regretted his decision. More recently, Diana, the Princess of Wales, is reported to have sought a separation from Charles, the Prince of Wales, on the basis of her need for the emotional intimacy she found difficult to achieve amid ritual and obligation, which accompany the position of royalty. Had she been operating from an absolutist perspective she would have continued to live with the prince.

Whether or not two unmarried people should have intercourse may be viewed differently by absolutists and relativists. Whereas an absolutist would say that it is wrong for unmarried people to have intercourse and right for married people to do so, a relativist would say, "It depends on the situation." For example, suppose a married couple do not love each other and intercourse is an abusive, exploitative act. Also, suppose an unmarried couple love each other, and that their intercourse experience is an expression of mutual affection and respect. A relativist might conclude that, in this particular situation, it is "more right" for the unmarried couple to have intercourse than the married couple.

NATIONAL DATA ℘ When U.S. adults aged 18 to 74+ were asked whether they felt premarital sexual relations were "always wrong," about a fourth responded "yes" (GSS News, 1992).

CONSIDERATION

It is sometimes difficult to make sexual decisions on a case-by-case basis. The statement, "I don't know what's right anymore," reflects the uncertainty of a relativistic view. Once a person decides that mutual love is the context justifying intercourse, how often and how soon is it appropriate for the person to fall in love? Can love develop after two hours of conversation? How does one know that love feelings are genuine? The freedom that relativism brings to sexual decision making requires responsibility, maturity, and judgment. In some cases, individuals may deceive themselves into thinking that they are in love so they will not feel guilty about having intercourse with someone.

Hedonism

Hedonism suggests that the ultimate value and motivation for human actions lie in the pursuit of pleasure and the avoidance of pain. The hedonistic value is reflected in the statement, "If it feels good, do it." Hedonism assumes that sexual desire, like hunger and thirst, is an appropriate appetite and its expression is legitimate.

When hedonism is defined as "what's in it for me" rather than "what's in it for us," men may be more prone to hedonism than women. Linn (1991) reviewed the work of Carol Gilligan (Gilligan, Ward, and Taylor, 1988) and suggested that men and women have different perspectives in making sexual decisions. Men look at deciding to have intercourse in a relationship as confirming their masculinity and autonomy; women are more likely to focus on the impact of such a decision on their relationship with their respective partners ("Will he love me in the morning?") Hence, women may be more relativistic.

Table 4.2 reflects how the absolutist (religious or legal), relativist, and hedonist might make various sexual decisions.

I am a tramp and proud of it.

MADONNA

It is that old-fashioned idea of familial obligation that so often gets short shrift in a society that places high value on the individual's pursuit of happiness.

CYNTHIA TUCKER

T A B L E 4.2
Value Perspectives and Sexual Choices

DILEMMA	VALUE PERSPECTIVE	SEXUAL CHOICE
1. Have premarital sex?	Religious Absolutism	No
	Relativism	Yes or No (Depends on Situation)
	Hedonism	Yes
2. Disclose HIV infection to new lover?	Legal Absolutism	Yes
	Relativism	Yes
	Hedonism	No
3. Have extramarital sex?	Religious Absolutism	No
	Legal Absolutism	No
	Relativism	Yes or No (Depends on Situation)
	Hedonism	Yes

CONSIDERATION

Are sexual values changing? A team of researchers (Robinson et al., 1991) studied the attitudes of college students toward premarital intercourse over a 20-year period. They found a "continuing liberalization for both males and females, with the larger shift for females" (216). Specifically, university men approving premarital intercourse increased from 65 percent in 1965 to 79 percent in 1985; the corresponding increases for university women were 28 percent and 63 percent. The actual rates for premarital intercourse may be even higher. In one study of 79 undergraduate men and 193 undergraduate women, 96 percent of the men and 93 percent of the women reported having experienced premarital intercourse (Knox & Schacht, 1992).

℘ Identifying Your Personal Sexual Values

You can clarify your own sexual values in several ways. These include completing the following value statements, using a scale designed to identify sexual values on an acceptable-unacceptable continuum, identifying the level of sexual guilt provoked by various conditions, and making choices when confronted with various sexual dilemmas.

Value Statements

Select one ending for each of the following statements:

1. For me, it is most important that a sexual experience:
   a. Be morally correct.
   b. Be fun and pleasurable.
   c. Increase the love feelings I have with my partner.
   d. Not result in my contracting an STD.
   e. Result in orgasm.

2. In a sexual relationship, it is most important that:
   a. My partner be in love with me.
   b. I be in love with my partner.
   c. Sex mean the same thing to both of us.
   d. We are married to each other.
   e. My partner is uninhibited.

3. If I am feeling the need for sexual release, I would rather (as my first choice):
   a. Have intercourse.
   b. Have my partner perform oral sex.
   c. Engage in vigorous physical activity.
   d. Masturbate.
   e. Have a sexual dream resulting in orgasm.

4. Intercourse is most appropriate under the following conditions:
   a. The partners are married.
   b. The partners are engaged.
   c. The partners are in love.
   d. The partners feel affection for each other.
   e. Both partners are consenting even though they do not feel affection for each other.

5. The worst thing that I could find out about my sexual partner is that he or she:
   a. Has a sexually transmissible disease.
   b. Is homosexual or bisexual.
   c. Has been unfaithful or has deceived me.

    d. Is sterile.

    e. Does not love me.

There are no right or wrong answers to these questions. Your selection reflects the focus of your sexual value in each area.

Acceptable-Unacceptable Continuum

Another way of clarifying your sexual values is to think of the degree to which you regard various sexual issues as acceptable. What category on the continuum below best reflects your sexual values about sex without love, abortion, group sex, oral-genital sex, anal sex, masturbation, intercourse, homosexuality for others, homosexuality for self, extramarital sex, and virginity at marriage?

Acceptable	Does Not Matter	Unacceptable

CONSIDERATION

An important dimension of values clarification is becoming aware that you may have different standards for yourself and others. For example, there is a distinction between "I would never have an abortion" and "I believe every woman should be able to choose whether to have an abortion." Some people separate their own values and choices from those they feel others "should" have; others do not.

Sexual Guilt

Sexual values may also be assessed by identifying how guilty a person anticipates feeling after engaging in various sexual behaviors (Knox, Walters, & Walters, 1991). Sexual guilt may be defined as feeling bad for engaging or thinking about engaging in a behavior because to do so is regarded as wrong. Table 4.3 reflects the average level of guilt on a four-point continuum for various sexual situations reported by 249 undergraduate university students. You might compare your answers with theirs.

    The degree of guilt that college students predict they would feel for engaging in various sexual behaviors varies by whether someone is likely to find out. Sexual guilt for various sexual behaviors tends to be higher when discovery by significant others is possible. Women and younger individuals also report being more guilty than men and older individuals (Knox et al., 1991).

    Sexual guilt also varies by culture. Japanese, Vietnamese, and Hispanic women are expected to feel more guilty for engaging in extramarital sexual behavior than their husbands for engaging in the same behavior (Mindel, Habenstein, & Wright, 1988). Researchers at Anadolu University, Eskisehir, Turkey, observed that those who engage in sexual behavior in spite of the

ACROSS CULTURES ∿

restrictive culture are likely to experience high proportions of guilt (Erkmen, Dilbaz, Serber, Kaptanoglu, & Tekin, 1990).

Finally, high sex guilt is associated with several other aspects of sexuality. Cado and Leitenberg (1990) found that high sex guilt was associated with sexual dissatisfaction and sexual dysfunction. Smith and Walters (1988), in their review of the literature, also found that the higher the sex guilt, the lower:

- the frequency of masturbation
- the frequency of female orgasm
- the use of reliable effective contraception
- the chance of selecting abortion to end an unwanted pregnancy
- the chance of avoiding a premarital pregnancy

T A B L E 4.3

How Guilty Would You Feel If?

HOW GUILTY WOULD YOU FEEL IF . . .	AVERAGE SCORE
1. You have intercourse with someone 18 years older than you. Both of you are unmarried.	2.04
2. You decide not to tell the person you are about to marry any information concerning your previous affectional relationships because you believe it will have no bearing on your marriage.	2.18
3. The person you are about to marry learns of a previous sexual affair with another person you did not particularly care for prior to your present relationship.	2.29
4. You reveal to an associate that a person who had invited you to dinner was gay and there were to be no other guests.	2.48
5. Your mother discovers that you, at age 16, are having intercourse with a member of the opposite sex.	2.76
6. You concealed from the person you are about to marry that you had earlier contracted and was cured of gonorrhea.	2.88
7. Your parents learn of your sexual relationship with someone of another race and you know they disapprove.	3.03
8. As a student, you are in love with a teacher who is fired because your sexual relationship has been brought to the attention of the instructor's dean.	3.51
9. You are in a committed relationship with a person, yet you had intercourse with someone else.	3.52
10. Your fiancé learns that you had a sexual encounter with your fiancé's best friend while your fiancé was away visiting her/his grandmother.	3.66

Scoring: 1 = No guilt; 2 = Little guilt; 3 = Moderate guilt; 4 = Considerable guilt

Source: Adapted from the original data collected for "Sexual Guilt Among College Students" by D. Knox, L. H. Walters, and J. Walters. *College Student Journal,* 1991, *25,* 432–433.

Sexual Values Dilemma

Still another way to assess sexual values is to develop an answer to a moral dilemma. For example, Katherine is involved in a mutual love relationship and plans to marry Bob in June, two months away. One evening Katherine and Bob's conversation drifts onto the topic of abortions. Bob states that "an abortion means the girl is promiscuous and irresponsible," and he is highly critical of a mutual friend who had had an abortion. Unknown to Bob, Katherine had an abortion two years before she met him. Should she tell him?

Another example of a value dilemma is in regard to the disclosure of infidelity. When Sherry was out of town, Ben met an old girlfriend, drank some wine, and had intercourse with her. They had dated for six years prior to his involvement with Sherry. He was not interested in rekindling the relationship with his old love, was sorry that he had sex with her, and told her that he would not see her again. He loved Sherry and was committed to a life with her (they were to be married when the semester was over). Should Ben tell Sherry of his encounter with an old love?

Finally, some couples face a dilemma over STDs. Madelyn contracted genital warts through sex with a previous partner. Now involved in a new relationship, she is undecided whether to tell him. If she does, she knows he will leave her because of his strong feelings about STDs. If she does not tell him, she feels he may never know since they practice safe sex. Should she tell him?

The goal in examining this and other value dilemmas is to explore our own sexual values. To assess the degree to which your sexual values are conservative or liberal, take the Conservative-Liberal Sexual Value Scale (Hudson, Murphy, & Nurius, 1983) in the following Self-Assessment. According to the scale, a liberal is one who feels that the expression of human sexuality should be open, free, and unrestrained; a conservative is one who feels that sexual expression should be considerably constrained and closely regulated. When the scale was administered to 689 students (primarily seniors and graduate students), both sexes tended to score borderline-low to high-liberal (Nurius & Hudson, 1982).

Whether your sexual values are liberal or conservative or somewhere midrange, they have been influenced by your family, peers, and society. Conservative parents and peers will have created a context conducive to the development of conservative sexual values. Liberal parents and peers will have created just the opposite context with a more liberal outcome. Societal influences are also involved. Our society is very liberal in terms of the sexual norms suggested in music, movies, and media. In contrast, strict sexual norms exist in Japan, where sexually explicit magazines are not readily available in the local convenience store and adolescents are expected to delay the expression of their sexuality.

> False face must hide what the false heart doth know.
>
> SHAKESPEARE

Conservative-Liberal Sexual Value Scale

This questionnaire is designed to measure the way you feel about sexual behavior. It is not a test, so there are no right or wrong answers. Answer each item as carefully and accurately as you can by placing the most appropriate number beside each one as follows:

1 Strongly disagree   4 Agree
2 Disagree   5 Strongly agree
3 Undecided

	SD	D	U	A	SA
1. I think too much freedom is given to adults these days.	1	2	3	4	5
2. I think that the increased sexual freedom seen in the past several years has done much to undermine the American family.	1	2	3	4	5
3. I think that young people have been given too much information about sex.	1	2	3	4	5
4. Sex education should be restricted to the home.	1	2	3	4	5
5. Older people do not need to have sex.	1	2	3	4	5
6. Sex education should be provided only when people are ready for marriage.	1	2	3	4	5
7. Premarital sex may be a sign of a decaying social order.	1	2	3	4	5
8. Extramarital sex is never excusable.	1	2	3	4	5
9. I think there is too much sexual freedom given to teenagers these days.	1	2	3	4	5
10. I think there is not enough sexual restraint among young people.	1	2	3	4	5

	SD	D	U	A	SA
11. I think people engage in sex too often.	1	2	3	4	5
12. I think the only proper way to have sex is through intercourse.	1	2	3	4	5
13. I think sex should be reserved for marriage.	1	2	3	4	5
14. Sex should be only for the young.	1	2	3	4	5
15. Too much social approval has been given to homosexuals.	1	2	3	4	5
16. Sex should be devoted to the business of procreation.	1	2	3	4	5
17. People should not masturbate.	1	2	3	4	5
18. Heavy sexual petting should be discouraged.	1	2	3	4	5
19. People should not discuss their sexual affairs or business with others.	1	2	3	4	5
20. Severely physically and mentally handicapped people should not have sex.	1	2	3	4	5
21. There should be no laws prohibiting sexual acts between consenting adults.	1	2	3	4	5
22. What two consenting adults do together sexually is their own business.	1	2	3	4	5
23. There is too much sex on television.	1	2	3	4	5
24. Movies today are too sexually explicit.	1	2	3	4	5
25. Pornography should be totally banned from our bookstores.	1	2	3	4	5

SELF-ASSESSMENT 〜

Conservative-Liberal Sexual Value Scale *continued*

SCORING: Reverse the scores for statements 21 and 22 in the following way; 1 = 5, 2 = 4, 4 = 2, 5 = 1. For example, if you wrote 1 for statement 21 ("There should be no laws prohibiting sexual acts between consenting adults"), change that number to five for scoring purposes. Reverse score statement 22 similarly. Add the numbers you assigned to each of the 25 statements. Your score may range from a low of 25 (strongly disagreed with all items; 1 × 25 = 25) to a high of 125 (strongly agreed with all items: 5 × 25 = 125). If you score between 25 and 50, you may be regarded as a high-grade liberal; if you score between 50 and 75, a low-grade liberal. If you score between 100 and 125, you may be regarded as a high-grade conservative; if you score between 75 and 100, a low-grade conservative.

(NOTE: This Self-Assessment is included in this chapter for the purpose of being fun and thought-provoking for the student.)

SOURCE: Hudson, W. W., G. J. Murphy, and P. S. Nurius. A short-form scale to measure liberal vs. conservative orientations toward human sexual expression. *Journal of Sex Research*, 1983, *19*, 258–272. A publication of the Society for the Scientific Study of Sex. Reprinted by permission.

🍂 Sexual Behaviors

Having examined the definitions, functions, and history of sexual values (as well as identifying alternative sexual values and one's own sexual values), we now turn to the behavioral expression of these values. After looking at gender and racial differences in sexual behavior, we briefly discuss masturbation, interpersonal noncoital sexual behavior, and sexual intercourse.

> **When the subject is sex, no one knows for sure who is telling the truth, who is lying, who is talking and who is silent.**
>
> **DIANE CRISP**

Gender and Racial Differences in Sexual Behavior

Are there differences between the sexual behaviors of men and women and between blacks and whites? In regard to the differences between men and women, a team of researchers (Billingham et al., 1989) analyzed the question-naires of 221 men and 220 women and found that men reported higher rates of sexual aggressiveness and orgasmic behavior than women. The researchers concluded that biological factors (higher testosterone levels) provided the best explanation for the differences between the sexes. Alternatively, social learning theorists would argue that men learn to be more sexually aggressive and orgasmic than women.

> **Dad told all the boys to get laid as often as possible.**
>
> **JOHN F. KENNEDY**

Men and women also differ in their motivations for sexual intercourse. Men report the desire for sexual pleasure, conquest, and relief of sexual tension more often than women who emphasize emotional closeness and affection (Townsend & Levy, 1990).One survey of 2,365 unmarried respondents ages 18 to 30 revealed that half the men, in contrast to a quarter of the women, could not recall the first and last names of everyone they have slept with (Rubenstein, 1993).

Men are also more approving of sex earlier in a relationship than women. Fifty-nine percent of all U.S. freshman men agreed that it was all right for two people who liked each other, but who had known each other for a very short time, to have sex. Thirty-two percent of U.S. college freshman women also agreed (American Council on Education and University of California, 1992). In the Rubenstein survey (1993), 60 percent of the men, in contrast to 16 percent of the women, felt that sex on the first date was all right.

Finally, men and women differ in regard to their tolerance of sexual infidelity. When 370 university students were asked to indicate what sexual behaviors were acceptable at what levels of the relationship, men were more tolerant of a man's sexual infidelity than of a woman's (Margolin, 1989). Also, men in this study tended to say that sexual infidelity in dating or marriage relationships was "moderately unacceptable," whereas women tended to say that sexual infidelity was "very unacceptable" in both dating and marriage relationships.

Even though there are considerable differences between the sexes, racial and ethnic groups exhibit considerable similarities. Baldwin et al. (1992) studied the sexual behaviors of whites, Asians, Blacks, and Latinos in a random sample of 1,173 college students and concluded that ethnicity had little effect on the behaviors studied, especially after controlling for background variables such as socioeconomic status. Individuals from lower income backgrounds reported higher frequencies of sexual behavior than those with higher income frequencies, regardless of the individuals' ethnic background.

However, a more recent national study of the sexual behavior of men found some racial differences. In regard to oral sex, 79 percent of white men in contrast to 43 percent of black men reported having performed oral sex; 81 percent of white men had received oral sex compared with 62 percent of black men. In regard to anal sex, 20 percent of white men reported having engaged in anal sex in contrast to 14 percent of black men (Billy et al., 1993). Of these findings, the authors concluded, "In general, black men's sexual activity tends to involve primarily vaginal sex and, to a limited extent, receiving oral sex" (p. 59). In another study comparing 199 black and 174 white newlywed couples, black spouses reported greater enjoyment in sexual relations than white spouses. The researchers suggested that blacks may be more open about enjoying sex than whites (Oggins et al., 1993).

Masturbation

Masturbation is defined as stimulating one's own body with the goal of experiencing pleasurable sexual sensations. In one study of 193 university women and 79 university men, 57 percent and 87 percent respectively reported having masturbated (Knox & Schacht, 1992).

NATIONAL DATA ✷ Of 1,275 respondents, three-fourths of the women and almost all of the men reported having masturbated before their first intercourse experience (Rubin, 1991).

I have this recurring fantasy when I have sex ... that I'm with someone.

LATENIGHT COMIC

NATIONAL DATA Two-thirds of almost 8,000 respondents reported that they viewed masturbation as a natural part of life (Janus & Janus, 1992).

Alternative terms for masturbation include autoeroticism, self-pleasuring, solo sex, and sex without a partner. Several older, more pejorative terms for masturbation are self-pollution, self-abuse, solitary vice, sin against nature, voluntary pollution, and onanism. The negative connotations associated with these terms are a result of various myths (e.g., masturbation causes insanity, blindness, and hair on the palms) about masturbation. These myths originated in religion, medicine, and traditional psychotherapy. Parents have also been instrumental in perpetuating a negative view of masturbation to their children.

Religion and Masturbation   Ancient Jews considered masturbation a sin so grave that it deserved the death penalty. Catholics regarded masturbation as a mortal sin, which, if not given up, would result in eternal damnation. Although Protestants felt that neither death nor eternal hellfire were appropriate consequences for masturbation, hell on earth (feeling anxious and guilty) was. The basis for these indictments was that masturbation is nonprocreative sex, and any sexual act that cannot produce offspring is morally wrong. The antidote for this evil behavior was abstinence and prayer (Money et al., 1991).

Medicine and Masturbation   The western medical community helped reinforce the negative associations of masturbation by bringing "scientific validity" to bear on its description of the hazards of masturbation. In 1758, Samuel Tissot, a Swiss physician, published *Treatise on the Diseases Produced by Onanism,* in which he implied that the loss of too much semen, whether by intercourse or masturbation, was injurious to the body and would cause debility, disease, and death (Tissot, 1766).

> **CONSIDERATION**
>
> Adding to the medical bias against masturbation was John Harvey Kellogg, M.D., who believed, as did the Reverend Sylvester Graham, that masturbation resulted in the loss of fluids that were vital to the body. In 1834, Graham wrote that an ounce of semen was equal to the loss of several ounces of blood. Graham believed that every time a man ejaculated, he ran the risk of contracting a disease of the nervous system. His solution was Graham crackers to help prevent the development of carnal lust, which resulted from eating carnivorous flesh (Graham, 1848). Kellogg suggested his own brand of cure—corn flakes. Kellogg's Corn Flakes were originally developed as a food to extinguish sexual desire and to help an individual curb masturbation desires.

The good thing about masturbation is that you don't have to get dressed up for it.

TRUMAN CAPOTE

In the nineties, it's sex with you and you.

ROBIN WILLIAMS

By the mid-nineteenth century, Tissot's theories had made their way into medical textbooks, journals, and books for parents. With no data, physicians added to the list of disorders resulting from masturbation—pimples, falling hair, weak eyes, and suicidal tendencies. Kinsey and his colleagues contributed the greatest challenge to the existing myths about masturbation by their disclosure that 92 percent of the men in their sample reported having masturbated (Kinsey, Pomeroy, and Martin, 1948). Yet the researchers found no evidence of the dire consequences that had been earlier predicted for those who masturbate.

Traditional Psychotherapy and Masturbation   In the early twentieth century, psychotherapy joined medicine and religion to convince people of the negative effects of masturbation. Psychotherapists, led by Freud, suggested that masturbation was an infantile form of sexual gratification. People who masturbated "to excess" could fixate on themselves as a sexual object and would not be able to relate to others in a sexually mature way. The message was clear: if you want to be a good sexual partner in marriage, don't masturbate; and if you do masturbate, don't do it too often.

> **Masturbation—it's sex with someone I love.**
>
> WOODY ALLEN

CONSIDERATION

The result of religious, medical, and therapeutic professions denigrating masturbation was devastating. Those who masturbated felt the shame and guilt they were supposed to feel. The burden of these feelings was particularly heavy since there was no one with whom to share the guilt. In the case of a premarital pregnancy, responsibility could be shared. But with masturbation, the "crime" had been committed alone.

Parents and Masturbation   While parents could have opted to counter the negative religious, medical, and psychotherapeutic attitudes toward masturbation, they have rarely done so. Rather, their silence on the subject communicates agreement that masturbation is shameful. Rubin (1991) observed:

> **Masturbation remains the activity that's least likely to be talked about, and even less likely to be named.**
>
> LILLIAN RUBIN

> Parents don't have to frown upon the masturbatory activities of the child; they have only to avoid noticing and labeling it for it to become suspect. By singling it out with silence, they send a message that the child interprets to mean that this nameless activity is something we don't talk about, one that calls for guilt and concealment (p. 22).

New attitudes toward masturbation have emerged. Although some religious leaders still view masturbation in negative terms, most health care providers and therapists today view masturbation as normal and healthy sexual behavior. Furthermore, masturbation has become known as a form of "safe sex" in that it involves no risk of transmitting diseases (such as HIV) or producing unintended pregnancy.

Interpersonal Noncoital Sexual Behavior

The term *petting* emerged in the early 19th century as premarital couples looked for ways to express their love and sexual attraction while confining intercourse to marriage (Rothman, 1987). Since the term *petting* is now outdated, we use the term *interpersonal noncoital sexual behaviors* which includes touching, kissing, breast stimulation, penile stimulation, and clitoral stimulation.

Whoever called it necking was a poor judge of anatomy.

GROUCHO MARX

CONSIDERATION

Most people define sex as intercourse. However, intercourse is "a form of lovemaking which is often well suited to men's orgasm and pleasure but is not necessarily well suited to [women's]" (*Boston Women's Health Collective*, 1984, 185). One woman commented:

> In high school we had long making-out periods and I had orgasms all the time. When we "graduated" to intercourse, I stopped having them so easily because he stopped doing all the other things (p. 186).

While the term *noncoital sexual behavior* is often referred to as "foreplay," this term suggests that touching, kissing, manual/oral stimulation are merely preludes to the "main act" of intercourse. Thus, we suggest replacing the term *foreplay* with the term *lovemaking*.

NATIONAL DATA ℘ In the Janus sample of almost 8,000 respondents, half of the men and a third of the women reported that a wide variety of sexual techniques was a must for maximum enjoyment (Janus & Janus, 1992).

Touching   Many regard touching as the most significant aspect of sex. The 3,000 women in Hite's (1977) study stated repeatedly that touching, holding, caressing, being close to, lying next to, and pressing bodies together was more important to them than intercourse or orgasms. For many, such physical closeness gives a feeling of emotional closeness that is satisfying whether or not intercourse or orgasm follow.

Another form of touching is massage. For many individuals, a body massage is more pleasurable than any other form of touching. While many forms of touching are stimulating, massage is relaxing. Being in a state of relaxation, however, can lead to interest in sexual activity. One student commented:

> When I'm finished working all day and taking classes at night, I'm exhausted and usually not interested in sex. But my husband has learned that if he spends twenty minutes massaging me, I feel relaxed, my body feels good, and that's the best time to have sex (Author's files).

❧ **IN FOCUS 4.1** ❧

The Origin of Mouth Kissing

Desmond Morris, a noted zoologist with an interest in the behavior of human animals, suggested that mouth kissing has its origins in mother-infant interactions of early human history.

In early human societies, before commercial baby food was invented, mothers weaned their children by chewing up their food and then passing it into the infantile mouth by lip-to-lip contact, which naturally involved a considerable amount of tonguing and mutual mouth-pressure. This almost bird-like system of parental care seems strange and alien to us today, but our species probably practiced it for a million years or more,

and adult erotic kissing today is almost certainly a Relic Gesture stemming from these origins. . . . Whether it has been handed down to us from generation to generation . . . or whether we have an inborn predisposition towards it, we cannot say. But, whichever is the case, it looks rather as though, with the deep kissing and tonguing of modern lovers, we are back again at the infantile mouth-feeding stage of the far-distant past. . . . If the young lovers exploring each other's mouths with their tongues feel the ancient comfort of parental mouth-feeding, this may help them to increase their mutual trust and thereby their pair-bonding (quoted in Ackerman, 1990, 112).

Behold the kiss is potent still.

JOHN RICHARD MORELAND

Kissing continues to be a way of being intimate.

Kissing There are different styles of kissing. In one style of kissing, the partners gently touch their lips together for a short time with their mouths closed. In another, there is considerable pressure and movement for a prolonged time when the closed mouths meet. In still another, the partners kiss with their mouths open, using gentle or light pressure and variations in movement and time. Kinsey referred to the latter as deep kissing (also known as soul kissing, tongue kissing, or French kissing).

How did the custom of mouth kissing come about? In Focus 4.1 describes one researcher's ideas concerning the origin of mouth kissing.

Kissing may or may not have emotional or erotic connotations. A goodnight kiss may be perfunctory or may symbolize in the mind of each partner the ultimate sense of caring and belonging. It may also mean different things to each partner.

CONSIDERATION

When writing a letter to a loved one, we sometimes write a row of XXXXXXs to represent kisses. This custom stems from the Middle Ages, when so many people were illiterate that a cross (X) was acceptable as a signature on a legal document. The cross (X) stood for "St. Andrew's mark," and people vowed to be honest by writing a cross that represented his sacred name. To pledge their sincere honesty, people would kiss their signature and, in time, the X became associated with the kiss alone (Ackerman, 1990).

Breast Stimulation   Breast stimulation, both manual and oral, is a common noncoital sexual behavior. Over 95 percent of the men and women at a Columbian university reported having engaged in breast stimulation (Alzate, 1989). In our society, the female breasts are charged with erotic potential. A billion-dollar pornographic industry encourages men to view women's breasts in erotic terms. Not all women share men's erotic feelings about breasts. Women may or may not manually stimulate their own breasts and often neglect the breasts of their male partners, even though male breasts have the same potential for erotic stimulation as female breasts. For some men, breast stimulation by their partners is particularly important.

Penile Stimulation   Caressing the penis is another noncoital sexual behavior.

MANUAL STIMULATION   Eighty-six percent of university females in one study reported that they had actively manually stimulated their partner's genitals (Alzate, 1989). Being in love or feeling strong affection was the condition under which most women reported feeling most comfortable engaging in this behavior.

> Some students think genitalia is an Italian airline.
>
> SYLVIA HACKER

FELLATIO   One of the most intimate forms of noncoital sexual behavior is fellatio, or oral stimulation of the man's genitals by his partner.

NATIONAL DATA ❦ Of 3,290 men aged 20–39, 79 percent reported ever having received oral sex. Twenty-four percent reported having received oral sex once or twice in the last month (Billy et al., 1993).

In spite of the reported high incidence of fellatio, it remains a relatively taboo subject for open discussion. In many states legal statutes regard fellatio as a "crime against nature." "Nature" in this case refers to reproduction and the "crime" is sex that does not produce babies.

Clitoral Stimulation   "Please take me clitorally" is the message most of the 3,000 women in Hite's (1977) study of female sexuality would like their lovers to act on. Again and again, the women in Hite's study, when asked how men made love to them, said their partners spent too little time (sometimes none at all) stimulating their clitoris and that they needed such stimulation to derive maximum pleasure from the sexual experience. The clitoris may be stimulated by hand, mouth, or the penis.

> 12 percent of men think they know where a woman's clitoris is, but two percent have no idea.
>
> CARIN RUBENSTEIN, *MADEMOISELLE* SURVEY

MANUAL STIMULATION   Ninety-six percent of 128 university males reported that they had actively manually stimulated their partner's genitals (Alzate, 1989). Such stimulation may be to ready the woman for intercourse or as an end in itself and may or may not include insertion of the man's fingers.

CUNNILINGUS   Cunnilingus involves stimulating the clitoris, labia, and vaginal opening of the woman by her partner's tongue and lips. Seventy-two percent of 193 university women reported that they had been the recipient of cunnilingus (Knox & Schacht, 1992).

NATIONAL DATA 😵 Of 3,286 men aged 20–39, 75 percent reported having performed oral sex. Twenty-one percent reported having performed oral sex once or twice in the last month (Billy et al., 1993).

To what degree do women enjoy cunnilingus? In a study of women aged 27 to 49 in established sexual relationships, heterosexual cunnilingus was their preferred sexual activity (Kahn, 1983). The moist, warm, mobile tongue on their clitoris feels very good to most women. Those who find it unpleasant or repulsive often view their vaginal area as dirty and oral sex as obscene and unnatural. One woman said that her partner's mouth was for eating, drinking, speaking, and kissing those he loved—not for using on her genitals.

How do men feel about cunnilingus? In a study of 4,000 men, less than three percent said that cunnilingus was unpleasant or boring (Pietropinto & Simenauer, 1977). Some men perform cunnilingus because they want to rather than because their partners ask them to. Their enjoyment in cunnilingus may spring from doing something forbidden, from their enhanced self-image as a good lover, or just wanting to please their partner.

CLITORAL STIMULATION VIA PENIS   In addition to stimulating the clitoral-vulval area by hand and mouth, some women rub their partner's penis inside their vaginal lips. The penis may be rubbed in a circular motion, or up and down the vaginal lips, or directly on the clitoris. Such stimulation may or may not be followed by penetration. As suggested earlier, premarital couples who wish to avoid intercourse for moral reasons may enjoy such stimulation, yet stop short of intercourse to maintain their virginity. This has been referred to as "technical virginity," measured in millimeters!

CONSIDERATION

Although rubbing the penis on or near the clitoris is not the same as intercourse, it can result in the same outcome—pregnancy. If the man ejaculates near the woman's vaginal opening during penis-clitoral stimulation, pregnancy may occur. Even if the man does not ejaculate, his penis may emit a small amount of fluid from the Cowper's gland that contains sperm.

Two percent of women report that they have anal sex every time they have sex.

CARIN RUBENSTEIN *MADEMOISELLE* SURVEY

Anal Intercourse   Another form of noncoital sexual behavior is anal intercourse. Fifteen percent of a random sample of 1,173 college students reflecting white, black, Asian, and latino ethnicity reported having engaged in anal intercourse (Baldwin et al., 1992).

NATIONAL DATA ❧ Of 3,298 men aged 20–39, 20 percent reported having had anal sex. As noted earlier, white men were more likely to have experienced anal sex than black men (21 percent versus 14 percent) (Billy et al., 1993).

In *Anal Pleasure and Health,* Morin (1986) details the history of the anal taboo and suggests ways for those interested in anal sex to relax, desensitize their fears, and discover potential pleasure. However, damage to the rectum sometimes occurs which may require surgery to correct.

CONSIDERATION

Couples who engage in anal intercourse should use condoms during anal intercourse as a precaution against contracting HIV and other STDs. Switching from anal to vaginal intercourse also requires a new condom for hygiene.

Sexual Intercourse

Sexual intercourse, or *coitus,* refers to the sexual union of a man's penis in a woman's vagina. Eighty percent of a random sample of 1,173 college students reflecting white, black, Asian, and latino ethnicity, reported having engaged in vaginal intercourse (Baldwin et al., 1992). Similarly, Phillips (1992) reported that 82.3 percent of the first year students at a midsize southeastern university in her random sample were sexually active. Twenty percent of her respondents reported having had two or more sexual partners during the three months prior to the survey.

> It is as important to use a condom consistently as it is to use it correctly.
>
> BETSY RYAN

NATIONAL DATA ❧ Of 3,317 men aged 20–39, 95 percent reported having had vaginal intercourse. Eighty-eight percent of those who were never married reported having had vaginal intercourse (100 percent of the married and formerly married). Twenty-three percent of the never married had had more than 20 partners (Billy et al., 1993).

NATIONAL DATA ❧ In a national sample of women aged 15–44, 41 percent reported having had four or more partners, 23 percent six or more, and eight percent more than ten (Kost & Forrest, 1992).

Sexual intercourse may be viewed as a means of communication that occurs for various reasons and in different contexts—before marriage, during marriage, outside marriage, and after marriage, as well as independently of marriage. Each partner brings to the intercourse experience a motive (to express emotional intimacy, to have fun—see In Focus 4.2); a psychological state (contentment, excitement, hostility, boredom); and a physical state (aroused, relaxed, tense, exhausted).

~;· IN FOCUS 4.2 ·~

University Students' Motivations to Have Intercourse

In an attempt to identify the motivations university students have for engaging in intercourse and the gender differences that might exist, Brigman and Knox (1992) surveyed 163 students enrolled in "Courtship and Marriage" and "Marriage and the Family" classes at East Carolina University who reported having had intercourse.

The following table shows the percentages of respondents who reported each of several motivations for their last intercourse experience. The data emphasize that more than one motivation for intercourse is operative during each intercourse experience and that the emotional elements of sexuality take precedence over physical elements such as relief of sexual tension.

Motivations	% Reporting
Intimacy	67
Love	51
Fun	47
Please the partner	24
Relieve sexual tension	14

The importance of intimacy as a motivation for inter-course is different for women than for men (see the following Table). Women were significantly more likely to list intimacy as a motivation for intercourse than men. Similarly, men were less likely to regard intimacy as a motivation for intercourse than women. That women are more likely to prefer an emotional context for intercourse has been reported by previous researchers (Klassen et al., 1989).

Degree of Emotional Intimacy	Women (N = 87)	Men (N = 76)
High Emotional Intimacy	57%	43%
Low Emotional Intimacy	31	68

SOURCES: Brigman, B. and D. Knox. University students' motivations to have intercourse. *College Student Journal,* 1992, *26,* 406–408. Excerpts reprinted with the permission of *College Student Journal.* Dr. George E. Uhlig, Project Innovation of Mobile, P.O. Box 8508, Spring Hill Station, Mobile, Alabama 36608. Klassen, A. D., C. J. Williams, and E. E. Levitt. *Sex and morality in the United States: An empirical enquiry under the auspices of the Kinsey Institute.* Middletown, Conn.: Wesleyan University Press, 1989.

CONSIDERATION

The combination of motives and states may change from one sexual encounter to the next. Tonight, one partner may feel aroused and seek intercourse mainly for physical pleasure, but the other partner may feel tired and only have intercourse because of a sense of duty or to please the spouse. Tomorrow night, both partners may feel relaxed and loving and have intercourse as a means of expressing their feelings for each other.

First Intercourse Experiences

Because people attach a great deal of emotional and social significance to intercourse, the first experience is likely to be memorable. Some confusion, anxiety, and frustration about the when, who, why, and how of first intercourse are typical. The following statements reflect such feelings: "I'd like to get it over with"; "My closest friend has intercourse regularly. I wonder when I'll be doing it?" "I feel that I should already have had intercourse by now, but I haven't." Compounding these concerns are those about the partner ("Will my partner respect me?"), pregnancy ("Will a pregnancy occur?"), and sexually transmitted diseases ("Will I become infected?").

Orgasm during first intercourse occurs less often than might be expected. While 72 percent of 128 male undergraduate students reported having an orgasm during first intercourse, only 23 percent of 93 undergraduate females reported having an orgasm during the first intercourse (Alzate, 1989).

The degree to which a person is religiously devout also influences a person's decision about whether or not to have intercourse. Individuals who report having a strong religious faith are less likely to approve of premarital intercourse (Miller & Olson, 1988).

The age of the partner also has an effect on intercourse. Age 18 marks the time a person graduates from high school and leaves home and is regarded as the time sexual intercourse becomes socially approved. For college students, it is the time of "full premarital sexual rights" (Sprecher, 1989). However, the timing of first intercourse may vary. In one study of 126 males, the average age of first intercourse was 15.8. Of 93 females in the study, the average age of first intercourse was 19.2 (Alzate, 1989). In another study of over 800 female nurses, the average age of first intercourse was 19.2 (Davidson & Darling, 1988).

The timing of first intercourse also varies by race and cultural background. Table 4.4 identifies the ages of first intercourse from a national sample of youth residing in the United States.

As the table indicates, men, regardless of racial background, have first intercourse earlier than women. In addition the racial backgrounds from earliest to latest intercourse are black, Latino, white, and Mexican American. Of particular note is that Latinos and Mexican Americans are often lumped into the category of Hispanic. However, their timing of first intercourse is different suggesting that these subgroups must be examined separately (Day, 1992).

TABLE 4.4

Average Age for First Intercourse by Gender and Race

	MEXICAN/AMERICAN		LATINO		BLACK		WHITE	
	MEN	WOMEN	MEN	WOMEN	MEN	WOMEN	MEN	WOMEN
Age	16.3	17.6	15.4	17.8	14.3	16.8	16.3	17.4

Source: Day, Randal D. The transition to first intercourse among racially and culturally diverse youth. *Journal of Marriage and the Family,* 1992, *54,* 749–762. Adapted from Table 1 on p. 754. Reprinted by permission of the National Council on Family Relations. Copyright 1992. National Council on Family Relations, 3989 Central Avenue, NE, Suite 550, Minneapolis, MN 55421.

❦ Trends

As the HIV epidemic has become more visible, people have become slightly more selective in their sexual partners and the use of condoms has increased. Women, as well as men, have begun to take initiatives in purchasing condoms with nonoxynol-9 (see Choices section to follow) and having them available for use.

A team of researchers asked 312 college students to indicate whether they had changed their sexual behavior in response to the threat of contracting AIDS (Jurich et al., 1992). Response categories included the following: no effect, engaging in sex less frequently, more selective in choosing a sexual partner(s), and stopped having sex. Sixty-four percent of the respondents who were dating and had experienced sexual intercourse reported that they had changed their sexual behavior in response to AIDS; 35.9 percent reported that they had not done so. Those who were most likely to change their behavior perceived themselves to be most susceptible to contracting the virus. Hence, "perceived susceptibility is the key factor motivating individuals to change their behavior" (p. 103). In contrast, a major reason for *not* changing one's sexual behavior in reference to the fear of contracting HIV or other STDs is the belief that bad things happen to others, not to one's self (Brehm, 1992).

Finally, as the HIV epidemic continues, more people will decide to be tested for HIV and will request potential sexual partners do likewise. (HIV and other sexually transmitted diseases are discussed in Special Topics 1 at the end of the text.)

⤳ CHOICES ⤳

---

*D*eciding whether and when to have intercourse in a new relationship is a vital concern in regard to sexual values and relationships. In addition, individuals also make decisions about whether to masturbate with one's partner.

Intercourse with a New Partner?

Sexual values are operative in choosing whether to engage in sexual intercourse in a new relationship. The following might be considered in making such a decision.

Personal Consequences How do you predict you will feel about yourself after you have intercourse? An increasing number of individuals are relativists and feel that if they are in love and have considered their decision carefully, the outcome will be

❦ CHOICES ❧

positive. (The quotes in this section are from students in the authors' classes.):

> I believe intercourse before marriage is okay under certain circumstances. I believe that when a person falls in love with another, it is then appropriate. This should be thought about very carefully for a long time, so as not to regret engaging in intercourse. I do not think intercourse should be a one-night thing, a one-week thing, or a one-month thing. You should grow to love and care for the person very much before giving that "ultra" special part of you to your partner. These feelings should be felt by both partners; if this is not the case, then you are not in love and you are not "making love."

Those who are not in love and have sex in a casual context sometimes feel badly about the experience:

> I viewed sex as a new toy—something to try as frequently as possible. I did my share of sleeping around, and all it did for me was to give me a total loss of self-respect and a bad reputation. Besides, guys talk. I have heard rumors that I sleep with guys I have never slept with. The first couple of guys I had sex with pressured me, and I regret it. I don't believe in casual sex; it brings more heartache than pleasure. It means so much more when you truly love the partner, and you know your love is returned.

Another student said:

> The first time I had intercourse, I was in love and I thought he loved me. But he didn't. He used me, and I have always hated him for it.

Some students reported positive consequences for casual sex:

> We met one night at a mutual friend's party. We liked each other immediately. We talked, sipped some wine, and ended up spending the night together. Though we never saw each other again, I have very positive memories of the encounter.

The effect intercourse will have on you personally will be influenced by your personal values, religious values, and the emotional involvement with your partner. Some people prefer to wait until they are married to have intercourse and feel that this is the best course for future marital stability and happiness. Abstinence is an appropriate alternative choice. There is often, but not necessarily, a religious basis for this value. Strong personal and religious values against nonmarital intercourse plus a lack of emotional involvement usually results in guilt and regret following an intercourse experience. In contrast, values that regard intercourse as appropriate within the context of a love relationship are likely to result in feelings of personal satisfaction and contentment after intercourse.

The existence of a double sexual standard also influences how individuals will react to sexual intercourse with a new partner. A double standard suggests that there is one standard for men and another for women. Traditionally, men who had one night stands with various women could expect social approval for their behavior. But women who engaged in similar behavior were more likely to be disapproved of.

Partner Consequences Because a basic moral principle is to do no harm to others, it may be important to consider the effect of intercourse on your partner. Whereas intercourse may be a pleasurable experience with positive consequences for you, your partner may react differently. What are your partner's feelings about nonmarital intercourse and her or his ability to handle the experience? If you suspect your partner will regret having intercourse, then you might reconsider whether intercourse would be appropriate with this person.

One man reported that after having intercourse with a woman he had just met, he awakened to the sound of her uncontrollable sobbing as she sat on the end of the bed. She was guilty, depressed, and regretted the experience. He said of the event, "If I had known how she was going to respond, we wouldn't have had intercourse."

(continued)

One woman reported that she made a mistake in having intercourse with a friend. "To me," she said, "it was just a friendship and I knew that there was no romantic future. For him it was different. He fell in love and wanted us to be lovers. It destroyed him when he learned I had no such interest."

Relationship Consequences What is the effect of a couple having intercourse on their relationship? Cate et al. (1993) assessed the effect of the first intercourse experience of 366 students with a current partner or the last intercourse experience with a previous partner. The higher the guilt associated with having intercourse for the first time, the less positive the effect on the relationship for both women and men. Conversely, the more permissive the sexual values of the partners, the more likely they were to report that sexual intercourse had a positive impact on their relationship. In addition, the higher the quality of the physical aspect of the first intercourse with a partner, the greater the positive impact on the relationship for both women and men.

What is the effect on a couple's subsequent marital relationship if they have intercourse with each other before they are married? Ard (1990) studied couples who did and did not have intercourse and who subsequently married each other. The most prominent effect (67 percent) reported by those who had intercourse was "no

effect" with about 20 percent reporting a favorable effect and 13 percent reporting a negative effect. However, those NOT having intercourse reported that the most prominent effect on their subsequent marriage to each other was no effect (54 percent) with 39 percent reporting a favorable effect and seven percent reporting an unfavorable effect. Hence, almost twice as many of those who chose not to have intercourse before marriage with their partner reported a positive effect as compared with those who chose to have intercourse with their partner. Women were more likely than men to report favorable effects on the marriage for choosing not to have premarital intercourse (Ard, 1990).

Suppose individuals who have intercourse before marriage don't choose to marry each other but end up marrying someone else. What is the effect of having had intercourse on one's subsequent marriage to another person? Kahn and London (1991) examined national data on premarital intercourse and subsequent divorce of all U.S. women age 15–44 and found that divorce was more likely among individuals who had had premarital intercourse. The explanation for this correlation suggested by the researchers was that both premarital intercourse and divorce are nontraditional behaviors and that individuals who break traditional norms of intercourse before marriage are also more likely to

express their nontraditionality in regard to divorce. However, both the data analysis and interpretation have been questioned by Heaton (1993). After reviewing Heaton's concerns, both Kahn & London (1993) held firm on their data and interpretation.

Contraception Another potential consequence of intercourse is pregnancy. Once a couple decides to have intercourse, a separate decision must be made as to whether intercourse should result in pregnancy. Some couples want children and make a mutual commitment to love and care for their offspring. Other couples do not want children. If the couple wants to avoid pregnancy, they must choose and effectively use a contraceptive method. But many do not. Six percent of the 672 sexually active university first year students in the Phillips survey (1992) reported that they used no method of birth control. Six percent of these sexually active students also reported that they had become pregnant at least once. In many cases, pregnancy comes as a surprise. One woman recalled:

It was the first time I had intercourse, so I didn't really think I would get pregnant my first time. But I did. And when I told him I was pregnant, he told me he didn't have any money and couldn't help me pay for the abortion. He really wanted nothing to do with me after that (Author's files).

ᴠ᪣: CHOICES ᨄ

HIV and Other Sexually Transmissible Diseases Avoiding HIV infection and other sexually transmissible diseases (STDs) is an important consideration in deciding whether to have intercourse in a new relationship. Increasing numbers of people having more frequent intercourse with more partners has resulted in the rapid spread of the bacteria and viruses responsible for numerous varieties of STDs. Four and one half percent of 672 sexually active first year university students in the Phillips (1992) study reported that they had been diagnosed as having an STD.

Although no method is completely safe, a sexually active person can reduce the chances of getting (or giving) HIV and other STDs by getting tested for HIV and other STDs and by asking a potential sex partner to do likewise before engaging in sexual behavior with the partner. Since HIV antibodies may not be evident for six months after exposure, an important precaution is not to have sex with someone who has had multiple sexual partners. Finding such a partner is very difficult because people lie to each other about sexual matters. Cochran and Mays (1990) noted in a sample of 18- to 25-year-old college students that 34 percent of the men and 10 percent of the women who were sexually experienced reported having told a lie in order to have sex. Individuals are particularly likely to lie about their number of previous sexual partners. In one study, the most frequently reported lie told to potential sexual partners was in regard to the number of previous sexual relationships or partners they had had (Knox, Schacht, Holt, & Turner, 1993).

In addition to selectivity in choosing one's sexual partner and awareness of potential dishonesty in regard to information about a chosen partner's previous sexual partners, looking for sores or discharges before sex and washing exposed areas after contact may help to reduce exposure. A critically important precaution is the use of a latex resevoir tip condom, which is lubricated with non-oxynol 9 (shown to kill HIV in laboratory animals). Read the label on condoms to ensure that non-oxynol 9 is included. While this may be good advice, 1,173 students from a random sample of college students representing whites, blacks, Asians, and Latinos, reported that, when having vaginal intercourse during the past three months, they used condoms only 31.1 percent of the time (Baldwin et al., 1992, 203). In a national random sample of adults in the United States, only 17 percent of those with multiple sexual partners reported using a condom all the time (Catania, 1992). In the Phillips study of 672 sexually active university first year students, less than half reported using a condom their last intercourse experience (1992).

In a national sample of men aged 20–39, 39 percent of those who were single and sexually active reported that they had used a condom in the last month (Tanfer et al., 1993). Single black men were more likely to have used condoms than single white men (49 percent versus 36 percent) and men (both married and single) under 30 were more likely to have used condoms than men over 30 (36 percent versus 19 percent) (Tanfer et al., 1993). Those who had engaged in anal sex, homosexual sex, sex with a one-night stand partner, or sex with multiple partners were more likely to have used a condom.

These grim statistics emphasize the need to initiate a "safe sex" talk with a potential sex partner. Less than one-fourth of all college freshmen throughout the United States reported that they discussed "safe sex" with a partner in the past year (American Council on Education and University of California, 1992). One of the problems of doing so is that such talk is often felt to be a cold bucket of water on the excitement of anticipating sexual pleasure. One researcher emphasized the need to eroticize safe sex talk so that it becomes a turn on rather than a turn off. "In light of contemporary media coverage linking sexual activity with disease, death, incest, abuse, and rape, it is clearly time to consider interven-

(*continued*)

⌇ **CHOICES** ∾

---

tions that dangle carrots, not swords, before lovers" (Adelman, 1992, 492).

A nationwide survey of men's preferences in condoms showed that color, ribbing, and partner's preference were relatively unimportant in selecting a condom. Factors that were important included ease of putting it on, having the right amount of lubrication, and the quality of staying on. Men also stated that they thought the use of a condom sent a mixed message to their partners—that you care enough about them to use a condom but that either you have AIDS or you think you partner does (Grady et al., 1993).

Consider the Influence of Alcohol/Drugs on Choices A final consideration in regard to the decision to have intercourse in a new relationship is to be aware of the influence of alcohol and drugs on such a decision. Twenty-five percent of the 672 sexu-

ally active university first year students in the Phillips (1992) survey reported they had used alcohol or drugs before their last occasion of intercourse (men were more likely than women to have done so). In a survey of 2,365 readers of *Mademoiselle* and *Details* magazines, 48 percent of the women and 58 percent of the men reported that they had had sex only because they had too much to drink (Rubenstein, 1993). Other researchers have found that engaging in safe sex behavior is associated with having had fewer sexual partners in the past and not using drugs such as cocaine or amyl nitrate (poppers) (Exner et al., 1992).

Choose to Masturbate with One's Partner?

Some partners regard masturbation as a personal and private experience while others regard it as an experience

to share. Regarding the latter, Rubin (1991) noted that couples under 35 were particularly likely to share the experience: "We love to watch each other masturbate; it's a great turn on" (p. 186).

A positive view of masturbating with one's partner is reflected in the following (Boston Women's Health Collective, 1984, 178).

> When my fiancé asked if he could help me masturbate I thought it was kinky at first. Then I showed him how I do it and he showed me how he does. We watch each other to see what feels good. . . .

> My lover rubbed her breasts and clitoris while I made love to her yesterday. After I got over feeling a little inadequate (I should be able to do it all!), I found it was like having another pair of hands to make love to her with. It was a turn-on to both of us.

⅋ **Summary**

Sexual values are moral guidelines for sexual behavior. Sexual values vary by culture, help define who we are, provide direction in determining who we marry, and affect our risk of contracting HIV and other STDs.

Our sexual values have their heritage in Jewish and Christian religions. Early Jewish thought emphasized the importance of sex in marriage, stressed procreation, and noted that variations such as homosexuality were sinful. Christian thought varied from sex is sinful to sex is good. The Puritans emphasized a strong sense of the importance of being proper and God fearing in one's sexuality; the Victorians gave us a prudish sense of sexuality and divided women into two types. Those who loved sex were "bad" women;

"good" women were those who restricted their sexuality to marriage and who did not enjoy sexual feelings.

Three sexual value perspectives are absolutism ("rightness" is defined by an official code of morality), relativism ("rightness" depends on the situation—who does what, with whom, in what context), and hedonism ("if it feels good, do it").

You may assess your own sexual values by completing various value statements, identifying your sexual values on an array of topics from acceptable to unacceptable, identifying what situations make you feel guilty, and responding to various value dilemma situations.

Women and men differ in their sexual values and behaviors. Men are more aggressive sexually, have orgasms more often, and are more likely to have intercourse for sexual conquest and relief of sexual tension. Women are more passive sexually, have orgasm less frequently, and are more likely to have intercourse as an expression of emotional closeness and affection. Based on a study by Baldwin, the sexual behaviors of white, Asian, black, and Latino college students are very similar—particularly after controlling for background variables such as socioeconomic status. Those reflecting lower income backgrounds reported higher frequencies of sexual behavior than those with higher incomes.

Masturbation is defined as sexual self-stimulation with the goal of pleasuring one's self. Traditionally, masturbation has been viewed as immoral and harmful by religion, medicine, and psychotherapy. However, attitudes toward masturbation are changing. Although religious leaders may still express disapproval, most physicians and therapists are more positive about masturbation.

Interpersonal noncoital sexual behavior involves touching, kissing, breast stimulation, penile stimulation, clitoral stimulation, and anal intercourse. The latter remains a relatively taboo and infrequent behavior in contrast to vaginal intercourse. Trends in sexual values include more selectivity in sexual partners, HIV testing, and increased use of the condom for protection against STDs.

Questions for Reflection

1. How have your sexual values changed in the last five years. To what degree do you feel these changes are related to your peers and relationships?
2. To what degree has the HIV epidemic affected your sexual values and behavior? To what degree are you comfortable asking your partner about his or her previous sexual partners and about emphasizing the importance of using a condom?
3. How do you think you would feel about sex if you were reared in any of the societies mentioned in the In Focus 4.1 insert on sexual values from a cross-cultural perspective.

References

Ackerman, D. A natural history of the senses. New York: Random House, 1990.

Adelman, M. B. Sustaining passion: Eroticism and safe-sex talk. *Archives of Sexual Behavior,* 1992, *21,* 481–494.

Alzate, H. Sexual behavior of unmarried Colombian university students: A follow-up. *Archives of Sexual Behavior,* 1989, *18,* 239–250.

American Council on Education and University of California. The American freshman: National norms for fall 1992. Los Angeles, California: Los Angeles Higher Education Research Institute, 1992.

Ard, Ben Neal. *The sexual realm in long-term marriages: A longitudinal study following marital partners over twenty years.* San Francisco, Calif.: Mellen Research University Press, 1990.

Baldwin, J. D., S. Whiteley, and J. I. Baldwin. The effect of ethnic group on sexual activities related to contraception and STDs. *The Journal of Sex Research,* 1992, *29,* 189–205.

Bancroft, J., B. B. Sherwin, G. M. Alexander, D. W. Davidson, and A. Walker. Oral contraceptives, androgens, and the sexuality of young women: I. A comparison of sexual experience, sexual attitudes, and gender role in oral contraceptive users and nonusers. *Archives of Sexual Behavior,* 1991, *20,* 105–120.

Billingham, Robert E., Kelly A. Smith, and J. Keller. The effect of chronological and theoretical birth order on sexual attitudes and behaviors. *Archives of Sexual Behavior,* 1989, *18,* 109–116.

Billy, J. O. G., K. Tanfer, W. R. Grady, and D. H. Klepinger. The sexual behavior of men in the United States. *Family Planning Perspectives,* 1993, *25,* 52–60.

Brehm, S. S. *Intimate relationships,* 2d ed. New York: McGraw-Hill, 1992.

Brigman, B. and D. Knox. University students' motivations to have intercourse. *College Student Journal,* 1992, *26,* 406–408.

Bullough, V. L. A historical approach. *Theories of Human Sexuality,* J. H. Greer and W. T. O'Donohue, eds. New York: Plenum Press, 1987, 49–63.

Cado, S. and H. Leitenberg. Guilt reactions to sexual fantasies during intercourse. *Archives of Sexual Behavior,* 1990, *19,* 49–63.

Carswell, R. W. Historical analysis of religion and sex. *The Journal of School Health,* 1969, *39,* 673–684.

Catania, J. A., T. J. Coates, R. Stall, H. Turner, J. Peterson, N. Hearst, M. M. Dolcini, E. Hudes, J. Gagnon, J. Wiley, and R. Groves. Prevalence of AIDS-related risk factors and condom use in the United States. *Science,* 1992, *258,* 1101–1106.

Cate, R. M., E. Long, J. J. Angera, and K. K. Draper. Sexual intercourse and relationship development. *Family Relations,* 1993, *42,* 158–164.

Cochran, S. and V. Mays. Sex, Lies and HIV. *New England Journal of Medicine,* March 15, 1990, 774–775.

Darling, Carol Anderson, J. Kenneth Davidson, Sr., and Ruth P. Cox. Female sexual response and the timing of partner orgasm. *Journal of Sex and Marital Therapy,* 1991, *17,* 3–21.

Davidson, J. K., Sr. and C. A. Darling. The sexually experienced woman: Multiple sex partners and sexual satisfaction. *The Journal of Sex Research,* 1988, *24,* 141–154.

Day, R. D. The transition to first intercourse among racially and culturally diverse youth. *Journal of Marriage and the Family,* 1992, *54,* 749–762.

Ellis, A. *Sex without guilt.* New York: Lyle Stuart, 1966.

Erkmen, H., N. Dilbaz, G. Seber, C. Kaptanoglu, and D. Tekin. Sexual attitudes of Turkish university students. *Journal of Sex Education and Therapy,* 1990, *16,* 251–261.

Exner, T. M., H. F. F. Meyer-Bahlburg, and A. A. Ehrhardt. Sexual self-control as a mediator of high risk sexual behavior in a New York City cohort of HIV+ and HIV– gay men. *The Journal of Sex Research,* 1992, *29,* 389–406.

Frayser, S. G. *Varieties of sexual experience.* New Haven, Conn.: Human Relations Area Files Press, 1985.

Gilligan, C., V. W. Ward, and Taylor, eds. *Mapping the moral domain.* Cambridge, Mass.: Harvard University Press, 1988.

Grady, W. R., D. H. Klepinger, J. O. G. Billy, and K. Tanfer. Condom characteristics: The perceptions and preferences of men in the United States. *Family Planning Perspectives,* 1993, *25,* 67–73.

Graham, S. 1848. *Lecture to Young Men, On Chastity, Intended Also for the Serious Consideration of Parents and Guardians.* (10th ed.) Boston: C. H. Price.

GSS News. General Social Survey. NORC, 1155 East 60th Street, Chicago, Illinois 60637. September 1992, Number 6, page 5.

Heaton, T. B. Comment on "Premarital sex and the risk of divorce." *Journal of Marriage and the Family,* 1993, *55,* 240–241.

Hite, S. *The Hite report: A nationwide study of female sexuality.* New York: Dell, 1977.

Hudson, W. W., G. J. Murphy, and P. S. Nurius. A short-form scale to measure liberal vs. conservative orientations toward human sexual expression. *Journal of Sex Research,* 1983, *19,* 258–272.

Janus, S. and C. Janus. *The Janus report on sexual behavior.* New York: Wiley, 1992.

Johnson, W. S. *Living in sin: The victorian sexual revolution.* Chicago: Nelson-Hall, 1979.

Jurich, J. A., R. A. Adams, and J. E. Schulenberg. Factors related to behavior change in response to AIDS. *Family Relations,* 1992, *41,* 97–103.

Kahn, J. R. and K. A. London. Reply to comment on Kahn and London (1991). *Journal of Marriage and the Family,* 1993, *55,* 241.

Kahn, S. S. *The Kahn report on sexual preferences: What the opposite sex likes and dislikes—and why.* New York: St. Martin's Press, 1983.

Kinsey, A., W. Pomeroy, and C. Martin. *Sexual Behavior in the Human Male.* Philadelphia: Saunders, 1948.

Kinsey, A., W. Pomeroy, C. Martin, and P. Gebhard. *Sexual behavior in the human female.* Philadelphia: Saunders, 1953.

Klassen, Albert D., Colin J. Williams, and Eugene E. Levitt. *Sex and morality in the U.S.: An empirical enquiry under the auspices of the Kinsey Institute.* Middletown, Conn.: Wesleyan University Press, 1989.

Knox, D. and C. Schacht. Sexual behaviors of university students enrolled in a human sexuality course. *College Student Journal,* 1992, *26,* 38–40.

Knox, D., C. Schacht, J. Holt, and J. Turner. Sexual lies among college students. *College Student Journal,* in press, 1993.

Knox, D., L. H. Walters, and J. Walters. Sexual guilt among college students. *College Student Journal,* 1991, *25,* 432–433.

Kost, K. and J. D. Forrest. American women's sexual behavior and exposure to risk of sexually transmitted diseases. *Family Planning Perspectives,* 1992, *24,* 244–254.

Leigh, Barbara Critchlow. Reasons for having and avoiding sex: Gender, sexual orientation, and relationship to sexual behavior. *Journal of Sex Research,* 1989, *26,* 199–209.

Linn, R. Sexual and moral development of Israeli female adolescents from city and kibbutz: Perspectives of Kohlberg and Gilligan. *Adolescence,* 1991, *26,* 59–70.

Margolin, Leslie. Gender and the prerogatives of dating and marriage: An experimental assessment of a sample of college students. *Sex Roles,* 1989, *20,* 91–102.

Miller, Brent C., and Terrance D. Olson. Sexual attitudes and behavior of high school students in relation to background and contextual factors. *Journal of Sex Research,* 1988, *24,* 194–200.

Mindel, C. H., R. W. Habenstein, and R. Wright, Jr., eds. *Ethnic families in America: Patterns and variations,* 3d ed. New York: Elsevier Publisher, 1988.

Money, J., K. S. Prakasam, and V. N. Joshi. Semen-conservation doctrine from ancient Ayurvedic to modern sexological theory. *American Journal of Psychotherapy,* 1991, *XLV,* 9–13.

Morin, J. *Anal pleasure and health.* Burlingame, Calif.: Down There Press, 1986.

Nurius, P. S., and W. W. Hudson. A sexual profile of social groups. *Journal of Sex Education and Therapy,* 1982, *8,* no. 2, 15–30.

Oggins, J., D. Leber, and J. Veroff. Race and gender differences in black and white newlyweds' perceptions of sexual and marital relations. *Journal of Sex Research,* 1993, *30,* 152–160.

Phillips, Jennifer C. Self-reported health behaviors of college freshmen. Unpublished thesis. Department of Health, Physical Education, Recreation and Safety, May 1992. Used by permission of Jennifer C. Phillips, Health Educator, Student Health Service, East Carolina University, Greenville, North Carolina 27858.

Robinson, I., K. Ziss, B. Banza, S. Katz and E. Robinson. Twenty years of the sexual revolution, 1965–1985. *Journal of Marriage and the Family,* 1991, *53,* 216–220.

Rothman, E. K. *Hands and hearts: A history of courtship in America.* Cambridge: Harvard University Press, 1987.

Rubenstein, C. Generation sex. *Mademoiselle.* 1993, June, 130–137.

Rubin, L. B. *Erotic wars.* New York: Harper Collins Publishers, 1991.

Rubinson, Laurna and L. De Rubertis. Trends in sexual attitudes and behaviors of a college population over a 15-year period. *Journal of Sex Education and Therapy,* 1991, *17,* 32–42.

Seligmann, J., M. N. Peyser, L. Beachy, B. Fisher, D. Hannah, and A. Duignan-Cabera. The HIV dating game. *Newsweek,* October 5. 1992, 56–57.

Smith, R. and J. Walters. Sexual guilt. Unpublished paper, 1988, University of Georgia, Department of Child and Family Development, Athens, Georgia. Used by permission.

Special Committee on Human Sexuality. *Part I: Keeping body and soul together: Sexuality, spirituality, and social justice.* General Assembly, Presbyterian Church (USA), 1991.

Sprecher, S. Premarital sexual standards for different categories of individuals, *Journal of Sex Research,* 1989, *26,* 232–248.

Szasz, J. T. *Sex by prescription.* New York: Doubleday, 1980.

Tanfer, K., W. R. Grady, D. H. Klepinger, and J. O. G. Billy. Condom use among U.S. men, 1991. *Family Planning Perspectives,* 1993, *25,* 61–66.

Tannahill, R. *Sex in history.* New York: Stein and Day, 1982.

Tissot, S. A. *Onania, or a treatise upon the disorders produced by masturbation.* A. Hume, trans. London: J. Pridden, 1766. (Original work published in 1758.)

Townsend, J. M. and G. D. Levy. Effects of potential partner's physical attractiveness and socioeconomic status on sexuality and partner selection. *Archives of Sexual Behavior,* 1990, *19,* 149–164.

Williams, John D. and Arthur P. Jacoby. The effects of premarital heterosexual and homosexual experience on dating and marriage desirability. *Journal of Marriage and the Family,* 1989, *51,* 489–497.

Contents

5
CHAPTER
Dating and Mate Selection

Is It True?

1. Couples who are separated by a great distance should handle any big disagreements over the phone so that they won't spoil the time when they are together.

2. The criteria for choosing a partner for a first marriage are usually the same as choosing a partner for a second marriage.

3. Parents who discourage their offspring from dating and being involved with a particular person are usually successful in breaking up the couple.

4. Most people who join a videodating club say they are looking for a lot of people to date casually.

5. According to a recent study of college students, women are as likely as men to initiate dates and pay for dating expenses.

1 = F; 2 = F; 3 = T; 4 = F; 5 = F

Don't wait and find the person you can live with; wait and find the person you can't live without.

UNKNOWN

"Beverly Hills 90210" is a popular television program focusing on the interpersonal relationships of seven friends in late adolescence/early adulthood. A recurring theme of the show is the on and off love relationships among some of the characters. Other television programs ("Melrose Place," soap operas) reflect similar relationship content. The dating process becomes an interest for most individuals in their teens and early twenties. Those who divorce or become widowed may repeat the dating process later in life.

As noted earlier, a central goal of marriage from the viewpoint of society is to bond two people together who will produce, protect, nurture, and socialize children to be productive members of society. To ensure that this goal is accomplished, society must make some provision for sexually mature women and men to meet, interact, and pair off in long-term relationships for eventual parenthood. Traditionally, the dating process served to guide the woman-man interaction through an orderly process toward mate selection. Today, the term "dating" less often has the unique meaning of seeing one person with the goal of marriage.

NATIONAL DATA ✽ Only seven percent of all U.S. college and university first year students plan to marry while in college (American Council on Education and University of California 1992).

Different patterns of "dating" include dating in groups and/or dating in nonexclusive or exclusive relationships. Some people date by "hanging around" and "getting together" in groups of various sizes; others prefer one-to-one relationships. The latter may be "open" (each partner may date others) or "closed" (the partners date each other exclusively). Such exclusive dating may or may not be oriented toward marriage.

Relationships that lead to marriage are not necessarily permanent. Rather, some individuals will marry more than once. Also, the criteria for choosing a partner at one stage in life may be different from the criteria at another time. One divorced man said:

> The first time around, I wanted someone who was a visual knockout. I married a real beauty, and because we argued all the time, she began to look like Cyclops to me. The next time, I will choose someone with similar values and goals; looks aren't that important to me anymore.

After reviewing how the Industrial Revolution changed the courtship process of women and men, we will examine the realities of dating, selecting a marriage partner, and using the engagement period. We end with a discussion of the conditions under which you might prolong your engagement.

❦ Courtship in Historical Perspective

In colonial America, a man who wanted to marry a woman had to ask the father's permission to do so. The following letter, written around 1705, is from William Byrd to Daniel Parke, asking his permission to marry his daughter (Woodfin & Tinling, 1942).

> Since my arrival in this country, I have had the honour to be acquainted with your daughters, and was infinitely surpriz'd to find young ladys with their accomplishments in Virginia. This surprize was soon improv'd into a passion for the youngest, for whom I have all the respect and tenderness in the world. However, I think it my duty to intreat your approbation before I proceed to give her the last testimony of my affection. And the young lady her self, whatever she may determine by your consent, will agree to nothing without it. If you can entertain a favourable opinion of my person, I dont question but my fortune may be sufficient to make her happy, especially after it has been assisted by your bounty. If you shall vouchsafe to approve of this undertaking, I shall indeavour to recommend myself by all the dutiful regards to your Excellency and all the marks of kindness to your daughter. Nobody knows better than your self how impatient lovers are, and for that reason I hope youll be as speedy as possible in your determination, which I passionately beg may be in favour of your & c.

The Industrial Revolution

The transition from a courtship system controlled by parents to the relative freedom of mate selection experienced today occurred in response to a number of social changes. The most basic change was the Industrial Revolution, which began in England in the middle of the eighteenth century. No longer were women needed exclusively in the home to spin yarn, make clothes, and process food from garden to table. Commercial industries had developed to provide these services, and women transferred their activities in these areas from the home to the factory. The result was that women had more frequent contact with men.

Women's involvement in factory work decreased parental control; parents were unable to dictate the extent to which their offspring could interact with those they met at work. Hence, values in mate selection shifted from the parents to the children. In the past, parents had approved or disapproved of a potential mate on the basis of their own values: Was the person from "good stock"? Did the man have property or a respectable trade? Did the woman have basic domestic skills? In contrast to these parental concerns, the partners focused more on love feelings. Finally, the Industrial Revolution created more leisure time for dating.

Having someone wonder where you are when you don't come home at night is a very old human need.

MARGARET MEAD

The '90s version of the dating scene has taken on a whole new plot line—boy meets girl and they go out . . . along with six of their friends.

LINDA SHRIEVES

Parental Influence Today

As a result of the Industrial Revolution and the gradual loss of parental control, young American women not only became acquainted with young men outside the family circle but also felt free to consider them as possible mates. With the development of the automobile in the twentieth century came a radical change in the conditions of social interaction of unmarried men and women. Couples could now escape from their respective parents to do as they wished. Movies provided an additional place to share an evening away from friends. Within one generation, courtship had changed from parental to couple control.

However, parents still try to influence the dating and mate selection choices of their offspring. Some do it directly by encouraging or discouraging the relationship with a particular person. Sprecher and Felmlee (1992) noted that when parents disapproved of and discouraged a relationship with a particular person, a breakup was more likely.

Parents also influence those with whom their children pair off by choosing the neighborhoods in which their children will live and the schools they will attend. This influence is more subtle but helps control the "pool of eligibles" from which their offspring will select.

While American parents are relatively restrained in their attempts to influence the mate selection preferences of their children, Asian American parents may wield a heavy influence. Particularly among first generation immigrants, some Chinese, Japanese, Korean, and Philippine men and women will not marry someone if their parents disapprove of their choice. Second and third generation offspring are more likely to have been influenced by American culture and to be less constrained by their parents' wishes.

> **CONSIDERATION**
>
> Parental interference sometimes drives dating partners to be together more often—even to marry. If your parents don't want you to date someone, try to separate the issue of why they disapprove of the person from the issue of whether you can see your partner. You can date and marry whomever you like. In a power struggle with your parents, you will win. The more important concern is why do they object? Your parents know you fairly well, love you, and probably have your best interests in mind. You may still decide to go against their wishes (it is your life), but do so because you genuinely disagree with their perceptions and concerns—not because you want to show them you can marry whomever you want whether they like it or not.

ꝃ Contemporary Functions of Dating

Because most people regard dating or "getting together" as a natural part of getting to know someone else, the other functions of dating are sometimes

A maid marries to please her parents; a widow to please herself.

WILLIAM SCARBOROUGH

overlooked. There are at least five of these—confirmation of a social self; recreation; companionship, intimacy, and sex; socialization; and mate selection.

Confirmation of a Social Self

One of the ways we come to be who we are is through interaction with others who hold up social mirrors in which we see ourselves and get feedback on how others view us. When you are on a first date with a person, you are continually trying to assess how that person sees you: Does the person like me? Will the person want to be with me again? When the person gives you positive feedback through speech and gesture, you feel good about yourself and tend to view yourself in positive terms. Dating provides a context for the confirmation of a strong self-concept in terms of how you perceive your effect on other people.

If I am not worth the wooing, I surely am not worth the winning.
LONGFELLOW

Recreation

Dating, hanging around, or getting together is fun. These are things we do with our peers, away from our parents, and we select the specific activities because we enjoy them. "I get tired of studying and being a student all day," a straight-A major in journalism said. "Going out at night with my friends to meet guys really clears my head. It's an exciting contrast to the drudgery of writing term papers."

CONSIDERATION

In spite of the trend toward egalitarian roles, some traditional role expectations and behavior persist in dating. Based on data from 418 students at a large state university two researchers observed that men were more likely to initiate dates, to pay for date expenses, and to encourage sexual intimacy than women. In addition, women were more concerned about the career potential of their male dating partners than vice versa (Asmussen & Shehan, 1992).

Companionship/Intimacy/Sex

Major motivations for dating are companionship, intimacy, and sex. The impersonal environment of a large university makes a secure dating relationship very appealing. "My last two years have been the happiest ever," remarked a senior in interior design. "But it's because of the involvement with my fiancé. During my freshman and sophomore years, I felt alone. Now I feel loved, needed, and secure with my partner." In a study on "Romance in the Personal Ads," Fischer (1990) observed that men were more interested in "companionship" while women were more interested in "a commitment."

Socialization

Before puberty, boys and girls interact primarily with peers of their same sex. A boy or girl may be laughed at if he or she shows an interest in someone of the opposite sex. Even when boy-girl interaction becomes the norm at puberty, neither sex may know what is expected of them. Dating offers the experiences of learning how to initiate conversation and developing an array of skills in human relationships, such as listening and expressing empathy. Dating also permits an individual to try out different role patterns, like dominance or submission, and to assess the "feel" and comfort level of each.

Status Achievement

Some people date "to achieve, prove, or maintain status" (Rice, 1990, 359). Dating someone and being attached to someone are typically regarded as having more status than being unattached and alone. Other people may date for peer acceptance and conformity to gender roles, not for emotional reasons (Basow, 1992). Gay people are particularly aware of the need to date for peer acceptance and sometimes fake the heterosexual dating ritual for the "sake of appearances" (McNaught, 1983, 142).

Mate Selection

Finally, dating may serve to pair two people off for marriage. Eighty-nine percent of 80 clients at a Videodating Service said that they were looking for a serious, permanent relationship rather than a casual relationship (Woll & Young, 1989).

Young Americans seem to be choosing their mates the same way they're choosing their cars: carefully.

ROBERT V. LEVINE

CONSIDERATION

Selecting a mate has become big business. B. Dalton is one of the largest book chains in the United States; they carry about 200 titles on relationships and about 50 of these are specifically geared toward finding a mate.

℘ Dating Realities

One of the first concerns in dating is finding someone to date. Other concerns include maintaining a dating relationship when the partners are separated, dealing with problems in dating, and terminating a dating relationship.

Finding a Dating Partner

Most people meet dating partners through friends, work, classes, or parties. Table 5.1 reflects the qualities sought in a dating partner by both women and

---

⌁ IN FOCUS 5.1 ⌁

How to Meet Someone on Your Campus

The following suggestion is a way for you to meet someone on your campus. Turn back to the Self-Assessment: Love Attitudes Scale, in Chapter 3 on Love Relationships. Hand your text to someone you are interested in meeting and say, "I'm enrolled in a marriage course on campus and have been requested to ask another person on campus to take this love test. Would you take a couple of minutes and complete it for me?"

Persons who are interested in some level of interaction with you will agree to complete the love scale. They may ask you questions about it ("What does the third statement mean?") establish eye contact, and indicate (through smiles and gestures) a willingness to interact with you.

Not all persons will be receptive. Think of your goal as being to find out how others score on the Love Attitudes Scale—not for him or her to fall in love with you. Indeed, if you ask 20 people to complete the scale, expect only one to show an interest in you beyond the scale.

---

men university students. In Focus 5.1 provides a structured way for you to meet someone in one of your classes or on campus.

Since an increasing number of individuals are waiting until they are out of school and in their mid-twenties to marry, the large pool of potential partners, present in both high school and college, may no longer be available. Work may offer few social contacts so other mechanisms of meeting a potential partner have become more acceptable. The stigma of advertising in magazines and newspapers, joining specialized dating clubs, and perusing videos at videodating clubs is declining (Ahuvia & Adelman, 1992). Rather than view themselves as "lonely losers," people may increasingly view themselves as "creative choosers."

TABLE 5.1
Qualities Sought in a Dating Partner, by Gender

QUALITY	FEMALES (N = 272)	MALES (N = 146)	AVERAGE PERCENT
Companionship	94.9	87.0	90.95
Physical attractiveness	87.5	92.5	90.00
Intelligence	91.9	87.7	89.80
Easy-going personality	86.8	80.1	83.45
Emotional support	86.0	63.7	74.85
Good career potential	67.6	34.9	51.25
Similar religious and political values	40.1	26.0	33.05
Family background	36.8	21.2	29.00

Source: Adapted from "Gendered Expectations and Behaviors in Dating Relationships," by Linda Asmussen and Constance L. Shehan. Paper, 54th Annual Conference of the National Council on Family Relations, Orlando, Florida, 1992. Used by permission.

Single's parties provide a context for meeting a new partner.

Learn to love the possible!

MILTON FISHER

Magazines and Newspapers In advertising for a new partner, people most frequently mention their age, avocation, and personality characteristics (Labeff et al., 1989). However, in describing themselves, women were more likely to mention age and men were more likely to mention personality characteristics.

In a review of studies on advertising for a partner, women received an average of 15 replies; men 11 (Ahuvia & Adelman, 1992). Factors associated with men receiving the most replies included (1) being older and taller, (2) having higher education/professional status, and (3) seeking an attractive woman but avoiding sexual references. For women, those factors associated with receiving the most replies included (1) physical attractiveness, (2) younger, physically fit and interested in sports, and (3) mentioning or alluding to sex. "For both men and women, writing an ad with originality or flair increased the number of respondents, as did seemingly trivial traits like possessing a certain hair color" (Ahuvia & Adelman, 1992, 457).

Some magazines feature ads marketed to a particular group of singles. Sparrow (1991) noted, "Increasingly, blacks are using personal ads in black and other singles magazines to meet members of the opposite sex. Such magazines include *Black Gold* in Chicago, *Chocolate Single* in New York, and *Positively Black Professionals* in New Jersey" (p. 105).

Another magazine, *Cherry Blossoms,* (now in its 20th year) is designed for the individual seeking a partner from another country. Each issue features ads from more than 500 women from 40 countries. A 12-month subscription is over $500.

Videodating Clubs The newest method of finding a partner is to be interviewed on videotape and let others watch your cassette in exchange for your watching those already on file. Eighty clients of a videodating service said that the opportunity to watch the videotapes others had made of themselves was the most attractive feature of videotaping (Woll & Young, 1989). Once they saw someone that they liked, the person was contacted by the service and invited in to review the potential partner's videocassette. If the interest was mutual, the partners would meet.

NATIONAL DATA ❦ Of America's approximately 2,000 firms specializing in finding a partner, about 600 use video technology (Ahuvia & Adelman, 1992). "Great Expectations" is the largest videodating service in the United States. It has over 21 centers and 65,000 clients nationwide. The cost for a lifetime membership (until you get married) in Los Angeles is about $2,000 (Goldberg, 1989).

CONSIDERATION

How successful are commercial dating services in matching people with others with whom they have something in common and eventually marry? Based on a review of the literature, the available evidence suggests that such avenues do help to screen out partners with whom one would have little or nothing in common; the result is that partners who end up meeting are fairly similar in their interests and characteristics. Persons who are matched in regard to optimism-pessimism and in abstract versus concrete thinking are the most likely to like the person with whom they are matched and to end up getting married (Ahuvia & Adelman, 1992).

Dating at a Distance

Partners who date may be separated for long periods of time. In a study of relationship problems of university students, 58 percent of the men (260) and 52 percent of the women (391) reported that "living away from each other" was a problem (Riggs, 1993). Because of their mutual enjoyment in the relationship, separated partners are motivated to continue the relationship at a distance. A team of researchers (Fielding, Clarke, & Llewelyn, 1991) studied long-distance relationships and had several recommendations for individuals involved in them.

1. Don't expect it to be easy. Learning to live in a long-distance relationship is difficult; but it can be done, and it can be worthwhile and successful.
2. Anticipate the various stages. The first stage of feelings associated with long-distance relationships involves assuming that they aren't different from other relationships. The second stage is anger and resentment and feeling "Why does this have to happen to me?" The third stage involves acceptance of the separation.

3. Identify the benefits of long-distance relationships. These include feeling greater personal freedom, a sense of personal enhancement, the enhancement of the relationship as a result of the enriched experience of both partners, and the greater importance that both partners attach to the relationship.

4. Find methods of maintaining a long-distance relationship. These include frequent contact by phone (daily) supplemented by letters, postcards, cassette tapes, and videotapes. In addition, it is important to be involved in worthwhile activities with friends, work, sports, and personal projects when apart.

5. Avoid unsettling phone content. Talking on the phone should involve the typical sharing of events. When the need to discuss a difficult topic arises, the phone is not the best place for such a discussion. Rather, it may be wiser to wait and do this face to face. If you decide to settle a disagreement over the phone, stick at it until you have a solution acceptable to both of you.

Problems in Dating

The course of true love never did run smooth.

SHAKESPEARE

Men and women are often confronted with problems or concerns in dating. Table 5.2 describes dating problems reported by university women and men. Note the differences between women and men. For example, more women than men are concerned about what to wear and discouraging sexual intimacy. More men than women are concerned about having enough money to pay for dating activities and encouraging sexual intimacy.

T A B L E 5.2
Most Difficult Problems in Dating, by Gender

PROBLEM	FEMALES (N = 272)	MALES (N = 146)	AVERAGE PERCENT
Deciding where to go or what to do	32.7	33.1	32.90
Not having enough money	21.7	36.6	29.15
Knowing how to say what I want to say	31.3	24.8	28.05
Knowing what to talk about	19.1	16.6	17.85
No problems	12.5	14.5	13.25
Worry about what to wear	18.0	4.1	11.05
Worrying about sexually transmitted diseases	12.1	9.0	10.55
Discouraging sexual intimacy	18.4	2.1	10.25
Encouraging sexual intimacy	2.6	15.9	9.25
Other problems	8.5	9.7	9.15

Source: Adapted from "Gendered Expectations and Behaviors in Dating Relationships," by Linda Asmussen and Constance L. Shehan. Paper, 54th Annual Conference of the National Council on Family Relations, Orlando, Florida, 1992. Used by permission.

Sexual coercion, date rape, and violence and abuse constitute more serious problems faced by some dating partners. These concerns are discussed in detail in Chapter 12, Violence and Abuse in Relationships. Here, we want merely to emphasize that the greater the number of problems (e.g., jealousy, lack of time together, interference of friends) the greater the occurrence of physical aggression in the relationship (Riggs, 1993).

Terminating a Dating Relationship

Sometimes relationship problems become so frequent and intense that one or both partners feels the need to terminate the relationship. Of 101 couples who had been dating for an average of 18 months, almost half (44.6 percent) had broken up within two years (Sprecher & Felmlee, 1992).

A number of steps might be considered in terminating a dating relationship.

1. Decide that terminating the relationship is what you want to do. In some cases, people terminate relationships and later regret having done so. Setting unrealisticly high standards may eliminate an array of individuals who might be superb partners, companions, and mates. If the reason for ending a relationship is conflict over an issue or set of issues, an alternative to ending the relationship is to attempt to resolve the issues through negotiating differences, compromising, and giving the relationship more time. However, in some cases, it may be wiser to terminate a wounded relationship than to try to keep it alive. As Rhett Butler says to Scarlett O'Hara in *Gone with the Wind,*

   I was never one to patiently pick up broken fragments and glue them together and tell myself that the mended whole was as good as new. What's broken is broken—I'd rather remember it as it was at its best than mend it and see the broken pieces as long as I lived (Mitchell, 1977, 945).

2. Acknowledge and accept that terminating a relationship may be painful for both partners. There may be no way you can stop the hurt. One person said, "I can't live with him any more, but I don't want to hurt him either." The two feelings are incompatible. To end a relationship with someone who loves you is usually hurtful to both partners.

3. After deciding that termination is the goal and accepting the inevitable pain, tell the partner that you do not want to continue the relationship for a reason that is specific to you ("I need more freedom," "I want to go to graduate school in another state," "I'm not ready to settle down," and the like). Don't blame your partner or give your partner a way to make things better. If you do, the relationship may continue because you may feel obligated to give your partner a second chance.

   Although some people prefer to tell the partner in person, others feel that a letter is easier. "I know it's chicken," said one history major, "but I just can't tell her to her face. I've tried twice and she's talked me out of it both

Last night I wrote I loved you and your oatmeal cookies; tonight I write I hate you but I still love your oatmeal cookies.

HAL J. DANIEL III

times." Still others prefer the phone. One person used a cassette tape. "I didn't want the coldness of a letter or to get trapped in a phone conversation and hear him start crying, so I made him a cassette tape and mailed it to him."

4. Cut off the relationship completely. If you are the person ending the relationship, you will be less involved in the relationship than your partner. Your lower level of involvement may make it possible for you to continue to see the other person without feeling too hurt when the evening is over. But the other person will have a more difficult time and will heal faster if you stay away completely. Alternatively, some people are skilled at ending love relationships and turning them into friendships. While the path to friendship may be painful, it is often rewarding across time for the respective partners. Being the person who has not chosen to terminate the relationship may make relating to the beloved as a friend not as a lover more painful.

5. Allow yourself to grieve about the end of the relationship. Ending a love relationship is painful. It is okay to feel this pain, to hurt, to cry. Allowing yourself to experience such grief is often functional in getting over a relationship and enhancing yourself as a person for the next relationship.

6. Learn from the terminated relationship. Stets (1993) observed that when past issues involved in terminated relationships remain unresolved, they reappear in later relationships and lead to consecutive relationship break-ups. Issues that remain unresolved may include problems of independence and commitment.

CONSIDERATION

The termination of a relationship may be necessary because of a behavior that the other person is engaging in (drug abuse) or not engaging in (never has anything positive to say). However, it is possible that you may want to end a relationship for reasons that have little to do with the other person. Being unable to love another person, being unable to make a commitment to another person, and not being able to negotiate differences are possible reasons for wanting to end a relationship. These are also issues which may surface in subsequent relationships. Recognizing one's own contribution to the breakup and working on any characteristics which may be a source of future relationship problems may be one of the benefits of terminating a relationship. Otherwise, one may repeat the process.

---

7. Start new relationships. Even though it is important for the individual to take time to grieve over the relationship that has ended and to analyze it for any important lessons, it is emotionally healthy to move on. By going out with others you force your ex-partner to acknowledge that you are serious about ending the relationship. You should also encourage your ex-partner to see others.

There is no remedy for love but to love more.

HENRY DAVID THOREAU

CONSIDERATION

Although you may not feel like initiating contact with others, it will eventually heal the pain to get back into the stream of life by doing so. Don't wait until you feel like seeing others; do it immediately. But watch the level of involvement in a new relationship. Because you have just come from a terminated relationship, you may be particularly vulnerable or susceptible to a new love. For now, the goal should be to see others and have fun—not to fall in love or find a new partner.

Individuals who report the easiest adjustments to the termination of a relationship are those who ended a very stressful relationship and became involved in a new relationship within a short time (Weaton, 1990).

ॐ Dating the Second Time Around

Over two million Americans get divorced each year (National Center for Health Statistics, 1993). Most people who divorce wish to become involved in another relationship (as evidenced by the fact that over three-quarters of the divorced remarry). Jane Fonda and Ted Turner are examples of individuals who dated and married the second time around. Some differences between the "single again" population and those dating prior to first marriage include the following:

Nothing grows again more easily than love.

SENECA

1. Divorced individuals are, on the average, ten years older when they begin to date again. When divorced men remarry, they are about age 37; divorced women, 34. When widowed men remarry, they are about age 63; widowed women, 54. In contrast, men and women marrying for the first time are 26 and 24 respectively. Widows and widowers are usually 40 and 30 years older respectively when they begin to date "the second time around" (*Statistical Abstract of the United States: 1993,* Table 143).
2. Most men and women who are dating the second time around find fewer partners from which to choose than when they were dating prior to a first marriage, since over sixty percent of the U.S. adult population is married (*Statistical Abstract of the United States: 1993,* Table 59). Divorced and widowed women, particularly, may have difficulty in finding a partner the second time around. Not only are there more women than men in our society, but it is normative for older men to date younger women. All the younger women are available to the older men but all the younger men are not available to the older women. The result is fewer partner choices for women.
3. The older an unmarried person, the greater the likelihood of having had multiple sexual partners (Thornton, 1990; Knox & Schacht, 1992), which

has been associated with increased risk of contracting HIV and other STDs. Therefore, individuals entering the dating market for the second time are advised to be more selective in choosing their sexual partners because the likelihood of those partners having had a higher number of sexual partners is greater. In addition, the divorced are much less likely to be monogamous than married adults (Greeley, Michael, & Smith, 1990), so dating an older divorced person may involve even greater risk of contracting an STD. As we will note in the trends section at the end of the chapter, an increasing number of individuals are becoming concerned about HIV and other infections and discuss being HIV tested with new partners before having intercourse with them. Such a discussion may be particularly important for those reentering the dating market.

4. More than half of those dating again have children from a previous marriage. How these children feel about their parents dating, how the partners feel about each other's children, and how the partners' children feel about each other are complex issues. Deciding whether to have intercourse when one's children are in the house, what the children call the new partner, and how terminations of relationships are dealt with are other issues familiar to many people dating for the second time.

    A team of researchers (Darling et al., 1989) studied the effects of children on dating the second time around as experienced by 155 single parents. They concluded, "The presence of children appears to be a major obstacle in the development of new relationships by parents" (p. 241). Mothers reported more interference than fathers since the former are more often the custodial parent.

5. Previous ties to the ex-spouse in the form of child support or alimony, phone calls, and the psychological memory-experience of the partner's first marriage will have an influence on the new dating relationship. If the separation/divorce was bitter, the partner may be preoccupied and/or frustrated in his or her attempts to cope with the past.

6. Divorced people who are dating again tend to have a shorter courtship period than first marrieds. In a study of 248 individuals who remarried, the median length of courtship was 9 months as opposed to 17 months the first time around (O'Flaherty & Eells, 1988). A shorter courtship may mean that sexual decisions are confronted more quickly—timing of first intercourse, discussing the use of condoms/contraceptives, and discussing when/if the relationship is to be monogamous.

7. The divorced and widowed who reenter the dating market often comment that they feel awkward about dating again. One 45-year-old widow commented:

    > After my husband's death I didn't even think of getting back into the dating game. The dating scene today is completely different from what it was earlier. I'm from the old school—one woman, one man. With the advent of AIDS, one has to be extra careful. I enjoy male companionship for dinner and conversation and I don't have time for games or insecure men (Sparrow, 1991, 108).

CONSIDERATION

It may be helpful to keep in mind that the awkwardness of dating again is not uncommon and may be a topic to facilitate open communication with a new partner. "I'm not sure how to date anymore," when said to a new partner on a first date acknowledges the awkwardness of the situation, exposes one's vulnerability, and provides an opportunity for the partner to share similar feelings.

Dating in the Middle Years

Some of those dating the second time around are in their middle years (defined by the U.S. Bureau of the Census as age 45 to 65). In general, fewer norms guide the dating behaviors of middle-age partners. In their twenties, it was usually clear who would call whom, how soon or late sexual intimacy would occur, and when parents would be involved. But in middle age, the norms are in flux. While one of the partners may be operating on the "old" norms, the other partner may be behaving in reference to a new set of dating norms. The latter imply that either sex calls the other, sexual intimacy usually occurs sooner rather than later, and parents are not consulted about involvement with the new partner.

Children are often an important consideration and influence in the courtship progress of remarriages, either through direct involvement (taking the kids to the beach) or through their opinions ("I don't like her/him"). Financial obligations to previous spouses and children can also have an impact on the new couple.

Public disclosure in terms of announcements and a large wedding are more common in first than in second marriages. The partners in a second marriage more often have a small wedding ceremony with a few selected friends. Announcements are sent out less often, and the couple are more likely to live together before getting married.

Dating in the middle years is also different from dating in the earlier years because the life experience of the respective partners often includes previous marriages, children, careers, financial independence, and experience with the death of one's parents. Guttman (1991) noted that unresolved grief associated with the death of one's parent(s) may have profound effects on the way an individual interacts in relationships. For example, unresolved grief may create negativity or difficulty in forming intimate interpersonal bonds.

> Middle age is when you begin to think about how many years you have left rather than how many years you have lived.
>
> BERNICE NEUGARTEN

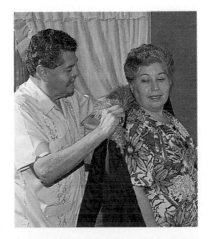

Dating in the middle years is both similar and different from the earlier years.

Dating in the Later Years

Due to divorce and late life widowhood, the number of elderly (over age 65) people without partners is one of the fastest growing segments of our population.

NATIONAL DATA &s In 1992, there were 1,730,000 unattached men (never married, widowed, divorced) and 4,780,000 unattached women (never married, widowed, divorced) between the ages of 65 and 74 in the United States (*Statistical Abstract of the United States: 1993*, Table 61).

Particularly vulnerable to being without a partner are the women over age 80 for whom there are only 53 men for every 100 women. Patterns that are developing to adjust to this lopsided man-woman ratio include women dating younger men, romance without marriage, and "share-a-man" relationships.

While Cher is a celebrity who is known for her dating younger men, over three million women are married to men who are at least ten years younger than they. Although traditional women were socialized to seek an older, financially "established" man, the sheer shortage of men has encouraged many women to seek younger partners.

Women in their later years have also moved away from the idea that they must remarry and have become more accepting of the idea that they can enjoy the romance of a relationship without the obligations of a marriage. Ken Dychtwald (1990) in his book *Age Wave* observed that many elderly women were interested in romance with a man but were not interested in giving up their independence. "Many say they do not have the same family-building reasons for marriage that young people do. For women especially, divorce or widowhood may have marked the first time in their lives that they have been on their own, and many now enjoy their independence" (p. 222). In addition, many elders are reluctant to marry because of a new mate's deteriorating health. "They would not want to become the caretaker of an ill spouse, especially if they had been through an emotionally draining ordeal before" (p. 222).

Faced with a shortage of men but reluctant to marry those who are available, some elderly women are willing to share a man. In elderly retirement communities such as Palm Beach, Florida, women count themselves lucky to have a man who will come for lunch, take them to a movie, or be an escort to a dance. They accept the fact that the man may have luncheon, movie, or dancing dates with other women. "The alternative may be no male companionship at all" (p. 226).

Men at this age are aware they are in demand. Cruise lines such as Royal Viking and the Royal Cruise Line provide older male "hosts" to compensate for the shortage of available male cruise passengers. In exchange for their services they are given free cruise passage, complimentary shore excursions, and $100 bar credit per trip (sexual activity with guests is strictly prohibited for hosts).

&s Mate Selection

The mutual selection of Whitney Houston and Bobby Brown, Paula Abdul and Emilio Estevez, Bruce Springsteen and Patti Scialfa, and Melanie Griffith and Don Johnson did not occur by chance. Various cultural, sociological, psychological, and—some sociobiologists say—biological factors combined to influence their meeting and marriage.

Cultural Aspects of Mate Selection

Cultural norms for mate selection vary. The degree of freedom individuals have in choosing a marriage partner depends on the culture of the society in which they live. In some cultures (parts of India, China, and Palestine) "marriages are arranged by parents, other relatives, or hired 'match makers' and often the young men and women have little say in the matter. The primary criteria considered in the matching process are often the families' religion, caste, and social class, and love is expected to develop after the marriage occurs" (Sprecher & Chandak, 1992, 59). A sample of Indians (from India) (71 percent of whom were between the ages of 17 and 21) identified the primary advantages of arranged marriages. These included experiencing support from the respective families, having a high quality and stable marriage, and having compatible or desirable backgrounds. The primary disadvantages were not knowing the partner well, greedy in-laws demanding a huge dowry from the woman's father, and incompatibility or unhappiness. The In Focus 5.2 insert reflects the experience of a Palestinian woman attending college in the United States. Her marriage was arranged by her father.

Aside from the legal restrictions, the United States theoretically has a mate selection system of free choice. However, some arranging by parents or others takes place in all cultures. A great many American marriages have been arranged up to modern times, both in poor rural areas and in high society (for example, the marriage of Consuelo Vanderbilt to the Duke of Marlborough in 1895). The Reverend Sun Myung Moon of the Unification Church personally matched and married 2,075 couples in a mass Madison Square Garden ceremony in New York in the early eighties.

Endogamous-Exogamous Pressures   Whereas some societies exert specific pressure on individuals to marry predetermined mates, other societies apply more subtle pressure. The United States has a system of free choice that is not exactly free. Social approval and disapproval restrict your choices so that you do not marry just *anybody*. *Endogamous pressures* encourage you to marry those within your own social group (racial, religious, ethnic, educational, economic); *exogamous pressures,* in the form of legal restrictions, encourage you to marry outside your family group (to avoid sex with and marriage to a sibling or other close relative).

The pressure toward an endogamous mate choice is especially strong when race is concerned. One white woman said, "Some of my closest friends are black. But my parents would disown me if I were to openly date a black guy." In contrast, a black man said, "I would really like to date a girl in my introductory psychology class who's white. But my black brothers wouldn't like

Endogamous pressures make it unlikely that this interracial couple will marry.

IN FOCUS

A Palestinian's Experience in Mate Selection

My name is Tahaia Brothers. I am a 19-year-old university student and moved to the United States when I was six. I was socialized as a Palestinian and never touched my husband until we were married.

In America, you date, have sex, and live together before you are married. Palestinian ways are very different—adolescents never date. We are never allowed to be alone with a member of the opposite sex unless we are in our parents' house (with our parents present).

Any physical contact before marriage is strictly prohibited. Sex before marriage is unheard of. If a girl has sex before she is married, her parents disown her. This means that she is thrown out of their house and not allowed to live with, see, or associate with them or other relatives again.

If a man knows that a woman has had sex before marriage, he will not want her. Men require that their brides be pure—this is the way I was until I met my husband. I have known only one man.

My father loves me very much but is very strict. He wants only what is best for me. He selected my husband-to-be and arranged a time I would meet with him in my house. This man (who was a stranger to me) and I talked and decided that we would tell our parents that we wanted to be engaged.

The engagement lasted five months during which time we only saw each other in the presence of my parents. After the wedding (the ceremony and celebration lasted seven hours) we took a short "honeymoon" before coming back to school.

People ask me about love. In my culture, love follows marriage, it does not precede it. I respected my husband before I married him—now I love him. People also ask me if I think about having sex with other men. Never. I am devoted to my husband, he is devoted to me, and that is the way it should be.

We have a "traditional marriage" as you would call it. I cook, clean, and serve my husband. My classmates sometimes laugh when I use the term *serve* but that is the way I was taught. My husband is good to me. He loves me and supports us financially. We are very happy.

SOURCE: Used by permission of Tahaia Brothers, Greenville, North Carolina. Developed exclusively for this text.

If you end up being my baby, it don't matter if you're black or white.

MICHAEL JACKSON

it, and while my parents wouldn't throw me out of the house, they would wonder why I wasn't dating a black girl."

These endogamous pressures are not operative on all people at the same level or may not work at all. Those who are older than 30, who have been married before, and/or who live in large urban centers are more likely to be color blind in their dating and marrying. In Hawaii, interracial dating and marriage are normative, and interracial marriage does occur throughout our society.

Endogamous dating and mating pressure is also evident among religious groups such as the Mormons. One researcher (Markstrom-Adams, 1991) compared 36 Mormon high school students with 47 non-Mormons and found only 22 percent of Mormons would "advise dating between Mormons and non-Mormons" in contrast to 45 percent of non-Mormons who would advise such dating.

In contrast to endogamous marriage pressures, exogamous pressures are mainly designed to ensure that individuals who are perceived to have a close biological relationship do not marry each other. Incest taboos are universal. In no society are children permitted to marry the parent of the opposite sex. In the United States, siblings and first cousins (in some states) are also prohibited from marrying each other.

Sociological Aspects of Mate Selection

Sociological aspects of mate selection include the concepts *homogamy* and *propinquity*.

Homogamy   The homogamy theory of mate selection states that we tend to be attracted to and become involved with those who are similar to ourselves in such characteristics as age, education, social class, race, and intelligence. Considerable research suggests that homogamy or "like marries like" in the selection of a marriage partner is associated with more satisfying relationships (Tzeng, 1992; Surra, 1991).

Marry yourself.

JACK WRIGHT

1. *Age.* When a friend gets you a date, you assume the person will be close to your age. Your peers are not likely to approve of your becoming involved with someone twice your age. A student who was dating one of her former teachers said, "He always comes over to my place, and I prepare dinner for us. I don't want to be seen in public with him. Although I love him, it doesn't feel right being with someone old enough to be my father." Such a concern for age homogamy is particularly characteristic of individuals who have never married. Those who have been married before are much more likely to become involved with someone who is less close to their age.

NATIONAL DATA ☙ The median age of first married females and males is 23.7 and 25.5 respectively. The median age at remarriage for divorced females and males is 33.6 and 37.0. The median age at remarriage for widowed females and males is 53.9 and 63.0 (*Statistical Abstract of the United States: 1993,* Table 143).

> **CONSIDERATION**
>
> One of the unique qualities of universities is that they provide an environment in which to meet hundreds or even thousands of possible partners of similar age, education, social class, and general goals. This opportunity will probably not be matched later in the work place or where one lives following graduation.

2. *Education.* The level of education you attain will also influence your selection of a mate. A sophomore who worked in a large urban department store during the Christmas holidays remarked, "The two weeks Todd and I spent selling record albums and tapes were great. But our relationship never gathered momentum. I was looking forward to my last two years of school, but Todd said college was a waste of time. I don't want to get tied to someone who thinks that way."

People are sometimes attracted to those who have the same interests.

If you would marry wisely, marry your equal.

OVID

This student's experience suggests that you are likely to marry someone who has also attended college. Not only does college provide an opportunity to meet, date, and marry another college student, but it also increases the chance that only a college-educated person will be acceptable. The very pursuit of education becomes a value to be shared and, when educational levels are similar, helps to insulate one's relationship against future divorce (Tzeng, 1992).

3. *Social Class.* You have been reared in a particular social class that reflects your parents' occupations, incomes, and educations as well as your residence, language, and values. If you were brought up in the home of a physician, you probably lived in a large house in a nice residential section of town. You were in a higher social class than you would have been if your parents were less educated and worked as grocery store check-out clerks.

The social class in which you were reared will influence how comfortable you feel with a partner. "I never knew what a finger bowl was," recalled one man, "until I ate dinner with my girlfriend in her parents' Manhattan apartment. I knew then that while her lifestyle was exciting, I was more comfortable with paper napkins and potato chips. We stopped dating." Indeed, women who have high incomes may either be less attractive as partners or have less need for a husband. Greenstein (1992) noted in a national sample of 2,375 never married women ages 14 to 22 that high-income women were less likely to marry.

CONSIDERATION

While it is difficult to know the reality of the relationship between the Diana and Charles, the Princess and Prince of Wales, the media suggested that social class background was one of the differences that led to their public separation in late 1992. The upper class socialization of Charles had led him to think in terms of duty, obligation, and propriety. Diana, who had not been socialized in this regard, tended to view such expectations as restricting her individual freedom.

The mating gradient refers to the tendency for husbands to be more advanced than their wives in regard to age, education, and occupational success. Two researchers assessed the expectations of 131 single female and 103 male college students and found that most women expected their husbands to be "superior in intelligence, ability, success, income, and education. Less than 10 percent of the women in this sample expected to exceed their marriage partner on any of the variables measured" (Ganong & Coleman, 1992, 61).

As a result of the mating gradient, some high-status women and low-status men remain single. Upper-class women typically receive approval from their parents and peers only if they marry someone of equal status. On the other hand, approval is less likely to be withheld from men who marry women who are younger and lower in social status. Educated, professional black females have a particularly difficult time finding black males of equal status.

> **CONSIDERATION**
>
> The mating gradient results in an oversupply of unmarried older, bright, educated, professional women. Men might consider the personal, social, and economic benefits of including such women in their pool of potential partners, and women might reconsider the idea that their mate must be older, educated, and professionally established. Solid happy relationships can result from a number of different pairings. The mating gradient may be an artificial restriction.

4. *Race.* Homogamy operates strongly in reference to race. In Chapter 8 we will discuss interracial marriages (black-white marriages specifically) in detail. Here, we merely point out that of the 53 million married couples in the United States less than one half of one percent consist of black-white couples (*Statistical Abstract of the United States: 1993,* Table 63).

5. *Intelligence.* Intelligence was the number one characteristic that 122 male and 210 female undergraduates said they looked for in the opposite sex (Daniel et al., 1985). "There are plenty of bimbos on campus," said one student. "I need someone whose cortical cells are active and who thinks about things other than drinking Bud Lite." Another said, "I think intelligent guys are just more fun. They are never boring and seem to know what is coming down."

6. *Physical Appearance.* In general, people tend to become involved with those who are similar in physical attractiveness. However, a partner's attractiveness may be more important for men than for women (Sprecher, 1989). In one study, at least 50 percent of women said that "attractiveness" was what men were interested in, but only 13 percent of the men felt that this was important for women (Woll & Young, 1989).

7. *Body Clock Compatibility.* Some of us are "morning people," some of us are "night people." Morning people arise early and feel most energetic in the morning. Night people sleep late and feel most energy late at night. Night people like to go to sleep at dawn—just the time when morning people are getting up.

   A team of researchers (Larsen et al., 1991) studied the marital relationships of 150 couples who were mismatched or matched in terms of body clocks. The mismatched couples reported significantly less marital adjustment, more marital conflict, less time spent in serious conversation, less time spent in shared activities, and less frequent sexual intercourse than matched couples. Loneliness was also a problem. For mismatched couples, both spouses commonly complained of feeling lonely. The morning person would wake up and have coffee alone since the partner was still asleep; similarly, the night person would watch late night TV alone since the partner was already asleep. Couples on different sleep patterns may work at

I see no marriages fail sooner than such as are concluded for beauty's sake.

MONTAIGNE

this aspect of their relationship through compromise or accommodation or develop new cognitions or patterns to reduce its negative influence.

8. *Other Factors.* Marital status and religion are other factors involved in homogamous mate selection. The never married tend to select the never married, the divorced tend to select the divorced, and the widowed tend to select the widowed as partners to marry. In addition, although religious homogamy is decreasing because we are becoming increasingly pluralistic and secularized as a society, this factor is still operative. Two researchers analyzed the couple formation of a sample of college students and observed that spirituality, Christianity, and a view that marriage is a lifetime commitment were important considerations in the selection of a partner. Some of the respondents also noted that God played a vital role in their formation as a couple (Young & Schvaneveldt, 1992).

Similarity of perceptions is another homogamous factor that researchers have found is related to marital happiness. Family therapists have found that spouses who have similar perceptions of themselves, each other, their relationship, their children, and family life in general, tend to report more marital satisfaction and more harmonious family functioning (Deal, Wampler, & Halverson, 1992).

> **The foundation of the marriage determines its duration.**
>
> JACK WRIGHT

CONSIDERATION

Even if all the homogamous factors discussed above were present in a couple's relationship, the couple would be unlikely to marry if they did not have love feelings. This is particularly true in the United States where couples are socialized to marry only those for whom they feel a deep emotional attachment. To marry without love, according to U.S. norms, is to begin a relationship with a missing psychological element.

This insistence on love before marriage is not true in all societies. In parts of rural China and India, marriages are still regarded as unions between families and are arranged by a matchmaker or go-between. Individuals are taught to expect love after, not before marriage (Lindsey, 1990).

Propinquity   Years ago, a sociologist found that one-sixth of 5,000 couples applying for marriage licenses in Philadelphia lived within one city block of each other. One-third of the couples lived within five blocks of each other and half lived within 20 blocks (Bossard, 1932). This study illustrates the principle of residential propinquity, or the tendency to select marriage partners from among those who live nearby.

Propinquity, which means nearness or proximity, may also refer to the workplace and school. Propinquity may be related to mate selection because living, working, or going to school near someone provides an opportunity to meet that person. In addition, being at the same school, working at the same job, or living close to one another may be related to sharing similar interests, values, life experiences,and characteristics.

Psychological Aspects of Mate Selection

Psychologists have focused on complementary needs, exchanges, parental images, and personalities in regard to mate selection.

Complementary Needs Theory   "In spite of the women's movement and a lot of assertive friends,I am a shy and dependent person," remarked a transfer student. "My need for dependency is met by Warren, who is the dominant, protective type." The tendency for a submissive person to become involved with a dominant person (one who likes to control the behavior of others) is an example of attraction based on *complementary needs*. Complementary needs theory states that we tend to select mates whose needs are opposite and complementary to our own needs. Partners can also be drawn to each other on the basis of nurturance versus receptivity. These complementary needs suggest that one person likes to give and take care of another, while the other likes to be the benefactor of such care. Other examples of complementary needs may involve responsibility versus irresponsibility and peacemaker versus trouble-maker. The idea that mate selection is based on complementary needs was suggested by Winch (1955), who noted that needs can be complementary if they are different (for example, dominant and submissive) or if the partners have the same need at different levels of intensity. As an example of the latter, two individuals may have a complementary relationship when they both want to do advanced graduate study, but both need not get Ph.D.s. The partners will complement each other if one is comfortable with his or her level of aspiration, represented by a master's degree, but still approves of the other's commitment to earn a Ph.D.

Winch's theory of complementary needs, commonly referred to as "opposites attract," is based on the observation of 25 undergraduate married couples at Northwestern University. The findings have been criticized by other researchers who have not been able to replicate Winch's study. Two researchers said, "It would now appear that Winch's findings may have been an artifact of either his methodology or his sample of married people" (Meyer & Pepper, 1977).

Three questions can be raised about the theory of complementary needs:

1. Couldn't personality needs be met just as easily outside the couple's relationship rather than through mate selection? For example, couldn't a person who has the need to be dominant find such fulfillment in a job that involved an authoritative role, such as head of a corporation or an academic department?
2. What is a complementary need as opposed to a similar value? For example, is desire to achieve at different levels a complementary need or a shared value?
3. Don't people change as they age? Could a dependent person grow and develop self-confidence so that they may no longer need to be involved

It ain't fiction;
It's a natural fact.
We come together
cuz opposites attract.

PAUL ABDUL

with a dominant person? Indeed, they may no longer enjoy interacting with a dominant person.

Exchange Theory *Exchange theory* suggests that mate selection is based on assessing who offers the greatest rewards at the lowest cost. Five concepts help to explain the exchange process in mate selection:

1. Rewards are the behaviors (your partner looking at you with the "eyes of love"), words (saying "I love you"), resources (being beautiful or handsome, having money), and services (driving you home, typing for you) your partner provides for you that you value and that influence you to continue the relationship.
2. Costs are the unpleasant aspects of a relationship. One man said, "I have to drive across town to pick her up, listen to her nagging mother before we can leave, and be back at her house by midnight."
3. Profit occurs when the rewards exceed the costs.
4. Loss occurs when the costs exceed the rewards.
5. No other person is currently available which offers a higher profit.

Most people have definite ideas about what they are looking for in a mate, about what categories of persons are "eligible" or "ineligible." Mate selection takes place in a marriage market. The merchandise consists of eligible males and females who can be "exchanged" for a given price. The currency used in the marriage market consists of the socially valued characteristics of the persons involved, such as age, physical characteristics, and economic status. In our free choice system of mate selection, we typically get as much in return for our social attributes as we can (Sparrow, 1991).

Exchange concepts operate at three levels of the dating relationship—who can date whom, the conditions of the dating relationship, and the decision to marry. As for whom you date, two researchers (Schoen & Woolredge, 1989) noted a pattern of exchange based on "a female emphasis on male economic characteristics and a male emphasis on female noneconomic characteristics" (p. 465). Hence, females tend to trade their youth and beauty for the male's economic resources. However, as women have become more economically independent, this pattern of exchange has lessened.

Once you identify a person who offers you a good exchange for what you have to offer, other bargains are made about the conditions of your continued relationship. Forty years ago, two researchers (Waller & Hill, 1951) observed that the person who has the least interest in continuing the relationship can control the relationship. This *principle of least interest* is illustrated by the woman who said, "He wants to date me more than I want to date him, so we end up going where I want to go and doing what I want to do." In this case, the woman trades her company for the man's acquiescence to her choices.

Additional exchanges take place as the partners move toward marriage. They make a marital commitment when they both feel they are getting the partner who offers the most rewards of all potential alternatives. A graduating senior and groom-to-be remarked, "It's easy. I've decided to marry Maria because sharing life with her is more fun than being with anyone else. And marriage is one way to help ensure that we will be together to share our lives across the years."

Another exchange occurring in relationships is that of information. As long as the information both partners learn about the other is consistent with their expectations of the other, the relationship will continue. One way to help become more secure in a relationship is to find out as much as possible about each other. If the relationship continues with full knowledge of each other's feelings on a variety of issues, it is more likely to be secure than if the partners stay together but know very little about each other. The Self-Assessment Relationship Inventory later in this chapter provides one way for partners considering marriage or living together to find out more about each other.

Parental Image Whereas the complementary and exchange theories of mate selection are relatively recent, Freud suggested earlier that the choice of a love object in adulthood represents a shift in libidinal energy from the first love objects—the parents. This means that a man looks for a wife like his mother and a woman looks for a husband like her father. In a study of almost 7,000 spouses, Jedlicka (1984) observed that selecting a partner similar to the opposite-sex parent occurs more often than can be expected by chance.

One of the reasons for selecting a person similar to the opposite-sex parent is the familiarity with the personality and values of the parent. Selecting someone who is similar to the parent provides a sense of comfort and predictability. Sharing similar values also helps to bond the partners to each other since most people like someone who agrees with them (Whyte, 1990).

Holt (1993) and Hendrix (1992) suggested that one's parents are involved in yet another way in regard to the selection of one's mate. They hypothesized that individuals who had unmet needs with a parent would select a partner with the same characteristics in an effort to correct the problems with the parent by correcting them with the mate. For example, a man with a cold and withdrawn mother would be attracted to a woman with similar characteristics for his wife. Subconsciously, he would feel that if he were able to develop a more nurturing and loving relationship with her, he would generalize these feelings to his mother and thereby resolve his feelings of being rejected and abandoned by her.

Desired Personality Characteristics for a Mate

In choosing a mate, we look for someone with particular personality characteristics that we find desirable. Eighty-five single professional women identified the top 19 characteristics they looked for in a mate. The most important was "honesty" followed by "intelligence" (Sparrow, 1991). Honesty was also identified by 443 university students as the most important quality they looked for in their "ideal partner" (Laner, 1989). Despite the fact that honesty is the

*I wanna girl
Just like the girl
that married dear ole Dad.*
SONG LYRICS

TABLE 5.3

Cultural, Sociological, and Psychological Filters of Mate Selection

CULTURAL FILTERS

For two people to consider marriage to each other,

Endogamous factors (same race, caste)	and ↓	Exogamous factors (not blood related)

must be met.
↓

After the cultural prerequisites have been satisfied, sociological and psychological filters become operative.

SOCIOLOGICAL FILTERS

Propinquity = the tendency to select a mate from among those who live, work, or go to school nearby.

Homogamy = the tendency to select a mate similar to oneself in regard to the following:

Age	Physical Appearance
Race	Body Clock Compatibility
Education	Religion
Social Class	Marital Status
Intelligence	

PSYCHOLOGICAL FILTERS

Desired Personality Characteristics
Complementary Needs
Cost-Benefit Ratio in Exchanges
Similarity to Opposite-Sex Parent

primary value sought in a potential partner, recent data suggests that interpersonal lies are not uncommon among university students (Knox, Schacht, Holt, & Turner, 1993). We will discuss this issue in detail in Chapter 9 on Communication and Conflict.

Sociobiological Aspects of Mate Selection

Sociobiology suggests a biological basis for all social behavior—including mate selection. Based on Charles Darwin's theory of natural selection, which states that the strongest of the species survive, sociobiologists contend that men and women select each other as mates on the basis of their concern for producing offspring who are most capable of surviving.

According to sociobiologists, men look for an attractive, bright, sexually conservative woman who will care for their offspring. Men also look for young women. Women, in contrast, look for an industrious man who has a good earning capacity to provide for her children. This pattern of men seeking physically attractive young women and women seeking economically ambitious men was also observed in 37 groups of men and women in 33 different societies (Buss et al., 1990).

CONSIDERATION

Sociobiologists also contend that voice quality is involved in mate selection. Daniel and McCabe (1992) studied the voice preferences of 244 undergraduates and observed that men rate women with low pitch voices as "least sexy" while women rate men with high pitch voices as "least sexy." The researchers suggested that "these ratings possibly reflect the respondents' perceptions of "hormonal imbalance" within the speakers" (p. 61).

The sociobiological explanation for mate selection is extremely controversial. Critics argue that women may show concern for the earning capacity of men because the women have been systematically denied access to similar economic resources, and selecting a mate with these resources is one of their remaining options. In addition, it is argued that both women and men, when selecting a mate, think more about their partners as companions than as future parents of their offspring.

✥ Becoming Engaged

An engagement to be married represents an intermediate stage between courtship and marriage. What are the implications of this stage, and how can you use it to increase future happiness?

Implications of an Engagement

The engagement period is usually regarded as a serious, monogamous, public, and preparatory time for the wedding.

Serious An engagement is a specific commitment to marry. Once the words "let's get married" are spoken and agreed to, the relationship assumes a different status.

The other person is no longer viewed as a casual partner but as a future spouse. Although a few regard engagement lightly, most take it seriously.

Monogamous Engagements tend to carry the expectation that both partners refrain from engaging in romantic or sexual activity with other individuals. This informal expectation for engaged couples to be monogamous becomes a

At last, my love has come along. My lonely days are over and life is like a song.

GENE WATSON

formal expectation once the couple is married, in that sex outside of marriage is a violation of the law.

Public   Some couples have the understanding that they are engaged, but choose to keep their engagement private and informal. For many couples, however, engagement involves a public, formal announcement of their intent to marry. Parents and peers become involved in the event and may communicate their evaluations of each partner's marital choice.

Preparations   Of first weddings, 80 percent take place in a traditional setting (a church or a synagogue) with bridesmaids and ushers. Such an event requires tremendous preparation and, for many couples, is a time of intense stress. "We were both under so much pressure preparing for the wedding," recalled one bride, "at one time we considered calling it off. My father told us if it was going to be that big of a hassle, to elope and he would give us the $5,000."

Using Your Engagement Period Productively

The engagement period is often regarded as a time to plan the wedding. But too often couples focus more on the wedding plans than on cementing their relationships. We suggest that the engagement period be used to systematically examine your relationship by asking each other specific questions, recognize dating danger signals, visit your future in-laws, and participate in premarital counseling.

Marry for money and starve for love.
UNKNOWN

Examine Your Relationship   In a commercial for an oil filter, a mechanic says he has just completed a "ring job" on a car engine that will cost the owner over $400. He goes on to say that a $5.98 oil filter would have made the job unnecessary, and ends his soliloquy with, "Pay me now, or pay me later." The same idea applies to the consequences of using or not using your engagement period to examine your relationship. At some point, you will take a very close look at your partner and your relationship; but will you do it now—or later? Doing so now may be less costly than doing so after the wedding.

Consider completing the Relationship Inventory (see Self-Assessment) to assess the degree to which you and your partner are compatible, similar, or dissimilar in terms of the issues and values that matter to each of you.

Recognize Dangerous Patterns   As you examine your relationship, you should be sensitive to patterns that suggest you may be on a collision course. Three such patterns include breaking the relationship frequently, constant arguing, and inequality resulting from differences in education, social class, and the like. A roller-coaster engagement is predictive of a marital relationship that will follow the same pattern.

SELF-ASSESSMENT
The Relationship Inventory

The following questions are designed to increase your knowledge of how you and your partner think and feel about a variety of issues. Each partner should ask the other the following questions:

CAREERS AND MONEY

1. What kind of job or career will you have? What are your feelings about working in the evening versus being home with the family? Where will your work require that we live? How often do you feel we will be moving? Where are the places you would refuse to move to? How much will your job require that you travel?

2. What are your feelings about joint versus separate checking accounts? Which of us do you want to pay the bills? How much money do you think we will have left over each month? How much of this do you think we should save?

3. When we disagree over whether to buy something, how do you suggest we resolve our conflict?

4. What jobs or work experience have you had in the past?

5. What is your preference for where we live? Do you want to live in an apartment or house? What are your needs for a car, compact disk player, video recorder, television, cable TV?

6. How do you feel about my having a career? Do you expect me to earn an income? If so, how much annually? To what degree do you feel it is your responsibility to cook, clean, and take care of the children? How do you feel about putting young children or infants in daycare centers? When they are sick and one of us has to stay home, who will that be?

7. Do you want me to account to you for the money I spend?

8. How much money do you think we should give to charity each year?

RELIGION AND CHILDREN

1. To what degree do you regard yourself as a religious person? What do you think about religion, a supreme being, prayer, and life after death?

2. Do you go to religious services? Where? How often? Do you pray? How often? What do you pray about? When we are married, how often would you want to go to religious services? In what religion would you want our children to be reared? What responsibility would you take to ensure that our children had the religious training you wanted them to have?

3. How do you feel about abortion? Under what conditions, if any, do you feel abortion is justified?

4. How do you feel about children? How many do you want? Why? When do you want the first child? At what intervals would you want to have additional children? What do you see as your responsibility for childcare—changing diapers, feeding, bathing, playing with children, and taking them to piano lessons? To what degree do you regard these responsibilities as mine?

5. Suppose I did not want to have children or couldn't have them, how would you feel? How do you feel about artificial insemination, surrogate motherhood, in-vitro fertilization (see Chapter 14), and adoption?

6. To your knowledge, can you have children? Are there any genetic problems in your family history that would prevent us from having normal children?

7. Do you want our children to go to public or private schools?

8. How should children be disciplined? How were you disciplined as a child?

9. To what degree should marriage be adult or child oriented?

(continued on next page)

SEX

1. How much sexual intimacy do you feel is appropriate in casual dating, involved dating, and engagement?
2. What do you think about masturbation, oral sex, homosexuality, S & M, and anal sex?
3. What type of contraception do you suggest? Why? If that method does not prove satisfactory, what method would you suggest next?
4. What are your values regarding sex outside of marriage? If I were to have an affair and later tell you, what would you do? Why? If I had an affair, would you want me to tell you? Why?
5. What sexual behaviors do you most and least enjoy? How often do you want to have intercourse? How do you want me to turn you down when I don't want to have sex? How do you want me to approach you for sex? How do you feel about just being physical together—hugging, rubbing, holding, but not having intercourse?
6. What does an orgasm feel like to you? By what method of stimulation do you experience an orgasm most easily?
7. What is pornography and/or erotica to you? How do you feel about it?

RELATIONSHIPS WITH FRIENDS/COWORKERS

1. How do you feel about my spending one evening a week from 6:00 to 11:00 with my friends or coworkers?
2. How do you feel about my spending time with friends of the opposite sex during this time?
3. What do you regard as appropriate and inappropriate affectional behaviors with friends?

RECREATION AND LEISURE

1. How do you feel about golf, surfing, swimming, boating, horseback riding, jogging, lifting weights, racquetball, basketball, football, baseball, tennis, soccer, wrestling, fishing, hunting? How often do you engage in each of these activities? What recreational activities would you like me to become interested in?
2. What hobbies do you have?
3. What do you like to watch on TV? How often do you watch TV and for what periods of time?
4. What is the amount and frequency of your current alcohol and drug (i.e., marijuana, cocaine, crack, speed) consumption? What, if any, have been your previous alcohol and drug behaviors and frequencies? What are your expectations of me regarding the use of alcohol and drugs?
5. How often will you want to go on vacation? Where will you want to go? How will we travel? How much money do you feel we should spend on vacations each year?

PARTNER FEELINGS

1. If you could change one thing about me, what would it be?
2. What would you like me to do to make you happier?
3. What would you like me to say or not say to make you happier?
4. What do you think of yourself? Describe yourself with three adjectives.
5. What do you think of me? Describe me with three adjectives.
6. What do you like best about me?
7. Do you think I get jealous easily? How will you cope with my jealousy?
8. How do you feel about me emotionally?
9. To what degree do you feel we each need to develop and maintain outside relationships so as not to focus all of our interpersonal expectations on each other?

FEELINGS ABOUT PARENTS/FAMILY

1. How often do you have contact with your father/mother? How do you feel about your parents?
2. What do you like and dislike about my parents?

3. What is your feeling about living near our parents? How would you feel about my parents living with us? What will we do with our parents if they can't take care of themselves?
4. How do your parents get along? Rate their marriage on a 0–10 scale (0-unhappy; 10-happy). What are your parents' role responsibilities in their marriage?
5. To what degree did members of your family enjoy spending their free time together? What are your expectations of our spending free time together?
6. To what degree did members of your family consult each other on their decisions? To what degree do you expect me to consult you on the decisions that I make?
7. How close were your family members to each other? To what degree do you value closeness versus separateness in our relationship?
8. Who was the dominant person in your family? Who had more power? Who do you regard as the dominant partner in our relationship? How do you feel about this power distribution?

OTHER QUESTIONS

1. Do you have any history of abuse or violence, either with your being abused as a child or your being abused or being the abuser in an adult relationship?

2. If we could not get along, would you be willing to see a marriage counselor? Would you see a sex therapist if we were having sexual problems?
3. What is your feeling about prenuptial agreements?
4. What value do you place on the opinions or values of your parents and friends?
5. What are your feelings about our living together?
6. To what degree do you enjoy getting and giving a massage? How important is it to you that we massage each other regularly?

It would be unusual if you agreed with each other on all of your answers to the previous questions. You might view the differences as challenges and then find out the degree to which the differences are important for your relationship. You might need to explore ways of minimizing the negative impact of those differences on your relationship. It is not possible to have a relationship with someone where there is total agreement. Disagreement is inevitable; the issue becomes how you and your partner manage the disagreements.

NOTE: This Self-Assessment is intended to be thought-provoking and fun. It is not intended to be used as a clinical or diagnostic instrument.

The same is true of frequent arguments in a relationship. If arguing is a pattern, the engaged couple may want to consider learning more productive communication techniques (see Chapter 9 on Communication and Conflict).

Lovers' quarrels become marital quarrels.

EDGAR M. ARENDELL

CONSIDERATION

A relationship pattern characterized by lack of communication may be just as unhealthy as a relationship pattern characterized by arguments. One divorced man said, "My wife and I never fought and never argued. We communicated very little of our real feelings to each other and over the years we drifted into separate lives."

Relationships in which the partners are regarded as being unequal to each other are precarious. Consider the case of Bill and Susan. He was a divorced physician with two children. She was a nurses' aide, and although she held him in awe, they had little in common. Although lovers may view each other with awe, spouses rarely do. Eventually, Bill may feel cheated because he does not have a companion equal to his life and educational experience. Susan may feel stress at continually trying to be what she is not to appease Bill. So persons who are radically different in age, education, social class, and values should be cautious about marrying. Friends select each other because they have something in common and will maintain their relationship for the same reason. Lovers may select each other on the basis of love feelings, but when these feelings dissipate, what they have in common is crucial in determining whether they maintain their interest in each other.

Recognize Potentially Problematic Personality Characteristics   Just as relationships may have qualities that predict future difficulty, individuals may have characteristics that should be viewed with concern. Snyder and Regts (1990) identified three such personality characteristics, which predispose individuals toward impaired functioning in marriage: poor impulse control, hypersensitivity to perceived criticism, and exaggerated self-appraisal.

Persons who have poor impulse control have little self restraint and may be prone to aggression and violence. Lack of impulse control is also problematic in marriage because the person is less likely to consider the consequences of their actions. For example, having an affair might sound like a good idea at the time but have devastating consequences for the marriage.

Hypersensitivity to perceived criticism involves getting hurt easily. Any negative statement or criticism is received with a greater impact than intended by the partner. The disadvantage of such hypersensitivity is that the partner may learn not to give feedback for fear of hurting the hypersensitive partner. Such lack of feedback to the hypersensitive partner blocks information about what the person does that upsets the other and might do to make things better. Hence, the hypersensitive one has no way of learning that something is wrong and the partner has no way of alerting the hypersensitive partner. The result is a relationship in which the partners can't talk about what is wrong.

An exaggerated sense of one's self is another way of saying the person has a big ego and always wants things to be his or her way. A person with an inflated sense of self may be less likely to consider the other person's opinion in negotiating a conflict and prefer to dictate an outcome. Such disrespect for the partner can be damaging to the relationship.

Observe Your Future In-Laws   Engagements often mean more frequent interaction with each partner's parents, so you might seize the opportunity to assess the type of family your partner was reared in and the implications for your marriage. When visiting your in-laws-to-be, observe their standard of living, the way they relate to each other, and the degree to which your partner is

Don't let your in-laws become out-laws.

ED HARTZ

similar to your future in-laws. How does their standard of living compare with that of your own family? How does the emotional closeness (or distance) of your partner's family compare with that of your family? Such comparisons are significant because both you and your partner will reflect your respective home environments to some degree. If you want to know what your partner may be like in 20 years, look at his or her parent of the same sex. There is a tendency for a man to become like his father and a woman to become like her mother.

Consider Premarital Counseling or Marriage Preparation Course

Most clergy offer three premarital sessions before marrying a couple. These sessions may consist of information about marriage, an assessment of the couple's relationship, or resolving conflicts that have surfaced in the relationship. Those who do not plan to be married in a church or a synagogue or who do not choose to see a clergyman for premarital counseling sometimes see a marriage counselor. A professional can be helpful in assisting a couple to assess their relationship. Although the couple might deny the existence of a problem for fear that looking at it will break up the relationship, the counselor can help them examine the problem and work toward the goal of solving it.

Some premarital counselors use inventories to help identify couples who are likely to get divorced. Larsen and Olson (1989) developed an inventory, Premarital Personal and Relationship Evaluation (PREPARE) which assesses expectations, communication, conflict resolution skills, and background origins. They gave the inventory to 164 premarital couples and conducted a follow-up three years later. They found that couples who had unrealistic expectations, poor communication patterns, absence of conflict resolution skills, etc., were more likely to have separated than those scoring high in these areas. Couples who take the PREPARE are able to predict their probability of divorce with an 80 to 85 percent accuracy (Davis, 1992).

Some premarital couples attend the Prevention and Relationship Enhancement Program (PREP) offered in selected sites in the United States, Canada, and Europe. PREP is designed to "teach premarital couples the skills associated with marital success" (Renick et. al., 1992, 142). It is offered in two formats. In the extended version, couples attend a weekly 2 to 2-½ hour in groups of four to eight couples who hear brief lectures on communication or relationship issues. "Each couple is assigned a communication consultant who works with the individual couple as they privately practice the skills" (p. 142). In the alternative weekend format, 20 to 40 couples hear the communication lectures in a group setting and practice the skills on their own.

Outcome research over ten years on the effectiveness of PREP is impressive. Not only have couples who learned how to communicate and negotiate conflict been less likely to divorce or separate than a control group (8 percent versus 16 percent), they reported greater marital satisfaction, fewer conflicts, and less physical violence (Renick et al., 1992). Couples who want to help insulate themselves against divorce might well consider such preventive

Keep your eyes wide open before marriage, half shut afterwards.

BEN FRANKLIN

Examining one's relationship with a counselor before marriage is one way to increase the chance of a durable happy marriage.

programs, which focus on communication and negotiation skills. (The names of the programs may vary, for example, Premarital Relationship Enhancement also focuses on learning specific relationship skills: Ridley and Sladeczek, 1992.)

Another marriage preparation program is The Marriage Project, located in the Vancouver, B.C., area. Although church affiliated, its focus is on relationship issues and skill development. Based on questionnaires from 193 couples who completed the course (average age of the men, 30; women, 28), Russell and Lyster (1992) noted that most reported satisfaction with the course and would recommend it to others. Older couples benefited from communications training while younger couples benefited more from concrete information about finances and parenting (Russell & Lyster, 1992B).

Prolong Your Engagement If . . .

Even though you and your partner may have examined your relationship, seen a counselor, and feel confident about your impending marriage, there are five conditions under which you might consider prolonging your engagement. In combination, these conditions argue against getting married at this time.

> It is good to marry late or never.
>
> JOHN CLARK

Age 18 or Younger The strongest predictor of getting divorced is getting married as an adolescent. Individuals who marry in their teens may disrupt their ability "to resolve crises of intimacy and identity formation, and may thus lead to problems in the formation and maintenance of intimate relationships" (Teti & Lamb, 1989, 209). The effect is true for both whites and blacks.

> Marry in haste and repent at leisure.
>
> JOHN RAY

Short Courtship Although Julia Roberts and Lyle Lovett knew each other seriously for less that a month before their wedding in June 1993, a short courtship is associated with divorce. Partners who date each other for at least two years before making a marital commitment report the highest level of marital satisfaction (Grover, 1985). A short courtship does not allow the partners to observe and scrutinize the behavior of the other in a variety of settings.

CONSIDERATION

Suggestions to maximize learning about each other include taking a three-day "primitive" camping trip, taking a 15-mile hike together, wallpapering a small room together, and/or spending 24 hours together when one partner has the flu. Time should also be spent with each other's friends and family. If the couple plans to have children at some future point, they may want to observe how each other relates to infants and children.

Financial Stress Two researchers (Johnson & Booth, 1990) observed that spouses who were economically stressed reported that it had a negative effect on their marital happiness and that they thought about divorce more often. Being economically stressed does not necessarily mean having a low income. Many couples with high incomes are under financial stress. Two researchers suggested that marital satisfaction depends not on the income itself, but rather on the couple's feelings that their income is adequate (Berry & Williams, 1987). Some research suggests that black women are more likely than white women to insist on economic resources being in place before the marriage and resist a marital commitment to someone who has limited resources (Bulcroft & Bulcroft, 1993).

Parental Disapproval   A parent recalled, "I knew when I met the guy it wouldn't work out. I told my daughter and pleaded that she not marry him. She did, and they are divorced." Such parental predictions (whether positive or negative) often come true. If the predictions are negative, they may contribute to stress and conflict once the couple marries.

Even though parents who reject the commitment choice of their offspring are often regarded as unfair, their opinions should not be taken lightly. The parents' own experience in marriage and their intimate knowledge of their offspring combine to help them assess how their child might get along with a particular mate. If the parents of either partner disapprove of the marital choice, the partners should try to evaluate these concerns objectively. The insights may prove valuable.

Premarital Pregnancy   Premarital pregnancies and births are not unusual.

NATIONAL DATA ❧ Twenty-seven percent of all births to U.S. women are to unmarried mothers (*Statistical Abstract of the United States: 1993*, Table 98).

Marriages that begin when the woman is pregnant are associated with higher marital unhappiness and divorce than those who do not conceive children before marriage. Combined with adolescence, a short premarital period, lack of money, and parental or in-law hostility, premarital pregnancy may be an ominous beginning for newlyweds.

CONSIDERATION

Should you call off the wedding? If you are having second thoughts about getting married to the person to whom you have made a commitment, you are not alone. It is not uncommon for engagements to be broken. Although some anxiety about getting married is normal (you are entering a new role), constant questions to yourself, such as "Am I doing the right thing?," or thoughts, such as "This doesn't feel right," are definite caution signals that suggest it might be best to call off the wedding. Before marriage, you will be breaking an engagement; after marriage, you will be getting a divorce. Although calling off the wedding will create anxiety, calling off the marriage (divorce) will create even more. "When in doubt, don't go through with the wedding," says one marriage counselor.

℘ Developing a Prenuptial Agreement

The primary purpose of a prenuptial agreement (also referred to as a premarital agreement, marriage contract, or antenuptial contract) is to specify ahead of time how property will be divided and who will be responsible for paying what to whom if the marriage ends in divorce. Persons who have been married before are often concerned that money and property be kept separate in a second marriage. An example of a premarital agreement is provided in Appendix B at the end of the text.

Individuals in first marriages are less likely to draw up a prenuptial agreement. They view it as unromantic and want to avoid tying the relationship to money. "When marriage succeeds, it's by muting the relationship between money and power. Indeed, if marriage is to work, it must operate more like a mutual fund" (Goodman, 1992, A-6).

Some individuals who do sign an agreement later regret it. Sherry, a never married 22-year-old, signed such an agreement:

> Paul was adamant about my signing the contract. He said he loved me but would never consider marrying anyone unless we signed a prenuptial agreement stating that he would never be responsible for alimony in case of a divorce. I was so much in love, it didn't seem to matter. I didn't realize that basically he was and is a selfish person. Now, five years later, after a divorce, I go to the court begging for alimony while he lives in a big house overlooking the lake with his new wife.

The husband viewed it differently. He was glad that she had signed the agreement and that his economic liability to her was limited. He could afford the new house by the lake with his new wife because he was not sending money to Sherry.

Pepper Schwartz, a sociologist at the University of Washington, noted that the economic worth of a spouse

> . . . is a very hypocritical, unexamined and always dangerous topic in a marriage. If you want to know what people really want to give each other, look at the terms in prenuptial agreements—there's a notable lack of generosity. The message of these contracts is, "I will keep you in the style in which I want to live but only while I feel good about you" (quoted in Goodman, 1992, A-6).

CONSIDERATION

Couples who do decide, for whatever reason to develop a prenuptial agreement, need an attorney to draw up the agreement. The laws regulating marriage and divorce vary by state and only an attorney can help ensure that the document drawn up will be honored.

Prenuptial contracts do have a value beyond the legal implications. Their greatest value may be that they facilitate the partners discussing together their expectations of the relationship. In the absence of such an agreement, many couples may never discuss the issues they may later face.

❦ Predicting Your Marital Happiness

It is not possible to predict with 100 percent accuracy what your level of marital satisfaction will be even days after your wedding. There are several reasons why.

Illusion of the Perfect Mate

The illusion that you have found the perfect partner—one who will be all things to you, and vice versa—will carry you through courtship and the early part of your marriage (Marano, 1992). However, reality can be very different. You have not found the perfect mate—there isn't one. Anyone you marry will not have a quality you value, and the one quality that your partner lacks may become the only one you come to regard as important (Sammons, 1993). When some people discover their partner lacks something they think is essential (empathy, dependability, being faithful,) they may consider a divorce. Although it is important to find a partner with whom you are compatible, the expectation that your partner and/or your relationship be perfect will set you up for disappointment and relationship instability.

> Just because you don't see shooting stars
> Doesn't mean it isn't perfect.
> Can't you see
> It's the stuff that dreams are made of.
>
> CARLY SIMON

Deception During the Premarital Period

Your illusion of the perfect mate is helped along by some deception on the part of your partner. At the same time, you are presenting only favorable aspects of yourself to the other person. These deceptions are often not deliberate but are merely attempts to withhold the undesirable aspects of yourself for fear that your partner may not like them. One male student said he knew he drank too much and if his date found out, she would be disappointed and might drop him. He kept his drinking hidden throughout their courtship. They married and are now divorced. She said of him, "I never knew he drank whiskey until our honeymoon. He never drank like this before we were married."

Courtship elicits the most positive aspects of an individual. Marriage elicits more (and sometimes less positive) aspects of the individual.

> It does not much signify whom one marries, as one is sure to find next morning that it is someone else.
>
> SAMUEL ROGERS

> There are more lies told in courtship than at any other time in life.
>
> JACK TURNER

Confinement of Marriage

Another factor that makes it impossible to predict marital happiness is the different circumstances of the premarital period and marriage. Although premarital norms permit relative freedom to move in and out of relationships, marriage involves a legal contract. One recently married person described marriage as an iron gate that clangs shut behind you, and "getting it open is almost impossible." One's freedom to leave a relationship is transformed by the wedding ceremony. Thereafter, there is tremendous social pressure to work things out and a feeling of obligation to do so that was not previously present. The new sense of confinement to one person and a routine set of activities may bring out the worst in partners who seemed very cooperative before marriage.

> When you marry, you go into captivity.
>
> SADIE WRIGHT

If you don't have time for your relationship, do you have time for a divorce?

LOUISE SAMMONS

Do not think that years leave us and find us the same!

OWEN MEREDITH

We marry someone who is ideally suited to us NOW, in our present "headspace," present "need," and present environment. All are likely to change and it is expected that we accommodate to the changes and remain devoted to our partners.

TIM BRITTON

Balancing Work and Relationship Demands

Predicting marital happiness is also difficult because the partners must necessarily shift their focus from each other to the business of life. Careers and children emerge as concerns that often take precedence over spending time with each other, going to parties, and seeing movies. Time and energy spent on jobs and childrearing often leave marriage partners too tired to interact with each other. "I never see my partner" is a statement often heard by marriage counselors. Also, the more abrasive communication encouraged by conditions of stress has negative consequences for the way partners feel about each other. "Whenever we do get together, we fight," said one partner. (We will discuss work and leisure in greater detail in Chapter 11 on Work and Leisure in Relationships.)

Inevitability of Change

One of the major themes of this text is that you are continually changing. Just as you are not the same person you were 10 years ago, you will be different 10 years from now. The direction and intensity of these changes are not predictable for you or for your partner. You, your partner, and your relationship will not be the same two years (or two days) in a row. Reflecting on change in her marriage, one woman recalled:

> When we were married we were very active in politics. Now I have my law degree and am enjoying my practice. But Jerry is totally immersed in meditating and taking health food nutrients. He also spends four nights a week playing racketball. I never imagined that we'd have nothing to say to each other after only three years of marriage.

Other spouses may maintain similar interests across years of marriage, but either or both may undergo a dramatic change in mental functioning. In recent years, Alzheimer's disease and its attendant problems for interpersonal relationships have been featured in the media (Wasow, 1986). One spouse said:

> We've lived together for 36 years, and now she has Alzheimer's disease. It means that the last of life we were looking forward to sharing has become a nightmare. She sometimes forgets my name and resents it when I try to help dress her. But if I don't she'll put her bra on backwards and she literally forgets where the bathroom is. I know that her brain has deteriorated and that the person I once knew is no longer inside, but it hurts me so much.

Spouses who are subjected to combat stress are also changed, and the effect on their marriages is evident. A team of researchers interviewed wives of combat veterans who were experiencing CSR (combat stress reaction) from the 1982 Lebanon War. They found that these couples were "found to be characterized at all points in time by more conflict, less intimacy, less consensus, less cohesion, and less expressiveness than non-CSR couples" (Solomon et al., 1992, 316).

> **CONSIDERATION**
>
> Whether or not you will be happily married after your wedding cannot be predicted. Although selecting a compatible partner is basic, other factors that are crucial to a successful marriage include giving up any illusions of finding a perfect mate, minimizing premarital deception, accepting (and enjoying) the confinement of marriage, balancing work and relationship demands, and adapting to whatever changes occur.

ஜ Trends

Modern dating relationships are characterized by "hanging out" in groups as well as paired-off couples, a gradual shift away from traditional dating practices, increased interracial, interreligious, and interethnic dating, and increased confusion about roles in dating relationships. As we will note in the next chapter, both women and men are marrying later than in previous years. The result of such delay is that individuals today have more time to become involved with a variety of people before marriage. More time spent dating also has implications for how dating is perceived—initially, more for fun and recreation than for commitment and mate selection.

Other trends in dating include greater use of mate-selection technology. As our society becomes more populated, urban, and industrial, there will be fewer personal networks within which to meet eligible mates. Increasingly, individuals who might not otherwise meet through traditional dating patterns will be linked through advertisements in newspapers or magazines and videotape dating clubs. The $40 billion dating service industry will also become more specialized. Individuals seeking a Jewish person, vegetarian, or music lover may use a specialized dating service to target these individuals (Kaplan, 1990).

With more than 50 percent of all marriages ending in divorce, some couples are becoming more cautious about entering into marriage. The growing possibility that "divorce may happen to me, too" may reduce the number of hasty, ill-conceived marriages. The fact that age at marriage is inching upward may reflect a greater determination to marry when the conditions are right, not when the emotions are ready. Also, the use of marriage agreements reflects a concern that each partner be aware of the other's expectations to prevent misunderstandings.

In addition to exercising greater caution in entering into marriage, alternatives to the traditional formal engagement are becoming more acceptable. Although the engagement ring and wedding announcement will continue to be the script for most people, a growing number, particularly those who live together, are bypassing the formality of an engagement period.

☙ CHOICES ☙

---

*T*he three major decisions in deciding on a mate are who, when, and why?

Who Is the Best Person to Marry?

While there is no perfect mate, some individuals are more suited to you as a marriage partner than others. As we have seen in this chapter, persons with a big ego, poor impulse control, and an over-sensitivity to criticism should be considered with great caution. Equally important as avoiding someone with undesirable personality characteristics is selecting someone with whom you share a great deal in common. "Marry yourself" may be a worthy guideline in selecting a marriage partner. Homogamous matings in regard to race, education, age, intelligence, religion, social class, body clock, and marital status (e.g., never marrieds marry never marrieds; divorced with children marry those with similar experience) tend to result in more durable satisfying relationships.

Finally, marrying someone with whom you have a relationship of equality and respect is associated with marital happiness. Relationships in which one partner is exploited or always made to feel intimidated engender negative feelings of resentment and distance. One man said, "I want a co-chair not a committee member for a mate." He was saying that he wanted a partner with whom he related as an equal.

When Is the Best Time to Marry?

There are three factors to consider in selecting the "best" time to get married—age, education, and career plans.

Age   Your age and that of your partner at the time of marriage are predictive of your future happiness. Individuals who wait until they are into their twenties are much more likely to stay married than those who marry in their teens (Tzeng, 1992). Teen marriages are particularly vulnerable to divorce because of premarital pregnancies, insufficient income, and lack of parental support. Indeed, the teen divorce rate is two to three times greater than the divorce rate among people who marry in their twenties.

Education   The more education men and women have at the time of their marriage (and the greater the similarity of their educations), the greater their chance of staying married (Tzeng, 1992). Individuals who go to college are older than those who marry in high school, and have a greater income-earning potential. The mean annual income of a woman who completes high school is $11,316; who completes college is $20,376; who earns a master's degree is $31,368. The corresponding salaries for men are $22,236; $38,820; and $44,976. (*Statistical Abstract of the United States: 1993*, Table 234).

However, education may become a liability when the woman has more than the man. A team of researchers observed that women who marry down in education have a higher divorce rate than those who marry a man who has an education equal to or above hers (Bumpass et al., 1991).

Career Plans   The timing of your marriage will also depend on your career plans. Some individuals feel that they want to be established in a career for a couple of years and be economically independent before they get married. Not only do they want to get settled, they want to know that they can take care of themselves. This may be particularly true for some women. One student in the authors' classes said, "My sister married this guy in college and threw her career plans to the wind. She's now divorced with two children with no child support and is on the job market for the first time at age 31. Establishing myself in a career first is simply a way of protecting myself if something goes wrong."

Waiting to marry until your twenties when your education is behind you and you are established in a career is one course of action. Others choose to marry before they finish school and before their career plans have solidified. Some are glad they did. One student noted, "Yes, there are times I have thought that it might have been better if we had waited to get married. But we were in love and simply didn't want to live apart or deal with a long-distance romance. We had to make a decision to marry when we were both available to each other before we drifted off into separate careers in separate states. We are glad we made our relationship a priority."

Why?—Choosing to Avoid Marrying for the Wrong Reasons

While people often marry for reasons of love, companionship, and personal fulfillment, they sometimes marry for the wrong reasons. In a survey of over 56,000 *Woman's Day* readers, 41 percent said that they married for the wrong reasons (Lear, 1986). The following are some of the negative motivations for marriage that may be operative for one or both partners.

Rebound A rebound marriage results when you marry someone immediately after another person has terminated a relationship with you. It is a frantic attempt to reestablish your desirability in your own eyes and in the eyes of the partner who just dropped you. One man said:

> After she told me she wouldn't marry me, I became desperate. I called up an old girlfriend to see if I

could get the relationship going again. We were married within a month. I know it was foolish, but I was very hurt and couldn't stop myself.

To marry on the rebound is questionable because the marriage is made in reference to the previous partner and not to the partner being married. In reality, you are using the person you intend to marry to establish yourself as the winner in the previous relationship. To avoid the negative consequences of marrying on the rebound, you might wait until the negative memories of your past relationship have been replaced by positive aspects of your current relationship. In other words, marry when the satisfactions of being with your current partner outweigh any feelings of revenge.

Escape A partner may marry to escape an unhappy home situation in which the parents are often seen as oppressive and overbearing and their marriage as discordant. Their continued bickering may be highly aversive, causing the partner to marry to flee the home. A family with an alcoholic parent may create an escape situation. One woman said:

> I couldn't wait to get away from home. Ever since my dad died, my mother has been drinking and watching me like a hawk. "Be home early, don't drink, and watch out for those horrible men," she would always say. I admit it. I married the

first guy that would have me. Marriage was my ticket away from that woman.

Marriage for escape is a poor idea. It is far better to continue the relationship with the partner until mutual love and respect, rather than the desire to escape an unhappy situation, become the dominant forces propelling you toward marriage. In this way you can evaluate the marital relationship in terms of its own potential and not solely as an alternative to an unhappy situation.

Next Logical Step Partners who have dated each other for several years may feel that marriage is the next logical step in their relationship. They may not be particularly enamoured with each other and may even have a very conflictual relationship, but feel that since they have already invested a significant amount of time into the relationship, they may as well marry each other. Partners might consider that marriage is optional, that it does not alter their relationship for the better, and that feeling very positive about each other and the relationship is important before making a commitment to marry.

Psychological Blackmail Some individuals get married because their partner takes the position that "I can't live without you" or "I will commit suicide if you leave me." Because the
(continued)

◡: CHOICES :◡

person fears that the partner may commit suicide, the wedding occurs. The problem with such a marriage is that the partner has learned to manipulate the relationship in such a way to get what he or she wants. Use of this power often creates resentment in the other partner who feels trapped in the marriage. Escaping from the marriage becomes even more difficult.

One way of coping with a psychological blackmail situation is to get the person to go with you to a counselor to "discuss the relationship." Once inside the therapy room, you can tell the counselor that you feel pressured to get married because of the suicide threat. Counselors are trained to respond to this situation.

Pity Some partners marry because they feel guilty about terminating a relationship with someone whom they pity. The boyfriend of one woman got drunk one Halloween evening and began to light fireworks on the roof of his fraternity house. As he was running away from a Roman candle he had just ignited, he tripped and fell off the roof. He landed on his head and was in a coma for three weeks. A year after the accident his speech and muscle coordination were still adversely affected. The woman said she did not love him any more but felt guilty about terminating a relationship now that he had become physically afflicted. She was ambivalent. She felt it was her duty to marry her fiancé, but her feelings were no longer love feelings.

Pity may also have a social basis. For example, a partner may fail to achieve a lifetime career goal (for example, flunks out of medical school). Regardless of the reason, if one partner loses a limb, becomes brain damaged, or fails in the pursuit of a major goal, it is important to keep the issue of pity separate from the advisability of contracting the marriage. The decision to marry should be based on factors other than pity or gratitude to the partner.

Delaying marriage until all of the "right" conditions are met may be extremely difficult. Most of us assume that *our* marriage will be different, that it will not end in divorce, and that love is enough to compensate for such factors as premarital pregnancy or financial stress.

Even if all of the indications for a successful marriage are present, either you or your partner may be reluctant to make a commitment. In this case, the individual may want to explore the source of the reluctance and remember that marriage is only one lifestyle option among several.

℘ Summary

Dating is the primary mechanism by which men and women pair off into exclusive, committed relationships. Contemporary functions of dating involve confirmation of a social self, recreation, companionship, intimacy, sex, socialization, status achievement, and mate selection.

Relatively new methods of finding dating partners include advertising or joining a videodating club. Most people who use a videodating club do so as a way of meeting an exclusive mate rather than a means of attracting a wide range of partners.

Persons who are dating "the second time around" are different from young people dating for the first time. These individuals are older, have fewer available partners, and over half have children from a previous marriage.

As dating moves toward mate selection, the partners are influenced by various cultural, sociological, psychological, and perhaps biological factors.

Although marriages in some cultures are arranged by parents or other relatives, our culture relies mainly on endogamous and exogamous pressures to guide mate choice.

Sociological aspects of mate selection include homogamy (people prefer someone like themselves) and propinquity (people are more likely to find a mate who lives in close proximity).

Psychological aspects of mate selection include complementary needs, exchange theory, and parental image. Complementary needs theory suggests that people select others who have opposite characteristics to their own. They may also seek each other out if they both have the same need at different levels of intensity. Most researchers find little evidence for complementary needs theory.

Exchange theory suggests that one individual selects another on the basis of rewards and costs. As long as an individual derives more profit from a relationship with one partner than another, the relationship will continue. Exchange concepts influence who dates whom, the conditions of the dating relationship, and the decision to marry.

The parental image theory of mate selection says that a man looks for a wife like his mother and a woman looks for a husband like her father.

The sociobiological view of mate selection suggests that men and women select each other on the basis of their biological capacity to produce and support healthy offspring. Men seek young women with healthy bodies, and women seek ambitious men who will provide economic support.

You can use the engagement period productively by systematically examining your relationship, observing your future in-laws for clues about your partner's background and character, and going for premarital counseling. Conditions under which you might want to prolong your engagement include having known each other for less than two years, having an inadequate or unstable source of income, having parents who disapprove of your marriage, and being pregnant.

Some couples decide to write a marriage agreement to specify the understandings of their relationship. If these involve the disposition of property and assets, a lawyer should be asked to draw up the agreement. Otherwise, the document may not be in legal terms recognized by the courts.

Regardless of what you do, you will not be able to guarantee yourself and your partner a happy marriage. The illusion of the perfect mate, deception during the premarital period, the confinement of marriage, the demands of careers and children, and the inevitability of change make prediction of future marital happiness impossible.

Trends in dating relationships include a longer period of dating, a gradual shift from the traditional dating pattern to a more informal one, increased interracial, interreligious, and interethnic dating, and greater availability of technological means of finding dates. In addition, trends in marital commitments include the possibility of greater caution entering marriage (the fact that people are marrying later is some evidence for this) and the increasing use of prenuptial agreements.

Questions for Reflection

1. How does exchange theory help to explain your involvement in your most recent relationship? What specifically are or were the rewards and costs of that relationship?
2. What kinds of influence do your parents (or children) have on your dating relationships?
3. What are your feelings about prenuptial agreements? Would you want a prenuptial agreement? Why or why not?

References

Ahuvia, A. C. and M. B. Adelman. Formal intermediaries in the marriage market: A typology and review. *Journal of Marriage and the Family,* 1992, 54, 452–463.

American Council on Education and University of California, the American Freshman: National Norms for Fall, 1992. Los Angeles, Calif.: Los Angeles Higher Education Research Institute, 1992.

Asmussen, L. and C. L. Shehan. Gendered expectations and behavior in dating relationships. Paper, 54th Annual Conference of the National Council on Family Relations, Orlando, Florida, 1992. Used by permission.

Basow, S. A. *Gender stereotypes and roles,* 3d ed. Pacific Grove, Calif.: Brooks/Cole, 1992.

Berry, R. E. and F. L. Williams. Assessing the relationship between quality of the life and marital income satisfaction: A path analytic approach. *Journal of Marriage and the Family,* 1987, 49, 107–116.

Bossard, J. H. S. Residential propinquity as a factor in marriage selection. *American Journal of Sociology,* 1932, 38, 219–224.

Bulcroft, R. A. and K. A. Bulcroft. Race differences in attitudinal and motivational factors in the decision to marry. *Journal of Marriage and the Family,* 1993, 55, 338–355.

Bumpass, L. L., T. Castro Martin, and J. A. Sweet. The impact of family background and early marital disruption. *Journal of Family Issues,* 1991, 12, 22–42.

Buss, D. M. et al. International preferences in selecting mates: A study of 37 cultures. *Journal of Cross-Cultural Psychology,* 1990, 21, no. 4, 5–47.

Daniel, H. J., Jr. and R. B. McCabe. Gender differences in the perception of vocal sexiness. In *The nature of the sexes: The sociobiology of sex differences,* J. N. G. van der Dennen, ed. Groningen, The Netherlands: Origin Press, 1992, 55–62.

Daniel, H.J., III, K.F. O'Brien, R.B. McCabe, and V.E. Quinter. Values in mate selection: A 1984 campus survey. *College Student Journal,* 1985, 19, 44–50.

Darling, C. A., J. K. Davidson, and W. E. Parish, Jr. Single parents: Interaction of parenting and sexual issues. *Journal of Sex and Marital Therapy,* 1989, 15, 227–245.

Davis, W. A. Psychological tests help couples spot pitfalls before the big step. *The Daily Reflector,* November 6, 1992, d-6.

Deal, J. E., K. S. Wampler, and C. F. Halverson, Jr. The importance of similarity in the marital relationship. *Family Process,* 1992, 31, 369–382.

Dychtwald, J. E., K. S. Wampler, and C. F. Halverson, Jr. The importance of similarity in the marital relationship. *Family Process,* 1992, 31, 369–382.

Fielding, Guy, Sue Clarke, and Sue Llewelyn. Long-distance relationships: The use of communication media to maintain intimate relationships during brief and extended nonpermanent separations, An exploratory research investigation. Department of Communication and Media, Bournemouth Polytechnic, United Kingdom, 1991, unpublished paper. Used by permission.

Ganong, L. W. and M. Coleman. Gender differences in expectations of self and future partner. *Journal of Family Issues*, 1992, *13*, 55–64.

Goldberg, Bernard Matchmaker. "48 Hours: Lonely Street" CBS News, October 5, 1989.

Goodman, Ellen. Finances challenge modern relationships. *The Daily Reflector*, August 14, 1992, a-6.

Greeley, Andrew M., Robert T. Michael, and Tom W. Smith. Americans and their sexual partners. *Society*, July/August 1990, 36–42.

Greenstein, T. N. Delaying marriage: Women's work experience and marital timing. Paper, 54th Annual Conference, National Council on Family Relations, Orlando, Florida, 1992. Used by permission of the author.

Grover, K.J., C.S. Russell, W.E. Schumm, and L.A. Paff-Bergen. Mate selection processes and marital satisfaction. *Family Relations*, 1985, *34*, 383–86.

Guttman, H. A. Parental death as a precipitant of marital conflict. *Journal of Marital and Family Therapy*, 1991, *17*, 81–87.

Hendrix, H. *Keeping the love you find*. New York: Pocket Books, 1992.

Holt, J. Expanding self knowledge in love relationships: An extension of behavioral counseling. Thesis, Department of Sociology, East Carolina University, 1993. Used by permission.

Jedlicka, D. Indirect parental influence on mate choice: A test of the psychoanalytic theory. *Journal of Marriage and the Family*, 1984, *46*, 65–70.

Johnson, D. R. and A. Booth. Rural economic decline and marital quality: A panel study on farm marriages. *Family Relations*, 1990, *39*, 159–165.

Kaplan, Steven. Looking for love in all the right places. *The World and I*, February 1990, 224–229.

Knox, David and C. Schacht. Sexual behaviors of university students enrolled in a human sexuality course. *College Student Journal*, 1992, *26*, 38–40.

Knox, D., C. Schacht, J. Holt, and J. Turner. Sexual lies among college students. *College Student Journal*, 1993, (in press).

LaBeff, Emily E., John H. Hensley, Deborah A. Cook, and Christy L. Haines. Gender differences in self-advertisements for dates: A replication using college students. *Free Inquiry in Creative Sociology*, 1989, *17*, 45–50.

Larsen, Andrea S. and David H. Olson. Predicting marital satisfaction using PREPARE: A replication study. *Journal of Marital and Family Therapy*, 1989, *15*, 311–322.

Larson, J. H., D. R. Crane, and C. W. Smith. Morning and night couples: The effect of wake and sleep patterns on marital adjustment. *Journal of Marital and Family Therapy*, 1991, *17*, 53–65.

Lear, M.W. How many choices do women have? *Woman's Day*, November 11, 1986, 109 et passim.

Lindsey, L. L. *Gender roles: A sociological perspective*. Englewood Cliffs, N.J.: Prentice-Hall, Inc., 1990.

Marano, H.E. The reinvention of marriage. *Psychology Today*, January/February 1992, 48 et passim.

Markstrom-Adams, C. Attitudes on dating, courtship, and marriage: Perspectives on in-group versus out-group relationships by religious minority and majority adolescents. *Family Relations*, 1991, *40*, 91–96.

McNaught, B. R. Overcoming self-hate through education: Achieving self-love among gay people. *Promoting Sexual Responsibility and Preventing Sexual Problems*, G. Albee, S. Gordon, and H. Leitenberg, eds. Hanover: University Press of New England, 1983, 133–145.

Meyer, J.P., and S. Pepper. Need compatibility and marital adjustment in young married couples. *Journal of Personality and Social Psychology*, 1977, *35*, 331–342.

Mitchell, M. *Gone With the Wind*. New York: Macmillian, 1977.

National Center for Health Statistics: 1993. Births, Marriages, Divorces, and Deaths for March 1993. Monthly Vital Statistics Report, vol 42, no. 13. Hyattsville, Md.: Public Health Service.

O'Flaherty, Kathleen M. and L. W. Eells. Courtship behavior of the remarried. *Journal of Marriage and the Family,* 1988, *50,* 499–506.

Renick, M. J., S. L. Blumberg, and H. J. Markman. The prevention and relationship enhancement program (PREP): An empirically based preventive program for couples. *Family Relations,* 1992, *41,* 141–147.

Rice, F. P. *The adolescent,* 6th ed. Boston: Allyn and Bacon, 1990.

Ridley, C. A. and I. E. Sladeczek. Premarital relationship enhancement: Its effect on needs to relate to others. *Family Relations,* 1992, *41,* 148–153.

Riggs, D. S. Relationship problems and dating aggression. *Journal of Interpersonal Violence,* 1993, *8,* 18–35.

Russell, M. N. and R. F. Lyster. Consumer satisfaction with an interchurch marriage preparation program: Implications for program design and development. *Proceedings: Family and Work* 54th Annual Conference, National Council on Family Relations, Orlando, Florida, 1992B Vol 2, #1, p. 93

Russell, M. N. and R. F. Lyster. Marriage preparation: Factors associated with consumer satisfaction. *Family Relations,* 1992, *41,* 446–451.

Sammons, R. A., Jr. Personal communication. Mesa Behavioral Medicine Clinic, Grand Junction, Colorado, 1993. Used by permission of Dr. Sammons.

Schoen, Robert and John Woolredge. Marriage choices in North Carolina and Virginia, 1969–71 and 1979–81. *Journal of Marriage and the Family,* 1989, *51,* 465–481.

Snyder, D. K. and J. M. Regts. Personality correlates of marital dissatisfaction: A comparison of psychiatric, maritally distressed, and nonclinic samples. *Journal of Sex and Marital Therapy,* 1990, *90,* 34–43.

Solomon, Z., M. Waysman, R. Belkin, G. Levy, M. Mikulincer, and D. Enoch. Marital relations and combat stress reaction: The wives' perspective. *Journal of Marriage and the Family,* 1992, *54,* 316–326.

Sparrow, K. H. Factors in mate selection for single black professional women. *Free Inquiry in Creative Sociology,* 1991, *19,* 103–109.

Sprecher, S. and R. Chandak. Attitudes about arranged marriages and dating among men and women from India. *Free Inquiry in Creative Sociology,* 1992, *20,* 59–69.

Sprecher, S. and D. Felmlee. The influence of parents and friends on the quality and stability of romantic relationships: A three-wave longitudinal investigation. *Journal of Marriage and the Family,* 1992, *54,* 888–900.

Statistical Abstract of the United States: 1993, 113th ed. Washington, D.C.: U.S. Bureau of the Census, 1993.

Stets, J. E. The link between past and present intimate relationships. *Journal of Family Issues,* 1993, *14,* 236–260.

Surra, C. A. Research and theory on mate selection and premarital relationships in the 1980s. *Contemporary Families,* Alan Booth, ed. Minneapolis, Minn.: National Council on Family Relations, 1991, 54–75.

Thornton, Arland. The courtship process and adolescent sexuality. *Journal of Family Issues,* 1990, *11,* 239–273.

Tzeng, M.S. The effects of socioeconomic heterogamy and changes on marital dissolution for first marriages. *Journal of Marriage and the Family,* 1992, *54,* 609–619.

Waller, W., and R. Hill. *The family: A dynamic interpretation.* New York: Holt, Rinehart & Winston, 1951.

Wasow, M. Support groups for family caregivers of patients with Alzheimer's disease. *Social Work,* 1986, *31,* 93–97.

Weaton, B. Life transitions, role histories, and mental health. *American Sociological Review,* 1990, *55,* 209–223.

Whyte, M. K. *Dating, mating, and marriage.* Hawthorne, N.Y.: Aldine de Gruyter, 1990.

Winch, R.F. The theory of complementary needs in mate selection. Final results on the test of the general hypothesis. *American Sociological Review,* 1955, *20,* 552–555.

Woll, Stanley B. and Peter Young. Looking for Mr. or Ms. Right: Self-presentation in Videodating. *Journal of Marriage and the Family,* 1989, *51,* 483–488.

Woodfin, M. H., and J. Tinling, eds. *Another secret diary of William Byrd of Westover, 1739–1741.* Richmond, Va.: 1942.

Young, M. H. Ph.D and J. D. Schvaneveldt Ph.D. The effects of religious orientation on couple formation among college students. Paper, 54th Annual Conference, National Council on Family Relations, Orlando, Florida. 1992. Used by permission. Both Young and Schvaneveldt are in the Dept. of Family and Human Development, Utah State University, Logan, Utah.

Contents

6
CHAPTER

Living Together

Is it True?

1. Our society is becoming less tolerant of people who live together before marriage.

2. Most living together individuals are under age 25.

3. Cohabitants have intercourse more frequently, have more egalitarian sexual relationships, and are less monogamous than marrieds.

4. Individuals who live together before marriage are more likely to get divorced than individuals who do not live together before marriage.

5. Common law marriages are recognized in all 50 states.

1 = F; 2 = F; 3 = T; 4 = T; 5 = F

Cohabitation is clearly not for everyone, but for those who, as a function of age or circumstance, feel lonely at the thought of singlehood or trapped at the thought of traditional marriage, cohabitation offers a unique alternative.

MICHAEL D. NEWCOMB

One of the major changes in our society is the gradual acceptance of and toleration by the larger society of couples who live together (Axinn & Thornton, 1993). This new attitude toward living together has increased among people of all ages, races, and social classes.

In this chapter, we will examine the characteristics of those who live together, their motivations for doing so, and how they evaluate the experience. In addition, we will assess the potential benefits and disadvantages of becoming involved in a living-together relationship. Finally, because the courts are indicating increased concern, we look at the legal implications of living together as an unmarried couple.

Most unmarried couples [who live together] are not reckless, licentious people out of control.

SAMUEL S. HILL

☙ Definition and Prevalence of Living Together

In research, over 20 definitions of living together (also referred to as **cohabitation**) have been used. These different definitions involve different criteria that may be used to identify live-in couples, including duration of the relationship, frequency of overnight visits, emotional/sexual nature of the relationship, and sex of the partners. Most research on cohabitation has been conducted on heterosexual live-in couples. We define living together (or cohabitation) as two unrelated adults involved in an emotional and sexual relationship who sleep overnight in the same residence on a regular basis. The terms used to describe live-ins include *cohabitants* and POSSLQ (People of the Opposite Sex Sharing Living Quarters), the latter term used by the U.S. Bureau of the Census.

The idea of living together did not catch on until the early sixties, when half a million couples were cohabiting. By the mid-nineties the number had increased over four times.

NATIONAL DATA ☙ Over three million U.S. couples are cohabiting (*Statistical Abstract of the United States: 1993,* Table 62).

Reasons for the increase in cohabitation include delay of marriage, fear of marriage, career or educational commitments; increased tolerance from society, parents, and peers; improved birth control technology and the desire for a stable emotional and sexual relationship without legal ties. Cohabitation has

Cohabitation unions themselves are highly unstable and relatively short-lived, because they either result in marriage or dissolve.

CATHERINE SURRA

become both an alternative lifestyle as well as a stage in a couple's relationship sometimes involving both commitment and eventual marriage.

NATIONAL DATA ಜಿ In a national study of U.S. adults, 28 percent reported that they had cohabitated (Thomson & Colella, 1992).

ಜಿ Types of Living Together Relationships

There are various types of living together relationships. One type of living together relationship may be viewed as a stage in the courtship process that may eventually lead to marriage between the partners. Another type of living together relationship may be considered an alternative to marriage, rather than as a stage leading to marriage. Finally, some living together relationships are based on economic convenience. Next, we look more closely at these various types of living together relationships.

Living Together as a Stage in Courtship

According to sociologist Ronald Rindfuss,

There is no single answer to whether cohabitation is a late stage of courtship or an early stage of marriage.

LARRY BUMPASS AND
JAMES SWEET

> Cohabitation is a new stage in the American courtship process. In an earlier time, they would have gotten married or simply continued dating. (quoted in Larson, 1991, 20)

Couples who view living together as a stage in courtship differ in regard to their motivations for living together. Some cohabitants are definitely committed to marriage; they may even be formally engaged. These couples may live together because they consider themselves practically married, even though the formal wedding has not yet taken place. These couples feel sure they will marry, yet they may be delaying getting married until the time is "right," that is, until they finish school, get settled in a new job, or adjust to a move or change of residence.

Other cohabitants are romantically involved and think that they want to get married, but they are not formally engaged. Before these couples formally commit to marriage, they want to live together to confirm that getting married is the right decision. These couples feel that living together will help them assess their compatibility over time. In essence, these couples view living together as a trial marriage. These couples may have the understanding that they will eventually marry, but only if they feel that their relationship continues to be strong and fulfilling after living together for a period of time. In one study of women and men who had lived together, 73 percent of the men and 68 percent of the women reported that living together was a way of having a trial marriage (Glezer, 1991).

CONSIDERATION

In the 1920s, Judge B. B. Lindsey suggested the living together alternative out of his concern for the number of divorcing couples he saw in his court. He reasoned that if couples lived together before marriage, they might be better able to assess the degree to which they were compatible with each other. Similarly, Margaret Mead suggested a "two-stage marriage." The first stage would involve living together without having children. If the partners felt that their relationship was stable and durable, they would get married and have a family.

Finally, some cohabitants are emotionally and sexually involved and want to live together because they enjoy each other. They do not view living together as a trial marriage, although they have not ruled out the possibility of future marriage. Rather, they feel that living together may enhance their relationship. As for the future of the relationship, these couples have a "let's wait and see" attitude.

CONSIDERATION

Some research suggests that most living together relationships do not lead to marriage but rather are terminated. In one study of living together relationships, 75 percent of the couples had terminated their relationship within four years (Glezer, 1991).

Living Together as a Permanent Alternative to Marriage

Whereas most people regard living together as a stage to a future marriage (although not necessarily with the person with whom they currently live), some people view living together as a permanent alternative to marriage. They enjoy living together, but they do not plan to marry anyone–ever.

There are various reasons and motivations for living together as a permanent alternative to marriage. Those who select living together as a permanent alternative to marriage may have been married before and don't want the entanglements of another marriage. Others feel that the "real" bond between two people is (or should be) emotional. They contend that many couples stay together because of the legal contract, even though they do not love each other any longer. "If you're staying married because of the contract," said one partner, "you're staying for the wrong reason." Some couples feel that they are "married" in their hearts and souls and don't need or want the law to interfere with what they feel is a private act of commitment. While this arrangement is relatively rare on the U.S. mainland, it is common among Puerto Ricans (Landale & Fennelly, 1992). In Puerto Rico, it is not uncommon for individuals with children to live together throughout their lives without ever formally getting married.

A first union, be it a marriage or a cohabitation, is increasingly likely to dissolve. Societal changes are making it less and less likely that the first union will be the last union.

ROBERT SCHOEN

The acceptance of cohabitation without marriage may lead to a substitution of cohabitation for marriage.

WILLIAM AXINN
ARLAND THORNTON

Some individuals who live together are very satisfied with their relationship and feel no need to change it. Although they are emotionally and physically involved, they fear that marriage will change their relationship. Many of those in this category have been married before and are cautious about a remarriage. "If our relationship is great the way it is, why change it by getting married?" is their motto. Some people in this category fear that their relationship will become worse if they marry. Jill Boles has been married several times and is currently living with her partner. She commented why living together may have benefits for keeping the relationship more interesting.

> Each of my husbands was a wonderful human being, but somewhere along the line we took each other for granted, we misunderstood each other and we lost communication. When you're living with someone you share more (Wessel, 1992, g-10).

Some women reject marriage for philosophical reasons:

> I have enough trouble with my identity as a woman starting her own business that I don't need to confuse it with _____'s business. I don't like the stigma. . . . I don't want to be a "Mrs." in any way (Kotkin, 1985, 167).

Other individuals feel that living together permanently allows you to keep your own identity:

> . . . right now, we can take vacations separately; we can do things separately. It seems that once you're married, . . . the two of you become one identity—the way people look at you (Kotkin, 1985).

> **CONSIDERATION**
>
> It is sometimes suggested that "living together is the same as being married." However, Rindfuss and VandenHeuvel (1992) observed that living together is closer to being single than being married. They noted that "Cohabitors' fertility expectations, nonfamilial activities, and home ownership rates resemble those of the singles" (p. 136).

Homosexual couples also live together as a permanent alternative to marriage. Our cultural bias against homosexuality is reflected in the law which prohibits homosexual couples from marrying. In some states, homosexual couples are being granted legal entitlements that have traditionally been reserved for married couples. However, homosexual living together couples are still not allowed to be legally married, which gives them no choice but to live together as a permanent alternative to marriage.

> **CONSIDERATION**
>
> Some living together homosexual couples may think of themselves as "married" in the sense that they view their relationship as a long-term, monogamous

Marriage is a lottery, but you can't tear up your ticket if you lose.

F. M. KNOWLES

commitment. Homosexual couples may buy houses together, celebrate "anniversaries" together, and in some cases, rear children together.

Living Together for Economic Convenience

Sometimes people live with a partner out of economic convenience. They may not be deeply in love with each other but feel good enough friends to live together to share expenses. They may have sex together but are not necessarily exclusively bonded to each other. They may live together primarily to save on rent, utilities, and other living expenses.

Other cohabitants may prefer to get married, but live together unmarried in order to maintain their social security benefits. Widows and widowers may lose half of their social security entitlements if they remarry. Consequently, some widows and widowers live with a new partner without getting married.

CONSIDERATION

Another reason why some people decide to live together is that it represents independence from one's parents and rebellion against tradition.

🦢 Characteristics of Cohabitants

People who cohabitate tend to be older, childfree, and less educated. Cohabitants tend to be over the age of 25.

NATIONAL DATA 🦢 In a national study of cohabitation, almost 70 percent of individuals who were living together were between the ages of 25 and 34. Only 24 percent were between the ages of 19 and 24 (Bumpass & Sweet, 1989).

CONSIDERATION

Living together is not limited to young and middle aged couples. Some elderly live together both in and out of nursing homes.

As one 63-year-old retiree said, "My girlfriend (age 64) lives just down the hall from me. . . . When she spends the night, she usually brings her cordless phone. . . . just in case her daughter calls." One 61-year-old woman told us that even though her 68-year-old boyfriend has been spending three or four nights a week at her house for the past year, she has not been able to tell her family. "I hide his shoes when my grandchildren are coming over." (Dychtwald, 1990, 221).

With the exception of cohabitants in Puerto Rico, where living together is more akin to marriage with children, most cohabitants in the United States tend not to have young children living with them.

NATIONAL DATA ❧ About 66 percent of unmarried couples who live together do not have children under the age of 15 living with them (*Statistical Abstract of the United States: 1993*, Table 62).

Finally, cohabitants also differ by education with the highest rates of cohabitation among the least educated. Surra (1991) identified other characteristics of cohabitators and found that they tend to be never married rather than previously married and divorced (53 percent versus 34 percent), whites rather than blacks, and less conventional (greater drug abuse, less religiosity).

Buunk and Van Driel (1989) reviewed the literature and noted an array of other characteristics typical of individuals who were living together. When compared to noncohabitors, cohabitors were less religious, had first intercourse earlier, had more sexual partners, used more illicit drugs, and had parents they described as unhappy or divorced. Axinn & Thornton (1993) also found that women who cohabitated tended to have mothers who approved of cohabitation. Stets (1993) also reviewed the literature and found that being black, involved in an interracial relationship, having a drinking problem, and having previously cohabited were correlated with cohabitation.

C O N S I D E R A T I O N

Cohabitants have been stereotyped as being unconventional. However, researchers DeMaris and MacDonald (1993) compared a national sample of marrieds and cohabitants and concluded that cohabitants "hold a variety of family attitudes and beliefs, some of which are conventional, some of which are unconventional, and many of which are somewhere in between" (p. 496). Examples of conventional attitudes of cohabitants include women who value traditional families and men who take parental obligations seriously. Unconventional attitudes occur with respect to sexual behavior, gender equality, and having children out of wedlock.

❧ The Experience of Living Together

In the following section we look at the decision to live together, feelings about marriage, sexuality, division of labor, money, and problems that couples who live together report.

Deciding to Move in Together

In a study of 98 individuals who were living together, 20 percent of the respondents had known each other for three months before moving in together; 25 percent had known each other four to six months; 28 percent seven to twelve months; 18 percent between one and two years; 7 percent had known each other more than two years (Glezer, 1991).

Sometimes, living together is the result of both partners making a conscious decision to do so. However, many partners become emotionally involved with each other, spend increasingly larger amounts of time together, and gradually drift into a living together arrangement. The typical pattern is to spend an occasional night together, then a weekend, then a night before or after the weekend, and so on. This escalation usually takes place over a period of months. In a study of 58 divorced women, Montgomery et al. (1992) found that ninety-one percent lived with their new husband before marrying him. The typical sequence was "dated but lived apart," to "lived together several days a week" or "almost every day" to "combined residence" before marriage (Montgomery et al., 1992).

"We just enjoyed spending time together and the more, the better. We weren't aware that we were gradually moving in together—but that's what was happening," an English major recalls.

Another couple remember their experience:

> We were at his place fooling around when I said how nice it would be to have my stereo to listen to. We decided to go to my dorm and get it. Doing so was symbolic, because in the next few days we had moved my other stuff into his apartment. We never talked about living together, only "getting my stuff."

Feelings about Marriage

What do couples who cohabit feel about marriage in general and about marriage to each other? In a study of 40 American college living together couples, 93 percent of the women and 85 percent of the men reported that they would eventually marry (Risman et al., 1981). When 98 Australian cohabitants were asked about marriage, 54 percent of the men and 46 percent of the women reported that they eventually planned to marry, sometime in their lives (though not necessarily each other). Those who had been married before and who were cohabitating (in contrast to the never married cohabitants) were much less likely to report that they would eventually marry (28 percent versus 47 percent). "It appears that those who had previously been in an unsuccessful relationship were more likely to be wary about making legally binding commitments" (Glezer, 1991, 26).

Sexuality in Living Together Relationships

Cohabitants have intercourse more frequently, have more egalitarian sexual relationships, and are less monogamous than marrieds. One explanation for more frequent intercourse among cohabitants is that, in general, they are younger and have been together fewer years than marrieds. And since the older the couple and the longer the couple have been in a relationship, the less

Although marriage may increase commitment and foster greater acceptance by relatives and society, it may also bring more role playing, possessiveness, and a reduced sense of independence and autonomy. Some might wonder if this is a fair exchange.

MICHAEL NEWCOMB

frequently they have intercourse, it is not surprising that cohabitants report more frequent intercourse.

In addition, cohabitants (as compared to marrieds) are more equal in terms of initiating intercourse with each other. Forty-two percent of 646 cohabitants versus 33 percent of 3,612 spouses have relationships in which the initiation of sexual activity is equal (Blumstein & Schwartz, 1983). This, too, is not surprising in that cohabitants by virtue of their willingness to live outside of conventional norms and marriage might also be expected to develop less traditional patterns of interaction.

Cohabitants, when compared to marrieds, also tend to be less monogamous than marrieds. In one study, twenty-five percent of male cohabitors (in contrast to 11 percent of husbands) reported at least one instance of nonmonogamy in the last year. The corresponding percentages for female cohabitors and wives were 22 percent and 9 percent (Blumstein & Schwartz, 1990). The norms of fidelity in marriage may be much more controlling of spouses than the norms of faithfulness in cohabiting relationships. Homosexual cohabiting couples are less likely to be monogamous than heterosexual couples (Glezer, 1991).

Division of Labor

Who does the work in living together relationships? Although many cohabitants share the work in their relationships, there seems to be a drift toward traditional roles, the woman doing more of the work. This traditional division of labor may be the unconscious replication of the role relationships the respective partners observed in their parents' marriages. One woman who cooks, cleans, and does the laundry said, "I really don't mind. I'd rather be

He doesn't cook, he barbecues. Men will cook as long as danger's involved.

RITA RUDNER

Although men in cohabitation relationships do a lot of domestic work early in the relationship, over time they tend to do considerably less than the woman.

taking care of things around the apartment than just sitting around." One might predict that her mother also takes care of her father in a similar manner and feels guilty "just sitting around."

Some women feel frustrated and angry about the traditional drift toward conventional male-female roles in a living together situation. One graduate student who had recently moved in with her partner said:

> Moving in together has caused some unanticipated problems. Things prior to that had been quite egalitarian, and I liked the way Bob treated me. After we moved in, the boxes had not even been unpacked and I became a *housewife!* I worked all day on *our* house while he went to school. It was horrible, and I was miserable. We talked about it, and two days later I was the housewife again. I'm hoping that since we're moved in and things are unpacked and cleaned, this problem will be resolved.

Money and Property

Unmarried cohabiting couples are faced with issues concerning their money and property. Dealing with such matters may be difficult for cohabiting couples. A financial planner noted, "People don't feel comfortable talking about money in a relationship because it reduces love to numbers and dollar signs" (quoted in Scherreik, 1993, 33).

Experts recommend that in the beginning of a cohabitating relationship, money should be kept separate (Scherreik, 1993). This means that each partner should maintain individual checking and savings accounts and credit cards. Ideally, partners should share expenses equally. In addition, both names should be on the apartment lease if the couple is renting.

In a study of Australian cohabitants, fewer than half (46 percent) reported that they had a joint bank account, 71 percent reported that they shared housing costs, and 66 percent reported that they bought things jointly. The previously married were more likely to share housing costs and to buy things jointly than the never married (Glezer, 1991). This pattern may reflect the pattern of joint spending characteristic of marrieds.

According to the authors of *The Living Together Kit* (Ihara & Warner, 1990), when unmarried couples buy a house, car, furniture, or other costly items (worth $500.00 or more), they should consider developing a written and signed legal agreement. The written agreement should include a description of the assets, how they were acquired, how the couple will meet their financial obligations, and what will happen to their assets if the relationship terminates. Purchasing real estate together may require a separate agreement, which should include how the mortgage, property taxes, and repairs will be shared. The agreement should also specify who gets the house if the couple part and how the value of the departing partner's share will be determined. If the couple have children, another agreement may be helpful in defining custody, visitation, and support issues in the event the couple terminates their relationship.

There are a lot of hot arguments over "cold cash."

E. C. MCKENZIE

ACROSS CULTURES ❧

Potential Problems Experienced by Cohabitants

Partners who live together report certain problems including parents, children, loss of freedom, and violence and abuse.

Parents   Most college students are reluctant to tell their parents they are living together. They fear their parents' disapproval and, in some cases, retribution. "My dad would cut off my money if he knew Mark and I were living together," said one junior.

Some live-in partners do not care if their parents know they are living together. Those who do hide it feel guilty about the deception. "I don't feel good about being dishonest with my folks, but I tell myself it would hurt them more if they knew," one partner said.

Still others are sorry they can't share their feelings about their companion with their parents. "I've never been happier than since I moved into Carl's apartment. But the fact that my folks don't know and would be disappointed if they did bothers me. Carl is a very important part of my life, and I feel sad that I can't share him with my parents," observed a music major.

Older, noncollege, divorced people who live together also have parental concerns. "No matter how old I am," said one 36-year-old woman, "I'm still my mother's child, and she thinks living together is wrong." Expecting parents to change their values is probably unrealistic. Most cohabiting couples who have disapproving parents are tolerant of their parents' values, yet respect their own values by continuing to live together.

Children   Youngsters of unmarried parents who live together may also create problems. These include rejecting the parent's new live-in partner by ignoring, direct attacks, or being disrespectful. These issues are similar to those experienced by partners in new stepfamilies.

Adult children of parents who cohabit may also be a problem. They may disapprove of the selection of their parent's partner and, like the youngster, ignore, attack, or be disrespectful. Whether a young child or older adult, children may affect the happiness of the partners who live together.

Loss of Freedom   Some partners complain that a live-in relationship restricts their freedom. One woman said:

> Last week I hit a new low point. I felt very trapped and that all my independence and freedom were gone. I had earlier insisted that we have an open relationship (sex with others allowed), but it didn't occur to me until now that I am part of a *couple* and no one's going to be interested in me. Also, I felt I'd have no alone time except when I'm working (we do not have separate bedrooms and we use one car to go back and forth to school). I've had nightmares about being married and even awakened one night terrified because I had rolled over and felt someone in bed with me (guess I'd been dreaming I was "single" again).

Violence and Abuse   Cohabitants are twice as likely as married couples to report physical abuse in their relationships (Stets & Straus, 1989). The precipitating factors most frequently related to violence in cohabiting relationships are jealousy and arguments over sex (Makepeace, 1989). The problem of violence and abuse in relationships is examined in detail in Chapter 12, Violence and Abuse in Relationships.

Living Together: A Cross-Cultural View

ACROSS CULTURES ❧

Living together is more frequently practiced and much more accepted in Denmark and Sweden than in the United States. These countries regard living together as a social institution in that individuals may live together with or without children and without social disapproval. Rather, cohabitants as well as marrieds, are treated by close friends and relatives, as well as by society, as a unit (Gibbons, 1992). In Denmark and Sweden, more young people aged 20–24 are cohabiting than are married (Coleman & Salt, 1992). A unique aspect of the Danes and Swedes is that they have a strong belief in the sanctity of private life. Since living together represents a private choice, there is social approval for that choice.

Australia also has an element of individualism but not to the same degree as Denmark and Sweden. About seven percent of the couples in Australia are living together (Glezer, 1991). Australian cohabitants tended to have left home earlier and to have become sexually active before age 18, suggesting less normative control and nonconventionality respectively. They were also more likely than noncohabitants to have egalitarian sex roles, to have no religious affiliation, and to come from an urban background (Glezer, 1991).

In Great Britain, cohabitation is a common preliminary to marriage, especially to remarriage, and is to some extent a replacement for it (Coleman & Salt, 1992). As is true in the United States, "cohabitation before marriage is becoming normal" (p. 137); 50 percent of never-married couples who were married in 1988, and 74 percent of couples marrying for a second time cohabited before marriage.

❧ Potential Advantages and Disadvantages of Living Together

Although living together before marriage does not ensure a happy, stable marriage, there are some potential advantages of living together. Next, we look at some of these advantages, as well as potential disadvantages, of becoming involved in a living together relationship.

Potential Advantages of Living Together

Many unmarried couples who live together report that it is an enjoyable, maturing experience. There are other potential benefits as well.

Sense of Well-Being   When cohabitating persons (in a national sample) were compared with individuals who lived alone, the cohabitants reported a greater sense of well-being. However, when they were compared with marrieds, they were less happy (Kurdek, 1991). One explanation suggests that living together affords the companionship that living alone does not but that cohabitation does not afford the security often associated with marriage.

Delayed Marriage   Individuals who marry in their middle and late twenties are more likely to stay married and to report higher levels of marital satisfaction than those who marry earlier. To the degree that living together functions to delay the age at which a person marries, it may therefore be considered beneficial. "I married when I was 20," remarked one woman, "because you just didn't live together in those days. I wish I had waited to get married and had had the option of living together in the meantime." Lana Turner, the Hollywood actress of the forties, said one of the reasons she had seven marriages was that when two people became involved, they were not expected to live together—they were expected to marry.

Many cohabitants report that they enjoy the companionship of a live-in partner.

Gain Information about Self and Partner   Living with an intimate partner provides an opportunity for individuals to learn more about themselves and their partner. For example, individuals in living together relationships may find that their role expectations are more (or less) traditional than they had previously thought.

Learning more about one's partner is a major advantage of living together. A person's values, habits, reactions, and behavior patterns, as well as their relationship expectations, are more fully revealed in a living together context than in a traditional dating context.

Easier Adjustment to Stepfamily for Children   Children who have mothers who choose to cohabit with their future husband before getting married may have an easier adjustment to stepfamily living than children who have mothers who do not cohabit. A team of researchers studying remarriages of mothers—with children—who lived with their partner before marrying him found that cohabitation served as a way of introducing her children to the new stepdad (and the sooner after the divorce the better). A quick transition from divorce to cohabitation minimizes the time that children must adjust to routines in a single parent home (Montgomery et al., 1992).

Terminate Unsatisfactory Relationship Before Marriage   Even though ending a living together relationship may be a difficult and stressful experience, it is probably more traumatic to end a relationship after a couple has married. Since living together relationships usually involve fewer legal ties, it may be easier to disengage from a living together relationship than a marriage. According to Rindfuss and VandenHeuvel (1992), discord is more likely to lead to the termination of a cohabiting relationship than a marital relationship.

> Living together is a sure way to avoid a possible disaster.
>
> ABIGAIL VAN BUREN (DEAR ABBY)

Potential Disadvantages of Living Together

"Never again" said a man who had formerly had a living together relationship. "I invested myself completely and felt we would eventually get married. But she never had that in mind and just took me for a ride. The next time, I'll be married before moving in with someone." Living together may have negative consequences for some people—they may feel used or tricked. In addition, cohabitants may (as noted earlier) experience problems with their parents. Finally, living together couples are often not granted the same economic benefits bestowed by a marriage license.

Feeling Used or Tricked   When levels of commitment are uneven in a relationship, the partner who is most committed feels used. "I always felt I was giving more than I was getting," said one partner. "It's not a good feeling." Cohabitants may also feel used when they find themselves in a one-sided convenience relationship (Ridley et al., 1978). Although some live-in relationships involve mutual convenience, others do not. In a one-sided convenience

---

⤳ IN FOCUS 6.1 ⤳

Living Together as Preparation For Marriage

One of the motivations for living together is the opportunity to screen out a partner with whom marriage might not work. But do couples who live together before they get married have a greater chance of staying married than couples who do not live together before they get married? The answer is no. Based on a comparison of national samples of couples who did and did not live together before they got married, "the proportion separating or divorcing within 10 years is a third higher among those who lived together before marriage than among those who did not—36 versus 27 percent" (Bumpass & Sweet, 1989, 10). These results are similar to those reported by Demaris and Vaninadha Rao (1992) and by Booth and Johnson (1988) for U.S. couples and by Balakrishnan and colleagues for Canadian couples (1987). Other researchers have also found lower quality marriages (less happy, more conflict), lower commitment to the institution of marriage (belief that marriage is not a lifetime commitment), and greater perceived likelihood of divorce among couples who had cohabitated (Thomson & Colella, 1992; Stets, 1993).

One explanation for why cohabitants may have lower quality relationships, lower institutional commitment, and less hope for the future of their relationships is that cohabitation may draw people who are not ready to commit to each other or to the institution of marriage. Cohabitants may also have developed "bad habits with respect to the development and maintenance of a relationship, and these problems get imported into subsequent relationships" (Stets, 1993, 255). For example, they may have a greater tendency to withdraw from a relationship and separate rather than negotiating disagreements. Alternatively, "cohabitation may adversely affect relationship quality and/or weaken institutional commitment" (Thomson & Colella, 1992, 267).

Schoen (1992) also found higher divorce risks among first time marrieds who had previously cohabitated but noticed that this phenomenon was largely true of persons who were born before the late forties. Those who were born 1948–52 and 1953–57 who lived together and married did *not* show a significantly higher divorce risk. Schoen argued that this may be due to the fact that in earlier decades, cohabitation was practiced primarily by persons

who were less conventional and stable—characteristics that may be related to relationship instability. In more recent decades, cohabitation has been practiced by a wider range of individuals—not only those who are less conventional and stable. However, the respondents in the DeMaris and Vaninadha Rao (1992) study of cohabitation were from a 1972 high school cohort. This cohort did evidence a greater divorce rate, which is contrary to what Schoen (1992) would have predicted.

Divorce rates are higher among couples who live together before marriage for various reasons:

1. *Weaker commitment to marriage.* A Swedish study of 4,966 women found that "dissolution rates of women who cohabit premaritally with their future spouse are, on average, nearly 80 percent higher than the rates of those who do not live together" (Bennett et al., 1988, 132). In explaining this finding, the researchers suggested that persons who cohabit "may be unsure about, or ideologically opposed to, the institution of marriage itself, but who marry perhaps due to mounting external pressure" (p. 134). In other words, cohabitants may have a "weaker commitment to the institution of marriage" (p. 137).

   In another study, Schoen and Weinick (1993) compared partners in 157 cohabitations and 349 marriages and concluded that there is a "looser bond" between cohabitant partners than married partners. Specifically, the researchers observed that cohabitants (in contrast to marrieds) were less likely to be concerned about age, race, and religion in selecting a partner. ". . . we would argue that while cohabitors anticipate time together, married persons anticipate a lifetime. A different kind of relationship calls for a different kind of partner" (p. 413).

2. *False image.* In the chapter on Dating and Mate Selection, we noted that during courtship, individuals tend to selectively present their best self—they exaggerate their positive qualities and behaviors and minimize or conceal their negative ones. This tendency to present a false image in courtship also applies to living together couples who cohabit as a stage in the courtship process. After marriage, their real self may emerge and be a shock to the partner.

(continued on next page)

Cohabitants assume that because they are living with their partner that this is the way the partner is and will behave in marriage. This is not necessarily true.

3. *Role change.* When live-in lovers become spouses, they may find that their roles change. For example, cohabitants who had egalitarian role relationships may drift into traditional gender stereotyped roles after marriage. In addition, once live-ins assume the role of spouse, they may discover that they do not interact as well in the context of social and legal constraints as they did in a context of relative freedom.

4. *Willingness to violate social norms.* As we noted earlier, cohabitants tend to be people who are willing to violate social norms and live together before marriage. Once they marry, they may be more willing to break another social norm and divorce if they are unhappy than

unhappily married persons who tend to conform to social norms and have no history of unconventional behavior.

5. *Previous experience in terminating a relationship.* DeMaris and MacDonald (1993) found that the chance of divorce was higher when a spouse had been involved in a previous cohabiting relationship. The researchers suggested that the experience of having terminated a previous cohabiting relationship "enables one to be more willing to dissolve a subsequent cohabiting relationship—namely marriage" (p. 406).

These studies suggest that you should not live with a partner before marriage if your sole goal in doing so is to help ensure a happy marriage with that partner. There are no data to support such a causal relationship.

---

relationship, one partner manipulates the other in order to fulfill sexual, domestic, or other needs while withholding any semblance of commitment. There is little reciprocity, and the relationship becomes exploitative.

Living together partners may also feel used or tricked if their relationship does not lead to marriage. "I always felt we would be getting married, but it turns out that she was seeing someone else the whole time we were living together and had no intention of marrying me," recalled one partner.

> **CONSIDERATION**
>
> Because cohabitation is often an ambiguous relationship with partners attributing different meanings to the experience, the potential for feeling tricked or deceived is higher than in a marriage relationship, which usually has more clearly defined expectations.

Problems with Parents Some living together couples must contend with parents who disapprove of or do not fully accept their living arrangement. For example, cohabitants commonly report that when visiting their parents' homes, they are required to sleep in separate beds in separate rooms. Some cohabitants who have parents with traditional values respect their parents'

values and sleeping in separate rooms is not a problem. Other cohabitants feel resentful of parents who require them to sleep separately.

Some parents express their disapproval of their child cohabiting by cutting off communication, as well as economic support, from their child. Other parents display lack of acceptance of cohabitation in more subtle ways. One woman who had lived with her partner for two years said that her partner's parents would not include her in the family's annual photo portrait. Emotionally, she felt very much a part of her partner's family and was deeply hurt that she was not included in the family portrait (Authors' files).

Economic Disadvantages While some couples live together for economic convenience or advantages, other couples are economically disadvantaged by living together. For example, the tax structure and health care system tend to favor married couples over unmarried individuals.

When cohabiting couples split up, each partner is typically entitled only to assets in their own name, regardless of whether or not the partner helped to purchase the assets or contributed to the relationship in noneconomic ways (such as performing domestic tasks). Married couples who divorce generally have a right to an equitable share of any property acquired during the marriage.

Finally, if one member of a cohabiting couple dies, the other partner is typically not entitled to the social security or retirement benefits of the

SELF-ASSESSMENT ⚮

Living Together Consequences Scale

This inventory is designed to measure the degree to which living together may have positive or negative consequences for you and your partner. There are no right or wrong answers. After reading each sentence carefully, circle the number that best represents your feelings.

1 Strongly disagree   4 Mildly agree
2 Mildly disagree   5 Strongly agree
3 Undecided

	SD	D	U	A	SA
1. I have a fairly liberal background and living together is not against my values.	1	2	3	4	5
2. If we break up after living together without getting married, I will not be devastated.	1	2	3	4	5
3. I have thought a lot about the pros and cons of living together and feel that it is right for me and my partner.	1	2	3	4	5
4. I will not feel used if my partner breaks up with me and doesn't marry me.	1	2	3	4	5
5. I would not live with my partner as a way of getting back at my parents.	1	2	3	4	5
6. I want to live with my partner out of love, not out of convenience.	1	2	3	4	5
7. My partner and I have known each other for a long time.	1	2	3	4	5
8. I am not counting on living together to help us have a stronger relationship.	1	2	3	4	5
9. My partner and I have discussed our future.	1	2	3	4	5
10. My parents would not disown me if they found out that I was living with my partner.	1	2	3	4	5

SCORING: Add the numbers you circled. 1 (strongly disagree) is the most negative response, and 5 (strongly agree) is the most positive response. The lower your total score (10 is the lowest possible score), the greater the potential negative consequences of living together; the higher your score (50 is the highest possible score), the greater the potential positive consequences of living together. A score of 30 places you at the midpoint between the positive and negative consequences of living together.

NOTE: This Self-Assessment is intended to be thought-provoking and fun; it is not intended to be used as a clinical diagnostic measuring instrument.

deceased partner. The exception is if the couple have a common law marriage. (Common law marriages are discussed later in the section on legal rights of cohabiting partners.)

To assess the degree to which living together may have a positive or negative outcome for you and your partner, you can rate yourself according to the Living Together Consequences Scale in the Self-Assessment.

ॐ Legal Rights of Cohabiting Partners

In recent years, the courts and legal system have become increasingly involved in living together relationships. Some of the legal issues concerning cohabiting partners include common law marriage, domestic partnership, palimony, and child support.

Common Law Marriage

Despite the widespread assumption that heterosexual couples who live together a long time have a common law marriage, only 13 states and the District of Columbia recognize common law marriage. In these states (Alabama, Colorado, Georgia, Idaho, Iowa, Kansas, Montana, Ohio, Oklahoma, Pennsylvania, Rhode Island, South Carolina, and Texas), a heterosexual couple may be considered married if they are legally competent to marry and if there is agreement between the couple to live together with the intention of being husband and wife. A ceremony or compliance with legal formalities is not required. The amount of time a couple must live together before they are considered to have a common law marriage varies from state to state.

Domestic Partnership

In 1984, the city of Berkeley, California became the first municipality to enact domestic partner legislation. As of May 1993, about 25 cities, counties, and states allow unmarried partners to register as domestic partners (Scherreik, 1993). Domestic partnerships offer limited benefits and rights. For example, in New York City, domestic partner status extends unpaid maternity leaves to city employees and tenancy rights in rent-regulated housing.

The entitlements granted to registered domestic partners vary from place to place. Entitlements may include bereavement, sick, and/or parenting leaves as well as medical and/or dental health insurance benefits. Retirement benefits, family assistance, and discount buying privileges (e.g. "family memberships" to health clubs) are other benefits that may be given to registered domestic partners.

Palimony

A take-off on the word *alimony*, palimony refers to the amount of money one "pal" who lives with another "pal" may have to pay if the partners terminate their relationship. Palimony received national visibility in the early 1980s when Lee Marvin was ordered to pay Michelle Triola Marvin (with whom he had lived for seven years) $104,000 by the Los Angeles Superior Court for "rehabilitative purposes." Although the award was later overturned by the California Second District Court, a new era of palimony suits had begun.

Choosing to marry after cohabiting is usually based on personal desires (e.g. to increase commitment or have children) or social pressures (e.g. from parents).

MICHAEL NEWCOMB

In the past, partners in living together relationships had no legal rights in reference to each other. Today, such arrangements may be recognized as licit, and the parties can be held liable to each other and forced to pay money at the court's discretion. The primary factor in the court awarding palimony is the existence of a contract or agreement (written or implied) between the parties regarding their relationship.

Child Support

Individuals who live together and conceive children are responsible for those children whether they are married or not married. In most cases, the custody of the child will be given to the mother, and the father will be required to pay child support. In effect, living together is irrelevant in regard to parental obligations.

CONSIDERATION

Couples who live together or have children together should be aware that laws traditionally applying only to married couples are now being applied to many unwed relationships. Palimony, distribution of property, and child support payments are all possibilities once two people cohabit or parent a child.

℘ Trends

Living together has continued to increase over the last few decades. In 1970, 523,000 individuals in the United States were living together. By 1993, over three million were living together. This represents an increase of over 400 percent since 1970. Reasons for the increased rate of living together include people waiting until they are older to get married, becoming hesitant about marriage in the age of divorce, feeling that living together may not strain a relationship the way marriage does (Joe Pesci is living with his ex-wife and says that they get along better), and the increasing acceptance of living together by parents and institutions. As an example of institutional acceptance of cohabitating, Trinity College of Cambridge University has permitted unmarried students of the opposite sex to share two-bedroom apartments on campus. However, living together will probably not replace marriage, at least in the foreseeable future. Having children and being married are still very normative and many people who live together will most likely marry before they have a child.

Those who decide to live together are becoming more aware of the legal and economic implications of their doing so. This is particularly true of those who live together for a considerable period of time or who suggest to others that they consider themselves "married" in a spiritual sense. In such relationships and depending on the state, implied agreements between the partners may be enforceable. William Hurt, Nick Nolte, and Alice Cooper have all been sued by their former live-in partners.

Another trend is that "in recent years, employers—most in the nonprofit sector—have begun to offer the live-in partner of unmarried workers the same health-care and other employee benefits long available to spouses and children" (Scherreik, 1993, 33). These employers, which include the Manhattan newspaper *The Village Voice,* Levi Strauss & Co., and Ben & Jerry's Homemade Inc. may be setting a trend for other employers to extend benefits to cohabiting partners of employees.

~ CHOICES ~

Choices about living together include whether to live together, whether to maintain two residences, whether to tell parents, and how long to live together. Careful decision making may help to make living together a more positive experience.

Should I Live with My Partner?

There are three conditions under which you should probably not live together. First, if your values are such that you believe living together is wrong, the arrangement will probably have negative consequences for you. You may lose respect for yourself, your partner, and your relationship. Second, if you expect that marriage will result from living with your partner and you will be devastated if it does not, you should probably not live together. Living together is not equivalent to engagement, and it is not unusual for the partners who live together to have different goals about marriage. Even partners who view themselves as being engaged and who plan to marry may not do so after they have lived together. "I found out that I couldn't live with him," "I found out I didn't want to live with her," and "I found out I wasn't ready for marriage" are some of the comments made by those who live together but do not end up getting married. Third, it is unwise to live with someone you feel is exploiting you.

Aside from these three cautions, living together seems to have limited harmful effects and some beneficial ones. The primary benefit is that it may help partners to discover they are unsuited for marriage before they get married.

Should We Have One Residence or Two?

When partners drift into or decide to live together, they sometimes decide to maintain two residences. This arrangement furnishes a cover story for both sets of parents, a place for her to get her mail, and a haven to retreat to when conflict erupts in the relationship. One woman who maintained her own apartment said:

> I needed a place I could go back to—to call my own—and to see my friends. Having a place of your own is expensive, but it gives you flexibility by not putting all your eggs into the living together basket. I ended up breaking up with my partner, and I'm sure the adjustment was a lot easier because I had a place to retreat to when I needed it.

⌁ CHOICES ⌁

The disadvantage of maintaining a separate place may be the flip side of the advantages. If you have a place to retreat to, the skills of managing conflict with your partner may not be as easily learned. You can walk out when you want to, and your motivation for working things out may be lower. "I'm sure we would be apart," said one cohabitant "if I had not given up my dorm room. But because I had no place to escape to, we worked out our differences and have a stronger relationship for it."

Should I Tell My Parents I Am Living with My Partner?

The decision to tell parents about the living together relationship will depend on the parents, the relationship with them, the values of honesty and kindness, and the ability to hide the living together experience.

Some parents are very conservative and are devastated to learn that their son or daughter is in a living together relationship. One mother said:

> When we found out our daughter was living with her boyfriend, we were hurt more than we were shocked. We have a Christian home and always thought we had brought her up right. Her behavior was a slap in the face at everything that we had taught her.

Other parents don't approve of their children living together but view their doing so as part of the liberalization of our whole society. One father said:

> We know that a lot of young folks are living together these days. Our son went to one of these liberal colleges and learned all sorts of things we don't approve of. But we trust his judgment and don't figure that living together will hurt him. Besides, we would rather he live with his girlfriend than get married as young as he is.

Just as some parents are conservative and others are more liberal, the relationships offspring have with their parents will vary. "I've always been fairly open with my parents no matter what it was," said one cohabitant. But another said, "I can't tell my parents anything without them criticizing me, so I've learned to live my life and let them know as little as possible." Whether you tell your parents about your living together relationship will depend not only on who they are but also on your relationship with them.

The values of honesty and kindness are often in conflict when it comes to making a decision about telling parents about a living together relationship. If you value being honest with your parents, you will tell them you are living with your partner. But doing so may hurt them and give them a problem to live with. As an alternative to being honest, you might choose to be kind and not tell them, sparing them the burden of living with such information.

Axinn and Thornton (1993) predicted that children's experiences in cohabitation relationships would result in more positive parental attitudes toward cohabitation. Their prediction was based on the belief that parents who saw positive consequences for their cohabitating offspring and who did not wish to sever their relationship with their children would drift toward a positive view.

How Long Should I Live with My Partner?

There is no evidence to suggest that living together before marriage for any length of time is predictive of a successful marriage relationship. However, it is known that any relationships in which the partners have known each other for at least a year have a higher chance of marital success than relationships of shorter duration.

& Summary

Living together may be defined as two unrelated adults involved in an emotional and sexual relationship who sleep overnight in the same residence on a regular basis. Over three million unmarried U.S. couples currently live together (the percentage of individuals living together has increased over 400 percent since 1970).

Some unmarried couples live together as a stage in courtship or trial marriage. Others live together as a permanent alternative to marriage or for economic convenience. Increasingly, living together is being used as a trial marriage.

Couples who live together are more likely to be over 25, to be childfree, and to have less education than couples who do not live together. Some live-ins drift into living together relationships; others formally discuss living together first. Live-in partners tend to report high levels of satisfaction in their relationships and often divide housework along traditional lines. Many seem troubled that their parents do not know of their relationship but feel they would be disappointed if they did know. Other problems that live-in partners may experience involve children, loss of freedom, and violence or abuse.

Living together before marriage may be associated with marital instability because those who live together may be more prone to breaking norms. People who are willing to break social norms by living together may also be more willing to break social norms by divorcing if their marriage is not working for them. In addition, those who live together may have a weaker commitment to marriage.

Potential benefits of living together include a sense of well-being, delaying marriage until one is older, ending unsatisfactory relationships before marriage, gaining information about one's self and partner, and providing an easier adjustment to stepfamily living. Potential disadvantages include feeling used or tricked, problems with parents, and economic disadvantages.

A small percentage of unmarried couple households consist of those who are living together as a permanent alternative to marriage. These relationships may involve legal problems if they terminate, because the courts are increasingly willing to enforce implied agreements made by live-ins. Homosexual couples are prohibited by law to marry, and therefore have no choice but to view living together as a permanent alternative to marriage.

Trends in living together include an increase in the number of couples who live together and more lawsuits between those who live together and break up.

Questions for Reflection

1. To what degree do you feel that living together helps you to get to know a person? How willing would you be to live together before getting married?

2. To what degree do you feel our society should encourage people to live together before they get married?
3. What effect do you think living together might have on your subsequent marital relationship?
4. How much do you think the government should be involved in the enforcement of agreements between individuals who live together?

References

Axinn, W. G. and A. Thornton. Mothers, children, and cohabitation: The intergenerational effects of attitudes and behavior. *American Sociological Review,* 1993, *58,* 233–246.

Balakrishnan, T. R., K. V. Rao, E. Lapierre-Adamyck, and K. J. Krotki. A hazard model analysis of the covariates of marriage dissolution in Canada. *Demography,* 1987, *24,* 395–406.

Bennett, Neil G., A. K. Blanc, and D. E. Bloom. Commitment and the modern union: Assessing the link between premarital cohabitation and subsequent marital stability. *American Sociological Review,* 1988, *53,* 127–139.

Blumstein, Philip and Pepper Schwartz. *American couples: Money, work, and sex.* New York: William Morrow, 1983.

Blumstein, Philip and Pepper Schwartz. Intimate relationships and the creation of sexuality. *Homosexuality/Heterosexuality: Concepts of Sexual Orientation.* David P. McWhirter, Stephanie A. Sanders, and June Machover Reinish, eds. New York: Oxford University Press, 1990, 307–320.

Booth, Alan and D. Johnson. Premarital cohabitation and marital success. *Journal of Family Issues,* 1988, *9,* 255–272.

Bumpass, Larry and James Sweet. National Estimates of Cohabitation: Cohort Levels and Union Stability. NSFH Working Paper No. 2, 1989. Center for Demography and Ecology, University of Wisconsin–Madison, 4412 Social Science Building, 1180 Observatory Drive, Madison, WI, 53706.

Buunk, B. P. and B. Van Driel. *Variant lifestyles and relationships.* Newbury Park, Calif.: Sage Publications, 1989.

Coleman, D. and J. Salt. The British Population: Patterns, trends, and processes. Oxford: Oxford University Press, 1992.

DeMaris, A. and W. MacDonald. Premarital cohabitation and marital instability: A test of the unconventionality hypothesis. *Journal of Marriage and the Family,* 1993, *55,* 399–407.

DeMaris, A. and K. Vaninadha Rao. Premarital cohabitation and subsequent marital stability in the United States: A reassessment. *Journal of Marriage and the Family,* 1992, *54,* 178–190.

Dychtwald, Ken. *Age wave.* New York: Bantam Books, 1990.

Gibbons, J. A. Alternative lifestyles: Variations in household forms and family consciousness. *Family and Marriage: Cross-Cultural Perspectives,* K. Ishwaran, eds. Toronto, Ontario: Thompson Educational Publishing, Inc., 1992, 61–74.

Glezer, H. Cohabitation. *Family Matters,* 1991, *30,* 24–27.

Ihara, Tony and Ralph Warner. *The living together kit.* Berkeley, CA: Nolo Press.

Kotkin, M. To marry or live together. *Life Styles: A Journal of Changing Patterns,* 1985, *7,* 156–170.

Kurdek, L. The relations between reported well-being and divorce history, availability of proximate adults, and gender. *Journal of Marriage and the Family,* 1991, *53,* 71–78.

Landale, N. S. and Katherine Fennelly. Informal unions among mainland Puerto Ricans: Cohabitation or an alternative to legal marriage? *Journal of Marriage and the Family,* 1992, *54,* 269–280.

Larson, Jan. Cohabitation is a premarital step. *American Demographics,* 1991, *13,* 20–21.

Makepeace, James. Dating, living together, and courtship violence. *Violence in Dating Relationships,* M. A. Pirog-Good and Jan E. Stets, eds. New York: Greenwood Press, 1989, 94–107.

Montgomery, M. J., E. R. Anderson, E. M. Hetherington, and W. G. Clingempeel. Patterns of courtship for remarriage: implications for child adjustment and parent-child relationships. *Journal of Marriage and the Family,* 1992, 54, 686–698.

Ridley, C. A., D. J. Peterman, and A. W. Avery. Cohabitation: Does it make for a better marriage? *Family Coordinator,* 1978, 27, 129–136.

Rindfuss, R. R. and A. VandenHeuvel. Cohabitation: A precursor to marriage or an alternative to being single? *The Changing American Family,* S. J. South and S. E. Tolnay, eds. Boulder, Colo.: Westview Press, 1992, 118–142.

Risman, B. J., C. T. Hill, Z. Rubin, and L. A. Peplau. Living together in college: Implications for courtship. *Journal of Marriage and the Family,* 1981, 43, 77–83.

Scherreik, Susan. The practical part of living together. *The New York Times,* March 6, 1993, 142, 33(L).

Schoen, R. First unions and the stability of first marriages. *Journal of Marriage and the Family,* 1992, 54, 281–284.

Schoen, R. and R. M. Weinick. Partner choice in marriages and cohabitations. *Journal of Marriage and the Family,* 1993, 55, 408–414.

Statistical Abstract of the United States: 1993, 113th ed. Washington, D.C.: U.S. Bureau of the Census, 1993.

Stets, J. E. The link between past and present intimate relationships. *Journal of Family Issues,* 1993, 14, 236–260.

Stets, J. E. and M. A. Straus. The marriage as a hitting license: A comparison of assaults in dating, cohabiting, and married couples. *Violence in Dating Relationships,* M. A. Pirog-Good and Jan E. Stets, eds. New York: Greenwood Press, 1989.

Surra, C. A. Research and theory on mate selection and premarital relationships in the 1980s. *Contemporary Families,* Alan Booth, eds. Minneapolis, Minn.: National Council on Family Relations, 1991, 54–75.

Sweet, J. A. and L. L. Bumpass. Young adults' views of marriage, cohabitation, and family. *The Changing American Family.* S. J. South and S. E. Tolnay, eds. Boulder, Colo.: Westview Press, 1992, 143–170.

Thomson, E., and U. Colella. Cohabitation and marital stability: Quality or commitment? *Journal of Marriage and the Family,* 1992, 54, 259–267.

Wessel, H. Some live with those they divorced. *The Daily Reflector,* October 18, 1992, g-10.

Contents

7
CHAPTER

Lifestyle Alternatives

Is It True?

1. Marriage is no longer the preferred lifestyle among university students.

2. Commuter marriages are more likely to benefit the respective careers than the marriages of the spouses involved.

3. Homosexuality is more prevalent in the United States than in other countries and societies.

4. There are over 1,000 communes in the United States.

5. Lack of money is one of the biggest disadvantages of single parenthood.

1 = F; 2 = T; 3 = F; 4 = T; 5 = T

The way I remember it, traditional family values was encouraging children to be the best they can be. If your parents are black and white, if your parents are the same sex, that's still traditional family values to me.

GARTH BROOKS

"𝒟iverse" is the most accurate way to describe lifestyle alternatives today. The marriage of Julia Roberts and Lyle Lovett, the singlehood of Arsenio Hall, the homosexuality of Martina Navratilova, the commuter marriage of Phil Donahue and Marlo Thomas (until recently), and the single parenthood of over 9 million individuals are reminders that there is no relationship lifestyle chosen by all people. In this chapter we review the major alternatives and begin with marriage.

The fact that individuals define themselves in a significant way through their intimate sexual relationships with others suggests, in a Nation as diverse as ours, that there may be many "right" ways of conducting those relationships, and that much of the richness of a relationship will come from the freedom an individual has to choose the form and nature of these intensely personal bonds.

SUPREME COURT JUSTICE
HARRY BLACKMAN

𝒮 Marriage

Of all lifestyles, marriage is the most preferred. In a study of 821 undergraduate women and 535 undergraduate men (mean age of 20.2), 92 percent of the women and 83 percent of the men stated that they would like to marry by age 35 (Schroeder et. al., 1993).

Desire to marry may vary by race. In a national study comparing whites, blacks, and Hispanics ages 19 to 25, Hispanic men (4.61 on a five point scale) were the most interested in getting married and black men (3.88) were the least interested in getting married (South, 1993). Hispanic men saw marriage "as part of the *machismo* concept which stresses the importance of raising a family as an indicator of personal accomplishment and adult responsibility" (p. 368). Black men, on the other hand, saw marriage as restricting their sexual freedom and limiting their personal friendships. White women (4.40) wanted to marry more than white men (4.25) and black women (4.29) wanted to marry more than black men. Hispanic women also evidenced considerable interest in marriage (4.32). While there are variations, most people eventually marry.

NATIONAL DATA 𝒮 Of all American men (white, black, hispanic, and asian) age 75 and older, 96.5 percent have been married. Of all American women (white, black, hispanic, and asian) age 75 and older, 94.6 have been married (*Statistical Abstract of the United States: 1993*, Table 60).

Functions of Marriage

Marriage and the family have traditionally served several main functions in our society: to replace old members with new, socialized members; to regulate sexual behavior; and to stabilize adult personalities by providing companionship.

CONSIDERATION

The companionship-intimacy function of marriage has become more important as the form of marriage has changed. Unlike the traditional marriage, which was formal and authoritarian, emphasizing ritual and discipline, the egalitarian marriage is based on emotion, mutual affection, sympathetic understanding, and comradeship. The need for intimacy and companionship has become so strong that many couples consider divorce when they no longer feel "in love" or "able to communicate" with their partners. Other differences between the traditional and egalitarian marriage are presented in Table 7.1 It should be kept in mind that these are stereotypical marriages and that only a small percentage of today's marriages have all of the listed characteristics. This is particularly true of egalitarian marriages.

Recently, the traditional justifications for marriage have been questioned. There is little concern now that our society will "disappear" if people stop marrying. Children will continue to be born, and the increase in single-parent families suggests that the wife and husband team is not the only pattern for rearing children.

The argument that marriage tends to regulate sexual behavior is true, as most spouses have intercourse with each other most of the time. But again, the issue is children, and the development of contraceptive technology has made it possible for individuals to make love without making babies. It is the use of contraceptives, not marriage, that now prevents unwanted children.

Marriage has no natural relation to love. Marriage belongs to society; it is a social contract.

S. T. COLERIDGE

TABLE 7.1

Traditional and Egalitarian Marriages Compared

TRADITIONAL MARRIAGE	EGALITARIAN MARRIAGE
Emphasis on ritual and roles.	Emphasis on companionship.
Couples do not live together before marriage.	Couples may live together before marriage.
Wife takes husband's last name.	Wife may keep her maiden name.
Man dominant; woman submissive.	Neither spouse dominant.
Rigid roles for husband and wife.	Flexible roles for spouses.
One income (the husband's).	Two incomes.
Husband initiates sex; wife complies.	Sex initiated by either spouse.
Wife takes care of children.	Parents share childrearing.
Education important for husband, not for wife.	Education equally important for both.
Husband's career decides family residence.	Family residence decided by career of either spouse.

The emotional support each spouse derives from the other in the marital relationship remains one of the strongest and most basic functions of marriage. In our social world, which consists mainly of impersonal, secondary relationships, living in a context of mutual emotional support may be particularly important. Smart (1992) observed that spouses are particularly nurturing and supportive of each other at times of personal crises such as the death of an infant.

CONSIDERATION

Proponents of singlehood are quick to point out that not all spouses are emotionally nurturing and supportive of each other and that many nonmarital intimate relationships may be superior to marital relationships in regard to these characteristics.

Physical and Psychological Health Benefits of Marriage

Marriage (as compared to singlehood) is associated with higher levels of physical and psychological well-being. Coombs (1991) reviewed 130 studies comparing married people with those who were unmarried (never married, separated, divorced, widowed) and concluded:

> The published research on personal well-being reveals a consistent pattern: Married individuals, especially married men, experience less stress and emotional pathology than their unmarried counterparts. Studies of alcoholism, suicide, mortality and morbidity, schizophrenia, other psychiatric problems, and self-reported happiness generally support this thesis (p. 100).

One explanation of the correlation between being married and psychological well-being is that happy, cheerful, well-adjusted people are attractive marriage partners and are more likely to marry than are people who are psychologically or emotionally distressed (Mastekaasa, 1992).

Coombs (1991) identified another explanation for the correlation between marriage and physical and psychological well-being:

> Married individuals experience less physical and emotional pathology than the unmarried because they have continuous companionship with a spouse who provides interpersonal closeness, emotional gratification, and support in dealing with daily stress (p. 100).

Marriage may have more health benefits for men than women because "from childhood women are conditioned to look forward to marriage and, once wed, to be nurturing and provide supportive services for their husbands" (p. 100).

CONSIDERATION

When married men are compared to single men, they are happier, have higher incomes, and are healthier. However, when married women are compared with single women, the former have lower (personal) income, less occupational prestige, and worse mental health. Hence, marriage may be better for men than for women when compared to the alternative of being single.

Not all research has found that marriage is associated with higher levels of physical health. White (1992) studied the psychological and physical well-being of over 11,000 Canadians and found that while single individuals reported less subjective life satisfaction than marrieds, singles were more healthy (fewer ailments, fewer visits to physician) than marrieds.

In another study, Anson (1989) analyzed data from the National Health Interview Survey and found that individuals who live with another adult have fewer acute conditions and a lower frequency of being ill. The research by Anson clearly indicated the importance of a "proximate adult," not necessarily a marriage partner, for one's health.

Motivations for Marriage

Not only do the majority of women and men eventually marry, most women and men feel that marriage is important.

NATIONAL DATA ❧ When asked about the importance of marriage, 93 percent of adult women and 87 percent of adult men reported that marriage is "extremely" or "quite" important (Thornton, 1989).

The reasons most people are drawn to marriage include personal fulfillment, companionship, parenthood, and security.

Personal Fulfillment We are socialized as children to believe that getting married is what adult women and men do. Even if our parents are divorced, we learn that being married is what they wanted, but it didn't work out. Marriage often becomes a goal to achieve. Achieving that goal is assumed to give us a sense of personal fulfillment.

Companionship Many people marry primarily for companionship—for a primary group relationship. Primary groups are characterized by relationships that are intimate, personal, emotional, and informal (and hopefully happy). The family in which you grew up is a primary group.

Although marriage does not ensure it, companionship is the greatest expected benefit of marriage. Companionship is talking about and doing things with someone you love; it is creating a history with someone. "Only my partner and I know the things we've shared," said one spouse. "The shrimp dinner at

I do not . . . pretend to have discovered that life has anything more to be desired than a prudent and virtuous marriage.

SAMUEL JOHNSON BOSWELL

the ocean, the walk down Bourbon Street, and the robins that built the nest in our backyard are part of our joint memory bank."

Parenthood   Most people want to have children. In a study of 888 university students, 95 percent reported the intent to have children. This percentage has remained fairly consistent over a 15-year period at a large midwestern university (Rubinson & DeRubertis, 1991). Although some people are willing to have children outside of marriage (in a cohabitating relationship or in no relationship at all), most Americans desire to have children in a marital context. There is strong norm in our society (particularly among whites) that only spouses should have children.

NATIONAL DATA ❧ Eighty percent of all births to white women are to those who are married (*Statistical Abstract of the United States: 1993,* Table 101).

If money is all you want, money is all you'll get.

E. C. MCKENZIE

Security   People also marry for the emotional and financial security marriage can provide. However, marriage may no longer be a secure place. Since divorce in the United States can now be obtained by any spouse who wants one, marriage no longer provides the security—financial or otherwise—that it once did. Weitzman (1990) documented, and we will discuss in the chapter on divorce, that as a consequence of divorce law reform, women's economic status plummets following divorce.

The desire to have and rear children with a partner is an important motivation for marriage for some people.

Even though the security of marriage is declining, if divorce occurs the individuals are likely to remarry and to do so within three years (Ahlburg & De Vita, 1992). Regardless of the reason, marriage seems to offer what many people want and miss once they have experienced it.

CONSIDERATION

Although individuals may be drawn to marriage for reasons of security, companionship, etc., on the conscious level, unconscious motivations may also be operative. Individuals reared in a happy family of origin may seek to duplicate this perceived state of warmth, affection, and sharing. Alternatively, individuals reared in unhappy, abusive families may seek their own relationship to improve on what they observed in their parents' marriage.

Singlehood

Most adults in the United States eventually marry or remarry. While some adults never marry, even those who do may spend a significant part of their adult lives in singlehood.

Categories of Singles

When we think of the 50 million individuals in the United States who are currently not married, it is important to note that they are not alike. The different categories of single (i.e. unmarried) individuals include the never married, the separated or divorced, and the widowed.

Never Married Singles   Although most of the never marrieds will eventually marry, they represent the largest proportion of singles in the United States. Since 1980, there has been a dramatic increase in the percentage of men and women between the ages of 25 and 29 who are single. In 1980, 33 percent of the men and 21 percent of the women in these age ranges had never married; by 1991, these percentages had jumped to 49 and 33 percent respectively (*Statistical Abstract of the United States: 1993*, Table 60).

The never married singles include those who want to marry someday but not now, those who never want to marry, and those who want to get married but cannot find a partner. Some in this latter group are no longer young and the chance of their getting married is low. They would like to be married but are resigned to the fact that they probably never will be (Buunk & Van Driel, 1989).

Difficulty finding a marriageable partner accounts for singlehood among many black women. "Black women outnumber men in the ages when most people marry and start families, age 20 to 49" (O'Hare et al., 1991, 18). Not

> Advice to persons about to marry—Don't.
>
> HENRY MAYHEW

> Young people are marrying at older ages and more are foregoing marriage altogether.
>
> DENNIS A. AHLBURG
> CAROL J. DE VITA

only are there fewer black men available, those who are available may be victims of racial discrimination in hiring, firing, and salary advancement.

> The deteriorating economic position of black men has been blamed for further discouraging the formation of married-couple families. Black men, with low wages and little job security, have difficulty fulfilling the traditional role as the major breadwinner for a family (p. 18).

Black men that are single may be reluctant to marry. Indeed, the greater the number of available women, the less apt black men are to marry (Fossett & Kiecolt, 1993) since they may view marriage as restricting their sexual opportunities. The result is a high proportion of single black women when compared to single white women.

NATIONAL DATA   In 1990 the percent of never married black women age 30 to 34 was 35 percent in contrast to 17 percent of never married white women of similar age (O'Hare et al., 1992).

Never married adults also include homosexual women and men who are prohibited from being legally married.

CONSIDERATION

Some gay pair-bonded couples think of themselves as married, even though they are not legally wed. Some gay couples have formal ceremonies in which they exchange rings and vows of love and commitment. They may even refer to each other as their "husband," "wife," or "spouse."

It is better to be laughed at for not being married than to be unable to laugh because you are.

UNKNOWN

The dramatic increase in the number of singles is probably more due to those who would like to be married someday but, for now, are pursuing their education and employment opportunities. They also have considerable peer and societal support for remaining single. In addition, they have an array of contraceptives available, which means that many no longer feel the need to be married in order to have intercourse and avoid pregnancy.

CONSIDERATION

Two researchers suggested that singlehood has become a viable alternative and represents a revolution in what is going on outside the family.

> . . . unmarried people are experiencing the privacy, dignity, and authority (and sometimes the loneliness) of living in their own home rather than living in a family as a child, relative, or lodger (Goldscheider & Waite, 1991, xii).

In effect there is a new wave of youth who feel that their commitment is to themselves in early adulthood and to marriage only later, if at all. This translates into staying in school, establishing one's self in a career, and becoming economically and emotionally independent. The old pattern was to leap from school into marriage. The new pattern is to look, wait, and prepare before leaping.

Another reason for delaying marriage is the knowledge that some singles are very happy and some marrieds are very unhappy. Indeed, marrieds are reporting less satisfaction with being married.

NATIONAL DATA ❧ The percentage of U.S. husbands age 18 and older who reported that their marriages were "very happy" declined from 69.5 percent in the years 1973–1977 to 63.7 in the years 1984–1988. The corresponding percentages for wives in the respective years were 65.5 and 61.5 (Glenn, 1991).

> **CONSIDERATION**
>
> One of the explanations for a trend toward decreasing happiness reported by marrieds is that increasingly, "marrieds" are more often the serially married who report less happiness with each successive marriage (Kurdek, 1991).

Separated and Divorced Singles   There is a tendency to think of single people as only those who have never married. But statistics show otherwise.

NATIONAL DATA ❧ As a group, the divorced represent 8.8 percent of our adult population. In the United States, 8.6 percent of all white adults, 10.8 percent of all black adults, and 7.3 percent of all Hispanic adults are divorced (*Statistical Abstract of the United States: 1993,* Table 59).

For many of the divorced, the return to singlehood is not an easy transition. The separated and divorced are the least likely to say that they are "very happy" with their life: only 18 percent of divorced men compared to 36 percent of married men said they were "very happy." Only 19 percent of divorced women compared to 40 percent of married women said they were "very happy" (Glenn & Weaver, 1988). The divorced are also more likely to commit suicide than the married (Stack, 1990). However, after the initial impact of separation and divorce, most people remarry or adjust to and enjoy singlehood.

Widowed Single   Whereas some separated and divorced people choose to be single rather than remain in an unhappy marriage, the widowed are often forced into singlehood.

NATIONAL DATA ❧ In the U.S. adult population, 2.8 percent are widowed men; 10.3 percent are widowed women (*Statistical Abstract of the United States: 1993,* Table 59).

Living alone is not a great loss for many women, compared with a traditional marriage based on exchange (assuming they can maintain themselves financially); they have fewer rooms to clean and people to cook for, balanced against the loss of their partner's income.

FRANCES GOLDSCHEIDER
LINDA WAITE

Marriage is something the bachelor misses and the widower escapes.

F. M. KNOWLES

As a group, the widowed are happier than the divorced but not as happy as the married. Twenty-one percent of widowed men in contrast to 18 percent of divorced men and 36 percent of married men reported that they were "very happy." For women, 29 percent of the widowed compared to 19 percent of the divorced and 40 percent of the married reported that they were "very happy" (Glenn & Weaver, 1988).

Singlehood as a Lifestyle Choice

Singlehood may have different meanings to the never married, the separated, the divorced, and the widowed. While some view it as a lifestyle, others view it as a stage leading to marriage or remarriage.

Gibbons (1992) noted that singlehood in the Netherlands is viewed much more positively than in the United States. The "new ideologies that emphasize individual fulfillment over the importance of commitment to others may be making some impact on this alternative lifestyle" (p. 63). Alternatively, singlehood in Japan is not only viewed negatively but is associated with a higher mortality rate. Indeed, the death rate for the single person in Japan is three times as high as for the married person. Goldman (1993) suggested that this finding is an effect of the physically and mentally handicapped not being selected as spouses.

Some of the reasons why individuals elect to remain single and avoid marriage are reflected in Table 7.2

> I love the freedom that I have. I don't have to worry about a man's wardrobe, or his relatives, or his schedule, or his menu, or his allergies. I would not be married again.
>
> ANN LANDERS

~ ACROSS CULTURES

Single people are more free to do what they want, when they want.

TABLE 7.2
Reasons to Remain Single

BENEFITS OF SINGLEHOOD	DISADVANTAGES OF MARRIAGE
Feeling of self-sufficiency	Potential to feel dependent
Close friends of both sexes	Pressure to avoid opposite sex friendships
Spend money as wish	Expenditures influenced by needs of partner and children
Freedom to move as career necessitates	Restriction of career mobility
Freedom to travel	Travel restricted by family considerations
Responsibility for one's self only	Responsibility for spouse and children
Spontaneous lifestyle	Lifestyle sometimes too routine
Freedom to do as one wishes	What you do is restricted or influenced by spouse and children
Avoid emotional/financial stress of divorce	Possibility of divorce

---

↩ IN FOCUS 7.1 ↪

My Life as a Never Married Woman

At this point in my life, I enjoy being single. Of course, there are disadvantages to singlehood, but I like the privacy and independence that it affords me.

Singlehood gives me a tremendous amount of freedom and time. Since I am responsible only for myself, I can decide to relocate and/or continue my education. This freedom allows me to change, grow, and develop as a person. Part of my growth is dependent on maintaining diverse relationships, including male friendships. Being single, I can consciously choose to become romantically involved with males who would not be threatened by my male friends. Singlehood permits all sorts of small but important freedoms. For example, I can sleep late, read in bed, travel, visit with friends after work, and eat odd meals at unusual times. I also have the option not to prepare meals, clean the house, or answer the phone.

Being single has made me more aware of the importance of developing a positive self-image and learning to "pat myself" on the back. It has been essential for my mental health to develop a good support system and to confide in close friends. I have also discovered the need to be competent in traditionally male areas of expertise, such as car and house repairs. Learning simple tasks like replacing a windowpane, repairing the lawn mower, and tuning the car engine increases my self-confidence and sense of independence.

I feel comfortable with my single status after listening to some of my married female friends discuss what is expected of them in terms of their role as a wife and mother. This is not a feeling of superiority because being comfortable with my choice does not prevent an occasional sense of ostracism for not being married. Also, feeling good about myself does not eliminate all the anxiety I have about singlehood. For example, I wonder if I am possibly missing something wonderful by not having children.

One of the most difficult aspects of singlehood to cope with is the attitude and behavior of a few of my peers. The belief that being single indicates a personality defect makes me defensive about my lifestyle. Occasionally, I feel that I am viewed as a threat to married females, particularly if I have a professional relationship with their husbands. Also, my family is not completely supportive of my single status. Although my father was pleased and proud of my independence, his death removed much of my family support, and I believe that my mother and sisters would be relieved if I married.

The fact that I am single does not mean that I do not want a serious long-term relationship. However, being single is a challenge because, to be independent and to be comfortable enough to live alone, I have to like myself. So even though there are times I am lonely, overall I enjoy being single.

CONSIDERATION

However, there is a downside to staying single. One single woman observed, ". . . I am never invited to parties where there are married people and I don't have the constant emotional support when it is needed. I feel ostracized by the community and my relatives—grandparents, uncles, and aunts—urge me to settle down and get married" (Sparrow, 1991, 108).

In the past, if a man wasn't married, he must be gay; if a woman wasn't married, she must be undesirable. Now, going it alone has become socially acceptable, even chic.

JEAN SELIGMANN
TOM BARRETT

At the time this book went to press, Arsenio Hall, Linda Ronstadt, Al Pacino and Janet Reno (Attorney General under Clinton) are examples of individuals who had never married. The In Focus inserts 7.1 and 7.2 describe

---

IN FOCUS 7.2

My Life as a Never Married Man

I am not opposed to marriage. I am not opposed to courtship. I like women. I approve of women. I approve of men and women together. Despite much that I see to destroy my faith in old-fashioned love, I still believe in love—even if I have to admit I believe in that very outdated thing called "romantic love!"

I am 59 years old and I have never been married. I am an only child. I did not ever sit down and make a decision that I was never going to marry. I did not begin my life with the idea that I wanted to end it unmarried. I often think how nice it might have been had I married and had a family; but, perhaps I am something of a coward, for I often thank my lucky stars that I do not have a nagging "bitchy" wife and a house full of mean and ungrateful children! Somewhere along the line, I quietly decided that I did not wish to marry and I do not regret that decision. There is no history of divorce in my family. My parents and my grandparents were very happily married and well-adjusted people.

I do believe very much in the sacredness of marriage. I believe that marriage is a serious legal institution. I think of it as a legal commitment made by two people who have bonded themselves together—through vows or "oaths"—who have promised mutual respect, admiration, friendship, and love.

I am appalled at people today who seem to consider marriage as nothing more than an amusing arrangement that can be broken, discarded, and forgotten. I am shocked at people who, after 25–30 years of marriage, are seeking separations and divorces. I am constantly amazed at parents and children who do not seem to have any avenue of communication.

I must confess that I often feel grateful that I do not run the risk of falling "out" of love with a married partner. I have observed that far too many husbands and wives are strangers to one another and to their children. I have observed that often, today, only a fraction of life is actually lived in the home. When I was young, people still thought of their home as their "castle." Today, alas, castles and homes do not seem to provide the security they once did. I am an "old fogey" for I am shocked at the growing number of abortions and out-of-wedlock births, and the acceptance of unromantic and permissive sex.

I see so much so-called "love" that seems to be merely infatuation or sexual excitement. I am certainly very much aware of the "facts of life" but I still find myself shocked at the openness of today's "sexual freedom." I was reared in a long-ago era when one was still taught that it was not a sin to have sexual intercourse with one's marriage partner but it was a sin to have sexual relations outside of marriage. I was taught that marital partners should always be true to one another.

I think one of my "problems" is that I am an incurable romantic and romantics find it hard to adjust to the cold hard facts of the real world! Just as people who have never had children often feel they can give advice to parents as to how to rear their children, perhaps I, who have never been married, might be presumptuous and share with you my extremely "old-fashioned" ideas about love, courtship, and marriage.

In my own romantic, perhaps "foolish" way, I have always thought that courtship was a time when two people, attracted to one another, enjoyed each other's company and the company of their friends and if the friendship began to develop into love, then one began to think seriously of the other person as a lifetime mate and one gave careful consideration to mutual interests, backgrounds, goals in life, compatibility. One became increasingly aware of the possibility of uniting two lives, of trying to arrive at a complete understanding, a perfect partnership of democratic planning and mutual sharing. I have always felt that people who get married should be friends as well as lovers, that they should "like" one another as well as "love" or desire them.

I see many people (who are in marital situations) who take one another for granted. In my own romantic way, I have always felt that husbands and wives should remain affectionate, considerate, understanding, loving—even after the honeymoon is over. Somehow, I have thought that the "ideal" couple would always be as polite and courteous to one another as they were to their friends.

(continued on next page)

✄ IN FOCUS 7.2 ✄

I look about me and see parents who are deeply pained and hurt by the indifference and the rudeness and embarrassing behavior of their children and I am selfish enough to be glad that I will never have that problem. I see many parents as passive bystanders and others who are not sure how to go about being a parent. I see parents who work and sacrifice in order to provide their children with things the children often do not want or need or even appreciate and I am glad I will never have that experience.

I will never have to worry about dividing property—especially land and inherited possessions and I am glad I will not have to experience the bitterness, humiliation, and pain of divorce.

Philip Roth's autobiography relates that the author whistled on the way to his former wife's funeral and said at her casket: "You're dead and I didn't have to do it."

There was a time when a certain amount of pity and amused ridicule was felt toward the single person—the proverbial "old maid" or "sour old bachelor." Such people were thought of as eccentric and peculiar and "unwanted." The day of feeling sorry for the unmarried members of the family has long since passed away. Today, we see single people who lead perfectly happy and content lives, who maintain households and get along very well all alone. They have a freedom often envied by their married relatives. They have an affluence which is often a target of jealousy from those who have others to consider. It is not at all uncommon today to see a single man pushing a cart in a grocery store, washing clothes at a laundromat, cooking a meal for guests, setting a table, cleaning with a vacuum, entertaining guests.

One of my favorite modern plays is Arthur Miller's *The Price*. The theme of that drama is that for every decision we make in life, we pay a price. I chose not to marry and I have paid a price for it. I do sometimes think how nice it would be to have a family and I often wonder what will become of the things that I cherish—those things left to me as family heirlooms and those things which I have acquired. Since I am an only child, I have no one to leave the family items to who would appreciate them from the family standpoint. What I have will, very likely, at my death be sold at auction or distributed by lawyers amongst largely indifferent cousins.

The irony, of course, is that I would not have been able to travel throughout Europe, into Africa and Asia, Mexico and throughout the United States or been able to do so many of the things I have been able to do had I had a family!

So, indeed a "price" has been paid.

---

the experience of being single from the perspectives of a woman and a man who have chosen to be single.

Singlehood as a Stage

For most people, singlehood is not a permanent choice but a stage between various lifestyle choices they make throughout their lives. A fairly common pattern is for a person to experience singlehood, marriage, divorce (return to singlehood), living together, and remarriage. The decision to opt for any of these at any given time may be complex. Contributing to the selection of one lifestyle alternative is the perception of the positive and negative consequences of doing so compared to those of the other alternatives. The single person may be free but lonely and perceive marriage as worth the cost of lost freedom to gain

> It's a hard call to say whether living alone is a consequence of choice or a consequence of circumstance.
>
> JEANNE WOODWARD

companionship. The married person may be secure but bored and view the variety of singlehood as worth the cost of security. The person who lives with another may enjoy the spontaneity of "a relationship based on love, not law" but not like the lack of permanence of the relationship. Legitimizing the relationship through marriage may be worth risking the loss of some spontaneity.

Singlehood and HIV Infection Risk

Unmarried individuals who are not living with someone are at greater risk for contracting HIV and other STDs. In a national study comparing those who were not married (never married, divorced, separated, widowed) to those who were married or who were living together, the not married reported having more sexual partners and more "risky" sexual partners (Catania et al., 1992). While women typically report having fewer sexual partners than men, the men they have sex with have usually had multiple sexual partners. Hence, women are more likely to get infected from men than men are from women. In addition to the social reason, there is a biological reason—sperm, which may be HIV infected, is deposited into the woman's body.

Single Parenthood

The lifestyle alternative of single parenthood achieved national visibility during the 1992 presidential campaign when Vice-President Dan Quayle criticized the television sitcom, *Murphy Brown* for "glamorizing" what he viewed as a trend away from traditional family values. Murphy had made a creative choice to have a child without being married. Indignation from the CBS network to Tanya Tucker (a single mom) at Quayle's criticism reemphasized the value of alternative lifestyles.

Compared to previous decades, there are more single-parent families.

NATIONAL DATA ⚬ In 1991, there were over 9 million single-parent families, or one in eight families; these figures are double those of 1970. Women are five times more likely than men to be rearing a family alone; African-Americans are almost three times more likely than whites to be single parents (Ahlburg & De Vita, 1992).

> **Lone-parent families are families in their own right, and do not need reconstituting like a packet of mashed potatoes by adding the missing ingredient—in this case a man.**
>
> SANDRA SHAW

> **Middle–class social acceptance of unwed motherhood has grown.**
>
> JEAN SELIGMANN
> KENDALL HAMILTON

CONSIDERATION

In the past, single-parent families were regarded as "deviant" from the two parent norm. Derogatory terms such as "unmarried mothers," "fatherless families," and "incomplete families" suggested that such families were havens for delinquency and pathological development of children. More recently, single-parent families have begun to be considered by some as variations rather than deviations from the two-parent family.

The increase in single–parent families is related to three factors: the increased acceptance of children who are born outside of marriage, the changing sex ratio (there are currently 60 single men for every 100 single women), and the biological clock issue (Miller, 1993). In regard to the latter, the normal reproductive age of 15 to 44 (with the optimal years being 25 to 29), has meant that unmarried women (with no partner) near the outer range had to either give up the idea of having a traditional family or quickly decide to have and rear a child without a husband. Increasingly, they have chosen the latter.

Single-parent families develop from five avenues: involuntary unmarried childbirth, separation, divorce, widowhood, and by choice. While most women become single mothers by default, "many single women are having children by choice" (Sapiro, 1990, 313).

Single Mothers By Choice   While some single mothers by choice are in their teens, an increasing number of children are being conceived by single women over 30.

> For some of these women the reason for their choice is age. As they move into and through their thirties they worry that their biological aging will take away the choice to have a child. These women face important moral dilemmas: Is it right to marry a man just because one wants a child? Is this fair to the man? . . . Is it fair to the woman? (Sapiro, 1990, 313).

Many women who choose to be a single parent are either tired of waiting for "Mr. Right" or have no interest in finding him. "Most are women who have achieved a measure of economic self-sufficiency but have delayed childbearing to the point where they hear their biological clocks approaching midnight" (Smolowe, 1990, 76).

In 1989, one child in three was born to a mother over the age of 30 (Ahlburg & De Vita, 1992). One woman said:

> I could imagine going through life without a man, but I couldn't imagine going through life without a child. My biological clock started sounding like a time bomb (quoted in Smolowe, 1990, 76).

Another single mother by choice explained:

> My relationships were not developing along the course I had hoped. . . . I really love kids and feel I have a lot to offer (quoted in Smolowe, 1990, 76).

Jean Renvoize (1985) interviewed 30 unmarried women who made a conscious choice to have a baby with the intent of rearing their child alone. Of these women, the researcher said:

> I expected to find a group of tough-minded, militant women somewhat on the defensive; instead I found mostly happy, fulfilled, strong, but gentle individuals who gave out warmth and a readiness to share with others. There were women

An increasing number of women who are smart and educated are finding that there aren't enough men who are up to their standards.

ANDREW HOCKER

who had made their choice after much deliberation, mostly at a mature age, and who knew in advance that nothing in life comes free (p. 5).

The typical profile of the single mother by choice follows:

> . . . a white, educated, financially stable, professional woman who may have a prior history of marriage and/or pregnancy. She usually comes from an intact traditional family, although the parental marriage may have been conflictual (Miller, 1993, 22).
>
> . . . They are personable and have been able to develop strong and lasting friendships. They are sensitive and thoughtful and all too aware of the potential pitfalls that confront them and their children. They are also highly committed to their role as parents (p. 49).

Once a single woman has decided to have a child, she faces a choice of methods, including adoption, intercourse with a selected partner, insemination by a selected donor, or insemination by an unknown donor. Each of these methods may present certain problems. Adoption may involve an exhausting process of bureaucratic red tape and long waits. Adoption also means the woman has no biological ties to the child and does not experience pregnancy and childbirth, which she may view as advantages or disadvantages. If the father is known, there may be future legal conflicts over custody or access to the child. If the father is unknown, the woman may have less information about his background (although some sperm banks provide detailed medical and personal histories of donors). When the father is an unknown donor, many mothers wonder what to say to the child who asks who her or his father is.

An organization for women who want children and who may or may not marry is Single Mothers By Choice. The organization has more than 1,000 members and provides support for unmarried women who are contemplating the decision of whether to have a child. The organization also has "thinkers' groups" for women contemplating whether to have a child. Most women attending these groups decide *not* to have children after they have considered the various issues.

Challenges Faced by Single Parents   The single parent lifestyle involves numerous challenges. These may include the following issues:

1. Satisfaction of the emotional and disciplinary needs of the child. Perhaps the greatest challenge for single parents is to satisfy the emotional needs of their children—alone. Children need love, which a parent may express in numerous ways—from hugs to helping with homework. But the single parent who is tired from working all day and who has no one else with whom to share parenting at night may be less able to meet the emotional needs of a child.

   Single mothers also have no one to help them with disciplining their children. (It is recognized that there are also many coupled mothers who

The key thing for me in being a single parent was just wanting to have a child in my life, to love that child, and to understand what my priorities were.

A SINGLE MOTHER BY CHOICE

work outside the home and receive limited or no parenting help from their partner.) A single mother of three teenagers stated (Richards & Schmiege, 1993):

> In this day and age of child rearing it sure would be nice to be sharing the responsibility with someone else. I get tired of being a full-time policeman and everything else (p. 280).

When single mothers are compared with mothers living with partners, single mothers report more stress and more behavior problems with children. These single mothers also report more conflict with their daughters than with their sons (Webster-Stratton, 1989).

2. Satisfaction of adult emotional needs. Single parents have emotional needs of their own that children are often incapable of satisfying. The unmet need to share an emotional relationship with an adult can weigh heavily on the single parent. Shaw (1991) interviewed 25 single parent women and noted that loneliness was one of their concerns.

> Loneliness means lack of an adult companion to talk to, to hold, to be with, who loves them, who understands them, and puts them first, before anything else. . . . However, the fact that these women feel a need for "someone special" does not mean that they are more unhappy than other individuals in society who experience the same feelings. . . . On the contrary, they are for the most part extremely positive about themselves, and optimistic about their futures (p. 145).

Freedom means choosing your burden.

HEPHZIBAH MENUHIN

Custodial fathers comprise over 15 percent of all single-parent families.

3. Satisfaction of adult sexual needs. Some single parents regard their parental role as interfering with their sexual relationships. They may be concerned that their children will find out if they have a sexual encounter at home or be frustrated if they have to go away from home to enjoy a sexual relationship. A single mother explained her feelings (Richards & Schmiege, 1993):

> For a while, after being married for so long, it was difficult to adjust to being single, and I really . . . don't like the dating scene and all of that. So that was difficult to get used to. I would ask my single friends, "How do you have regular sex?" You know, what do you do? It was really major, after being with someone through my early adulthood; it was really difficult (p. 280).

Some choices with which they are confronted include: "Do I wait until my children are asleep and then ask my lover to leave before morning?" "Do I openly acknowledge my lover's presence in my life to my children and ask them not to tell anybody?" "Suppose my kids get attached to my lover, who may not be a permanent part of our lives?"

4. Lack of money. Lack of money is "the worst thing about being a single parent" (Shaw, 1991, 144). The problem is particularly acute when the single parent is a woman (Richards & Schmiege, 1993). The mean income for female-headed, single-parent families is considerably less than the mean income for two-parent families ($16,692 versus $40,000) (*Statistical Abstract of the United States: 1993,* Table 727). Male-headed, single-parent families are less economically stressed because men typically make more money than women ($28,351 versus $16,692) (Table 727).

5. Guardian. Single parents need to appoint a guardian to take care of their child in the event of death or disability.

6. Prenatal care. Women who decide to have a child without a male partner might be particularly sensitive to the prenatal care needs of their baby. In a national study of 56,596 infants, those who were born to single mothers were more likely to be born prematurely, to have low birthweights, and to die shortly after birth than those born to married mothers (Manderbacka et al., 1992). The researchers hypothesized that the reason for such findings may have been the lack of social support for the pregnancy or the working conditions of the mother. Alternatively, the researchers considered that it is possible that healthier people are more likely to be selected as married partners (p. 514).

There is no place like home if you haven't got the money to go out.

E. C. MCKENZIE

CONSIDERATION

Single motherhood is often discussed in negative terms. However, Shaw's (1991) respondents all reported positive aspects about being a single parent. These included being in control of their own lives and not having to answer to a husband, feeling independent and self confident, and an array of other issues such as . . .

> being able to watch what you want to on television, going to bed to sleep, not waking up every morning with someone's head on the pillow next to you, and not having someone there all the time, under your feet (p. 149).

In another study of single parents (Richards & Schmiege, 1993), 58 of 60 mothers and all 11 fathers were able to identify at least one strength of single parenthood. These included parenting skills (e.g. fostering independence), family management (e.g. coordinating schedules), communication (e.g. building trust and honesty), growing personally, and providing financial support.

Olson and Haynes (1993) interviewed 26 "successful" single parents (i.e. divorced men, divorced women, widowed men, widowed women, and individuals who had never been married) and identified seven themes (p. 262):

1. *Acceptance of the responsibilities and challenges presented in single-parent families:* Positive attitude toward parenting and life in general; problems neither minimized nor maximized, but solutions were sought.
2. *Prioritization of the parental role:* Focus on being the best possible single parent; sacrifices of time, money, and energy were evident.
3. *Employment of consistent, nonpunitive discipline:* Provide structure, democratic empowerment of children, and logical consequences for behaviors.
4. *Emphasis on open communication:* Promotion of trusting relationships and expression of feelings.
5. *Ability to foster individuality within a supportive family unit:* Fostering of individuality and independence; each member having own interests and skills.
6. *Recognition of need for self-nurturance:* Despite lack of time to take care of themselves, parents recognized the importance of self-nurturance and attempted to achieve it through physical, spiritual, emotional, or social means.
7. *Rituals and traditions:* Bedtime routines, special family activities, holiday celebrations.

℘ Homosexual Lifestyles

Considerable controversy surrounds the acceptability of homosexuality as an appropriate lifestyle. A *Newsweek* poll (1992) revealed that 53 percent of the respondents felt that homosexuality was *not* an acceptable lifestyle; 41 percent felt that it was an acceptable lifestyle. In Oregon, citizens were asked to vote on Measure 9, which would amend the state constitution to declare homosexuality as "abnormal, wrong, unnatural and perverse" (Foster, 1992). (The measure did not pass but a similar one did pass in Aspen, Colorado.)

Opposition to homosexuality as a lifestyle option has also been expressed by some citizens in response to the Rainbow Curriculum which is part of the instructional material for New York City's first graders. As part of the curriculum, lesbian mothers and homosexual fathers with their respective children are presented as appropriate alternative families. Those against the curriculum feel that it sends the "wrong message" to youth.

In spite of the opposition, some people are homosexual and prefer a homosexual lifestyle. In this section, we review the definition of homosexuality (and heterosexuality) and look at the nature of homosexual relationships.

Definition of Homosexuality/Heterosexuality

We define *homosexuality* or homoeroticism as the predominance of cognitive, emotional, and sexual attraction to those of the same sex. The term *gay* is synonymous with the term *homosexual;* it may refer to either males or females who have a same-sex orientation. More often the term *gay men* is used to refer to male homosexuals and the term *lesbian* is used to refer to homosexual women. The term *lesbian* originates from the ancient Greek island of Lesbos, where the poet Sappho taught young women to share the delights of their minds and bodies.

Heterosexuality or heteroeroticism refers to a predominance of cognitive, emotional, and sexual attraction to those of the opposite sex. Another term that refers to heterosexual is the word *straight,* from the expression "straight as an arrow," denoting adherence to conventional values and standards of behavior.

The primary distinguishing features of one's sexual orientation are one's cognitions (thoughts/fantasies), emotions (feelings), and sexual attractions (desires to touch/enjoy physically). However, other elements of sexual orientation may include sexual preference ("I choose a particular orientation"), recurring basis or stability ("My sexual preference is relatively stable"), and self-concept or self-identity ("I regard myself as having a particular sexual orientation"). One's behaviors may also be used to distinguish sexual orientation.

The distinction between homosexuality and heterosexuality is not as clear cut as it appears. In 1948, Kinsey and his colleagues suggested that sexual orientation may be understood as a continuum (see Figure 7.1, The Heterosexual-Homosexual Rating Scale).

Based on Kinsey's continuum, individuals with ratings of 0 or 1 are entirely or largely heterosexual; 2, 3, or 4 are more bisexual (also referred to as "omnisexual"); and 5 or 6 are largely or entirely homosexual. Using this continuum, it becomes clear that few people are entirely heterosexual or homosexual, but have gradations of thoughts, emotions, and behaviors in

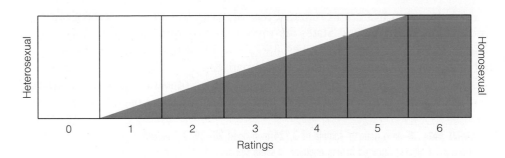

FIGURE 7.1
The Heterosexual-Homosexual Rating Scale
Source Kinsey, et al., 1953.

reference to the opposite and same sex. The following questions illustrate that "dividing people up into classes such as homosexual or heterosexual . . . ignores evidence suggesting that sexuality exists on a continuum" (Ross, 1987, 250). Which of the following individuals would you categorize as homosexual?

> Is it the young person who fantasizes about someone of their same sex in their class or on their school's swimming team? Is it the young person who has had a few sexual experiences with someone of the same sex? Is it the man who is married to a woman for years who occasionally has sex with men? Is it the woman who is married but unhappy with her sexual relationships with her husband and who has very close but non-sexual attachments to other women? What about the person who struggles against but never acts on desires for members of the same sex? What about those who feel an occasional sexual attraction to people of the other sex? (Blumenfeld & Raymond, 1989, 84).

CONSIDERATION

A symposium on the origins of homosexuality at Harvard Medical School was attended by a group of gay, lesbian, and bisexual students who referred to themselves as the "Kinsey 2-to-6-ers." They took their name from the one-to-six scoring Kinsey system mentioned above that identified "ones" as those who were exclusively heterosexual in both fantasy and actions (Wheeler, 1993). The existence of the group reflects the ambiguity of one's sexuality and the prevalence of those who do not conveniently fall into a 1 or 6 category.

Prevalence of Homosexuality/Heterosexuality

Accurate estimates of the prevalence of homosexuality are difficult to obtain because "societal intolerance [of homosexuality] may cause some survey respondents to conceal histories of same-gender sexual contact" (Fay, Turner, Klassen, & Gagnon, 1989, 338). Kinsey and his associates were the first to report same sex behavior.

NATIONAL DATA 🙠 Of 8,000 American women, 19 percent reported having had some sexual contact with other women, and 13 percent had experienced orgasm with another woman (Kinsey et al., 1953). Of 12,000 American men, 46 percent reported having had varying amounts of sexual activity with both men and women (Kinsey et al., 1948).

Homosexuality is neither mental illness nor mental depravity. It is simply the way a minority of our population express human love and sexuality.

BRYANT WELCH

Although it has been estimated that between five and ten percent of adult individuals in the United States are predominantly homosexual (Smith, 1991; Harry, 1990; Whitehead & Nokes, 1990), and that these rates are the same in all societies (Whitam, as quoted in Gelman & Foote, 1992, 52), more recent research has begun to suggest that the prevalence of same sex sexual behavior and exclusivity is much lower than previously thought (Rogers, 1993).

NATIONAL DATA   In a national sample of 3,224 men aged 20–39, 2.3 percent (2.4 percent of whites and 1.3 percent of blacks) reported having engaged in same sex sexual activity during the last ten years. Only 1.1 percent reported that they had only engaged in homosexual activity (1.3 percent of whites and 0.2 percent of blacks) (Billy et al., 1993).

Gay people (as well as straight people) are young and old, single and married, from all educational levels, occupations, income levels, races, and religions, and live in both large and small towns in all countries (Harry, 1990). There is a myth that a homosexual person is instantly recognizable because, it is believed, homosexual men are effeminate and lesbians are masculine. However, sexual orientation does not determine one's personality or mannerisms.

CONSIDERATION

Although gay marriages are effectively recognized in Denmark, nowhere in the United States are gay marriage licenses issued (Sherman, 1992). In addition, pair bonded gays are not allowed to receive annuity/pension plan and social security benefits. Discrimination against gays has its basis in history (only heterosexual unions have been officially recognized) and procreation (gays do not procreate and therefore do not help replenish the population).

"Causes" of Homosexuality: Biological or Social?

The predominant view regarding the development of sexual orientation is both biological and social. While individuals may be biologically predisposed to a particular sexual orientation, their social learning experiences may also influence their orientation. Any explanation that does not acknowledge the interaction of the biological and social components is incomplete.

Biological Explanations   Biological explanations focus on heredity and hormones. Regarding heredity, 87 percent of 402 parents of homosexuals believe that their children were "born that way" (Robinson, Walters, & Skeen, 1989, 69). The explanation that homosexuals are "born that way" reflects the theory that there is a genetic basis for homosexuality. Simon LeVay (1991) suggested such a basis as a result of scanning the brains of 41 cadavers (19 homosexual men, 16 heterosexual men, and 6 heterosexual women). He found that the portion of the brain thought to control sexual activity was half the size in homosexual men when compared with heterosexual men.

Temptation to flee into some sort of simplifying theory is a very old temptation.

MARTHA NUSSBAUM

The Lord is my shepherd and he knows I'm gay.

REVEREND TROY PERRY

CONSIDERATION

LeVay's research suggests more questions than answers. While he did document a difference in the brain structures of the hypothalamus, is this the basis for what makes people homosexual or heterosexual? Do the differences occur as a result of heredity or as a result of living a gay lifestyle? (Social influences may affect brain structure as people reading Braille after becoming blind have brains with increased size of the area controlling the reading finger.) If the differences occur routinely, when do they occur—prenatally, neonatally, during childhood, puberty, adulthood?

Another study that suggests a heredity basis for sexual orientation was conducted by J. Michael Bailey of Northwestern University (Department of Psychology) and R. C. Pillard of Boston University (School of Medicine). They found that of 56 identical male twins, if one was gay the other was almost three times more likely to be gay than if the twins were fraternal (Gelman & Foote, 1992). Similarly, in their study of 108 lesbians with twin sisters, almost half (48 percent) of the identical twin sisters were also lesbians. Only 16 percent of the lesbians' fraternal twin sisters and 14 percent of other biological sisters were also homosexual (Bailey, Pillard, Neal, & Agyei, 1993).

While these findings are impressive, they also create questions. What about the identical twins whose sexual orientations were different? If sexual orientation is genetic and two individuals have the same genetic makeup, their sexual orientation should be the same. Social or family differences might be suggested for the differences. But since both lesbians and nonlesbians as well as gay men and heterosexual men came from the same families, if social background is the determining factor, there should be a consistent sexual orientation produced by the same family background. We are left with the conclusion mentioned earlier that both biological and social factors are involved and how much of which is more critical is unknown. Social disapproval for homosexuality certainly accounts for a lack of expression for some individuals. "Men may have to have an overwhelming desire for other men, some social scientists say, to risk the scorn they may face if they express that desire" (Wheeler, 1993, a12).

There is also some evidence (as well as questions) about the degree to which hormones influence one's sexual orientation. Ellis and Ames (1987) believe that hormonal and neurological factors operating prior to birth (between the second and fifth month of gestation) are the "main determinants of sexual orientation" (p. 235). While these researchers do not deny that environmental factors also play a role, they assert that "very unusual postnatal experiences would be required to overcome strong predispositions toward either heterosexuality or homosexuality" (p. 235). According to Ellis and Ames, individuals do not learn to be heterosexual or homosexual; rather, they learn how, when, and where their sexual orientation is expressed.

Homosexuality has been a significant part of human sexual activity ever since the dawn of history, primarily because it is an expression of capacities that are basic in the human animal.

ALFRED KINSEY
WARDELL POMEROY
CLYDE MARTIN

Byne and Parsons (1993) reviewed recent research on the biological origin of sexual orientation and concluded, "there is no evidence at present to substantiate a biologic theory" (p. 228). Rather, they suggested that "personality traits interact with the familial and social milieu as the individual's sexuality emerges" (p.228).

Social Learning Explanations   Social learning theory emphasizes that individuals learn their sexual orientation. Many of these learning experiences occur in childhood. Money (1988) suggested that heterosexual children have been rewarded for expressing heterosexual scripts (playing house where the assigned roles are "mommy" and "daddy") and punished for same sex behavior (playing doctor with a same sex peer). Likewise, children who are punished for playing heterosexual games and acting out heterosexual scripts may suppress their heterosexual orientation. Without an outlet for heterosexual expression, they may drift toward homosexuality. Since homosexual behavior often occurs out of the sight of the parental eye, it goes unpunished and may develop as an alternative to heterosexual expression.

CONSIDERATION

Although some childhood and adolescent experiences may predispose a person to homosexuality, no one specific background characteristic seems to cause a person to become homosexual. Some heterosexual males played with dolls and were called sissy by their peers, and some heterosexual women were tomboys. In essence, childhood and adolescent experiences alone account for very little of the variance in explaining how a person becomes a homosexual (Boxer & Cohler, 1989).

The development of one's sexual orientation may also be explained by social psychological variables such as the self-concept and self-fulfilling prophecy. For example, an early adolescent homosexual experience may be influential in encouraging a person toward homosexuality if the experience is labeled by the adolescent or by others as evidence of homosexuality. Homosexual contacts in childhood and adolescence are not unusual in the process of growing up. However, some children who have sexual experiences with persons of their own sex may see these experiences as evidence of their homosexuality. Once individuals label themselves or are labeled by others as homosexuals, they may become locked into a self-fulfilling prophecy whereby their actions and identity conform to the label *homosexual*.

Gay Male Relationships

One common stereotype about gay men is that they are sexually promiscuous and do not have long-term committed relationships. However, many gay men do establish long-term committed relationships. In a study of 560 long-term gay male relationships, the average length of their relationship was seven years. Ninety-six percent reported that they were committed to be together "a long time," and 76 percent reported that they were committed for "life" ("National Survey Results," 1990).

Unlike heterosexual couples, homosexual couples receive little social support for continuing long-term relationships. For example, gay couples do not have the institutional support of legal marriage. Family members, who may provide support for heterosexual unions, often do not provide such support to homosexual couples. With 1 = strong support and 7 = hostility, the 560 couples in the long-term relationship survey gave their fathers and mothers 2.98 and 3.37 ratings respectively ("National Survey Results," 1990).

> **CONSIDERATION**
>
> Being sexually active with numerous partners is often condoned or approved in heterosexual men, yet the same behavior is condemned in homosexual men. "This double standard becomes clear when we consider terms which our culture uses to refer to promiscuous heterosexual men: 'Don Juan,' 'lady-killer,' or 'stud,' . . . (Blumenfeld & Raymond, 1988, 376). In contrast, the term promiscuous, when applied to gay males, has a negative connotation.

When gay male couples in one study were asked about the degree to which they had a monogamous or sexually open relationship, 96.4 percent reported that they were monogamous. Most also acknowledged a significant impact from the AIDS crisis on their decision to be sexually exclusive. "Many couples said the crisis had brought them closer together and increased appreciation for their partner" (Berger, 1990, 44). However, 69 percent of the couples said that they did not use condoms—they either felt that they were safe (because of a negative HIV test) or that they had already been exposed and subsequent exposure would make no difference (Berger, 1990).

Gay Female Relationships

Like many heterosexual women, most gay women value stable, monogamous relationships that are emotionally, as well as sexually satisfying. Transitory sexual encounters among gay women do occur, but they are the exception; not the rule. In a study of long-term gay relationships, five years was the average length of the relationship of 706 lesbian couples; 18 percent reported that they had been together 11 or more years. Ninety-one percent reported that they were sexually monogamous ("National Survey Results," 1990). The majority (57 percent) of the women in these lesbian relationships noted that they wore a ring to symbolize their commitment to each other. Some (19 percent) acknowledged their relationship with a ceremony. Most met through friends or at work. Only four percent met at a bar.

Maintaining a relationship in a society which discourages permanence is difficult enough for heterosexuals, but for gay people who generally receive no support for their efforts from family, employers, the church, or the state, the task can seem impossible.

BRIAN MCNAUGHT

Why is it that people are willing to go to a movie and watch someone get blown to bits for no reason and nobody wants to see two girls kissing or two men snuggling?

MADONNA

Like most heterosexual women, gay women emphasize the emotional/intimate aspects of their relationships.

Women in our society, gay and straight, are taught that sexual expression "should" occur in the context of emotional or romantic involvement. Ninety-three percent of 94 gay women in one study said their first homosexual experience was emotional; physical expression came later (Corbett & Morgan, 1983). Hence, for gay women the formula is love first; for gay men sex first—just as for their straight counterparts.

While gay female relationships normally last longer than gay male relationships, long-term relationships (20 years or more) are rare. Of 706 lesbian couples, only one percent had been in relationships lasting over twenty years ("National Survey Results," 1990). Serial monogamy—one relationship at a time—was the predominant pattern and 6.6 years was the average relationship duration.

When lesbians engage in extrapartner sexual relations, they (like heterosexual women) are likely to have emotional/sexual affairs rather than just sexual encounters. Nonmonogamy among lesbian couples is also likely to be related to dissatisfaction with the primary relationship. In addition, both lesbians and gay men are more likely than heterosexual couples to be open with their partners about their extrapartner activity (Nichols, 1987a).

Sexual Orientation and HIV Infection

HIV infection remains the most threatening STDs for male homosexuals and bisexuals. While homosexual males and bisexuals are at great risk for HIV infection, lesbians are at virtually no risk from female-to-female contact.

In an effort to document the degree to which homosexuals are at risk, Connell and Kippax (1990) interviewed 535 gay and bisexual men in New South Wales, Australia. When asked what percent had anal intercourse without condoms with a regular partner and with a casual partner, the percentages were 31 and 24 percent respectively. These percentages suggest that these gay men evidenced greater caution with casual partners. In addition, there is evidence that increased use of safe sex practices are increasing regardless of who the partner is. When asked if they had ever had anal intercourse without using a condom, 95 percent of the males responded "yes." When asked if they had done so in the last six months, 48 percent had done so.

More recent data on gay men, lesbian women, and heterosexuals who frequent bars further emphasize that sexual behavior is changing (Juran, 1991). Based on data from 71 gay men, 94 percent reported that they had changed their sexual behavior with 61 percent reporting use of condoms in the last two years and a quarter reporting they no longer engage in casual sex. Of 65 lesbians and bisexual women, one quarter said that they have less frequent casual sex and one quarter said that they no longer have sex with men. Heterosexual men and women also reported decreasing casual sexual contacts and increasing condom use (Juran, 1991). These data give support for the belief that homosexuals and heterosexuals are increasing their use of safer sex practices.

🥀 Other Lifestyle Alternatives

In this section we review other lifestyle alternatives, including communes, group marriage, and commuter marriage. At the end of this section, the Self-Assessment (Lifestyle Preference Inventory) allows you to assess the lifestyle that you prefer.

Communes

Single individuals and married couples (with or without children) may choose a lifestyle that includes living with numerous others and join a *commune*. Also referred to as an *intentional community*, a *collective*, or a *cooperative*, a commune is a group of three or more adults with no legal or blood ties who live together by their own choosing.

NATIONAL DATA 🥀 There are over 1,000 communes in the United States (Pitzer, cited in Quatrella, 1990).

> We will discover the nature of our particular genius when we stop trying to conform to our own or other people's models, learn to be ourselves, and allow our natural channel to open.
>
> SHAKTI GAWAIN

A listing of 350 North American communes and more than 50 communes on other continents is available in the *Directory of Intentional Communities,* from Sandhill Farm, Route 1, Box 155, Rutledge, Missouri 63563. Groups may have as many as 300 members such as the Farm in Summertown, Tennessee. More often, communes are much smaller. One of the most enduring communes is Twin Oaks Community in Louisa, Virginia which has been in existence over twenty years. One of the notable characteristics of Twin Oaks is that the decision to have a child must be approved by the 60 to 75 adult members of the community.

Individuals who decide to join a commune have a philosophical perspective compatible with contemporary communities. Some of the principles common to today's communes include (Quatrella, 1990):

- commitment to personal and planetary transformation
- cooperation
- respect for the environment
- experimentalism in work and relationships
- common sense approach in solving problems of pollution, inflation, violence, and alienation
- holistic health
- positive vision and setting an example for a better society
- self-government by consensus

CONSIDERATION

Most individuals who become involved in a communal lifestyle do so for only a brief time (a year or two) in their lives. "It appears that after the initial high levels of dedication and intense participation wear off, members often become disenchanted" (Buunk & Van Driel, 1989, 131). Indeed, it is rare that a commune survives at all. According to Dr. Donald E. Pitzer, executive director of the National Historic Communal Societies Association, 100,000 communal groups have formed in the United States since 1965. Of these only a small percentage have survived (Quatrella, 1990).

For individuals who want a communal like experience during the summer, The Omega Institute provides a retreat for 10,000 participants every summer. Stefan Rechtschaffen, the co-founder and director, noted that it is "a place of spirit where people can come and feel nurtured and learn on all levels of their being" (The Omega Institute, 1993, 52).

Group Marriage

While the principles listed above are common to many communes, sexual sharing is rare. When individuals in a group living arrangement (minimum of 3) agree to open sexual access to each other, they are involved in a group marriage (these are not legal). As noted in Chapter 1, the Oneida Community featured group marriage. John Humphrey Noyes, its founder, made clear his nonexclusive view of marriage:

> We can enter into no engagements with each other which shall limit the range of our affections as they are limited in the matrimonial engagements by the fashion of this world (Noyes, 1931, 17).

In the 1870s there were about 300 adults in the Oneida Community each of whom was considered married to each other. They called their arrangement *complex marriage* and used withdrawal as a form of birth control. Unique pair bonding did not occur and the decision of who would bear children was decided by a committee. Being young and beautiful were the primary qualifications for getting permission to conceive as a woman; being spiritually mature was the chief qualification for being selected as a father. *Stirpiculture* ("the breeding of special stocks or races") was the term used to describe Oneida's eugenics program. Fifty-eight children were born under this system (Sill, 1990).

Because of dissatisfaction among some of the members preferring conventional marriage and pressure from the outside by local clergy, the idea of complex marriage was dropped. Many members subsequently married. This commune existed from 1846 to 1880, a period of over 30 years.

A modern day example of group marriage is the Kerista commune in San Francisco founded by Bro Jud in 1971. It currently has 28 members who practice what they call *polyfidelity*.

It calls for a lifetime commitment not to one partner but to a group called a Best Friend Identity Cluster (B-FIC). The commune thus is not one large group marriage as the Oneida, but currently includes three Best Friend Identity Clusters as well as some persons not affiliated with any B-FIC. A new member of Kerista may apply for membership in a B-FIC. Membership in a cluster is granted only with unanimous agreement of B-FIC members. A three-month period of transitional celibacy is observed by a new member before beginning sexual relations within the B-FIC. This period allows time for STD and HIV tests (Sill, 1990).

Eve, who helped in the development of the commune, observed the advantages of polyfidelity:

1. It combines the best features of traditional marriage (lasting intimacy, trust, depth of relationships, secure home life) with the best features of the open lifestyle (variety and excitement).
2. It's a way for nonmonogamous persons to avoid STDs, as all members are screened for HIV and other STDs and there is fidelity within the group (Sill, 1990).

In spite of its presumed advantages, group marriage seems to hold little interest for college students. Out of 526 college students, five percent of the men and one percent of the women reported a willingness to participate in a group marriage (Billingham & Sack, 1986).

> To appreciate openness, we must have experienced encouragement to try the new, to seek alternatives, to view fresh possibilities.
>
> SISTER MARY LUKE TOBIN

Commuter Marriage*

As a result of more women pursuing careers (and men being supportive of wives who do so), some couples will have two careers in one marriage. When the careers of the respective partners are in different geographic locations, the couple may choose a commuter marriage. One of the most visible commuter marriages in our society was between Phil Donahue (in Chicago) and Marlo Thomas (in New York), who commuted to and from one another for four years until Donahue moved his program to New York.

NATIONAL DATA ❧ It is estimated that over 600,000 couples (one percent of all U.S. married couples) have commuter marriages (Carter, 1992).

Characteristics of Commuter Marriages   Four characteristics help to define commuter marriages: equal career commitment, distance, and a preference for living together (Gerstel & Gross, 1984).

EQUAL CAREER COMMITMENT.   In commuter marriages, both spouses are equally dedicated to the advancement and success of their respective careers. Her career is as important as his career. Like Brutus, who said of Caesar in Shakespeare's *Julius Caesar,* (Act III, Scene two) it's "not that I loved Caesar less, but that I loved Rome more," spouses in commuter marriages might say it's not that they love each other less but that they love their careers more.

The degree to which work represents a meaningful part of a commuter spouse's life is illustrated by a wife who said:

> I go to pieces when I don't work. I get bored when I am not working. We probably work too hard and occasionally feel guilty about it. But we're not the kind of people who can just relax. We think we have to do something (Gerstel & Gross, 1984, 33).

DISTANCE.   In commuter marriages, the distance between the spouses is great enough to require the establishment of two separate households. Commuter spouses cannot live in the same place and commute to their separate work places. They must live near their work and commute to see each other. The distance can range from 200 miles for domestic marriages to 5,500 miles for bicoastal marriages.

PREFERENCE FOR LIVING TOGETHER.   Although separated in reference to their careers, spouses in commuter marriages wish they could be together. They are not separated because they are having marital problems or are drifting toward a divorce. They look forward to an undefined time in the future when they can

---

*Information from Gerstel and Gross (1984) based on and reprinted by permission of the publisher of *Commuter Marriage* by N. Gerstel and H. Gross. Copyright © 1984 by The Guilford Press, New York.

have their careers and live together, too. In the meantime, they spend a lot of time, energy, and money traveling across the country so that they can be together. It is not unusual for commuter partners to spend about $6,000 per year traveling to be with each other (Gerstel & Gross, 1984).

Commuters also recognize the costs of not pursuing their careers. Each spouse feels as though both partners, individually and as a couple, would suffer if they did not pursue their career interests independently. One commuting wife said:

> I'd be miserable if I knew I gave up the opportunity to reach my career potential. I was reared in a home in which my mother had a career, and I was taught to pursue my career goals to the fullest. My dad was always supportive of my mother's career, so I always expected my husband to be supportive of my career.

Unique Problems in Commuter Marriages   When dual career couples in commuter marriages are compared with dual career couples who have the same residence, the former report less marital and family happiness (Bunker et al., 1992). Some of the problems experienced by commuter couples are examined in the following sections.

FRAGMENTED CONVERSATIONS.   Because commuters don't return to the same house each evening, their spouse is not there to share the intimate details of life and work. Most miss the presence of their partner and use the telephone as a substitute for face-to-face interaction. In one study, 42 percent of commuter spouses phoned each other every day, and 30 percent called every other day (Gerstel & Gross, 1984).

But just as spouses who live together don't always view their communication positively, neither do commuters. One husband recalls:

> Sometimes she will call me, and I'll be really tired. I just won't have any life in me. And she'll want something more from the call. There's a clashing. Or it happens the other way around. I'll feel good, and she'll be focused on something she's doing. It's hard to shift gears to get into someone else's mood when there is no forewarning and the phone call will soon be over (Gerstel & Gross, 1984, 58).

LACK OF SHARED LEISURE.   Each partner in a commuter marriage can talk with the other during the week, but going out to dinner, seeing a movie, or attending a concert or play with the spouse is not an option. Each spouse often misses not being able to spend leisure time with the other partner. Due to this high companionship need, most commuter spouses get together on weekends.

MARITAL SEX.   Commuter spouses obviously are not sexually available to each other every evening. But even spouses who live together rarely have intercourse every night. In commuter marriages, however, the partners' options of when they can have sex are compressed into smaller time periods. Even when the partners are not in the mood, they may feel that they should have sex because the weekend will soon be over. This places the unrealistic burden on the relationship that the limited time the couple does spend together should be perfect.

Some commuting women and men also experience the "stranger effect," reporting that they need a period of time to reacquaint themselves with their partner before they feel comfortable about having sex. "It takes me at least a day to feel close to him again," said one woman.

CHILDREN. Children may be an additional problem for the commuter couple. In most cases, young children will stay in the home of one parent, in effect making a single parent out of one spouse. Although some spouses enjoy the role of primary caregiver, others feel resentful of the spouse who is unhampered by the responsibilities of childrearing.

Benefits of Commuter Marriages In spite of the problems, there are benefits to a commuter marriage. We will address some here.

HIGHER HIGHS. "I'd rather have two terrific evenings a week with my spouse than five average ones," illustrates the view that the time commuter spouses have for each other is, in some ways, like courtship time—more limited but definitely enjoyable. Each spouse makes a special effort to make the time they have together good time. Some commuter partners feel the periods of separation enhance the love feelings in their relationship. One woman said:

> It's added some romance. There are a lot of comings and goings. We give each other presents. When I come home, there's a huge welcome. And there are tears at parting. I usually arrive looking exhausted. Show up completely collapsed. And my husband has a bottle of wine, no kidding, with a bow around it and flowers or a bottle of Chanel. And he makes a bath for me (Gerstel & Gross, 1984, 76).

LIMITED BICKERING. To ensure that the limited time is positive, commuters often make a point of avoiding petty bickering that sometimes creeps into the relationships of spouses who see each other every day. "We just don't want to argue over the laundry when we're together. We don't want to spoil the time we have together," said one commuter.

GREATER SATISFACTION WITH WORK. In one study, 90 commuters (defined as apart overnight for more than two nights a week) and 133 single resident dual career respondents were asked how satisfied they were with their work situation, their job, the time they have available for their work, the ability to be the worker they want to be, and the degree to which they meet the supervisor's work expectations (Bunker et al., 1992). Commuters gave more positive answers to each of the questions suggesting much greater job satisfaction than two earner couples in the same residence.

Lifestyle Preference Inventory

Below is a list of lifestyle choices. To indicate your preference, assign a number from 0 to 10 for each lifestyle (0 = no desire to experience this lifestyle; 10 = a strong desire).

Lifestyle	Preference
Sexually monogamous	_____
Sexually open	_____
Singlehood	
Single until meet "right" person	_____
Single until establish career	_____
Single forever	_____
Marriage	
Be married	_____
Traditional roles	_____
Shared roles	_____
One income or career	_____
Two incomes or careers	_____
Group marriage	_____
Sexual Orientation	
Heterosexual	_____
Homosexual	_____
Bisexual	_____
Children	
None	_____

Lifestyle	Preference
One	_____
Two	_____
Three	_____
Four or more	_____
Live Together	
To further assess relationship	_____
As a prelude to marriage	_____
As a permanent alternative to marriage	_____
For economic convenience	_____
Housing	
Live alone	_____
Live with someone of same sex	_____
Live with someone of opposite sex	_____
Live in commune	_____

Based on the preferences you selected, write a brief description of the lifestyle you prefer. If you are involved in a relationship, also ask your partner to indicate her or his preferences for each of these lifestyles.

NOTE: This Self-Assessment is intended to be fun and thought provoking, it is not a clinical or diagnostic instrument.

MORE PERSONAL TIME.   In the same study above, spouses in commuter marriages also reported that having more personal time to do what they want was a benefit of their lifestyle (Bunker et al., 1992). The presence of a spouse in the evening necessarily involves negotiation with the spouse about how time is to be spent. With no one else there, one's personal time is not compromised by family relationships or obligations.

Several factors influence the degree to which commuter couples are satisfied with their lifestyle. Based on a study of 39 commuter couples, Anderson (1992) found that couples who are satisfied with the commuter lifestyle tend to respond well to spending time by themselves and are able to

---

Lifestyle Patterns in Korea

My name is Kwangho Choe and I was born in Korea. Our country is very different than yours in a number of ways.

SCHOOL

Boys and girls, even in high school, are rarely ever in the same classroom. As a result, they establish close friendships with same-sex peers and have little opportunity to interact in opposite-sex contexts.

DATING

Most Korean boys and girls do not date in the sense of going out alone together. They mostly go out in same-sex groups. Korean men must go away for a three-year military service, which results in few close relationships before male military service is complete. Most men marry around age 28; women around age 23. Korean couples never live together before marriage. It is unheard of.

PREMARITAL SEX

Only about 15 percent of college students will have sex before marriage. It is important for women to be virgins. If they aren't, their chance of getting married is much lower. Nonvirgins must move out of town in order to get married.

ARRANGED MARRIAGE

The parents select the spouse for their son or daughter on the basis of that person's family. Once the families agree, the offspring must meet and decide if they want to marry. The husband's parents give the woman's parents a dowry to compensate them for the loss of their daughter. Love is expected to follow marriage rather than precede it.

EXTRAMARITAL SEX

Most husbands (90 percent plus) have sex with other women. It is often a woman whom they pay for sex. The wife knows but does not threaten to divorce the husband because she is economically dependent on him and her status in the community is highest as a married woman. A divorced woman with children has virtually no chance of getting remarried and often must return to her parents' home to survive.

MARRIAGE RELATIONSHIPS

In Korean marriages, men are dominant; women are submissive. Wives are expected to tolerate the extramarital affairs of their husbands.

HOMOSEXUALITY

Homosexuals are viewed very negatively. Homosexuality is "almost illegal" and they must stay invisible.

SOURCE: Kwangho Choe, Fayetteville, North Carolina. Used by permission and developed exclusively for this text.

---

afford the financial costs of commuting. Further, "families who are at later stages of the family life cycle when children are older and less dependent, simply have more flexibility and fewer day-to-day burdens when implementing a commuter lifestyle" (p. 19). Finally, couples who use a systematic or planned decision-making style tend to be more satisfied with their decision to commute. In using a systematic decision-making style, couples consider the alternatives to commuting, collect and evaluate information regarding their decision, mutually choose a plan of action, and make specific plans to reevaluate their decision at a later date.

Throughout this chapter, we have been discussing various lifestyle alternatives. A theme we would like to reemphasize is that various lifestyle patterns are permitted in some societies and not in others. The In Focus 7.3 insert reflects some of the lifestyle patterns operative in Korea. Notice the degree to which their culture is restrictive when compared to ours.

As we have seen in this chapter, there are a variety of lifestyles in the United States. The Lifestyle Preference Inventory may assist you in assessing the lifestyle that you prefer.

Trends

While marriage will continue to be the dominant lifestyle choice for heterosexual citizens in the United States, individuals are increasingly opting to delay getting married for personal preference, educational, or career reasons. The effect of individuals being older at the time they enter a first marriage is a slight increase in those remaining single (Brubaker & Kimberly, 1993; Surra, 1991).

Increased singlehood, living together, childfree marriages, divorce, and single parenthood suggest that traditional marriage may become one of several lifestyles individuals will experience at some time in their lifespan. Unlike in previous generations, there has been a growing acceptance of those who participate in these lifestyle alternatives.

While single parenthood has traditionally meant single motherhood, increasingly more men have begun to be in the role of single parent. Most enter this role through divorce but some choose to be single and choose to adopt or engage a surrogate mother. Indeed, fathers rearing their children without a wife has increased dramatically. In 1970, only one percent of households with children were headed by a male (with no spouse present); in 1992, the percentage had risen to four percent. The corresponding figures for female householder (no spouse present) were 10 and 22 percent in 1970 and 1992 respectively (*Statistical Abstract of the United States: 1993,* Table 75).

Custodial fathers now comprise more than 15 percent of all single-parent families. While most have been divorced, about a quarter have never been married and about eight percent are widowed. Of those who have been previously married, 60 percent have not remarried (Meyer & Garasky, 1993). The children in father only homes are more likely to be older and to be boys. Trends include fathers getting custody of younger children and female children.

Finally, we earlier noted that as women age, fewer men partners are available with whom they may pair off. One effect of an increasing number of elderly widowed and divorced women without men will be a binding and bonding together of women with other women for companionship.

In an increasingly "feminized" society, it's likely that many women will extract those nonromantic social and companionship needs that were fulfilled by a heterosexual mate and learn to satisfy them with their women friends. Pairs and groups of women will increasingly band together for companionship, for mutual support in times of need, and for the economic advantages that cohabitation and lifestyle sharing offers (Dychtwald, 1990, 228).

⌁ CHOICES ⌁

---

*B*ecause our society is becoming more tolerant of alternative lifestyles, a number of choices are realistic options for you. The basic choices and issues to consider follow.

Is Marriage for You?

The decision to marry or not might be based on the perceived consequences (positive and negative) of the respective lifestyles. The primary benefits of marriage include increased companionship, security, parenthood, and the development of a shared history. Although cohabitants may have made an emotional commitment to each other, spouses additionally have made a social and legal commitment. The blend of these commitments results in married people feeling more secure with each other and their relationship.

Marriage also furnishes the traditionally approved context for children. Although some individuals opt for single parenthood, most want to be married when they become parents. Persons who are not married and who choose parenthood will receive less social support than those who are married.

The experience of parenthood is one of numerous events spouses share over the course of their life together. Partners who don't get divorced may have 50 or so years of memories. One 40-year-old husband said:

> My wife and I have been seeing a movie a week since we began dating more than 20 years ago. We have already seen close to 1,000 movies together, and some of them have become a part of us. We still enjoy *Casablanca.*

In his play *Chapter Two,* Neil Simon likened a relationship to the alphabet. People who have just met are in the *As* and *Bs;* those who have known each other for years are in the *Rs* and *Ss.* One of the frustrating aspects of divorce is that we lose the shared history with a person and must begin at the *As* and *Bs* with a new person.

The disadvantages of marriage include interference with the achievement of other goals and relationships, risk of becoming divorced or widowed, and financial responsibility for others. The person who travels fastest, travels alone. If you have a career goal or want career success, the involvement of another person in your life can hinder your achievement of that goal. Not only may marriage restrict your career mobility, it may also interfere with the development of other relationships.

At least 50 percent of all brides and grooms in the United States become divorced; by not marrying, individuals can avoid the traumatic experience of divorce. In addition, most women outlive their husbands by eight years or so, so most wives have inadvertently signed up for several years in the widow role.

Financial responsibility for children, for homes, and for all the things married people buy is part of the marital package. Some people don't like to get in debt or to be obligated to pay for things that someone else (the spouse) wants. If you marry, you will incur the financial obligations of your partner and vice versa.

The decision to marry may not be a one-time decision. Many of us will make the basic decision between marriage and singlehood many times throughout our lives. The single decide whether to marry, and the married decide whether to stay married. For the divorced, the question is whether to remain single or to remarry.

⤳ CHOICES ⤴

Is Singlehood for You?

Singlehood is not a unidimensional concept. There are many styles of singlehood from which to choose. As a single person, you may devote your time and energy to career, travel, privacy, heterosexual or homosexual relationships, living together, communal living, or a combination of these experiences over time. The essential difference between traditional marriage and singlehood is the personal and legal freedom to do as you wish.

Although singlehood offers freedom, single people must deal with the issues of loneliness, money, education, and identity.

Loneliness   For some singles, being alone is a desirable and enjoyable experience. "The major advantage of being single," expressed one 29-year-old man, "is that I don't have to deal with another person all the time. I like my privacy." Henry David Thoreau, who never married, spent two years alone on 14 acres bordering Walden Pond. He said of the experience, "I love to be alone. I never found the companion that was so companionable as solitude."

It is sometimes assumed that most unmarried people are unhappy because they live alone—that to be alone is to be unhappy. But in one study, more than 400 older never married men and women said that their happiness depended not on whether they interact with others but on their stan-

dard of living and level of activity (Keith, 1986). Those who had adequate enough incomes to avoid having to always worry about money and who had enough things to do that they enjoyed (either through employment or self-generated activity) were happy.

Economic Concerns   Having social relationships or developing an enjoyment for being alone are not the only prerequisites to successful single living. It takes money. Money is less likely to be a problem for a man who has been socialized to expect to work all of his life and who usually earns about one-third more than a woman. A woman who decides not to marry is giving up the potentially larger income her husband might earn. Also, both men and women who decide not to marry give up the possibility of a two-income family.

Education   Since higher incomes are often associated with higher education, the person who is considering singlehood as a lifestyle might stay in school. Women and men who complete four years of high school can expect to earn about 30 percent less than those who complete four years of college. "It earns to learn" is a phrase that is used to promote the importance of education.

Personal Identity   Single people must establish an identity—a role—that helps to define who they are and what they do. Couples eat together,

sleep together, party together, and cooperative economically. They mesh their lives into a cooperative relationship that gives them the respective identity of being on their own marital team. On the basis of their spousal roles, we can predict what they will be doing most of the time. For example, at noon on Sunday, they are most likely to be having lunch together. Not only can we predict what they will be doing, their roles as spouses tell them what they will be doing—interacting with each other.

The single person must find other roles. A meaningful career is the avenue most singles pursue. A career provides structure, relationships with others, and a strong sense of identity ("I am an interior decorator"). To the degree that singles find meaning in their work, they are successful in establishing autonomous identities independent of the marital role.

In evaluating the single lifestyle, to what degree, if any, do you feel that loneliness would be a problem for you? What are your educational and career plans to ensure that you will be employed in your chosen field and maintain the standard of living you desire?

The old idea that you can't be happy unless you are married is no longer credible. Whereas marriage will be the first option for some, it will be the last option for others. One 76-year-old single-by-choice said, "A husband would have to be very special to be better than no husband at all."

ℰ Summary

Traditionally, marriage has existed to replenish society with socialized members, to regulate sexual behavior, and to stabilize adult personalities. However, the problem of overpopulation and the availability of convenient, effective contraception have undermined the first two functions. Emotional support is the primary function of marriage today.

The decision to marry often involves assessing the advantages and disadvantages of marriage compared to singlehood. Marriage offers a potentially intense primary relationship over time and avoids the potential loneliness associated with singlehood. But singlehood offers freedom to do as one wishes and avoids the obstacles to personal fulfillment associated with marriage. For many Americans, the decision to marry or to be single is not permanent. Many singles contemplate marriage, and many marrieds ponder whether they should stay married and, indeed, many people eventually divorce.

About 25 million Americans are homosexual. These individuals are victims of considerable social ridicule and prejudice. Nevertheless, many homosexuals establish fulfilling emotional and sexual relationships with each other.

Communal living is another infrequently chosen lifestyle option. There are hundreds of communes to select from, including those that emphasize religion, ideology, or group marriage. The advantages of communal arrangements include living with several people in an intimate environment and sharing expenses.

Group marriage also has few followers. This lifestyle has limited social support and considerable legal sanctions against it.

Commuter marriages reflect the desire of spouses to pursue their respective careers and maintain their marriage. Doing so is difficult and may provide more benefit to the career than to the marriage. Most couples view this lifestyle as temporary until they can manage their work lives so that they can live together.

Single parenthood is an alternative lifestyle experienced by over nine million parents. Although most of these are women who are either separated, divorced, or widowed, some have chosen to have a child without a husband. The primary disadvantage of single parenthood is the lack of money; the primary advantage is a sense of pride and self-esteem that results from being independent.

Trends in lifestyle alternatives include more people choosing singlehood, more people experiencing an array of alternative lifestyles throughout their life, more single fathers, and a closer emotional/social/economic bonding of women who may find themselves without men (particularly in later life).

Questions for Reflection

1. Which lifestyle do you feel offers the most benefits? Why?
2. How would you defend your involvement in each lifestyle choice to your grandparents?
3. What do you think will be the dominant lifestyle in the year 2020? Why?

References

Ahlburg, D. A. and C. J. De Vita. New realities of the American family. *Population Bulletin,* 1992, *47,* no. 2, 2–44.

Anderson, Elaine A. Decision-making style: Impact on satisfaction of the commuter couples' lifestyle. *Journal of Family and Economic Issues,* 1992, *13,* 5–21.

Anson, O. Marital status and women's health revisited: The importance of a proximate adult. *Journal of Marriage and the Family,* 1989, *51,* 185–194.

Bailey, J. M., R. C. Pillard, M. C. Neal, and Y. Agyei. Heritable factors influence sexual orientation in women. *Archives of General Psychiatry,* 1993, *50,* 217–223.

Berger, Raymond M. Men together: Understanding the gay couple. *Journal of Homosexuality,* 1990, *19,* 31–49.

Billingham, R. E. and A. R. Sack. Gender differences in college students' willingness to participate in alternative marriage and family relationships. *Family Perspective,* 1986, *20,* 37–44.

Billy, J. O. G., K. Tanfer, W. R. Grady, and D. H. Klepinger. The sexual behavior of men in the United States. *Family Planning Perspectives,* 1993, *25,* 52–60.

Blumenfeld, Warren J. and Diane Raymond. *Looking at gay and lesbian life.* Boston: Beacon Press, 1989.

Boxer, Andrew M. and Bertram J. Cohler. The life course of gay and lesbian youth: An immodest proposal for the study of gay lives. *Journal of Homosexuality,* 1989, *17,* 315–355.

Brubaker, T. H. and J. A. Kimberly. Challenges to the American family. *Family Relations: Challenges for the Future,* T. H. Brubaker, ed. Newbury Park, Calif.: Sage Publications, 1993, 3–16.

Bunker, B. B., J. M. Zubek, V. J. Vanderslice, and R. W. Rice. Quality of life in dual-career families: Commuting versus single-residence couples. *Journal of Marriage and the Family,* 1992, *54,* 399–407.

Buunk, B. P. and B. Van Driel. *Variant lifestyles and relationships.* Newbury Park, Calif.: Sage Publications, 1989.

Byne, William and Bruce Parsons. Human sexual orientation: The biological theories reappraised. *Archives of General Psychiatry,* 1993, *50,* 228–239.

Carter, J. H. Commuter marriages. *Black Enterprise,* 1992, *22,* 246–250.

Catania, J. A., T. J. Coates, R. Stall, H. Turner, J. Peterson, N. Hearst, M. M. Dolcini, E. Hudes, J. Gagnon, J. Wiley, and R. Groves. Prevalence of AIDS-related risk factors and condom use in the United States. *Science,* 1992, *258,* 1101–1106.

Connell, R. W. and S. Kippax. Sexuality in the AIDS crisis: Patterns of pleasure and practice in an Australian sample of gay and bisexual men. *The Journal of Sex Research,* 1990, *27,* 167–198.

Coombs, R. H. Marital status and person well-being: A literature review. *Family Relations,* 1991, *40,* 97–102.

Corbett, S. L. and K. D. Morgan. The process of lesbian identification. *Free Inquiry in Creative Sociology,* 1983, *11,* 81–83.

Directory of Intentional Communities, 1990 Sandhill Farm, Route 1, Box 155, Rutledge, Missouri 63563.

Doell, Ruth. Comments on John Money's 1988 *Gay, Straight, and In-Between: The Sexology of Erotic Orientation.* (New York: Oxford University Press, 1988). *Journal of Homosexuality,* 1990, *19,* 121–125.

Dychtwald, Ken. *Age wave.* New York: Bantam Books, 1990.

Ellis, Lee and M. Ashley Ames. Neurohormonal functioning and sexual orientation: A theory of homosexuality–heterosexuality. *Psychological Bulletin,* 1987, *101,* no. 2, 233–258.

Fay, Robert E., Charles F. Turner, Albert D. Klassen, John H. Gagnon. Prevalence and patterns of same-gender sexual contact among men. *Science,* 1989, *243,* 338–348.

Fossett, M. A. and K. J. Kiecolt. Mate availability and family structure among African Americans in U.S. metropolitan areas. *Journal of Marriage and the Family,* 1993, *55,* 288–302.

Foster, D. Anti-gay measure rocks Oregon. *The Daily Reflector,* October 18, 1992, E-6.

Gelman, D. and D. Foote. Born or bred. *Newsweek,* February 1992, 46–53. See also Marcia Barinaga. Is homosexuality biological? *Science,* 1992, *253,* 956–957, which details LeVay's study.

Gerstel, N. and H. Gross. *Commuter marriage.* New York: The Gilford Press, 1984.

Gibbons, J. A. Alternative lifestyles: Variations in household forms and family consciousness. *Family and Marriage: Cross-Cultural Perspectives.* K. Ishwaran, ed. Toronto, Ontario: Thompson Educational Publishing, Inc., 1992, 61–74.

Gladue, Brian A. Psychobiological contributions. *Male and Female Homosexuality: Psychological Approaches,* Louis Diamant, ed. New York: Hemisphere Publishing Corporation, 1987.

Glenn, N. D. The recent trend in marital success in the United States. *Journal of Marriage and the Family,* 1991, *53,* 261–270.

Glenn, N. D. and C. N. Weaver. The changing relationship of marital status to reported happiness. *Journal of Marriage and the Family,* 1988, *50,* 317–324

Goldman, N. The perils of single life in contemporary Japan. *Journal of Marriage and the Family,* 1993, *55,* 191–204.

Goldscheider, F. K. and L. J. Waite. *New families, no families?* Berkeley, Calif.: University of California Press, 1991.

Hammer, J. and J. Gordon. The new bicoastals: Love on Tokyo time. *Newsweek,* February 13, 1989, 50.

Harry, Joseph. A probability sample of gay males. *Journal of Homosexuality,* 1990, *19,* 89–104.

Juran, S. Sexual behavior changes among heterosexual, lesbian and gay bar patrons as assessed by questionnaire over an 18-month period. *Journal of Psychology and Human Sexuality,* 1991, *4,* 111–121.

Keith, P. M. Isolation of the unmarried in later life. *Family Relations,* 1986, *35,* 389–396.

Kinsey, A. C., W. B. Pomeroy, and C. E. Martin, *Sexual behavior in the human male.* Philadelphia: Saunders, 1948.

Kinsey, A. C., W. B. Pomeroy, C. E. Martin, and P. H. Gebhard. *Sexual behavior in the human female.* Philadelphia: W. B. Saunders, 1953. Reprinted by permission of the Kinsey Institute for Research in Sex, Gender, and Reproduction, Inc. (Book reprinted in 1970 by Pocket Books.)

Klassen, Albert D., Colin J. Williams, and Eugene E. Levitt. 1989. *Sex and morality in the United States.* Middletown, Conn.: Weselyan University Press.

Klein, F. Sexual orientation: A multi-variable dynamic process. *Journal of Homosexuality,* 1985, *11,* 35–49.

Kurdek, L. A. The relations between reported well-being and divorce history, availability of a proximate adult, and gender. *Journal of Marriage and the Family,* 1991, *53,* 71–78.

LeVay, S. News and Comment. *Science,* 1991, *253,* 956–957.

Lever, J., D. E. Kanouse, W. H. Rogers, S. Carson, and R. Hertz. Behavior patterns and sexual identity of bisexual males. *The Journal of Sex Research,* 1992, *29,* 141–167.

Manderbacka, K., J. Merilainen, E. Hemminki, O. Rahkonen, and J. Teperi. Marital status as a predictor of perinatal outcome in Finland. *Journal of Marriage and the Family,* 1992, *54,* 508–515.

Mastekaasa, A. Marriage and psychological well-being: Some evidence on selection into marriage. *Journal of Marriage and the Family,* 1992, *54,* 901–911.

McWhirter, D. P. and A. M. Mattison. *The male couple: How relationships develop.* Englewood Cliffs, N.J.: Prentice-Hall, 1984.

Meyer, D. R. and S. Garasky. Custodial fathers: Myths, realities, and child support policy. *Journal of Marriage and the Family,* 1993, *55,* 73–89.

Miller, N. *Single parents by choice: A growing trend in family life.* New York: Insight Books, 1993.

Money, John. *Gay, straight, and in-between: The sexology of erotic orientation.* New York: Oxford University Press, 1988.

National Center for Health Statistics. Annual summary of births, marriages, divorces, and deaths: United States, 1991. Monthly vital statistics report; vol. 40 no. 13. Hyattsville, Md.: Public Health Service, 1992.

Bryant, S. and Demian. National survey results of gay couples in long-lasting relationships. *Partners: Newsletter for Gay & Lesbian Couples,* May/June 1990, 1–16.

Newsweek Poll on Homosexuality. Newsweek, September 14, 1992. In "Gays Under Fire" by B. Turque, C. Friday, J. Gordon, D. Glick, P. Annin, F. Vhideva, A. Duignan-Cabrera, and L. Haessly, 35–40.

Nichols, Margaret. Lesbian sexuality: Issues and developing theory. *Lesbian Psychologies: Explorations and Challenges,* Boston Lesbian Psychologies Collective, eds. Chicago: University of Illinois Press, 1987a, 97–125.

Noyes, G. W. 1932, *John Humphrey Noyes: The Putney community.* Cited in John S. Sill, Utopian group marriage in the 19th and 20th centuries: Oneida community and Kerista commune. *Free Inquiry in Creative Sociology,* 1990, *18,* 21–28.

O'Hare, W. P., K. M. Pollard, T. L. Mann, and M. M. Kent. African Americans in the 1990s. *Population Bulletin,* 1991, *46,* 1–40.

Olson, M. R. and J. A. Haynes. Successful single parents. *Families in Society.* 1993, *74,* 259–267

The Omega Institute. A site visit of Psychology Today. *Psychology Today,* January/February 1993, *26,* 52–55.

Quatrella, L. Cooperative alternative community education. *Communities,* May 1990, *76,* 4–8.

Renvoize, Jean. *Going solo: Single mothers by choice.* London: Routledge and Kegan Paul, 1985.

Richards, Leslie N. and Cynthia Schmiege. Problems and strengths of single parent families: Implications for practice and policy. *Family Relations,* 1993, *42,* 277–285.

Robinson, Bryan E., Lynda Henley Walters, and Patsy Skeen. Response of parents to learning that their child is homosexual and concern over AIDS: A national study. *Journal of Homosexuality,* 1989, *18,* 59–80.

Rogers, P. How many gays are there? *Newsweek,* February 15, 1993, 46.

Ross, Michael W. Gay youth in four cultures: A comparative study. *Journal of Homosexuality,* 1989, *17,* 299–314.

Roush, M. Finally, Murphy fires back at Quayle. *USA Today,* September 21, 1992, D1.

Rubinson, L. and L. DeRubertis. Trends in sexual attitudes and behaviors of a college population over a 15-year period. *Journal of Sex Education and Therapy,* 1991, *17,* 32–42.

Sapiro, V. *Women in American society, 2d ed.* Mountain View, Calif.: Mayfield, 1990.

Schechter, M. T., K. J. P. Craib, B. Willoughby, B. Douglas, W. A. McLeod, M. Maynard, P. Constance, and M. O'Shaughnessy. Patterns of sexual behavior and condom use in a cohort of homosexual men. *American Journal of Public Health,* 1988, *78,* 1535–1538.

Schroeder, K. A., L. L. Blood, and D. Maluso. Gender differences and similarities between male and female undergraduate students regarding expectations for career and family roles. *College Student Journal,* 1993, *27,* 237–249.

Shaw, S. The conflicting experiences of lone parenthood. *Lone Parenthood,* Michael Hardey and Graham Grow, ed. Toronto, Ontario: University of Toronto Press, 1991, 143–145.

Sherman, S., ed. *Lesbian and gay marriage: Private commitments, public ceremonies.* Philadelphia: Temple University Press, 1992.

Silberstein, L. R. *Dual-career marriage: A system in Transition.* Hillsdale, N.J.: Lawrence Erlbaum Associates, 1992.

Sill, John. Utopian group marriage in the 19th and 20th centuries: Oneida community and Kerista commune. *Free Inquiry in Creative Sociology,* 1990, *28,* 21–28.

Smart, L. S. The marital helping relationship following pregnancy loss and infant death. *Journal of Family Issues,* 1992, *13,* 81–98.

Smith, T. W. Adult sexual behavior in 1989: Number of partners, frequency of intercourse and risk of AIDS. *Family Planning Perspectives,* 1991, *23,* 102–107.

Smolowe, Jill. Last call for motherhood. *Time* (Special Issue: Women: The Road Ahead), Fall, 1990, *136,* no. 19, 76.

South, S. J. Racial and ethnic differences in the desire to marry. *Journal of Marriage and the Family,* 1993, *55,* 357–370.

Sparrow, K. H. Factors in mate selection for single black professional women. *Free Inquiry in Creative Sociology,* 1991, *19,* 103–109.

Stack, S. New micro-level data on the impact of divorce on suicide, 1959–1980: A test on two theories. *Journal of Marriage and the Family,* 1990, *52,* 119–127.

Statistical Abstract of the United States: 1993, 113th ed. Washington, D.C.: U.S. Bureau of the Census, 1993.

Surra, C. A. Research and theory on mate selection and premarital relationships in the 1980s. *Contemporary Families,* Alan Booth, ed. Minneapolis, Minn.: National Council on Family Relations, 1991, 54–75.

Thornton, A. Changing attitudes toward family issues. *Journal of Marriage and the Family,* 1989, *51,* 878–893.

Webster-Stratton, Carolyn. The relationship of marital support, conflict, and divorce to parent perceptions, behaviors, and childhood conduct problems. *Journal of Marriage and the Family,* 1989, *51,* 417–430.

Weitzman, L. J. Women and children last: The social and economic consequences of divorce law reforms. *Issues in Feminism: An Introduction to Women's Studies,* S. Ruth, ed. Mountain View, Calif.: Mayfield, 1990, 312–335.

Wheeler, D. L. Study of lesbians rekindles debate over biological basis for homosexuality. *The Chronicle of Higher Education,* March 17, 1993, A6–A13.

White, J. M. Marital status and well-being in Canada. *Journal of Family Issues,* 1992, *13,* 390–409.

Whitehead, Minnie M. and Kathleen M. Nokes. An examination of demographic variables, nurturance, and empathy among homosexual and heterosexual big brother/big sister volunteers. *Journal of Homosexuality,* 1990, *19,* 89–101.

Contents

8
CHAPTER

Marriage Relationships

Is It True?

1. The laws regulating domestic relations are the same throughout the various states.

2. Black-white interracial marriages are increasing.

3. Age-discrepant marriages are more likely to end in divorce than marriages in which the spouses' ages are within three years of each other.

4. About 20 percent of spouses in the United States report that they are in a stable but unhappy relationship.

5. The relationship with in-laws is likely to improve after marriage.

1 = F; 2 = T; 3 = T; 4 = T; 5 = T

One does not find happiness in marriage, but takes happiness into marriage.

E. C. MCKENZIE

The media attention given to the marriages of Jane Fonda and Ted Turner, Richard Gere and Cindy Crawford, and Hume Cronyn and Jessica Tandy constantly reminds us that a marriage relationship is the context in which many American adults—61 percent (*Statistical Abstract of the United States: 1993,* Table 59)—live. While we get only glimpses of the private life behind the public image, we learn enough to know that marriage relationships are incredibly diverse. Indeed, there is no one marriage relationship—only marriage relationships that differ by social class, ethnicity, religion, physical ability (or disability), presence or absence of children, age and education of spouse, first or subsequent marriage, and degree of freedom or intimacy among other variables.

In this chapter we discuss various types of marriage relationships including college marriages, mixed marriages (interfaith, interracial, cross-national, age-discrepant), black marriages, Mexican-American marriages, Native American marriages, Asian and Pacific Islander marriages, successful marriages, and unhappy but stable marriages. We begin by noting that marriage is a commitment and involves various rites of passage (wedding, honeymoon) and changes (personal, social, sexual, legal).

Marriage as a Commitment

Maxim Gorky said, "When a woman gets married, it's like jumping into a hole in the ice in the middle of winter; you do it once, and you remember it for the rest of your days." One of the reasons getting married leaves such an indelible memory is the significance of the commitment. Marriage represents a multi-level commitment—person to person, family to family, and couple to state.

Person to Person

Commitment in American marriages may be defined as an intent to maintain the relationship. Saying "I do" in a marriage ceremony implies that you and your partner are making a personal commitment to love, support, and negotiate differences with each other. You are establishing a primary relationship with your partner. Although other existing relationships with parents and friends may continue to be important, they may become secondary.

The primacy of the marriage relationship over family relationships is not shared by all societies. Traditional Chinese, Japanese, and Korean marriages are regarded less as commitments of the spouses to each other and more as

---

The American family does not exist. Rather, we are creating many American families, of diverse styles and shapes. In unprecedented numbers, our families are unalike.

JERROLD K. FOOTLICK

Only one in five married couples fits the popular stereotype of having one or more children, the breadwinning husband, and the homemaking wife.

DENNIS A. AHLBURG
CAROL J. DE VITA

Marital happiness is the most important determinant of overall happiness.

MARY BENIN
BARBARA NIENSTEDT

ACROSS CULTURES

commitments of the respective partners to maintain the family unit. Family harmony and stability take precedence over marital harmony and stability.

CONSIDERATION

Despite the high divorce rate in our society, our cultural expectation of marriage is that it is a lifelong commitment. One hundred years ago, it was typical for married partners to stay together until one of them died. But the average life span then was only about 45. Today, because of an increased life span, "till death do us part" could mean being married for 50, 60, or more years. Because people today live longer than in the past, they have more years to grow and change in terms of their feelings and values. This is one reason why a lifelong commitment to marriage may be more difficult to achieve today than a hundred years ago.

While commitment is usually defined in terms of personal dedication to stay together, commitment may also be defined as an obligation to continue a relationship. Two researchers (Stanley & Markman, 1992) noted that when personal dedication wanes, the feeling of obligation (which often surfaces when children are born) is sometimes enough to keep partners together. Commitment based on obligation may be linked not only to one's own children but also to other family members. Obligatory commitment may also be felt towards one's spouse, especially when that spouse is extremely dependent on the marital relationship.

Family to Family

Marriage also involves commitments by each of the marriage partners to the family members of the spouse. Married couples are often expected to divide their holiday visits between both sets of parents. In addition, each spouse becomes committed to help his or her in-laws when appropriate and to regard family ties as part of marital ties. For some older couples, this means caring for disabled parents who may live in their home. "We always said that no parent was ever going to live with us," said one spouse. "But my wife's father died, and her mother had no place to go. Her living here was an initial strain, but we've learned to cope with the situation quite well."

Not all couples accept the family to family commitment. Some spouses have limited contact with their respective parents. "I haven't seen my folks in years and don't want to," said one woman in her second marriage.

Family Commitments among the Hmong The Hmong of Laos live in extended families (over 60,000 have immigrated to the United States) where marriage commitments are formally negotiated between the respective families through mediators. Once the man and the woman decide that they would like to marry, the parents of the man send two mediators to the parents of the woman with a formal marriage proposal. "Upon the mediators' arrival at the girl's parents'

> Remember, your relatives had no choice in the matter either.
>
> E. C. MCKENZIE

ACROSS CULTURES ∾

residence, they will announce their mission and request permission to enter the home. The girl's parents will also find two able mediators who would come to the negotiation table with the other mediators" (Thao, 1992, 56). One of the issues they discuss is the bride price (an amount of money) the man is to pay the family of the girl for their hardship of raising a child they are now giving up. The agreements are written down and signed, not necessarily by the man and the woman but by the parents. "The proposal will become a binding contract between the two parties, the young man and his family on one side and the girl and her family on the other, witnessed by the mediators themselves" (p. 56).

Couple to State

> **The trouble with wedlock is, there's not enough wed and too much lock.**
>
> CHRISTOPHER MORLEY

In addition to person to person and family to family commitments, spouses become legally committed to each other according to the laws of the state in which they reside. This means they cannot arbitrarily decide to terminate their own marital agreement.

NATIONAL DATA ✜ About 2.3 million marriage licenses are issued to U.S. couples every year. These represent a legal bond—not only between individuals, but also between the couple and the state (*Statistical Abstract of the United States: 1993*, Table 91).

Just at the state says who can marry (not close relatives, the insane, or the mentally deficient) and when (usually at age 18 or older), legal procedures must be instituted if the couple want to divorce. The state's interest is that a couple stay married, have children, and take care of them.

✜ Rites of Passage

A *rite of passage* is an event which marks the transition from one social status to another. The first day in school, getting a driver's license, and graduating from high school/college are all events which mark major transitions in status (to student, driver, and graduate). Weddings and honeymoons are also rites of passage which mark the transition from being single to being married.

Weddings

> **I hope you will be as happy as we all thought we would be.**
>
> SAID TO A BRIDE AT HER WEDDING RECEPTION

The wedding is a rite of passage that is both religious and civil. To the Catholic church, marriage is a sacrament which implies that the union is both sacred and indissoluble. According to Jewish and Protestant faiths, marriage is a special bond between the husband and wife sanctified by God but divorce and remarriage are permitted.

While love is a personal feeling, marriage is a public commitment from person to person, family to family, and couple to state.

Regardless of the religious group, there are certain commonalities in most weddings:

> Four parties are represented in the service: the couple, the religious group (clergy), the state (witnesses), and the parents (usually through the father). Each party to the marriage rite covenants [enters into an agreement] with the other parties in fulfilling his or her obligations so that the marriage will be blessed "according to the ordinances of God and the laws of the state." The denomination, through the clergy, pledges God's grace, love, and blessing. The man and woman make vows to each other "in the presence of God and these witnesses." The state grants the marriage license once the laws have been fulfilled (the witnesses are present to see that the law is obeyed). The parents (through the father) pledge to give up their daughter to her new husband, no longer coming between the bride and groom. After giving the bride away, the father sits down beside his wife, leaving the couple standing together (Rice, 1993, 208).

Societies differ in regard to what constitutes a wedding ceremony. Among the Trobriand Islanders, it is the sharing of a meal.

While love is a private experience, marriage is a public experience in the United States. This is emphasized by the wedding in which family and friends of both parties are invited to participate. The wedding is a time for the respective families to learn how to cooperate with each other for the benefit of the respective daughter and son. Conflicts over number of bridesmaids and

ACROSS CULTURES ∿

ushers, number of guests to invite, and place of the wedding are not uncommon. While some families harmoniously negotiate all differences, others become so adamant about their preferences that the prospective bride and groom elope to escape or avoid the conflict. However, most families recognize the importance of the event in the life of their daughter or son and try to be helpful and nonconflictual.

In preparation for the wedding, some states require each partner to have a blood test to certify that neither has a sexually transmitted disease. This document is then taken to the county courthouse, where the couple applies for a marriage license. Two-thirds of the states require a waiting period between the issuance of the license and the wedding. Eighty percent of the couples are married by a clergyman; 20 percent (primarily remarriages) go to a justice of the peace or judge.

CONSIDERATION

Custom dictates that the bride wear something old, new, borrowed, and blue. The "old" (e.g., gold locket) is something that represents the durability of the impending marriage. The "new," in the form of new unlaundered undergarments emphasizes the new life to begin. The "borrowed" (e.g., a wedding veil) is something that has already been worn by a currently happy bride, and the "blue" (e.g., ribbons) represents fidelity (those dressed in blue have lovers true). The bride throwing her floral bouquet signifies the end of girlhood; the rice thrown by the guests at the newly married couple signifies fertility.

The divorce rate would be lower if, instead of marrying for better or worse, people would marry for good.

UNKNOWN

It is no longer unusual for couples to have weddings that are neither religious nor traditional. Only friends of the couple and members of the immediate families may gather in the bride-to-be's backyard. Rather than the traditional white gown, the bride may wear her favorite dress. The groom may wear a suit instead of a tuxedo, and everyone else wears whatever they think is appropriate. In the exchange of vows, neither partner promises to obey the other, and their relationship is spelled out by the partners rather than by tradition. Vows often include the couple's feelings about equality, individualism, humanism, and openness to change.

Part of the preference for less lavish, less traditional weddings is economic. A couple can easily spend $20,000 on a wedding for the reception, rings, clothes, photographer, clergy person, and other related expenses. This amount does not include the honeymoon. As couples marry at a later age, more of them assume the financial responsibility of the wedding rather than the bride's parents paying for it.

NATIONAL DATA ✖ The average cost of a 200-guest wedding is between $15,000 and $30,000 *(Cook, 1990).* Of course, this size wedding may also be arranged less expensively.

CONSIDERATION

One alternative to spending such large sums on a wedding is elopement. Some couples make a deal with their parents either to elope or to have a small wedding in the backyard. One bride said, "The marriage license cost us $10, and we're using the $4,000 my dad gave us as a down payment on a mobile home." However, other couples want the experience of a big wedding. "I'm only going to get married once," said one bride-to-be. "And I want it to be a big church wedding with a horse-drawn carriage to take us away after the reception."

Honeymoons

Traditionally, another rite of passage follows immediately after the wedding—the honeymoon. The functions of the honeymoon are both personal and social. The personal function is to provide a period of recuperation from the usually exhausting demands of preparing for and being involved in a wedding ceremony and reception. The social function is to provide a time for the couple to be alone to solidify their identity from that of an unmarried to a married couple. And, as a married couple, their sexual expression with each other achieves full social approval and legitimacy. Now they can have children with complete societal approval.

> The honeymoon is a period of doting between dating and debating.
>
> UNKNOWN

❧ Changes After Marriage

After the wedding and honeymoon the new spouses begin to experience the stark realities of marriage. This involves learning that they have been taught certain myths (see In Focus 8.1) about marriage. In addition, the partners become aware that changes occur in their personal, social, legal, and sexual relationship.

> Keep your eyes wide open before marriage, half shut afterwards.
>
> BEN FRANKLIN

Personal Changes

One initial consequence of getting married may be an enhanced self-concept. Parents and close friends usually arrange their schedules to participate in your wedding and give gifts to express their approval. In addition, the strong evidence that your spouse approves of you and is willing to spend a lifetime with you also tells you that you are a desirable person.

The married person also begins adopting new values and behaviors consistent with the married role. Although new spouses often vow that "marriage won't change me," it does. For example, rather than stay out all night at a party, which is not uncommon for singles who may be looking for a partner, spouses (who are already paired off) tend to go home early. Their roles of spouse, employee, and parent, force them to adopt more regular hours. The

> Marriage is the difference between painting the town and painting the back porch.
>
> UNKNOWN

Myths About Marriage

One of the reasons we are surprised by the actual experience of marriage is that we have a poor idea of what day-to-day living together in marriage is really like. Our assumptions are often distortions of reality. Some of the more unrealistic beliefs our society perpetuates about marriage are discussed here.

MYTH 1: OUR MARRIAGE WILL BE DIFFERENT

All of us know married people who are bored, unhappy, and in conflict. Despite this, we assume our marriage will be different. The feeling before marriage that "it won't happen to us" reflects the deceptive nature of courtship. If we are determined that our marriage will be different, what steps are we taking to ensure that it is? This question is relevant because many of us who enter marriage believing that it will be different for us blindly imitate the marriage patterns of others instead of making a conscious effort to manage our own relationship to make it as fulfilling as we expect it to be.

MYTH 2: WE WILL MAKE EACH OTHER HAPPY

We also tend to believe that we are responsible for each other's happiness. One woman recalls:

> When my husband tried to commit suicide, I couldn't help but think that if I had been the right kind of wife he wouldn't have done such a thing. But I've come to accept that there was more to his depression than just me. He wasn't happy with his work, he drank heavily, and he never got over his twin brother's death.

Although you and your partner will be a tremendous influence on each other's happiness, each of you has roles (employee, student, sibling, friend, son or daughter, parent, and so on) beyond the role of spouse. These role relationships will color the interaction with your mate. If you have lost your job or flunked out of school, your father has cancer, your closest friend moves away, or your mother can no longer care for herself, but is resisting going to a retirement home, it will be difficult for your spouse to "make you happy." Similarly, although you may make every effort to ensure your spouse's happiness, circumstances can defeat you. Waiting for someone else to make you happy is quite likely to be a lifelong wait.

MYTH 3: OUR DISAGREEMENTS WILL NOT BE SERIOUS

Many couples acknowledge that they will have disagreements, but they assume theirs will be minor and "just part of being married." However, "insignificant" conflict that is not resolved can threaten any marriage. "All I wanted was for him to spend more time with me," recalls a divorced woman. "But he said he had to run the business because he couldn't trust anyone else. I got tired of spending my evenings alone and got involved with someone else."

MYTH 4: MY SPOUSE IS ALL I NEED

All of us have needs that require the support of others. These needs range from wanting to see a movie with someone to needing someone to talk to about personal problems to needing the physical expression of a partner's love. Although it is encouraging to believe that our partner can satisfy all of our intellectual, physical, and emotional needs, it is not realistic.

A more optimistic way to think of these four beliefs about marriage is to recognize that our marriage *may* be different, that we will be *one* important influence on our partner's happiness, that our disagreements *may* not be serious (or if they are serious, we may develop skills to resolve them), and that we will be able to satisfy many of our partner's needs.

role of married person implies a different set of behaviors than the role of single person. Although there is an initial resistance to "becoming like old married folks," the resistance soon gives way to the realities of the role.

Spouses who did not live together before marriage must also learn how to share living space with someone (e.g., both want the desk by the window), cope with various habits (e.g., leaving the toothpaste cap off, towels on bathroom floor) and adjust to each other's body clocks (e.g., one likes to watch late night TV). Financial issues must also be worked out in regard to who spends how much on what, a separate or joint account, and who will balance the checking account and prepare the income tax forms? The number of interactions, decisions, and negotiations also escalates—purchases, time away from each other, meetings for lunch, vacations, and entertaining guests. Future plans in terms of a house and children also come into play. None of these issues alone has much influence on the perception of one's happiness in marriage. However, being confronted with a barrage of differences on a daily basis may begin to influence one's marital happiness.

Another common result of getting married is disenchantment. It may not happen in the first few weeks or months of marriage, but it is almost inevitable. Farrah Fawcett once said, "Marriage—that's when the blazing torch of love slowly turns into a pilot light." Whereas courtship is the anticipation of a life together, marriage is the day-to-day reality of that life together—and reality does not always fit the dream. Daily marital interaction exposes both partners as they really are: human beings.

Disenchantment after marriage may be related to each partner shifting their focus of interest away from each other and toward their work. When children come, their focus shifts to the children. In any case, each partner usually gives and gets less attention in marriage than in courtship. If the partners do not discuss these changes, they may define each other's interests that are external to the relationship as betrayal. "The task is then to start down the rocky road of accepting differentness as enhancing the relationship" (Marano, 1992, 51).

Parents, In-Laws, and Friendship Changes

Marriage affects relationships with parents, in-laws, and the friends of both partners. Parents are likely to be more accepting of the partner following the wedding. "I encouraged her not to marry him," said the father of a recent bride, "but once they were married, he was her husband and my son-in-law, so I did my best to get along with him."

Just as acceptance of the mate by the partner's parents is likely to increase, interaction with the partner's parents is likely to decrease. This is particularly true when the newly married couple moves to a distant town. "I still love my parents a great deal," said a new husband, "but I just don't get to see them very often." Parents whose lives have revolved around their children may feel

> After the wedding, moonlight and roses become daylight and dishes.
>
> EDGAR ARENDALL

particularly saddened at the marriage of their last child and may be reluctant to accept the reduced contacts. Frequent phone calls, visits, invitations, and gifts may be their way of trying to ensure a meaningful place in the life of their married son or daughter (Goetting, 1990). Such insistence by the parents and in-laws may be the basis of the first major conflict between the spouses. There is no problem if both spouses agree on which set of in-laws or parents they enjoy visiting and the frequency of such get-togethers. But when one spouse wants his or her parents around more often than the partner does, frustration will be felt by everyone.

Two researchers (Serovich & Price, 1992) examined in-law relationships of 309 spouses. They found that most reported high relationship quality with in-laws, that wives reported equally satisfying relationships with both mothers- and fathers-in-law, and that how close one lived to one's in-laws was not a significant factor in satisfaction with in-law relationships.

CONSIDERATION

Most marriage counselors believe that when the spouses must choose between their partner and parents, more long-term positive consequences are associated with choosing the partner rather than the parents. Ideally, of course, such choices should be avoided. For partners to try to deny their mate access to the mate's parents is risky. When a person marries, that individual inherits an already existing family; parent and in-law relationships come with the marriage.

Time separates the best of friends, and so does money—and marriage!

UNKNOWN

Marriage also affects relationships with friends of the same and opposite sex. Less time will be spent with friends because of the role demands from the spouse. In addition, friends will assume that the newly married person now has a built-in companion and is not interested in (or would be punished by the spouse for) going barhopping, to movies, or whatever. More time will be spent with other married couples, who will become powerful influences on the new couple's relationship.

CONSIDERATION

What spouses give up in friendships they gain in developing a close relationship with each other. "We still enjoy our friends, but we end up spending more time with each other than with anyone else. We like it that way," said an elementary school teacher.

However, it is a mistake to abandon friendships after getting married. The spouse cannot be expected to satisfy all social needs, and friends can often relieve some of the spouse's burden. Also, since many marriages end in divorce, friends who have been maintained throughout the marriage can become vital support systems when adjusting to a divorce.

Legal Changes

Unless the partners have signed a prenuptial agreement specifying that their earnings and property will remain separate, the wedding ceremony is associated with an exchange of property. Once two individuals become husband and wife, each spouse automatically becomes part owner of what the other earns in income and accumulates in property. Although the laws on domestic relations differ from state to state, courts typically award to each spouse half of the assets accumulated during the marriage (even though one of the partners may have contributed a smaller proportion). For example, if a couple buy a house together, even though one spouse invested more money in the initial purchase, the other will likely be awarded half of the value of the house if they divorce. (Having children complicates the distribution of assets since the house is often awarded to the custodial parent). In the event of death, the spouses are legally entitled to inherit between one-third and one-half of the partner's estate, unless a will specifies otherwise.

Should the couple divorce after having children, each is legally responsible to provide for the economic support of their children. In the typical case, the mother assumes primary physical custody of the children and the father is required by court order to pay about one-fourth of his gross income (usually through the children's graduations from high school) if there are two children or 18 percent for just one child. Although child support awards to the custodial parent (usually the mother) are common, only about half of the fathers pay the full amount ordered (Buehler, 1987). Legally, failure to pay child support is regarded as contempt of court and punishable by jail.

Wedlock is a padlock.
JOHN RAY

Sexual Changes

Sex will also undergo some changes during the first year of marriage. The frequency declines for most married couples, but the quality may improve. According to one wife:

> The urgency to have sex disappears after you're married. After a while you discover that your husband isn't going to vanish back to his apartment at midnight. He's going to be with you all night, every night. You don't have to have sex every minute because you know you've got plenty of time. Also, you've got work and other responsibilities, so sex takes a lower priority than before you were married.

Love me like you want to, not like you have to.
PAT COOPER

NATIONAL DATA ॐ Two-thirds of the married people in a national sample reported that their sex lives improved after marriage (Janus & Janus, 1992).

Division of Labor Changes

One result of the feminist and women's movement is that an increasing number of couples share the domestic work in their relationship. However, research consistently shows that household work is largely performed by women (Mederer, 1993). During courtship, couples may share equally in household work. After marriage, however, there is a tendency for women and men to drift into traditional roles. One woman remarked,

> When we were dating, Joe cooked elaborate meals on the weekends, did his own laundry, and we went grocery shopping together. Now that we are married, he hardly ever cooks, and I'm the one who ends up doing his laundry and going to the grocery store.

NATIONAL DATA &c; Using data from the National Survey of Families and Households, Shelton (1992) reported that unmarried women spend 32.2 hours per week on housework while married women spend 41.7 hours per week on housework. However, for men, being married is not associated with a significant increase in time spent doing housework. Unmarried men spend 21.6 hours per week doing housework while married men spend 21.9 hours per week doing housework.

CONSIDERATION

The fact that wives put in almost twice the hours as their husbands, has a negative impact on their marital happiness. The greater the wives' relative contribution to household labor, the less satisfied they are about their marriages (Suitor, 1991).

Interactional Changes

The way wives and husbands perceive and interact with each other continues to change throughout the course of the marriage. Two researchers studied 238 spouses who had been married over thirty years and observed that (across time) men changed from being patriarchal to collaborating with their wives and that women changed from deferring to their husband's authority to challenging their authority (Huyck & Gutmann, 1992).

&c; College Marriages

Today, the proportion of college students who are married is much higher than in earlier years. Before 1940, it was not uncommon for a college or university to deny admission to married students or to require enrolled students to drop out if they married. It was believed that married students would influence single students to be less committed to academics. After World War II, the return of married veterans to college established the social legitimacy of the college marriage. (Even high school marrieds are acceptable now.)

Young Married College Students

Although most college students prefer to finish their degrees before getting married, others seem compelled by the desire to be married while still attending school. If they decide to marry, they will soon confront role conflict and economic issues.

NATIONAL DATA ❦ Seven percent of U.S. college students reported that "chances are very good that they will marry while in college" (American Council on Education and University of California, 1992).

Role Conflict Married students have two major roles to fulfill—student and spouse. In addition, the married student may also take on the role of parent and employee. Trying to fulfill all these roles may lead to *role conflict,* which exists when the expectations of one role are in conflict with the expectations of another role. For example, the role of student involves spending time writing term papers, studying for exams, and going to class. These role expectations may conflict with spending time with one's partner, caring for a child, or meeting one's job responsibilities. Role conflict may also be greater for women than for men because women typically assume primary responsibility for childcare and other domestic tasks.

CONSIDERATION

Although role conflict is not unique to the college marriage, one role is more likely to be added to another without sufficient time to adjust to the previous role. Stacking the roles of student, spouse, employee, and possibly parent requires a greater degree of adaptation than is required of the single college student, who has fewer roles to juggle. Aware of the role-stacking effect, most students opt to delay marriage until after graduation.

Money Problems Some parents disapprove of their offspring getting married while still in college and stop financial support after the wedding. Lack of money is not unique to the young and newly married college couple, but it introduces a variable that was not present when they were single and engaged. A sophomore who married in his freshman year wrote:

> We began our marriage without any help from our parents. The result was a tremendous strain on our once happy relationship. Not having enough money put us both under tensions that neither of us had known before. We struggled to make rent, utilities, tuition, and other payments. We squeezed our budget for money to buy food with. Our recreational lifestyle had changed drastically because we rarely had money to eat out or to see a movie. We bought no new clothes—birthdays were the only times we got new ones. The result was unhappiness which we would not let others know about because of our pride. We were both from middle-class families, but we were poor.

Older Married College Students

A look around any college classroom reveals a number of older students, many of whom are married (also referred to as nontraditional students). In contrast to most of the younger college marrieds, many of these spouses have been or are employed in full-time jobs and have children.

How does returning to school affect the marriage relationship? In a study of 361 women age 26 and older who were married and had at least one child, one-half of those who dropped out before completing their degree and one-third of those who did complete their degree reported that their return to school had resulted in some strain on the marriage (Berkove, 1979). This showed itself in the husband's jealousy in competing with his wife's new interest and his annoyance over occasional late meals and a cluttered house. One student wife said of her husband:

> He mentions how much money my education is costing (even though I've worked part time off and on) and how much time I spend away from the family (he spends as much time away from the family as I do). He has stopped commenting on the state of the house, since I told him that if it was too dirty to suit him, he was welcome to clean it, because it suited me just fine.

Benefits also resulted from the wife's return to school. Most of the wives reported increased personal and intellectual development, and one-half reported that their husbands showed greater appreciation of, satisfaction with, and pride in the fact that they had returned to school (Berkove, 1979).

Student wives who are also mothers report positive benefits for their children. In a study of 40 such women (Kelly, 1982), more than half said the relationships with their children had improved since they had returned to school. Their children showed an increased interest in their own schoolwork, and there was a new mutuality of interest—both mother and child would talk about "having to get homework done."

Making good grades and spending time with family is often accomplished at the expense of the student wife's sleep. In essence, the wife and mother "added her study (sometimes a full-time student load) to her existing program, and what she cut back on was sleep and leisure time. It is little wonder that one of the main problems cited by mature-age female students is chronic tiredness" (Kelly, 1982, 291).

What happens when the older married husband returns to school? McRoy and Fisher (1982) studied 20 couples in which only the husband was in graduate school and compared them with 20 couples in which only the wife was in graduate school and 20 couples in which both spouses were in graduate school. Results showed that the husband being in school was associated with less money and less marital satisfaction than either of the other two groups. It seems that when the husband does not contribute economically to the marriage and family, everyone suffers. "But that's not true of us," said one student husband who is being supported by his wife. "I put her through school, and now it's her turn to earn the money. We both agreed on this plan, and it hasn't been a problem for either of us."

It seem a bit odd for a college to give a man with a wife and three kids a Bachelor's Degree.

E.C. MCKENZIE

Mixed Marriages

Mixed marriages are those in which the partners differ in regard to one or more variables such as religion, race, national heritage, or age. Interreligious, interracial, cross-national, and age-discrepant marriages are examples of marriages in which the partners differ from each other in a particular way.

Interreligious Marriages

NATIONAL DATA   In the 1960s, 90 percent of Jewish marriages were between two persons of the Jewish faith. More recently, the percentage has dropped to 30 percent. The American Jewish Committee estimates there are 300,000 interfaith couples in the United States and more than 600,000 children with both Jewish and Christian parents (Kantrowitz & Witherspoon, 1987).

Are people in interreligious marriages less satisfied with their marriages than those who marry someone of the same faith? The answer depends on a number of factors. First, people in marriages in which one or both spouses profess to "no religion" tend to report lower levels of marital satisfaction than those in which at least one spouse has a religious tie. People with "no religion" are often more liberal and less bound by traditional societal norms and values— they feel less constrained to stay married for reasons of social propriety.

Second, men in interreligious marriages tend to report less marital satisfaction than men in marriages in which the partners have the same religion. This may be due to the fact that children of interreligious marriages are typically reared in the faith of the mother, so that the father's influence is negligible. Third, wives who marry outside their faith do not seem any less happy than wives who marry inside their faith. Catholics who marry someone of a different faith are just as likely to report being happily married as Catholics who marry Catholics (Shehan et al., 1990).

CONSIDERATION

The impact of a mixed religious marriage may depend more on the devoutness of the partners than the fact that the partners are of different religions. If both spouses are devout in their religious beliefs, they may expect some problems in the relationship (although not necessarily). Less problematic is the relationship in which one spouse is devout but the partner is not. If neither spouse in an interfaith marriage is devout, problems regarding religious differences may be minimal or nonexistent.

Interracial Marriages

"I give up. It's not worth it," said "Flipper" to Angie in Spike Lee's *Jungle Fever.* They were interracial lovers who had experienced severe social disapproval for their relationship from their respective families. Such social pressure contributes to the fact that less than one percent of all U.S. married couples are black-white couples.

NATIONAL DATA ❧ Of the more than 53 million married couples in the United States, only 246,000 (about one-half of one percent) are black-white couples (*Statistical Abstract of the United States: 1993*, Table 63). The husband is usually black, the wife, white.

Interracial marriages may involve many combinations, including, American white, American black, Indian, Chinese, Japanese, Korean, Mexican, Malaysian, and Hindu mates. Examples of black men who married white women include Montel Williams, Quincy Jones, Gregory Hines, and Charles Barkley. Roger Ebert (of Siskel and Ebert "Sneak Previews") is an example of a white man married to a black woman. Black-white spouses are more likely to have been married before, to be age-discrepant, to live far away from their place of birth, to have been reared in a racially tolerant region of the country, and to have some education beyond high school (Taylor et al., 1991).

Both sets of parents tend to reject the interracial marriage of their son or daughter. Such parental rejection springs from a concern about how the marriage will affect the parents' own status and their fear for the couple and the problems they must face. Lack of social support, overt hostility, and lack of similar backgrounds may contribute to a higher divorce rate for interracial couples. Black singer Lena Horne said of the divorce from her white husband, "We had a good life together and I loved him, but he didn't know what it meant to be black." By this she made reference to the cultural heritage of racial prejudice and discrimination with which whites may be empathetic but cannot identify with experientially.

Parents are also concerned about the children the interracial couples may have. However, their fears may be unwarranted. Two researchers (Stephan & Stephan, 1991) compared children of mixed heritage (Asian-Americans, Hispanic-Americans) with those of single heritage (Caucasians) and found no evidence of negative effects on an array of measures. "Positive effects were found for intergroup contact and attitudes, language facility, and enjoyment of the culture of minority groups. Mixed-heritage students appeared to have better relations with single-heritage groups than the single-heritage groups have with one another" (p. 241).

> **CONSIDERATION**
>
> Lovers considering an interracial relationship might consider moving to a social context that is more approving of such relationships. Hawaii has a large number of interracial relationships which make such relationships more the norm than the exception. While moving to Hawaii might not be feasible, people in larger cities are also much more approving of interracial relationships than people in rural areas. Some interracial couples prefer to work, play, and shop where they do not have to contend with constant prejudice and discrimination.

Cross-National Marriages

The number of international students studying at American colleges and universities is considerable.

NATIONAL DATA ❧ Approximately 420,000 foreign students are enrolled at more than 2,500 colleges and universities in the United States. Over half (263,000) are from Asia (*Statistical Abstract of the United States: 1993,* Table 277).

The proportion of foreign students in the total enrollment at the Massachusetts Institute of Technology, Columbia University, and the University of Southern California is 20, 13, and 12 percent respectively (Open Doors, 1988). Since American students take classes with foreign students, it often happens that dating and romance lead to marriage. When the international student is male, more likely than not, his cultural mores will prevail and will clash strongly with his American bride's expectations, especially if they should return to his country.

One female American student described her experience of marriage to a Pakistani, who violated his parents' wishes by not marrying the bride they had chosen for him in childhood. The marriage produced two children before the four of them returned to Pakistan. She felt that her in-laws did not accept her and were hostile toward her. The in-laws also imposed their religious beliefs on her children and took control of their upbringing. When this situation became intolerable, she wanted to return to the United States. Because the children were viewed as being "owned" by their father, she was not allowed to take them with her and was banned from even seeing them. Like many international students, the husband was from a wealthy, high-status family, and she was powerless to fight them. She has not seen her children in six years.

Some cross-national couples solve their cultural differences by making as complete a break as possible from their cultural past. In the previous case, the American woman could have accepted the traditions of her husband. However, Cottrell (1993) emphasized that for her to do so would be quite difficult:

> . . . the Western wife does not know how to play her primary role in a traditional society, that of mother and wife. She does not know the heritage which is her responsibility to transmit to her children, and she does not understand the institutional arrangements for cultural transmission (p. 97).

Alternatively, the couple could have stayed in America and reared their children here. Doing so would be difficult for the Pakistani husband since he would have to give up his family ties. He is not likely to do this since he was reared with familistic values. Due to the potential problems faced by cross-national couples, it may be advisable for the partners to spend considerable time in each other's cultural home before making a marital commitment.

Age-Discrepant Marriages

Regarding my love for Soon-Yi—it's real and happily all true.

WOODY ALLEN, IN REGARD TO HIS RELATIONSHIP WITH THE 21-YEAR-OLD ADOPTED DAUGHTER OF MIA FARROW

Age-discrepant relationships received nationwide visibility when Woody Allen, age 57, made public his love for Soon-Yi, age 21. While the future of that relationship is unknown, it is not unusual for men to be older than the partners they select. Celebrities and the number of years they are older than their spouses include Hugh Hefner, 37; Johnny Carson, 26; and Frank Gifford (married to Kathie Lee), 23. While less common, some women are significantly older than their husbands. Mary Tyler Moore is 16 years older than her husband; Olivia Newton-John is 11 years older than her husband.

Based on a national sample of over 46,000 women age 16 and over residing with their husbands, a team of researchers (Shehan, Berardo, Vera, & Carley, 1991) identified the background characteristics of those most likely to be involved in age-discrepant marriages:

1. *Race.* Blacks are 1.5 times more likely than whites to be in marriages in which the husbands are ten or more years older than the wives. Similarly, wives of Spanish origin are 1.5 times more likely than non-Spanish women to be in marriages in which the husbands are ten or more years older than the wives.

2. *Interracial and interethnic marriages.* Compared to nonmixed unions, interracial and interethnic marriages are more likely to involve relationships in which the husbands are ten years older than the wives.

3. *Remarriage.* Wives in second or subsequent marriages are 2.7 times more likely to be younger than their husbands and 7.05 times more likely to be older than their husbands.

The prospect of dating someone in her twenties becomes less appealing as you get older. At some point in your life, your tolerance level goes down and you realize that, with someone much younger, there's nothing really to talk about.

CLINT EASTWOOD
AGE 60

Some issues common to individuals in age-discrepant marriages revolve around interests, children, sex, and early widowhood.

Interests Although partners of very different ages may develop mutual interests, their interests are more likely to be different. The younger partner might enjoy Van Halen; the older partner, Glenn Miller. The younger partner may want to engage in strenuous recreation, such as skiing or hiking. Even if the older partner has an interest in such activity, this partner may be physically unable to engage in such recreation.

Children   The May-December couple may experience difficulties concerning children. For example, the younger partner may want children, but the older partner may feel too old to be a parent to a young child. In addition, children from the older partner's previous marriage may require financial support, limiting the money available to the couple to start a new family.

Sex   An older man may not be able to meet the sexual demands of a much younger woman. As a consequence, she may seek a sexual companion outside the marriage. The husband may be threatened by such competition, and the marriage relationship may be jeopardized. Sex is not necessarily a problem, however. The younger partner may have a sex drive that is equal to (or even less than) that of the older partner. Also, partners with the lower sex drive (usually older partners) may learn to satisfy their mate's sexual needs in a variety of ways.

Early Widow   American men die approximately seven years earlier than American women. The younger wife in the May-December marriage is therefore more likely to be a widow longer than the wife who is married to someone closer to her age. Indeed, the woman married to a man older than herself is more likely to die at an earlier age than her counterpart who marries a younger man. Two researchers (Klinger-Vartabedian & Wispe, 1989) observed this phenomenon and speculated:

> Perhaps marital partners set their own social or biological clocks in accordance with their spouses' age, thus creating a mortality mean. In the hypothetical averaging of ages, the older person becomes "younger" and lives longer than expected, while the younger person becomes "older" and dies sooner than expected (p. 201).

> Better be an old man's darling, than become a young man's slave.
>
> J. R. PLANCHE

Some age discrepant marriages are those in which the woman is older than the man.

CONSIDERATION

None of these concerns are necessarily unique to the May-December marriage. Conflicts over sex, children, and recreation may occur in marriages in which the partners are the same age, and newlyweds are not guaranteed that their spouse will be healthy and alive tomorrow. However, data comparing spouses whose ages are within three years of each other with spouses whose ages are more than three years apart suggest that age-discrepant marriages are more likely to end in divorce (Tzeng, 1992).

❦ Black Marriages

The black family has often been described in negative terms such as low income, births to unmarried mothers, one-parent families, and spouses with limited educations. Such a negative pathological model of black family life is a result of researchers approaching "the African-American family as a deviation

I'm reminded that I'm black every day.

SPIKE LEE

"... and you know who is the first to be hit by bad economic times ... you people."

H. ROSS PEROT

Black America and black families can be understood only in the context of a white racist America.

JOYCE E. WILLIAMS

A racially integrated community is a chronological term timed from the entrance of the first black family to the exit of the last white family.

SAUL ALINSKY

from the white norm. The African-American family should be viewed as a distinct cultural form that has been shaped by unique social, historical, economic, and political forces, rather than as a deficient White family" (Mirande, 1991, 56).

In addition, in contrast to the negative images of the African American family, these families may just as well be described in terms of their positive aspects or strengths. These include strong kinship bonds, favorable attitudes toward the elderly, adaptable roles, strong achievement orientations, strong religious orientations, and a love of children (Rice, 1993). Indeed, Taylor et al. (1991) emphasized that research on black family life is increasingly reflecting an appreciation for the "variability in the status of black families overall" (p. 232).

The Context of Racism

Black marriages occur in the context of continued racism, discrimination, and economic insufficiency. *Racism* is the belief that some groups are, as a result of heredity, inferior to other groups. Blacks live in a white racist society in which whites, as a group, are prejudiced against blacks. This prejudice manifests itself in discrimination against blacks. Jaynes and Williams (1989) observed evidence of the fallacy that overt discrimination has virtually vanished in the last 20 years. They note that as soon as the workday ends, blacks and whites retreat to different worlds. Whites can, if they choose, buy their way into a world of racially homogeneous schools, shopping areas, and recreational facilities.

The figures on economic inequality in the United States emphasize the extent of discrimination. The median family income is about 25 percent less for blacks than whites (*Statistical Abstract of the United States: 1993*, Table 715). Some of this economic strain is due to racial discrimination, which limits the employment opportunities and earning capacity of blacks.

Kinship Ties

Kinship (blood) ties were significantly important in the West African societies from which blacks were brought to be slaves in the United States. In these societies, an individual's social and economic status, as well as means of subsistence, depended on the maintenance of both nuclear and extended kinship ties. In spite of the efforts of many slaveowners to sever kinship ties among blacks, the African pattern of family relationships, which consists of the cooperation and mutual support of mother, father, children, grandparents, brothers, sisters, nieces, nephews, and cousins, persisted and is regarded by scholars today as the major force contributing to the survival of black people in the United States.

As discrimination and economic insufficiency continued to plague black society, the need for kinship ties and community support became increasingly crucial and necessary to black survival. Today, black spouses continue to maintain close ties with their parents and kin after they are married. In some cases, they may live with their parents in extended family households (Taylor et al., 1991). Even if they do not, their parents continue to be important sources of emotional and economic support.

NATIONAL DATA ✖ In a national study of black Americans, 86.9 percent said that they sought informal assistance for a serious personal problem. Mothers and sisters were those most often asked for help (Chatters, 1989). Another national study focusing on black mothers (both never married and married) emphasized that they tended to live in close proximity to their families, have daily contact with kin, and report feelings of closeness to and satisfaction with their families (Jayakody et al., 1993).

Marital Roles

The strong emphasis on ties to one's parents and the larger kinship system seems to affect the black marriage relationship. In many cases, the mother-child relationship seems to take precedence over the wife-husband relationship. It is uncertain whether this tie is maintained because the black wife feels that her economically disadvantaged husband will not be able to support her or that he will not stay around to do so (desertion rates among black men are higher than among white men).

Although not all black wives prioritize the mother role over the spouse role, the precedence seems well established. "In the colonial period of Africa, missionaries often observed and reported the unusual devotion of the African mother to her child" (Staples, 1988). This bond also extends to grandchildren as extended households among black women are primarily due to the presence of grandchildren residing within their households (Taylor et al., 1991).

Many analysts argue that the modern African-American family has always differed from European-American families and should not be expected to conform to the married-couple pattern.

WILLIAM P. O'HARE

Not all black wives prioritize their mother role over their marital role.

Black men labor under negative stereotypes. Some of these stereotypes become self-fulfilling prophecies because the dominant society is structured in a way that prevents many black men from achieving socially approved goals. In spite of their disadvantaged socioeconomic status, most black men function in a way that gains the respect of their mates, children, and community (Staples, 1988). In regard to the parenting role, Mirande (1991) reviewed the literature and observed that in spite of the traditional view that the father in the African American family is absent or insignificant, many fathers play an integral role in the family and "typically assume an authoritative role" (p. 58).

Marital Satisfaction

While married blacks report being happier than never married, separated, and divorced blacks (Taylor et al., 1991), black spouses tend to be less happy than white spouses (Staples, 1988). Reasons for their lower sense of marital satisfaction are primarily in reference to economic and social discrimination. Black wives may be particularly unhappy because, with fewer partners to select from, they may be forced to settle for husbands who have less education than they do. The sense of inadequacy the black husband may feel, coupled with the black wife's feeling that she has selected someone who is less than her ideal mate, may have a negative impact on both partners (Ball & Robbins, 1986). Black husbands are also influenced by economic concerns: the higher the family income, the greater the satisfaction with family life (Staples, 1988). Finally, data from the National Survey of Black Americans reveal that black spouses who do not have children report being happier than black spouses who do have children (Broman, 1988). However, other researchers have found that parental status is unrelated to both life and family life satisfaction (Taylor et al., 1991), and African-American and white spouses report similar levels of marital satisfaction (McAdoo, 1992). The latter finding is based on a study of 208 parents living in the Baltimore/Washington area.

Ꝙ Mexican American Marriages

Approximately 22 million Mexican Americans (about nine percent of our population) live in the United States, primarily in the five southwestern states close to Mexico (California, Texas, New Mexico, Arizona, and Colorado) (*Statistical Abstract of the United States: 1993*, Table 18). The term *Mexican American* refers to those of Mexican origin or descent living in America. The term is sometimes used synonymously with Chicanos, Spanish Americans, Hispanics, Mexicanos, Californios, and Latin Americans.

When America annexed Texas in 1845, Mexico became outraged and the Mexican War followed (1846–1848). In the Treaty of Guadalupe Hidalgo, Mexico recognized the loss of Texas and accepted the Rio Grande as the boundary between Mexico and the United States. Although the war was over,

We still don't have enough of the right kind of information to adequately explain the complexity and volatility of Hispanic families.

WILLIAM VEGA

hostilities continued, and the negative stereotyping of Mexican Americans as a conquered and subsequently inferior people became entrenched. Such stereotyping and discrimination has had implications for the stress to which Mexican American spouses have been exposed. Compared to Anglos, Mexican Americans have less education, lower incomes, and work in lower-status occupations (Becerra, 1988).

The Husband-Wife Relationship

There is great variability among Mexican American marriages. What is true in one relationship may not be true in another, and the same relationship may not resemble itself at two different points in time. Nevertheless, some "typical" characteristics of Mexican American relationships are detailed here.

Male Dominance   Although role relationships between women and men are changing in all segments of society, traditional role relationships between the Mexican American sexes are characterized by male domination.

> Male dominance is the designation of the father as the head of the household, the major decision maker, and the absolute power holder in the Mexican American family. In his absence, this power position reverts to the oldest son. All members of the household are expected to carry out the orders of the male head (Becerra, 1988, 148).

Female Submissiveness   The complement to the male authority figure in the Mexican American marriage is the submissive female partner. Traditionally, the Chicana is subservient to her husband and devotes her time totally to the roles of homemaker and mother. As more wives begin to work outside the home, the nature of the Mexican American husband-wife relationship is becoming more egalitarian in terms of joint decision making and joint parental childrearing (Vega, 1991).

While previous researchers (Becerra, 1988) have suggested that the divorce rate among Mexican Americans is lower than the rate for whites, more recent research suggests that, when separation is included in marital disruption, such differences disappear (Vega, 1991). Hence, the presumed strong family orientation and influence of the Catholic church (a disproportionate number of Mexican Americans are Catholic), does not have the effect dropping the divorce rate among Hispanics.

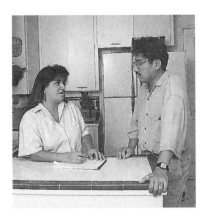

As more wives become employed, the nature of the Mexican American husband-wife relationship is becoming more egalitarian.

The Parent-Child Relationship

In the past, Mexican Americans have valued close relationships with both nuclear and extended family members (*familism*). Although members of the extended family (aunts, uncles, and grandparents) may still be regarded with great affection, Mexican Americans are becoming more Americanized and nuclear-oriented (Becerra, 1988). Those families that enjoy large extended-family social networks do so because they are geographically located in the same area, which permits frequent visiting and behavioral exchange.

The relationship between Mexican American children and their parents has traditionally been one of respect. This respect results not from fear but from parents (including fathers) being warm, nurturing, and companionable (Mirande, 1991). In addition, it is common for the younger generation to pay great deference to the older generation. When children speak to their elders, they are expected to do so in a formal way.

Native American Marriages

About two million individuals define themselves as Native Americans (*Statistical Abstract of the United States: 1993*, Table 52). The term refers not only to American Indians but Inuit (Eskimos) and Aleuts (native people of Aleutian Islands). American Indians comprise over 95 percent of all Native Americans and are the group to which we will refer.

Native Americans as a group are young (half are under 35), Protestant, and Democrat (Hoffman, 1989). At the present time, there are about 300 tribal groups with over 160 different languages. "In reality, terms such as 'American Indian' and 'Native American' encompass a variety of cultures, nationality groups, languages, and family systems. It is, thus, very difficult to generalize about such groups" (Mirande, 1991, 69). When the various forms are viewed across time, Native American families have been patrilineal (heritage traced through males), matrilineal (heritage traced through females), monogamous, polygynous, and polyandrous. Tribal identity has consistently taken precedence over family identity and the values of a family reflect those of the particular tribe.

Given these caveats, John (1988) and Yee (1992) made some observations about Native American families.

1. Mate selection is based on romantic love.
2. There is little stigma attached to having a child whether the woman is married or single. Children are highly valued in the Native American community.
3. Intermarriage rates are the highest of any racial group. The most frequent intermarriage involving a Native American is between a white husband and an Indian wife.
4. Divorce among Native Americans is regarded as a less traumatic event and is usually not associated with guilt, recriminations, or adverse effects.
5. Elders are viewed as important and are looked up to. They are given meaningful economic, political, religious, and familial roles within the tribe.
6. Extended families are the norm.
7. Role relationships between husbands and wives are becoming less traditional as Native American women become increasingly involved in working outside the home.

What is certain about Native American families is that there is great cultural conflict between their values and those of the larger American society. Native Americans are very present oriented whereas mainstream (white) society is future oriented and concerned with schedules and plans. John (1988) commented on the outcome of the conflicts between the cultures:

> Despite the fact that Native American families are not immune to the larger, social structural forces in operation in the United States, I believe that Native American families continue to exhibit a unique character attributable to long-standing cultural differences from American culture as a whole . . . they will adapt their family practices to meet their own needs (pp. 356, 358).

ॐ Asian and Pacific Islander American Marriages

Asian and Pacific Islander Americans comprise over seven million individuals (three percent of the U.S. population) and represent one of the fastest growing minority groups in the United States (O'Hare & Felt, 1991; *Statistical Abstract of the United States: 1993*, Table 18). These groups include Chinese, Filipino, Japanese, Korean, Vietnamese, Cambodian, Thai, LaoHmong, Burmese, Samoan, and Guamanian. Each group is different depending on their cultural heritage, immigration history, American response to their arrival or presence and their resulting socioeconomic and social adaptation (Yee, 1992). Immigration history is relevant to family patterns in that, historically, immigration laws restricted whole families from immigrating. Rather only men were permitted entry because they were a source of inexpensive labor, which resulted in splintered families (wives and children later joined the immigrated men).

The cultural heritage brought to the states included Confucian philosophy and the importance of familism. Confucian principles emphasized superiority of husbands and elders over wives and children. These values often clashed with Asian children who were socialized in America toward more egalitarian roles. Familism as a value emphasized the importance of the family group over the individual with the result of a much lower divorce rate among Asians and Pacific islanders. The next section provides a closer look at how generations of Japanese families change as a result of being in the United States.

Japanese American marriages differ in regard to how long the spouses have lived in the United States. Issei or first generation Japanese Americans were born in Japan and immigrated to the United States in the early 1900s. They are now in their eighties and live with their children, in nursing homes, or in senior citizen housing projects such as the Little Tokyo Towers in Los Angeles. Their values, beliefs, and patterns reflect those of traditional Japanese families. These beliefs include (Kitano, 1988): (1) offspring not allowed to select their own spouse, (2) a stronger parent-child bond than the bond between husband and wife, (3) male dominance, (4) rigid division of labor by sex, and (5) precedence of family values over individual values.

The Nisei or second generation children "are products of a variety of influences—their Issei parents, Japanese American peers, other minorities, and the American mainstream" (p. 266). The younger Nisei believe in romantic love, select their own mates, regard the husband-wife relationship as more important than the parent-child relationship, and have egalitarian sex roles. However, family gatherings of extended kin are common.

The Sansei are the third generation children and reflect even greater Americanization than the Nisei. The Sansei marry for love (Mirande, 1991) and do not hesitate to marry someone who is not Japanese (about 60 percent of marriages are out-group marriages). Most of these interracial marriages are to whites. "The increase in out-group marriage rates is the result of the breakup of the ghetto, loss of family control over marital choices, changes in the law, and more liberal attitudes toward interracial unions on the behalf of both the ethnic and majority communities" (Kitano, 1988, 274).

Black, Mexican American, Native American, and Asian and Pacific Islands marriages emphasize the diversity of marriage patterns in the United States. In the next section we focus on goals common to Americanized marriages—marital stability and happiness.

❧ Successful Marriages

One year of joy, another of comfort, and all the rest of content.

JOHN RAY

There is substantial evidence that marriage disproportionately benefits men.

JOHN GOTTMAN

The view that is so widely held that marriage is good for men and bad for women should be debunked as a myth.

DAVID MYERS

Most people who marry do so with a common goal—to have a successful marriage. Marital success is measured in terms of marital stability and marital happiness. Stability refers to how long the spouses are married and how permanent they view their relationship, whereas marital happiness refers to more subjective aspects of the relationship. In describing marital success, researchers have used the terms *satisfaction, quality, adjustment, lack of distress,* and *integration.* Marital success is often measured by asking spouses how happy they are, how often they spend their free time together, how often they agree about various issues, how easily they resolve conflict, how sexually satisfied they are, and how often they have considered separation or divorce (see Self-Assessment: Marital Success Scale).

Figure 8.1 provides the retrospective marital enjoyment evaluation of 52 white, college educated husbands and wives over a period of 35 years together. They reported the most enjoyment with their relationship in the beginning, followed by less enjoyment during the childbearing stages, and a return to feeling more satisfied after the children left home. Husbands also reported being more satisfied throughout the marriage than the wives (Vaillant & Vaillant, 1993).

One problem encountered in measuring marital success is that people tend to answer questions the way they think they should rather than the way things are. This tendency to give socially desirable answers (also referred to as conventionalization) makes it difficult for researchers to know what relationships are actually like behind closed doors. Nevertheless, 27 percent of 15,000 married respondents reported they had "excellent"—and 34 percent reported

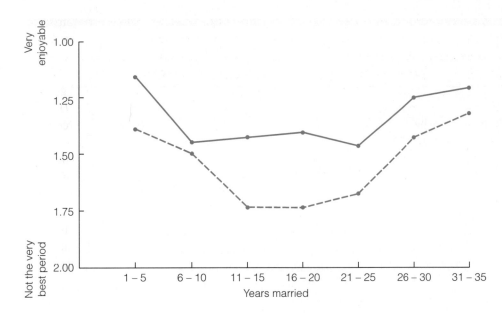

FIGURE 8.1

Retrospective Marital Enjoyment

Source: Caroline O. Vaillant and George E. Vaillant. Is the U-curve of marital satisfaction an illusion? A 40-year study of marriage. *Journal of Marriage and the Family,* 1993, 55, 237, Figure 6. Copyrighted 1993 by the National Council on Family Relations, 3989 Central Avenue NE, Suite 550, Minneapolis, MN 55421. Reprinted by permission.

Note: The figure divides length of intact marriages into seven consecutive 5-year periods and compares the retrospectively assessed marital satisfaction of 52 husbands and their wives; 1 = very enjoyable, 2 = not the very best. —— = husbands, - - - = wives.

that they had "very good" marriages (Schwartz & Jackson, 1989). The respondents had been married an average of about six years, most in their first marriage, and had an average of 2.7 children living with them. Very happy marriages tend to exhibit three primary characteristics.

1. *Quality Time Together.* A national study of over 1,200 married adults revealed that happily married spouses spend a lot of time interacting (Zuo, 1992). In the Schwartz and Jackson (1989) study, the spouses with "excellent" or "very good" marriages "had a close friendship and did all the little, daily things together. They were always there for each other" (70).

> **CONSIDERATION**
>
> In one study, 55 couples wore electronic pagers for one week and provided reports on their companionship, activity, and affect for an average of 45 random times when signaled by the pagers. Based on this study, the researcher concluded that the amount of time couples spent together did not by itself predict marital satisfaction. Rather, marital satisfaction was associated with the quality of the affect experienced by couples when they were together (Larson, 1992).

2. *High Affection and High Sex Frequency.* Schwartz and Jackson (1989) found that spouses in very happy relationships showed a great deal of affection in public. The spouses also reported being sexually passionate in private with

If I'm in the garage all night working on my cars and she's in the house reading, we're still together. But if I'm in the garage all night and she's not in the house, it seems terribly lonely to me.

JAY LENO

Marital Success Scale

This scale is designed to measure the degree to which you have a successful relationship. There are no right or wrong answers. After reading each sentence carefully, circle the number that best represents your feelings.

1 Strongly disagree
2. Mildly disagree
3 Undecided

4 Mildly agree
5 Strongly agree

		SD	MD	U	MA	SA
1.	I am in love with my partner.	1	2	3	4	5
2.	I am happy with my partner.	1	2	3	4	5
3.	My partner and I can usually negotiate our differences and feel good about the solution.	1	2	3	4	5
4.	My partner and I spend most of our free time together.	1	2	3	4	5
5.	I would rather be with my partner than with anyone else.	1	2	3	4	5
6.	I have not thought of separating from or divorcing my partner.	1	2	3	4	5
7.	I enjoy sex with my partner.	1	2	3	4	5
8.	My partner is a good lover.	1	2	3	4	5
9.	My partner and I agree on most issues.	1	2	3	4	5
10.	My partner and I communicate easily with each other.	1	2	3	4	5
11.	My partner and I have similar values.	1	2	3	4	5
12.	My partner and I treat each other as equals.	1	2	3	4	5

		SD	MD	U	MA	SA
13.	My partner and I are affectionate with each other.	1	2	3	4	5
14.	My partner and I are committed to make our relationship work.	1	2	3	4	5
15.	My partner is supportive of my interests.	1	2	3	4	5
16.	I can tell my partner when something is bothering me.	1	2	3	4	5
17.	My partner can tell me when something is bothering him or her.	1	2	3	4	5
18.	My partner and I rarely argue.	1	2	3	4	5
19.	My partner lets me know that I am loved.	1	2	3	4	5
20.	I let my partner know that I love him or her.	1	2	3	4	5

Score _____

Scoring: Add the numbers you circled. The response that suggests the most successful relationship is 5 (strongly agree), and the response that suggests the most problematic relationship is 1 (strongly disagree). Therefore, the higher your total score (100 is the highest possible score), the more successful your relationship. The lower your total score (20 is the lowest possible score), the more difficult you view your relationship. A score of 60 places you at the midpoint between the extremes.

NOTE: This Self-Assessment is designed to be thought provoking: it is not intended as a clinical evaluation device.

A successful marriage requires falling in love many times, always with the same person.

MIGNON MCLAUGHLIN

the happiest of spouses reporting the highest frequency of intercourse of all the couples—with 8 to 12 occasions of intercourse each month. One woman reported, "My husband satisfies my sexual needs; he is a sexually exciting partner" (p. 68).

❧ **IN FOCUS 8.2** ❧

The Family Life of Centenarians

There are over 50,000 centenarians (individuals over 100 years old) living in the United States. Over half of these people live with family members (outside of an institution). Over half can attend to themselves (go to the bathroom, get out of the bed, walk) unassisted and over 80 percent can converse easily (Sanders, 1993). While stereotypes of centenarians are predominately negative, centenarians represent a great reservoir of information about life in the later years.

Only a small percentage (8 percent) of individuals over 100 are married. Most married centenarians are men in their second or third marriages. Many have outlived some of their children.

Marital satisfaction in these elderly marriages is related to a high frequency of expressing love feelings to one's partner. While it is assumed that spouses who have been married for a long time should know how each other feels, this is often not the case. Telling each other "I love you" is very important to the respective spouses.

A good relationship with one's elderly parents seems to be more related to the life satisfaction of the offspring than to the life satisfaction of the elderly parent. Hence, the caregiver benefits as well as the person receiving the care.

The elderly, often stereotyped as nonproductive and in wheelchairs, provide enormous contributions to our society. They not only provide love, a sense of history, and economic support to their children/stepchildren, they contribute to their community. A study of North Dakota elderly revealed that they contributed 2.5 million hours annually of volunteer work to the citizens of the state. That the elderly only receive help from others is blatantly inaccurate. Their contribution to themselves, their families, and their society is enormous.

SOURCE: Sanders, Greg. The family in later life. Presentation on behalf of the Center on Aging, Department of Sociology, and Department of Child Development and Family Relations, East Carolina University, April 23, 1993. Used by permission of Dr. Sanders.

---

3. *Equality and Respect for Each Other's Needs.* Very happy spouses in the Schwartz and Jackson (1989) study also reported fairness, cooperation, and sharing of cooking, cleaning, childrearing, and breadwinning. Each partner felt that they worked together and that neither was the dominant partner. The wives also reported that they shared equal financial authority. Decisions to purchase big ticket items such as cars and refrigerators were always discussed ahead of time. Eighty-eight percent of the women who reported having excellent marriages said that they shared decision making equally (Schwartz & Jackson, 1989). Equal decision making is important because it communicates to each partner that individual opinions and feelings are valued. Ward (1993) also found an association between marital happiness and household equity.

> The married life is the only life.
>
> GEORGE PETTIE

The Schwartz and Jackson (1989) study reported the characteristics of marriages that had endured an average of six years. Robinson and Blanton (1993) identified the marital strengths in enduring marriages of 15 couples who had been married over 30 years. These strengths included:

● Intimacy—closeness with the spouse which permeated the relationship encompassing the emotional, physical, and spiritual aspects.

⤳ IN FOCUS 8.3 ⤳

An Arrangement of Marriages*

Tolstoy wasn't even half right. Happy couples are not all alike. Nor is every unhappy family unhappy in its own way.

If David H. Olson, Ph.D., is correct, there are seven basic types of marriage. In three of them, where happiness abounds, the couples held together by the smooth working of most or all factors intrinsic to relationships—personality compatibility, communication, conflict resolution, and sexuality. In the other four, the marriage hinges more on external elements, leisure activities, religious attitudes, financial management, children, family and friends, and distress predominates.

Unfortunately, Olson finds, most people today live in distressed marriages. But his studies of over 15,000 couples point the way to happier futures for many.

Head of family social science at the University of Minnesota, Olson evaluated marital partners—both as individuals and the consensus between them—along the nine dimensions that previous studies had shown to be areas of trouble and conflict. He also looked at their global assessment of satisfaction, and their cohesion and adaptability. When he compiled all the data, families naturally clustered into seven distinct profiles.

Type 1—Devitalized marriage: 40 percent of couples. There is pervasive unhappiness with all relationship dimensions and considerable instability. Both partners have considered divorce. They are critical of each other's personality. Their marriage is strictly utilitarian. They tend to be younger, married a shorter time, and have a lower income than other couples. Many are minorities. More of them come from divorced homes, and more of them were previously divorced themselves. They stay together for lack of alternatives.

Type 2—Financially focused: 11 percent of couples. These couples have conflict and are unhappy in their communication and the way conflicts are resolved. They are dissatisfied with the personal characteristics of their partner, and there may be bitter personal attacks. Their careers come before the relationship, and money or financial rewards hold them together. Their single relationship strength is financial management. A high number of husbands and wives in such utilitarian relationships have considered divorce.

Type 3—Conflicted: 14 percent. They are dissatisfied in many facets of the relationship—personality issues, communication, conflict resolution, and sexuality—and they may avoid or fail to settle issues between them. Instead, they focus on and gain satisfaction from outside experiences

---

- Commitment—divorce was not considered an option; the couples were committed to each other for personal reasons rather than societal pressure.
- Communication—sharing thoughts and feelings, discussing problems together, listening to each other's point of view.
- Congruence—similarity of perceptions in regard to their relationship.
- Religious orientation—strong religious orientation provided couples with social support from church members, spiritual support, emotional support, and moral guidance in working out problems (Robinson, in press).

Marry, and with luck it may go well. But when a marriage fails, then those who marry live at home in hell.

EURIPIDES

𝒮 Unhappy But Stable Marriages

Unhappy but stable marriages are those in which the spouses describe their marriages as unhappy yet predict there is a low chance that they will divorce.

❧ IN FOCUS 8.3 ❧

such as leisure, the children, religious life. But a high percentage of both partners have considered divorce.

Type 4—Traditional: 10 percent. They are moderately satisfied with many relationship elements, while their sexual relationship and the way they communicate are sources of distress. They are not as critical of each other's personality as Types 1, 2 and 3. Their strength lies in a satisfying religious life and good interaction with extended family and friends. The marriages are relatively stable. These couples tend to be older, married longer, white, and Protestant.

Type 5—Balanced: 8 percent. They are moderately satisfied with most relationship areas, with real strengths in communication and problem-solving. The biggest problem is financial management. They have higher than average agreement on leisure, childrearing, and sexuality. They place a high value on the nuclear family. Still, over a quarter have considered divorce.

Type 6—Harmonious: 8 percent. They are highly satisfied with each other, the expression of affection, and their sexual life. But they are self-centered, viewing children as a burden and parenting as a source of distress. It may be that, when a problem develops in this family, it shows up in the child.

Type 7—Vitalized: 9 percent. They are highly satisfied with almost every dimension of their relationship and get along well. They are personally integrated, have strong internal resources, and agree in most external areas. They develop difficulties but resolve them well. They are economically better off than most others, and tend to be older, married longer, white, Protestant. They tend to be in their first marriage and come from intact families.

There were a few surprises in the study. Even the best-adjusted couples are not immune to marital shakiness; nearly one in four wives in Type 7 marriages had at some point considered divorce. In fact, wives were generally less satisfied than husbands in all seven marriage types.

While recognizing the complexity of marriage relationships, the typology points to the specific strengths families can build upon in times of crisis. And it indicates weaknesses that need to be addressed if and when couples seek therapy.

*SOURCE: "An Arrangement of Marriages" (PT Staff, Jan/Feb). Reprinted with permission from *Psychology Today* magazine. Copyright © 1993. (Sussex Publishers, Inc)

NATIONAL DATA ❧ Based on a national sample of U.S. marrieds, 7.4 percent of the husbands and 7.0 percent of the wives reported they were involved in unhappy but stable marriages (Heaton & Albrecht, 1991).

The characteristics of individuals involved in unhappy but stable relationships include being older, being committed to marriage as an institution, having few social contacts, feeling little control over one's life, and believing that divorce would make them even more unhappy. Factors that have little effect on the continuity of unhappy marriages include socioeconomic status, economic assets, ethnicity, household division of labor, and religious affiliation and participation (Heaton & Albrecht, 1991).

Penance and matrimony are the same.

RICHARD DUKE

The relatively low percentage of respondents who report being unhappy in and who intend to remain in unhappy marriages reflects attrition of unhappy marriages through dissolution at an unprecedented rate. The predominant belief is that marriages should be happy and that divorce is an acceptable solution to dissatisfaction (p. 757).

This chapter has focused on various marriage relationships in which couples are involved. Another way to describe marriage relationships is by arrangement type. These types are reviewed in the In Focus 8.3: An Arrangement of Marriages.

♋ Trends

Marriage relationships in the United States will continue to be very diverse. No single family form, sex role relationship, or set of values will represent "the" American family. Racial, ethnic, and cultural differences will ensure that marital life is rich and varied.

The rate of intermarriage (age-discrepant, religious, and racial) has increased and may continue to do so. This trend is partly due to a weakening of the influence nuclear families have over enforcing the norms of endogamy. That families have become more liberal with each succeeding generation was illustrated in the earlier discussion of Japanese American marriages.

Finally, colleges and universities have begun to accommodate the needs of married students. The availability of housing on campus for married students has increased and more day–care and preschool facilities have become available on college and university campuses. Evening classes have also become more common to accommodate the student (married or single) who is employed during the day.

> **What the coming multicultural, polyethnic, pluralistic—unarguably diverse—America will be no one knows for certain. There are no models anywhere for what is happening here.**
>
> ITABARI NJERI

⤳ CHOICES ⤳

Marriage partners may be confronted with decisions about the partners' "night out," parents as live-ins, and who manages the money.

Partners' Night Out?

Although recently married individuals may want to spend all of their time together, this need often diminishes over the years and the need to spend time without the spouse increases. Frequently one or both partners want to spend time with their friends. This may mean going to happy hour on Wednesdays with their coworkers, bowling, shopping, playing bridge, fishing, golfing, or seeing a movie.

Some spouses have a policy of trust with each other. One wife said:

> I tell John to go anywhere he wants to with anyone he wants to just as long as he is emotionally and sexually faithful to me. I'm not going to try to restrict what John does. If he wants to be unfaithful to me, he will. But I have no reason to distrust him,

❧ CHOICES ❧

and I'm sure he doesn't get involved with other women when we're apart.

Other spouses are very suspicious of each other. One husband said:

> I didn't want her having lunch or after work drinks with her boss. I don't think it's a healthy situation. Before you know it they would be talking about getting together at the beach.

For partner's night out to have a positive impact on the couple's relationship, it is important that the partners maintain emotional and sexual fidelity to each other, that each partner have a partner's night out, and that the partners spend some nights alone with each other. Friendships can enhance a marriage relationship by making the individual partners happier; but friendships cannot replace the marriage relationship. Spouses must spend time alone to nurture their relationship.

Parents as Live-Ins?

As the parents of the spouses get older, a decision must often be made by the spouses about whether to have the parents live with them. Usually it is the mother of either spouse; the father is the most likely to die first. One wife said:

> We didn't have a choice. His mother is 82 and has Alzheimer's disease. We couldn't afford to put her in a nursing home at $1,200 a month, and she couldn't stay by herself. So we took her in. It's been a real strain on our marriage, since I end up taking care of her all day. I can't even leave her alone to go to the grocery store.

Some elderly persons do have resources for nursing home care or the spouses can afford it. But even in these circumstances, some spouses decide to have their parents live with them. "I couldn't live with myself if I knew my mother was propped up in a wheelchair eating Cheerios when I could be taking care of her," said one spouse.

When spouses disagree about parents in the home, the results can be devastating. According to one wife:

> I told my husband that mother was going to live with us. He told me she wasn't and that he would leave if she did. She moved in, and he moved out (we were divorced). Five months later, my mother died.

Who Will Manage the Money?

Marriage is a partnership of two people who cooperate economically. It is like a small business. Money comes in (income), and money goes out (expenses). Someone must be responsible for seeing that expenses do not consistently exceed income (to avoid going deeply into debt), bills are paid (to keep the lights and water on), and accurate records are kept (to pay taxes and for Internal Revenue Service audits). Couples differ in who manages the money. In some marriages, one spouse is responsible; in others, the partners may do so jointly. Joint bookkeeping works only if role responsibilities are clear and each person is disciplined enough to fulfill his or her responsibility.

How many checking and savings accounts to have is another issue. No pattern works best for all people. One couple may have one savings and one checking account; another may have three checking and three savings accounts. In an instance of the latter, the husband, wife, and child each had their own checking and savings accounts, and each was responsible for keeping the books for their accounts. "It is really easier if everyone keeps up with his or her own," said the wife.

⌇ Summary

All marriage relationships represent a commitment between the partners, between the respective families, and between the couple and the state. The wedding is a rite of passage signifying the change from the role of single individual to the role of married spouse. Marriage involves various personal, social, legal, sexual, and interactional changes for the spouses. Personal changes include an enhanced self-concept that results from entering into a committed, loving relationship. Society also approves of a couple's marriage and encourages them to feel good about their decision. But the reality of marriage also involves disenchantment—the gradual process whereby each spouse becomes aware that the other person in courtship is not always the same person in marriage.

Marrying while still in college may lead to role conflict. Trying to fulfill the roles of student, spouse, employee, and perhaps parent may introduce strain in some relationships.

An increasing number of marriages are interreligious. Although mixed religious marriages do not necessarily imply a greater risk to marital happiness, marriages in which one or both spouses profess no religion are in the greatest jeopardy. Also, husbands in interreligious marriages seem less satisfied because children are usually reared in the faith (or nonfaith) of the wife.

Divorce is greater among black marriages than white marriages. This is partly due to economic insufficiency and the social context of racism. It is a myth that overt discrimination has virtually vanished in the last 20 years. As soon as the workday ends, blacks and whites retreat to different worlds.

Mexican American marriages have traditionally been characterized by male dominance and female submissiveness. As more wives work outside the home, the power of the Chicana will increase and the balance of power will continue to shift.

Native American marriages are not so easily categorized. Since tribal identity supersedes family identity and the values and beliefs vary widely among and between the 300 federally recognized tribes, there are few fixed characteristics of Native American marriages.

Japanese American marriages differ depending on the degree of socialization of the spouses in the United States. Issei (first generation) marriages are very traditional in contrast to Sansei (third generation) marriages in which the spouses are very Americanized.

Marital success refers to both marital stability and marital happiness. Marital success may be assessed by examining how much time the couple spend together, how they evaluate the time they spend together, the absence of conflict, and the similarity of values. Very happy spouses report that they spend the majority of their leisure time together, that they are affectionate in public and passionate in private, and that they value equality in their relationships.

Questions for Reflection

1. How has the adult relationship in which you have been involved the longest changed over time?
2. How do you feel about entering interreligious, interracial, and age-discrepant marriages?
3. How do the characteristics of your relationship compare with those of very happy marriages?

References

American Council on Education and the University of California. The American freshman: National norms for fall, 1992. Los Angeles, Calif.: Los Angeles Higher Education Research Institute, 1992.

Ball, R. E. and L. Robbins. Marital status and life satisfaction among black Americans. *Journal of Marriage and the Family,* 1986, *48,* 389–394.

Becerra, R. M. The Mexican American family. *Ethnic families in America: Patterns and variations,* C. H. Mindel, R. W. Habenstein, and R. Wright, Jr., eds. New York: Elsevier, 1988, 141–159.

Berkove, G. F. Perceptions of husband support by returning women students. *Family Relations,* 1979, *28,* no. 4, 451–457.

Boston, Thomas D. *Race, class, and conservatism.* Boston: Unwin Hyman, 1988.

Broman, C. L. Satisfaction among blacks: The significance of marriage and parenthood. *Journal of Marriage and the Family,* 1988, *50,* 45–51.

Buehler, C. Initiator status and divorce transition. *Family Relations,* 1987, *36,* 82–86.

Chatters, L. M., J. J. Taylor, and H. W. Neighbors. Size of informal helper network mobilized during a serious personal problem among black Americans. *Journal of Marriage and the Family,* 1989, *51,* 667–676.

Cook, A. The $60,000 wedding. *Money,* May 1990, 118–132.

Cottrell, A. B. Cross-national marriages. *Next of Kin,* L. Tepperman and S. J. Wilson, eds. Englewood Cliffs, N.J.: Prentice-Hall, 1993, 96–100.

Finkel, J. S. and F. J. Hansen. Correlates of retrospective marital satisfaction in long-lived marriages: A social constructivist perspective. *Family Therapy,* 1992, *19,* 1–16.

Glenn, N. D. Quantitative research on marital quality in the 1980s: A critical review. *Contemporary families: Looking forward, looking back,* Alan Booth, ed. Minneapolis, Minn.: National Council on Family Relations, 1991, 28–41.

Goetting, A. Patterns of support among in-laws in the United States. *Journal of Family Issues,* 1990, *11,* 67–90.

Heaton, T. B. and S. L. Albrecht. Stable unhappy marriages. *Journal of Marriage and the Family,* 1991, *53,* 747–758.

Hoffman, Thomas J. Native Americans, public spending issues, incumbent support and political cynicism: A comparative analysis. *Free Inquiry in Creative Sociology,* 1989, *17,* 33–40.

Huyck, M. H. and D. L. Gutmann. Thirtysomething years of marriage: Understanding experiences of women and men in enduring family relationships. *Family Perspective,* 1992, *26,* 249–265.

Janus, S. and C. Janus. *The Janus Report on sexual behavior* New York: Wiley, 1992.

Jayakody, R., L. M. Chatters, and R. J. Taylor. Family support to single and married African American mothers: The provision of financial, emotional, and child care assistance. *Journal of Marriage and the Family,* 1993, *55,* 261–276.

Jaynes, Gerald D. and Robin M. Williams, Jr. *A common destiny: Blacks and American society.* Washington, D.C.: National Academy Press, 1989.

John, R. The native American family. *Ethnic families in America,* 3d ed., C. H. Mindel, R. W. Habenstein, and R. Wright, Jr., eds. New York: Elsevier, 1988, 325–367.

Johnson, D. R., T. O. Amoloza, and A. Booth. Stability and developmental change in marital quality: A three-wave panel analysis. *Journal of Marriage and the Family,* 1992, *54,* 582–594.

Kantrowitz, Barbara and D. Witherspoon. The December dilemma: How to reconcile two faiths in one household. *Newsweek,* December 28, 1987, 56.

Kelly, S. Returning to college. *Family Relations,* 1982, *31,* no. 2, 287–294.

Kitano, H. L. The Japanese American family. *Ethnic Families in America: Patterns and Variations,* 3d ed., Charles H. Mindel, Robert W. Habenstein, and Roosevelt Wright, Jr., eds. New York: Elsevier, 1988, 258–276.

Klinger-Vartabedian, Laurel and L. Wispe. Age differences in marriage and female longevity. *Journal of Marriage and the Family,* 1989, *51,* 195–202.

Larson, R. The time husbands and wives spend together: A shadowy quantity. Paper, 54th Annual Conference, National Council on Family Relations, Orlando, Florida, 1992. Used by permission.

Marano, H. E. The reinvention of marriage. *Psychology Today,* January/February 1992, 49 et passim.

McAdoo, J. L. Ethnic and gender differences in work, family and interrole conflict. *Proceedings: Work and Family* 54th Annual Conference of National Council on Family Relations, 1992, 2, 1, p. 42.

McRoy, S. and V. Fisher. Marital adjustment of graduate student couples. *Family Relations,* 1982, *31,* no. 1, 37–41.

Mederer, H. J. Division of labor in two–earner homes: Task accomplishment versus household management as critical variables in perceptions about family work. *Journal of Marriage and the Family,* 1993, *55,* 133–145.

Mirande, A. Ethnicity and fatherhood. *Fatherhood and Families in Cultural Context,* F. W. Bozett and S. M. H. Hanson, eds. New York: Springer Publishing Co., 1991, 33–82.

O'Hare, W. P. and J. C. Felt. Asian Americans: American's fastest growing minority group. *Population Trends and Public Policy,* 1991, *19,* 1–16.

Olson, D. H. An arrangement of marriages. *Psychology Today,* January/February 1993, *26,* 22.

Open Doors, 1978–1988. Institute of International Education, 809 United Nations Plaza, New York, NY.

Rice, F. P. *Intimate relationships, marriages and families.* Mountain View, Calif.: Mayfield Publishing Co., 1993

Robinson, L. Religious orientation in enduring marriages: An exploratory study. *Review of Religious Research,* in press.

Robinson, Linda C. and Priscilla W. Blanton. Marital strengths in enduring marriage. *Family Relations,* 1993, *42,* 38–45.

Schwartz, Pepper and Donna Jackson. How to have a model marriage. *New Woman,* February 1989, 66–74.

Serovich, J. and S. Price. In-law relationships: A role theory perspective. Paper, 54th Annual Conference, National Council on Family Relations, Orlando, Florida, 1992. Used by permission. Julianne Serovich is an assistant professor of marriage and family therapy at Texas Tech University. Sharon Price is professor and chair of the Department of Child and Family Development at the University of Georgia.

Shehan, C. L., F. M. Berardo, H. Vera, S. M. Carley. Women in age-discrepant marriages. *Journal of Family Issues,* 1991, *12,* 291–305.

Shehan, C. L., E. W. Bock, and G. R. Lee. Religious heterogamy, religiosity, and marital happiness: The case of Catholics. *Journal of Marriage and the Family,* 1990, *52,* 73–79.

Shelton, Beth Anne. *Women, men, and time: Gender differences in paid work, housework, and leisure.* New York: Greenwood Press, 1992.

Stanley, S. M. and H. J. Markman. Assessing commitment in personal relationships. *Journal of Marriage and the Family,* 1992, *54,* 595–608.

Staples, Robert. The Black American family. *Ethnic families in America: Patterns and variations,* C. H. Mindel, R. W. Habenstein, and R. Wright, Jr., eds. New York: Elsevier, 1988, 303–324.

Statistical Abstract of the United States: 1993, 113th ed. Washington, D.C.: U.S. Bureau of the Census, 1993.

Stephan, W. G. and C. W. Stephan. Intermarriage: Effects on personality, adjustment, and intergroup relations in two samples of students. *Journal of Marriage and the Family,* 1991, *53,* 241–250.

Suitor, J. J. Marital quality and satisfaction with the division of household labor across the family life cycle. *Journal of Marriage and the Family,* 1991, *53,* 221–230.

Taylor, R. J., L. M. Chatters, M. B. Tucker, and E. Lewis. Developments in research on black families: A decade review. *Contemporary Families,* Alan Booth, ed. Minneapolis, Minn.: National Council on Family Relations, 1991, 275–296.

Thao, T. C. Among customs on marriage, divorce and the rights of married women. *Cultural Diversity and Families,* K. G. Arms, J. K. Davidson, Jr., and N. B. Moore, ed. Dubuque, Iowa: Brown and Benchmark, 1992, 54–66.

Tzeng, Meei-Shenn. The effects of socioeconomic heterogamy and changes on marital dissolution for first marriages. *Journal of Marriage and the Family,* 1992, *54,* 609–619.

Vaillant, C. O. and G. E. Vaillant. Is the U-curve of marital satisfaction an illusion? A 40-year study of marriage. *Journal of Marriage and the Family,* 1993, *55,* 230–239.

Vega, W. A. Hispanic families in the 1980s: A decade of research. *Contemporary Families,* Alan Booth, ed. Minneapolis, Minn.: National Council on Family Relations, 1991, 297–306.

Ward, R. A. Marital happiness and household equity in later life. *Journal of Marriage and the Family,* 1993, *55,* 427–428.

Yee, B. W. K. Gender and family issues in minority groups. *Cultural Diversity and Families,* K. G. Arms, J. K. Davidson, Sr., and N. B. Moore, eds. Dubuque, Iowa: Brown and Benchmark, 1992, 5–10.

Zuo, J. The reciprocal relationship between marital interaction and marital happiness: A three-wave study. *Journal of Marriage and the Family,* 1992, *54,* 870–878.

Contents

9
CHAPTER

Communication and Conflict

Is It True?

1. The most frequently told lie reported by a sample of college students was the number of previous sexual partners they had had.

2. According to Deborah Tannen, women and men focus on basically the same content when they are having a conversation.

3. Conflict in a relationship is sometimes healthy for the partners and their relationship.

4. Most states license or certify marriage and family therapists.

5. Telling your partner everything you think and feel is probably better for your relationship than tempered honesty.

1 = T; 2 = F; 3 = T; 4 = F; 5 = F

If you're married for more than ten minutes you will have to forgive someone for something.

HILLARY CLINTON

One of the primary characteristics of all successful relationships is effective communication. In a study of 451 families, the researchers (Rueter & Conger, 1992) noted that it is the quality of the communication exchanged between family members rather than the amount of communication that is crucial to effective problem solving. Levine and Busby (1992) analyzed data on 800 couples and concluded that being flexible and negotiating differences are more important than similarities between the partners in creating a shared reality.

> **Speech is the voice of the heart.**
> KAIBARA EKKEN

Another researcher (Yandoli, 1989) looked at sources of stress in medical marriages (marriages in which one or both partners were medical doctors) and found that problems in these relationships were not necessarily associated with the number of hours spent working; rather, being satisfied in the relationship seemed to be associated with communication and intimacy between the partners.

Noller and Fitzpatrick (1991) reviewed the literature in regard to the communication patterns between happy and unhappy couples. They found that the couples differed with the happy couples spending more time talking, more time talking about personal topics, greater disclosure of positive feelings about the partner, more agreement, more use of humor, and less focus on "winning a conflict."

In this chapter we define communication as both content (verbal and nonverbal) and process and look at principles and techniques of effective communication. We also look at how women and men differ in their communication styles, communication and intimacy, and various theories of communication. We end the chapter with a review of marital conflict, principles and techniques of conflict resolution, and the different styles of marital therapy that are available.

ℬ Definition of Effective Communication

Communication may be defined as the process of exchanging information and feelings between two individuals. Communication involves not only spoken words but nonverbal messages. The latter are conveyed by tone of voice and body language. For example, assume two individuals are saying goodnight at the end of their first date. One says to the other, "I'll call you." Depending on the tone of voice (excitement or sullenness) and body language (looking into the eyes of the person and holding hands with the person or looking down and avoiding hand contact), the nonverbal message will mean different things.

> **An argument usually consists of two people each trying to get the last word—first.**
> LAURENCE PETER

Good communication is essential for a happy and durable relationship.

Sweet discourse makes short the days and nights.

GEORGE HERBERT

Effective communication may be defined as the exchange of information and feelings that is timely, accurate, and precise (Turner, 1993). Timely information means that you tell your partner information at a time that allows him or her to make an appropriate response. Suppose you want your partner to be aware that your birthday is a week from Saturday and that you would like to go out to dinner. Giving timely information, in this case, involves telling your partner *before* your birthday that you would like to go out to dinner on your birthday. If you wait until after your birthday to alert your partner to your desire to go out to dinner on your birthday, your partner is unable to respond to the request. Similarly, if you are resentful about something your partner has done or failed to do, telling your partner about your feelings and expectations when you are having these feelings provides an opportunity for effective change on the part of your partner.

Effective communication also involves conveying information that is accurate. Simply stated, accurate information is information that is true. If you tell your partner that you have not had contact with a previous lover, when in fact you have had such contact, you are giving inaccurate information.

C O N S I D E R A T I O N

In some cases, we may unintentionally provide inaccurate information (for example, when we, ourselves, have been misinformed). When we intentionally convey false information, we are being dishonest. Honesty is a trait that most individuals value in their intimate relationships. Unfortunately, dishonesty is surprisingly common in such relationships (see In Focus 9.1).

Effective communication implies not only that information be timely and accurate but also precise. Precise information is information that is clearly expressed with specificity and detail. In relationships, communicating precise information implies revealing exactly how you feel and what you want. For example, if you would like to eat a particular food or at a particular place with your partner ("Grilled chicken at Wendy's would be terrific"), you need to make your wishes known. Otherwise, your partner may assume that chicken McNuggets at McDonalds would be fine with you.

Being precise about one's emotions may be more difficult than being precise about one's preferred food. For example, consider a woman whose partner has been invited to a bachelor party, complete with stripper. The woman feels she would be very upset if her partner goes to this party; she may even feel she does not want to be involved with "the kind of man who goes to those kinds of parties." If she tells her partner she prefers that he not go to the bachelor party, she is providing accurate information. However, she is not communicating information that is precise in that she is not telling him the full weight of her feelings about his going to a bachelor party.

CONSIDERATION

Although the words *accurate* and *precise* are often used interchangeably, there is an important distinction in the respective meanings. Accurate means "true." While precise has several meanings (see any dictionary), our usage of the word *precise* in this chapter means "clearly expressed." An important implication of this distinction is that accurate information is not necessarily precise; and precise information is not necessarily accurate.

While communication involves verbal content that is hopefully timely, accurate, and precise, equally important is the nonverbal content. Nonverbal aspects of spoken verbal communication include tone of voice, volume, pitch, and rate of speech. Nonverbal aspects of written verbal communication include style of writing (handwritten, printed, typed, sloppy, neat) and medium (personal stationary, card, napkin).

There are many forms of nonverbal communication, which include the following (Argyle, 1988):

1. facial expression
2. gestures and bodily movements
3. spatial behavior (e.g. how close you stand to a person)
4. gaze and pupil dilation
5. bodily contact
6. nonverbal vocalizations (e.g. sighs, grunts)
7. clothes, and other aspects of appearance
8. posture
9. smell

Distressed spouses are less accurate at decoding the nonverbal communication of their partners than that of strangers.

PATRICIA NOLLER

⌁ IN FOCUS 9.1 ∿

Dishonesty in Intimate Relationships

In a study of 85 single professional women, honesty was ranked as the most important quality in a mate (Sparrow, 1991). Honesty was also identified by 443 university students as the most important quality they looked for in their "ideal partner" (Laner, 1989). However, Saxe (1991) observed that deception is "a ubiquitous feature of human social interaction" (p. 409). And, as suggested by a number of studies, dishonesty may be particularly rampant among single university students.

Shusterman and Saxe asked 50 undergraduate students who were involved in relationships whether they had ever lied to their partners (reported in Saxe, 1991).

More than 85 percent reported that they had done so. Examples of lies that students reported follow:

● I kissed another guy at a party and never told my boyfriend.
● I cheated on her with an attractive friend of mine.
● I was sexually involved with a friend of his for about a month.

In the Shusterman and Saxe study, 41 percent of the lies reported by students involved extradyadic sex. Almost all of the subjects reported that the reason for the deception was

(continued on next page)

LIES UNIVERSITY STUDENTS REPORTED HAVING TOLD TO CURRENT OR PAST PARTNER (N = 137)

Lie	Male	Female	Total Number of Students Reporting Lie	Percent of Sample Reporting Lie
Number of previous partners	11%	20%	42	30.6
Had an orgasm	1	23	33	24.1
You're the best	8	8	22	16.1
It was good	2	15	23	16.8
I love you	7	8	21	15.3
I'm a virgin	3	5	11	8.0
No lies	1	6	9	6.6
You're the biggest	0	7	10	7.3
I like oral sex	4	1	8	5.8
On my period	0	4	6	4.4
I've never cheated	1	3	5	3.6
Yes, I want to	0	1	2	1.5
Age	1	2	3	2.2
I'll call	2	.01	3	2.2
I've got a headache	1	2	3	2.2
No, I don't have AIDS or an STD	1	.01	2	1.5
I'll pull out	2	0	2	1.5
Too tired	1	.01	2	1.5
I'm on the pill	0	.01	1	0.75
I don't have protection	1	0	1	0.75
You're beautiful	1	0	1	0.75

℘ **IN FOCUS 9.1** ℘

---

to protect their partners or their relationship. For example, students who lied to their partners said they did so for the following reasons:

- The other guy didn't matter to me at all, so I didn't want to risk the relationship.
- I wouldn't want the hassle of breaking her trust in me.
- I didn't want to hurt him.

Other studies have been conducted in regard to dishonesty in relationships. In one study of 18- to 25-year-old students attending college in California, 34 percent of men and 10 percent of women reported having told a lie to someone in order to have sex with that person (Cochran & Mays, 1990). Another study found that lying was one of the strategies university men use to obtain sexual intimacy (Gray et al., 1988). In still another study, 39 percent of 252 women reported that they "sometimes-to-always" pretended to have an orgasm when they did not (Darling, Davidson, & Cox, 1991).

Knox, Schacht, Holt, and Turner (1993) studied sexual lies among 137 college students. The table reflects the nature and frequency of the lies they reported telling. Notice the gender differences in lying behavior.

REFERENCES:

Cochran, S. and V. Mays. Sex, lies and HIV. *New England Journal of Medicine,* March 15, 1990, 774–775.

Darling, Carol Anderson, J. Kenneth Davidson, Sr., and Ruth P. Cox. Female sexual response and the timing of partner orgasm. *Journal of Sex and Marital Therapy,* 1991, *17,* 3–21.

Gray, Michael D., Diane Lesser, Howard Rebach, Brenda Hooks, and C. Bounds, Sexual aggression and victimization: A local perspective. *Response to the Victimization of Women and Children,* 1988, *11,* no. 3, 9–13.

Knox, D., C. Schacht, J. Holt, and J. Turner. Adapted from Sexual lies among university students. *College Student Journal,* 1993, *27,* 269–272. Used by permission of *College Student Journal.*

Laner, M. R. Competitive vs. noncompetitive styles: Which is most valued in courtship? *Sex Roles,* 1989, *20,* 168.

Saxe, Leonard. Lying: Thoughts of an applied social psychologist. *American Psychologist,* 1991, *46,* no. 4, 409–415.

Sparrow, Kathleen Handy. Factors in mate selection for single black professional women. *Free Inquiry in Creative Sociology,* 1991, *19,* no. 1, 103–109.

A review of some research on nonverbal communication and marital satisfaction appears in the In Focus 9.2.

℘ Effective Communication: Basic Principles and Techniques

Effective communication involves various principles and techniques which include the following:

1. *Make Communication a Priority.* Communicating effectively implies making communication an important priority in a couple's relationship. When communication is a priority, partners make time for communication to occur in a setting without interruptions—they are alone; they do not answer the phone; they turn the television off. Prioritizing communication results in more information being exchanged between the partners, which

It is extremely easy for us to give our major attention to minor matters.

E. C. MCKENZIE

∽ **IN FOCUS 9.2** ∽

Nonverbal Communication and Marital Satisfaction

Researchers L'Abate and Bagarozzi (1993) reviewed the literature on nonverbal communication and marital satisfaction.

Some of their findings follow:

- Behaviors exhibited between spouses carry symbolic messages concerning the sender's evaluations of the receiver. When Dan smiles (a nonverbal behavior) at Sharon, he attempts to convey to her his positive feelings about her.
- The nonverbal part of a message carries more weight when the verbal and nonverbal components conflict. For example, if Sharon tells Dan, "I love you" but crosses her arms, stands back and looks at the floor when saying so, Dan is likely to feel that she doesn't really mean what she says.
- Dissatisfied couples tend to attribute hurtful intent to their spouses more frequently than satisfied couples. Melissa and Chad are an unhappy couple. If Melissa forgets to leave the porch light on for Chad, he is likely to assume that her doing so is to convey her displeasure with him and their relationship. If the couple were happy with each other, her not leaving the porch light on would probably not be interpreted negatively by Chad.

In summary . . .

How one perceives one's mate; how one interprets the spouse's behavior; how one experiences the partner's intentions and the hidden, symbolic meanings that one attributes to the spouse's verbal statements, coupled with one's unspoken assumptions and expectations for the mate- all play a part in the degree to which the message received is consistent with the message sent. These factors can be considered to be noise in the communication channel. The more noise, the more distorted the message (L'Abate & Bagarozzi, 1993, 43).

The same nonverbal behavior is also subject to multiple interpretations. For example, crying may be viewed as the manipulation of one's partner, the sharing of hurt feelings, or the expression of one's openness and vulnerability. Interpersonal conflict might occur when one partner interprets crying as manipulation while the other interprets it is an expression of vulnerability.

SOURCE: Based on Luciano L'Abate and Dennis A. Bagarozzi. *Sourcebook of marriage and family interaction.* New York: Brunner/ Mazel, Publishers, 1993.

The heart's letter is read in the eyes.

HERBERT

increases the knowledge each partner has about the other. In relationships where communication is a priority, partners may be more willing to communicate about difficult, but important topics.

2. *Establish and Maintain Eye Contact.* Shakespeare noted that one's eyes are the "mirrors to the soul." Partners who look at each other when they are talking not only communicate an interest in each other but are able to gain information about the partner's feelings and responses to what is being said. Not looking at your partner may be interpreted as lack of interest and prevents you from observing nonverbal cues.

3. *Ask Open-Ended Questions.* When your goal is to find out what your partner's thoughts and feelings are about an issue, it is best to use open-ended questions. An open-ended question encourages your partner to give an answer that contains a lot of information. A closed-ended question elicits a one-word answer, such as "yes" or "no." Closed-ended

T A B L E 9.1

Open-Ended and Closed-Ended Questions

OPEN-ENDED QUESTIONS	CLOSED-ENDED QUESTIONS
How do you feel about living together?	Do you think living together is wrong?
How do you feel about my going out with my friends without you?	Do you think we should have a "boys/girls night out?"
Tell me about your previous relationships.*	Have you been involved with a lot of people before me?
What are your religious beliefs?	Do you believe in God?
What are your feelings about marriage?	Do you ever want to get married?

*Although this is technically a statement, it may be considered a question because it asks for information.

questions that can be answered with a "yes" or "no" do not provide the opportunity for the partner to express feelings and preferences in detail. Table 9.1 provides examples of open-ended and closed-ended questions.

4. *Use Reflective Listening*. To be a good communicator, one must be a good listener, and to be a good listener, one must use reflective listening. The technique of reflective listening involves paraphrasing or restating what the person you are listening to has said to you. Reflective listening involves restating both the content of what the person has said and the feeling(s) that the person is conveying. Because feelings are often conveyed nonverbally, it is important to "listen to" a person's nonverbal messages (tone of voice, facial expression, gestures, gaze, spatial behavior—how close) and to reflect the feelings that one observes. You may have to ask an open-ended question (e.g., "How does that make you feel?") in order to find out what a person is feeling and be able to reflect back their feelings.

Reflective listening serves the following functions: (a) creates the feeling for the speaker that she or he is being listened to and is being understood and (b) increases the accuracy of the listener's understanding of what the speaker is saying. If a reflective statement does not accurately reflect what the speaker thinks and feels, the speaker can correct the inaccuracy by restating her or his thoughts and feelings.

An important quality of reflective statements is that they are nonjudgmental. For example, suppose two lovers are arguing about spending time with their respective friends and one says, "I'd like to spend one night each week with my friends and not feel guilty about it." The partner may respond by making a statement that is judgmental (critical or evaluative). Judgmental responses serve to punish or criticize someone for what he or she thinks, feels, or wants and often result in frustration and resentment. Table 9.2 provides several examples of judgmental statements and nonjudgmental reflective statements.

TABLE 9.2

Judgmental and Nonjudgmental Reflective Responses to One Partner Saying "I'd Like to Spend One Evening Each Week with My Friends"

NONJUDGMENTAL REFLECTIVE STATEMENTS	JUDGMENTAL STATEMENTS
You have a preference for us to be with our respective friends.	You only think about what *you* want.
You think it is healthy for us to be with our friends some of the time.	You value "us" less than I do.
You really enjoy your friends and want to spend some time with them.	You just want a night out so that you can meet someone new.
You think it is important that we not abandon our friends just because we are involved.	You just want to get away so you can drink.
You think that our being apart one night each week will make us even closer.	You are selfish.

TABLE 9.3

Examples of Phrases Used in Making Reflective Statements

1. It sounds like you're feeling . . .
2. What I hear you saying is that . . .
3. You are angry when . . .
4. So, from your point of view . . .
5. It's important to you that . . .
6. You feel hurt because . . .
7. Your feeling is that . . .
8. When I come home late, you feel . . .
9. What you would like is . . .
10. You feel that . . .

CONSIDERATION

Reflective listening is a simple technique, but many individuals find it difficult to incorporate into their communication style. Reflective listening is particularly difficult when the speaker is angry at the listener and has said something hurtful or critical. For example, your partner may say to you: "I'm sick and tired of you being late all the time. The only person you think of is yourself. You are the most inconsiderate person I know." Because you feel attacked and criticized, you may respond by defending yourself ("I am not always late!") or by attacking back ("You are so rigid!"). It might be more difficult to simply reflect back what your partner has said to you: "It sounds like you feel really hurt and angry that I was late tonight. You feel that my being late means that I don't care about you and that it is inconsiderate to be late. It is important to you that I be on time in the future." Table 9.3 lists several phrases that may be used in making reflective statements.

5. *Use "I" Statements.* "I" statements focus on the feelings and thoughts of the communicator, without making a judgment on others. Because "I" statements are a clear and nonthreatening way of expressing what you want and how you feel, they are likely to result in a positive change in the listener's behavior. In contrast, "You" statements blame or criticize the listener and often result in increasing negative feelings and actions in the relationship.

6. *Say Positive Things About Your Partner.* Everyone likes to hear others say positive things about them. Communication in any relationship feels better when it contains many positive references to the individuals involved. These positive references may be in the form of compliments.

For example, a spouse who tells a partner that "You deserved a raise, you're the best!" or "You smell wonderful" is giving positive feedback to the partner. Positive feedback may also be in the form of words of gratitude. "I'm so glad you remembered to put gas in the car" and "Thank you for that delicious dinner" are examples of expressions of gratitude.

7. *Make Positive Requests for Change.* In addition to telling their partner what pleases them, partners who communicate effectively give feedback about what displeases them. Communication is more effective when this type of feedback is expressed in terms of positive requests for future change. Rather than say, "Don't be late," it may sound better if the partner hears, "Please meet me at 4:00." Rather than say, "You always leave the bathroom a wreck," it may sound better if the partner hears, "Please hang up your towel after you take a shower."

8. *Make Specific Resolutions to Disagreements.* To prevent the same issues or problems from continuing to happen, it is important to agree on what each partner will do in similar circumstances in the future. For example, if going to a party together results in one partner drinking too much and drifting off with someone else, what needs to be done in the future to ensure an enjoyable evening together?

   Coming to such a resolution is not easy, especially when each partner blames the other, is defensive, or hopes that the conflict will go away. Resolving disagreements takes time, energy, and skill. The result is a sense of pride the partners may have about their relationship in regard to their ability to resolve conflict.

9. *Give Congruent Messages.* A message is congruent when the verbal and nonverbal behavior match. A person who says, "O.K. You're right" and smiles as he or she embraces the partner with a hug is communicating a congruent message. In contrast, the same words accompanied by leaving the room and slamming the door communicate a very different message.

10. *Share Power.* "By far the most common source of problems in a relationship involves the distribution of power" (Duncan & Rock, 1993, 50). Power is the ability to impose one's will on the partner and to avoid being influenced by the partner. Power is a subtle element in communication and is often operative without awareness. Partners exercise power by several means:

    Withdrawal—(Not speaking to the partner.)
    Guilt induction—("How could you ask me to do this?")
    Being pleasant—("Kiss me and help me move the sofa.")
    Being dependent—("Don't leave me—I need you.")
    Negotiation—("I'll go with you to your parents if you will let me golf for a week with my buddies.")
    Deception—(Running up bills on charge card.)
    Blackmail—("I'll tell your parents you do drugs if you do.")
    Physical Abuse—(or verbal threats)

As noted in Chapter 2 on Gender Roles, egalitarian relationships have the greatest capacity for satisfaction because neither partner feels

Courtship in a marriage can be a lot better than court.

DEAN EDELL

Despite our celebration of openness, in the power struggle, it's the person who's most vulnerable, most generous, most committed who loses.

ROBERT KAREN

Although difficult, the man might respond by saying, "You are very angry at me and feel that I like her better than you. I'm glad you told me your feelings. I haven't made myself clear about how much I like your sense of humor."

There is no good arguing with the inevitable. The only argument available with an east wind is to put on your overcoat.

J. R. LOWELL

exploited by the other, not guilty for taking advantage of the partner. "In a good relationship, ideally there is a balance of power" (Duncan & Rock, 1993, 51).

11. *Choose Your Reaction Carefully.* Because people influence each other, the way you respond to your partner influences the way your partner responds to you. If your partner accuses you of being unfaithful, rather than defend yourself, ask what you have done to elicit these feelings. Listen nondefensively (Duncan & Rock, 1993). If your partner is worried about how you spend your time, rather than shout that you resent not being trusted, keep a detailed diary of what you do and share it with your partner daily (p. 95).

12. *Keep the Process of Communication Going.* Communication is both content (verbal and nonverbal) and process (the couple continue to interact so as to find a resolution to the conflict). It is important not to allow difficult content to shut down the communication process (Turner, 1993). In order to ensure that the process continues, the partners should focus on the fact that the sharing of information is essential and reinforce each other for keeping the process alive. For example, if your partner tells you something that you do, which bothers him or her, it is important to thank him or her for telling you that rather than becoming defensive. In this way, your partner's feelings about you stay out in the open rather than hidden behind a wall of resentment. Otherwise, if you punish such disclosure because you don't like the content, subsequent disclosure will stop.

One of the most frustrating experiences is when one partner wants and tries to communicate, but the other partner will not communicate. If your partner will not communicate with you, you might try the following (Duncan & Rock, 1993):

1. Do something that's a noticeable change from your previous strategies. Become less available for conversation and do not try to initiate or maintain discussion. Cut it short if a discussion does start. This not only removes but reverses all pressure on the partner. The entire pattern changes and the power shifts.

2. Interpret silence in a positive way: "We are so close we don't always have to be talking." "I feel good when you're quiet because I know that it means everything is all right between us." This negates any power your partner might be expressing through silence.

3. Focus less on the relationship and more on satisfying yourself. When you do things for yourself, you need less from others in the way of attention and assurance.

The Self-Assessment: Effective Communication Scale may help you to assess the degree to which your relationship is characterized by effective communication.

Effective Communication Scale

This scale is designed to predict the degree to which you and your partner have communication patterns that may be conducive to a positive relationship. There are no right or wrong answers. After reading each item carefully, circle the number that applies to you.

1 Never   4 Frequently
2 Rarely   5 Very Frequently
3 Occasionally

	N	R	O	F	VF
1. My partner and I make sure we address issues that are bothering one or both of us.	1	2	3	4	5
2. We look at each other when we are talking.	1	2	3	4	5
3. We ask open- rather than closed-ended questions.	1	2	3	4	5
4. We use reflective listening when we talk about an issue over which we disagree.	1	2	3	4	5
5. We use "I" statements.	1	2	3	4	5
6. We compliment each other frequently.	1	2	3	4	5
7. We resolve disagreements in such a way that we both feel good.	1	2	3	4	5

	N	R	O	F	VF
8. We share the power in our relationship.	1	2	3	4	5
9. We make positive requests for change in each other.	1	2	3	4	5
10. We have a good track record for resolving conflicts so that the same problem does not recur.	1	2	3	4	5

SCORING: Add the numbers you circled. 1 (never) represents a pattern that does not reflect effective communication and 5 (very frequently) represents a pattern that reflects effective communication. The lower your total score (10 is the lowest possible score), the less effective is the communication between you and your partner. The higher your total score (50 is the highest possible score), the more effective is your communication pattern. A score of thirty places you at the midpoint between having ineffective and effective communication patterns.

NOTE: This Self-Assessment is intended to be fun and thought provoking. It is not intended to be used as a clinical diagnostic instrument.

❧ Gender Differences in Communication

Tannen (1990) observed that men and women, in general, focus on different content in their respective conversations. Men tend to focus on activities; women, relationships. To men, talk is information; to women, it is interaction. To men, communication should emphasize what is rational; to women, communication is about emotion and relationships. To men, conversations are negotiations in which they try to "achieve and maintain the upper hand if they can, and to protect themselves from others' attempts to put them down and push them around" (p. 25). However, to women, conversations are negotiations for closeness in which they try "to seek and give confirmations and

Every sociolinguistic study of men's and women's conversation, and particularly men in conversation with women, has found that men almost entirely dominate the conversation.

W. NEIL ELLIOT

support, and to reach consensus" (p. 25). Their goal is to preserve intimacy and avoid isolation.

A team of researchers reviewed the literature on intimacy in communication and observed that men approach a problem in the relationship cognitively while women approach it emotionally (Derlega et al., 1993). The reaction of a husband to a seriously ill child is to put pressure on the wife to be mature (stop crying) about the situation and to encourage stoicism (asking her not to feel sorry for herself). Wives, on the other hand, want their husbands to be more emotional (by asking them to cry to show that they really care that their child is ill).

Swain (1989) also observed that men and women have different communication patterns in same sex relationships. Men feel more comfortable communicating with other men. "I'm more relaxed around guys. You don't have to watch what you say," (p. 75) reported one man. Men also feel that they are communicating with each other and being intimate when they are sharing an activity (e.g. sports) together. "The closeness is in the 'doing'—the sharing of interests and activities" (Swain, 1989, 77). In contrast, women friends are more likely to talk and not depend on an activity to generate comfortable feelings or dialogue.

Men and women are also socialized to express their nonverbal emotions differently. For example, many women are socialized not to express anger so that when they are angry, they cry. Men, on the other hand, are socialized not to display hurt feelings so they often become angry when they are hurt (L'Abate & Bagarozzi, 1993).

Men and women also differ in the way they read cues to assess each others' interest in physical intimacy (Reiss & Reiss, 1990). For example, a man might assess his date's interest in physical intimacy by looking to see if she had another drink, agreed to go to his apartment, laughed at a dirty joke, and permitted him to touch her breast. A woman might assess her date's interest in physical intimacy according to whether he smiled at her in a friendly way, laughed at her jokes, listened to her opinions, and kissed her tenderly. Both may guess the intentions of the other without engaging in direct clear communication about physical intimacy.

℘ Communication and Emotional Intimacy

Communication plays a major role in the level of emotional intimacy experienced by couples. The level of intimacy in a couple's relationship can be described by the eight facets described below (Russel, 1990; Waring, 1988). As you will note, four of these eight facets of intimacy relate to communication. The facets related to communication are marked with an asterisk (*).

*1. Conflict resolution—the ease with which differences of opinion are resolved.

Sometimes I wonder if men and women really suit each other. Perhaps they should live next door and just visit now and then.

KATHARINE HEPBURN

Men and women are so vastly different. There will always be a struggle between them.

GLENN CLOSE

If we are honest with ourselves, our [women and men] emotional landscapes are as strikingly different as the Sahara and Kilimanjaro.

HARRY STEIN

*2. Affection—the degree to which feelings of emotional closeness are expressed by the couple.
3. Cohesion—a feeling of commitment to the relationship.
*4. Sexuality—the degree to which sexual needs are communicated and fulfilled by the partner.
5. Identity—the couple's level of self-confidence and self-esteem.
6. Compatibility—the degree to which the couple is able to work and play together comfortably.
7. Autonomy—the degree to which the couple is successful in gaining independence from their families of origin and their offspring.
*8. Expressiveness—the degree to which thoughts, beliefs, attitudes, and feelings are shared within the relationship.

The Importance of Self–Disclosure in Intimate Relationships

One aspect of intimacy in relationships is self-disclosure. This involves revealing personal information and feelings to another person about one's self. According to Waring (1988), "self-disclosure is the single factor which most influences a couple's level of intimacy" (p. 38).

Individuals in Japan are taught that quick self-disclosure in social relationships is inappropriate. They are much less likely to disclose information about themselves than individuals socialized in the United States (Nakanishi, 1986).

How may couples facilitate self-disclosure in their relationship? Almost 25 years ago, R. D. Laing (1970) identified a communication method whereby couples can facilitate self-disclosure. The procedure involves the partners looking at an event or issue from four perspectives: his perspective, her perspective, his perspective of her perspective, and her perspective of his perspective. For example, suppose you and your partner are thinking about living together. Each of you will have different perspectives and feelings about moving in together. By each presenting his and her perspective and each identifying what he or she thinks is the perspective of the partner, they disclose a great deal about this issue. As a result the couple can, with full knowledge, decide what they want to do about living together.

Confiding—the ability to reveal yourself fully, honestly, and directly—is the lifeblood of intimacy.

LORI GORDON

ACROSS CULTURES

Productive Versus Nonproductive Communication

Productive communication increases the emotional closeness of the partners and brings their respective expectations and behaviors into alignment. Suppose one partner expects the other to be punctual, and the partners discuss the issue. Their communication will be productive to the degree that they feel closer as a result of the discussion and either one partner agrees to be more punctual or the other partner decides the issue isn't worth getting upset about and drops the expectation. Productive communication patterns imply that each partner

Trouble is a part of your life, and if you don't share it, you don't give the person who loves you enough chance to love you enough.

DINAH SHORE

will participate in stopping negative interaction from escalating, in focusing on issues rather than on personalities, and in responding to each other with supportive comments to create a context of positive regard for the other (Halford et al., 1990). Here is an example of productive communication:

> Mary and Bob have been living together for about six months. When they first moved in together, they agreed that because they were both in school and had part-time jobs, they would share the housekeeping chores—cooking, washing dishes, doing laundry, and keeping the apartment neat. It seemed to Mary that she was gradually drifting into the role of housewife, which she thought was counter to her agreement with Bob. She felt Bob wasn't going to start doing his share of the housework unless she brought it up, so she mentioned the subject one evening as she was preparing dinner.

MARY: You know, I thought we agreed that we would do the cooking and other stuff together.

BOB: Well, I guess we did . . . [feeling somewhat guilty for not living up to his part of the deal]. What do you want me to do?

MARY: Since I've got classes Tuesday and Thursday nights, it would be nice for you to take care of the cooking and washing the dishes on those nights. I'll handle it Monday, Wednesday, and Friday, and we can worry about the weekend later."

BOB: Okay. I guess I'm cooking Thursday night, eh? What would you like?

Nonproductive communication increases the emotional distance between the partners and leaves the discrepancy between their respective expectations and behaviors unchanged. An example follows:

That's my opinion and ought to be yours.

PAT COOPER

> Alice and Jeff have the same problem as Mary and Bob. Jeff hasn't been helping around the apartment, and Alice is upset.

ALICE: Jeff, I'm really fed up with your lying around the apartment while I do all the work. Didn't we agree to do this stuff together?

JEFF: Maybe we did, but I've got all I can do with school and work, so you'll just have to do it yourself.

ALICE: You aren't being very sensitive to my needs—I go to school and work, too. You're so lazy.

JEFF: What would you know about sensitivity?

ALICE: You're being hateful and mean.

JEFF: I guess you're being real sweet when you talk like that aren't you? And when are you going to pay back the money you owe me, hypocrite?

ALICE: I'm not listening to this crap.

JEFF: Yeah! What are you going to do about it?

ALICE: Leave—that's what.

JEFF: Go ahead.

If you fight frequently, something is not being worked out.

RONALD KESSLER

What began as a discussion about Jeff helping Alice around the apartment has escalated into a decision to terminate the relationship. Blaming/belittling/attacking, insisting on the rightness of one's own position, and being unwilling to consider the other person's point of view inevitably leads to a breakdown in communication. Both partners become resentful and want to distance themselves from the relationship. Table 9.4 compares productive and nonproductive communication styles.

❧ Theories of Marital Communication

Various theories, or models, have been developed to help us understand the processes of communication in relationships. Five major theories of marital communication include behavioral exchange, behavioral competency, social learning, relational control, and systems (Fitzpatrick, 1988; Duncan & Rock, 1993).

Behavioral Exchange Model

The behavioral exchange model assumes that marital satisfaction is based on the ratio of rewards to costs in the relationship. Rewards are positive exchanges, such as compliments, compromises, and agreements. Costs refer to negative exchanges, such as critical remarks, complaints, and disagreements. According to this model, the greater the ratio of positive to negative exchanges, the happier the marriage is presumed to be.

"Do unto others as they would have you do unto them" is the Platinum rule.

JACK TURNER

TABLE 9.4

Characteristics of Productive and Nonproductive Communication

PRODUCTIVE COMMUNICATION (MARY AND BOB)	NONPRODUCTIVE COMMUNICATION (ALICE AND JEFF)
1. Avoidance of behaviors in column 2.	1. Blaming: ". . . you're lying around the house while I do the work."
2. Neutral statement rather than accusation: "I thought we agreed . . . ."	2. Name calling: "lazy," "hypocrite."
3. Acknowledgment of responsibility for partner's discomfort: "Well, I guess we did discuss my sharing the work."	3. Threatening: "I'm going to leave."
4. Expression of willingness to alleviate problem: "What do you want me to do?"	4. Using sarcasm: "What would you know about sensitivity?" "I guess you're being real sweet when you talk like that."
5. Positive labeling of suggestion—"It would be nice if. . . ."	5. Being judgmental: "You're being hateful and mean."
6. Reciprocity: "I'll handle it Monday, Wednesday, and Friday."	6. Changing issues: ". . . When are you going to pay back the money you owe me. . . ?"
7. Positive expression at end of conflict: "Okay. I guess I'm on for Thursday night, eh?"	7. No attempt to stop escalation of conflict.
8. Brief: Mary and Bob took two turns each speaking.	8. Lengthy: Alice and Jeff took six turns each speaking.

The behavioral exchange model emphasizes the importance of positive interaction in marital satisfaction. However, it does not resolve the issue of whether positive interaction leads to marital happiness, or marital happiness leads to positive interaction.

Behavioral Competency Model

This model views marital unhappiness as resulting from the spouses' lack of skill in communication, conflict resolution, and stress management. This model views communication as a skill that can be learned and continually improved.

The behavioral competency model predicts that couples who have and use skill in arguing constructively will have a high level of relationship satisfaction. But this model does not seem to apply to couples in courtship or in the early stages of a relationship. That is, inability to argue constructively in courtship does not seem to affect satisfaction with the relationship at the time, but it does predict unhappiness in the marriage after several years.

Social Learning Theory

Reward it is, that makes us good or bad.

ROBERT HERRICK

Social learning theory emphasizes how communication patterns between partners are learned. A partner who discloses sexual fantasies of another and who is berated for having such fantasies learns not to be open about fantasies. In contrast, a partner who is reinforced for such disclosure ("I appreciate your telling me your fantasies about others") is likely to disclose in the future.

Social learning theory also describes how partners decrease a behavior by punishing it. The wife who criticizes her husband's cooking is punishing her husband's cooking behavior, making him less likely to cook in the future.

CONSIDERATION

Sometimes people in relationships make the mistake of punishing the very behaviors they want to occur. The wife in the above example complained that her husband didn't do his share of the cooking. If she wants his cooking behavior to increase, she might consider reinforcing it ("It's so nice to come home and have dinner already made") rather than punishing it ("You overcooked the broccoli again," "Why didn't you put fresh garlic in the spaghetti?")

Social learning theory is sometimes criticized for being too focused on observed behavior, and not attentive to internal states, such as thoughts and feelings. This model is particularly useful, however, not only in understanding behavior, but in changing it as well.

Relational Control Model

The relational control model views the communication between partners as reflective of the distribution of power in the relationship. One aspect of this model focuses on how the parties either assert or relinquish control through their communication. Hence, communication patterns reveal who has the power in the relationship and how this power is used. Power refers to the ability of individuals to carry out their will, even in the face of resistance by others.

This model may be criticized on two grounds. First, the "chicken and the egg" problem exists—does the power structure in a relationship determine the communication pattern? Or does the communication pattern in the relationship determine the power structure in that relationship? Second, this model does not acknowledge that one partner may have more power in some areas of the relationship, whereas the other partner may have more power in other aspects of the relationship. In addition, power in relationships is not fixed, but rather may change over time.

Systems Model

A systems view of communication emphasizes that each person in a relationship continually influences the other. Because of this, "you are not acting completely of your own free will" (Duncan & Rock, 1993, 48). For example if you refuse to get into an argument by not yelling back, your partner's choice of continuing to argue with you is muted.

A systems perspective suggests that communication between partners often involves attempts to influence each other. Statements made by a partner often convey a message regarding that partner's needs. Implicit in this message is a command or directive intended to influence the behavior of the other partner.

> "My back itches" may mean "Scratch my back." "I had a rough day" may mean "Leave me alone," "I need your support," or "Fix me a drink." Even "I love you" can be an implicit command, depending upon the circumstances. It may mean "Tell me that you love me" (pp. 49–50).

One criticism of the systems model is that it places responsibility for a behavior on someone other than the person who engages in the behavior. For example, according to the systems model, a wife who is abused by her husband must be doing something to elicit or contribute to his behavior. While this may be true, it is the husband who is ultimately responsible for his behavior.

Each of these theories provide a unique focus when observing interaction in relationships. A summary of the basic perspective, key concepts, and criticisms of each theory are presented in Table 9.5.

Healthy relationship systems exhibit disagreement but they manage (qua "process") their disagreement more functionally.

**MICHAEL KOLEVZON
LORI JENKINS**

TABLE 9.5

Theories of Marital Communication

THEORY	PERSPECTIVE	KEY CONCEPTS	CRITICISMS OF THE THEORY
Behavior Exchange	Ratio of positive to negative exchanges determines marital satisfaction.	Ratio of exchanges Rewards Costs	Causal direction is unclear. (Is positive interaction the cause or result of marital satisfaction?)
Behavior Competency	Communication is a behavioral skill that can be learned.	Expression of feelings Conflict resolution Negotiation	May not apply to courtship or early stages of the relationship.
Social Learning	Positive verbal behavior must be rewarded to be maintained.	Positive reinforcement Negative reinforcement Punishment	Focuses on behavior, does not address internal thoughts and feelings.
Relational Control	Communication between partners reflects the distribution of power in the relationship.	Power	Causal direction is unclear. (Is power in a relationship the cause or result of communication patterns?) Power structure changes over time. Each partner may have power in some aspects of the relationship.
Systems	Partners influence each other by what they say and do.	Relational system influence, control interaction	Misplaces responsibility for behavior.

℘ Conflicts in Relationships

Conflict may be defined as the process of interaction which results when the behavior of one partner interferes with the behavior of the other partner. A professor in a marriage and family class said, "If you haven't had a conflict with your partner, you haven't known him or her long enough." In this section, we will explore the inevitability, desirability, sources, and styles of conflict.

Inevitability of Conflict

If you are alone this Saturday evening from six o'clock until midnight, you are assured of six conflict-free hours. But if you plan to be with your partner, roommate, or spouse during that time, the potential for conflict exists. Whether you eat out, where you eat, where you go after dinner, and how long you stay must be negotiated. Although it may be relatively easy for you and your companion to agree on one evening's agenda, marriage involves the meshing of desires on an array of issues for potentially 60 years or more.

Although most men and women reach agreement on many issues before marriage, new needs and preferences will arise throughout the marriage.

We sleep in separate rooms, we have dinner apart, we take separate vacations—we're doing everything we can to keep our marriage together.

RODNEY DANGERFIELD

Changed circumstances sometimes call for the adjustment of old habits. A wife of three years recalls:

> I can honestly say that before we got married, we never disagreed about anything, but things were different then. Both my husband and I got money from our parents and never worried about how much we spent on anything. Now I'm pregnant and unemployed, and Neal still acts like we've got someone to pick up the tab. He buys expensive toys like a computer and all the games and software he can carry. He thinks that because he uses VISA we can pay the monthly premium and still live high. We're getting over our heads in debt, and we're always fighting about it.

Desirability of Conflict

Conflict can be healthy and productive for a couple's relationship. In one study of how spouses cope with marital distress, ignoring and resigning one's self to a problem actually increased the stress level experienced by the spouses. Although negotiating differences may not reduce immediate stress (it is often upsetting and uncomfortable to discuss a conflict in the relationship), such discussions were associated with fewer problems at a later time among the 758 interviewed spouses (Menaghan, 1982).

> Conflict in itself is not bad but conflict avoided or unresolved is. Once recognized and resolved, conflict can give disputants a positive feeling and may even lead to building a relationship between them. Conflict offers an opportunity.
>
> MARIAN L. EHLERS

CONSIDERATION

When you or your partner are concerned about an issue in your relationship, discussing it may have more positive consequences than avoiding it. You may not like what your partner has to say about the reason you are upset (and vice versa), but resolving the conflict becomes a possibility. Brooding over an unresolved issue may lead to further conflict.

By expressing your dissatisfactions, you alert each other to the need for changes in your relationship to keep your satisfactions high. One husband said he was "sick and tired of picking up his wife's clothes and wet towels from the bathroom floor." She, on the other hand, was angered by her husband talking on the phone during mealtime. After discussing the issues, she agreed to take care of her clothes in exchange for his agreement to take the phone off the hook before meals. The payoff for expressing their negative feelings about each other's behavior was the agreement to stop those behaviors.

Confronting relationship conflict may be good for your health. In one study, spouses with high blood pressure who suppressed their anger at their husbands or wives were twice as likely to die earlier than spouses who talked about what upset them (Julius, 1986). Furthermore, it is critical to discuss an issue rather than to become angry, confrontational, resentful or persistent with one's point of view. These latter expressions among spouses are associated with an increase in systolic blood pressure, which may contribute to cardiovascular disease (Brown & Smith, 1992).

Sources of Conflict

There are numerous sources of conflict. Some of these are easily recognized; others are hidden inside the web of marital interaction.

Act so as to elicit the best in others and thereby in thyself.

FELIX ADLER

Behavior   The behavior of the partners can sometimes create negative feelings and set the stage for conflict. In your own relationship, you probably become upset when your partner does things you do not like (is late or tells lies). On the other hand, when your partner frequently does things that please you (is on time, is truthful) you tend to feel good about your partner and your relationship.

We can choose how to interpret a given communication. Words or behaviors that have hurt us before no longer have this power.

BARRY DUNCAN
JOSEPH ROCK

Cognitions and Perceptions   Aside from your partner's actual behavior, your cognitions and perceptions of a behavior can be a source of satisfaction or dissatisfaction. One husband complained about the fact that his wife "was messy and always kept the house in a wreck." The wife suggested to her husband that rather than focus on the messy house, he might focus on the thought that she enjoys spending time with him rather than spending time cleaning the house. Thus, the husband replaces the cognition "What a messy house" with the cognition "Isn't it wonderful that my wife would rather go fishing with me than stay home and clean house."

*The mind is its own place,
And in itself can make
A heaven of hell,
A hell of heaven.*

JOHN MILTON

C O N S I D E R A T I O N

When dissatisfaction with your partner results from your partner engaging in behavior you do not like, consider if it may be easier for you to change your perception of the behavior rather than asking your partner to change the behavior.

Changing one's perception is also helpful in adjusting to negative events in one's family of origin. Easley and Epstein (1991) noted that ACOAs (Adult Children of Alcoholics) often feel helpless in coping with alcoholism in their families and adopt a pessimistic view of all intimate relationships. Alternatively, the researchers suggested that ACOAs adopt a frame of mind that allows them to make deliberate choices to survive in spite of the alcoholism in their families and to keep as many positives going in their families as possible. The latter includes continuing to maintain family rituals such as vacations, celebrations of holidays, birthdays, etc.

Value Differences   Because you and your partner have had different socialization experiences, some of your values will be different. One wife, whose parents were both physicians, resented her mother not being home when she grew up. She vowed that when her own children were born she would stay home and take care of them. But she married a man who wanted his wife to actively pursue a career and contribute money to the marriage. This is only one value conflict a couple may have. Other major value differences may be about religion (one feels religion is a central part of life; the other does not), money (one feels uncomfortable being in debt; the other has the buy-now-and-pay-later philosophy), and in-laws (one feels responsible for parents when they are old; the other does not).

CONSIDERATION

Value differences in a relationship are not bad in and of themselves. What happens depends less on the degree of difference in what is valued than on the degree of rigidity with which each partner holds his or her values. Dogmatic and rigid thinkers, feeling threatened by value disagreement, try to eliminate varying viewpoints and typically produce more conflict. But partners who recognize the inevitability of difference usually try to accept in each other what they cannot successfully compromise (Scoresby, 1977).

Inconsistent Rules   Partners in all relationships develop a set of rules to help them function smoothly. These unwritten but mutually understood rules include what time you are supposed to be home after work, whether you should call if you are going to be late, how often you can see friends alone, and when and how you make love. Conflict results when the partners disagree on the rules or when inconsistent rules develop in the relationship. For example, one wife expected her husband to take a second job so they could afford a new car. But she also expected him to spend more time at home with the family.

Leadership Ambiguity   Unless a couple has an understanding about which partner will make decisions in which area (for example, the husband will decide over which issues to "ground" teenage children; the wife will decide how much money to spend on vacations), each partner may continually try to "win" a disagreement. All conflict is seen as an "I win–you lose" encounter because each partner is struggling for dominance in the relationship. "In low-conflict marriages, leadership roles vary and are flexible, but they are definite. Each partner knows most of the time who will make certain decisions . . ." (Scoresby, 1977, 141).

Job Stress   When you are scheduled to take four exams on one day you are under a lot of pressure to prepare for them. The stress of such preparation may cause you to be irritable in interactions with your partner. A similar effect occurs when spouses are under job stress; they are less easy to get along with. When spouses are happy and satisfied with their employment, they are much

When married couples say, "We never argue," it's an incomplete sentence. "We never argue in public/in front of the children/during sex," maybe.
ERMA BOMBECK

more likely to report satisfaction in their marriages and in the relationships with their children (Belsky et al., 1985). One husband said:

> If I've been on the road all week and haven't made any sales, I feel terrible. And I'm on edge when the wife wants to talk to me or touch me. I seem like I get obsessed with how things are at work, and if they aren't okay, nothing else seems okay either. But if I've made a lot of sales and the commission checks are rolling in, I'm a great husband and father.

Styles of Conflict

Spouses develop various styles of conflict. If you were watching a videotape of various spouses disagreeing over the same issue, you would notice at least three styles of conflict. These styles are described in *The Marriage Dialogue* (Scoresby, 1977).

Complementary In the *complementary style* of conflict, the wife and husband tend to behave in opposite ways: dominant–submissive, talkative–quiet, active–passive. Specifically, one person lectures the other about what should or should not occur. The other person says little or nothing and becomes increasingly unresponsive. For example, a husband was angry because his wife left the outside lights of their house on all night. He berated her the next morning, saying she was irresponsible. She retreated in silence.

Some evidence suggests that the complementary style of conflict is more characteristic of Southern husbands and Southern wives than is true of Northern spouses. This is a potential result of the legacy of patriarchy in the Southern culture, which suggests that wives accept rather than question (Wilson & Martin, 1988).

People who fight fire wtih fire usually end up with ashes.

ABIGAIL VAN BUREN

Symmetrical In the *symmetrical style* of conflict, both partners react to each other in the same way. If she yells, he yells back. If one attacks, so does the other. The partners try to "win" their positions without listening to the other's point of view. In the preceding incident, the wife would blast back at the husband, stating he lived there too and was equally responsible for seeing that the lights were out before going to bed.

Parallel In the *parallel style* of conflict, both partners deny, ignore, and retreat from addressing a problem issue. "Don't talk about it, and it will go away" is the theme of this conflict style. Gaps begin to develop in the relationship, neither partner feels free to talk, and both partners believe that they are misunderstood. Both eventually become involved in separate activities, rather than spending time together. In the outside-light example, neither partner said anything about the lights being left on all night, but the husband resented the fact that they were.

This couple may be engaging in parallel conflict in which each is avoiding discussing an issue and retreating into another activity.

Condie (1989) identified three other styles of conflict. These include blowing off steam, alternating anger, and talking it out.

1. *Blowing Off Steam.* "Several couples indicated that the unfettered ventilation of emotions had been their preferred modus operandi for resolving differences" (p. 149).
2. *Alternating Anger.* Some couples have an agreement that if one of them gets angry, the other stays calm. One spouse said, "It is not good for two hotheads to be together" (p. 149).
3. *Talking It Out.* Couples agreed that this was the method they should use but that the "silent treatment" was the fastest avenue to peaceful coexistence" (p. 149). The longer the couple was married, the more likely they were to talk things out rather than use the silent treatment.

✿ Resolving Interpersonal Conflict: Basic Principles and Techniques

Every relationship experiences conflict. If left unresolved, conflict may create tension and distance in the relationship with the result that the partners stop talking, stop spending time together, and stop being intimate. Developing and

Two sets of skills necessary for living satisfactorily as individuals, dyads, and families are the ability to love and the ability to negotiate.

LUCIANO L'ABATE
DENNIS BAGAROZZI

using conflict resolution skills is critically important for the maintenance of a good relationship.

Howard Markman is head of the Center for Marital and Family Studies at the University of Denver. He and his colleagues have been studying 150 couples at yearly intervals (beginning before marriage) to determine those factors most responsible for marital success. They have found that communication skills that reflect the ability to handle conflict, which they call "constructive arguing," is the single biggest predictor of marital success over time (Marano, 1992). According to Markman:

> Many people believe that the causes of marital problems are the differences between people and problem areas such as money, sex, children. However, our findings indicate it is not the differences that are important, but how these differences and problems are handled, particularly early in marriage (p. 53).

There is also merit in developing and using conflict negotiation skills before problems develop. Not only are individuals more willing to work on issues when things are going well, they have not developed negative patterns of response that are difficult to change.

The following section describes principles and techniques that are helpful in resolving interpersonal conflict. Such principles and techniques permit a couple to manage present and future conflict by emphasizing on the "process" of their interaction and negotiation and not on "fixing" a specific problem (Kolevzon & Jenkins, 1992).

Address Recurring, Disturbing Issues

If you or your partner are upset about a recurring issue, talking about it may help. Pam was jealous that Mark seemed to spend more time with other people at parties than with her. "When we go someplace together," she blurted out, "he drops me to disappear with someone else for two hours." Her jealousy was also spreading to other areas of their relationship. "When we are walking down the street and he turns his head to look at another woman, I get furious." If Pam and Mark don't discuss her feelings about Mark's behavior, their relationship may deteriorate due to a negative response cycle: he looks at another woman, she gets angry, he gets angry at her getting angry and finds that he is even more attracted to other women, she gets angrier because he escalates his looking at other women, and so on.

To bring the matter up, Pam might say "I feel jealous when you spend more time with other women at parties than with me. I need some help in dealing with these feelings." By expressing her concern in this way, she has identified the problem from her perspective and asked her partner's cooperation in handling it.

When discussing difficult relationship issues, it is important to avoid attacking, blaming, or being negative. Such negative emotions reduce the motivation of the partner to talk about an issue and reduce the probability of a positive outcome (Forgatch, 1989).

> **C O N S I D E R A T I O N**
>
> It is important to use good timing in discussing difficult issues with your partner. In general, it is best to discuss issues or conflicts when (1) you are alone with your partner in private, rather than in public, (2) you and your partner have ample time to talk, and (3) you and your partner are rested and feeling generally good; avoid discussing conflict issues when you and your partner are tired, upset, and/or under unusual stress.

Focus on What You Want (Rather Than What You Don't Want)

Dealing with conflict is more likely to result in resolution if the partners focus on what they want, rather than what they don't want. For example, rather than tell Mark she doesn't want him to spend so much time with other women at parties, Pam might tell him that she wants him to spend more time with her at parties. Table 9.6 provides more examples of resolving conflict by focusing on "wants" rather than on "don't wants."

Find Out Your Partner's Point of View

We often assume that we know what our partner thinks and why our partner does things. Sometimes we are wrong. Rather than assume how people think and feel about a particular issue, we might ask our partner open-ended questions in an effort to get him or her to tell us thoughts and feelings about a particular situation. Pam's words to Mark might be, "What is it like for you when we go to parties?" "How do you feel about my jealousy?"

Once your partner has shared his or her thoughts about an issue with you, it is important for you to summarize your partner's perspective in a nonjudgmental way. After Mark told Pam how he felt about their being at parties together, she summarized his perspective by saying, "You feel that I cling to you more than I should and you would like me to let you wander

TABLE 9.6
Examples of Focusing on "Wants" Rather Than "Don't Wants"

DON'T WANTS	WANTS
I don't want to go to your parents for spring break.	I would like for us to go to the beach over spring break.
I don't want to see the Clint Eastwood movie.	I would like to see the Whoopi Goldberg movie.
I don't like heavy metal music.	I like new age music.
I don't want you to stay up so late at night.	I would like you to come to bed earlier.
I don't want to have sex in the morning before going to work.	I really prefer to have sex in the evening when we can relax and take our time.

around without feeling like you're making me angry." (She may not agree with his view, but she knows exactly what it is—and Mark knows that she knows.)

Generate Win-Win Solutions to the Conflict

The argument you just won isn't over yet.

UNKNOWN

There are various issues to keep in mind when searching for solutions to interpersonal conflict. For effective conflict resolution, couples may see the importance of focusing on interests rather than on positions, brainstorming, and looking for win-win solutions.

Interests and Needs vs. Positions   In order to both understand and resolve interpersonal conflict, individuals need to focus on the interests, rather than on the positions, of the individuals involved (Fisher & Ury, 1981). In this context, positions refer to statements about what an individual has decided. For example, Pam wants Mark to spend more time with her at parties and less time with other women; that is Pam's position. Let's assume that Mark wants to continue to spend a lot of time with other women at parties; that is Mark's position.

Interests, in this context, refer to the underlying needs and concerns of the individuals involved. Interests represent why a person wants something or takes a particular position. Many possible interests may underlie any one position. In the example we have been using, Pam's position that Mark should not spend so much time with other women at parties may be based on a number of different needs, including (1) Between school and work, Pam has little time with Mark and needs to spend more time with him; (2) Pam views Mark's spending time with other women as evidence that he does not find her attractive and prefers their company and needs to feel that Mark views her as attractive; and (3) Pam admires Mark's ability to converse and be sociable, but feels alone and anxious when he does because she feels shy and inadequate in social settings, and therefore needs to feel more secure interacting with others at a party.

By identifying the interests that underlie the positions, one can generate solutions that satisfy the needs and concerns of the individuals involved in the conflict. Below, we outline different possible solutions to Pam and Mark's conflict, depending on what the underlying interest is.

1. Interest: Pam feels the need to spend more time with Mark.
   Solution: Pam and Mark agree to go out alone twice weekly in addition to the amount of social time they already spend together.
2. Interest: Pam needs to feel that Mark finds her attractive.
   Solution: Mark agrees to say something positive about how Pam looks every day.
3. Interest: Pam wants to avoid feeling isolated at parties.
   Solution: Pam agrees to sign up for an Assertiveness Training workshop. Her goal is to develop social skills so that she is comfortable interacting with others at a party.

Brainstorming The technique of brainstorming involves suggesting as many alternatives as possible, without evaluating them. Brainstorming is crucial to conflict resolution because it shifts the partners' focus from criticizing each others' perspective to working together to develop alternative solutions. Alternatives that might be suggested by Pam and Mark include the following:

1. Change cognitions: Pam might change the way she views Mark's interaction with others at parties. Rather than view him as neglecting and rejecting her at parties, she might choose to view his desire to interact with others as evidence that he likes people and is socially skilled in interacting with others (both are positive qualities). She might also choose to view his being across the room as an opportunity for her to meet new people or to talk with those she already knows. Finally, she might view his looking at other women as evidence that he has a strong sex drive and remind herself that he values monogamy (two more positive qualities).

2. Change behaviors: Mark might spend more time with Pam at parties, reduce the frequency with which he looks at other women, and point out good-looking men for Pam. Alternatively, Pam might begin to encourage Mark to talk with others at parties and initiate conversations with new people herself.

3. Stop going to parties.

4. Stop seeing each other for two weeks.

5. Stop talking about the issue.

6. Break up.

Any solution may be an acceptable one as long as the solution is one of mutual agreement.

CONSIDERATION

Anderson (1992) observed that only 40 percent of couples in her study who were faced with the need to establish a commuter marriage generated any alternatives as to how they might resolve the issue of two careers in one marriage with job opportunities in different towns. She also noted that those who were systematic about making their decisions (i.e. generated and examined alternative solutions) reported more satisfaction.

Win-Win Solutions A win-win solution is one in which both people involved in a conflict feel satisfied with the agreement or resolution to the conflict. Finding a win-win solution requires that the interests (needs and concerns) of both parties be addressed. Each person should feel that his or her needs are being met through whatever solution they agree on.

Some couples view the resolution of their conflicts in win-lose terms (one person wins, the other one loses) rather than as opportunities for win-win solutions (both people win). In one study, 60 spouses (representing 30 marriages) were interviewed about relationship conflicts and their outcomes

(Bell et al., 1982). The results showed that husbands "win most conflicts, regardless of the strategies they or their wives employ" (p. 111). However, among couples in which the wife was a member of NOW (National Organization for Women), seven in 10 of the conflicts were "won" by the wife. We suggest that unless both win, both lose because all the winner gets is someone waiting to get back at him or her.

CONSIDERATION

If the goal is to develop and/or maintain a satisfying intimate interpersonal relationship, it is imperative to look for win-win solutions to conflicts. Solutions in which one person wins and the other person loses imply that one person is not getting his or her needs met. Consequently, the person who "loses" may develop feelings of resentment, anger, hurt, and hostility toward the winner and may even look for ways to get even. In this way, the winner is also a loser. It is important to remember that, in intimate relationships, one winner really means that there are two losers.

Evaluate and Select a Solution

After generating a number of solutions, each solution should be evaluated and the best one selected. In evaluating solutions to conflicts, it may be helpful to ask the following questions:

1. Does the solution satisfy both individuals? (Is it a win-win solution?)
2. Is the solution specific? Does the solution specify exactly who is to do what, how, and when?
3. Is the solution realistic? Can both parties realistically follow through with what they have agreed to do?
4. Does the solution prevent the problem from recurring in the future?
5. Does the solution specify what is to happen if the problem recurs?

Pam and Mark, for example, selected aspects from several alternatives from which they derived specific actions. They agreed that they would spend 45 minutes of each hour at a party talking and dancing together; Mark would be responsible for initiating and maintaining their time together, and Pam would be responsible for initiating their time away from each other. They also agreed that Pam would say nothing about the time they were apart unless Mark brought it up. They further agreed that it was okay for each of them to look at members of the opposite sex when they were with each other.

CONSIDERATION

Most of the agreements to resolve conflict that partners feel good about are either compromises or contain elements of each other's input. Both partners must be

Defense Mechanisms

Defense mechanisms are unconscious techniques that function to protect individuals from anxiety. Defense mechanisms temporarily minimize anxiety and avoid emotional hurt, but they also interfere with conflict resolution.

ESCAPISM

Escapism is the simultaneous denial and withdrawal from a problem. The usual form of escape is avoidance. The spouse becomes "busy" and "doesn't have time" to think about or deal with the problem, or the partner may escape into recreation, sleep, alcohol, marijuana, or work. Denying and withdrawing from problems in relations offer no possibility for confronting and resolving the problems.

RATIONALIZATION

Rationalization is the cognitive justification for one's own behavior that unconsciously conceals one's true motives. For example, one wife complained that her husband spent too much time at the health club in the evenings. The underlying reason for the husband going to the health club was to escape an unsatisfying home life. But the idea that he was in a "dead marriage" was too painful and difficult for the husband to face, so he rationalized to himself and his wife that he spent so much time at the health club because he made a lot of important business contacts there. Thus, the husband concealed his own true motives from himself (and his wife).

PROJECTION

Projection occurs when one spouse unconsciously attributes their own feelings, attitudes, or desires to their partner. For example, the wife who desires to have an affair may accuse her husband of being unfaithful to her.

Projection may be seen in statements like "You spend too much money" (projection for "I spend too much money") and "You want to break up" (projection for "I want to break up"). Projection interferes with conflict resolution by creating a mood of hostility and defensiveness in both partners. The issues to be resolved in the relationship remain unchanged and become more difficult to discuss.

DISPLACEMENT

Displacement involves shifting your feelings, thoughts, or behaviors from the person who evokes them onto someone else. The wife who is turned down for a promotion and the husband who is driven to exhaustion by his boss may direct their hostilities (displace them) onto each other rather than toward their respective employers. Similarly, spouses who are angry at each other may displace this anger onto someone else, such as the children.

By knowing about defense mechanisms and their negative impact on resolving conflict, you can be alert to their appearance in your own relationships. When a conflict continues without resolution, one or more defense mechanisms may be operating.

willing to assume responsibility for changing their own behavior first as a gesture of commitment and good faith toward each other and the relationship. Once partners feel that their partner feels good about them, they are more willing to move toward what the partner wants (Marano, 1992).

In spite of the motivation, knowledge, and skills to resolve conflict, some couples seem unable to do so. In such cases, defense mechanisms may be operative (see In Focus 9.3).

§ Marital Therapy

Sometimes it is difficult for spouses to resolve conflict by themselves. Becoming involved in marriage therapy is an alternative. Examples of problems spouses bring to marriage therapy are described in table 9.7.

Cost and Success of Marriage Therapy

The cost of private marriage therapy is around $100 per hour (a therapist in a local mental health center is less expensive). You can obtain a list of marriage therapists who are members of the American Association for Marriage and Family Therapists in your area by looking in the Yellow Pages under Marriage Therapists—Certified, or by writing to AAMFT at 1100 17th Street N.W., 10th Floor, Washington, D.C. 20036-1906, (202/452-0109).

Most marital therapy sessions last about 50 minutes, during which the spouses are usually seen together in what is referred to as *conjoint marriage therapy*. Some therapists (Gurman & Kniskern, 1986) feel strongly that it is important for couples to attend marriage therapy together; others (Wells & Giannetti, 1986) feel it may be productive for one partner to participate in marital therapy without the other partner present.

To what degree is involvement in marriage or family therapy beneficial? Based on reviews of research on marital and family research, Piercy and Sprenkle (1991) reported that beneficial outcomes occur in about two-thirds of the cases and that these effects are superior to receiving no treatment at all. The most beneficial outcomes are usually obtained in treatment that involves both spouses in conjoint therapy (both partners are seen in the same session) and treatment that is relatively short term (one to twenty sessions) as opposed to individual therapy for the respective partners (including traditional psychoanalytic therapy), which may take years.

Whether a couple in therapy remain together will depend on their motivation to do so, how long they have been in conflict, the severity of the problem, and whether one or both partners is/are involved in an extramarital affair. Two moderately motivated partners with numerous conflicts over several years are less likely to work out their problems than a highly motivated couple with minor conflicts of short duration. Beyond these factors, Allgood and Crane (1991) studied couples who had dropped out of marital therapy and noted that those least likely to drop out had more than two children and reported problems other than with the children.

Research suggests that about two-thirds of couples who become involved in marital therapy report positive outcomes.

> **CONSIDERATION**
>
> Spouses most likely to benefit from marriage therapy come to therapy when they experience recurrent conflicts they have been unable to communicate about and resolve. Spouses who wait until they are ready to divorce have usually waited too long.

TABLE 9.7

Problems Couples Bring to Marriage Therapy

COMMUNICATION AND EMOTIONS

Don't feel close to spouse
Rarely alone with spouse
Spouse complains/criticizes
Don't love spouse
Not loved by spouse
Spouse is impatient
Too little time spent communicating
Nothing to talk about
Intellectual gaps
Unhappiness with type of
    conversation
Spouse is unhappy and depressed
Arguments end in spouse
    abuse/violence

SEX

Lack of sexual desire
Infrequent or no orgasm
Pain during intercourse
Vagina too tight for penetration
Early ejaculation
Difficulty achieving or maintaining
    erection
No ejaculation
Differences over how sex occurs:
    Too little non-genital sexual
    behavior
    Spouse crude in approach
    Oral sex
    Positions
    Too little affection
Disagreement about frequency of
    intercourse
Disagreement about when sex
    occurs
Extramarital affair
One or both partners has STD

IN-LAWS

Talking over the phone to in-laws
How often in-laws visit

Borrowing money from in-laws
Living with in-laws
How often to visit in-laws
In-laws' dislike of spouse
In-laws' interference in children's
    lives
Loaning/giving money to in-laws

RECREATION

No sharing of leisure time
Desire of spouse for separate
    vacations
Competition (egos may be hurt if
    one spouse is, say, more athletic
    than partner)
Disagreement over amount of
    money to allocate for vacation
Spouse doesn't like family vacations
Disagreement over what is fun
Where to spend vacation

CHILDREN

Discipline of children
Care of children
Time with children
Number of children
Spacing of children
Infertility
Whether or not to adopt
Rivalry for children's love
Activities in which children should
    be involved
Sex education for children
Distress at children's behavior
Child abuse by one spouse
Retarded, autistic, or otherwise
    handicapped child
Stepchildren

MONEY

Too little money
Wife's job
Husband's job
Conflict over who buys what
Gambling
Borrowing
Excessive debts

RELIGION

Which church to attend
Spouse too devout
Spouse not devout enough
Religion for children
Church donations
Observance of religious holidays
    and rituals, such as circumcision
Breaking of vows

FRIENDS

Too few friends
Too many friends
Different friends
Confidence to friends
Time with friends
Jealousy

ALCOHOL OR DRUGS

Spouse drinks too much
Spouse smokes too much marijuana
Spouse takes too many pills
Amount of money spent on
    alcohol/drugs
Flirting as a consequence of
    drinking
Influence of drinking/drug habits on
    children
Violence as a consequence of
    drinking

People from different cultures may view marriage therapy differently from the way Americans do. For example, Wang (1992) noted that, in contrast to Americans, Chinese attach more stigma to seeing a therapist, are less likely to seek therapy unless court ordered to do so, and do not respond well to group therapy. Marriage therapists, sensitive to cross-cultural variations, need to provide more assurance to Chinese clients of confidentiality and provide more time for them to become comfortable in the sessions to open up.

Approaches to Marriage Therapy

Marriage therapists represent a range of theoretical orientations. They differ in the ways in which they identify the causes of marital problems and the ways in which they resolve the problems. The various approaches to marriage therapy include the following:

Systems Therapy   Systems therapists view marriage and the family as systems (or relational units) that are maintained by the behaviors (both healthy and unhealthy) of its members (Brehm, 1992). For example, a drug abusing teenager is viewed as one part of a family system. *Systems therapy* focuses on how the behavior functions within the family. For example, a drug abusing teenager may function to bond the parents together in their efforts to deal with the problem. Drug abuse may function as an attention-getting device for the teenager.

Behaviors that are problematic for couples or families may be understood by examining the purpose they serve within the family. How is the behavior benefiting the family as a whole? Does the behavior serve to deflect attention away from some other problem in the family? Once couples and families understand how problem behaviors serve a purpose by fulfilling a need, they can identify other ways of meeting that need and change or eliminate the problem behavior.

Behavior Therapy   Behavior therapists believe that unhappiness between spouses is caused by behavior they respectively engage in that upsets the partner. *Behavior therapy* is based on the assumptions that attitudes and feelings are based on behavior, that behavior is learned, and that behavior can change. Behavior marriage therapy focuses on identifying the kind (verbal and nonverbal) and frequency of behavior each partner would like the other to engage in. Behavior contracts (see table 9.8) are sometimes drawn up at the end of each session specifying what each partner has agreed to do. In addition to developing contracts, behavior therapists teach spouses communication and negotiation skills.

> I discovered I always have choices and sometime it's only a choice of attitude.
>
> JUDITH M. KNOWLTON

Cognitive Therapy   Based on the theories of Aaron Beck and Albert Ellis, *cognitive therapy* (sometimes known as rational-emotive therapy or cognitive-

TABLE 9.8

Behavior Contracts for Wife and Husband

After having identified what we would like each other to do, we agree to engage in the following behaviors, to keep records, and to take this sheet with us to our next therapy session.

WIFE	M	T	W	Th	F	S	S
Compliment Ted twice per day.	—	—	—	—	—	—	—
Make no negative statements to Ted each day.	—	—	—	—	—	—	—
Be ready to go out alone with Ted Saturday evening at 7:00.	—	—	—	—	—	—	—
Ensure that car has at least ¼th tank of gas after I drive.	—	—	—	—	—	—	—
HUSBAND							
Make two positive statements to Sue every day.	—	—	—	—	—	—	—
Say nothing negative to Sue each day.	—	—	—	—	—	—	—
Make reservations and be ready to go out with Sue Saturday evening at 7:00.	—	—	—	—	—	—	—
Not smoke in the house.	—	—	—	—	—	—	—

behavioral therapy) suggests that spouses are unhappy as a result of irrational beliefs they have about themselves and each other (Baucom & Epsten, 1989). The rational-emotive therapist encourages partners to examine their beliefs and to change them if they have a negative impact on the marriage. For example, the belief that "My spouse should care more about me than anything or anyone else" would be examined for its potential negative consequences on the relationship.

Other beliefs that may interfere with marital happiness include "People can't change," "Disagreements are destructive," "We should still have romance and passion in our relationship," and "I will get hurt if I get too close" (Brehm, 1992; Burns, 1989).

Strategic Therapy Using elements of both the behavioral and cognitive therapies, *strategic therapy* focuses on the presenting problem as the focus of therapy rather than viewing the presenting problem as a symptom of a larger problem. "Strategic therapy mirrors the pragmatic, result-centered technological spirit of the decade" (Piercy & Sprenkle, 1991, 447). Strategic family therapists focus on strategies of promoting change, coping, or solutions (Held, 1992).

Psychodynamic Therapy *Psychodynamic therapy* emphasizes unconscious conflicts as the cause of individual and family problems. For example, a wife who feels she should have the right to look at her husband's mail, and a husband who is horrified at her doing so are provided insight by the psychodynamic therapist as to their unconscious feelings that create the conflict. In examining the respective families in which the spouses grew up, the therapist might discover that the wife's parents never openly talked or shared anything with her. Hence, she learned that snooping was the only way she would be informed. In regard to the husband, he felt violated by his wife's snooping because during his adolescence, his parents would often snoop through his room. He resented his parents' snooping behavior and was hurt that they didn't trust him. After the spouses become aware that their behaviors and reactions are tied to earlier unresolved conflicts, they can use this insight to resolve their differences.

Adlerian Therapy　　Applying the theories of Austrian psychiatrist Alfred Adler, *Adlerian therapy* views marital discord as a result of power struggles between spouses. The individual is seen as trying to compensate for feelings of inferiority that began with the helplessness of infancy. The Alderian therapist seeks to improve marital relationships by helping couples to feel secure and to regard their power struggles as unnecessary.

Systems, behavioral, cognitive, strategic family, pyschodynamic, and Adlerian therapy are only a few of the different approaches used by marriage therapists. Other approaches include gestalt, humanistic, Rogerian, reality, and paradoxical therapy. Although systems and cognitive therapy are currently in vogue, no one therapy is unanimously regarded as superior.

C O N S I D E R A T I O N

All marital therapy modalities work best when both spouses are relatively free of psychopathology, alcohol/drug abuse, and depression. William Styron (1990), who was suffering from severe biochemically induced suicidal depression, noted the inability of his wife to help him and their relationship.

> Physically, I was not alone. As always, Rose was present and listened with unflagging patience to my complaints. But I felt an immense and aching solitude (pp. 45-46).

As Styron's experience illustrates, individual issues must be dealt with before relationship issues can be resolved.

❦ Marriage Enrichment

Spouses who are having marital difficulties often see a marriage therapist as a last resort—their final choice before seeking a divorce. Marriage counselors are thought of as an emergency medical team at the bottom of a cliff that ministers to those who have fallen in the hope of reviving them—but why not a guardrail at the top to prevent couples from slipping off the edge? Such preventive intervention is the goal of marriage enrichment programs, which are designed "to strengthen couples or families so as to promote a high level of present and future harmony and strength, and hence the long-term psychological, emotional, and social well-being of family members" (Guerney & Maxson, 1991, 457). Spouses who become involved in marriage enrichment when compared to those who become involved in therapy are less nervous and less depressed. They also tend to view their mates more positively (Markowski, 1991). When compared to the general population, couples who attend enrichment programs tend to be more educated. Most participants have had about three years of college (Guerney & Maxson, 1991).

More than 50 marriage enrichment programs are operative in the United States. All are designed to serve a large segment of the population and are conducted in a time-limited, group format. Some enrichment programs have a specific focus such as those for couples who are dating, dual-earner couples, remarried couples, couples confronted with stepparenting issues, and families coping with a member's life-altering disease.

Outcome studies suggest that participants benefit most from enrichment programs that are longer (more than 12 hours), structured, and emphasize learning behavioral skills through practice. Programs may create more harm than harmony if they emphasize complete openness or if the leaders of the program do not have adequate training. Also, severely distressed couples profit more from marriage therapy than marriage enrichment.

Complete openness during an encounter weekend may be dysfunctional. One husband felt that to be honest he needed to disclose a previous affair to his wife. The encounter weekend was over before the effects of his disclosure were resolved by the couple.

CONSIDERATION

To minimize the negative effects of exposure to a marriage enrichment program, the partners should not regard the experience as an opportunity to solve problems or to deal with difficult issues in their relationship. Such issues should be dealt with alone or in marriage therapy. Instead, a marriage enrichment program should be regarded as a place to improve communication skills between spouses who feel good about themselves and each other. Spouses also might consider contacting a therapist after an encounter weekend if they feel worse as a result of the experience.

When positive gains from marriage enrichment programs are achieved, they are usually sustained over a period of months. Regarding the validity of the marriage enrichment movement, Guerney and Maxson (1991) concluded, "On the whole, enrichment programs work and the field is an entirely legitimate one" (p. 463).

§ Trends

The most significant trend regarding communication in marriage is the increased willingness of couples to go public with their problems (many television talk shows depend on this willingness). When people realize how normal it is for couples to be faced with problems in their relationships, they abandon the myth that happy couples don't have conflicts.

Another trend involves the age of the couples and the nature of the problems brought to therapy. In the past, the majority of couples in marriage therapy were young, in their first marriages, and focused on dyad issues. Increasingly, they are middle age, in their second marriages, and conflicted with stepfamily issues.

Regardless of their age or problem, couples today are more likely to look for a therapist specializing in short-term rather than long-term therapy (Bloomfield et al., 1989). The relief offered by cognitive behavioral approaches coupled with the fact that insurance companies and employers will pay for only a limited number of sessions has helped to solidify the trend toward short-term therapy.

A fourth trend involves raising the standards that marriage and family therapists must meet. More states are enacting laws to create a classification of "certified marriage therapist" to denote that a counselor has the equivalent training and background required for admission to the American Association for Marriage and Family Therapy. This requires a minimum of a master's degree and specific training in marriage and family therapy, human sexuality, and ethics. Furthermore, the counselor must have conducted 1,500 hours of marriage and family therapy; at least 200 of these hours must be under the supervision of an approved supervisor. The hoped-for result will be a sufficient supply of highly trained and experienced marriage therapists to meet the growing demand for such services. Currently most states do not have adequate laws to protect the public from untrained marriage therapists.

↜ CHOICES ↝

A basic choice of individuals in a relationship is deciding how honest to be with each other. After examining how much openness is productive for a relationship we look at the issues of talking about one's past, disclosing attraction to others to one's partner, and whether to seek marital therapy.

Is Honesty Always the Best Policy?

Good communication often implies open communication, but how much honesty is good for a relationship? Duncan and Rock (1993) emphasized that it is a myth that always being honest is critical for a relationship to work.

> Being open with someone who will use the information to manipulate you or gain power over you is like playing poker and showing your cards before you bet. An open and honest expression must be interpreted as such by the receiver of the message for it to be truly open and honest. Openness is not the only way, and in some situations, not the best way (p. 49).

When the issue is an extramarital affair, spouses might consider the consequences before disclosing. Dr. Pepper Schwartz cautions women especially to think twice before confessing. "According to my research, only confess if you want to end your marriage, or if the relationship is so bad that you are willing to risk ending it in order to help it" (quoted by Van Matre, 1992, d-8).

Some couples, however, may find that the disclosure of an affair by one partner forces them to examine problems in their relationship and/or seek marriage therapy. In these cases, such disclosure may ultimately result in bringing the couple closer together in an emotional sense.

While complete dishonesty in the form of withholding may or may not be an advisable option in the case of an extradyadic indiscretion, other situations might call for tempered honesty. A particular situation in which tempered honesty may be the best policy is when you are extremely upset. In this situation, you may honestly feel and think horrible things about your partner. If you express such thoughts and feelings, they may be difficult to retract later when you are calm. At such times it may be best to not be totally honest with your thoughts and feelings. Instead, admit you are upset and either wait until you are calm to talk about the problem or refrain from expressing thoughts that are hurtful to your partner.

Though honesty may be tempered with kindness in some situations, in others it is probably best to be completely honest. Specific information that should not be withheld from the partner include previous marriages and children, a sexual orientation different from what the partner expects, alcohol or drug addiction, having a sexually transmitted disease, such as HIV or genital herpes, and any known physical disabilities, such as sterility. Disclosures of this nature include anything that would have a significant impact on the relationship.

Do I Tell My Partner About My Past?

Because of the fear of HIV infection and other STDs, some partners want to know the details of each other's previous sex life, including how many partners they have had sex with and in what contexts. Those who are asked will need to make a decision about whether to disclose the requested information, which may include one's sexual orientation, present or past sexually transmitted diseases, and any proclivities or preferences the partner might find bizarre (e.g., bondage and discipline). As noted earlier in the chapter, ample evidence suggests that individuals are sometimes dishonest in regard to the sexual information they provide to their partners.

In deciding whether or not to talk honestly about your past to your partner, you may want to consider the following questions: How important is it to your partner to know about your past? Do you want your partner to tell you (honestly) about her or his past?

(continued)

⌁ CHOICES ∾

Disclose Attractions to Others to One's Partner?

If partners stay together for a long time, they will likely, at some time and at some level, be attracted to someone outside the relationship. Whether such attractions or interests are to be disclosed to the partner may depend on the nature of the personalities of the individuals, the nature of the relationship with the partner, and the nature and extent of the attraction. Some couples decide to share such feelings and have relationships in which the partners are not insecure or defensive about such disclosures. Other couples decide it is much too painful to disclose or to hear of such interests. Still other couples ignore the issue. No one strategy might be considered best since different strategies may have both positive and negative outcomes for different couples. However, it is important for couples to acknowledge such attractions are likely to occur and to agree on the nature and extent of the desired disclosure.

Consult a Marriage Therapist?

Most people are reluctant to consult a marriage therapist. Most spouses have been taught that seeing a therapist about personal problems means they are mentally ill. "It's the crazy folks that see those counselors," said one woman. Other spouses feel their marriage is private and nobody else's busi-

ness. "You don't talk to strangers about those kinds of things," said another spouse. Still other spouses feel that if couples are really in love with each other, they will be able to work out anything. They assume only the people who don't love each other can't work out their problems.

Each of these beliefs is a myth. Seeing a therapist does not mean that you are mentally ill. On the contrary, we are never more mentally and emotionally healthy than when we can acknowledge that we have a problem and seek help for it.

The fact that marriage is a personal and private affair does not mean we cannot discuss our concern with a specialist. Our bodies are also personal and private, but this does not stop us from seeing a physician when we have a physical problem. Our mental health is as important to our feeling good as is our physical health. Both physicians and marriage therapists can be expected to treat the information we share with them with strict confidentiality. This is required by their code of professional ethics.

Finally, as we have seen earlier in this chapter, love is not enough to ensure the resolution of all conflicts. Two people can love each other intensely and not be able to resolve their conflicts or to live together happily. "We loved each other," said one spouse, "but we just couldn't make a go of it together."

Signs to look for in your own relationship that suggest you might consider seeing a therapist include feeling distant and not wanting to or being unable to communicate with your partner, avoiding each other, drinking heavily or taking drugs, privately contemplating separation, being involved in an affair, and feeling depressed.

If you are experiencing one or more of these concerns with your partner, it may be wise not to wait until it reaches a stage beyond which repair is impossible. Relationships are like boats. A small leak will not sink it. But if left unattended, the small leak may grow larger or new leaks may break through. Marriage therapy sometimes serves to mend relationship problems early by helping the partners to sort out values, make decisions, and begin new behaviors so that they can start feeling better about each other.

However, in spite of the potential benefits of marriage therapy, there are some valid reasons for not consulting a counselor.

Not all spouses who become involved in marriage therapy regard the experience positively. Some feel that their marriage is worse as a result. Saying things the spouse can't forget, feeling hopeless at not being able to resolve a problem "even with a counselor," and feeling resentment over new demands made by the spouse in

---

CHOICES

therapy are reasons some spouses cite for negative outcomes.

Therapists also may give clients an unrealistic picture of loving, cooperative, and growing relationships in which partners always treat each other with respect and understanding, share intimacy, and help each other become whomever each wants to be. In creating this idealistic image of the perfect relationship, therapists may inadvertently encourage clients to focus on the shortcomings in their relationship and to expect more of the therapist than is realistic. Couples in therapy must also be on guard against assuming that therapy is a quick and easy "fix." In order for therapy to be effective, a great deal of personal effort is required (Bloomfield et al., 1989).

Summary

Communication is the process of exchanging information and feelings between two individuals. Communication involves both verbal and nonverbal messages. What partners say and do are sometimes discrepant. While honesty in a relationship is highly valued by both women and men, many studies suggest that partners lie to each other about other relationships.

Basic principles and techniques of effective communication include prioritizing communication, maintaining eye contact, asking open-ended questions, using reflective listening, using "I" statements, complimenting each other, and sharing power. Partners must also be alert to keep the dialogue (process) going even when they don't like what is being said (content).

Women and men differ in the focus of their communication. Women tend to focus on relationships, emotions, and intimacy. Men tend to focus on activities, agendas, and achieving. In general, women try to negotiate; men try to win.

Theories of marital communication include behavioral exchange (good communication is based on ratio of positives and negatives), behavioral competency (negotiating is a skill), social learning (communication patterns are learned), relational control (communication patterns reflect and create power issues), and systems (the partners influence each other) models.

Marital conflict can erupt at any time. It is both inevitable and, under certain conditions, desirable. The causes of interpersonal conflict include behavior, perception, and value differences. Spouses also develop various styles of conflict—complementary (one dominant, the other submissive), symmetrical (both partners react the same way to each other), and parallel (both partners avoid confronting the problem).

Having a plan to communicate about conflicts is essential. Such a plan includes deciding to address recurring issues rather than suppressing them, asking the partner for help in resolving the issue, finding out the partner's point of view, summarizing in a nonjudgmental way the partner's perspective, brainstorming for alternative win-win solutions, and selecting a plan of action. To the degree that the plan of action includes suggestions made by each partner, the potential for success in resolving the problem is maximized. When we participate in a solution, we are more committed to seeing it work.

Some couples who can't resolve a conflict by themselves contact a marriage therapist. These therapists are not regulated by law in all states, so care should be exercised in selecting one. Also, there are many theoretical approaches; it is important to select a therapist who offers the style of therapy the couple wants. Most spouses report positive outcomes from their involvement in marriage therapy.

Marriage enrichment programs are for couples who have good marriages and who want to keep them that way. However, some couples do report negative experiences from their involvement in these programs. Although such experiences are rare, couples should be careful about the type of marriage encounter program they select.

Trends in resolving conflict include increasing numbers of women and men willing to "go pubic" with their problems, more couples in second marriages with stepfamily issues seeking therapy, and higher training standards for becoming a marriage and family therapist.

Questions for Reflection

1. Have you been able to reinforce your partner for telling you things (process) even though you felt uncomfortable hearing the words (content)?
2. Which of the theories of communication process best describe the communication pattern you have with your partner?
3. Would you be willing to become involved in marriage enrichment or marriage therapy? Why or why not?
4. If you were to consult a marriage therapist, which approach would you prefer?

References

Allgood, S. M. and D. R. Crane. Predicting marital therapy dropouts. *Journal of Marital and Family Therapy,* 1991, *17,* 73–79.

Anderson, E. A. Decision-making style: Impact on satisfaction of the commuter couples' lifestyle. *Journal of Family and Economic Issues,* 1992, *13,* 5–21.

Argyle, M. *Bodily communication.* New York: Methuen, Inc., 1988.

Baucom, D. H. and N. Epsten. *Cognitive-behavioral marital therapy.* New York: Brunner/Mazel, 1989.

Bell, D. C., J. S. Chafetz, and L. H. Horn. Marital conflict resolution: A study of strategies and outcomes. *Journal of Family Issues,* 1982, *3,* 111–132.

Belsky, J., M. Perry-Jenkins, and A. C. Crouter. The work-family interface and marital change across the transition to parenthood. *Journal of Family Issues,* 1985, *6,* 205–220.

Bloomfield, H. H., S. VeHese, and R. B. Kory. Healthy love. *Health,* 1989, *21,* 24–26.

Brehm, S. S. *Intimate relationships.* New York: McGraw-Hill, Inc., 1992.

Brown, P. C. and T. W. Smith. Social influence, marriage, and the heart: Cardiovascular consequences of interpersonal control in husbands and wives. *Health Psychology,* 1992, *11,* 88–96.

Burns, David D. *The good feeling handbook.* New York: William Morrow & Co., 1989.

Condie, Spencer J. Older married couples. *Aging and the Family,* Stephen J. Bahr and Evan T. Peterson, eds. Lexington, Mass.: Lexington Books, 1989, 143–158.

Derlega, V. J., S. Metts, S. Petronio, and S. T. Margulis. *Self–disclosure.* Newbury Park, Calif.: Sage Publications, 1993.

Doherty, W. J., M. E. Lester, and G. Leigh. Marriage encounter weekends: Couples who win and couples who lose. *Journal of Marriage and Family Therapy,* 1986, *12,* 49–61.

Duncan, B. L. and J. W. Rock. Saving relationships: The power of the unpredictable. *Psychology Today,* January/February 1993, *26,* 46–51, 86, 95.

Easley, M. J. and N. Epstein. Coping with stress in a family with an alcoholic parent. *Family Relations,* 1991, *40,* 218–224.

Fisher, Roger, and William Ury. *Getting to yes: Negotiating agreement without giving in.* Boston: Houghton Mifflin, 1981.

Fitzpatrick, M. A. *Between husbands & wives: Communication in marriage.* Beverly Hills, Calif.: Sage Publications, 1988.

Forgatch, Marion S. Patterns and outcome in family problem solving: The disrupting effect of negative emotion. *Journal of Marriage and the Family,* 1989, *51,* 115–124.

Guerney, Benard and Pamela Maxson. Marital and family enrichment research: A decade review and look ahead. *Contemporary Families: Looking Forward, Looking Backward,* Alan Booth, ed. Minneapolis, Minn.: National Council on Family Relations, 1991, 457–465.

Gurman, A. S. and D. P. Kniskern. Commentary on Wells and Giannetti article on individual marital therapy. *Family Process,* 1986, *25,* 51–62.

Halford, W. K., K. Hahlweg, and M. Dunne. Cross-cultural study of marital communication and marital distress. *Journal of Marriage and the Family,* 1990, *52,* 487–500.

Held, B. S. The problem of strategy within the stystemic therapies. *Journal of Marital and Family Therapy,* 1992, *18,* 25–34.

Julius, M. Marital stress and suppressed anger linked to death of spouses. *Marriage and Divorce Today,* 1986, *11,* no. 35, 1–2.

Kolevzon, M. S. and L. A. Jenkins. The relationship self-assessment inventory (RSAI): A guide to resolving conflict in couples therapy. Paper, 54th Annual Conference, National Conference on Family Relations, Orlando, Florida, 1992. Used by permission.

L'Abate, L. and D. A. Bagarozzi. *Sourcebook of marriage and family interaction.* New York: Brunner/Mazel, Publishers, 1993.

Laing, R. D. *Knots.* New York: Random House, 1970.

Levine, L. B. and D. M. Busby. Co-creating a shared reality with couples. Paper, 54th Annual Conference of the National Council on Family Relations, Orlando, Florida, 1992. Used by permission.

Marano, H. E. The reinvention of marriage. *Psychology Today,* January/February 1992, 49 et passim.

Menaghan, E. G. Coping with marital problems: Assessing effectiveness. Paper presented at the annual meeting of the American Sociological Association, 1982. Used with permission.

Markowski, E. M. Temperament differences in enrichment and therapy couples. Paper, American Association for Marriage and Family Therapy, Dallas, 1991. Used by permission.

Nakanishi, M. Perceptions of self-disclosure in initial interaction: A Japanese sample. *Human Communication Research,* 1986, *13,* 167–190.

Noller, P. and M. A. Fitzpatrick. Marital communication in the eighties. *Contemporary Families,* Alan Booth, ed. Minneapolis, Minn.: National Council on Family Relations, 1991, 42–53.

Piercy, Fred P. and Douglas H. Sprenkle. Marriage and family therapy: A decade review. *Contemporary Families: Looking Forward, Looking Backward* Alan Booth, ed. Minneapolis, Minn.: National Council on Family Relations, 1991, 446–456.

Reiss, Ira L. and Harriet M. Reiss. *An end to shame: Shaping our next sexual revolution.* New York: Prometheus Books, 1990.

Rueter, M. A. and R. D. Conger. The relationship between family problem solving interaction and family problem solving effectiveness. *Family Perspective,* 1992, *26,* 331–360.

Russell, Lila. Sex and couples therapy: A method of treatment to enhance physical and emotional intimacy. *Journal of Sex and Marital Therapy,* 1990, *16,* 111–120.

Scoresby, A. L. *The marriage dialogue.* Reading, Mass.: Addison-Wesley, 1977.

Sparrow, Kathlenn Handy. Factors in mate selection for single black professional women. *Free Inquiry in Creative Sociology,* 1991, *19,* no. 1, 103–109.

Styron, W. *Darkness visible: A memoir of madness.* New York: Random House, 1990.

Swain, Scott. Covert intimacy: Closeness in men's friendships. In *Gender in Intimate Relationships,* edited by B. J. Risman and P. Schwartz. Belmont, Calif.: Wadsworth Publishing Co., 1989, 71–86.

Tannen, D. *You just don't understand: Women and men in conversation.* London: Virago Press, 1990.

Turner, A. J. Effective communication. Presentation to Courtship and Marriage class, East Carolina University, October 14, 1992, and revised for this text in 1993. Used by permission of Dr. Turner, Huntsville, Alabama.

Van Matre, L. Honesty can be worst policy in affair. *The Daily Reflector,* August 28, 1992, d-8.

Wang, L. How to do marriage and family therapy with people from China. Paper, 54th Annual Conference of the National Council on Family Relations, Orlando, Florida, 1992. Used by permission.

Waring, Edward M. *Enhancing marital intimacy through facilitating cognitive self-disclosure.* New York: Brunner/Mazel, 1988.

Wells, R. A. and V. J. Giannetti. Individual marital therapy: A critical reappraisal. *Family Process,* 1986, *25, 43–51.*

Wilson, K. and P. Y. Martin. Regional differences in resolving family conflicts: Is there a legacy of patriarchy in the South? *Sociological Spectrum,* 1988, *8,* 197–211.

Yandoli, A. H. Stress and medical marriages. *Stress–Medicine,* 1989, *5,* 213–219.

Contents

ℬ **10** ℬ

CHAPTER

Sexuality in Relationships

Is It True?

1. The frequency of marital intercourse remains relatively constant across the duration of the marriage.

2. In a study of university men and women, over half said that they would insist on using a condom during intercourse.

3. Over 150 symptoms of premenstrual syndrome (PMS) have been identified.

4. Women who have an affair are more likely to be dissatisfied with their marriage than men who have an affair.

5. In one study of U.S. adults, one–fourth reported that they had engaged in group sex.

1 = F; 2 = F; 3 = T; 4 = T; 5 = T

A room with a view is in the dark with you.

CARLY SIMON

*I*n a study of over 9,000 spouses who rated their marriage as either "excellent" or "very good," physical affection in public and sexual passion in private were among the most important qualities in these relationships (Schwartz & Jackson, 1989). The absence of sexual dysfunctions also contributes to a good sexual relationship. In this chapter we review some unique aspects of marital sexuality, some facts about and prerequisites to sexual fulfillment, causes and types of sexual dysfunctions, and sexuality in the middle and later years.

If it weren't for pickpockets, I'd have no sex life at all.

RODNEY DANGERFIELD

🦋 Marital Sexuality

There are some unique aspects of marital sexuality. In our society, marital intercourse is the most legitimate form of sexual behavior. Homosexual, premarital, and extramarital intercourse do not enjoy society's complete approval, although attitudes and laws are changing. It is not only okay to have intercourse when married, it is expected. People assume that married couples make love and that something is "wrong" if they do not.

∿ **ACROSS CULTURES**

Virginity among Mangaian girls and boys in the Polynesian islands is looked upon with disdain. Virgins are viewed as not knowing how to provide sexual pleasure. Both girls and boys are encouraged at a young age to develop their sexuality through sex play and masturbation (Marshall, 1971).

Marital sexuality is characterized by declining frequency of sexual interactions.

NATIONAL DATA 🦋 Forty-five percent of couples married two years or less reported they had intercourse three or more times a week in contrast to 18 percent of couples who had been married ten years or more (Blumstein & Schwartz, 1990). Sixteen percent of 6,029 spouses reported that they had been sexually inactive during the month prior to the study (Donnelly, 1993).

Reasons for declining frequency include careers or jobs, children, and satiation. As we will note in the next chapter on Work and Leisure in Relationships, working full time and taking care of children can be exhausting. Even for spouses who are not employed but who have children, exhaustion is a problem. One woman said, "I'll tell you straight out. After taking care of a 3-year-old and a 9-month-old, I'm in no mood for sex."

Satiation, in psychology, means that repeated exposure to a stimulus results in the loss of its ability to reinforce. For example, the first time you listen to a new cassette tape or CD, you derive considerable enjoyment and satisfaction from it. You may play it over and over during the first few days. But after a week or so, listening to the same music is no longer new and does not give you the same level of enjoyment that it first did. So it is with intercourse. The thousandth time that a person has intercourse with the same person is not as new and exciting as the first few times. Although intercourse can remain very satisfying for couples in long-term relationships, satiation may result in decreased frequency of intercourse.

Sexual Satisfaction Over Time

How do spouses rate their sex lives throughout the marriage? Ard (1990) conducted a longitudinal study of 161 marital partners over a 20-year period. Eighty-five percent of the husbands reported "great enjoyment" in their sexual relationship the first three years of marriage; 54 percent of the wives reported likewise. When asked about the last three years of marriage, 70 percent of the husbands reported "great enjoyment" in contrast to 57 percent of the wives. Hence, husbands had overall greater enjoyment, which decreased across the 20-year span; wives had lower enjoyment than men but increased their level of enjoyment slightly with the passage of time.

> **Frequency of intercourse:**
> **Age 20–40, tri-weekly**
> **Age 40–60, try weekly**
> **Age 60–80, try weakly**
>
> UNKNOWN

In another study, a team of researchers interviewed both husbands and wives who were married to each other and found that while both reported relative satisfaction with their sexual relationship, the husbands saw themselves as more interested and gratified by the couple's sex life than the wives. In contrast, the wives tended to perceive both themselves and their husbands as having similar sexual desires and sexual pleasures in their relationship (Julien et al., 1992).

Monogamy in Marriage

Although spouses may differ in their perceptions of sexual satisfactions in the relationship, spouses tend to be sexually faithful to each other in a given year. Based on data from more than 1,510 husbands and a similar number of wives, Blumstein and Schwartz (1990) observed that 89 percent of the husbands and 91 percent of the wives reported they had been sexually faithful to their spouse during the past year. These percentages are considerably higher than those for individuals who were living together (74 percent). The researchers commented that these data emphasize that "sexual behavior is created by relationship expectations and traditions rather than by sexual essences" (p. 318). In other words, spouses expect each other to be sexually faithful. Committed live-ins are also expected to be sexually faithful but the expectation is less strong.

> **Too much of a good thing can be wonderful.**
>
> MAE WEST

& Sexual Fulfillment: Some Facts

The last two decades have brought remarkable advances in our knowledge of human sexuality.

HELEN KAPLAN

Individuals who have a good sexual relationship with their partners are often aware of some basic facts about human sexuality. Some of these facts include those discussed in the following sections.

Learned Sexual Attitudes and Behaviors

Whether you believe that "Sex is sinful" or "If it feels good, do it," your sexual attitudes have been learned. Your parents and peers have had a major impact on your sexual attitudes, but there have been other influences as well: school, church or synagogue, and the media. Your attitudes about sex would have been different if the influences you were exposed to had been different.

The same is true of sexual behavior. The words you say, the sequence of events in lovemaking, the specific behaviors you engage in, and the positions you adopt during intercourse are a product of the learning history you and your partner have had. The fact that learning accounts for most sexual attitudes and behaviors is important because negative patterns can be unlearned and positive patterns can be learned.

ACROSS CULTURES

It is also important to be aware that you have been reared in American society and that your thoughts, feelings, attitudes, and behaviors have been shaped by this culture. Had you been reared in another culture, your perceptions of sexuality would be different. For example, having intercourse with a brother or sister is likely to induce feelings of shame or disgust in our society, but the Dahomey of West Africa and the Inca of Peru have viewed such a relationship as natural and desirable (Stephens, 1982).

Time and Effort Needed for Effective Sexual Communication

Most of us who have been reared in homes in which discussions about sex were infrequent or nonexistent may have developed relatively few skills to employ in talking about sex. Talking about sex with our partner may seem awkward. Overcoming our awkward feelings requires retraining ourselves so that sex becomes as easy for us to talk about as what we had for lunch. Some suggestions that may be helpful in developing effective sexual communication follow.

Say Sex Words   Effective sexual communication involves using words to refer to sexual anatomy and sexual behaviors. You might develop a list with your partner that contains all of the technical and slang words you can think of about sex. Then alternate with your partner, reading one word after the other from the list. As you read these sex words, take turns sharing your feelings about and reactions to each word. The goal is to find out which sex words you and your partner feel most comfortable using. Some individuals prefer technical terms for sexual acts and sexual anatomy. Others prefer certain slang terms. Many individuals are offended or uncomfortable with some slang terms because they have a negative connotation. As a result of doing this exercise, you and your partner should know which sex words are preferred and which sex words are to be avoided.

An intimate relationship provides a comfortable context in which to learn positive attitudes toward sexual expression.

CONSIDERATION

Some individuals do not like any of the technical or popular slang words for certain sexual anatomy or sexual behaviors. In this case, the partners may invent another word or term that they both feel good about. For example, one woman said she did not like any of the popular slang words for vagina. She also did not want her partner to use the word "vagina" in their sexual communication because it sounded too "medical." The woman suggested that she and her partner invent another term to refer to "vagina." They decided to use the word "mango" as their personal slang word for vagina.

Ask Open-Ended Questions   Open-ended questions are questions that may elicit detailed answers, rather than one-word answers such as "yes" or "no." To learn more about your partner, ask specific questions that cannot be answered with a yes or no. Examples include "What does orgasm feel like to you?," "Tell me about the sexual activities you like best," and "How can I be a better sex partner?"

Give Reflective Feedback   When your partner shares with you very intimate details concerning sexuality, it is important to respond in a nonjudgmental way. One way to do this is to reflect back what your partner tells you.

Suppose Mary tells Jim that the best sex for her is when he is holding and caressing her, not when they are actually having intercourse. An inappropriate response by Jim to her disclosure would be "Something must be the matter with you." This would undoubtedly stop Mary from telling Jim anything more about her feelings. But Jim's reflective statement, "Our being close is what you like best in our relationship," confirms for Mary that he understands how she feels and that her feelings are accepted.

Effects of Physical and Mental Health on Sexual Performance

Effective sexual functioning requires good physical and mental health. Physically, this means regular exercise, good nutrition, lack of disease, and lack of fatigue. Regular exercise, whether walking, jogging, aerobics, swimming, or bicycling, is related to higher libido, sexual desire, and intimacy (Ash, 1986). Performance in all areas of life does not have to diminish with age—particularly if people take care of themselves physically (Bronte, 1989).

Good health also implies being aware that some drugs may interfere with sexual performance. Alcohol is the most frequently used drug by American adults. Although a moderate amount of alcohol can help a person become aroused through a lowering of inhibitions, too much alcohol can slow the physiological processes and deaden the senses. Shakespeare may have said it best: "It [alcohol] provokes the desire but it takes away the performance" (Macbeth, Act II, Scene three). The result of the excessive intake of alcohol for women is a reduced chance of orgasm; for men, it is an increased chance of experiencing difficulty attaining or maintaining erection.

The reactions to marijuana—a drug also used during sexual arousal—are less predictable than the reactions to alcohol. Some individuals report a short-term enhancement effect; others say that marijuana just makes them sleepy. In men, chronic use may decrease sex drive because marijuana may lower testosterone levels.

ଝ Sexual Fulfillment: Some Prerequisites

There are several prerequisites for having a good sexual relationship.

Self-Knowledge and Self-Esteem

Being sexually fulfilled implies having knowledge about yourself and your body. To be in touch with yourself and your own body is to know how you can best experience sexual pleasure. "I've read all the books on how to get the most out of sex," said one man, "and I've concluded that the experts know a lot about what some people like sexually, but nothing about what *I* like. Good sex for me is more related to the context than to the technique. And I'm sure that for the next person it's something else."

Sexual fulfillment also implies having a positive self-concept. To the degree that you have good feelings about yourself, you will regard yourself as a person someone else would enjoy touching, being close to, and making love with. If you do not like yourself, you may wonder how anyone else would either.

A Good Relationship

A guideline among therapists who work with couples who have sexual problems is "Treat the relationship before focusing on the sexual issue." The

Acquaint thee with thyself.

M. F. TUPPER

sexual relationship is part of the larger relationship between the partners, and what happens outside the bedroom in day-to-day interaction has a tremendous influence on what happens inside the bedroom. The statement "I can't fight with you all day and want to have sex with you at night" illustrates the social context of the sexual experience. Oggins et al. (1993) observed in a sample of 199 black and 174 white couples that, particularly for women, perceptions of sexual enjoyment were associated with reports of relationship satisfaction.

The type of relationship the partners have may also be important. Two researchers observed that spouses who are androgynous (each person reflects a blend of masculine and feminine traits) in their sexual interaction report higher levels of sexual satisfaction (Rosenweig & Dailey, 1989).

The effects of a couple's overall and sexual relationships are intertwined. According to an old adage, when sex goes well, it is 15 percent of a relationship, when it goes badly, it is 85 percent. Undoubtedly, many partners agree. The sexual relationship positively influences the couple's overall relationship in several ways: (1) as a shared pleasure, a positively reinforcing event; (2) by facilitating intimacy, as many couples feel closer and share their feelings before or after a sexual experience; and (3) by reducing tension generated by the stresses of everyday living and couple interaction (McCarthy, 1982).

Sex is the salt of life.
JAMES HUNEKER

CONSIDERATION

Sexual interaction communicates how the partners are feeling and acts as a barometer for the relationship. Each partner brings to a sexual encounter, sometimes unconsciously, a motive (pleasure, reconciliation, procreation, duty), a psychological state (love, hostility, boredom, excitement), and a physical state (tense, exhausted, relaxed, turned on). The combination of these factors will change from one encounter to another. Tonight the wife may feel aroused and loving and seek pleasure, but her husband may feel exhausted and hostile and only have sex out of a sense of duty. Tomorrow night, both partners may feel relaxed and have sex as a means of expressing their love for each other.

The verbal and nonverbal communication preceding, during, and after sexual interaction also may act as a barometer for the relationship. One wife said:

> I can tell how we're doing by whether or not we have intercourse and how he approaches me when we do. Sometimes he just rolls over when the lights are out and starts to rub my back. Other times, he plays with my face while we talk and kisses me and waits till I reach for him. And still other times, we each stay on our side of the bed so that our legs don't even touch.

Open Sexual Communication

Sexually fulfilled partners are comfortable expressing what they enjoy and do not enjoy in the sexual experience. Unless both partners communicate their needs, preferences, and expectations to each other, neither is ever sure what the other wants. In essence, the Golden Rule ("Do unto others as you would have them do unto you") is not helpful because what you like may not be the

Open sexual communication includes being explicit about what one likes the partner to do and not do to provide pleasure.

Take responsibility for hearing and being heard correctly.

JACK TURNER

same as what your partner wants. A classic example of the uncertain lover is the man who picks up a copy of *The Erotic Lover* in a bookstore and leafs through the pages until the topic on how to please a woman catches his eye. He reads that women enjoy having their breasts stimulated by their partner's tongue and teeth. Later that night in bed, he rolls over and begins to nibble on his partner's breasts. Meanwhile, she wonders what has possessed him and is unsure what to make of this new (possibly unpleasant) behavior. Sexually fulfilled partners take the guesswork out of their relationship by communicating preferences and giving feedback. This means using what some therapists call the touch-and-ask rule. Each touch and caress may include the question "How does that feel?" It is then the partner's responsibility to give feedback. If the caress does not feel good, the partner can say what does feel good. Guiding and moving the partner's hand or body are also ways of giving feedback.

But open sexual communication is more than expressing sexual preferences and giving feedback. Women wish that men were more aware of a number of sexual issues. Some comments from students in the authors' classes follow:

- It does not impress women to hear about other women in the man's past.
- If men knew what it is like to be pregnant, they would not be so apathetic about birth control.
- Most women want more caressing, gentleness, kissing, and talking *before* and *after* intercourse.

- Some women are sexually attracted to other women, not to men.
- Sometimes the woman wants sex even if the man does not. Sometimes she wants to be aggressive without being made to feel that she shouldn't be.
- Intercourse can be enjoyable without a climax.
- Many women do not have an orgasm from penetration only; they need direct stimulation of their clitoris by their partner's tongue or finger. Men should be interested in fulfilling their partner's sexual needs.
- Most women prefer to have sex in a monogamous love relationship.
- When a woman says "no," she means it. Women do not want men to expect sex every time they are alone with their partner.
- Many women enjoy sex in the morning, not just at night.
- Sex is *not* everything.
- Women need to be lubricated before penetration.
- Men should know more about menstruation.
- Many women are no more inhibited about sex than men.
- Women do not like men to roll over, go to sleep, or leave right after orgasm.
- Intercourse is more of a love relationship than a sex act for some women.
- The woman should not always be expected to supply a method of contraception. It is also the man's responsibility.
- Women tend to like a loving, gentle, patient, tender, and understanding partner. Rough sexual play can hurt and be a turnoff.
- Men should know that all women are not alike in what pleases them sexually.

Men also have a list of things they wish women knew about sex:

- Men do not always want to be the dominant partner; women should be aggressive.
- Men want women to enjoy sex totally and not be inhibited.
- Men enjoy tender and passionate kissing.
- Men really enjoy fellatio.
- Women need to know a man's erogenous zones.
- Oral sex is good and enjoyable, not bad and unpleasant.
- Many men enjoy a lot of romantic foreplay and slow, aggressive sex.
- Men cannot keep up intercourse forever. Most men tire more easily than women.
- Looks are not everything.
- Women should know how to enjoy sex in different ways and different positions.
- Women should not expect a man to get a second erection right away.
- Many men enjoy sex in the morning.
- Pulling the hair on a man's body can hurt.
- Many men enjoy sex in a caring, loving, exclusive relationship.
- It is frustrating to stop sex play once it has started.
- Women should know that all men are not out to have intercourse with them. Some men like to talk and become friends.

The widespread availability of condoms has not been met with consistent use.

Fifty-seven percent of 2,058 individuals over age 18 reported that AIDS had no effect on sexual behavior.

BARBARA LEIGH

The pressure on individuals to be sexually interested, responsive, and enthusiastic within a committed relationship is at an all-time high in our society.

SANDRA R. LEIBLUM
RAYMOND C. ROSEN

Address Safer Sex Issues

Sexuality in an age of HIV and STD infections demands talking about safer sex issues with a new potential sexual partner. Two researchers (Gray & Saracino, 1991) asked 252 university women and 207 university men whether it was "very likely" they would bring up a variety of issues with new potential sexual partners. The issues and percentages follow (p. 261).

Issue	Percent
Discuss condom before having intercourse.	54
Ask to have a monogamous relationship.	49
Insist on using a condom before intercourse.	40
Ask how many sexual partners he/she has had.	27

These percentages reflect the ambivalence college students have about increasing the degree to which they engage in safer sex behavior. While over half say that they would discuss condoms, only 40 percent report that they would insist on a condom. And while almost half would ask for sexual exclusivity, only a fourth would ask about previous sexual partners. Only five percent of this sample reported it was "very likely" that both they and their partners would be tested for HIV before having intercourse (p. 262).

CONSIDERATION

Part of the ambivalence in asking others about the number of sexual partners they have had is the fear that one will be asked to reciprocate the disclosure. Over three-fourths of the college students referred to in Gray and Saracino's study, reported up to four sexual partners in the last 12 months preceding the study. Three-fourths also reported they had not changed their sexual behavior in spite of the new cultural emphasis on AIDS awareness. Even when the sexual behavior being engaged is ultra high risk (anal intercourse), 71 percent of 114 heterosexuals reported that they never used a condom (Catania et al., 1992).

Realistic Expectations

To achieve sexual fulfillment, expectations must be realistic. A couple's sexual needs, preferences, and expectations may not coincide. It is unrealistic to assume that your partner will want to have sex with the same frequency and in the same way that you do on all occasions. It may also be unrealistic to expect the level of sexual interest and frequency of sexual interaction in long-term relationships to remain consistently high.

CONSIDERATION

Sexual fulfillment means not asking things of the sexual relationship that it cannot deliver. Failure to develop realistic expectations will result in frustration and resentment.

Debunking Sexual Myths

Sexual fulfillment also means not being victim to sexual myths. Some of the more common myths include that sex equals intercourse and orgasm, that women who love sex don't have values, and that the double standard is dead. Zilbergeld (1992) identified some sexual myths unique to men. Some of these include that men are totally liberated and comfortable with sex, that real men don't have sex problems, and that men are always interested in and ready for sex. He also challenged the myth that "good sex is spontaneous with no planning and talking." Indeed, individuals with busy and hectic schedules most often plan their lovemaking if it is to occur at all. See Table 10.1 for other sexual myths.

It ain't so much the things we don't know that get us in trouble. It's the things we know that ain't so.

ARTEMUS WARD

A Healthy Attitude Toward Sex

Sexual fulfillment also depends on having a positive attitude toward sex. Traumatic sexual experiences such as rape or child sexual abuse may create an intense negative attitude toward sex. Any sexual advance or contact can cause the individual to become anxious and engender the desire to escape or avoid the situation. Such negative reactions to sex are best dealt with through therapy.

I still have a problem as a result of growing up in Catholic Ireland, brought up to believe that sex is something dirty.

SINÉAD O'CONNER

People can be viewed on a continuum from feeling uncomfortable and wanting to avoid sex (erotophobia) to enjoying and wanting to be involved in sex (erotophilia). The erotophobic may feel nauseated by erotic material; the

TABLE 10.1
Sexual Myths

THE FOLLOWING ARE SOME OF THE MORE COMMON SEXUAL MYTHS.

Masturbation is sick.
Masturbation will make you go blind and grow hair on your palm.
Sex education makes children promiscuous.
Sexual behavior usually ends soon after age 60.
People who enjoy pornography end up committing sexual crimes.
Most "normal" women have orgasms from penile thrusting alone.
Extramarital sex always destroys a marriage.
Extramarital sex will strengthen a marriage.
Simultaneous orgasm with one's partner is the ultimate sexual experience.
My partner should enjoy the same things that I do sexually.
A man cannot have an orgasm unless he has an erection.
Most people know a lot of accurate information about sex.
Using a condom ensures that you won't get HIV.
Most women prefer a partner with a large penis.
Few women masturbate.
Women secretly want to be raped.

SELF-ASSESSMENT

Index of Sexual Satisfaction (ISS)

This questionnaire is designed to measure the degree of satisfaction you have in the sexual relationship with your partner. It is not a test, so there are no right or wrong answers. Answer each item as carefully and accurately as you can by placing a number beside each one as follows:

1 Rarely or none of the time
2 A little of the time
3 Some of the time
4 Good part of the time
5 Most or all of the time

1. I feel that my partner enjoys our sex life. _____
2. My sex life is very exciting. _____
3. Sex is fun for my partner and me. _____
4. I feel that my partner sees little in me except for the sex I can give. _____
5. I feel that sex is dirty and disgusting. _____
6. My sex life is monotonous. _____
7. When we have sex it is too rushed and hurriedly completed. _____
8. I feel that my sex life is lacking in quality. _____
9. My partner is sexually very exciting. _____
10. I enjoy the sex techniques that my partner likes or uses. _____

11. I feel that my partner wants too much sex from me. _____
12. I think that sex is wonderful. _____
13. My partner dwells on sex too much. _____
14. I try to avoid sexual contact with my partner. _____
15. My partner is too rough or brutal when we have sex. _____
16. My partner is a wonderful sex mate. _____
17. I feel that sex is a normal function of our relationship. _____
18. My partner does not want sex when I do. _____
19. I feel that our sex life really adds a lot to our relationship. _____
20. My partner seems to avoid sexual contact with me. _____
21. It is easy for me to get sexually excited by my partner. _____
22. I feel that my partner is sexually pleased with me. _____
23. My partner is very sensitive to my sexual needs and desires. _____
24. My partner does not satisfy me sexually. _____
25. I feel that my sex life is boring. _____

erotophilic may feel aroused by it. The Self-Assessment above provides a way to measure the level of sexual satisfaction with a partner.

Sexual Dysfunctions: Onset, Situations, Causes

It is not uncommon for couples who are very satisfied with their relationship to have one or more sexual problems. Sex therapists refer to such problems as *sexual dysfunctions*. The existence of a sexual dysfunction implies that the partners want something to happen that is not happening (for example, orgasm) or want to stop something from happening that is happening (for example, rapid ejaculation).

The primary objective of all sex therapy is to relieve the patient's sexual dysfunction.

HELEN KAPLAN

Index of Sexual Satisfaction (ISS) *continued*

Scoring Items 1, 2, 3, 9, 10, 12, 16, 17, 19, 21, 22, and 23 must be reverse-scored. (For example, if you answered 5 on the first item, you would change that score to 1.) After these positively worded items have been reverse-scored, if there are no omitted items, the score is computed by summing the item scores and subtracting 25.

Interpretation Scores can range from 0 to 100, with a high score indicative of sexual dissatisfaction. Hudson, Harrison, and Crosscup (1981) suggested that a score of approximately 30 or above is indicative of dissatisfaction in one's sexual relationship. However, they cautioned,

> Actually, no single score for the ISS (or any such scale) should be taken too seriously. . . . In all cases it is important to evaluate the obtained ISS score in relation to all other clinical evidence that is available concerning the presence and severity of difficulties in the sexual component of a dyadic relationship. (pp. 166–167)

Psychometric Information Hudson et al. (1981) demonstrated good construct validity for the ISS. The ISS correlated 0.68 with the Index of Marital Satisfaction, 0.47 with the Generalized Contentment Scale, and 0.44 with the Sexual Attitude Scale. The reliability of the scale was examined in three study samples. The average value of Coefficient Alpha for the three samples was 0.916, showing excellent reliability over three separate and heterogenous samples. Two of the samples consisted of adults who were not seeking counseling. Their mean ISS score was 15.2 (SD=11.28). The third sample was composed of people seeking counseling for personal or relationship problems. The counseling group's mean was 41.5 (SD=18.13). The test-retest reliability was 0.93 (in an additional sample of graduate students in social work).

REFERENCE

Hudson, W. W., Harrison, D. F., & Crosscup, P. C. (1981). A short-form scale to measure sexual discord in dyadic relationships. *Journal of Sex Research, 17,* 157–174.

NOTE: This reproduction of the ISS includes the replacement items recommended by the authors following their analysis of the scale's item-total correlations.

SOURCE: Published by permission of the *Journal of Sex Research,* a publication of the Society for the Scientific Study of Sex.

Sexual dysfunctions are classified by time of onset, situations in which they occur, and cause. Regarding onset, a *primary dysfunction* is one that a person has always had. A *secondary dysfunction* is one which a person is currently experiencing, after a period of satisfactory sexual functioning. For example, a woman who has never had an orgasm with any previous sexual partner has a primary dysfunction whereas a woman who has been orgasmic with previous partners but not with a current partner has a secondary sexual dysfunction.

A *situational dysfunction* occurs in one context or setting and not in another, while a *total dysfunction* occurs in all contexts or settings. For example, a man who is unable to become erect with one partner but who can become erect with another has a situational dysfunction.

Finally, a sexual dysfunction may be classified according to whether it is caused primarily by biological (or organic) factors, such as insufficient hormones or physical illness, or by psychosocial or cultural factors such as negative learning, guilt, anxiety, or an unhappy relationship.

CONSIDERATION

In most cases, sexual dysfunctions are caused by more than one factor (Goldman, 1992; Hawton, 1985). In addition, factors are often contributory rather than causal. Each by itself may not ensure the development of a sexual problem, but a problem may result from a complex interaction of factors (Hawton, 1985).

In the following sections we discuss various sexual dysfunctions as they relate to desire, arousal, and/or orgasm (of the sexual response cycle), which involve an objective physiological impairment (e.g., loss of erection) and/or a disturbance in both the subjective sense of pleasure or experience of pain (APA, 1987).

CONSIDERATION

Although we will discuss treatments for both female and male sexual dysfunctions, these discussions are not intended to be a replacement for sex therapy. We recommend that partners experiencing sexual problems for a prolonged period of time who have been unable to resolve the concerns themselves consider consulting a sex therapist. The name of a certified sex therapist in your area can be located by calling 312/644–0828 or by writing to the American Association of Sex Educators, Counselors, and Therapists (435 North Michigan Avenue, Suite 1717, Chicago, Illinois 60611).

ACROSS CULTURES | Although consulting a therapist is something most citizens of the United States would be willing to do, Asians and Chinese Americans would probably not consider this option. Rather, they have been socialized that problem solving is to occur within the family and that bringing a problem to an outsider (i.e., therapist) may be very shameful. Other cultural variations also occur. For example, the Irish would turn first to a priest for diagnosis and treatment (Lavee, 1991).

Desire Phase Dysfunctions

The *Diagnostic and Statistical Manual* (DSM–III–R), published by the American Psychiatric Association classifies two types of desire phase dysfunctions: hypoactive sexual desire and sexual aversion.

Hypoactive Sexual Desire   The term *hypoactive sexual desire* refers to a low interest in sexual activities or fantasies. Other terms that are used to refer to a

T A B L E   10.2

Types of Sexual Dysfunctions in Women and Men

ASPECTS OF SEXUALITY AFFECTED	SEXUAL DYSFUNCTION	
	WOMEN	MEN
Sexual Desire	Hypoactive Sexual Desire Sexual Aversion	Hypoactive Sexual Desire Sexual Aversion
Arousal	Female Sexual Arousal Dysfunction	Erectile Dysfunction Rapid Ejaculation
Orgasm	Inhibited Female Orgasm	Inhibited Male Orgasm
Sexual Pain	Dyspareunia Vaginismus	Dyspareunia

low interest in sex include "inhibited sexual desire," "low sexual desire," and "impaired sexual interest." Like other sexual dysfunctions, hypoactive sexual desire may be primary, secondary, situational, or total.

Both women and men may experience hypoactive sexual desire.

NATIONAL DATA 🐾 One estimate suggests that about 20 percent of the total adult population in Europe and the United States have low sexual desire (APA, 1987).

Assessing whether you or your partner has hypoactive sexual desire is problematic. First, there are no clear criteria for determining "abnormal" levels of sexual desire. Two people can vary greatly in the degree to which they experience sexual interest or desire, and each may feel comfortable with his or her level of sexual desire. Furthermore, as we have noted, sexual desire in couples predictably decreases over time; in general, the longer a couple has been together, the less sexual desire they report (Carroll & Bagley, 1990). It is important to be cautious and not label one's self or partner as abnormal since there are wide variations in sexual interest.

Among the women of the island of Inis Beag (off the coast of Ireland), it is expected that they have no sexual desire or needs. Any woman who finds pleasure in sex is viewed as a deviant (Messenger, 1971).

A C R O S S   C U L T U R E S 〜

C O N S I D E R A T I O N

When a desire discrepancy occurs, the person who desires less frequent sexual activity is often labeled as having a "problem" (i.e., low sexual desire); rarely is the partner who desires more frequent sexual activity labeled as having "hyperactive" sexual desire.

Hypoactive sexual desire may be caused by one or more of a variety of factors, including restrictive upbringing, relationship dissatisfaction (e.g., anger or resentment toward one's partner), nonacceptance of one's sexual orientation, learning a passive sexual role, and physical factors such as stress, illness, drugs, and fatigue. In addition, abnormal hormonal states have been shown to be associated with low sexual desire. For example, androgen deficiency is associated with low sexual desire in men (hormonal effects on women's libido are not clearly understood) (Segraves, 1988).

Treatment of hypoactive sexual desire varies, depending on the underlying cause(s) of the problem. Some of the ways in which lack of sexual desire may be treated include the following:

⤳ ACROSS CULTURES

1. *Increase Relationship Satisfaction.* This usually involves couple therapy. However, an open, egalitarian relationship which has mutual satisfaction as its goal is not shared by couples everywhere. Indeed, Hispanics, Mexicans, and Puerto Ricans tend to emphasize male superiority and focus on the needs of the male to the exclusion of the female. The pleasure and satisfaction of the woman is not considered important (Lavee, 1991).

2. *Identify and Implement Conditions for Satisfying Sex.* Bass (1985) suggested that many people who believe they have a low sexual drive have mislabeled the problem. In many cases, the "real" problem (according to Bass) is not that the person has low sexual desire, but rather, the person has not identified or implemented the conditions under which he or she experiences satisfactory sex. Bass tells his clients who believe they have a low sex drive that "just as their desire to eat is only temporarily diminished when confronted with certain unappetizing foods, so too their sexual desire is only temporarily inhibited through their failure to identify and implement their requirements for enjoyable sex" (p. 62).

3. *Practice Sensate Focus.* Sensate focus is a series of exercises developed by Masters and Johnson used to treat various sexual dysfunctions. Sensate focus may also be used by couples who are not experiencing sexual dysfunction, but want to enhance their sexual relationship.

    In doing the *sensate focus* exercise, the couple (in the privacy of their bedroom) remove their clothing and take turns touching, feeling, caressing, and exploring each other in ways intended to provide sensual pleasure. In the first phase of sensate focus, genital touching is not allowed. The person being touched should indicate if he or she finds a particular touching behavior unpleasant, at which point the partner will stop or change what is being done.

    During the second phase of sensate focus, the person being touched is instructed to give positive as well as negative feedback (i.e., to indicate what is enjoyable as well as what is unpleasant). During the third phase, genital touching can be included, without the intention of producing orgasm. The goal of progressing through the three phases of sensate focus is to help the couple reestablish positive, pleasurable sensations, promote trust and communication, and reduce anxiety related to sexual performance.

4. *Openness to Reeducation.* Reeducation involves the person being open to examining the thoughts, feelings, and attitudes she or he was taught as a child and reevaluating them. The goal is to redefine sexual activity so it is viewed as a positive, desirable, healthy, and pleasurable experience.

5. *Other Treatments.* Other treatments for lack of sexual desire include rest and relaxation. This is indicated where the culprit is chronic fatigue syndrome (CFS), the symptoms of which are overwhelming fatigue, low-grade fever, and sore throat. Other treatments for lack of sexual desire include hormone treatment and changing medications (if possible) in cases where medication interferes with sexual desire. In addition, sex therapists often recommend that people who are troubled by a low level of sexual desire engage in masturbation as a means of developing positive sexual feelings. Therapists also recommend the use of sexual fantasies. Women who do not have sexual fantasies or who report feeling guilty about having them report higher levels of sexual dissatisfaction (Cado & Leitenberg, 1990).

Sexual Aversion   Another desire phase dysfunction is *sexual aversion* (also known as "sexual phobia" and "sexual panic disorder"), which is characterized by the individual wanting nothing to do with genital contact with another person. The immediate cause of sexual aversion is an irrational fear of sex. Such fear may result from negative sexual attitudes acquired in childhood or sexual trauma such as rape or incest. Some cases of sexual aversion may be caused by fear of intimacy or hostility toward the other sex.

Treatment for sexual aversion involves providing insight into the possible ways in which the negative attitudes toward sexual activity developed, increasing the communication skills of the partners, and sensate focus. Understanding the origins of the sexual aversion may enable the individual to view change as possible. Through communication with the partner and through sensate focus exercises, the individual may learn to associate more positive feelings with sexual behavior.

Arousal Phase Dysfunctions

Some relationship partners who experience desire for sexual activity have difficulty experiencing sexual arousal. The arousal phase of the sexual response cycle involves numerous physiological changes, including vaginal lubrication, nipple erection, and genital vasocongestion. Problems of sexual arousal are characterized by failure of the physiological responses that normally occur during this phase and/or by lack of pleasurable sensations usually associated with sexual arousal. The DSM–III–R (APA, 1987) classifies two types of arousal phase dysfunctions: female sexual arousal disorder and male erectile disorder.

> **CONSIDERATION**
>
> The terms *frigid* and *impotent* have been commonly used to refer to women who are sexually unresponsive and men who have difficulty achieving or maintaining an erection. Because being labeled as frigid or impotent has negative connotations, sex therapists avoid using these terms, and instead use more neutral terms with their clients such as *arousal difficulties* or *erectile difficulties.*

Female Sexual Arousal Dysfunction *Female sexual arousal dysfunction* (also known as "impaired sexual arousal" and "general sexual dysfunction") is defined as not becoming physiologically aroused (lubrication) or not labeling one's arousal in positive terms. Like other sexual dysfunctions, female sexual arousal dysfunction may be primary, secondary, situational, or total. In a review of five small surveys on the incidence of sexual dysfunctions, the percentage of women reporting low arousal ranged from 10 percent to 50 percent (Schover & Jensen, 1988).

Factors that may cause sexual arousal difficulties are similar to those factors associated with hypoactive sexual desire. Thus, relationship dissatisfaction, restrictive upbringing, and nonacceptance of one's sexual orientation are possible factors associated with arousal difficulties.

Female sexual arousal dysfunction may also result from estrogen deficiency; the most common cause of estrogen deficiency is menopause. Other biological factors that may be related to lack of sexual arousal in women include neurogenic disorders (e.g., multiple sclerosis) and some drugs (e.g., antihistamines and antihypertensives). Strong emotions, such as fear, anger, and resentment as well as feeling stress may also interfere with the autonomic reflex, which controls genital vasocongestion (Kaplan, 1974, 1983).

Treatment of women who have difficulty experiencing sexual arousal is similar to treatment for hypoactive sexual desire. Thus, treatment may include some combination of the following: increase relationship satisfaction, sensate focus, reeducation, rest and relaxation, hormone treatment, masturbation and fantasy, and changing medication.

> **CONSIDERATION**
>
> In describing a woman's lack of arousal, it is important to consider that the problem may not be the woman's inability to become aroused but her partner failing to provide the kind of stimulation required for arousal to occur. Goldsmith (1988) notes that "an insensitive partner, whose sexual arousal techniques are too rough or too fast, is thought to contribute greatly to a woman's lack of ability to become aroused" (p. 21). When this is the case, the woman may benefit from identifying and implementing conditions for satisfying sex—the same treatment Bass (1985) suggested for hypoactive sexual desire discussed earlier.

Male Erectile Dysfunction   Male erectile dysfunction is defined as a man's inability to get and maintain an erection or labeling such an erection in negative terms. Like other sexual dysfunctions, erectile dysfunction may be primary, secondary, situational, or total. Occasional, isolated episodes of the inability to attain or maintain an erection are not considered dysfunctional; these are regarded as normal occurrences. In order to be classified as an erectile dysfunction, the erection difficulty should last continuously for a period of at least three months (Sonda, Mazo, & Chancellor, 1990). A review of five small survey studies on the incidence of sexual dysfunctions revealed that the rate of erectile dysfunction in men ranged between 0 and 27 percent (Schover & Jensen, 1988).

It has been estimated that, in at least 50 percent (and up to 80 percent) of men complaining of erectile dysfunction, the primary cause of the erection difficulty is biological (Carroll & Bagley, 1990; Sohn & Sikora 1991). Biological causes of erectile dysfunction include fatigue and stress, diabetes, antihypertensive medication, and narcotics. Chronic alcohol abuse may also result in erectile dysfunction (Schiavi, 1990). Neurological disease, such as multiple sclerosis or other illnesses and injuries that impair the lower spinal cord, endocrinological disease that results in androgen deficiency, vascular disease, and some prostatic surgical procedures may also cause erectile dysfunction.

Psychosocial factors associated with erectile dysfunction include fear (e.g., of unwanted pregnancy, intimacy, HIV or other STDs), guilt, and relationship dissatisfaction. For example, the man who is having an extradyadic sexual relationship may feel guilty. This guilt may lead to difficulty in achieving or maintaining an erection in sexual interaction with the primary partner and/or the extradyadic partner. A man may also feel guilty if he does not love his partner, yet says he does in order to persuade the partner to have sexual relations. In addition, a man with a sexually transmitted disease may feel guilty about having sex with someone. Finally, religious or parental teachings that sex is dirty or sinful may produce guilt associated with sex that can lead to erection difficulties.

Anxiety may also inhibit the man's ability to create and maintain an erection. One source of anxiety is "performance pressure," which may be self-imposed or imposed by a partner. In self-imposed performance anxiety, the man constantly "checks" (mentally or visually) to see that he is erect. Such self-monitoring (also referred to as "spectatoring") creates anxiety since the man fears he may not be erect.

Partner imposed performance pressure involves the partner communicating to the man that he must get and stay erect to be regarded as a good lover. Such pressure usually increases the man's anxiety, thus ensuring no erection. Whether self or partner imposed, the anxiety associated with performance pressure results in a vicious cycle—anxiety, erectile difficulty, embarrassment, followed by anxiety, erectile difficulty, and so on.

Performance anxiety may also be related to alcohol use. After consuming more than a few drinks, the man may initiate sex but may become anxious

The erection is considered by almost all men as the star performer in the drama of sex and we all know what happens to a show when the star performer doesn't make an appearance.

BERNIE ZILBERGELD

after failing to achieve an erection (too much alcohol will interfere with erection). Although alcohol may be responsible for his initial "failure," his erection difficulties continue because of his anxiety.

CONSIDERATION

Some men are not accustomed to satisfying their partners in any other way (cuddling, cunnilingus, digital stimulation) than through the use of an erect penis. Most of the women in one study (86 percent) who had male partners with erectile dysfunction reported that their partners never engaged in any sexual activities other than intercourse (Carroll & Bagley, 1990). However, when these women were asked, "What is your favorite part of sexual behavior?" 60 percent said foreplay and 3 percent said afterplay; only 37 percent said sexual intercourse was their favorite part of sexual interactions.

Treatment of erectile dysfunction (like treatment of other sexual dysfunctions) depends on the cause(s) of the problem. When erection difficulties are caused by psychosocial factors, treatment may include improving the relationship with the partner and/or removing the man's fear, guilt, or anxiety (i.e., performance pressure) about sexual activity. These goals may be accomplished through couple counseling, reeducation, and sensate focus exercises. A sex therapist would instruct the man and his partner not to engage in intercourse, so as to remove the pressure to attain or maintain an erection. During this period, the man is encouraged to pleasure his partner in ways that do not require him to have an erection (e.g., cunnilingus, manual stimulation of partner). Once the man is relieved of the pressure to perform and learns alternative ways to satisfy his partner, his erection difficulties (if due to psychosocial factors) often disappear.

Treatment for erectile dysfunction related to biological factors may include rest and relaxation, modification of medication, alcohol, or drug use, or hormone treatment. Surgical occlusion of venous drainage leakage may also be an effective treatment for some men with erectile difficulty (Bancroft, 1989).

Another option for treating biologically caused erectile dysfunction is a penile prosthesis (or penile implant). These may be an inflatable prosthesis or a permanent semirigid rod. In a study of 27 men (who had had an implant) and their partners, the majority of the men (72 percent) and their partners (65 percent) would recommend penile implants for men with erectile dysfunction (McCarthy & McMillan, 1990). However, restoration of erectile competence may not improve the overall relationship between the man and his partner.

Another treatment alternative for erectile dysfunction is "injection therapy" whereby the patient injects premixed solutions of papaverine or prostaglandin E combined with phentolamine into the corpora cavernosa of the penis via a syringe. The injection results in a firm erection 5–10 minutes after the injection and lasts 30 to 40 minutes (Kaplan, 1990). In a study of 42 men who used papaverine hydrochloride and phentolamine mesylate, the quality of erections, sexual satisfaction, and frequency of intercourse were all improved (Althof, et al., 1991). Disadvantages of injection therapy include discomfort and bruising associated with self-injections; side effects such as sustained or recurring erections, fibrotic nodules, and abnormal liver function values; and lack of research data on long-term effects of injection therapy (Althof, et al., 1989; Althof et al., 1991).

Cultures differ in terms of how they treat sexual dysfunctions. In China, men with erectile dysfunction are regarded as "suffering from deficiency of Yang elements in the kidney" and are treated with drinking a solution prepared with water and several chemicals designed to benefit kidney function. They may also be given accupuncture therapy (Shikai, 1990, 198).

An alternative to penile prostheses, injections and various medications for the treatment of erectile dysfunction is the use of a vacuum device, which produces an erection that lasts for 30 minutes. Vacuum devices contain a chamber large enough to fit over the erect penis, a pump, connector tubing, and tension rings.

> When the pump is activated, negative pressure is created within the system, which pulls blood into the penis to produce either erectile augmentation or an erection-like state. After adequate tumescence is achieved, the tension band is guided from the chamber to the base of the penis to produce entrapment of blood (Witherington, 1991, 73).

ACROSS CULTURES ❧

Orgasm Phase Dysfunctions

Orgasm phase dysfunctions include inhibited orgasm and rapid ejaculation.

Inhibited Female Orgasm   *Inhibited female orgasm,* also known as "anorgasmia," "orgasmic dysfunction," and "orgastic dysfunction," occurs when the woman does not experience orgasm after a period of adequate sexual stimulation. Difficulty achieving orgasm may be primary, secondary, situational, or total. Situational orgasmic difficulties, in which the woman is able to experience orgasm under some circumstances but not others are the most common. Many women are able to experience orgasm during manual or oral clitoral stimulation, but are unable to experience orgasm during intercourse (i.e., in the absence of manual or oral stimulation).

NATIONAL DATA ❧ It is estimated that 30 percent of American women have difficulty experiencing an orgasm during intercourse (APA, 1987). Schover & Jensen (1988) reported that between 4% and 15% of women are unable to orgasm under any conditions.

Biological factors associated with orgasmic dysfunction may be related to fatigue, stress, alcohol, and some medications, such as antidepressants and antihypertensives. Regarding stress and fatigue, 61 percent of 65 married women identified fatigue as an important reason why they had difficulty achieving an orgasm (Davidson & Darling, 1988). Diseases or tumors that affect the neurological system, diabetes, and radical pelvic surgery (e.g., for cancer) may also impair a woman's ability to experience orgasm.

CONSIDERATION

Women who have difficulty achieving orgasm tend to report having experienced their first menstruation later than women who report having no difficulty. Raboch and Raboch (1992) suggested "that biological factors are important for insufficient orgasmic capacity" (p. 118). In other words, women may have different biological capacities for orgasm.

Psychosocial and cultural factors associated with orgasmic dysfunction are similar to the causes of lack of sexual desire. Causes of orgasm difficulties in women include restrictive childrearing and learning a passive female sexual role. Guilt, fear of intimacy, fear of losing control, ambivalence about commitment, and spectatoring may also interfere with the ability to experience orgasm. Other women may not orgasm because of their belief in the myth that women are not supposed to enjoy sex.

Relationship factors, such as anger and lack of trust, may also produce orgasmic dysfunction. For some women, the lack of information may result in orgasmic difficulties, (i.e., some women do not know that clitoral stimulation is important for orgasm to occur). Some women may not orgasm with their partners because they do not tell their partners what they want in terms of sexual stimulation because of shame and insecurity (Kelly, Strassberg, & Kircher, 1990).

CONSIDERATION

A woman who does not orgasm because of lack of sufficient stimulation is not considered to have a sexual dysfunction. In one study, 64 percent of the women who did not experience orgasm during sexual intercourse said that the primary reason was lack of noncoital clitoral stimulation. The type of stimulation most effective in inducing orgasm was manual and oral stimulation and manipulation of the clitoral and vaginal area (Darling, Davidson, & Cox, 1991).

Because the causes for primary and secondary orgasm difficulties vary, the treatment must be tailored to the particular woman. Treatment may include rest and relaxation and change of medication or limiting alcohol consumption prior to sexual activity. Sensate focus exercises may be beneficial in helping a woman explore her sexual feelings and to increase her comfort with her partner. Treatment may also involve improving relationship satisfaction and teaching the woman or the couple how to communicate their sexual needs.

Masturbation is a widely used treatment for women with orgasm difficulties. LoPiccolo and Lobitz (1972) developed a nine-step program of masturbation for women with orgasm difficulties. The rationale behind masturbation as a therapeutic technique for anorgasmic women is that masturbation is the technique that is most likely to produce orgasm. Masturbation gives the individual complete control of the stimulation, provides direct feedback to the woman of the type of stimulation she enjoys, and eliminates the distraction of a partner. Kinsey, Pomeroy, Martin, and Gebhard (1953) reported that the average woman reached orgasm in 95 percent or more of her masturbatory attempts. In addition, the intense orgasm produced by masturbation leads to increased vascularity in the vagina, labia, and clitoris, which enhances the potential for future orgasms.

Inhibited Male Orgasm Difficulty experiencing orgasm also occurs in men. Inhibited male orgasm (formerly referred to as retarded ejaculation) is defined as not being able to ejaculate after prolonged stimulation. Like other sexual dysfunctions, inhibited male orgasm may be primary, secondary, situational, or total. In most cases of inhibited male orgasm, the man is unable to reach orgasm during sexual intercourse, but is able to reach orgasm through other means, such as masturbation. Orgasm difficulties are much less common in men than they are in women.

Several medications may interfere with ejaculation, including some hormone-based medications, tranquilizers, barbituates, antidepressants, and antihypertensives (Hawton, 1985). Injury or disease that impairs the neurological system may also interfere with orgasm in the male.

Most cases of inhibited male orgasm are believed to be caused by psychosocial factors (Goldman, 1992; Kaplan, 1974; Weinstein & Rosen, 1988). Psychosocial causes of inhibited male orgasm include anxiety, fear, spectatoring, negative attitudes toward sexuality, and conflict or power struggles in the relationship. For example, traumatic experiences, such as being discovered by parents while masturbating, can lead to fear, anxiety, and punishment associated with impending orgasm. Thus, the sensation of impending orgasm can become conditioned to produce the response of fear and anxiety, which inhibits orgasm (Kaplan, 1974). Some men are obsessed with trying to become aroused and pleasing their partners, which may lead to anxiety and spectatoring which inhibits the ejaculatory reflex (Shaw, 1990). Fear of pregnancy and guilt may also interfere with a man's ability to orgasm and ejaculate. Learning negative messages about sexual genitals or sexual activities from one's parents or religious training may also lead to ejaculation difficulties. Regarding relationship power struggles, a man's inability to achieve orgasm may be conceptualized as "an expression of the penis's refusal to be commanded interpersonally" (Shaw, 1990, 160).

Just as many women are unable to orgasm because of lack of sufficient stimulation, some men with inhibited male orgasm are unable to orgasm because of lack of sufficient stimulation. These men may have developed a pattern of masturbation that involves vigorous stimulation and are unable to obtain sufficient stimulation from the vagina (Bancroft, 1989).

> If you use the electric vibrator near water, you will come and go at the same time.
>
> RICHARD PRYOR

Treatment for inhibited male orgasm may involve changing medications. More frequently, treatment focuses on the psychosocial origins, consists of exploring the negative attitudes and cognitions that interfere with ejaculation, and reeducation to change such negative attitudes.

Treatment may also involve sensate focus exercises, which allow the couple to experience physical intimacy without putting pressure on the man to perform sexually. Eventually, the man's partner helps him ejaculate through oral or manual stimulation. After they are confident he can be brought to orgasm orally or manually, the partner stimulates him to a high level of sexual excitement and, at the moment of orgasm, inserts his penis into her vagina so that he ejaculates inside her. After several sessions, the woman gradually reduces the amount of time she orally or manually manipulates her partner and increases the amount of time she stimulates him with her vagina (Masters & Johnson, 1970). Alternatively, the goal in treating inhibited male orgasm may be to enjoy sexual activities with a partner without the expectation that ejaculation must occur inside the vagina (Leiblum & Rosen, 1989).

Rapid Ejaculation   Rapid ejaculation, formerly known as "premature ejaculation," is defined as "persistent or recurrent ejaculation with minimal sexual stimulation before, upon, or shortly after penetration and before the person wishes it" (APA, 1987, 295). Rapid ejaculation is the most common sexual dysfunction in men.

> As far as the ability to satisfy their mates goes, "nice guys finish last."
>
> ANTHONY WALSH

NATIONAL DATA   One estimate suggests that 30 percent of the adult male population has rapid ejaculation (APA, 1987).

Whether a man ejaculates too soon is a matter of definition, depending on his and his partner's desires. Some partners define a rapid ejaculation in positive terms. One woman said she felt pleased that her partner was so excited by her that he "couldn't control himself." Another said, "The sooner he ejaculates, the sooner it's over with, and the sooner the better." Other women prefer that their partner delay ejaculation. Thirty-one percent of 709 female nurses reported that their partners ejaculated before they had an orgasm, and 23 percent wanted their partners to delay their ejaculation (Darling et al., 1991). Some women regard a pattern of rapid ejaculation as indicative of selfishness in their partners. This feeling can lead to resentment and anger.

 **ACROSS CULTURES**

On the island of Inis Beag, off the coast of Ireland, men are expected to ejaculate as fast as they can. By doing so it is believed that they spare the woman as much unpleasantness as possible by getting the sex over with as quickly as possible. Only the men are thought to have sexual needs and to enjoy sex (Messenger, 1971).

Rapid ejaculation is rarely caused by biological factors. However, a biological explanation of rapid ejaculation suggested by Assalian (1991) is that some men have a hypersensitive sympathetic system, which leads to rapid ejaculation. Kaplan (1974, 1983) suggested that rapid ejaculation is the result of the absence of voluntary control over the ejaculatory reflex.

Psychosocial factors associated with rapid ejaculation include early learning experiences, anxiety, and conflict or power struggles in the relationship between the man and his partner. Some examples of early learning experiences include prostitutes who rush their clients and men who use withdrawal before ejaculation as a birth control method so that ejaculation outside the vagina is trained (Masters & Johnson, 1970).

Treatment of rapid ejaculation may involve exploring relationship factors underlying the man's rapid ejaculation. If anxiety about his rapid ejaculation is a contributing factor, sensate focus exercises and pleasing his partner through oral or manual sexual stimulation may remove the pressure to delay ejaculation.

Another procedure used for treating rapid ejaculation is the "squeeze technique," developed by Masters and Johnson. The partner stimulates the man's penis manually until he signals that he feels the urge to ejaculate. At his signal, the partner places her thumb on the underside of his penis and squeezes hard for three to four seconds. The man will lose his urge to ejaculate. After 30 seconds, the partner resumes stimulation, applying the squeeze technique again when the man signals. The important rule to remember is that the partner should apply the squeeze technique whenever the man gives the slightest hint of readiness to ejaculate. (The squeeze technique can also be used by the man during masturbation to teach himself to delay his ejaculation).

Another technique used to delay ejaculation is known as the "pause technique," also referred to as the "stop-start technique." This technique involves the man stopping penile stimulation (or signaling his partner to stop stimulation) at the point that he begins to feel the urge to ejaculate. After the period of preejaculatory sensations subside, stimulation resumes. This process may be repeated as often as desired by the partners.

Another method in increasing the delay of ejaculation is for the man to ejaculate often. In general, the greater the number of ejaculations a man has in one 24-hour period, the longer he will be able to delay each subsequent ejaculation.

Medications have also been used to help men delay ejaculation. In a study of five men who took clomipramine, all "reported significant delays and heightened control of ejaculation with a small nighttime dose" (Assalian, 1988). Since ejaculation is dependent on the sympathetic component of the autonomic nervous system, clomipramine's effectiveness results from its ability to inhibit receptors in this area. Minor side effects include sleepiness, a dry mouth, and a tendency toward constipation.

Sexual Pain Dysfunctions

Two types of sexual pain dysfunctions are dyspareunia and vaginismus.

Dyspareunia *Dyspareunia* refers to "recurrent or persistent genital pain in either a male or a female before, during, or after sexual intercourse" (APA, 1987, 295). Dyspareunia is more common in women than in men. In a review of five small survey studies on the prevalence of sexual dysfunctions, the percentage of women reporting dyspareunia ranged from 8 percent to 21 percent; in men the percentage ranged from zero to 6 percent (Schover & Jensen, 1988).

Dyspareunia in women may be caused by biological factors such as vaginal or pelvic infections or inflammations, vaginitis, and allergic reactions to substances such as deodorant, douches, and contraceptive devices. In rare cases, the woman with dyspareunia is allergic to her partner's semen (Hawton, 1985). Coital pain may also result from tender scarring following an episiotomy, which is a surgical slit sometimes made in the vaginal area to ease the childbirth process (Bancroft, 1989). Dyspareunia may also be caused by lack of lubrication, a rigid hymen, or an improperly positioned uterus or ovary. In men, dyspareunia may be caused by inflammations of or lesions on the penis (often caused by herpes), Peyronie's disease (which causes a bending in the penis during erection), and urethritis (Kaplan, 1983). Because dyspareunia is often a symptom of a medical problem, a physician should be consulted.

Dyspareunia may also be caused by psychosocial factors, including guilt, anxiety, or unresolved feelings about a previous trauma, such as rape or childhood molestation. Religious and parental prohibitions against sexual activity and relationship conflicts may also result in dyspareunia.

Dyspareunia caused by biological factors may be treated by evaluating the medical condition causing the coital pain. If medical or surgical procedures cannot resolve the pain, the person with dyspareunia may try different intercourse positions or other sexual activities that provide pleasure with no or minimal pain.

When dyspareunia is caused by psychosocial factors, treatment may involve reeducation to replace negative attitudes with positive attitudes toward sexual activity. Individual therapy may help the person resolve feelings of guilt or anxiety associated with sexual activity. Couple therapy may be indicated to resolve relationship conflicts. Sensate focus exercises may help the individual relax and enjoy sexual contact.

Vaginismus *Vaginismus,* a sexual dysfunction that occurs in women, refers to "recurrent or persistent involuntary spasm of the musculature of the outer third of the vagina that interferes with coitus" (APA, 1987, 295). Vaginismus is classified as a "sexual pain dysfunction" because the involuntary spasm of the vagina causes the woman to experience pain if she were to attempt sexual intercourse.

In women who experience dyspareunia (which may be caused by biological or psychosocial factors), vaginismus may be a protective response to prevent pain. In other words, if a woman anticipates coital pain, she may involuntarily constrict her vagina to prevent painful intercourse.

Vaginismus may also be related to psychosocial factors such as restrictive parental and religious upbringing in which the woman learns to view intercourse as dirty and shameful. Other psychosocial factors include rape, incest, and childhood molestation.

Treatment for vaginismus should begin with a gynecological examination to determine if an organic or physical problem is producing the vaginismus. If the origin of the vaginismus is psychological, the treatment may involve teaching the woman relaxation techniques. When relaxation is achieved, the woman is instructed to introduce her index finger into her vagina. The use of lubricants, such as K-Y jelly may be helpful. After the woman is able to insert one finger into her vagina, she is instructed to introduce two fingers into the vagina, and this exercise is repeated until she feels relaxed enough to contain the penis. Some therapists use graduated dialators. Once the woman learns she is capable of vaginal containment of the penis, she is usually able to have intercourse without difficulty. Therapy focusing on the woman's cognitions and perceptions about sex and sexuality with her particular partner may precede and/or accompany the finger exercises.

Another problem some women experience is premenstrual syndrome. Although premenstrual syndrome is not a sexual dysfunction, it can be problematic for some women and their relationships with their sexual partners (See In Focus 10.1).

℘ Extradyadic Sexual Involvements

Aside from specific sexual problems, dating, cohabitating, and marital couples may also be confronted with the issue of extradyadic involvements. These may be defined as spending emotional and/or sexual time with someone other than the primary partner (of the dyad) who often feels threatened.

The terms "cheating," "unfaithfulness," and "infidelity," which are used to describe extradyadic sexual behavior, reflect societal disapproval of such behavior. Disapproval for extradyadic sexual activity among dating and cohabitating partners is not as strong as for marrieds. In a study of college undergraduates, Lieberman (1988) found that about two-thirds of the students expressed that extradyadic sexual intercourse in dating couples was wrong while 80 percent thought extramarital sex was wrong. In another study, only three percent of 188 university students reported approval of extramarital intercourse (Rubinson & De Rubertis, 1991).

While extradyadic sexuality may occur among dating and cohabiting partners, we will discuss sexual involvements married individuals have with someone other than their own spouse. (The consequences of engaging in extradyadic sex are discussed in the Choices section at the end of this chapter.)

Studies differ on the extent of extramarital intercourse. In a review of the literature on extramarital intercourse, Thompson (1983) concluded that half of all husbands and about the same percentage of wives have intercourse at least

How strange it is when you're up front and tell about problems (in a marriage), and you're so glad to have put it back together. Then it's amazing that the burden of proving that it's really working shifts to you. If you quit and pack it in, nobody asks any other questions.

BILL CLINTON

↶ IN FOCUS 10.1 ↷
Premenstrual Syndrome

Premenstrual syndrome (PMS) refers to the physical and psychological problems some women experience from the time of ovulation to the beginning of, and sometimes during, menstruation. Shaughn O'Brien (1987) emphasized that knowledge about PMS is plagued by anecdote, opinion, and a mass of uncontrolled therapeutic studies.

There are over 159 symptoms, which may include the following:

Psychological	**Dermatological**
Tension	Acne
Depression	Herpes
Irritability	**Orthopedic**
Lethargy	Joint pains
Altered sex drive	Backaches
Excessive energy	**Behavioral**
Mood swings	Increased drug use
Suicidal thoughts	Increased alcohol use
Indecision	Impulsive
Confusion	Accident prone
Poor judgment	Crying
Feeling insecure	**Physical**
Neurological	Weight gain (due to in-
Migraine	creased appetite
Epilepsy	and water retention)
Respiratory	Breast tenderness
Asthma	Change in metabolism
Rhinitis	

In a study of 702 women with PMS symptoms, the most frequently reported symptoms were negative affect (crying, irritability, depression, tension, restlessness, wordy quarrel), problems with concentration (decreased efficiency, difficulty concentrating, confusion, avoiding social activity, accidents), pain (headache, cramps, backache, feeling sick), and water retention (weight gain, swelling, change eating habits) (Van Der Ploeg, 1991).

Almost all women experienced at least one premenstrual symptom. Those experiencing two or three symptoms not severe enough to affect daily functioning were regarded as having premenstrual syndrome. Premenstrual disorder, de-fined by the American Psychiatric Association, involves having five or more symptoms severe enough to impair daily functioning. Some people have attributed instances of child abuse, alcoholism, divorce, and suicide to PMS. In Great Britian, PMS has been used successfully as a defense for criminal behavior. A court ruled that PMS was a factor to consider in the mitigation of punishment, not as an excuse for violent, assaultive criminal behavior (Lewis, 1990). Such a defense has not been tried, but likely will, in the United States.

The following example from the authors' files is of a woman experiencing premenstrual disorder.

Alice A., a 35-year-old housewife and mother, is usually a friendly and productive person, but two weeks out of each month she is overwhelmed by extreme irritability, tension, and depression.

It's as if my mind can't keep up with my body. I cook things to put in the freezer, clean, wash windows, work in the yard—anything to keep busy. My mind is saying slow down, but my body won't quit. When I go to bed at night, I'm exhausted. And everything gets on my nerves—the phone ringing, birds singing—everything! My skin feels prickly, my back hurts, and my face feels so tight that it's painful. I scream at my husband over ridiculous things like asking for a clean pair of socks. I hate myself even when I'm doing it, but I have no control. I can't stand being around people, and the only way I can even be civil at parties is to have several drinks.

This lasts for about a week, and then I wake up one morning feeling as if the bottom has dropped out of my life. It's as if something awful is going to happen, but I don't know what it is and I don't know how to stop it. I don't even have the energy to make the beds. Every movement is an effort.

I burst out crying for no reason at crazy times, like when I'm fixing breakfast or grocery shopping. My husband thinks I'm angry with him, and I can't explain what's wrong because I don't know myself. After about four days of fighting off the depression, I just give up, take the phone off the hook, and stay in bed. It's terrifying. I feel panicky—trapped.

IN FOCUS 10.1

Then one morning I wake up and suddenly feel like myself. The sun is shining, and I like life again.

While the media demonstrate a strong bias in favor of reporting negative menstrual cycle changes (Chrisler & Levy, 1990), less than five percent of women experience premenstrual disorder (Gise, 1991).

Other women experience a milder form of PMS, including different symptoms in varying degrees. Because more than 150 symptoms have been associated with PMS, there is little agreement about whether or when a person is experiencing the phenomenon. In a study (McFarlane, Martin, & Williams, 1988) of the menstrual cycles of 21 women who were "normally cycling" and 21 women who were taking oral contraceptives, the researchers concluded:

> Our results indicate that the women in this study did not actually experience the classic menstrual mood pattern. . . . The evidence regarding their actual moods suggests that the stereotype that most women are victims of their raging hormones is wrong (p. 216).

Indeed, men in the same study were also asked to keep daily mood and symptom diaries. They also reported great variability in their irritability, energy, and creativity throughout the month (McFarlane et al., 1988).

While PMS is associated with negative symptoms, some women report positive changes associated with their premenstrual period. In a study of 100 women, 66 percent reported at least one positive premenstrual change in the premenstrual week (Stewart, 1984). Positive changes included increased sexual interest, increased sexual enjoyment, more attractive breasts, more energy, tendency to get things done, and increased creativity.

PMS symptoms may be exacerbated by social influences. For example, in a study of 150 married women, those with careers and primary childrearing responsibility reported the highest PMS distress (Coughlin, 1990). Tavris (1992) observed that both men and women tend to attribute a woman's depression, hostility, or anger during her premenstrual phase to biological explanations like PMS. However, the real problems that "PMS sufferers" have may not be biological or hormonal in nature; the real problems include family conflicts, low pay, long hours, unsupportive partners, and "housework blues."

Various treatments of PMS have been suggested. Some physicians view PMS as an imbalance of hormones and prescribe progesterone. Still others focus on nutrition and exercise. Diet changes include eliminating alcohol, sugar, salt, and caffeine. Eating several small meals every two to four hours is also suggested. Dr. Leslie Hartlye Gise, Director of the Premenstrual Syndrome Program at Mount Sinai School of Medicine, recommends group meetings with other women, regular aerobic exercise, and medications such as alphrazolam (Gise, 1991).

SOURCES:

Chrisler, J. C. and K. B. Levy. The media construct a menstrual monster: A content analysis of PMS articles in the popupress. *Women and Health,* 1990, *16,* 89–104.

Coughlin, P. Premenstrual syndrome: How marital satisfaction and role choice affect symptom severity. *Social Work,* 1990, *35,* 351–355.

Gise, L. H. Premenstrual Syndrome: Which treatments help? *Medical Aspects of Human Sexuality.* February 1991, 62–68.

Lewis, J. W. Premenstrual syndrome as a criminal defense. *Archives of Sexual Behavior,* 1990, *19,* 425–442.

McFarlane, J., C. L. Martin, and T. M. Williams. Mood fluctuations: Women versus men and menstrual versus other cycles. *Psychology of Women Quarterly,* 1988, *12,* 201–228.

Shaughn-O'Brien. *Premenstrual syndrome.* Oxford: Blackwell Scientific Publications, 1987.

Stewart, D. E. Positive changes in the premenstrual period. *Acta-Psychiatrica-Scandinavica,* 1984, *79,* 400–405.

Tavris, C. *The mismeasure of women.* New York: Simon and Schuster, Inc., 1992.

Van Der Ploeg, H. M. The factor structure of the menstrual distress questionnaire—Dutch. *Psychological Reports,* 1991, *66,* 707–714.

once with someone other than their spouse at some time during the marriage. However, only 11 percent of husbands and 9 percent of wives in a national sample reported at least one occasion of extramarital intercourse in the last year (Blumstein & Schwartz, 1990). More recent figures are even lower.

NATIONAL DATA   Only 1.5 percent of a random sample of married U.S. adults reported having a sexual partner other than their spouse in the past 12 months (Smith, 1991).

Types of Extradyadic Sexual Involvements

Various types of extradyadic encounters include "brief encounters," "romantic affairs," "open marriages," "swinging" (mate swapping), and "group sex."

Brief Encounters   We refer to extradyadic sexual involvements that are brief and involve little to no emotional investment as "brief encounters." The lyrics to the song, "Strangers in the Night" describe two people exchanging glances who end up having intercourse "before the night is through." Although the partners may see each other again, their sexual encounter is a "one-night stand" more often than not. Sexual involvement with prostitutes or women who offer sexual activity in massage parlors may also be viewed as extradyadic sexual involvement of the "brief encounter" variety.

Husbands are more likely to have brief encounters than wives. In one study, 28 percent of the husbands and 5 percent of the wives who had had an extramarital encounter said that the last encounter was a one-night stand (Spanier & Margolis, 1983). In another study, of 59 married women who reported having had an affair, almost half reported meeting the man through a friend and 20 percent on their own. In addition, of these 59 married women who had had an affair, 36 percent reported that it was more sexual than emotional. And the more they enjoyed the sexual aspect of the relationship the less likely they were to terminate the affair (Hurlbert, 1992).

> **CONSIDERATION**
>
> A brief encounter may occur as a "one time mistake" for which the individual feels sorry and never repeats the event. Or brief encounters may become a goal and a way of life. Some therapists characterize the constant search of new brief sexual encounters as an "addiction" (Carnes, 1991).

Romantic Affairs   Intense reciprocal emotional feelings characterize many affairs. Such feelings are partly a function of the conditions under which the relationship exists. For example, lovers have very little time together. Like Romeo and Juliet who were restricted by their parents, married lovers are restricted by their spouses and other family responsibilities. Such limited access makes the time they spend together very special. In addition, the lover is not associated with the struggles of marriage—bills, childcare, washing dishes, cleaning house, mowing the lawn—and so may be experienced from a more romantic perspective. We consider the effects of extramarital affairs on marriage relationships in the choices section at the end of this chapter.

CONSIDERATION

Single women may be increasingly willing to have affairs with married men not only because single men are scarce, but also because a relationship with a married man requires less commitment and leaves more time for the single woman to devote to her career. Single women are primarily motivated by the emotional attraction to the married man, but usually do not envision being married to the man with whom they have an affair. One single woman remarked:

> Where else could I have exactly what I want from a relationship? I have my freedom and my own life separate from him. I have certain wants and he meets those, and on my own terms (Trotter, 1989, 215).

Open Marriages   In the book *Open Marriage* (O'Neill & O'Neill, 1972), the authors suggested that some couples are able to integrate extramarital sex into marriage. Sexually open marriages are those marriages in which both spouses have a positive attitude toward extramarital relationships and give each other the freedom to pursue such relationships (Buunk & Van Driel, 1989). In an open marriage, each partner is aware of the other having sex with someone outside the relationship (in contrast to an affair that occurs without the partner's knowledge). The concept of open marriage may also apply to committed dating and cohabiting relationships.

When 35 couples in sexually open marriages were compared with 35 married couples who did not have sexually open marriages, the open marriage couples reported greater satisfaction with their marital sexual relationship. The researchers (Wheeler & Kilmann, 1983) commented that for some couples:

> . . . engaging in recreational sexual activities with outside partners apparently does not interfere with each member's perception of a positive marital sexual relationship; for these couples, it may be that their marital sexual relationship is enhanced by agreed-on sexual contact with outside partners. This may not be the case for couple members who engage in covert extramarital sexual relationships, often as an "escape" from a dysfunctional marital relationship (p. 304).

While one of the motivations for becoming involved in an open marriage is to enhance the couple's sexual/marital relationship, most of these relationships do not last. Couples in sexually open relationships sometimes discuss and agree on various guidelines in order to reduce the risk of divorce. Buunk (1980) studied married couples in open relationships and identified some guidelines:

1. *Marriage primacy.* Most participants in Buunk's sample emphasized the importance of prioritizing the marital relationship, showing respect for

feelings, being honest, and devoting sufficient time and energy to the spouse.

2. *Restricted intensity.* About one-third of Buunk's sample agreed to restrict the intensity and degree of extradyadic sexual involvement. One-third of the couples had agreed that an extradyadic sexual relationship would be terminated at the request of the partner.

3. *Visibility.* Many couples in Buunk's sample agreed to keep each other informed about any extradyadic sexual relationships. Some also agreed to restrict such relationships to those persons the partner knew. Others agreed to consult and obtain consent from their spouse before engaging in extradyadic sexual activity.

Swinging   Swinging, also referred to as comarital sex, exists when the partners of one marriage or committed relationship have sexual relations with the partners of another relationship. Swinging is similar to sexually open relationships in that it involves mutual consent between the partners for extradyadic sexual activity. However, swinging is unique in that it is a more couple-oriented activity. Bringle and Buunk (1991) describe swinging as:

> extramarital sexual relationships [that] occur with both persons present and only within specified times and settings. The actual sexual contact may be open (occurs in the presence of others) or closed (occurs in separate rooms); in either case, the participants most typically arrive as a couple and depart as a couple. Furthermore, the sexual activity is, to a greater extent than with open marriages, engaged in for its own sake. The philosophy is one of recreational, body-oriented sexuality rather than emotional involvement and personal growth (p. 148).

CONSIDERATION

Although swinging is viewed as a couple-oriented activity, "it is probably instigated by the man's desire for sexual variety, for the benefit of the man, and the wife serves the function of creating the opportunity (why else would it be known as 'wife swapping'?)" (Bringle & Buunk, 1991, 149). It is not surprising then that in a study of ex-swingers, the most common reason couples discontinued swinging was the wives' dissatisfaction with this form of extradyadic sex (Murstein, Case, & Gunn, 1985).

Group Sex   While swinging involves couples swapping partners, group sex involves sexual encounters involving three or more individuals. Group sex may occur in the context of an on-going intimate relationship among the participants or among recently acquainted individuals who mutually agree to have group sex. In some cases, a pair-bonded or married couple may invite one or more people to engage in group sex.

NATIONAL DATA ℘ In one study of 1,275 respondents in the United States, one-fourth reported they had experienced group sex (Rubin, 1991).

Motivations of the respondents in Rubin's sample for engaging in group sex were mixed. Some sought a novel experience, others thought it would be fun, and still others viewed it as the symbol of total sexual freedom. One respondent noted:

> Like I said, it's hard to describe, but there's something about the kind of freedom you feel. You know, sex is a very possessive thing, and when you're having sex with more than one person, no one can possess you or think they're possessing you. Do you know what I mean? (Rubin, 1991, 127).

Motivations for Extradyadic Sexual Encounters

Partners involved in committed relationships report a number of reasons why they become involved in extradyadic sexual relationships. Some of these reasons include:

Variety, Novelty, and Excitement Extradyadic sexual involvement may be motivated by the desire for variety, novelty, and excitement (Bringle & Buunk, 1991). One of the characteristics of sex in long-term committed relationships is the tendency for it to become routine. Early in a relationship, the partners cannot seem to have sex often enough. But with constant availability, the partners may achieve a level of satiation and the attractiveness and excitement of sex with the primary partner seems to wane. The *Coolidge Effect* is a term used to describe this waning of sexual excitement and the effect of novelty and variety on sexual arousal:

> One day President and Mrs. Coolidge were visiting a government farm. Soon after their arrival, they were taken off on separate tours. When Mrs. Coolidge passed the chicken pens, she paused to ask the man in charge if the rooster copulated more than once each day, "Dozens of times," was the reply. "Please tell that to the President," Mrs. Coolidge requested. When the President passed the pens and was told about the rooster, he asked, "Same hen every time?" "Oh no, Mr. President, a different one each time." The President nodded slowly and then said, "Tell that to Mrs. Coolidge" (Bermant, 1976, 76–77).

> An affair is like Christmas morning—a marriage is like Christmas afternoon.
>
> TIM BRITTON

CONSIDERATION

The Coolidge Effect illustrates the effect of novelty and variety on the copulation behavior of roosters, not humans. Varying levels of sexual novelty and variety may, indeed, be important for achieving sexual satisfaction for many individuals. However, unlike roosters, humans need not have multiple sexual partners in order to experience novelty and variety. Rather, humans may create sexual novelty and variety within a monogamous relationship by having sex in novel places, exploring different intercourse positions, engaging in a variety of noncoital petting behaviors, wearing a variety of erotic clothing, and utilizing sexual fantasies in their sexual encounters.

Don't leave the job half done—leave nothing behind. You took her off my hands, now please take her off my mind.

GENE WATSON

I didn't leave my husband for someone else, I left for myself.

JOAN LUNDEN

Friendship   Extradyadic sexual involvements may develop from friendships. The extramarital involvements of women are more likely to develop out of friendships than those of men (Atwater, 1979). Friendships that develop into extradyadic sexual relationships often begin in the workplace. Co-workers share the same world 8–10 hours a day and over a period of time may develop good feelings for each other that eventually lead to a sexual relationship. In the next chapter we will discuss managing attractions in the workplace. The skill of having a nonsexual relationship with a close and intimate friend may be useful in a variety of contexts.

Relationship Dissatisfaction   It is commonly believed that people who have affairs are not happy in their marriage, but this is more likely to be true of wives than of husbands. Men who have affairs often are not dissatisfied with the quality of their marriage or their sexual relationship with their wife (Yablonsky, 1979). Rather, men often seek extramarital relationships as an additional life experience.

One source of relationship dissatisfaction is an unfulfilling sexual relationship. Some people engage in extradyadic sex because their partner is not interested in sex. Others may go outside the relationship because their partners will not engage in the sexual behaviors they want and enjoy. The unwillingness of the partner to engage in oral sex, anal intercourse, or a variety of sexual positions sometimes results in the other partner looking elsewhere for a more cooperative partner.

Most wives "appear to seek extramarital sex when they experience some deficit—sexual, emotional, or perhaps, economic—in their marriage, or perceive another man as being superior to (not merely different from) their husbands" (Symons, 1979, 238). Women who feel trapped in a bad marriage may not want a divorce. "So they turn to an affair or a series of them as a means of treading water, keeping the marriage afloat for the time being until their children grow up or they (the wives) earn a degree, etc." (Schaefer, 1981).

In a study of premarital extradyadic sexual behavior, the most frequently reported justifications for such behavior were: dissatisfaction with the relationship, boredom, revenge, anger or jealousy, being unsure of the relationship and variety (Roscoe et al., 1988).

Revenge   Some extradyadic sexual involvements are acts of revenge against one's partner for engaging in extradyadic sexual activity. When partners find out that their mate has had, or is having, an affair, they are often hurt and angry. One response to this hurt and anger is to have an affair to "get even" with the unfaithful partner.

Desire for Homosexual Relationship   Some individuals in heterosexual committed relationships engage in extradyadic sex because they desire a homosexual relationship. Some gay individuals marry as a way of denying their homosexuality or creating a social pretense that they are heterosexual. These individuals are likely to feel unfulfilled in their marriage and may seek involvement in an extramarital homosexual relationship. Other individuals may marry and then discover later in life that they desire a homosexual relationship. Such individuals may feel that (1) they have been homosexual or bisexual all along; (2) their sexual orientation has changed from heterosexual to homosexual or bisexual; (3) they are unsure of their sexual orientation and want to explore a homosexual relationship; or (4) they feel predominately heterosexual but wish to experience a homosexual relationship for variety.

Spouses in heterosexual marriages who engage in an extramarital homosexual relationship may or may not be happy with their marital partner. Blumstein and Schwartz (1990) provide an example of a woman:

> . . . unhappily married for 23 years but feeling a profound absence of a real "soul mate." She met a woman at her son's college graduation ceremony, and over a long period of time, the two women gradually fell in love and left their husbands. Not only did the respondent's sense of self change but so did her sexual habits and desires (p. 314).

Aging A frequent motive for intercourse outside of marriage is the desire to reexperience the world of youth. Our society promotes the idea that it is good to be young and bad to be old. Sexual attractiveness is equated with youth, and having an affair may confirm to an older partner that he or she is still sexually desirable. Also, people may try to recapture the love, excitement, adventure, and romance associated with youth by having an affair.

One writer (Gordon, 1988) interviewed men who had left their wives for a younger woman. These men focused not on the physical youth of their partners, but on the youthful attitude of their new partners—the openness, innocence, unscarred emotions. They also emphasized the uncritical love they felt from their younger partner. Gordon labeled these men as having "Jennifer Fever"—they had developed a pattern of denying the aging process by seeking a youthful partner to create the illusion that they were not getting older. Gordon suggested the term *Jennifer* because she found that the name of the younger woman was often Jennifer. Gordon further warned that they would seek another "Jennifer" as the current one aged.

Absence from Partner One factor that predisposes a person to an extradyadic sexual encounter is prolonged separation from the partner. Some wives whose husbands are away for military service report that the loneliness can become unbearable. Some husbands who are away say it is difficult to be faithful. Partners in commuter relationships may also be vulnerable to extradyadic sexual relationships.

It's hard for an old rake to turn over a new leaf.

LAURENCE PETER

CONSIDERATION

The spouse who chooses to have an affair is often judged as being unfaithful to the vows of the marriage, as being deceitful to the partner, and of inflicting

(continued on next page)

enormous pain on the partner (and children). What is often not considered is that when an affair is defined in terms of giving emotional energy, time, and economic resources to something or someone outside the primary relationship, there are other types of "affairs" that are equally as devastating to a relationship. Spouses who choose to devote their lives to their children, careers, parents, friends, or recreational interests may deprive the partner of significant amounts of emotional energy, time, and money and create a context in which the partner may choose to become involved with a person who provides more attention and interest.

§ Sexual Fulfillment in the Middle and Later Years

As individuals progress through the family life cycle, their sexuality changes during the middle and later years.

Sexuality in the Middle Years

> The most frightening thing about middle age is the knowledge that you'll outgrow it.
>
> DORIS DAY

When does a person become middle-aged? The U.S. Census Bureau regards you as middle-aged when you reach 45. Family life specialists define middle age as that time when the last child leaves home and continues until retirement or either spouse dies. Changes in sexuality are different for women and for men during this time.

Women and Menopause Menopause is the primary physical event for the middle-aged woman. Defined as the permanent cessation of menstruation, menopause is caused by the gradual decline of estrogen produced by the ovaries. It occurs around age 50 for most women but may begin earlier or later. Signs that the woman may be nearing menopause include decreased menstrual flow and a less predictable cycle. After 12 months with no period, the woman is said to be through menopause. During this time the woman should use some form of contraception. Women with irregular periods may remain at risk of pregnancy up to 24 months following their last menstrual period (Boston Women's Health Book Collective, 1984). Which one she uses (including the Pill and IUD) should not be dictated by her age since age, by itself, is not considered a contraindication for the use of hormonal contraceptive or the IUD (Connell, 1991).

The term *climacteric* is often used synonymously with menopause. But menopause refers only to the time when the menstrual flow permanently stops, while climacteric refers to the whole process of hormonal change induced by the ovaries, pituitary gland, and hypothalamus. Reactions to such hormonal changes may include hot flashes in which the woman feels a sudden rush of heat from the waist up. Hot flashes are often accompanied by an increased reddening of the skin surface and a drenching perspiration. Other symptoms may include heart palpitations, dizziness, irritability, headaches, backache, and weight gain. Wing et al. (1991) noted that weight gain is a normal occurrence for women during menopause, which increases their risk of coronary heart disease.

Many women also report other physiological and behavioral changes as a result of the aging process and of decreasing levels of estrogen: (1) a delay in the reaction of the clitoris to direct stimulation, (2) less lubrication during sexual excitement, (3) a less intense orgasm, (4) a smaller vaginal opening, (5) decreased sexual desire, and (6) decreased sexual activity (Sarrel, 1990; Sherwin, 1991). Decreases in both desire and sexual activity may not only be caused by decreasing estrogen levels but also by beliefs that middle-aged women should not be interested in sex and that the woman who is no longer fertile should no longer be sexual (Bachmann, 1991). In addition, decreases in sexual desire and activity among middle-aged women is related to lack of a confiding relationship, alcoholism on the part of the spouse, and major depression (Hallstrom & Samuelsson, 1990).

To minimize the effects of decreasing levels of estrogen, some physicians recommend estrogen replacement therapy (ERT), particularly to control hot flashes during the climacteric. Also referred to as HRT (hormone replacement therapy), researchers disagree on the benefits. Hunter (1990) suggested that HRT does not have significant effects on mood or sexual behavior over and above placebo effects.

A cross-cultural look at menopause suggests that a woman's reaction to this phase of her life may be related to the society in which she lives. For example, among Chinese women, fewer menopausal symptoms have been observed. Researchers have suggested this may occur because older women in China are highly respected, as are older people generally. Researchers Karen Matthews and Nancy Avis conducted a longitudinal study of 541 women as they progressed through menopause and found that the negative expectations our society has of the menopausal years "may cause at least some of the problems women experience" (quoted in Adler, 1991, 14).

ACROSS CULTURES ꙩ

Men and the Decrease in Testosterone   The profound hormonal changes and loss of reproductive capacity, which occur in women during menopause, do not occur in men (Keogh, 1990). However, production of testosterone usually begins to decline around age 40 and continues to decrease gradually until age 60 when it levels off. A 20-year-old man usually has about twice the amount of testosterone in his system as a 60 year old man (Young, 1990). The decline is not inevitable but is related to general health status.

The consequences of lowered testosterone include (1) more difficulty in getting and maintaining a firm erection, (2) greater ejaculatory control with the possibility of more prolonged erections, (3) less consistency in achieving orgasm, (4) fewer genital spasms during orgasm, (5) a qualitative change from an intense, genitally focused sensation to a more diffused and generalized feeling of pleasure, and (6) an increase in the length of the refractory period, during which time the man is unable to ejaculate or have another erection.

CONSIDERATION

These physiological changes in the middle-aged man, along with psychological changes, have sometimes been referred to as male menopause. During this period the man may experience nervousness, hot flashes, insomnia, and no interest in sex. But these changes most often occur over a long period of time, and the anxiety and depression some men experience seem to be as much related to their life situation as to hormonal alterations.

A middle-aged man who is not successful in his career is often forced to recognize that he will never achieve what he had hoped but carry his unfulfilled dreams to the grave. This knowledge may be coupled with his awareness of diminishing sexual vigor. For the man who has been taught that masculinity is measured by career success and sexual prowess, middle age may be particularly traumatic.

The best insurance for continued sexual activity in later years appears to be frequent sexual activity in the earlier years.

WILLIAM YOUNG

Sexuality in the Later Years

Middle age women and men become the elderly.

NATIONAL DATA ❧ Thirteen percent of all Americans (over 32 million individuals) are over the age of 65 (*Statistical Abstract of the United States, 1993*, Table 14).

Sexuality of Elderly Men Data based on 427 male veterans (randomly selected) ages 30 to 99 revealed that sexual interest, activity, and ability decline with age. Sexual interest declined from a mean of 4.4 (5 = extremely interested; 4 = very interested) in men aged 30–39, to 2.0 (2 = slightly interested; 1 = not interested) in men age 90–99 (Mulligan & Moss, 1991). Note that while sexual interest declined, it did not stop. No respondent reported a total absence of interest.

Just as interest declined, so did intercourse frequency. It dropped from a mean of once per week in those 30–39 years old to once per year in those 90–99 years old (Mulligan & Moss, 1991). Part of the decline among the 90-to 99-year-old group may be attributed to the lack of a spouse or sexual partner. Regarding the ability of these elderly men to perform sexually, the frequency, rigidity, and duration of erections decreased dramatically with age. Of men 90 to 99, they reported a mean of 1.9 in terms of rigidity of erection with 1 = flaccid erection never lasting long enough for intercourse and 5 = extremely rigid and always lasting long enough for intercourse. (In contrast, men aged 30 to 39 reported a mean rigidity of 4.5). Even though these

Expressing physical affection continues in later years.

90-year-olds achieved an erection, only 21 percent of them were able to orgasm.

Other research supports the view that sexual behavior declines with age. Schiavi et al. (1990) observed that of 65 healthy married men aged 45–74, those who were 65–74 reported less sexual desire (thought about sex less frequently and could comfortably go without sex for longer periods of time), engaged in intercourse less often, masturbated less frequently, and had fewer orgasms than the men aged 45–65. The older group also reported lower arousal, fewer erections, and more difficulty becoming aroused. Getting an erection was their most frequently reported sexual problem.

CONSIDERATION

However, the enjoyment of sex reported by these men did not change with age. Their satisfaction with their own sexuality remained substantially the same. In another study of 61 elderly men (average age = 71) both with and without sexual partners, sexual satisfaction was rated at an average of 6.3 on a scale where 1 = no satisfaction and 10 = extremely high satisfaction (Mulligan & Palguta, 1991).

Sexuality of Elderly Women Fewer studies have been conducted on the sexuality of elderly women (Morley & Kaiser, 1989). However, Bretschneider and McCoy (1988) collected data from 102 white women (and 100 white men) ranging in age from 80 to 102 who lived in residential treatment centers in Northern California. Some of the findings follow:

1. Thirty-eight percent of the women in contrast to 66 percent of the men reported that sex was currently important to them.
2. Thirty percent of the women and 62 percent of the men reported they had sexual intercourse sometimes.
3. Of those with sexual partners, 64 percent of the women in contrast to 82 percent of the men said that they were at least mildly happy with their partners as lovers.
4. Forty percent of the women and 72 percent of the men reported they currently masturbated.
5. Touching and caressing without sexual intercourse was the most frequently engaged in behavior by women (64 percent) and men (82 percent).

> We have no role models, no guidebooks that affirm the new strengths that are emerging in ourselves as we age.
>
> BETTY FRIEDAN

These findings suggest declines in sexual enjoyment and frequencies are greater for women in the later years than men.

Another study emphasized the importance of a partner for the sexual activity of women. Of elderly women, age 60 and over, 56 percent of the married women reported that they were still sexually active. However, of the unmarried women, only five percent reported being sexually active (Diokno et al., 1990). Seventy-five percent of the women in the retirement homes studied by Bretschneider and McCoy (1988) reported they had no regular sexual partner.

❦ Trends

Trends in sexual fulfillment include greater access to information about sexual fulfillment, a wider range of expression in sexual fulfillment, increased emphasis on sexuality in the middle and later years, and more extramarital affairs by women. Magazines like *Cosmopolitan, Redbook, Ladies Home Journal, McCall's,* and *Family Circle* regularly feature articles on sexual aspects of the woman-man relationship. Research on sexuality is no longer available only to academics. It is available to every person who stands in line to pay for groceries. Such visibility of sexual topics is not limited to magazines but includes movies, television, and radio. The openness with which the media treats sex will continue.

One consequence of this visibility is an awareness of the widening range of sexual behaviors expressed by different people. "Donahue" and "Geraldo" once featured discussions on "safe" topics only; more recent programs have included such topics as polygamy, bisexual marriage, celibacy, and transsexuality. Exposure to media-mediated sex alerts us to the tremendous variations in sexual experience.

Because our population is gradually getting older, they are tending to move away from a focus on sexuality in youth to sexuality in the middle and later years. A life-span focus on sexuality gives more visibility to sexuality issues and concerns for older individuals.

❧ CHOICES ❧

One can make a number of choices in regard to sexual fulfillment. These include choices in whether to engage in sexual behavior when sexual desire is minimal, to minimize the focus on orgasm, or to participate in extradyadic sex.

Engage in Sexual Behavior When Desire Is Low?

Individuals often bring to therapy the problem of having minimal sexual de-sire yet wanting such desire and wanting to engage in sexual behavior with one's partner. Moser (1992) noted:

> People may engage in sex, even frequently, but for reasons other than their own desire (e.g., marital duty, to prove that they can, as a form of self-treatment, to become pregnant, to promote intimacy, to please the partner, for self-esteem, etc.) (p. 66).

Data collected by Beck, Bosman, and Qualtrough (1991) also suggests that, indeed, individuals sometimes engage in sexual behavior even though they may have minimal sexual desire at the time. The researchers observed that 82 percent of 86 college women and 60 percent of 58 college men reported doing so and that their primary motivation was to please the partner.

Aside from pleasing the partner, another potential positive outcome from choosing to engage in sexual behavior independent of desire is that the individual may discover desire fol-

⚘ CHOICES ⚘

lows involvement in sexual behavior. Cognitive behavior therapists conceptualize this phenomenon as "acting one's self into a new way of feeling rather than feeling one's self into a new way of acting." Rather than wait for the feelings of sexual desire to occur before engaging in sexual behavior, the person "acts as though there is feeling" only to discover that the feelings sometimes follow. An old French saying reflects this phenomenon: "L'appetite viens avec mangent," which translates into "the appetite comes with eating."

We are not suggesting that individuals who lack sexual desire should routinely initiate sexual behavior with their partners. Individuals should respect their own feelings and preferences and should not feel coerced into engaging in sexual behavior when they do not want to. However, when one is generally comfortable engaging in sexual behavior with a particular person with whom coercion is not an issue, the person may choose to engage in sexual behavior with minimal desire for the potential positive outcomes mentioned above.

Minimize Focus on Orgasm?

For many individuals in our society, the focus of sex is orgasm. One choice individuals can make is to selectively attend to the emotional, affectional, nongenital aspects of sexual interaction. Choosing a focus other than orgasm allows the respective partners to define their sexual encounter in positive terms independent of an orgasmic experience. Such a choice has a win-win outcome. Not only do the partners enjoy the benefits of other than an orgasm focus, each encounter is "successful" since it does not depend on an orgasm.

Participate in Extradyadic Sex?

Beginning in adolescence, individuals are confronted with the decision to be monogamous and faithful.

No to Extradyadic Sex. When 672 spouses were asked if they had been monogamous during the last 12 months, 96 percent reported affirmatively (Greeley et al., 1990). While not all spouses have the opportunity (an available partner) and a context (out of town or away from the spouse) for extradyadic sex, regardless of the reason, the overwhelming majority are faithful in any given year.

Some of those deciding not to have extramarital sex feel that it causes more trouble to themselves and to their partners than it is worth. "I can't say I don't think about having sex with other women, because I do—a lot," said one husband, "but I would feel guilty as hell, and if my wife found out, she would kill me." Spanier and Margolis (1983) found that more women who engaged in extradyadic sex reported more guilt feelings than did men (59 percent versus 34 percent).

Partners who engage in sex with someone else risk hurting their mate emotionally. Extradyadic intercourse not only involves a breach of intimacy by having sex with someone else, it also involves deceit. As a result, the partner may develop a deep sense of distrust, which often lingers in the relationship long after the affair is over.

Another reason why having an affair hurts the partner and the relationship is that "it represents a regressive transformation from the person considering the couple's joint outcomes to decisions being made on appraisals that are based on individualistic outcomes" (Bringle & Buunk, 1991). In other words, choosing to engage in sex with someone other than the primary partner is a decision based on what the individual wants (individualism), not on what the couple want (familism).

In addition to guilt, distrust, and emotional pain as potential outcomes of an affair, another danger is the development of a pattern of having affairs. "Once you've had an affair, it's easier the second time," said one spouse. "And the third time, you don't give it a thought." Increasingly, the spouse looks outside the existing relationship for sex and companionship.

Engaging in extradyadic sex may result in the termination of the primary relationship. In a study on how dating partners would cope with learning their partner had been unfaithful,

(continued)

⌐ CHOICES ∾

respondents revealed they would (in descending order of frequency): terminate the relationship, confront and find out the reason, talk it over, consider terminating the relationship, and work to improve the relationship (Roscoe et al., 1988). Another study found that extramarital affairs played a role in one-third of divorces (Burns, 1984). It is interesting to note that, according to Spanier and Margolis (1983), most persons described their own affairs as being a consequence of marital problems. However, spouses' affairs were described as being the cause of marital problems. Regardless of who has the affair, Pittman (1993) observed, "However utopian the theories, the reality is that infidelity, whether it is furtive or blatant, will blow the hell out of a marriage" (p. 35).

If the partner finds out the spouse wants a divorce because of an affair, the "adulterer" may also pay an economic price. In some states, adultery is grounds for alimony.

Another potential danger in having extradyadic sex is the potential to contract a sexually transmitted disease. The HIV epidemic has increased the concern over this possibility. A spouse who engages in extradyadic sex may not only contract a sexually transmitted disease, but also transmit the disease to their partner (and potentially their unborn offspring). In some cases, extradyadic sex may be deadly.

Finally, spouses who engage in extradyadic sex relationships risk the possibility of their partner finding out

and going into a jealous rage. Jealousy may result in violence and even the death of the unfaithful spouse and/or the lover involved. Another possible tragic outcome of extramarital relationships is that the spouse who has been "cheated on" becomes depressed and commits suicide.

Partners who decide to avoid extradyadic encounters might focus on the small choices that lead to a sexual encounter. Since extradyadic sex occurs in certain relationships and structural contexts, the person can choose to avoid these. For example, choosing not to become involved in intimate conversations and choosing not to have lunch or to drink alone in a bar with someone to whom you are attracted decreases the chance a relationship will develop or that a context will present itself where a sexual encounter becomes a possibility. The person who chooses to talk intimately with others, have lunch with them, and "happy hour" drinks is increasing the chance an extramarital relationship will develop.

Yes to Extradyadic Sex. A small percentage of spouses who have had an affair feel it had positive consequences for them, their marriage, and/or their partners. In one instance, a woman, whose husband constantly criticized her, said of her extramarital relationship, "He made me feel loved, valued, and worthwhile again." This woman eventually divorced her husband and said that she never regretted

moving from an emotionally abusive relationship to one in which she was loved and nurtured.

In a study by Atwater (1982), 60 percent of women reported that they enjoyed sex more with their extramarital partners than with their husbands. In addition to good sex, other potential positive consequences of engaging in extradyadic sex include personal growth and self-discovery.

For some spouses who have an affair and who stay married, the marriage may benefit. Some partners become more sensitive to the problems in their marriage. "For us," one spouse said, "the affair helped us to look at our marriage, to know that we were in trouble, and to seek help." Couples need not view the discovery of an affair as the end of their marriage; it can be a new beginning.

Another positive effect of a partner discovering an affair is that the partner may become more sensitive to the needs of the spouse and more motivated to satisfy them. The partner may realize that if the spouse is not satisfied at home, he or she will go elsewhere. One husband said his wife had an affair because he was too busy with his work and did not spend enough time with her. Her affair taught him that she had alternatives—other men who would love her emotionally and sexually. To ensure that he did not lose her, he cut back on his work hours and spent more time with his wife.

Britton (1984) interviewed 276 spouses who had had an affair and

---

✣ CHOICES ✣

---

noted the conditions under which extradyadic sex is likely to have the least negative consequences. These included having a solid marriage relationship, being able to compartmentalize one's life, not telling the partner, having infrequent contacts with the lover, and having extradyadic sex for recreation (not emotion) only.

ℬ Summary

Marital intercourse is characterized by its social legitimacy, declining frequency, and monogamy. Spouses tend to regard their level of interest, sexual satisfaction, and pleasure differently. Husbands regard themselves as more interested and more satisfied than their wives.

Sexual fulfillment involves self-knowledge, self-esteem, a good out-of-bed relationship, open sexual communication, safe sex, not believing various sex myths, and creativity. Previous traumatic sexual experiences (rape, child sexual abuse) can create negative feelings and reactions toward sexual interaction.

Spouses who rate their relationships as "very good" or "excellent" may also tend to have an absence of sexual dysfunctions. Such dysfunctions may be described as primary (always been present), secondary (present now but not always), situational (present with one partner but not with another), or total (present with all partners). Causes may also be biological (insufficient hormones, fatigue, physical illness), psychosocial (unhappy relationship, fear of intimacy, fear of pregnancy), or a combination of the two.

Sexual dysfunctions occur at different points along the sexual response cycle of desire, arousal, or orgasm. Desire phase dysfunctions include too little desire (hypoactive sexual desire) or none at all (sexual aversion). Causes may be biological or social. Negative past sexual experiences usually account for sexual aversion.

Arousal phase dysfunctions include inability to become aroused as a female (female sexual arousal dysfunction) or inability to create and maintain an erection (male erectile dysfunction). Orgasm phase dysfunctions include not being able to orgasm (inhibited female orgasm, inhibited male orgasm) or ejaculating before desired (rapid ejaculation). Sexual pain dysfunctions involve pain during sexual engagement (dyspareunia) or constriction of the vagina (vaginismus).

While most spouses are sexually monogamous within a 12-month period, research suggests that about half of husbands and wives have intercourse with someone other than their partner at least once during the marriage. Motivations for extradyadic sexual involvements include variety, aging, or an unhappy relationship. Men and women generally have different motives for extradyadic involvements.

Regarding the middle and later years, women are challenged by menopause and men by lower testosterone levels. Elderly individuals report less interest, activity, and ability in regard to sexual activity. They also report a shift in their view of sexuality from genital to affection.

Questions for Reflection

1. How do you define sexual fulfillment?
2. What sexual dysfunctions have you or your partners experienced and to what degree do you regard the causes as biological or psychosocial?
3. Would you be willing to consult a sex therapist for a sexual problem?

References

Adler, T. Women's expectations are menopause villains. *Monitor,* July 1991, 14.

Althof, Stanley E., Louisa A. Turner, Stephen D. Levine, Candace Risen, Elroy Kursh, Donald Bodner, and Martin Resnick. Why do so many people drop out of autoinjection therapy for impotence? *Journal of Sex and Marital Therapy,* 1989, *15,* 121–129.

Althof, S. E., L. A. Turner, S. D. Levine, C. B. Risen, D. Bodner, E. D. Kursh, and M. I. Resnick. Sexual, psychological, and marital impact of self-injection of papaverine and phentolamine: A long-term prospective study. *Journal of Sex and Marital Therapy,* 1991, *17,* 101–112.

American Psychiatric Association. *Diagnostic and statistical manual of mental disorders,* 3d ed. rev. Washington, D.C., 1987.

Ard, Ben N. *The sexual realm in long-term marriages: A longitudinal study following marital partners over twenty years.* San Francisco, Calif.: Mellen Research University Press, 1990.

Ash, P. Healthy sexuality and good health. *Sexuality Today,* 1986, *9,* no. 24, 1.

Assalian, Pierre. Clomipramine in the treatment of premature ejaculation. *Journal of Sex Research,* 1988, *24,* 213–215.

Assalian, Pierre. *Premature ejaculation: Is it really psychogenic?* Paper presented at the annual meeting of the Society for the Scientific Study of Sex, New Orleans. Used by permission, 1991. Write to author at Department of Psychiatry, Montreal General Hospital, 1650 Cedar Avenue, Montreal, Quebec, Canada H3G1A4.

Atwater, L. *The extramarital connection: Sex, intimacy, identity.* New York: Irvington, 1982.

Atwater, L. Getting involved: Women's transition to first extramarital sex. *Alternative Lifestyles,* 1979, *2,* 33–68.

Bachmann, G. Sexual dysfunction in the older woman. *Medical Aspects of Human Sexuality,* February 1991, 42–45.

Bancroft, J. *Human sexuality and its problems,* 2d ed. New York: Churchill Livingstone, 1989.

Bass, B. A. The myth of low sexual desire: A cognitive behavioral approach to treatment. *Journal of Sex Education and Therapy,* 1985, *11,* 61–64.

Beck, J. G., A. W. Bozman, and T. Qualtrough. The experience of sexual desire: Psychological correlates in a college sample. *Journal of Sex Research,* 1991, *28,* 443–456.

Bermant, G. Sexual behavior: Hard times with the Coolidge Effect. *Psychological Research: The Inside Story,* M. H. Siegel and H. P. Zeigler, eds. New York: Harper & Row, 1976.

Blumstein, P. and P. Schwartz. Intimate relationships and the creation of sexuality. *Homosexuality/ Heterosexuality: Concepts of Sexual Orientation,* David P. McWhirter, Stephanie A. Sanders, and June M. Reinish, eds. New York: Oxford University Press, 1990, 307–320.

Boston Women's Health Book Collective. *The new our bodies, ourselves.* New York: Simon & Schuster, 1984.

Bretschneider, Judy G. and Norma L. McCoy. Sexual interest and behavior in healthy 80 to 102 year olds. *Archives of Sexual Behavior,* 1988, *17,* 109–129.

Bringle, R. G. and B. T. Buunk. Extradyadic relationships and sexual jealousy. *Sexuality in Close Relationships,* K. McKinney and S. Sprecher, eds. Hillsdale, N. J.: Lawrence Erlbaum, 1991, 135–152.

Britton, T. Lenoir Community College, Kinston, N.C. Personal communication, 1984.

Bronte, Lydia. *Head first: The biology of hope.* New York: E. P. Dutton, 1989.

Burns, A. Perceived causes of marriage breakdown and conditions of life. *Journal of Marriage and the Family,* 1984, *46,* 551–562.

Buunk, B. Sexually open marriages: Ground rules for countering potential threats to marriage. *Alternative Lifestyles,* 1980, *3,* 312–328.

Buunk, B. and B. Van Driel. *Variant lifestyles and relationships.* Newbury Park, Calif.: Sage, 1989.

Cado, S. and H. Leitenberg. Guilt reactions to sexual fantasies during intercourse. *Archives of Sexual Behavior,* 1990, *19,* 49–63.

Carnes, P. *Don't call it love.* New York: Bantam, 1991.

Carroll, J. L. and D. H. Bagley. Evaluation of sexual satisfaction in partners of men experiencing erectile failure. *Journal of Sex and Marital Therapy,* 1990, *16,* 70–78.

Catania, J. A., T. J. Coates, R. Stall, H. Turner, J. Peterson, N. Hearst, M. M. Dolcini, E. Hudes, J. Gagnon, J. Wiley, and R. Groves. Prevalence of AIDS-related risk factors and condom use in the United States. *Science,* 1992, *258,* 1101–1106.

Connell, Elizabeth B. Contraceptive options for the woman over 40. *Medical Aspects of Human Sexuality,* April 1991, 20–24.

Darling, C. A., J. K. Davidson, and R. P. Cox. Female sexual response and the timing of partner orgasm. *Journal of Sex and Marital Therapy,* 1991, *17,* 3–21.

Davidson, J. K. and C. A. Darling. The stereotype of single women revisited: Sexual practices and sexual satisfaction among professional women. *Health Care for Women International,* 1988, *9,* 317–336.

Diokno, A. C., M. B. Brown, and A. R. Herzog. Sexual function in the elderly. *Archives of Internal Medicine,* 1990, *150,* 197–200.

Donnelly, Denise A. Sexually inactive marriages. *The Journal of Sex Research,* 1993, *30,* 171–179.

Goldman, H. H. *Review of general psychiatry,* 3d ed. Norwalk, Conn.: Appelton & Lange, 1992.

Goldsmith, L. Treatment of sexual dysfunction. E. Weinstein and E. Rosen, eds. *Sexuality counseling: Issues and implications,* Pacific Grove, Calif.: Brooks/Cole, 1988, 16–34.

Gordon, B. *Jennifer fever.* New York: Harper & Row, 1988.

Gray, L. A. and M. Saracino. College students' attitudes, beliefs, and behaviors about AIDS: Implications for family life educators. *Family Relations,* 1991, *40,* 258–263.

Greeley, Andrew M., Robert T. Michael, and Tom W. Smith. Americans and their sexual partners. *Society,* July/August 1990, 36–42.

Hallstrom, T. and S. Samuelsson. Changes in women's sexual desire in middle life: The longitudinal study of women in Gothenburg. *Archives of Sexual Behavior,* 1990, *19,* 259–268.

Hawton, K. *Sex therapy: A practical guide.* Oxford: Oxford University Press, 1985.

Hunter, M. S. Emotional well-being, sexual behavior and hormone replacement therapy. *Maturitas,* 1990, *12,* 299–314.

Hurlbert, D. F. Factors influencing a woman's decision to end an extramarital sexual relationship. *Journal of Sex and Marital Therapy,* 1992, *18,* 104–114.

Julien, D., C. Bouchard, M. Gagnon, and A. Pomerleau. Insider's views of marital sex: A dyadic analysis. *The Journal of Sex Research,* 1992, *29,* 343–360.

Kaplan, H. The classification of the female sexual dysfunctions. *Journal of Sex and Marital Therapy,* 1974, *1* no. 2, 124–138.

Kaplan, H. S. *The evaluation of sexual disorders.* New York: Brunner/Mazel, 1983.

Kaplan, H. S. Sex, intimacy, and the aging process. *Journal of the American Academy of Psychoanalysis,* 1990, *18,* 185–205.

Kelly, M. P., D. S. Strassberg, and J. R. Kircher. Attitudinal and experiential correlates of anorgasmia. *Archives of Sexual Behavior,* 1990, *19,* 165–177.

Keogh, E. J. The male menopause. *Australian Family Physician,* 1990, *19,* 833–840.

Kinsey, A. C., W. B. Pomeroy, C. E. Martin, and P. H. Gebhard. *Sexual behavior in the human female.* Philadelphia: W. B. Saunders, 1953.

Lavee, Yoav. Western and non-western human sexuality: Implicatons for clinical practice. *Journal of Sex and Marital Therapy,* 1991, *17,* 203–211.

Lawson, A. *Adultry: An analysis of love and betrayal.* New York: Basic Books, 1988.

Lieberman, B. Extrapremarital intercourse: Attitudes toward a neglected sexual behavior. *Journal of Sex Research,* 1988, *24,* 291–299.

Leiblum, S. R. and R. C. Rosen. Couples therapy for erectile disorders: Conceptual and clinical considerations. *Journal of Sex and Marital Therapy,* 1989, *17,* 147–159.

LoPiccolo, J. and C. Lobitz. The role of masturbation in the treatment or orgasmic dysfunction. *Archives of Sexual Behavior,* 1972, *2,* 163–171.

Masters, W. H. and V. E. Johnson. *Human sexual inadequacy.* Boston: Little, Brown, 1970.

Marshall, D. Sexual behavior on Mangaia. In D. Marshall & R. Suggs (Eds.) *Human sexual behavior: Variations in the ethnographic spectrum.* New York: Basic Books, 1971, 103–162.

McCarthy, B. W. Sexual dysfunctions and dissatisfactions among middle-years couples. *Journal of Sex Education and Therapy,* 1982, *8,* no. 2, 9–12.

McCarthy, J. and S. McMillan. Patient/partner satisfaction with penile implant surgery. *Journal of Sex and Marital Therapy,* 1990, *16,* 25–37.

Messenger, J. C. Sex and repression in an Irish folk community. In D. S. Marshall and R. C. Suggs (Eds.) *Human sexual behavior: Variations in the ethnographic spectrum.* New York: Basic Books, 1971, 3–37.

Morley, J. E. and F. E. Kaiser. Sexual function with advancing age. *Medical Clinics of North America,* 1989, *73,* 1483–1495.

Moser, C. Lust, lack of desire, and paraphilias: Some thoughts and possible connections. *Journal of Sex and Marital Therapy,* 1992, *18,* 65–69.

Mulligan, Thomas and C. Renne Moss. Sexuality and aging in male veterans: A cross-sectional study of interest, ability, and activity. *Archives of Sexual Behavior,* 1991, *20,* 17–25.

Mulligan, T. and R. F. Palguta, Jr. Sexual interest, activity, and satisfaction among male nursing home residents. *Archives of Sexual Behavior,* 1991, *20,* 199–204.

Murstein, B. I., D. Case, and S. P. Gunn. Personality correlates of ex-swingers. *Lifestyles,* 1985, *8,* 21–34.

Oggins, J. D. Leber, and J. Veroff. Race and gender differences in black and white newlyweds' perceptions of sexual and marital relations. *Journal of Sex Research,* 1993, *30,* 152–160.

O'Neill, N. and G. O'Neill. *Open marriage: A new life style for couples.* New York: Avon Books, 1972.

Pietropinto, A. Sex and the elderly. *Medical Aspects of Human Sexuality,* June 1987, 110–117.

Pittman, F. Beyond betrayal: Life after infidelity, *Psychology Today,* May/June 1993, 33 et passi.

Raboch, J. and J. Raboch. Infrequent orgasms in women. *Journal of Sex and Marital Therapy,* 1992, *18,* 114–120.

Roscoe, B., L. E. Cavanaugh, and D. R. Kennedy. Dating infidelity: Behavior, reasons, and consequences. *Adolescence,* 1988, *13,* 35–43.

Rosenweig, Julie M. and Dennis M. Dailey. Dyadic adjustment/sexual satisfaction in women and men as a function of psychological sex role self-perception. *Journal of Sex and Marital Therapy,* 1989, *15,* 42–56.

Rubin, L. B. *Erotic wars*. New York: Harper Perennial, 1991.

Rubinson, L. and L. DeRubertis. Trends in sexual attitudes and behaviors of a college population over a 15-year period. *Journal of Sex Education and Therapy*, 1991, *17*, 32–42.

Sarrel, P. M. Sexuality and menopause. *Journal of Obstetrics and Gynecology*, 1990, *75*, 26s–30s.

Schaefer, L. Women and extramarital affairs. *Sexuality Today*, 1981, *4*, no.13, 3.

Schiavi, R. C., P. Schreiner-Engle, and J. Mandeli. Healthy aging and male sexual function. *American Journal of Psychiatry*, 1990, *147*, 766.

Schover, L. R. and S. B. Jensen. *Sexuality and chronic illness: A comprehensive approach*. New York: Guilford Press, 1988.

Schwartz, P. and D. Jackson. How to have a model marriage. *New Woman*, February 1989, 66–74.

Segraves, R. T. Hormones and libido. *Sexual Desire Disorders*, S. R. Leiblum and R. C. Rosen, eds. New York: Guilford Press, 1988, 271–312.

Sexual Addiction Survey Results Released. *Siecus Report*, 1988, *17*, 20.

Shaw, J. Play therapy with the sexual workhorse: Successful treatment with twelve cases of inhibited ejaculation. *Journal of Sex and Marital Therapy*, 1990 *16*, 159–164.

Sherwin, B. B. The impact of different doses of estrogen and progestin on mood and sexual behavior in postmenopausal women. *Journal of Clinical Endocrinology and Metabolism*, 1991, 336–343.

Sherwin, B. B. The psychoendrocrinology of aging and female sexuality. *Annual Review of Sex Research*, vol II. J. Bancroft, C. M. Davis, and H. J. Ruppel, eds. Lake Mills, Iowa: Stoles Graphic Services, 1991.

Shikai, X. Treatment of impotence in traditional Chinese medicine. *Journal of Sex Education and Therapy*, 1990, *16*, 198–200.

Smith, Tom W. Adult sexual behavior in 1989: Number of partners, frequency of intercourse and risk of AIDS. *Family Planning Perspectives*, 1991, *23*, 102–107.

Sohn, M. and R. Sikora. *Ginkgo bilaba* extract in the therapy of erectile dysfunction. *Journal of Sex Education and Therapy*, 1991, *17*, 53–61.

Sonda, L. P., R. Mazo, and M. B. Chancellor. The role of yohimbine for the treatment of erectile impotence. *Journal of Sex and Marital Therapy*, 1990, *16*, 15–21.

Spanier, G. B. and R. L. Margolis. Marital separation and extramarital sexual behavior. *Journal of Sex Research*, 1983, *19*, 23–48.

Statistical Abstract of the United States: 1993, 113th ed. Washington, D.C.: U.S. Bureau of the Census, 1993.

Stephens, W. N. *The family in cross-cultural perspective*. Washington, D.C.: University Press of America, 1982.

Symons, D. *The evolution of human sexuality*. New York: Oxford University Press, 1979.

Tavris, C. *The mismeasure of woman*. New York: Simon and Schuster, 1992.

Thompson, A. P. Emotional and sexual components of extramarital relations. *Journal of Marriage and the Family*, 1984, *46*, 35–42.

Thompson, A. P. Extramarital sex: A review of the research literature. *Journal of Sex Research*, 1983, *19*, 1–22.

Trotter, S. Single women/married men. *Free Inquiry in Creative Sociology*, 1989, *17*, 213–217.

Weinstein, E. and E. Rosen. Introduction: Sexuality counseling. *Sexuality counseling: Issues and implications*, E. Weinstein and E. Rosen, eds. Pacific Grove, Calif.: Brooks/Cole, 1988, 1–15.

Wheeler, J. and P. R. Kilmann. Comarital sexual behavior: Individual and relationship variables. *Archives of Sexual Behavior*, 1983, *12*, 295–306.

Wing, R. R., K. A. Matthews, L. H. Kuller, E. N. Meilahn, and P. L. Plantinga. Weight gain at the time of menopause. *Archives of Internal Medicine*, 1991, *151*, 97–102.

Witherington, R. Vacuum devices for the impotent. *Journal of Sex and Marital Therapy*, 1991, *17*, 69–80.

Yablonsky, L. *The extra-sex factor: Why over half of America's married men play around*. New York: Times Books, 1979.

Young, William R. Changes in sexual functioning during the aging process. *Sexology: An independent field*, F. J. Bianoco and R. Hernandez Serrano, eds. New York: Elsevier Science Publishers, 1990, 121–128.

Zilbergeld, B. *The new male sexuality: The truth about men, sex and pleasure.* New York: Bantam, 1992.

Contents

❧ 11 ❧
CHAPTER
Work, Leisure, and Relationships

Is it True?

1. Women's employment may have a positive impact on the quality of marriages since fewer women will either enter into or remain in marriages for financial reasons.

2. Most current studies on the effect of both spouses being employed on the couple's marriage have found either a positive effect for both spouses or no effect at all.

3. During the 1930s, 26 states had laws prohibiting the hiring of married women.

4. Unmarried women spend more time each week doing housework than married women.

5. About 21 percent of wives employed full time have higher earnings than their husband.

1 = T; 2 = T; 3 = T; 4 = F; 5 = T

Individual lives are defined by the weaving together of three strands: work, family, and leisure.

KARLA A. HENDERSON
M. DEBORAH BIALESCHKI
SUSAN M. SHAW
VALERIE J. FREYSINGER

Money may be the husk of many things, but not the kernel. It brings you food, but not appetite; medicine but not health; acquaintances but not friends; servants, but not faithfulness; days of joy, but not peace or happiness.

HENDRIK HOSEN

bumper sticker that reads, "I owe, I owe, it's off to work I go" reflects the recognition that earning an income is a necessary part of life. In this chapter, we examine how employment and unemployment affect women, men, marriages, and families. We also explore who does what in terms of unpaid work, or housework. Strategies that women and men use to balance work and family demands are also described. Lastly, we discuss the aspect of family life that makes many Americans look forward to Fridays (TGIF—Thank God It's Friday)—leisure.

℘ A Look at Paid Employment and U.S. Families

Without my money none careth for me.

THOMAS DELONEY

More and more women are also leaving the household to earn money. After exploring the meanings of money, we look at employed wives in the past and present and examine dual-earner families.

The Meanings of Money

Economists view money as the medium of exchange for the distribution and consumption of goods and services in our society. But money has more personal meanings that relate to self-esteem, power, security, love, and conflict.

Women who are economically independent report a positive effect on their self esteem.

Self-Esteem   Money affects self-esteem because, in our society, human worth, particularly for men, is sometimes equated with financial achievement. A young husband and father mused:

> I've been working for seven years, and I've got nothing to show for it. I can't even pay the light bill, let alone buy the things we want. My two closest friends are making a lot of money in their jobs. It makes me feel bad when I know that I can't provide for my family the way they provide for theirs. I'm a failure. (Author's files)

Of course, the self-esteem of women is also influenced by money. Employed wives often report an enhanced self-esteem as a result of increased economic independence.

Power in Relationships Money is a central issue in relationships because of its association with power, control, and dominance (Riza et al., 1992). Blumstein and Schwartz (1991) found that "the greater the husband's income, the greater his decision-making and leadership power relative to his wife's. Likewise, the greater the wife's income, the greater her relative power on these two dimensions" (p. 273).

CONSIDERATION

According to Yoger and Brett (1989), employed women are more likely to feel that they have more power in relationship decisions regarding how money is spent if they keep their own savings and checking accounts.

Sharing the power over how money is spent is associated with increased marital satisfaction. Schwartz and Jackson (1989) found that wives who had equal or greater influence in deciding how much cash to keep on hand, paying bills, and keeping track of expenditures, reported being much happier in their marriage. When the husband dominated the economic decisions, wives reported being much more unhappy in their marriage.

Money also provides women and men with the power to be independent. The higher a spouse's income, the more power that spouse has to leave the relationship. Indeed, some economically dependent unhappy wives may seek employment so that they can afford to leave.

Money translates into power not only between spouses but in other family relationships. Parents use money to influence their children's decisions and behavior. For example, parents may threaten to withdraw their financial support from a son or daughter whom they discover is living together with a girlfriend or boyfriend. And, some divorced parents complain that their ex-spouse uses money to "buy" the affections of the children or to influence the children's preference concerning physical custody arrangements.

Security Oscar Wilde once said, "When I was young, I used to think that money was the most important thing in life; now that I am older, I know it is." Money represents security. People without money often feel that they live on the verge of disaster. "My car has four slick tires," said a single parent of two children who had returned to college, "and when one of those pops, I've had it. I don't have the money for new tires, and I can't walk to work."

Buying life insurance expresses the desire to provide a secure future for loved ones. "If something happens to me," one wife said, "my husband and children will need more than the sympathy they'll get at my funeral. They'll need money." Without money, there is no security—either present or future. Money also secures us against ill health. Because medical care often depends on the ability to pay for it, our health is directly related to our financial

> Husbands listen more to a wife who is employed, and employed wives listen more to themselves.
>
> ROBERT BLOOD

> I always tell women to have money of their own, or a way to earn it. Because you never know what's going to happen.
>
> JOAN LUNDEN

resources. Money buys visits to the physician, as well as food for a balanced diet.

Love   To some individuals, money may also mean love. While admiring the engagement ring of her friend, a woman said, "What a big diamond! He must really love you." The assumption is that big diamond equals high price equals deep love feelings.

Similar assumptions are often made when gifts are given or received. People tend to spend more money on presents for the people they love, believing that the value of the gift symbolizes the depth of their emotion. People receiving gifts may make the same assumption. "She must love me more than I thought," mused one man. "I gave her a CD for Christmas, but she gave me a CD player. I felt embarrassed." His feeling of embarrassment is based on the idea that the woman loves him more than he loves her because she paid more for her gift to him than he did for his gift to her.

Similarly, the withdrawal of money may mean the absence of love. When two people get divorced, aside from what the court may order in alimony and child support, it is assumed that their economic sharing is over.

Conflict   Money may also be a source of conflict in relationships. Seventy-seven percent of 15,000 spouses reported that money was the greatest problem in their marriage—outranking sex, in-laws, or infidelity (Schwartz & Jackson, 1989). Couples argue about what to spend money on (new car? vacation? pay off credit card?) and how much money to spend. One couple in marriage therapy reported that they argued over whether to buy orange juice that was fresh squeezed or from concentrate (Author's files). As noted earlier, conflicts over money in a relationship often signify conflict over power in the relationship.

Family conflicts over money sometimes surface when a parent dies. One older brother noted that his father's death resulted in all of his siblings arguing over who was due how much. "It has splintered the otherwise close family completely," he remarked.

> ### CONSIDERATION
>
> Although money can create conflict it can also be used to reduce stress and provide recreational family time. For example, partners who argue over who is to clean the house may hire a person to clean it for them. Money may also enable couples to take vacations and pay for recreational activities, allowing them to escape day-to-day pressures and have fun as a family.

Another potential conflict related to money may arise when spouses disagree about whether the wife, especially if she has young children, should earn an income. Despite the increasing numbers of women in the workplace, husbands are expected to be employed, while wives are sometimes viewed as

---

How do I love thee? Let me count your money.

UNKNOWN

I married for love and got a little money along with it.

ROSE KENNEDY

There are a lot of hot arguments over "cold cash."

E. C. MCKENZIE

having the option to be employed or not.. Next, we take a brief look at employed women in the past and present.

Employed Women: Past and Present

Before 1940, a married woman's place was in the home, and although she might sell her wares, sewing, laundry, and cooking skills (this work could be done without leaving home), she was not expected to earn an income working outside the home. The exception was the black, immigrant, rural woman, who has always tended to work outside the home out of economic necessity.

World War II marked the point at which employment became normative for all classes of women. Their participation in the labor force became a national necessity. While most middle-class, wartime, employed women were expected to return to the traditional roles of wife and mother after the war was over, a Women's Bureau survey conducted in 1944 and 1945 revealed that between 75 and 80 percent of all women war workers wanted to remain on the job after the fighting had stopped (Chafe, 1976). Although demobilization resulted in the loss of jobs for many women (and men), the trend toward increased participation of women in the labor force had been established.

The increase in U.S. women's participation in paid employment has been dramatic. In 1900, only 20 percent of U.S. women were employed; this figure had risen to 37.7 percent in 1960, 43.3 percent in 1970, 51.5 percent in 1980, and 57.3 percent in 1991 (see Figure 11.1).

CONSIDERATION

Moen (1992) suggested that, "The trend in women's employment may have a positive impact on the quality of marriages, since fewer women will either enter into or remain in marriages simply for financial reasons" (p. 68). Because many women earn their own money, they do not need to marry a man for money and they can afford to leave a husband who mistreats them.

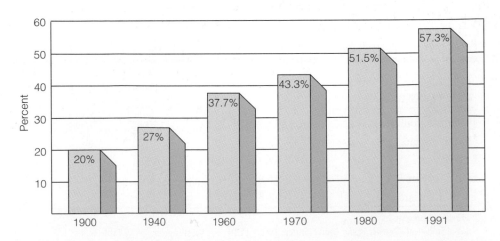

FIGURE 11.1

PERCENTAGE OF U.S. WOMEN EMPLOYED: 1900 TO 1991

Sources: Moen, P. Women's two roles: A contemporary dilemma. New York: Auburn House, 1992, 12. An imprint of Greenwood Publishing Group, Inc., Westport, CT. Reprinted with permission; Statistical Abstract of the United States, 1992, 112th edition, Washington D.C., Table 612

The increase in women's workforce participation in general included a radical jump in wives working outside the home.

NATIONAL DATA ⚮ In 1960, only 31.9 percent of married women were employed. In 1980, for the first time in U.S. history, half of all wives were employed. By 1992, 59.3 percent of U.S. wives (husbands present) were employed (*Statistical Abstract of the United States: 1993*, Table 633).

CONSIDERATION

During the Great Depression of the 1930s, 26 states enacted laws prohibiting the hiring of married women. These laws stemmed from the concern that wives were or would be taking jobs away from men.

Twenty years ago, a wife's and mother's employment pattern primarily followed the development of her children; her times of peak employment were before her children were born and after they left home. This pattern has changed; more mothers with children of all ages now work outside the home.

NATIONAL DATA ⚮ In 1975, 43.8 percent of married mothers with children under 18 were employed. This figure rose to 60.8 percent in 1985 and 67.9 percent in 1992 (*Statistical Abstract of the United States:* 1993, Table 634).

Table 11.1 shows that the labor force participation rate of married mothers of children of all ages has increased over the last two decades. However, many women still prefer to stop working when their children are young. Fifty-three percent of 821 undergraduate university women said that their ideal lifestyle preference was (assuming that they had graduated, gotten a job, and were married) to "stop working at least until the youngest child is in school, then pursue a full time job" (Schroeder et al., 1993, 243). Many women who return to their jobs soon after their baby is born do so primarily for financial reasons (Volling & Belsky, 1993).

TABLE 11.1

Percentage of Employed Married* Mothers by Age of Youngest Child: 1975 to 1992

AGE OF YOUNGEST CHILD	1975	1985	1992
1 year or younger	30.8	49.4	56.7
Under 3 years	32.7	50.5	57.5
3 to 5 years	42.2	58.4	63.5
6 to 13 years	51.8	68.2	74.9
14 to 17 years	53.5	67.0	76.6

* Husband present

Source: Statistical Abstract of the United States: 1993, 113th ed. Washington, D.C., Table 634.

CONSIDERATION

There seems to be a discrepancy between the role women want for themselves in regard to employment and childcare and the role men want for their wives. Although only 6 percent of 821 undergraduate women in one study indicated a preference for leaving the workforce when their baby is born and never returning, half of 535 undergraduate men at the same university reported this preference for their future wives (Schroeder et al., 1993).

A woman's paid work role varies from one society to another. The proportion of women in the labor force ranges from a low of three or four percent in parts of Western Africa to as much as 85 percent in Sweden (Tepperman & Wilson, 1993).

Cultural norms often dictate the extent to which women are employed. In a study of the labor patterns of women in Queretaro, Mexico, Chant (1993) identified three reasons men gave for not wanting their wives to work. First, the men were fearful that their wives would earn more money than they did and "get ahead of them." Second, if a wife worked it might be interpreted that her husband was unable to fulfill his role as breadwinner and that he was unable to exercise his authority over his wife. Third, the employed wife would have more freedom and her risk of being unfaithful would increase.

ACROSS CULTURES 〜

Obstacles to Women Pursuing Careers   Although there are many women who have successful careers, women are less likely than men to have careers and are more likely than men to have jobs (Silberstein, 1992). Careers usually require formal training/education, commitment (to work long hours for many years), and, oftentimes, mobility to relocate or travel.

Obstacles to the wife's pursuing a career include responsibility for children and housework, lack of support from the husband, and lack of role models. Although there are exceptions, both wives and husbands tend to expect that the wife will be primarily responsible for childcare—an expectation that may hinder a wife's career advancement (Floge, 1989).

Many women find it extremely difficult to decide whether they are mothers who happen to work, or workers who happen to be mothers.

MARTIN O'CONNELL
DAVID E. BLOOM

NATIONAL DATA 🎇 Almost 40 percent of U.S. mothers of preschool children combine employment and caregiving by working part time (Folk & Beller, 1993).

In addition to childcare, women still do most of the housework. Over half of the 20 dual-career women in Silberstein's (1992) study perceived their husbands' lack of help or low level of help with household and childcare responsibilities to be the major way in which their husbands had hurt their careers.

Another obstacle to some wives pursuing careers is lack of support from the husband. If the husband is not supportive of his wife's career, he may make it difficult for her to be successful and happy in her work.

Lastly, many women today have mothers who did not have a career; therefore, these women do not have a role model for how to be a successful career woman and a wife and mother at the same time (Silberstein, 1992). These women were post war baby boomers whose mothers were born/grew up during the Great Depression.

CONSIDERATION

The number of women pursuing careers is increasing. A 1990 national poll found that 45 percent of women view their work as a career, up from 41 percent in 1985 (Townsend & O'Neil, 1990). This poll also found that, in 1990, 57 percent of women reported that the ideal lifestyle involved combining marriage, career, and children; only 27 percent preferred marriage and children, but no career.

Dual-Earner Marriages

As we have seen, an increasing number of women have entered the workforce. Today, most husbands have working wives and most children have employed mothers as well as fathers.

NATIONAL DATA ✄ Only 20 percent of married couples fit the traditional model with the breadwinning husband, the stay-at-home wife, and two children (Ahlburg & De Vita, 1992).

> The fundamental challenge to women—and to men—is to build a life that includes both family and work roles.
>
> PHYLLIS MOEN

Because women still bear most of the childcare and other household responsibilities, women in dual-earner marriages are more likely than men to want to be employed part time, rather than full time, or to work full time but not year round, such as teachers who are not employed in the summer. In a study of 949 Australian men and women in two-parent families, 80 percent of the men in contrast to 18 percent of the women reported that they wanted to work full time (Glezer, 1991).

NATIONAL DATA ✄ In 1991, only 10 percent of employed U.S. men worked part-time. In contrast, 25 percent of employed U.S. women worked part-time (*Statistical Abstract of the United States: 1993*, Table 639).

> The modern couple is willing to sacrifice some of its time alone, some of its leisure, some of its commitment to work for a shot at the new true American Dream: A balanced work and home life with an equitable distribution of tasks, resulting in honest, healthy, successful family relationships.
>
> MARCIA BYALICK
> LINDA SASLOW

Some dual-earner marriages are dual-career in that both spouses have a career. Three types of dual-career marriages are those in which the husband's career takes precedence, the wife's career takes precedence, or both careers are regarded equally. When couples hold traditional gender role attitudes, the husband's career is likely to take precedence. This situation translates into the wives being willing to relocate and to disrupt their careers for the advancement of their husband's career (Bielby & Bielby, 1992).

For couples who do not hold traditional gender role attitudes, the wife's career may take precedence. In such marriages, the husband is willing to relocate and to disrupt his career for his wife's. Such a pattern is also likely to occur when the wife earns considerably more money than her husband.

NATIONAL DATA ❧ About 21 percent of wives employed full time have higher earnings than their husbands (Crispell, 1989).

Studies disagree on the happiness of spouses in marriages where the wife's career is given priority over the husband's. In a small sample of marriages in which the wife's career was given priority over the husband's, almost all of the husbands (95 percent) and most of the wives (77 percent) felt that their marriages were "very happy" or "somewhat happy" (Atkinson & Boles, 1984). However, based on interviews with 20 dual-career couples and a review of the literature, Silberstein (1992) noted that many women feel that "to surpass their husbands in occupational success would provoke marital unease as well as intrapersonal dissonance with expectations of both husbands and wives" (p. 160).

Some dual-career spouses prioritize neither his nor her career but view both careers equally. When 135 married women professionals with preschool children were asked whose career took precedence, 42 percent said "both— about the same" (34 percent said that their husband's career took precedence and 24 percent said their own career took precedence) (Emmons et al., 1990). The view that the careers of wives and husbands are equally important will probably become more prevalent as more women pursue careers, and egalitarian role relationships replace traditional gender role relationships.

❧ Effects of a Dual-Earner Lifestyle

What are the effects on women, men, their marriages, and their children of couples involved in a dual-earner family?

Effects on Women

Various researchers have reviewed the literature on the effects of employment on women and found generally positive effects on their psychological well-being (Crosby, 1993; Menaghan & Parcel, 1991; Moen, 1992). Beneficial outcomes include enhanced self-esteem, power, and independence resulting from earning an income. Employed women also have increased social interaction with a wider network of individuals, which is in contrast to full-time homemakers who may experience isolation and lack of social ties.

> Women have adjusted to the necessity of working for pay, but there has been little reciprocal adjustment on the part of other family members.
>
> **LORNE TEPPERMAN**
> **SUSANNAH WILSON**

CONSIDERATION

Some married women work because two incomes are required to meet the basic financial needs of the family. However, the rewards of working for many women extend beyond the income. About half (51 percent) of over 3,000 working mothers agreed with the statement, "I wouldn't quit working even if I could afford to" (Rubenstein, 1991).

Benefits may also surface when the children leave home. Adelmann et al. (1989) found, compared to full-time homemakers, employed women adjust more easily to their children leaving home. When the parenting role subsides, employed women still have meaningful work roles on which to focus their energy.

On the negative side, employed wives, as well as employed single mothers, often experience what sociologists call *role overload*—not having the time and/or energy to meet the demands of one's role responsibilities. Because women have traditionally been responsible for most of the housework and childcare, employed women come home from work to what Hochschild (1989) calls the *second shift*: an "extra month of twenty-four hour days a year" cooking, cleaning, doing laundry, and feeding/bathing/doing homework with kids (p. 3).

> As a result, women tend to talk more intently about being overtired, sick, and "emotionally drained." Many women I could not tear away from the topic of sleep. They talked about how much they could "get by on" . . . six and a half, seven, seven and a half, less, more. . . . Some apologized for how much sleep they needed. . . . They talked about how to avoid fully waking up when a child called them at night, and how to get back to sleep. These women talked about sleep the way a hungry person talks about food (p. 9).

Another stressful aspect of employment for employed mothers, either in dual-earner or single-parent families, is *role conflict*—being confronted with incompatible role obligations. In a study of 135 married female professionals, over 75 percent of the women reported experiencing frequent conflict between work and family responsibilities. The average occurrence of role conflict was "two or three times a week" (Emmons et al., 1990). The most frequently reported role conflict situations were having to rush their children in the morning so that the women would not be late for work, having to leave work earlier than they would have liked to because of their children, and having to work during times usually reserved for the family.

Role conflict may also create feelings of guilt. In a survey of over 3,000 employed mothers, about 40 percent reported that they felt guilty about not spending enough time with their children and not being home when their children got out of school (Rubenstein, 1991). Other situations that tended to produce role conflict included going to work when one's child was sick and missing school events due to work obligations. Other sources of guilt were also mentioned. Twelve percent of the wives reported feeling guilty over not spending enough time with their husbands.

> The few things that I regret in my life are not having put enough time into mothering, wiving, taking care of the inner life.
>
> JANE FONDA

> At work, you think of the children you have left at home. At home, you think of the work you've left unfinished.
>
> GOLDA MEIR

CONSIDERATION

Researchers suggest that women who are most likely to benefit from employment are those who want to be employed and who enjoy their work (Moen, 1992; Spitze, 1991). Conversely, "women who dislike their work and have little control over it suffer the most conflict over their roles as wife, mother, and worker" (Rubenstein, 1991, 55). Studies also show that "unlike with men, part-time employment is associated with higher levels of well-being among women, since it presumably permits a better coordination of work and family responsibilities" (Moen, 1992, 50). In addition, women whose husbands participate in housework and childcare are more likely to benefit psychologically from employment.

I'm a hard worker as opposed to a workaholic because I do my best in both categories: family and taking care of business. Fortunately, I love both things but family does take priority.

REBA MCENTIRE

Effects on Men

Men may also benefit from being in a dual-earner marriage (Crosby, 1993; Spitze, 1991). Benefits for the husband include being relieved of the sole responsibility for the financial support of the family and more freedom to change jobs or go to school. Men also benefit by having a spouse with whom to share the daily rewards and stresses of employment. And, to the degree that women find satisfaction in their work role, men benefit by having a happier partner. Finally, men benefit from a dual-earner marriage by increasing the potential to form a closer bond with their children through active childcare.

NATIONAL DATA ॐ Fathers are the primary childcare provider in 15 percent of dual-earner families (Ahlburg & DeVita, 1992).

Phil Jones sometimes cares for his son, Alexander, at work.

However, just as employed women often experience role overload and role conflict, so do many men. Regarding role overload, many men work overtime or have more than one job. Men may also have difficulty combining work and family roles. A 1989 *New York Times* poll found that 72 percent of employed fathers (with children under 18) felt torn between the demands of their jobs and their desire to spend more time with their families (cited in Moen, 1992).

Not all men want their wives to work outside the home. Depression has been found in husbands whose wives work when they prefer that they not. In addition, husbands may experience distress if they interpret their wives' employment as an indication that the husband is not an adequate provider (Menaghan & Parcel, 1991; Spitze, 1991).

Effects on Marriages

The effects of employment on marital satisfaction have been studied extensively. Most current studies have found either a positive effect of both marital partners being employed or no effect at all (Spitze, 1991). Thomas (1990) studied 41 dual-career black couples; 98 percent of the husbands and 85 percent of the wives reported that they were happy with their marriage.

The dual-income lifestyle benefits spouses by providing them with similar experiences and concerns to share. Having two earners in a marriage also allows couples to achieve a higher family income, although for many couples two incomes are necessary to meet the basic financial needs of the family.

CONSIDERATION

Part of the income of working mothers is spent on work-related expenses. Estimates of work-related expenses are between 25 and 50 percent of women's take-home pay, with childcare the largest expense for those who have young children (Israelsen, 1991). Fees at urban childcare centers often run $750.00 a month or higher (Schellenbarger, 1993). From another source, the cost of a daycare center ranges from $140.00 to $800.00 a month (Caminiti, 1992). Other expenses include taxes, transportation, and lunch money. In addition, when both spouses work, they often spend a larger portion of their family income on housecleaning services, eating out, and convenience foods such as frozen dinners.

When both spouses earn an income, they tend to experience more joint decision making and more consensus on decisions (Godwin & Scanzoni, 1989). However, Moen (1992) noted that "couple decisions—whether to move, when to have a child—become more complicated when two jobs are involved" (p. 69).

On the negative side, Moen (1992) noted that the marriage suffers in "terms of the availability and flexibility of time" (p. 68). In a study of 20

Men feel that they receive relatively little credit for being involved fathers or role-sharing husbands.

LISA SILBERSTEIN

dual-career couples, many women reported being stressed and exhausted, which resulted in little time together, lack of quality time, and less sex (Silberstein, 1992).

Decrease in family size is another effect of a dual-earner lifestyle. The percentage of women ages 40–44 who had only one child rose from 9.6 percent in 1980 to 16.9 percent in 1990—a 76 percent increase. Martha Farsworth Riche of the Population Reference Bureau noted that this change is partly the result of "mothers and fathers who have equally demanding careers." Career women delay having kids, and "people who delay tend to have smaller families" (Peterson, 1993, D1).

Regarding marital stability, researchers have linked the rise in women's employment and rising divorce (Spitze, 1991). One explanation is that couples are better able to financially afford divorce if both spouses earn an income. Another explanation is that the stresses of a dual-earner lifestyle contribute to divorce.

CONSIDERATION

Three researchers compared 75 one-earner and 184 two-earner families and found that one-earner families reported more satisfaction with family life but less satisfaction with finances. Conversely, two-earner families reported more satisfaction with finances but less satisfaction with family life (Hilton, Baird, & Haldeman, 1992). As we noted in Chapter 1, all choices involve trade-offs.

A third explanation is that the rise in women's employment may be, in part, a response to women's perception of the increased divorce risk—they may seek employment to become financially independent in case the marriage does not work out.

Several factors may influence whether a dual-earner lifestyle has negative or positive effects on a marital relationship. One factor that influences marital happiness in dual-earner marriages is the degree to which spouses experience stress in their jobs. In a study of 86 dual-earner couples, wives who reported higher levels of work stress also reported lower levels of marital adjustment (Sears & Galambos, 1992). Bolger et al. (1990) found that stress and arguments in the workplace lead to stress and arguments at home (the reverse is also true—stress at home leads to stress at the workplace). Jobs that involve high pressure and little support from co-workers may result in more frequent marital arguments (Hughes, Galinsky, & Morris, 1992). Such jobs may be more characteristic of the working class than the middle class. Edwards et al. (1992) found that the wife's employment had a negative effect in working class marriages, but not in middle class marriages.

Another factor that affects marital quality among dual-earner couples is the amount of support the spouses give each other for working and the degree to which both spouses are satisfied with the division of housework and childcare in the marriage (Vannoy & Philliber, 1992). Husbands are more

It is now more widely understood that work–family problems are a result of families changing faster than institutions—than the workplace with its last minute meetings or mandatory overtime, than the schools that provide little warning of events that parents are supposed to attend, than doctors and dentists who don't have evening hours or than banks that close at three o'clock.

ELLEN GALINSKY

likely to share housework and childcare if they have egalitarian gender role attitudes. It is not surprising then that in a study of 452 couples, the researchers found that gender role attitudes, particularly those of the husband, were important in determining marital quality (Vannoy & Philliber, 1992). "The husband's expectations determine the nature of the marriage. He must be willing to be married to an employed wife, and to share household and childcare tasks" (p. 391).

CONSIDERATION

When the husband does not share the work load and the wife feels that she is not being treated fairly, the marriage suffers (Blair, 1993). In addition, based on a national study of over 13,000 adults, Lye and Biblarz (1993) concluded that marital satisfaction in the dual–earner marriage is reduced when the husband and wife do not share similar attitudes about the wife's being employed. Hence, if marriages are to benefit from dual employment, husbands must value their wives' labor force participation and be willing to share the demands of housework and childcare.

Lastly, the happiness of dual-earner couples, as well as single-earner couples, depends on each spouse being committed to making time for their relationship. "The bottom-line of making a dual-earner marriage work," said one spouse, "is to help your partner and be committed to your relationship" (Author's files).

Effects on Children

How does being reared in a dual-earner family affect children? Before reading further, you may want to complete the following Self-Assessment to assess your beliefs regarding the consequences of maternal employment for children.

Parents want to know if maternal employment has negative consequences for their children. Spitze (1991) reviewed the research and concluded that there are no direct effects, positive or negative, of maternal employment on children. For example, Thornton (1992) reported finding no substantial or consistent effects of maternal employment on gender role attitudes, divorce attitudes, and premarital sexual behavior attitudes of adolescents. Research shows that children of employed mothers develop just as well emotionally, intellectually, and socially as children whose mothers stay at home (Berg, 1986).

Indeed, there are some potential advantages and disadvantages for children who are reared in dual-earner families or single-parent families in which the parent is employed (Gerson, 1991; Moen, 1992; Rubenstein, 1991; Silberstein, 1992).

1. *Economic advantages.* In some families, the incomes of two parents is necessary to cover the basic expenses of housing, clothing, medical care,

Beliefs About the Consequences of Maternal Employment for Children

Directions: Using the scale below, please mark a number on the blank line next to each statement to indicate how strongly you agree or disagree with it.

1	2	3	4	5	6
Disagree Very Strongly	Disagree Strongly	Disagree Slightly	Agree Slightly	Agree Strongly	Agree Very Strongly

_____ 1. Children are less likely to form a warm and secure relationship with a mother who is working full time.

_____ 2. Children whose mothers work are more independent and able to do things for themselves.

_____ 3. Working mothers are more likely to have children with psychological problems than mothers who do not work outside the home.

_____ 4. Teenagers get into less trouble with the law if their mothers do not work full time outside the home.

_____ 5. For young children, working mothers are good role models for leading busy and productive lives.

_____ 6. Boys whose mothers work are more likely to develop respect for women.

_____ 7. Young children learn more if their mothers stay at home with them.

_____ 8. Children whose mothers work learn valuable lessons about other people they can rely on.

_____ 9. Girls whose mothers work full time outside the home develop stronger motivation to do well in school.

_____ 10. Daughters of working mothers are better prepared to combine work and motherhood, if they choose to do both.

_____ 11. Children whose mothers work are more likely to be left alone and exposed to dangerous situations.

_____ 12. Children whose mothers work are more likely to pitch in and do tasks around the house.

_____ 13. Children do better in school if their mothers are not working full time outside the home.

_____ 14. Children whose mothers work full time outside the home develop more regard for women's intelligence and competence.

_____ 15. Children of working mothers are less well-nourished and don't eat the way they should.

_____ 16. Children whose mothers work are more likely to understand and appreciate the value of a dollar.

_____ 17. Children whose mothers work suffer because their mothers are not there when they need them.

_____ 18. Children of working mothers grow up to be less competent parents than other children, because they have not had adequate parental role models.

_____ 19. Sons of working mothers are better prepared to cooperate with a wife who wants both to work and have children.

_____ 20. Children of mothers who work develop lower self-esteem because they think they are not worth devoting attention to.

_____ 21. Children whose mothers work are more likely to learn the importance of teamwork and cooperation among family members.

_____ 22. Children of working mothers are more likely than other children to experiment with drugs, alcohol, and sex at an early age.

(continued on next page)

_____ 23. Children whose mothers work develop less stereotyped views about men's and women's roles.

_____ 24. Children whose mothers work full time outside the home are more adaptable: they cope better with the unexpected and with changes in plans.

Scoring Instructions: Items 1, 3, 4, 7, 11, 13, 15, 17, 18, 20, and 22 refer to "costs" of maternal employment for children and yield a Costs Subscale score. High scores on the Costs Subscale reflect strong beliefs that maternal employment is costly to children. Items 2, 5, 6, 8, 9, 10, 12, 14, 16, 19, 21, 23, and 24 refer to "benefits" of maternal employment for children and yield a Benefits Subscale score. To obtain a Total Score, reverse score all items in the Benefits Subscale so that 1 = 6, 2 = 5, 3 = 4, 4 = 3, 5 = 2, and 6 = 1. The higher one's Total Score, the more one believes that maternal employment has negative consequences for children.

SOURCE: Greenberger, E., W. A. Goldberg, T. J. Crawford, and J. Granger. Beliefs about the consequences of maternal employment for children. *Psychology of Women Quarterly,* 1988, *12,* 35–59. Used by permission of Cambridge University Press.

NOTE: This Self-Assessment is included in this text to be thought–provoking. It is not intended to be used by students or instructors as a clinical evaluation device.

and food. In other families, having two incomes provides resources to give children "extras," such as private lessons (e.g., music, dance, swimming, karate), travel and vacation experiences, home computers, and a college education.

2. *More independence.* One mother said that because she was not at home to chauffeur her children everywhere, they had to learn how to get from point A to point B on their own (Silberstein, 1992). Children in homes in which there is not a full-time homemaker may also learn to prepare food for themselves and take care of their own laundry.

3. *Greater family contribution.* Children in dual-earner families and single-parent families may be required to contribute more to household tasks.

> Over the years, we've trained the kids to share all the work around the house. They've had to get used to not having us there to do it for them. And I think that's been good for them (Silberstein, 1992, 139).

4. *Positive role models.* In dual-earner families, boys may learn more egalitarian gender role attitudes so that they will be more supportive of their wives' employment. Daughters may also learn egalitarian gender role attitudes and will have a role model for combining work and family roles.

5. *Happier parents.* Dual-career wives in Silberstein's study said that they were less dependent on their children to meet their emotional needs and less likely to be resentful of the demands of the children than if they were not

employed. One employed mother said, "Being away from my kids makes me appreciate them more" (Rubenstein, 1992, 55).

6. *Wider exposure to caretakers.* Parents in Silberstein's study viewed the people who helped to take care of their children as enhancing the lives of their children.

There are also potential disadvantages for children reared in dual-earner (or single-parent) families. These include the following:

1. *Less time with parents.* Employed parents don't have as much time to spend with their children as do unemployed parents. However, Spitze (1991) reviewed research that suggests "the gap is least among the more educated, who spend time with their children at the expense of sleep and leisure" (p. 394).
2. *Parents more stressed.* Children in dual-earner families may not only complain that they don't see enough of their parents, but that they must contend with stressed out parents. One parent noted, "They don't like it when I'm overstressed or tired. They notice if I'm in a fog. They'll say, 'Dad, pay attention' " (Silberstein, 1992, 143). Another parent noted, "Some days I'm just so beat after the day that I'm only half there."
3. *Restricted activities.* Children's activities may be curtailed if there is no parent available to transport the child. Thus, children with both parents working may have less opportunity to participate in organized sports, clubs, and extracurricular activities.

Various factors influence how the dual-earner lifestyle affects children. These factors include the child's personality, gender, the family's resources and stage in the life cycle, parental attitudes and values, and the parents' working conditions (Moen, 1992). For example, in a study of 60 infants and their mothers, Willie (1992) found that mothers who felt forced to return to work for financial reasons or who reported that returning to work was very difficult "provided their infants with inappropriate verbal and physical reassurance . . . and showed an ambivalent and needy tone" (p. 275).

The effects on children with both parents in the workforce also depend on the quality of childcare arrangements provided for the children. Some children are cared for by one parent who works nights while the other parent works days. Other children are cared for by relatives. Another option, which is not affordable to some, is to pay for childcare (daycare is discussed in Chapter 15, Rearing Children). Many children stay at home by themselves for a period of time while the parents are at their jobs. However, 92 percent of a national sample of 83 self-care school-aged children had access to at least one adult in case they needed help. They also had contact with siblings, friends, or both during self-care (Hobbs & Rodman, 1992).

In the Choices section at the end of this chapter, we discuss the issues parents might consider in deciding whether to leave their children home alone.

$\mathcal{E}$ Housework in U.S. Families

One of the issues with which spouses (and children to some degree) in dual-earner families must contend is housework, which includes childcare, food preparation, shopping for food/clothes/other household items, repairing car/house, yard work, laundry, and housecleaning. In this section we look at the division of household labor in the family and explore cultural forces that influence the nature and amount of household labor performed in modern households.

CONSIDERATION

To what degree does being married affect the number of hours women and men spend doing housework? For women, being married means spending more time doing household labor. Using data from the National Survey of Families and Households, Shelton (1992) reported that married women spent 41.7 hours per week on housework while unmarried women spent 32.2 hours per week on housework. However, for men, being married is not associated with time spent doing household labor. Married men spent 21.9 hours per week on housework, while unmarried men spent 21.6 hours.

Division of Household Labor Between Women and Men

Research consistently shows what most couples can attest to: household work is largely performed by women (Mederer, 1993). Based on data from the National Survey of Families and Households, Shelton (1992) reported that employed women reported doing an average of 38.1 hours of housework per week, compared to 21.9 hours per week for employed men. In a study of 697 married couples in which one-third of the women and most of the men were employed full time, Hardesty and Bokemeier (1989) found that about three-fourths of the women and men reported that the wife always or usually performs the grocery shopping, prepares breakfast, and makes doctor and dental appointments. In addition, 85 percent of the respondents reported that the wife usually or always writes letters to relatives and takes care of general housecleaning.

In a nationwide survey of 2,200 male-female households, about 75 percent of the households reported that the women usually performed the shopping, 5 percent the man, and 20 percent both the woman and the man (Blaylock & Smallwood, 1987). Younger, better-educated couples were more likely to share shopping tasks than older, less-educated couples.

CONSIDERATION

The inequity between women and men regarding the distribution of household work has decreased somewhat in the last two decades. In 1975, men did 46

> percent as much household work as women. This figure rose to 54 percent in 1981 and 57 percent in 1987 (Shelton, 1992).

Employment of the Wife   How does employment of the wife affect the amount of time she spends doing housework? Hochschild (1989) suggested that employed women come home to a "second shift;" they are likely to spend three hours a day doing housework compared to their husbands who spend 17 minutes. Data from the National Survey of Families and Households revealed that unemployed married women spent an average of 46 hours per week on housework (not including childcare). Married women who worked part-time spent 42.7 hours and those who worked full-time spent 35.5 hours a week on housework (Shelton, 1992).

How does employment of the wife affect the amount of housework performed by her husband? Based on an extensive review of research, Israelsen (1991) concluded that regardless of employment status, women contribute significantly more time to housework and childcare than their spouses. Shelton (1992) reported that "men married to women employed full-time spend only one more hour per week on house cleaning (8.6 minutes per day) than men married to full-time homemakers" (p. 90).

Table 11.2 reflects that women do more housework and childcare regardless of whether they work outside the home. The exception is that men are more likely to take out the trash, mow the lawn, and repair things.

Employed women spend considerably more time in childcare than employed men.

TABLE 11.2

Division of Labor in Household Tasks of 1,057 Married Couples

	WIFE NOT WORKING %	WIFE WORKING PART TIME %	WIFE WORKING FULL TIME %	ALL COUPLES %
HOUSEWORK				
Doing the laundry				
Husband more	1	2	7	3
Both equally	5	5	16	9
Wife more	94	93	77	88
Cleaning the bathroom				
Husband more	3	3	9	5
Both equally	7	7	11	9
Wife more	90	90	80	86
Vacuuming the carpets				
Husband more	5	5	12	7
Both equally	12	11	21	15
Wife more	83	84	67	78
MEALS				
Cooking the evening meal				
Husband more	3	4	10	6
Both equally	8	12	19	13
Wife more	89	84	71	81
Doing the grocery shopping				
Husband more	3	5	8	5
Both equally	21	15	27	22
Wife more	76	80	65	73
Doing the dishes				
Husband more	6	8	12	9
Both equally	23	30	32	28
Wife more	71	62	56	63

What factors are associated with a husband's participation in household work? Several studies have found that husbands who had higher levels of educational achievement and egalitarian gender role attitudes tended to participate more in domestic work compared to husbands with lower levels of education and traditional gender role attitudes (Barnett & Baruch, 1987; Kamo, 1988; Ross, 1987). Another study also found that in dual-earner families, men who believed in the traditional male provider role were less involved in domestic tasks than men who viewed themselves as co-providers, rather than primary providers (Perry-Jenkins & Crouter, 1990). In one study,

TABLE 11.2

Division of Labor in Household Tasks of 1,057 Married Couples, *continued*

	WIFE NOT WORKING %	WIFE WORKING PART TIME %	WIFE WORKING FULL TIME %	ALL COUPLES %
MAINTENANCE				
Taking out rubbish				
Husband more	51	54	60	55
Both equally	24	28	24	25
Wife more	25	18	16	20
Taking care of the lawn				
Husband more	69	74	80	74
Both equally	21	15	14	17
Wife more	10	11	6	9
Repairing things around the house				
Husband more	83	78	81	81
Both equally	12	13	13	12
Wife more	5	9	6	7
CHILDREN				
Taking the children to their activities and appointments				
Husband more	5	4	7	5
Both equally	30	31	47	35
Wife more	65	65	46	60
Playing with the children				
Husband more	6	10	9	8
Both equally	71	68	71	70
Wife more	23	22	20	22
Punishing the children				
Husband more	7	10	12	9
Both equally	68	65	72	68
Wife more	25	25	16	23

Source: Australian Family Formation Project (Stage Two) 1990–1991. Table presented in Glezer, Helen. "Juggling work and family commitments." *Family Matters,* April 1991, no. 28, 10. Used by permission of the Australian Institute for Family Studies, 300 Queen Street, Melbourne, 30000, Victoria, Australia.

men who had high incomes as evidence of their provider role were also less likely to help prepare meals, wash dishes, do laundry, and clean the house (Brayfield, 1992).

While men with traditional gender role attitudes spend less time on household labor than men with egalitarian gender role attitudes the opposite is true for women. Women with traditional gender role attitudes spend more time on household labor than women with egalitarian gender role attitudes (Shelton, 1992).

Cleaning your house while your kids are still growing is like shoveling the walk before it stops snowing.

PHYLLIS DILLAR

Presence of Children In Table 11.3, you will note that the more children that live in the household, the more time employed women and men spend on household labor (Shelton, 1992). While the presence of children is associated with increased household labor for both women and men, the increase is greater for women.

Children's Participation in Housework

White and Brinkerhoff (1981) found that parents reported four reasons for involving children in housework:

1. Doing chores helps children build character.
2. Children have a duty to help the family.
3. Parents need help with household chores.
4. Children need to learn how to do household tasks.

Children of two–earner couples do more housework than children of couples in which only one parent is employed.

T A B L E 11.3

Household Labor Hours for Employed Women and Men by Number of Children

NUMBER OF CHILDREN	WOMEN	MEN	MEN AS A % OF WOMEN
None	28.2	18.5	65.6
One	43.8	26.1	59.6
Two or more	51.2	23.8	46.5

Source: Based on data from the 1987 National Survey of Families and Households, reported in Women, men and time: Gender differences in paid work, housework and leisure, Beth Anne Shelton. New York: Greenwood Press, 992, 68. An imprint of Greenwood Publishing Group Inc., Westport, Ct. Reprinted with permission.

While parents feel it is important for daughters and sons to participate in housework, daughters seem to do more of it than sons (Benin & Edwards, 1990). The researchers also found that daughters in dual-earner families do more housework than daughters in single-earner families (10.2 hours a week versus 8.2 hours a week).

Children also tend to perform gender stereotyped chores in the house. Girls tend to do more cooking, laundry, and cleaning, whereas boys tend to do more outdoor chores, such as taking out the garbage and mowing the lawn.

CONSIDERATION

If women and men are to achieve role sharing and equal responsibility in family domestic tasks, it may be important to recognize the importance of changing the attitudes of men and women toward family roles. Parents might consider socializing their children to view domestic tasks as a responsibility shared between women and men.

> Contemporary standards of housecleaning are a modern invention, like the vacuum cleaners and furniture polishes that make them possible.
>
> JULIET B. SCHOR

❧ Balancing the Demands of Work and Family

One of the major concerns of employed wives and husbands is how to juggle the demands of work and family simultaneously and achieve a sense of accomplishment and satisfaction in each area. In this section, we examine an array of strategies spouses use to cope with role overload and role conflict. These include: (1) the "superperson" strategy, (2) cognitive restructuring, (3) delegation of responsibility, (4) planning and time management, and (5) shift work.

> The lives of married women professionals with young children are complicated "juggling acts" in which conflicting role demands and time shortages often detract from overall quality of life.
>
> CAROL-ANN EMMONS
> MONICA BIERNAT
> LINDA BETH TIEDJE
> ERIC L. LANG
> CAMILLE B. WORTMAN

CONSIDERATION

In general, women tend to accommodate their work to their family rather than their family to their work (Glezer, 1991). While most men may be more likely to subordinate their family to their career, a recent study of two-earner couples found that the men were just as likely as women to cope with work and family demands by subordinating their work (Schnittger & Bird, 1990).

Superperson Strategy

The "superperson" strategy involves working as hard and as efficiently as possible to meet the demands of work and family. The person who uses the superperson strategy often skips lunch and cuts back on sleep and leisure in order to have more time available for work.

While both women and men may use this strategy, the term *superwoman* has been used to refer to women who attempt to "do it all." In a study of 135

> The joys of motherhood are never fully experienced until all the children are in bed.
>
> E. C. MCKENZIE

~: IN FOCUS 11.1 ~

Cultural Influences on the Nature of Household Labor

Cultural forces may influence the long hours women spend doing housework. Schor (1991) noted that studies of household labor spanning 1910 through the 1970s show that "the amount of time a full-time housewife devoted to her work remained virtually unchanged over fifty years—despite dramatic changes in household technology" (p. 8). This is largely because the development of labor-saving devices such as refrigerators, laundry machines, dishwashers, vacuum cleaners, and microwaves, and the availability of ready-made clothes and processed food, has been accompanied by increased cultural standards for cooking, shopping, cleaning, laundry, and care of children. For example, while washers and dryers have reduced the time required to wash and dry a load of clothes, increased standards of cleanliness and an increase in the size of the wardrobe increased the number of loads washed each week. Schor (1991) noted that,

> [In colonial times,] washing would be done once per month at most and, in many families, much less— perhaps four times per year. Nearly everyone wore dirty clothes nearly all the time. . . . When the electric washer was introduced (1925), many Americans enjoyed a clean set of clothes (or at least a fresh shirt or blouse) every Saturday night. By the 1950s and 1960s, we washed after one wearing (p. 89).

Married women may have higher standards regarding their participation in household work than their husbands have for them. In a study of 135 women professionals with preschool children (Emmons et al., 1990), wives tended to think that their husbands were satisfied with the amount of time they were currently spending on household work, whereas their husbands actually preferred that their wives spend "a little less time" on these activities. Instead, husbands in this study tended to "prefer their wives to relax alone more than they do and to spend less time on housework and meal preparation . . ." (p. 88).

The household labor of colonial women consisted of making yarn, cloth, candles, and soap; tending gardens and animals; sewing and mending clothes; baking bread and churning butter; and caring for the sick. Cleaning house was a chore that was typically performed only once a year (Margolis, 1984). Although colonial women had more children than women have today, standards of childrearing have increased making childcare more time consuming today than it was in the past. For example, while colonial women may have had nine children who were bathed once a week, women today may have two children who are bathed daily.

The cultural values of materialism and consumerism have also resulted in increased housework. As people strive for and acquire bigger homes, they also acquire more rooms to keep clean, more floors to sweep and polish and more rugs to vacuum. A bigger yard means more grass to mow. More furniture means more dusting and polishing. While some women and men may have the time for housework, and may enjoy doing it, others view housework as physically tiring, psychologically unfulfilling, and demanding of time that takes away from other pursuits.

---

professional women with preschool children, the superwoman strategy was the most common strategy used in both the workplace and in the home (Emmons et al., 1990).

Hochschild (1989) noted that the term *superwoman* or *supermom* is a cultural label that allows the woman to regard herself as "unusually efficient, organized, energetic, bright, and confident" (p. 32). However, Hochschild noted that this was a "cultural cover up" for an overworked and frustrated woman.

Nancy Holt, a social worker and the mother of a son named Joey, found the idea of a supermom curiously useful. She had to face a terrible choice between having a stable marriage or an equal one, and she was to choose the stable marriage. She was to struggle hard to suppress her conflict with her husband and to perform an emotional cover-up. The supermom image appealed to her because it offered her a cultural cover-up to go with her emotional one (p. 32).

Cognitive Restructuring

Another strategy used by some women and men experiencing role overload and role conflict is cognitive restructuring, which involves choosing to view the situation in positive terms. In a study of dual-career couples, some spouses coped with the stress by "believing that our family life is better because both of us are employed," "believing there are more advantages than disadvantages to our lifestyle," and "believing that my career has made me a better wife/husband than I otherwise would be" (Schnittger & Bird, 1990, 201). Other examples of cognitive restructuring include, "I told myself that it wouldn't be the end of the world if I didn't get all my work done on time," and "I tried to recognize that I'd have to lower my standards about such things as how clean the house is and how elaborate the meals are" (Emmons et al., 1990).

> Nothing is either good or bad but thinking makes it so.
>
> SHAKESPEARE

> I discovered I always have choices and sometimes it's only a choice of attitude.
>
> JUDITH M. KNOWLTON

Delegation of Responsibility

A third way couples manage the demands of work and family is to delegate responsibility to others for performing certain tasks. Because women tend to bear most of the childcare and housework responsibility, they may choose to ask their partners to contribute more or to take responsibility for these tasks. Parents may also involve their children more in household tasks, which not only relieves the parents, but also benefits children by requiring them to learn domestic skills and the value of contributing to the family. If it is financially possible, someone may be hired to clean the house.

> If you do not ask their help, all men are good-natured.
>
> H. H. HART

NATIONAL DATA ❦ Nine percent of married couples spend an average of $1,265 on domestic services (Schwenk & Lino, 1992).

Two California entrepreneurs offered a "Rent-A-Wife" service to employed women and bachelors and found that 95 percent of their clientele were employed women (Bounds, 1992). Parents may also obtain help with childcare responsibilities by asking family members or friends to help out or by hiring a babysitter or other childcare surrogate.

Another form of delegating responsibility involves the decision to reduce one's current responsibilities and not take on additional responsibilities. For example, women and men may give up volunteer work and/or avoid agreeing to additional volunteer responsibilities or commitments. In the realm of paid work, women and men can choose not to become involved in professional activities beyond that which is required.

> **CONSIDERATION**
>
> The increased work and family demands on contemporary women and men have led to a decrease in volunteer work in our society (Moen, 1992). Individuals are often conflicted about their desire to participate in volunteer work and their desire to reduce their responsibilities. For some individuals, the social and personal benefits of participating in volunteer work may outweigh the strain it places on their already busy schedules. However, for other individuals, the time and energy costs of doing volunteer work outweigh the benefits.
>
> One possible solution for the person who wants to participate in volunteer work, yet also wants to spend more time with the family, is to find volunteer work in which one's partner (e.g., both parents attend PTA meetings) and/or children want to participate. One mother said, "My children and I have become involved in a community recycling awareness program. It's great because we are spending time together doing something that we enjoy and that makes a contribution to society" (Author's files).

Planning and Time Management

It is a bad plan that cannot be altered.

PUBLILIUS SYRUS

Still another strategy for coping with the demands of work and family is the use of planning and time management. This involves setting priorities and making lists of what needs to be done each day. Time planning also involves allocating time for activities regarded as important and not letting other pressures interfere with those activities. In addition, time planning involves trying to anticipate stressful periods and planning ahead for them.

> **CONSIDERATION**
>
> Emmons et al. (1990) compared women who used various strategies (super-woman, cognitive restructuring, delegation of responsibility, and planning and time management) for coping with the demands of work and family. They found that the only coping strategy consistently associated with a decrease in marital/parenting/job stress and an increase in overall well-being was planning and time management.

Shift Work

Some dual-earner couples attempt to solve the problem of childcare by one parent working during the day and the other parent working at night so that one parent can always be with the children.

NATIONAL DATA $\mathcal{S}$ Approximately 20 percent of the U.S. work force works nonstandard hours, or shift work (Liskowsky, 1992). Demand of the job is the most reported reason for working the late shift (Ingrassia & Springen, 1993)

Shift workers often experience sleep deprivation and fatigue, which may make it difficult for them to fulfill domestic roles as a parent or spouse (Liskowsky, 1992). Shift work also has a negative effect on marital relations, due to the lack of time the couple has together (White & Keith, 1990).

> **Shift work is a good place to hide a bad marriage. Some people choose shift work because they would like more independence from their family.**
>
> LYNN WHITE

CONSIDERATION

One alternative to the problem of parents being torn between work and family is for Congress to change the Fair Labor Standards Act to mandate a six-hour work day and a 30-hour work week as full-time work with full-time pay and benefits. "A shorter work week would reduce unemployment and, if designed to correspond with the school day, allow all workers—men and women—time for children and housework" (Horn, 1990, 22).

💥 Unemployment and Family Life

Some spouses do not have the problem of juggling the responsibilities of work and home because they are unemployed. However, unemployment poses its own set of challenges.

NATIONAL DATA 💥 In 1992, the unemployment rate was 7.4 percent (*Statistical Abstract of the United States: 1993*, Table 652). This means that 7.4 percent of the U.S. civilian noninstitutionalized population age 16 and older had no employment for at least four consecutive weeks, during which they tried to find a job. Unemployment rates for minorities are higher than the national average. In 1991 the unemployment rate was 14.1 for blacks, and 11.4 for Hispanics.

While over 55 percent of individuals who are unemployed are without a job for 10 weeks or less (*Statistical Abstract of the United States: 1993*, Table 652), the nonvoluntarily unemployed often experience lowered self-esteem and confidence, anxiety, depression, and alcohol abuse (Feather, 1990; Jones, 1992; Liem & Liem, 1990). These effects may be more severe for men than for women, because our society expects men to be the primary breadwinner in the family and equates masculine self-worth and identity with job and income.

> **I have lifted sand and carried salt, and there is nothing heavier than debt.**
>
> AHIKAR

Unemployment affects not only the individuals who lose their jobs, but their spouses and families as well.

> Wives and children of unemployed men are hit particularly hard because their economic well-being is often dependent on the employment of male breadwinners. . . . Wives experience stress not only from the need to live on reduced income but also because they are exposed to changes in their husbands' psychosocial functioning (Jones, 1992, 59).

Liem and Liem (1990) studied 82 families in which the husbands had recently lost their jobs and found that the wives reported increases in hostility,

Unemployment means more than standing in line to collect an unemployment check. In addition to one's standard of living, one's self esteem and relationship with spouse and children are affected.

depression, and anxiety. The degree to which they experience these negative reactions depended on their perception of how much the unemployed partner contributed to the family in nonmonetary ways (e.g., housework and childcare).

CONSIDERATION

Voydanoff (1991) noted that unemployment may influence major family choices. For example, couples experiencing unemployment may decide to postpone childbearing, move in with relatives, or have relatives or boarders join the household.

A family out of debt is out of danger.

P. PERCIVAL

Unemployment has also been associated with increased family violence (Straus, Gelles, & Steinmetz, 1980), and the stress of unemployment may precipitate divorce (Glyptis, 1989). However, couples who have a strong relationship may find that dealing with the stresses of unemployment may strengthen their relationship even more; couples who are in relationships characterized by unhappiness and discord may find that the pressures of unemployment increase the unhappiness and conflict in their relationship (Glyptis, 1989).

Even with a strong marriage, unemployment on the part of the spouse can be difficult. The experiences of a couple coping with the husband's unemployment are described in In Focus 11.2. While this husband chose to quit his job, more often unemployment results from being fired or laid off.

IN FOCUS 11.2

Unemployment: One Couple's Experience

THE UNEMPLOYED HUSBAND'S VIEW

Two years ago I was employed in a job in which I earned over $40,000 per year, including health and retirement benefits. I felt I could no longer tolerate the incessant demands being made on me so I quit my job, thinking that I would find another job that was more satisfying. My wife of 21 years and three children were aware of my frustrations, but did not want me to stop working until I had another job arranged. Things haven't been the same since I resigned.

Sometimes I feel happier being unemployed in that I no longer have to live with the frustrations that went along with my job. However, I have also experienced depression and suicidal thoughts over being without work. Job opportunities for a middle-aged man are limited. The jobs that are available do not pay much. In the past year I have worked in a convenience store, cut grass, and painted houses. I have also sent out over 45 resumes and interviewed for about 10 jobs. Often, the interviewer doesn't even call back or write to say I don't have the job.

The impact on my family has been both good and bad. The good side has been my availability to spend time with my two teenage children. The bad side is that we have plunged deeply into debt and have to watch how every penny is spent. I often feel that my family blames me for the economic hardships we are experiencing. Although I contribute to the family by working odd jobs and doing things around the house, I don't feel that my efforts are recognized or appreciated.

It isn't easy to be an unemployed male in our society— it's as though I'm nothing if I don't earn money. I resent this view. I've seen plenty of wealthy men who are bankrupt in their interpersonal relationships. They have the "things,"

those outward signs that show others they are successful, but they are not happy in their marriages and have distant relationships with their children.

THE EMPLOYED WIFE'S VIEW

I did not approve of my husband resigning his position. All jobs have their frustrations. I have tried to be supportive, but the longer he has gone without a steady job, the more resentful I have become.

I do not require a lot of money to be happy. I can be thrifty and frugal. But lack of money is intolerable when I don't know where the next meal is coming from and am afraid to answer the phone because it is probably another bill collector.

My husband's anger and quick temper also scare me. There are times I feel he is upset with himself for not having a job and I know he takes it out on me and the children. He expects us to overlook the fact that we are in this mess because of a decision he made.

I have an enjoyable job teaching preschool children but it doesn't pay enough to keep us afloat. I've had friends ask me why I stay married to him and I get embarrassed when people ask me if my husband has found a job yet. It isn't easy being poor compared to the middle-class life to which we were accustomed.

In spite of our economic situation, we continue to have some good times as a couple and as a family. I guess my biggest fear and worry is that I don't know how long my husband will be without stable employment. We won't divorce over this but it has and continues to put a lot of strain on our relationship.

Leisure in Our Lives and Relationships

Most of us feel we don't have enough leisure in our lives. Consider the following survey results (reported in Collins, 1991, and Schor, 1991):

- 70% of respondents making $30,000 or more said that they would like to give up a day's pay each week for one or two days off.

How beautiful it is to do nothing, and then rest afterward.

SPANISH PROVERB

- 20% of respondents said they had called in sick to work at least once in the past year when they simply needed more time to relax.
- Nearly a third of respondents worried that they didn't spend enough time with family and friends.
- 74% of men and 82% of women declared that they would sacrifice career advancement in order to spend more time with their families.

After defining leisure, we look at the benefits of leisure for our lives and relationships and discuss various factors that prevent many women and men from achieving adequate leisure in their lives.

Defining Leisure

Leisure has been defined in various ways (Henderson, Bialeschki, Shaw, & Freysinger, 1989; Schor, 1991). According to one view, leisure may be defined as participation in certain activities including socializing, sports, arts, and media. The problem with this definition is that different activities may be perceived as leisure by different people in different situations. For example, some people consider reading to be a leisure activity, while others feel that reading is arduous work.

Leisure has also been equated with "free time," or unobligated time away from paid employment and housework in which a person may choose what to do. However, some people may regard "free time" as empty and unfulfilling, rather than as leisure. Hence, most definitions of leisure emphasize the importance of the person's subjective experience as a defining criteria for leisure.

According to Henderson et al. (1989), researchers have identified a number of components of the leisure experience, including free choice or freedom from constraint, enjoyment, relaxation, and self-expression. We define leisure as the use of time to engage in freely chosen activity perceived as enjoyable and satisfying.

Benefits of Leisure for Individuals and Families

Leisure fulfills important functions in our individual and interpersonal lives (Henderson et al., 1989; Schor, 1991). Leisure activities may relieve work-related stress and pressure; facilitate social interaction and family togetherness; foster self-expression, personal growth, and skill development; and enhance overall social, physical, and emotional well-being.

The old adage, "The family that plays together stays together" reflects the belief that shared leisure activities strengthen family bonds. A number of studies support the association of shared leisure activities with marital stability and satisfaction. In a five-year longitudinal study, Hill (1988) found that the amount of shared leisure time, especially outdoor recreation, was associated with marital stability. Parallel leisure activities, which involve sharing time but

Leisure time, not money, is the status symbol of the 90s.

JOHN ROBINSON

with minimal interaction (such as watching television) were also found to be associated with marital stability.

Smith, Snyder, and Monsma (1988) found that marital satisfaction could be predicted by the proportion of leisure time spouses spent together. In contrast, engaging in leisure activities alone or with persons other than the spouse was predictive of marital discord.

CONSIDERATION

While leisure represents a means of family togetherness and enjoyment, it may also represent an area of stress and conflict. In a national survey, one-third of U.S. families reported they experienced stress from conflicts over the use of leisure time. Conflicts related to the use of leisure time were reported to be more stressful than childrearing or finances (Straus, Gelles, & Steinmetz, 1980).

Spending leisure time together may also be beneficial only if communication patterns between the partners are good (Holman & Jacquart, 1988). Couples who are prone to physical violence, have differences in their respective values, and who exhibit disrespect have higher marital tension and lower marital quality the longer they spend time together (Rosenblatt, Titus, Nevalding, & Cunningham, 1979).

℘ Barriers to Leisure

As noted at the beginning of this section, individuals feel they do not have enough leisure. What factors have contributed to the "leisure shortage" many women and men complain about? Barriers to leisure include the rising demands of the workplace, traditional gender roles, materialistic values, and the commodification of leisure.

Demands of the Workplace

A major barrier to leisure has been the rising demands of the workplace. Many jobs demand employees work overtime; other jobs pay so little that an employee must take a second job or work two shifts in order to make ends meet.

The 5:00 Dads of the 1950s and 1960s (those who were home for dinner and an evening with the family) are becoming an "endangered species." Thirty percent of men with children under fourteen report working fifty or more hours a week. And many of these 8:00 or 9:00 Dads aren't around on the weekends either. Thirty percent of them work Saturdays and/or Sundays (Schor, 1991, 21).

Regarding women, studies estimate that the working time of employed mothers averages between 65 and 89 hours per week (Schor, 1991). Very little time is left over after the responsibilities of work and home have been met, and

There is no such thing as a workaholic if you enjoy what you are doing.
DONALD TRUMP

Either I can spend time with my family or support them—not both.
MASSACHUSETTS FACTORY WORKER

women and men have very little energy to participate in leisure activities after working for 9 to 16 hours a day.

CONSIDERATION

Adult women and men in the United States spend an average of 15 hours a week watching television (Robinson, 1990). According to Robinson's estimates, 38 percent of the total leisure time of women and men is spent watching TV. This may be partly due to the fact that people are too tired to engage in more active leisure activities. However, when a national sample of women and men were asked, "If there were one more hour in the day, how would you spend it?" the most common response was "participate in active sports;" only 1 percent said they would watch more TV.

Adults are not the only ones working long hours. Schor (1991) reported that by 1990, 53.7 percent of U.S. teens were in the workforce, nearly 10 points higher than it had been in 1965. While some lower-income families cannot survive economically without the income generated by teenage children, many middle-class teenagers work for consumeristic reasons—expensive clothes, the latest CD sound system, and a car. Participating in the workforce may teach the value of work and money and importance of education to avoid being stuck in low-wage jobs. However, working too many hours may interfere with one's education. "Teachers report that students are falling asleep in class, getting lower grades, and cannot pursue after-school activities" (Schor, 1991, 27).

Materialistic Values

The media bombards us daily with advertisements that increase our aspirations to have the things that money can buy. So we work long and hard hours to achieve a certain standard of living. Once we have achieved that standard of living, we may choose to scale back the time devoted to work and devote more time to leisure and our family. However, once we attain the goods that we desire, we often find we want more. Thus, many couples get caught up in a vicious cycle of working long hours to achieve a certain standard of living, only to find that their standard of living rises again.

Schor (1991) suggested that gaining leisure in our lives may mean "stepping off the consumer treadmill, which requires altering a way of life and a way of thinking" (p. 157). One person made a choice to scale back on lifestyle:

> You either have to make the money which will buy you the kind of life that you think you have to have, or you can change those expectations and you don't need the money anymore. And that's what I've done (Harriman, 1982, cited in Schor, 1991, 158).

Riches take away more pleasures than they give.

S. G. CHAMPION

CONSIDERATION

Many societies recognize the importance of leisure in everyday life. The *siesta* (afternoon time of rest) is a tradition in Mexico. In France, many workers and school children take two-hour lunch breaks. Even so-called primitive peoples, who are commonly thought to live a harsh life; spend relatively little time doing work. Schor (1991) noted that,

> If the Kapauku of Papua work one day, they do no labor on the next. !Kung Bushmen put in only two and a half days per week and six hours per day. In the Sandwich Islands of Hawaii, men work only four hours per day. And Australian aborigines have similar schedules. . . . They are materially poor by contemporary standards, but in at least one dimension—time—we have to count them richer (p. 10).

Traditional Gender Roles

Traditional gender roles may also create barriers to leisure in the lives of women and men. Whether employed or unemployed, women bear most of the responsibility for childrearing, housework, and general care of the family. The result is that women have little time for leisure. Women also tend to spend their leisure time engaged in hobbies related to household tasks, such as preserving and canning fruits and vegetables, cooking, and sewing (Henderson, 1990; Shelton, 1992). In addition, women's leisure is often combined with household chores (Henderson et al., 1989). For example, women often watch TV while they iron clothes, talk on the phone with a friend while cooking in the kitchen, socialize with neighbors while looking after the children, listen to music while cleaning house, or clip coupons and make a grocery list while riding a stationary bicycle. In addition, women's leisure activities are often constrained by the leisure needs of the family. For example, a woman may spend an afternoon at the pool, but may do so primarily to provide her children a fun day at the pool. Similarly, a woman may walk in the park primarily so her children may enjoy the playground or feed the ducks at the pond. (It is also true that some fathers schedule their leisure activities in reference to their children).

> As women seek to have choices in all aspects of their lives, they desire options and choices within leisure as well.
>
> KARLA A. HENDERSON
> M. DEBORAH BIALESCHKI
> SUSAN M. SHAW
> VALERIE J. FREYSINGER

CONSIDERATION

Many full-time housewives feel that, because they do not earn an income, they are not entitled to leisure (Henderson et al., 1989). Participation in the paid workforce may place increased demands on a woman's time and leave less time for leisure. However, Henderson et al. (1989) noted that employed women may be more likely to become involved in leisure activities because of their work affiliations, increased disposable income, and sense of entitlement to leisure.

Shaw (1990) noted that family recreational activities often represent a great deal of work for women—more so than for men. For example, a family picnic involves shopping for and packing the food and cleaning up the picnic site afterwards—tasks that are traditionally viewed as women's work. Going on a family vacation involves many tasks also done primarily by women, including packing the suitcases, canceling the newspaper delivery for the week, packing snacks for the car ride, making arrangements with the neighbors to feed the cat and get the mail, and unpacking the suitcases after returning from vacation. In addition, women may do more of the emotional work of trying to ensure that all family members have a good time. It is not uncommon to hear women say that after taking a family vacation, they need another vacation to recover!

Holidays provide another example of how gender roles constrain women's leisure. After the Thanksgiving holidays, many women are exhausted by the hours of cooking they did to achieve the perfect Thanksgiving meal. Christmas holidays also represent a great deal of work for women. Traditionally, women in our society who celebrate Christmas have learned it is their primary responsibility to do the Christmas shopping, mail the Christmas presents and cards, put up decorations, and bake Christmas cookies. Many women spend considerable time and energy to ensure that Christmas is a positive experience for the family. But many drive themselves to exhaustion during the process.

Women's leisure is also constrained by safety concerns. Women are less likely to use parks at certain hours or to participate in outdoor activities if they are fearful of their safety (Henderson, 1990).

Men's leisure is also affected by gender role expectations which equate a man's self-worth with his income and put men in the role of primary breadwinner. One man said,

> Being a man means being willing to put all your waking hours into working to support your family. If you ask for time off, or if you turn down overtime, it means you're lazy or you're a wimp (cited in Schor, 1991, 149).

> Organizing family activities and creating environments and situations conducive to family leisure takes effort and work, and this work falls disproportionately to women.
>
> SUSAN M. SHAW

Commodification of Leisure

Many leisure activities cost money that families simply do not have in their budget. One father said, "I used to take the family to a movie every weekend. Not anymore. After you add the cost of popcorn and drinks, I just can't afford it" (Author's files). Schor (1991) described the "commodification of leisure" in our society.

> Private corporations have dominated the leisure "market" encouraging us to think of free time as a consumption opportunity. Vacations, hobbies, popular entertainment, eating out, and shopping itself are all costly forms of leisure. How many of us, if asked to describe an ideal weekend, would choose activities that cost nothing? How resourceful are we about doing things without spending money? (p. 162)

৪ Trends

The trend toward women in the workforce will continue. In 1940, only one in four (25 percent) workers was a woman. By the twenty-first century, it is estimated that almost half (48 percent) of all workers will be women (Moen, 1992).

The increasing number of women in the workforce will be accompanied by increases in governmental and company policies designed to help women and men balance their work and family roles. In 1993, President Clinton signed into law the Family Leave Act, which states that all companies with 50 or more employees must provide up to 12 weeks of unpaid leave for reasons of family illness, birth, or adoption of a child. The time may be taken in short time units (e.g. an employee wants to cut back following the birth of a child). However, the U.S. still lags behind other countries in providing paid time off for new parents (e. g. Germany provides 14 weeks off with 100 percent salary replacement) (Caminiti, 1992).

Private companies and employers will adopt new personnel policies and benefits that address the family concerns of their employees. Such policies and benefits will include assistance with childcare, assistance with elderly parent care, part-time employment options (including job sharing), flextime, and relocation assistance (Deitsch, 1992; Dychtwald, 1990; Moen, 1992). PepsiCo Inc. in Purchase, New York has an on-site concierge to do personal chores for its 800 employees (Lopez, 1993). However, such a service is rare and, in general, companies currently do very little to provide help for parents and their children. A national survey of 875 workplaces where 50 or more people were employed revealed that only 7.2 percent had on-site or near-site child care programs (Shellenbarger, 1996).

An increasing number of employers will allow individuals to work at home (telecommuting). New technologies for data processing and electronic communication, such as the facsimile machine (fax), have made it possible for more and more people to work at home and simultaneously manage their work and family roles. In 1993 there were about 8 million telecommuters (Brau, 1993).

Another trend is to be self-employed in a home-based business. From 1988 to 1992, the self-employment figure for full-time home workers grew 9 percent (Washer, 1993). Working at home, whether for an employer or for one's own business, has some major advantages. These include "avoiding commuting," "wearing comfortable clothing," and "taking care of children while on the job" (Brau, 1993, 41–42). One self-employed woman who works at home commented that she liked the flexibility working at home allows: "I can pick up my daughter from school when I want to, or even get on the portable phone and go downstairs to knead some bread for dinner while I'm working" (cited in Washer, 1993, 46). According to Brau (1993), "as middle-aged baby boomers lose their enthusiasm for salaried jobs, working at home may become a more mainstream option" (p. 8).

Home workers claim that they are more relaxed, have a healthier diet, exercise more often, and have a better sex life than do nonhome workers.

PATRICIA BRAU

✦ CHOICES ✦

---

*A*mong the choices couples face is whether to allow their children to be "home alone" while the parents work, and responding to the possibility of involvement in a romantic relationship while at work.

Allow Children to Stay Home Without Adult Supervision?

Many dual-earner and single-parent families do not have the resources to afford childcare while the parent is working. While relatives and friends may help, over two million children aged 5 to 13 are not supervised by an adult for some time after school (Cain & Hofferth, 1989). While these self-care or "latch-key children" often fend for themselves very well, some are at risk. Over 230,000 are between the ages of five and seven and are vulnerable to a lack of care in case of an accident or emergency.

Children who must spend time alone at home should know the following:

1. How to reach their parents at work (the phone number, extension number, and name of the person to talk to if the parent is not there).
2. Their home address and phone number in case information must be given to the fire department or an ambulance service.
3. How to call emergency services, such as the police and fire departments.

4. The name and number of a relative or neighbor to call if the parent is unavailable.
5. To keep the door locked and not let anyone in.
6. Not to tell callers their parents are not at home. (They are busy or can't come to the phone.)
7. Not to play with appliances, matches, or the fireplace.

Parents should also consider the relationship of the children they leave alone. If the older one terrorizes the younger one, the children should not be left alone. Also, if the younger one is out of control, it is questionable to put the older one in a role of responsibility. If something goes wrong (there is an accident), the older child may be unnecessarily burdened with guilt.

Become Involved in a Romantic Relationship at Work?

Because the number of employed women has increased in recent years, and because more women are entering previously male-dominated professions, more men and women are working together. The workplace has become a major source of intimate interaction as women and men share the physical proximity of working side by side over a long period of time.

Marcy Crary (1988) conducted research on attraction and intimacy in the workplace. She interviewed men

and women whose workplaces included financial service companies, consulting groups, mental health clinics, state agencies, hospitals, and universities. She found that one aspect of managing relationship attraction at work involves the dilemma of whether to discuss the attraction to the other person. She suggested that "the difficulty of *not* discussing the attraction is that one can end up with pent-up energy, which can in turn lead to a preoccupation with the attraction . . ." (p. 464). However, some people fear that if they disclose their feelings of attraction to other person, they must not only deal with their feelings, but the feelings of the other person as well. The other person may also pressure the individual to act on their attraction. One woman consultant said:

I chose to tell him that I was attracted to him but that for a number of reasons I was not going to act on it. This was in response to his telling me that he found me very attractive. Well, it turned out that in telling him I was attracted to him I had made the situation much worse. He continued to pursue the issue, so much so that it almost felt like sexual harassment. I then chose to back off from working with him because he was making it so difficult (Crary, 1988, 464).

Being attracted to someone at work may or may not lead to the develop-

⌁ CHOICES ⌁

ment of an intimate relationship. Even if the relationship is emotionally intimate, it may not involve sex. But managing office attractions may be difficult. Crary (1988) identified the following basic issues involved in intimate relationships at work:

1. *Balancing intimacy and work with the same person.* Some people find it difficult to balance the role of lover with their work responsibilities. One financial services employee who had developed a romantic relationship with a female co-worker described the problem of balancing work responsibilities and relationship expectations:

   > She walks into my office unannounced, and I don't have the time to be with her. . . . This was interfering with my performance at work. I felt I should spend time with her and I couldn't; she didn't like that (Crary, 1988, 467).

2. *Dealing with outsiders' views of the relationship.* Co-workers in close relationships are subject to being negatively judged by others at work. Other workers may assume that a close relationship is sexual, whether it is actually true. Other workers also feel a lack of objectivity and unfairness to other workers may result from having too close relationships at work. Some women

The consequences of becoming involved in a romantic relationship at work must be carefully considered.

fear "the classic accusation that associates a woman's rise in an organization with her sexual activity rather than with her competence" (Crary, 1988, 468).

Another concern for those involved in "office romances" is how management views intimate relationships at work. While some organizations are not concerned about romantic relationships at work, other organizations view such relationships as inappropriate and have formal policies and sanctions against them. One study

found that 12.7 percent of the organizations surveyed have a formal policy against unmarried bosses dating subordinates and 13 percent have a formal policy against employees marrying each other and continuing to hold their same job. Only 1.2 percent have a formal policy against unmarried employees living together and 0.4 percent have a policy against unmarried co-workers dating each other (Ford & McLaughlin, 1988).

3. *Dealing with changes in the relationship.* Over time, all relationships experience various changes including varying degrees of involvement and commitment. Changes in the relationship may become particularly problematic in the work setting when one partner wants to make changes, but the other one does not. For example, in an intimate but nonsexual relationship, one partner may want to become sexually involved, but the other does not. Or, one partner in an ongoing sexual relationship may want to discontinue having sex or may become disinterested in continuing the relationship. While relationship changes may be problematic in general, in the workplace they may interfere with job security, job performance, and/or one's comfort and enjoyment at the workplace.

✋ Summary

Money is a source of self-esteem, power in relationships, security, and conflict. It may also be used as an expression of love or the absence of it. In regard to the latter, divorced people rarely give each other money unless ordered to do so by the court.

Women have entered the labor force with increasing frequency. In 1900 only 20 percent of U.S. women were employed. In 1994, the figure is likely to be over 60 percent. Women are least likely to work outside the home when their children are under one year of age and most likely to do so when their children reach the teen years.

The proportion of women who work for paid employment varies by society. In Western Africa labor force participation by women ranges from three or four percent to as much as 85 percent in Sweden. In the United States, women are more likely to have jobs than careers. Responsibility for children, lack of support from the husband, and lack of role models contribute to the fewer number of career women than men.

An increasing number of couples are in dual-earner relationships. Benefits for women being involved in paid employment include enhanced self-esteem, power in the relationship, and independence. Negatives for women include exhaustion due to role overload and frustration or guilt due to role conflict. Women who report the highest levels of employment satisfaction are those who want to work, work part time, and have husbands who are supportive of their employment.

Men benefit from their wives' employment by being relieved of full responsibility for the financial support of the family, freedom to change jobs, and having a partner with whom to share the concerns of the work world. Men who report being dissatisfied with their wives' employment interpret such employment as a reflection of their own inadequacy to support the family. Some men are also torn between their work and family responsibilities.

Couples in dual–earner relationships tend to report positive effects. Not only do they have a higher income, they report having similar experiences and concerns to talk about. A major drawback of involvement in a dual-earner marriage is the lack of time together.

Children seem to experience no direct negative effects from both parents being employed. Rather, children may enjoy having more money in the family (for cable TV, music lessons, karate training) and daughters may benefit from observing an employed mother as a role model. Disadvantages include less time with parents, a higher level of stress at home, and more restricted activities if parents are not available to transport children.

Housework is generally done by the wife. However, if the wife is employed, the husband is more likely to participate in housework and childcare. Men who help with housework are more likely to have egalitarian gender role attitudes, make less money than their wives, and are unemployed.

Strategies used for balancing the demands of work and family include the superperson strategy, cognitive restructuring, delegation of responsibility, and planning and time management. A researcher who compared the various strategies found that time management was the most effective.

Spouses and couples are increasingly beginning to value their leisure. Such leisure helps to relieve stress, facilitate social interaction and family togetherness, and foster personal growth and skill development. However, leisure may also create conflict over how to use leisure time.

Barriers to having enough leisure time include incessant demands of the workplace, materialistic values (which requires work to earn the money to buy "things"), traditional gender roles (women do most of the work during holidays), and commodification of leisure. The latter refers to the idea that you need to spend money in order to have a good time.

Trends in work and leisure include more women being employed, increased government support of dual-earner families in the form of unpaid leave for family-related concerns, increased profamily policies by private companies in the form of assistance in childcare/flex time/relocation, and more individuals working at home in response to the computer revolution.

Choices in regard to employment involve deciding the conditions under which children may be left alone at home and managing romantic feelings of attraction to a co-worker.

Questions for Reflection

1. Would you rather have a salary increase or a reduction in the number of hours your employer expects you to work?
2. In regard to the employment of both spouses, to what degree do you feel infants should or should not be taken care of by someone other than the parents?
3. What is your ideal lifestyle in regard to job or career, part-time or full-time employment, and one- or two-earner relationship?

References

Adelmann, P. K., T. C. Antonucci, S. E. Crohan, and L. M. Coleman. Empty nest, cohort, and employment in the well-being of midlife women. *Sex Roles*, 1989, 173–189.

Ahlburg, D. A. and C. J. DeVita. New realities of the American family. *Population Bulletin*, 1992, 47, 1–44.

Atkinson, M. P. and J. Boles. WASP (Wives as Senior Partners). *Journal of Marriage and the Family*, 1984, 46, 861–870.

Barnett, R. C. and G. K. Baruch. Determinants of fathers' participation in family work. *Journal of Marriage and the Family*, 1987, 49, 29–40.

Benin, H. and D. A. Edwards. Adolescents' chores: The differences between dual- and single-earner families. *Journal of Marriage and the Family*, 1990, 52, 361–373.

Berg, B. *The crisis of the working mother.* New York: Summit Books, 1986.

Bielby, W. T. and D. D. Bielby. I will follow him: Family ties, gender-role beliefs, and reluctance to relocate for a better job. *The American Journal of Sociology,* 1992, *97,* 1241–1268.

Blair, S. L. Employment, family, and perceptions of marital quality among husbands and wives. *Journal of Family Issues,* 1993, *14,* 189–212.

Blaylock, J. R. and D. M. Smallwood. Intrahousehold time allocation: The case of grocery shopping. *Journal of Consumer Affairs,* 1987, *21,* 183–201.

Blumstein, P. and P. Schwartz. Money and ideology: Their impact on power and the division of household labor. *Gender, Family, and Economy.* R. L. Blumberg, ed. Newbury Park, Calif.: Sage Publications, 1991, 261–288.

Bolger, Naill, A. DeLongis, R. C. Kessler, and E. Wethington. The contagion of stress across multiple roles. *Journal of Marriage and the Family,* 1989, *51,* 175–183.

Bounds, W. Rent-A-Wife is cleaning up. *The Daily Reflector,* Greenville, NC, September 2, 1992, d-3.

Brau, P. Homework for grownups. *American Demographics,* 1993, August, 38–42.

Brayfield, April A. Employment resources and housework in Canada. *Journal of Marriage and the Family,* 1992, *54,* 19–30.

Cain, Virginia S. and Sandra L. Hofferth. Parental choice of self-care for school-age children. *Journal of Marriage and the Family,* 1989, *51,* 65–77.

Caminiti, S. Who's minding America's kids? *Fortune,* 1992, August 10, 50–53.

Chafe, W. H. Looking backward in order to look forward: Women, work, and social values in America. *Women and the American Economy: A Look to the 1980s,* J. M. Dreps, ed. Englewood Cliffs, N.J.: Prentice-Hall, 1976, 6–30.

Chant, S. Family structure and female labour in Queretaro, Mexico. *Next of Kin,* L. Tepperman and S. J. Wilson, eds. Englewood Cliffs, N.J.: Prentice-Hall, Inc., 1993, 205–210.

Collins, Gail. Why no one wants to work anymore. *Working Woman,* November 1991, *16,* no. 11, 160.

Crary, M. Managing attraction and intimacy at work. *The Work and Family Sourcebook,* Fairles E. Winfield, ed. Greenvale, N.Y.: Panel Publishers, Inc., 1988, 459–474.

Crispell, Diane. Dual disparity (earnings of working women). *American Demographics,* 1989, *7,* 16–18.

Crosby, F. E. *Juggling: The unexpected advantages of balancing career and home for women and their families.* New York: The Free Press, 1993.

Deitsch, M. Work and family: What are companies doing? *Financial Executive,* 1992, *8,* 60–61.

Dychtwald, Ken. *Age wave.* New York: Bantam Books, 1990.

Edwards, John N., T. D. Fuller, S. Varkitphokatorn, and S. Sermsri. Female employment and marital instability: Evidence from Thailand. *Journal of Marriage and the Family,* 1992, *54,* 59–68.

Emmons, C., M. Biernat, L. B. Tiedje, E. L. Lang, and C. B. Wortman. Stress, support, and coping among women professionals with preschool children. *Stress Between Work and Family,* J. Eckenrode and S. Gore, eds. New York: Pienum Press, 1990, 61–93.

Feather, Norman T. *The psychological impact of unemployment.* New York: Springer-Verlag, 1990.

Floge, Liliane. Changing household structure, child-care availability, and employment among mothers of preschool children. *Journal of Marriage and the Family,* 1989, *51,* 51–63.

Folk, K. F. and A. H. Beller. Part-time work and childcare choices for mothers of preschool children. *Journal of Marriage and the Family,* 1993, 55, 146–157.

Ford, R. C. and F. S. McLaughlin. Should Cupid come to the workplace? An ASPA survey. *The Work and Family Sourcebook,* F. E. Winfield, ed. Greenvale, New York: Panel Publishers, Inc., 1988, 449–457.

Gerson, K. *Hard choices: How women decide about work, career and motherhood.* Berkeley, Calif.: University of California Press, 1991.

Glezer, H. Juggling work and family commitments. *Family Matters,* April 1991, *28,* 6–11.

Glyptis, S. *Leisure and unemployment.* Philadelphia: Open University Press, 1989.

Godwin, D. D. and J. Scanzoni. Couple consensus during marital joint decision making: A context, process, outcome model. *Journal of Marriage and the Family,* 1989, *51,* 943–956.

Hardesty, C. and J. Bokemeier. Finding time and making do: Distribution of household labor in non-metropolitan marriages. *Journal of Marriage and the Family,* 1989, *51,* 253–267.

Henderson, Karla A. The meaning of leisure for women: An integrative review of the research. *Journal of Leisure Research,* 1990, *22,* 228–243.

Henderson, K. A., M. D. Bialeschki, S. M. Shaw, and V. J. Freysinger. *A leisure of one's own: A feminist perspective on women's leisure.* State College, Penn.: Venture Publishing, Inc., 1989.

Hill, M. S. Marital stability and spouses' shared time: A multidisciplinary hypothesis. *Journal of Family Issues,* 1988, *9,* 427–451.

Hilton, J., L. Baird, and V. Haldeman. Comparison of finances, stress, and satisfaction in one-earner and two-earner rural families. Paper, 54th Annual Conference, National Council on Family Relations, Orlando, Florida, 1992. Used by permission.

Hobbs, B. and H. Rodman. Activities and social contact of self-care children. *Proceedings: Families and Work.* National Council on Family Relations, 54th Annual Conference, 1992, 2, no. 1, 51.

Hochschild, A. *The second shift.* New York: Viking Press, 1989.

Holman, T. B., and M. Jacquart. Leisure-activity patterns and marital satisfaction: A further test. *Journal of Marriage and the Family,* 1988, *50,* 69–77.

Horn, P. Creating a family policy. *Dollars & Sense,* January/February 1990, *22,* 6–8.

Hughes, Diane, E. Galinsky, and A. Morris. The effects of job characteristics on marital quality: Specifying linking mechanisms. *Journal of Marriage and the Family,* 1992, *54,* 31–42.

Ingrassia, M. and K. Springer. Living on dracula time. *Newsweek,* 1993, July 12, 68–69.

Israelsen, C. L. Family resource management. *Family Research: A Sixty-Year Review,* S. J. Bahr, ed. New York: Lexington Books, 1991, *1,* 171–234.

Jones, L. His unemployment and her reaction: The effect of husbands' unemployment on wives. *Affilia: Journal of Women and Social Work,* 1992, *7,* 7–20.

Kamo, Y. Determinants of household division of labor: Resources, power and ideology. *Journal of Family Issues,* 1988, *9,* 177–200.

Liem, J. H. and G. R. Liem. Understanding the individual and family effects of unemployment. *Stress Between Work and Family,* J. Eckenrode and S. Gore, eds. New York: Plenum Press, 1990, 175–204.

Liskowsky, David R. Biological rhythms and shift work. *Journal of the American Medical Association,* December 2, 1992, *268,* 3047.

Lopez, J. A. Undivided attention: How PepsiCo gets work out of people. *The Wall Street Journal,* April 1, 1993, *221,* 1.

Lye, D. N. and T. J. Biblarz. The effects of attitudes toward family life and gender roles on marital satisfaction. *Journal of Family Issues,* 1993, *14,* 157–158.

Margolis, Maxine. *Mothers and such: Views of American women and why they changed.* Berkeley: University of California Press, 1984.

Mederer, H. J. Division of labor in two-earner homes: Task accomplishment versus household management as critical variables in perceptions about family work. *Journal of Marriage and the Family,* 1993, *55,* 133–145.

Menaghan, E. G. and T. L. Parcel. Parental employment and family life: Research in the 1980s. *Contemporary Families: Looking Forward, Looking Back,* A. Booth ed. Minneapolis: National Council on Family Relations, 1991, 361–380.

Moen, Phyllis. *Women's two roles: A contemporary dilemma.* New York: Auburn House, 1992.

Perry-Jenkins, M. and A. C. Crouter. Men's provider-role attitudes: Implications for household work and marital satisfaction. *Journal of Family Issues,* 1990, *11,* 136–156.

Peterson, K. S. Kids without siblings get their due. *USA Today,* March 1, 1993, D1–D2.

Riza, W. R., R. N. Singh, and V. T. Davis. Differences among males and females in their perception of spousal abuse. *Free Inquiry in Creative Sociology,* 1992, *20,* 19–24.

Robinson, John P. The leisure pie. *American Demographics*, 1990, 12, no. 9, 39.

Rosenblatt, P. C, S. L. Titus, A. Nevaldine, and M. R. Cunningham. Marital system differences and summer-long vacations: Togetherness-apartness and tension. *American Journal of Family Therapy*, 1979, 7, 77–84.

Ross, C. E. The division of labor at home. *Social Forces*, 1987, 65, 816–833.

Rubenstein, C. Guilty or not guilty. *Working Mother*, May 1991, 53–56.

Schnittger, M. H. and G. W. Bird. Coping among dual-career men and women across the family life cycle. *Family Relations*, 1990, 39, 199–205.

Schor, Juliet B. *The overworked American: The unexpected decline of leisure.* (no place of publication given in book) Basic Books, 1991.

Schroeder, K. A., L. L. Blood, and D. Maluso. Gender differences and similarities between male and female undergraduate students regarding expectations for career and family roles. *College Student Journal*, 1993, 27, 237–249.

Schwartz, P. and D. Jackson. How to have a model marriage. *New Woman*, February 1989, 66–74.

Schwenk, F. N. and M. Lino. Purchase of domestic services by husband-wife households. Paper, 54th Annual Conference, National Council on Family Relations, Orlando, Florida, 1992. Used by permission.

Sears, H. A. and N. L. Galambos. Women's work conditions and marital adjustment in two-earner couples: A structural model. *Journal of Marriage and the Family*, 1992, 54, 789–797.

Shaw, Susan M. Deifying family leisure: An examination of women's and men's everyday experiences and perceptions of family time. *Leisure Sciences*, 1992, 14, no. 4, 271–286.

Shellenbarger, Sue. Work and family: So much talk, so little action. *The Wall Street Journal*, June 21, 1993b, et passim.

Shellenbarger, Sue. Longer commutes force parents to make tough choices where to leave the kids. *The Wall Street Journal*, August 18, 1993a, B1.

Shelton, Beth Anne. *Women, men, and time: Gender differences in paid work, housework, and leisure.* New York: Greenwood Press, 1992.

Silberstein, L. R. *Dual career marriage: A system in transition.* Hillsdale, N.J.: Lawrence Erlbaum Associates, 1992.

Smith, G. T., T. J. Snyder, and B. R. Monsma. Predicting relationship satisfaction from couples' use of leisure time. *American Journal of Family Therapy*, 1988, 16, 3–13.

Spitze, G. Women's employment and family relations: A review. *Contemporary Families: Looking Forward, Looking Back*, A. Booth, ed. Minneapolis: National Council on Family Relations, 1991, 381–404.

Statistical Abstract of the United States: 1993, 113th ed. Washington, D.C.: U.S. Bureau of the Census, 1993.

Strauss, M., R. Gelles, and S. Steinmetz. *Behind closed doors.* New York: Doubleday, 1980.

Tepperman, L. and S. J. Wilson. *Next of kin: An international reader of changing families.* Englewood Cliffs, N.J.: Prentice Hall, 1993.

Thomas, V. G. Determinants of global life happiness and marital happiness in dual-career black couples. *Family Relations*, 1990, 39, 174–178.

Thornton, A. The influence of the parental family on the attitudes and behavior of children. *The Changing American Family*, S. J. South and S. E. Tolnay, eds. Boulder, Co.: Westview Press, 1992, 247–266.

Townsend, B. and K. O'Neil. American women get mad. *American Demographics*, 1990, 12, 26–32.

Vannoy, D. and W. W. Philliber. Wife's employment and quality of marriage. *Journal of Marriage and the Family*, 1992, 54, 387–398.

Volling, B. L. and J. Belsky. Parent, infant, and contextual characteristics related to maternal employment decisions in the first year of infancy. *Family Relations*, 1993, 42, 4–12.

Voydanoff, P. Economic distress and family relations: A review of the eighties. *Contemporary Families: Looking Forward, Looking Back,* A. Booth, ed. Minneapolis: National Council on Family Relations, 1991, 429–445.

Washer, Louise. Home alone: The best home-based business strategies. *Working Woman,* March 1993, 45–50.

White, L. K., and D. B. Brinkerhoff. Children's work in the family: Its significance and meaning. *Journal of Marriage and the Family,* 1981, *43,* 789–798.

White, L. and B. Keith. The effect of shift work on the quality and stability of marital relations. *Journal of Marriage and the Family,* 1990, *52,* 453–462.

Willie, D. E. Maternal employment: Impact on maternal behavior. *Family Relations,* 1992, *41,* 273–277.

Yoger, S. and J. M. Brett. Professional couples and money. *Family Perspective,* 1989, *23,* 31–38.

❧ 12 ❧
CHAPTER

Violence and Abuse in Relationships

Contents

Is It True?

1. In most cases of rape, the offender is an acquaintance or dating partner of the victim.

2. Most women who are physically abused by their partners do not experience abuse until after they have married the abuser.

3. A cross-cultural study of family violence found that in most societies, alcohol plays a significant role in family violence.

4. Battering is the single major cause of injury to women in the United States.

5. In order to report child abuse or neglect to the authorities, one must have proof that child abuse or neglect has occurred.

1 = T; 2 = T; 3 = F; 4 = T; 5 = F

I was only nine years old when I was raped by my 19-year-old cousin. He was the first of three family members to sexually molest me.

OPRAH WINFREY

*A*n abused spouse lamented that she was drawn to her partner with deep feelings of love and intimacy. She detailed a long courtship which included "tender affection from the man I loved." But this haven of intimacy turned into a nightmare of violence and abuse.

How strange that relationships, which begin with such tenderness, can become so abusive. Indeed, relationships between dating partners, cohabiting lovers, spouses, siblings, and parents and their children provide some of the most rewarding and fulfilling experiences in our lives. Yet these same relationships may become the source of our deepest pain, anxiety, and despair. In this chapter we turn to the dark side of relationships and examine violence and abuse in dating, cohabitation, marriage, and family relationships.

> Although family violence receives considerably more attention today, it has been a part of the family throughout its history ..
>
> RICHARD GELLES

✦ Definitions of Violence and Abuse

Violence in relationships refers to the intentional use of physical force by an individual aimed at hurting or injuring another person (Busby, 1991). Violence, which may take the form of hitting, kicking, and the use of objects to hurt another person, is not uncommon in domestic relationships.

NATIONAL DATA ✦ In 1991, about 1.37 million domestic violent crimes were reported to police. About 83 percent of the victims were women. Over 20 percent of all aggravated assaults reported to the police are assaults involving domestic violence in the home (Majority Staff of the Senate Judiciary Committee, 1992).

Verbal abuse is a common form of abuse in relationships.

> **CONSIDERATION**
>
> Official reports of domestic violence do not reflect the actual number of incidents of domestic violence because most incidents are not reported. It is estimated that only 10 percent of violent episodes in the home are reported to police (National Clearinghouse for the Defense of Battered Women, 1990). Both men and women are reluctant to report abuse in the home.

Physical violence is only one form of abuse in relationships. Another form of abuse in relationships is verbal abuse, which causes mental or psychological distress. Although the traditional nursery rhyme teaches children that "Sticks and stones may break my bones, but words can never hurt me," words can and do hurt when they are used to denigrate or threaten another person. Straus and

> Many women perceive psychological abuse to be more painful and damaging than physical abuse.
>
> CHRISTOPHER MURPHY
> MICHELE CASCARDI

Sweet (1992) noted that abuse may also take the form of nonverbal symbolic behavior, which is "intended to cause psychological pain to another person, or perceived as having that intent" (p. 347). Examples of nonverbal symbolic abusive behavior include slamming a door, smashing an object or destroying a person's property, tearing up a photograph, and stony silence or sulking.

> ### CONSIDERATION
>
> Some research has found gender differences in perceptions of what constitutes abuse in relationships. For example, over 70 percent of men in an undergraduate class reported that "taking away my billfold" constituted "spousal abuse" whereas only 45 percent of women undergraduates in the same class agreed (Riza et al., 1992). Similarly, over 90 percent of the women compared to only 29 percent of the men agreed that "physically handles the other" is a phrase that describes abusive behavior (p. 20).

Force is not a remedy.

JOHN BRIGHT

Abuse may also involve neglecting to provide care (e.g., food, medical treatment, and personal hygiene) for a child or dependent adult. (In Illinois, neglect is defined separately from abuse) Lastly, abuse in relationships may involve using force or coercion to engage in sexual activity with a child or nonconsenting adult. We begin this chapter by exploring violence and abuse in dating relationships.

> ### CONSIDERATION
>
> In dating, cohabiting, and marital relationships, women are more likely than men to be victims of abuse. Women are six times more likely than men to be the victim of a violent crime committed by an intimate partner (Majority Staff of the Senate Judiciary Committee, 1992).

✇ Violence and Abuse in Dating Relationships

Distrust yourself and sleep before you fight.

JOHN ARMSTRONG

Many spouses who have been abused by their partners have noted that during dating and courtship, their partner never mistreated them. Indeed, in many cases, abuse in relationships does not occur until after the couple are married or living together. However, violent and abusive behavior may also be experienced in dating relationships.

Abuse in Dating Relationships

During courtship, women and men usually try to make the most positive impression possible on their dating partner. Despite the desire to present one's best qualities to one's dating partner, the display of violence and aggression sometimes occurs among dating partners.

NATIONAL DATA ❧ Using a nationally representative sample of college students, Stets and Henderson (1991) found that 30 percent reported behaving abusively and 31 percent reported being the recipient of abuse in courtship during the last 12 months.

In a study of 865 college students, DeMaris (1992) found that 25 percent reported violence in a current or previous relationship. Both the women and the men in the study reported that when one partner could be said to be the usual initiator of violence, that partner was most often the woman. This finding was true for both black and white respondents.

Verbal and symbolic abuse also occurs in dating relationships. One college student reported that his dating partner was angry that he chose to spend a Saturday afternoon with some friends watching a football game on TV, instead of with her. She expressed her anger by breaking his favorite CDs (Author's files).

As noted in Chapter 5, Riggs (1993) analyzed aggressive behavior in 653 university students who were involved in dating relationships and found that the more problems individuals reported the more likely they were to have experienced aggression in their relationship. Problems predictive of aggression (pushing, grabbing, slapping) were jealousy, break down of the relationship, and interference of friends.

Makepeace (1989) compared violence that occurs between partners on a first date, partners who are dating casually, and those who are in steady dating relationships. On first dates, violence is likely to be precipitated by disagreements over sex or jealousy. In casual dating relationships, violence is likely to be precipitated by arguments over sex or alcohol/drugs. Violence in steady dating relationships is likely to be precipitated by arguments over jealousy.

In the dating population, sexual abuse occurs more frequently than other types of physical abuse (Pirog-Good, 1992). Next we look at forms of sexual abuse that have gained increased attention in the media and on college campuses in the last decade—acquaintance and date rape.

The only thing we have to fear is not doing something about the fear we have.

E. C. MCKENZIE

Acquaintance and Date Rape

The word *rape* often evokes images of a stranger jumping out of the bushes or a dark alley to attack an unsuspecting victim. However, most rapes are not perpetrated by strangers.

NATIONAL DATA ❧ Only 15 percent of a national sample of rape victims reported they had been raped by a stranger; 85 percent had been raped by someone the victim knew (Koss et al., 1988).

Among the rape victims studied by Koss et al. (1988), 35 percent were attacked by their boyfriend or lover; 29 percent by a friend, co-worker, or neighbor; 25 percent by a casual date; and 11 percent by their husband. In a random sample of sorority women at Purdue University, 63 percent reported that since attending college they had experienced a man attempting to force sexual intercourse (get on top of her, attempt to insert penis) against their will;

⌣ IN FOCUS 12.1 ∾

A College Student's Experience with Date Rape

Last spring, I met this guy and a relationship started, which was great. One year later, he raped me. The term was almost over and we would not be able to spend much time together during the summer. Therefore, we planned to go out to eat and spend some time together.

After dinner we drove to a park. I did not mind or suspect anything for we had done this many times. Then he asked me into the back seat. I got into the back seat with him because I trusted him and he said he wanted to be close to me as we talked. He began talking. He told me that he was tired of always pleasing me and not getting a reward. Therefore, he was going to "make love to me" whether I wanted to or not. I thought he was joking so I asked him to stop playing. He told me he was serious and after looking at him closely, I knew he was serious. I began to plead with him not to have sex with me. He did not listen. He began to tear my clothes off and confine me so that I could not move. All this time I was fighting him. At one time I managed to open the door, but he threw me back into the seat, hit me, then he got on me and raped me. After he was satisfied, he stopped, told me to get dressed and stop crying. He said he was sorry it had to happen that way.

He brought me back to the dorm and expected me to kiss him good night. He didn't think he had done anything wrong. Before this happened, I loved this man very much, but afterward I felt great hatred for him.

My life has not been the same since that night. I do not trust men as I once did, nor do I feel completely comfortable when I'm with my present boyfriend. He wants to know why I back off when he tries to be intimate with me. However, right now I can't tell him, because he knows the guy who raped me (Author's files).

---

95 percent of the women reported that they knew their attackers (Copenhaver & Grauerholz, 1991). In a study of 171 college women (Pirog-Good, 1992), 26 percent reported that they had been the victim of sexual abuse by one or more dating partners within the prior 12 months. Respondents most frequently experienced necking (15 percent), chest fondling (12 percent), genital fondling (11 percent), oral sex (11 percent), and intercourse (9 percent) against their will. Koss (1992) reported in Senate testimony that five percent of college-aged women reported having been raped or the victim of an attempt in the last 12 months.

We went to Shoney's, ate apple pie and he took me back to my dorm room and raped me.

A COLLEGE STUDENT

These data reflect the fact that most rape is *acquaintance rape,* which may be defined as "nonconsensual sex between adults who know each other" (Bechhofer & Parrot, 1991, 12). One type of acquaintance rape is *date rape,* which refers to nonconsensual sex between people who are dating or on a date.

CONSIDERATION

Although it is the man who most often forces his dating partner to have sex, some women also force their dating partners to engage in sexual behaviors. Among 171 college women, 16 percent reported that they had inflicted sexually abusive behavior on a dating partner in the past 12 months. The most frequent forms of sexual behavior forced on their partners were necking (13 percent), genital fondling (6 percent), oral sex (4 percent), and intercourse (3 percent) (Pirog-Good, 1992).

Date rapes are usually not planned. Bechhofer and Parrot (1991) noted:

> He plans the evening with the intent of sex, but if the date does not progress as planned and his date does not comply, he becomes angry and takes what he feels is his right—sex. Afterward, the victim feels raped, while the assailant believes that he has done nothing wrong. He may even ask the woman out on another date (Bechhofer & Parrot, 1991, 11).

However, some date rapes are planned. The In Focus 12.1 insert describes such an experience as recalled by a woman who was raped by her boyfriend on a date.

ॐ Violence and Abuse in Cohabitation and Marriage Relationships

Violence and abuse occur not only in dating relationships but also in cohabitation and marriage relationships. Women as well as men may instigate the abuse (Riza et al., 1992).

Abuse in Cohabitation Relationships

NATIONAL DATA ॐ In a national sample of 5,768 couples, 35 percent of the cohabiting couples reported having been physically assaulted by their partner during the previous year (Stets & Straus, 1989).

Not only is the rate of physical violence highest among unmarried cohabiting couples, the severity of violence is greater among cohabiting couples compared to dating and marital partners (Stets & Straus, 1989). In living together relationships that experience violence, the precipitating disagreement is likely to be about jealousy or sex (Makepeace, 1989).

> Why is it that people are more likely to be assaulted, even killed in their own homes at the hands of someone they love?
>
> HARA ESTROFF MARANO

CONSIDERATION

Violence and abuse also occur among some gay and lesbian cohabiting couples. In one study of 100 battered lesbian partners, most reported they lived with their partners (Renzetti, 1989). In another study, twelve percent of gay men reported they were victims of forced sexual advances by their current partner (Waterman et al., 1989). This study also found that gay women were twice as likely to report experiencing violence in their relationships than gay men. The researchers suggested that gay women were more likely than gay men to report having been abused by their current partner because the relationships of gay women tended to be of longer duration.

Abuse in Marriage Relationships

NATIONAL DATA %% The National League of Cities estimates that as many as half of all women will experience violence during their marriage (Gibbs, 1993).

Most women (73–85 percent) do not experience physical abuse by their partner until *after* they have married the abuser (National Clearinghouse for the Defense of Battered Women, 1990). In some cases, marital abuse does not occur until after the couple has separated or divorced.

CONSIDERATION

The Department of Justice has found that, in almost three-quarters of reported spouse assaults, the battered was divorced or separated when the incident took place. This suggests that spouse abuse may be more prevalent than currently estimated, since most incidence surveys limit their sample to married couples (North Carolina Coalition Against Domestic Violence, 1991).

Available studies support the clinical impression that psychological and physical abuse go hand in hand.

CHRISTOPHER MURPHY
MICHELE CASCARDI

Flynn (1990) reported that both the husband and the wife are violent in half of all marriages experiencing violence. The most commonly held assumption is that when women are violent toward their partners, they are more likely than men to be acting defensively, rather than offensively. However, regardless of who initiates the violence, it usually results in more severe injuries for women than for men. DeMaris (1992) explained, "Because heterosexual pairing is characterized by differential size, strength, and fighting ability that favors the man, aggression initiated by him usually has far more serious implications" (118).

Verbal and symbolic aggression is even more common than physical abuse. In one study, three-quarters of both husbands and wives reported that they engaged in one or more acts of verbal or symbolic aggression with their spouse in the past year (Straus & Sweet, 1992).

Verbal and symbolic aggression are also known as psychological aggression. Examples of such aggression include the following (Murphy & Cascardi, 1993):

1. Isolation/restriction—one partner seeks to track, monitor, and control the other's activities and social contacts.
2. Humiliation/degradation—a partner denigrates, ridicules, or degrades the partner.
3. Threats to harm self, partner, friends, relatives, or pets.
4. Property violence—damage or destruction of personal property.
5. Jealousy and possessiveness—accusations or recriminations of infidelity.
6. Economic deprivation—attempts to control finances unilaterally or increase financial dependency.
7. Emotional withholding—refusals to provide emotional contact or support.

8. Minimization and denial—efforts to downplay the extent or impact of violence or abuse by questioning the partner's perceptions or sanity.

CONSIDERATION

Verbal aggression often precedes physical aggression in episodes of violence between intimate partners (Murty & Roebuck, 1992; Stets, 1990). One way to avoid physical violence in a relationship is for partners to withdraw from interaction that involves verbal aggression, before it escalates into physical abuse.

Rape in Marriage

Abuse in marital relationships may take the form of rape and sexual assault. In Russell's (1990) study of female San Francisco residents, 14 percent of married women revealed having been sexually assaulted by their husbands. Ten percent of married women in a Boston survey reported that they had been raped by their husbands (Finkelhor & Yllo, 1988). Such rapes may have included not only intercourse but also other types of sexual activities in which the wife did not want to engage, most often fellatio and anal intercourse. The various types of marital rape identified by the researchers include the following categories (Finkelhor & Yllo, 1988):

> The solution to the problem of wife rape starts with breaking silence about it.
>
> DIANA RUSSELL

1. *Battering Rape.* Battering marital rapes occur in the context of a regular pattern of verbal and physical abuse. The husbands yell at their wives, call them names, slap, shove, and beat them. These husbands are angry, belligerent, and frequently alcohol abusers. An example follows:

> One afternoon she came home from school, changed into a housecoat, and started toward the bathroom. He got up from the couch where he had been lying, grabbed her, and pushed her down on the floor. With her face pressed into a pillow and his hand clamped over her mouth, he proceeded to have anal intercourse with her. She screamed and struggled to no avail. Her injuries were painful and extensive. She had a torn muscle in her rectum, so that for three months she had to go to the bathroom standing up (pp. 144–145).

2. *Nonbattering Rape.* Nonbattering marital rapes often occur in response to a long-standing conflict or disagreement about sex. The violence is not generalized to the rest of the relationship but is specific to the sexual conflict. An example follows:

> Their love making on this occasion started out pleasantly enough, but he tried to get her to have anal intercourse with him. She refused. He persisted. She kicked and pushed him away. Still, he persisted. They ended up having vaginal intercourse. The force he used was mostly that of his weight on top of her. At 220 pounds, he weighs twice as much as she. "It was horrible," she said. She was sick to her stomach afterward. She cried and felt angry and disgusted. He showed little guilt. "He felt like he'd won something" (p. 145).

3. *Obsessive Rape.* Obsessive marital rapes may also be categorized as bizarre. The woman is used as a sex object to satisfy an atypical need of the husband. An example follows:

> "I was really his masturbating machine," one woman recalled. He was very rough sexually and would hold a pillow over her face to stifle her screams. He would also tie her up and insert objects into her vagina and take pictures, which he shared with his friends. The interviewee later discovered a file card in her husband's desk which sickened her. On the card, he had written a list of dates—dates that corresponded to the forced sex episodes of the past months. Next to each was a complicated coding system which seemed to indicate the type of sex act and a ranking of how much he enjoyed it (p. 146).

℘ Abuse in Intimate Relationships: Causes and Consequences

As noted in the beginning of the chapter, it seems ironic that individuals who care about each other are also the most likely to physically hurt each other. Next, we look at why some people in intimate relationships abuse their partners physically and sexually. We also examine the impact such abuse has on the victim and on children.

Factors That Contribute to Violence in Intimate Relationships

Our society promotes the expression of physical aggression.

Several factors help explain why some partners are violent in their relationships. These factors include cultural values, traditional gender roles, a family history of violence, and drug and alcohol use. In addition, a number of personality characteristics of abusers have been identified.

Cultural Values   We live in a culture that, in many ways, tolerates and even promotes violence. Violence in the family stems from acceptance of violence in our society as the legitimate means of enforcing compliance and solving conflicts at personal, national, and international levels (Viano, 1992).

Violence in the media reflects and perpetuates the cultural value of violence. By age 16, the typical child has witnessed 200,000 acts of violence on television (Toufexis, 1989).

Some evident suggests that violence is significantly more frequent among African American couples than white non-Hispanic couples. The explanation for this phenomenon is cultural in that blacks are more likely to represent lower social economic strata in which aggression and violent problem solving strategies are more common (Hampton & Washington Coner-Edwards, 1993).

> ### CONSIDERATION
>
> Rather than focus on blacks or whites as groups with different rates of vio- lence, it is helpful to look beyond to the social structures and inequalities which create the contexts for violence. "Couples become angry when unmet needs or unrealistic demands surface. Long-standing anger is often projected onto the partner, and violence erupts repeatedly in the marriage" (Hampton & Washington Coner-Edwards, 1993, 129). Indeed, when researchers compare blacks and whites in the same social class, the differences disappear, which suggests that violence is more a reflection of social class than race (Asbury, 1993).

Gender Roles   Violence between women and men may also stem from our culture's traditional gender roles. Straus (1980) noted,

> The cultural norms and values permitting and sometimes encouraging husband-to-wife violence reflect the hierarchical and male-dominant type of society that characterizes the Western world (p. 221).

Traditionally, men have viewed women (and children) as property. Prior to the late nineteenth century, it was a husband's legal right and marital obligation to discipline and control his wife through the use of physical force.

> ### CONSIDERATION
>
> The expression "rule of thumb" can be traced to an old English law which permitted a husband to beat his wife with a rod not thicker than his thumb. This "rule of thumb" was originally intended as a humane measure to limit how harshly men could beat their wives.

Traditional male gender roles have taught men to be aggressive. Tradition-ally, men have also been taught they are superior to women and so they may justify aggression toward women on the grounds that "women need to be put in their place." Traditional female gender roles have taught women to be submissive to their male partners' control.

Traditional gender role socialization may also explain some instances of physical aggression of women toward men. Shupe et al. (1987) explained that, because men are bigger and stronger than women, they are expected to treat women in a gentle and protective fashion. Women may feel justified in slapping a man when she is angry at him because she feels that men are tough and won't really be hurt by a slap. Men may be taught to accept the slap without retaliating, because it is men's role to be protective of women. In effect, society perpetuates a double standard, which says it is acceptable for a woman to hit a man but not acceptable for a man to hit a woman. Indeed, a sample of

Egalitarian couples have the lowest rates of violence and husband-dominated couples have the highest rates of spouse abuse.

MURRAY STRAUS

148 college students were much more tolerant of aggressive behavior in a dating relationship if it was initiated by the woman (Bethke & DeJoy, 1993).

Boye-Beaman et al. (1993) suggested a link between gender identity (instrumental quality of being goal oriented associated with masculinity and expressiveness quality of being action oriented toward maintaining interpersonal relationships associated with femininity) and premarital aggression and found that among white males, the greater the level of femininity, the lower the level of aggression. White husbands were also less likely than black husbands to score high on femininity.

Family History of Violence   Violence is learned primarily in the home. In a study of 328 couples who experienced abuse in their relationship, 75 percent of the women and 80 percent of the men reported being hit by their parents (Malone et al., 1989). This cycle of violence in which children observe and experience violence as a child and then inflict violence in their own adult relationships perpetuates itself; each generation tends to learn from the preceding one. According to Ney (1992), verbal abuse is more likely than physical abuse to be transmitted from one generation to the next.

CONSIDERATION

Pagelow (1992) questioned the cycle of violence as an explanation for partner abuse. She looked at a range of studies and observed that between 25 and 35 percent of individuals abused by their parents are estimated to be potential abusers of their children. She emphasized that this suggests that over two-thirds will *not* abuse their children and concluded, "There is sufficient reason to consider a family history of violence as only one factor out of many that may be associated with a greater probability of adult violence" (p. 111).

Drug and Alcohol Use   Drug and/or alcohol use may be related to some instances of abusive episodes in relationships. Indeed, Koss and Gaines (1993) identified regular use of alcohol and nicotine as the most important predictors of sexual aggression severity. According to Gelles and Straus (1988), almost half of all couples who engage in marital or parental violence reported it is associated with drinking by either the one who is violent, the victim, or both. In a study of crisis calls to the Atlanta Council for Battered Women (Murty & Roebuck, 1992), 30 percent of abuse victims reported that the perpetrators were intoxicated with alcohol at the time of their abuse. In a study of 320 young men who were married or living with their partner, 7 percent reported hitting their partner only after they had been drinking in contrast to 3.5 percent who reported the same event while sober (Leonard & Blane, 1992). Straus and Sweet (1992) found that drinking alcohol and using drugs were associated with higher rates of verbal and symbolic aggression among spouses. Although alcohol consumption is commonly believed to cause violent behavior, some research suggests otherwise (see In Focus 12.2).

Our understanding of the dynamics linking substance abuse and family violence is far from complete.

HEATHER R. HAYES
JAMES G. EMSHOFF

〜 **I N F O C U S   12.2** 〜

Does Alcohol Consumption Cause Violent Behavior?

As we have noted earlier, there seems to be a relationship between alcohol consumption and violent behavior. But does this relationship mean that alcohol is the *cause* of violent behavior? Some evidence suggests that the answer is "no."

If the chemical property of alcohol acts on the human organism in such a way as to produce violence, then drinking would produce violence in all people regardless of the culture in which they lived. But cross-cultural studies reveal that drunken behavior varies considerably across cultures. In some societies, drinking often leads to violence; in other societies, drinking leads to other behaviors, such as passivity and withdrawal (MacAndrew & Edgerton, 1969). The implication of this finding is that behaviors associated with alcohol consumption are learned from the culture.

In U.S. culture, we learn that drinking is associated with physical aggressiveness. In a worldwide study of 90 small-scale and peasant societies, Levinson (1989) found that alcohol plays little or no role in family violence in most societies around the world. Levinson found that alcohol consumption is a key factor in domestic violence in only a few of the societies he studied. Although alcohol no doubt has specific physiological effects on the human central nervous system, the behavioral manifestations of alcohol consumption are learned and culturally determined. However, in those cases where alcoholism is associated with violence, the person must be treated for alcoholism.

Personality Characteristics A number of personality characteristics have been associated with persons who are abusive in their intimate relationships. These include dependency, jealousy, need to control, unhappiness and dissatisfaction, and anger and aggressiveness (Vaselle-Augenstein & Ehrlich, 1992; Okun, 1986).

1. *Dependency.* Therapists who work with batterers have observed that they are extremely dependent on their partners. Because the thought of being left by their partners induces panic and "abandonment anxiety," batterers use physical aggression and threats of suicide to keep their partners with them.
2. *Jealousy.* Along with dependence, batterers exhibit jealousy, possessiveness, and suspicion. An abusive husband may express his possessiveness by isolating his wife from others; he may insist she stay at home, not work, and not socialize with others. His extreme, irrational jealousy may lead him to accuse his wife of infidelity and beat her for her presumed affair.
3. *Need to Control.* Batterers are often described as individuals who have an excessive need to be in control. They do not let their partners make independent decisions, and they want to know everything their partners do. They like to be in charge of all aspects of family life, including finances and recreation. In abusive relationships, one partner's need for control takes precedence over the needs of the other partner, who is submissive to the controlling partner (Stets, 1992).
4. *Unhappiness and Dissatisfaction.* Abusive partners often report being unhappy and dissatisfied with their lives, both at home and at work. Many

The question is not "why do they (the women) stay?" It's "why are they (the men) so vulnerable, so dependent?"

HARA ESTROFF MARANO

batterers have low self-esteem and high levels of anxiety, depression, and hostility. Extremely unhappy people often do not care how unhappy they make others.

5. *Anger and Aggressiveness*. Batterers are often described as aggressive individuals with a history of interpersonal aggressive behavior. They are also described as having poor impulse control in dealing with anger. Battered women report that episodes of violence are often triggered by minor events, such as a late meal or an unironed shirt.

> Anger is never without reason, but seldom a good one.
>
> BEN FRANKLIN

Factors That Contribute to Sexual Abuse in Adult Relationships

A number of factors may help explain why rape and sexual assault occurs between dating partners, cohabiting partners, and spouses. These factors include gender role socialization, rape-tolerant attitudes, and low self-esteem.

Gender Role Socialization In our society, some men are socialized to be sexually aggressive and to view women as objects for sexual gratification. To be sexually aggressive is, for some men, a part of the masculine role.

Historically, women have been viewed as the property of men. A husband forcing his wife to have sex was viewed as his right. Legal penalties for rape were initially based on property right laws designed to protect a man's property (wife or daughter) from forcible rape by other men; a husband "taking" his own property was not considered rape (Russell, 1990). This view of women as the sexual property of men has persisted. In essence, "the marriage license is a raping license" (Finkelhor & Yllo, 1988, 150).

> To understand more fully why people behave as they do, we have to look deep beneath their actions, beyond their automatic thoughts, and ferret out their basic beliefs.
>
> AARON T. BECK

Rape-Tolerant Attitudes Rape-tolerant attitudes, also called "rape-supportive attitudes" and "rape myths" are associated with self-reported rapes (Frank, 1991). Rape-tolerant attitudes, which may be learned from family, friends, and mass media, "are the mechanism that people use to justify dismissing an incident of sexual assault from the category of 'real' rape" (Burt, 1991, 27). For example, seventeen percent of all first-year college students throughout the United States *did not* agree with the statement, "Just because a man thinks that a woman has led him on, does not entitle him to have sex with her" (American Council on Education and University of California, 1992). Believing that a man is entitled to have sex with a woman that has led him on is an example of a rape-tolerant attitude. Such attitudes lead some individuals to initiate acts of forced sex and also serve as a subsequent justification for engaging in rape behavior.

In a study of rape-tolerant attitudes among college students, Holcomb et al. (1991) found that men are more likely than women to have rape-tolerant attitudes. Table 12.1 presents the percentages of college men and women who agreed with various rape-tolerant statements. (Six of the 20 statements used in the Holcomb et al. study are presented in Table 12.1).

TABLE 12.1

Percentage of College Men and Women Agreeing with Rape-Tolerant Statements

STATEMENT	MEN (N = 407)	WOMEN (N = 422)
1. A man sees sex as an achievement or notch in his belt.	47.9	67.8*
2. Deep down, a woman likes to be whistled at on the street.	54.8	38.9*
3. If a woman is heavily intoxicated, it is OK to have sex with her.	22.6	1.9*
4. Some women ask to be raped and enjoy it.	44.7	20.6*
5. Rape is often provoked by the victim.	30.5	14.7*
6. If a woman says "no" to having sex, she means "maybe" or even "yes."	36.9	21.1*

*Indicates a statistically significant gender difference.
Source: Holcomb, D. R., L. C. Holcomb, K. A. Sondag, and N. Williams. N. Attitudes about date rape: Gender differences among college students. *College Student Journal,* 1991, 25, 434–439. Reprinted by permission of *College Student Journal.*

Low Self-Esteem   Sexual abuse has been linked to low self-esteem. In a study of sexual abuse among college dating partners, Pirog-Good (1992) suggested that women with low self-esteem may be more likely to force sexual behaviors on their partners because the act of sex gives them the feeling of being wanted, desired, loved, "and thus important" (p. 108). Hence, when they have sex, even though they may force it, it has the effect of increasing their positive feelings about themselves. Women who are victims of sex abuse may also have low self-esteem and may feel that they deserve the abuse.

No one can make you feel inferior without your consent.

ELEANOR ROOSEVELT

The Impact of Abuse in Intimate Relationships

Not surprisingly, marital violence is associated with unhappy marital relationships (Bowman, 1990). Physical and emotional abuse is no doubt a factor in many divorces. In addition to affecting the happiness and stability of relationships, abuse affects the physical and psychological well-being of the victim. Abuse between parents also affects their children.

Effects of Partner Abuse On Victims   The most obvious effect of physical abuse by an intimate partner is physical injury. Indeed, Surgeon General Antonia Novella noted that battering is the single major cause of injury to women in the United States. As many as 35 percent of women who seek hospital emergency room services are suffering from injuries incurred by battering (Novello, 1992).

     When the abuse is sexual, it may be more devastating than sexual abuse by a stranger. The primary effect is to destroy the woman's ability to trust men in intimate interpersonal relationships. In addition, the woman raped by her husband lives with her rapist and may be subjected to repeated assaults. Most women raped by their husbands are raped on multiple occasions (Finkelhor & Yllo, 1988).

Violence among intimate partners or ex-partners may also include unintentional death and intentional murder. Each day, four women in the United States are killed by an abusing partner. The FBI reports that 30 percent of female homicide victims are killed by their husbands or boyfriends and six percent of male homicide victims are killed by their wives or girlfriends (North Carolina Coalition Against Domestic Violence, 1991).

> **Women are at greater risk of being killed by a male partner than by other family members or by any other persons outside the partnership.**
>
> ROBERT HAMPTON
> ALICE F. WASHINGTON CONER–EDWARDS

CONSIDERATION

Marital homicide differs by gender. For homicidal husbands, the act is nearly always offensive. For the homicidal wife, the act is usually defensive (Cazenave & Zahn, 1992; Goetting, 1989).

Many battered women who have killed their abusing husbands have been sent to prison. However, in 1990, Ohio Governor Richard Celeste commuted the sentences of 27 battered women serving time for killing or assaulting male companions (Gibbs, 1993). While society may be increasing its understanding of the desperation that drives a battered woman to kill her husband, it continues to be conflicted on how the legal system should respond to such acts.

Other less obvious effects of abuse by one's intimate partner include fear, feelings of helplessness, confusion, isolation, humiliation, anxiety, depression, stress-induced illness, symptoms of post-traumatic stress disorder, and suicide attempts (Gelles & Conte, 1991; Lloyd & Emery, 1993). In regard to the latter, about one-fourth of all female suicide attempts are preceded by abuse (North Carolina Coalition Against Domestic Violence, 1991).

Effects of Partner Abuse on Children   Abuse between adult partners also affects children. About 40 percent of battered women are abused during their pregnancy, resulting in a high rate of miscarriage and birth defects (North Carolina Coalition Against Domestic Violence, 1991). The March of Dimes has concluded that the physical abuse of pregnant women causes more birth defects than all the diseases put together for which children are usually immunized (Gibbs, 1993).

Witnessing marital violence is related to emotional and behavioral problems in children and subsequent violence in their own relationships (Busby, 1991). Children may also commit violent acts against a parent's abusing partner. Over half (63 percent) of males 11–20 years old in prison for homicide killed the person who abused their mother (North Carolina Coalition Against Domestic Violence, 1991).

Abusive Behavior Inventory

This inventory is designed to assess the amount of abuse occurring in a relationship. Circle the number that best represents your closest estimate of how often each of the behaviors happened in your relationship with your partner or former partner during the previous six months.

1 Never   4 Frequently
2 Rarely   5 Very frequently
3 Occasionally

1. Called you a name and/or criticized you.   1 2 3 4 5
2. Tried to keep you from doing something you wanted to do (e.g., going out with friends, going to meetings).   1 2 3 4 5
3. Gave you angry stares or looks.   1 2 3 4 5
4. Prevented you from having money for your own use.   1 2 3 4 5
5. Ended a discussion with you and made the decision himself/herself.   1 2 3 4 5
6. Threatened to hit or throw something at you.   1 2 3 4 5
7. Pushed, grabbed, or shoved you.   1 2 3 4 5
8. Put down your family and friends.   1 2 3 4 5
9. Accused you of paying too much attention to someone or something else.   1 2 3 4 5
10. Put you on an allowance.   1 2 3 4 5
11. Used your children to threaten you (e.g., told you that you would lose custody, said he/she would leave town with the children.)   1 2 3 4 5
12. Became very upset with you because dinner, housework, or laundry was not ready when he/she wanted it done the way he/she thought it should be.   1 2 3 4 5
13. Said things to scare you (e.g., told you something "bad" would happen, threatened to commit suicide).   1 2 3 4 5
14. Slapped, hit, or punched you.   1 2 3 4 5
15. Made you do something humiliating or degrading (e.g., begging for forgiveness, having to ask his/her permission to use the car or to do something).   1 2 3 4 5

16. Checked up on you (e.g., listened to your phone calls, checked the mileage on your car, called you repeatedly at work).   1 2 3 4 5
17. Drove recklessly when you were in the car.   1 2 3 4 5
18. Pressured you to have sex in a way you didn't like or want.   1 2 3 4 5
19. Refused to do housework or childcare.   1 2 3 4 5
20. Threatened you with a knife, gun, or other weapon.   1 2 3 4 5
21. Spanked you.   1 2 3 4 5
22. Told you that you were a bad parent.   1 2 3 4 5
23. Stopped you or tried to stop you from going to work or school.   1 2 3 4 5
24. Threw, hit, kicked, or smashed something.   1 2 3 4 5
25. Kicked you.   1 2 3 4 5
26. Physically forced you to have sex.   1 2 3 4 5
27. Threw you around.   1 2 3 4 5
28. Physically attacked the sexual parts of your body.   1 2 3 4 5
29. Choked or strangled you.   1 2 3 4 5
30. Used a knife, gun, or other weapon against you.   1 2 3 4 5

SCORING: Add the numbers you circled and divide the total by 30 to find your score. The higher your score, the more abusive your relationship.

The Inventory was given to 100 men and 78 women equally divided into groups of abusers/abused and nonabusers/nonabused. The men were members of a chemical dependency treatment program in a veteran's hospital and the women were partners of these men. Abusing or abused men earned an average score of 1.8; abusing or abused women earned an average score of 2.3. Nonabusing/abused men and women earned scores of 1.3 and 1.6 respectively (Shepard & Campbell, 1992).

SOURCE: Melanie F. Shepard and James A. Campbell. The Abusive Behavior Inventory: A Measure of Psychological and Physical Abuse. *Journal of Interpersonal Violence,* September 1992, 7, no. 3, 291–305. Inventory is on page 303–304. Used by permission of Sage Publications, 2455 Teller Road, Newbury Park, California 91320.

℘ Breaking the Cycle of Abuse

What choices do partners in abusive relationships have for breaking the cycle of violence in their lives? Next, we look at various options for abused partners and examine why abused partners stay in abusive relationships. We also look at how abusers may be helped to overcome their abusive behavior patterns.

Help for the Abused

Perhaps the first step in getting help for individuals in abusive relationships is for both partners to admit (rather than deny) that the abuse is occurring. The Abusive Behavior Inventory in the Self-Assessment provides a way to assess the degree to which both psychological and physical abuse is occurring in a relationship.

Once battered partners recognize they are being abused in their relationship, they may choose to leave the abusive relationship. However, some battered women who decide to leave such a relationship often do not have the economic means and/or the emotional strength to live independently. Thus, they may choose to stay with friends or relatives or may stay at a shelter for abused women and their children. Shelters for abused women offer an environment that empowers women by encouraging them to make independent choices about their abusive relationship and about their future. Most importantly, shelters provide a communal living situation in which abused women are encouraged to share their experiences, which reduces their sense of isolation and helps them express their anger and overcome feelings of guilt and inadequacy (Loseke, 1992). An alternative to shelters are "safe homes," which are private homes of individuals who volunteer to provide temporary housing to abused women who decide to leave their violent home.

NATIONAL DATA ℘ More than 700 battered women's shelters have been established in the United States (Johnson et al., 1992).

> **CONSIDERATION**
>
> Battered men are typically not allowed to stay at such shelters, but many shelters help battered men who want to escape their violent home find a motel room and offer these men counseling and supportive services.

Many professionals who counsel victims of relationship abuse recommend that the abused victim call the police and have the abusive partner arrested. Violence is more likely to stop if the abusive partner is arrested by the police than if the partner is not arrested (Ellis, 1992). Arresting the abuser communicates to the abuser that physical violence will not be tolerated. In addition, a judge may order the abuser to participate in counseling and may provide a

The idea is to restore personal power so that the battered woman will be capable of acting in her own best interest.

GARY BLAU
MARY BUTTEWEG DALL
LYNETTE ANDERSON

Abused women may need to seek temporary relief in an abuse shelter.

restraining order, which prohibits the abuser from having any physical contact with the victim.

However, most episodes of violent behavior in intimate relationships are not reported to the police. Even women who are abused to the extent they seek refuge in a shelter tend not to have the abuser arrested. In a study of shelters for abused women in Alabama, researchers found that only about one-fourth of the battered women obtained a warrant against their abuser and almost one-half of these women eventually dropped the charges (Johnson et al., 1992).

Some abuse victims fear that having their abusive partner arrested will result in retaliation and further abuse (this may indeed happen). Others hope that this time the abuser will change and stop the abuse. Others may simply not be emotionally ready to begin the process of separation from the abuser.

Men may be reluctant to report being abused by their female partner because they fear being viewed as weak and unmasculine. Men, who are stereotyped as being strong and tough, are assumed to be immune from any harm a woman (who is stereotyped as being weak) could inflict.

CONSIDERATION

Police officers are reluctant to intervene in domestic disputes because of the severe level of violence that occurs in the home. More than 25 percent of assaults on police officers occur during domestic disputes. About 20 percent of police officers killed each year meet their death while trying to intervene in a family dispute (Jaffe, 1990).

NATIONAL DATA ❧ In 1978, forty-seven states did not recognize marital rape as a crime. In July 1993, North Carolina became the fiftieth state to recognize marital rape as a crime (National Clearinghouse on Marital and Date Rape, 1993).

Women may be extremely reluctant to press charges against their husbands for marital rape. Those who do press charges are, in effect, challenging a large segment of society that still tends to view sex as the right of husbands. However, when women do prosecute raping husbands the conviction rate is high—88 percent conviction rate for victims of wife rape whose reports to the police result in arrest (Russell, 1991). Russell (1991) suggests that this high conviction rate is probably due to the fact that "wives who charge their husbands with rape have often been subjected to particularly brutal and/or deviant experiences" (p. 136).

In addition to seeking refuge at a shelter and having the abusive partner arrested, victims of abuse may find it helpful to participate in counseling. In counseling, the abuse victim may overcome feelings of self-blame and learn to place the responsibility on the perpetrator. Counseling may also help the abuse victim improve self-esteem and explore options for how to cope with the

Consistent with state law, the chief executive of every law enforcement agency should establish arrest as the preferred response in cases of family violence.

ATTORNEY GENERAL'S TASK FORCE ON FAMILY VIOLENCE

abuse. One option abuse victims struggle with is whether to stay in the relationship or whether to leave it. Next, we look at reasons why many abuse victims stay in the abusive relationship.

Why Do Some People Stay in the Abusive Relationship?

One of the most frequently asked questions to people who are abused by their partners is, "Why don't you get out of the relationship?" Reasons why abused partners stay in the abusive relationship include love, emotional dependency, commitment to the relationship, hope, view of violence as legitimate, guilt, fear, and economic dependency.

Love   Despite the physical and emotional pain abused partners are subjected to, they often feel love for the abusive partner. Love feelings may be maintained by the fact that abusive partners do not always behave in abusive ways; they may also act in positive and loving ways. In a study of abused women in dating relationships, those who were more likely to stay in the relationship had partners who engaged in a high frequency of positive behaviors (Kasian & Painter, 1992). The researchers hypothesized that "the presence of positive behaviors maintains a relationship regardless of the level of negative experiences" (p. 361). One woman said,

> Even though he slapped me around a lot, I never left him because when he wasn't hurting me he was so gentle and sweet. He would tell me that he loved me and that I was the only woman in the world who really understood him. Even though he hurt me, he always told me he was sorry, and was good to me right after the violence (Author's files).

Emotional Dependency   Just as abusive partners are often emotionally dependent on the person they abuse, so are abused partners emotionally dependent on their abuser. Such codependency was expressed by one woman who said,

> I know my boyfriend treats me badly, but I wouldn't know what to do without him. I need him. I would rather put up with the abuse than be alone without him (Author's files).

Commitment to the Relationship   Abused partners, especially those in marital relationships, may feel committed to the relationship. Some abused spouses stay in the relationship because they don't believe in divorce; they believe marriage is a permanent relationship, no matter what the quality of the marriage.

Hope   Abused partners may stay in the relationship because they hope the relationship will improve. In a study of 44 abused women who stayed in the abusive relationship, over 60 percent believed that "no matter how bad my partner's abuse gets, I believe there is a chance that our relationship will get

Ruthless love, great bane, great curse to mankind.

APOLLONIUS RHODIUS

better" and "If my partner promised never to abuse me again, I would believe him" (Herbert, Silver, & Ellard, 1991, 320).

View of Violence as Legitimate   Some abused partners stay in the relationship because they accept violence as a legitimate part of intimate relationships. This may be due to growing up in a home in which the parents abused each other, which may convey the message that marital violence is natural, inevitable, and to be expected.

Some abused partners may feel the violence directed toward them is legitimate because it is their fault; they either caused the abuse or they deserved it. Some abused partners feel if only they were a better partner or a better person, they would not be abused.

Guilt   Other abused partners stay in the abusive relationship because leaving would produce guilt. They may feel guilty about breaking up a family, especially if children are involved. Some abusers threaten suicide if their partners leave or use other verbal pleas to guilt-induce their partner into staying. For example, an abusive man may tell his partner the following:

> I know I'm a brute, but I'm on my knees asking for forgiveness. . . . How could you turn away from me when I most need you? . . . If you really loved me, you'd forgive and trust me. . . . Look how I'm hurting and how hard I'm trying. . . . I'm afraid I'll fall apart without you. . . . You're all I have, all I care about . . . (NiCarthy, 1986, 11).

He that knows no guilt can know no fear.

PHILIP MASSINGER

Fear   Abused partners may stay in the relationship because they fear the abuser will become even more violent if they leave. Often, such fear is the result of threats made by the abuser. In a study of physical abuse in lesbian relationships, one respondent said:

> I was afraid of leaving because she'd tried to kill me three times, each as more of a threat than an attempt, but I thought she'd be more serious if she knew I was serious about going (Renzetti, 1989, 161).

Some abused men fear if they leave the family, further violence will be directed at the children. Hence, men feel that by staying they are providing some protection for their children (Steinmetz & Lucca, 1988).

Economic Dependency   Some spouses may stay in an abusive relationship because they are economically dependent on their partner. They may feel that they have no place to go and no way to support themselves and their children.

CONSIDERATION

Men may also stay in abusive relationships for economic reasons. Even though men, as a group, have more economic resources than women, if a husband leaves a family he is still responsible for a certain amount of child support. Such cost is in addition to maintaining a separate residence for himself.

Feeling Stuck and Unable to Disengage   Dr. Karen Rosen and Dr. Sandra Stith (1992) of Virginia Polytechnic Institute and State University interviewed six young women who had stayed in violent dating relationships from three months to five and a half years and who reported they felt incapable of getting out. These women identified five variables they felt contributed to their being trapped, including

1. Romantic fantasies that their boyfriends would make things better for them or the reverse.
2. Traumatic bonding in that they felt closer to each other as a result of sharing the traumatic experience of relationship violence.
3. Illusions of control in that the woman felt she could control her partner's violence if she would just work hard enough to make the relationship work.
4. Seesaw coupling in which they felt trapped in oscillating cycles of ups and downs of emotional extremes and feelings of closeness and distance.
5. Peer and/or family collusion in which peers or family members would minimize or deny that the abuse was occurring.

Disengaging from an Abusive Relationship

All of the women Rosen and Stith (1992) interviewed were eventually able to free themselves from the abusive relationships in which they were involved. Doing so was a complex process that included the following factors.

Seeds of Doubt   Despite feeling stuck, each of the women had seeds of doubt that they should remain in the abusive relationship. One woman who had endured the relationship for five years reported "that a small voice somewhere inside her would occasionally whisper, 'You don't deserve this. You don't deserve this.' Although she stayed with him for all this time and felt that she loved him for most of those years, she never really trusted him fully after the first time he hit her" (p. 17).

Modest doubt is call'd the beacon of the wise.

SHAKESPEARE

Turning Points and Reappraisals   Turning points were events and reappraisals were reevaluations of the relationship that had a significant impact on the future direction of the relationship. Examples included graduating from high school (and thus the need to get on with one's life in a more healthy relationship), becoming pregnant (and regarding such abuse while pregnant with the man's child as intolerable), or becoming engaged (and recognizing it was now or never to get out of the abusive relationship).

    For one of the respondents, Alexandra, a turning point was moving from her parents' home to live in her own apartment. By doing so she was struck with the realization that "she alone was responsible for what happened to her now" (p. 21).

Self-Reclaiming Actions   These were self-empowering moves in which the abused woman took control of her life. One woman recognized that she had to save herself and began putting distance between her and her abusive partner. Her example follows:

> Two weeks before school started I decided, this is it. This whole relationship is driving me crazy. I've got to do something to get away from it. So in an attempt to get away from it, I decided to go away to school. So in a two-week span, I got accepted to a college that was a distance away, got registered, got an apartment and moved down there (p. 22).

Objective Reflection   Objective reflection occurred when the woman pulled back from the emotional context and reviewed her relationship and its consequences. Such reflection allowed the woman to see what was happening to her, which permitted her to move toward withdrawing. The objective reflection of one woman follows:

> It's just kind of thinking and looking at things. . . . I was still showing up and I was still very loyal, but part of me was sitting back and checking things out and making sure that I wasn't being real stupid by staying around (p. 24).

Paradigmatic Shifts and Last Straw Events   Paradigmatic shifts existed when the woman shifted her focus from staying in the relationship to getting out of it. "The initial position that the relationship is a means to meet her needs is replaced with the position that the relationship must be dissolved in order to meet her needs" (p. 25). Sometimes the shifts were prompted by last straw events. Being severely abused, being coldly rejected, or recognizing that the future was hopeless were examples. The experience of one woman reflected the process of finally deciding that something had to change.

> I had no more hope that things were going to work out. . . . And I saw Matt as the root of almost all of my problems. And I think that's part of what pushed me over the edge to decide that I couldn't be with him anymore. It was like, on one hand I had Matt, on the other I had hope. It was like which do I need more to survive. I needed the hope, so I had to get rid of him (p. 26).

Leaving and Moving On   Actually disengaging from the partner was difficult and painful. One woman recalled her feelings:

> I was talking to my girlfriend saying, "I feel like I'm going to die.". . . I was really scared. . . . I didn't know who I was. . . . I had no idea what life was outside all that craziness. . . . I was scared of what life offered, what was out there . . . (p. 28).

Researchers Rosen and Stith (1992) summarized their study by emphasizing the enormous strength abusive relationships have on holding the people involved in them and the difficulty of breaking through the cultural mandate to "stand by your man." Rather, women in abusive relationships must "manage to come to their senses and stand by themselves instead" (p. 31).

There must be fifty ways to leave your lover . . .

PAUL SIMON

TABLE 12.2

Perceived Reasons for Returning Home to Abusive Relationship

REASONS	MEAN
Give the abuser one more chance	10.0
Lack of financial resources	9.1
Emotional dependency on the abuser	9.0
Lack of housing resources	8.7
Lack of job opportunities	7.7
Denial of cycle of violence	7.6
Lack of support or follow-through by the legal system	7.6
Lack of childcare resources	7.1
Lack of transportation	6.7
Fear that the abuser will find her and do her harm	6.7
Lack of support from other family members	6.6
Fear that he will get custody of the children	5.8
Fear that the abuser will kidnap the children	5.8
Children miss the absent parent	5.6
Lack of professional counseling	5.1
Fear that the abuser will harm the children	4.6

Source: I. M. Johnson, J. Crowley, and R. T. Sigler. Agency response to domestic violence: Services provided to battered women. *Intimate Violence: Interdisciplinary Perspectives,* E. C. Viano, ed. 1992, 191–202 (Table on p. 199). Washington, D.C.: Hemisphere Publishing Co. Used by permission.

CONSIDERATION

Even when abused partners leave their abusers, they often return to the relationship. Seven out of ten shelters in Alabama reported that more than half of their clients return home to their abusive partner (Johnson et al., 1992). The shelter workers in this study were asked to rate their perceptions of important reasons for the victim's decision to return to the abusive relationship on a scale from most important (10) to least important (1). The results are listed in Table 12.2.

Help for the Abuser

Individuals arrested for acts of violence against their partners are often required by the court to participate in counseling. Some abusers seek counseling because it is the only condition under which their partners are willing to continue the relationship. Less frequently, some abusive individuals seek counseling on their own initiative.

Counselors work with abusers in individual, couple, and/or group counseling. Because abusers often deny the abuse or provide rationalizations

Violence is a series of dynamic processes between perpetrators and survivors . . . both groups are victims and need intervention and assistance.

ROBERT HAMPTON
ALICE F. WASHINGTON CONER–EDWARDS

for their violent behavior, a primary goal of counseling is for abusers to confront their rationalizations and denial, admit they have a problem, and take responsibility for their violent behavior. In a study of 50 women in a battered women's shelter, two researchers observed that the abuse decreased in those cases where the abuser apologized and took responsibility for the abuse. Alternatively, when the abuser denied responsibility and blamed the abuse on external factors such as alcohol, stress, or financial problems, the abuse continued (Wolf-Smith & LaRossa, 1992).

> **There is virtually no evidence that any form of couples therapy is effective in reducing violence. Individual or group therapy, which stresses the husband's responsibility may be more effective.**
>
> **NEIL JACOBSON**

C O N S I D E R A T I O N

Some abusers do not perceive their violent behavior as resulting from a deliberate choice they make to act in such a manner. Rather, they may describe their violent behavior as sudden, impulsive, and out of their control. However, in order to change violent behavior, abusers must recognize that they are in control of their behavior and are responsible for it. One counselor tells his clients,

> Violence is not like a bolt of lightning from a clear blue sky. There are storm clouds that gather beforehand that you can learn to notice so that you're not caught unaware by your own behavior (Okun, 1986, 217).

In cases where the abuser was abused as a child, the counselor may help the abuser explore how early family experiences served to teach violent behavior and values that "justify" such violence. Realizing that the violent behavior and values were learned may increase the possibility of learning new behaviors and values.

Counseling for the abuser involves learning alternatives to violence and learning to recognize internal and external signals associated with violent behavior. Alternatives to violence include leaving the situation, engaging in physical activity such as sports or exercise, and verbal problem solving. In counseling, the abuser may be taught effective communication and conflict negotiation skills as well as relaxation techniques. If substance abuse is a factor in the abuse, the abuser may be referred for substance abuse counseling.

C O N S I D E R A T I O N

Prevention of abuse in relationships involves continuing to increase public awareness about domestic violence, teaching couples how to communicate and to interrupt coercive cycles early, and encouraging couples to equalize the power in their relationship to encourage respect and avoid resentment (Murphy & Cascardi, 1993). Prevention of domestic violence may also be achieved by the following (Gelles, 1993):

1. Eliminate the norms that legitimize and glorify violence in the society and the family (e.g. eliminate spanking as a child-rearing technique, eliminate violence in the media, institute gun control).

(continued)

2. Reduce violence–provoking stress created by society by reducing poverty, inequality, and unemployment.
3. Change the sexist nature of society by promoting equality between women and men.

ॐ Child Abuse

Child abuse cases are serious and complex in nature and prosecution is neither the only solution nor a panacea. It does, however, recognize that children are as entitled to protection under the law as adults, and that offenders—whether parents, other caretakers, or strangers—are accountable for their behavior.

JAMES PETERS
JANET DINSMORE
PATRICIA TOTH

Child abuse may be defined as any interaction or lack of interaction between a child and his or her parents or caregiver that results in nonaccidental harm to the child's physical or psychological well-being. Child abuse includes physical abuse, such as beating and burning; verbal abuse, such as insulting or demeaning the child; and neglect, such as failing to provide adequate food, hygiene, medical care, or adult supervision for the child. Another type of child abuse is child sexual abuse. After looking at these various types of child abuse, we examine factors that cause or contribute to child abuse and how such abuse impacts the child.

Physical and Verbal Abuse and Neglect

The number of children who are physically abused, verbally abused, and/or neglected by their parents or caregivers is staggering.

NATIONAL DATA ॐ In 1991, almost two million cases of child abuse and neglect were reported (*Statistical Abstract of the United States:* 1993, Table 340).

> **CONSIDERATION**
>
> The actual number of children who are abused is much greater than the number reported because most cases of child abuse are not reported. One estimate suggests that only one in seven cases of child abuse is reported (Knudsen, 1989).

Twice as many cases of child neglect occur than cases of child physical and verbal abuse. In a review of the literature on child abuse, Lloyd and Emery (1993) noted that boys are more likely than girls to experience abuse. Other factors associated with an increased risk of child abuse include the following (Krugman et al., 1986; Lloyd & Emery, 1993; Oates et al., 1983; and Straus & Smith, 1990):

1. The pregnancy is premaritally conceived or unplanned and the father does not want the child.
2. Mother-infant bonding is lacking.
3. The child suffers from developmental disabilities or mental retardation.
4. Childrearing techniques are strict and harsh and include little positive reinforcement for the child.

5. The parents are unemployed.

6. Abuse between the husband and wife is present.

Intrafamilial Child Sexual Abuse

Another type of child abuse is child sexual abuse. Intrafamilial child sexual abuse (formerly referred to in professional literature as "incest") refers to exploitive sexual contact or attempted sexual contact between relatives before the victim is age 18. Sexual contact or attempted sexual contact includes intercourse, fondling of the breasts and genitals, and/or oral sex. Relatives include biologically related individuals but may also include stepparents and stepsiblings.

NATIONAL DATA   In a national survey of adults concerning child sexual abuse, 27 percent of the women and 16 percent of the men reported being victims. These percentages refer to both intrafamilial child sexual abuse and sexual abuse by nonfamily members (Finkelhor et al., 1990).

Female children are more likely than male children to be sexually abused. A study of almost 4,000 intrafamilial child sexual abuse cases revealed that 85 percent of the victims were female and 15 percent were male (Solomon, 1992).

> ### CONSIDERATION
>
> While many women may be reluctant to report they were sexually abused as children, men may be even more reluctant. If the child sexual abuse was perpetrated by an adult male (which is usually the case), the male victim may fear that admitting such abuse implies he is homosexual. Fearing others will stigmatize him for having experienced homosexual sex, the male victim of sexual abuse may not reveal the abuse to anyone.

Intrafamilial child sexual abuse, particularly when the perpetrator is a parent, involves an abuse of power and authority. The experience of a black woman who, as a child, was forced to have sexual relations with her father is described below (Author's files):

> I was around six years old when I was sexually abused by my father. He was not drinking at that time; therefore, he had a clear mind as to what he was doing. On looking back, it seemed so well planned. For some reason, my father wanted me to go with him to the woods behind our house to help him saw wood. Once we got there, he looked around for a place to sit and wanted me to sit down with him. He said, "Susan, I want you to do something for Daddy. I want you to lie down, and we are going to play Mama and Daddy." Being a child, I said, "Okay," thinking it was going to be fun. I don't know what happened next and I can't remember if there was pain or whatever. I was threatened not to tell, and remembering how he beat my mother, I didn't want the same treatment. It happened a few more times. I remember not liking this at all. But what could I do? Until age 18, I was constantly on the run, hiding from him when I had to stay

From the time I was 5 until I was 18 and moved away to college, my father sexually violated me.

MARILYN VAN DERBUR
FORMER MISS AMERICA

Even if one only takes the lowest estimates, it is clear that sexual abuse of children is a common experience of childhood and affects a large number of children.

JON R. CONTE

I was abused in every way, including sexually, by relatives.

ROSEANNE ARNOLD

home alone with him, staying out of his way so he wouldn't touch me by hiding in the corn fields all day long, under the house, in the barns, and so on until my mother got back home, then getting punished by her for not doing the chores she had assigned to me that day. It was a miserable life growing up in that environment.

Causes and Contributing Factors of Child Abuse

A variety of factors may cause or contribute to child abuse. These factors are discussed below:

Parental Psychopathology Some abusing parents may have a psychiatric condition. Symptoms of such conditions that may predispose the parent to abuse children include low frustration tolerance, inappropriate expression of anger, and emotional distress. Some child-abusing parents are dependent on alcohol or drugs, which may be associated with child abuse or neglect.

Some abusing parents have irrational perceptions or unrealistic expectations of their children's behavior. For example, a parent might view the crying of a baby as a deliberate attempt on the part of the child to irritate the parent. Or a parent may unrealistically expect a one-year-old child to be toilet trained and may beat the child for soiling or wetting his or her pants. One mother, unaware that most children are not developmentally ready to walk until age one, regarded her eight-month-old baby as "lazy" because he would not get up and walk (Blau et al., 1993). Changing parents' unrealistic expectations or irrational perceptions concerning their children's behavior is an important part of an overall plan to reduce child abuse (Martin & Walters, 1992).

History of Abuse Parents who were themselves physically or verbally abused, or neglected, tend to duplicate these patterns in their own families (Gelles & Conte, 1991). Some fathers who sexually abuse their children were sexually abused themselves.

> Child maltreatment is not committed by a parent in isolation, independent of the parent's past experiences and current circumstances.
>
> DONNA HARRINGTON
> HOWARD DUBOWITZ

CONSIDERATION

A man who attended a lecture on child abuse approached the speakers after the lecture ended. With tears in his eyes, the man told the speakers, "You said that people who are abused grow up to be abusers. Well, I was an abused child. I don't want to get married and grow up to abuse my children, so I will not get married" (Gelles & Straus, 1988, 49).

Although parents who were abused as children are more likely than parents who were not abused to abuse their own children, this does not mean that ALL people who are abused as children become abusers as adults. Indeed, some adults who were abused as children are dedicated to nonviolent parenting techniques precisely because they were abused as children and have experienced the physical and emotional consequences of abuse.

The use of corporal punishment in schools may also teach children that physical punishment is acceptable. Despite a growing sentiment that corporal punishment is damaging to children and a trend toward legislation banning such practices, corporal punishment still occurs. It is estimated that more than two million children receive corporal punishment each year (Pinkney, 1992).

Displacement of Aggression   One cartoon shows several panels consisting of a boss yelling at his employee, the employee yelling at his wife, the wife yelling at their child, and the child kicking the dog who chases the cat up a tree. Washburne (1983) observed, "Women's abuse of children stems directly from their own oppression in society and within the family. . . . Some women displace their frustration and anger on their children, the family members who are less powerful than they" (p. 291).

CONSIDERATION

The frustration and anger some parents displace onto their children may have its base in the larger society. Harrington and Dubowitz (1993) noted that "poverty, unemployment, lack of support for families and working parents, lack of health care, poor nutrition, substance abuse, and society's acceptance of violence are all related to child maltreatment" (p. 262). Indeed, the strategy to eliminate child abuse must include these broader issues.

Social Isolation   Unlike most societies of the world, many Americans rear their children in closed and isolated nuclear units. In extended kinship societies, other relatives are always present to help with the task of childrearing. Isolation means no relief from the parenting role as well as no supervision by others who might interfere in child abusing situations.

In a national survey of family violence, there was no difference between blacks and whites in the rate of abusive violence toward children (Gelles & Straus, 1988). This puzzled the researchers, as blacks in the United States have higher rates of unemployment and lower annual incomes compared to whites. Both unemployment and low income are associated with child abuse. The researchers concluded that, while blacks did suffer more economic problems and life stresses than whites, they were also more involved in family and community activities than whites, who tend to be more isolated from kinship networks. According to Gelles and Straus,

> Blacks reported more contact with their relatives and more use of their relatives for financial support and child care. . . . The extensive social networks that black families develop and maintain insulate them from the severe economic stresses they also experience, and thus reduce what otherwise would have been a higher rate of parental violence (p. 86).

If good and affordable child care is not available, parents may be unable to work or may leave their children in marginal or inadequate arrangements; child neglect and abuse are possible concerns.

DONNA HARRINGTON
HOWARD DUBOWITZ

The Stepparenting Factor   Children are much more likely to be abused if they are being reared in a home where there is a stepparent. In one study, preschoolers living with one natural and one stepparent were 40 times more likely to become child abuse cases than were like-aged children living with two natural parents (Daly & Wilson, 1985).

The researchers suggest that because stepparents do not have a biological tie with the stepchildren, they are less tolerant and altruistic toward them. This lack of tolerance, when coupled with stress in the marital and parental relationships, may result in abuse (Daly & Wilson, 1985).

CONSIDERATION

Although stepparents do not have a biological tie to their stepchildren, they may nevertheless develop strong, affectionate bonds with them. On the other hand, some stepparents may want a close emotional bond with their stepchildren, but are not accepted by the stepchildren. This lack of acceptance is, in some cases, related to the negative attitudes of divorced parents toward their ex-spouse's new partner. In order for children to develop strong bonds with their stepparent (and hence, reduce the likelihood of abuse by the stepparent), it is important that divorced parents encourage their children to have positive feelings for their stepparent.

The Impact of Child Abuse

How does being abused—physically, verbally, or sexually—impact the victim as a child and later as an adult? In general, the effects are negative and vary according to the intensity and frequency of the abuse.

Effects of Physical and Verbal Abuse   Reviews of research on the effects of child abuse suggest the following (Gelles & Conte, 1991; Lloyd & Emery, 1993):

1. Abused children have a number of cognitive, social, and emotional deficits believed to be the result of both their experience of abuse and their development in a socially impoverished environment.
2. Abused children tend to exhibit aggression, low self-esteem, depression, and low academic achievement.
3. Children who experience more severe abuse suffer more from intellectual deficits, communication problems, and learning disabilities.
4. Adults who were physically abused as children may exhibit low self-esteem, depression, unhappiness, anxiety, an increased risk of alcohol abuse, and suicidal tendencies.
5. Physical injuries sustained by child abuse cause pain, disfigurement and scarring, physical disability, and even death.

Effects of Sexual Abuse   Child sexual abuse may have serious, negative long-term consequences (Beitchman et al., 1992). Research on the effects of being sexually abused have found the following:

1. Among adolescent females, sexual abuse is associated with lower self-esteem, higher levels of depression, antisocial behavior (e.g., running away from home, illegal drug use), and suicidal attempts (Morrow & Sorrell, 1989).
2. The most devastating effects of being sexually abused occur when the sexual abuse is forceful, prolonged, and involves intercourse, and when the abuse was perpetrated by a father or stepfather (Beitchman et al., 1992; Morrow & Sorrell, 1989).
3. Sexually abused girls are more likely to experience teenage pregnancy (Boyer et al., 1991).
4. Fear, guilt, shame, sleep disturbances, and eating disorders have been associated with child sexual abuse (Browne & Finkelhor, 1986).
5. Adult males who were sexually abused as children by their mothers revealed several problems, including difficulty establishing intimate relationships, depression, and substance abuse (Krug, 1989). Sexually abused males also tended to develop negative self-perceptions, anxiety disorders, sleep and eating disturbances, and sexual dysfunctions such as decreased sexual desire, rapid ejaculation, and difficulty with ejaculation (Elliott & Briere, 1992).

Programs designed to prevent child sexual abuse emphasize a number of specific concepts:

> These include the concept that children own their *own bodies* and therefore can control access to their bodies; there is a *touch continuum,* which recognizes that there are different kinds of touches (e.g. safe and unsafe); *secrets about touching* can and should be told; children have a range of individuals in their *support systems* whom they can tell about touching problems; some programs encourage children to *trust their own feelings* so that, when a situation feels uncomfortable or strange, they should tell someone; and they can learn *how to say* 'no!' (Conte, 1993, 75).

> **Sexually abused children appear to function differently than do children who have not been abused.**
>
> JON R. CONTE

CONSIDERATION

If you have been the victim of sexual abuse and are experiencing difficulties as an adult because of your childhood victimization, you might consider getting help from your local mental health center or student counseling center. Alternatively, you might read self-help books such as *The Courage to Heal* (Bass & Davis, 1988) and *Victims No Longer: Men Recovering from Incest and other Sexual Child Abuse* (Lew, 1990). Finally, help for sex abuse victims is available nationwide through Childhelp USA (1–800–422–4453).

> **The foundation of child protection is found in state laws that require the reporting of known or suspected child abuse and neglect.**
>
> THEODORE J. STERN

& Parent, Sibling, and Elder Abuse

As we have seen, intimate partners and children may be victims of relationship violence and abuse. Parents, siblings, and the elderly may also be abused by family members.

Parent Abuse

Some people assume that because parents are typically physically and socially more powerful than their children, they are immune from being abused by their children. But parents are often targets of their children's anger, hostility, and frustration. It is not uncommon for teenage and even younger children to physically and verbally lash out at their parents. In a national survey of family violence, almost 10 percent of the parents reported that they have been hit, bit, or kicked at least once by their children (Gelles & Straus, 1988). The same researchers found that three percent of parents reported that they had been victimized at least once by a severe form of violence inflicted by a child age 11 or older. Children have been known to push parents down stairs, set the house on fire while their parents are in it, and use weapons such as guns and knives to inflict serious injuries or even kill a parent.

> **CONSIDERATION**
>
> Heide (1992) reported that about 300 parents in the United States are killed each year by their children. However, according to one attorney who specializes in defending adolescents who have killed a parent, over 90 percent of youths who kill their parents have been abused by them. "In-depth portraits of such youths have frequently shown that they killed because they could no longer tolerate conditions at home" (Heide, 1992, 6).

Sibling Abuse

Sibling abuse is a common form of abuse in the family.

Observe a family with two or more children and you will likely observe some amount of sibling abuse. Seventy-five percent of children with siblings have at least one violent episode of conflict with their siblings during a year's time. An average of 21 violent acts takes place between siblings in a family per year (Steinmetz, 1987).

Even in "well-adjusted" families, some degree of fighting among the children is expected. Most incidents of sibling violence consist of slaps, pushes, kicks, bites, and punches. However, serious and dangerous violent behavior between siblings occurs as well.

NATIONAL DATA & Each year, an estimated three percent of children in the United States use a weapon towards a brother or sister (Gelles & Straus, 1988).

Elder Abuse

Another form of family abuse involves abuse of the elderly. Although the definitions regarding what constitutes elder abuse vary, some forms of elder abuse include the following (Johnson, 1991):

1. Physical abuse (inflicting injury or physical pain)
2. Failure to provide basic health and hygiene needs, such as clean clothes, doctor visits, medication, and adequate nutrition
3. Sexual assault
4. Psychological abuse (verbal abuse, deprivation of mental health services, harassment, and deception)
5. Social abuse (unreasonable confinement and isolation, lack of supervision, unfit environment, and abandonment)
6. Legal abuse (improper or illegal use of the elder's resources)

> There is considerable evidence that abuse of the elderly, including patricide, has been present throughout history.
>
> FRANCES A. BOUDREAU

NATIONAL DATA ❧ The National Aging Resource Center on Abuse reports that neglect is the most frequent type of domestic elder abuse (37.2 percent), followed by physical abuse (26.3 percent), financial/material exploitation (20 percent), and emotional abuse (11 percent) (U.S. House of Representatives, Select Committee on Aging, 1991).

One type of elder abuse that has received recent media attention is "granny dumping." Adult children or grandchildren who feel burdened with the care of their elderly parent or grandparent drive the elder to the entrance of a hospital and leave him or her there with no identification. If the hospital cannot identify responsible relatives, the hospital is required by state law to take care of the abandoned elder or transfer the elder to a nursing home facility, which is paid for by the state funds. Relatives of the "dumped granny," hiding from financial responsibility, never visit or see "granny" again.

As is true of all forms of domestic violence, reliable estimates of the prevalence of elder abuse are difficult to obtain.

NATIONAL DATA ❧ Studies on the prevalence of elder abuse in the United States suggest that from 4 to 10 percent of the elderly population are abused (Johnson, 1991).

The abuser of the elderly tends to be an adult child or spouse of the victim. Some research suggests that the perpetrator of the abuse is more often the adult child (Boudreau, 1993) who is financially dependent on the elderly victim (Pillemer, 1985).

Adult children who are most likely to abuse their parents tend to be under a great deal of stress and to use alcohol or drugs. They also tend to be white, middle-aged, and lower-middle or upper-lower class (White, 1988). In some cases, parent abusers are "getting back" for their parents' maltreatment of them as children. In still other cases, the children are frustrated with the burden of having to care for their elderly parents. For the last category of parent abusers, local agencies throughout the nation provide such services as Meals on Wheels

Meals on Wheels is available in many localities to help adult children provide for their aging parents.

and elderly daycare to help children with their aging parents. The name of the agency nearest you may be obtained by writing the National Association of Area Agencies on Aging (600 Maryland Avenue, S.W., Suite 208, Washington, D.C. 20024). A newsletter, *Advice for Adults with Aging Parents,* is also available from Helpful Publications, Inc. (310 West Durham Street, Philadelphia, PA 19119–2901).

Family Violence: A Cross-Cultural Perspective

ACROSS CULTURES

David Levinson (1989) described the results of an extensive cross-cultural study of family violence in 90 non-Western societies. These societies represent the major cultural and geographical regions of the world. In this section, we look at the results of this study in order to gain a cross-cultural perspective on family violence.

Cross-Cultural Family Violence Statistics

Levinson reports that wife beating is the most common form of family violence, occurring in 84.5 percent of the 90 societies. Husband beating, on the other hand, occurs in only 26.9 percent of the 90 societies. In 15.5 percent of the societies, wife beating is rare or unheard of. In contrast, husband beating is rare or unheard of in 73.1 percent of the 90 societies. Adultery or sexual jealousy is a major reason for spouse abuse of both men and women.

In reference to child abuse, some form of physical punishment is used in 74.4 percent of societies. Physical punishment of children is rarely or never used in 26.5 percent of societies.

In our society, fighting among siblings is expected and common. However, physical violence between non-adult siblings is rare or absent in 56.2 percent of societies.

Societies with Minimal or No Family Violence

Out of the 90 societies in Levinson's study of family violence, 16 societies are virtually free of family violence. In these societies, spouse, child, and sibling abuse are rare or nonexistent. Levinson suggests that four factors explain the low rates of family abuse in these 16 societies.

1. Spouses have equal decision-making power in household and financial matters, equal freedom to divorce for both men and women, and no double standard regarding premarital sex.
2. Marriage is monogamous and the divorce rate relatively low, which suggests marital stability and emotional and economic dependence between spouses.
3. Disagreements between adults are resolved peacefully through mediation, disengagement, or avoidance of conflict situations.

4. Family members who are victims or are threatened with physical harm by a family member are offered immediate help by neighbors who intervene or provide shelter.

℘ Trends

Trends in violent and abusive relationships include greater public awareness that such behavior occurs in intimate relationships, an increased number of shelters for battered women, a less punitive and more rehabilitative approach to the sexuality of abusive fathers, and more weight being given to the preference of children in abusive families regarding where they want to live. In regard to the latter, 12-year-old Gregory Kingsley of Orlando, Florida, sued his biological mother for a "divorce" on grounds that he had not been properly taken care of. The court ruled in his favor and family ties with his biological mother were severed. While this is unusual and rare, the legal decision represents a precedent for future cases.

Another legal trend in the area of domestic violence is the adoption of policies that mandate the arrest of abusers. In 1981, Duluth, Minnesota, was the first U.S. city to institute mandatory arrests in domestic disputes, which means that even if a victim does not wish to press charges, the police are required to make an arrest if they see evidence of abuse. Since 1981, about half of the states and Washington, D.C., have established mandatory arrest policies (Dickinson & van der Merwe, 1992; Gibbs, 1993).

⌁ CHOICES ⌁

---

*C*hoices about abusive relationships include whether to report suspected cases of child abuse or neglect and whether to terminate an abusive dating relationship.

Report Suspected Cases of Child Abuse or Neglect?

Federal law requires all social workers, teachers, physicians, and other professionals to report suspected cases of child abuse or neglect to authorities, such as the police, Department of Social Services, or local office of Children's Protective Services. Failing to report suspected child abuse may result in criminal and civil liability.

Beyond the legal requirement of some professionals to report suspected child abuse, individuals may feel morally compelled to help a victimized child by reporting suspected abuse. But how does one decide whether there are grounds for suspected child abuse or neglect? Barker and Branson (1993) reported the following guidelines for determining whether there are grounds for reporting child abuse or neglect.

1. *Direct Evidence.* Direct evidence of child abuse or neglect includes:

(continued)

(a) eyewitness observations of a caregiver's abuse or neglect, (b) finding the child in physically dangerous circumstances, (c) the child or caregiver's own descriptions of abusive or neglectful behavior, (d) demonstrated inability by the parent to care for a newborn, and (e) disabilities by guardians so severe that the guardians are not likely to be able to provide needed care.

2. *Indirect Evidence.* Indirect evidence of child abuse or neglect includes: (a) suspicious injuries suggesting abuse, (b) supposedly accidental injuries that show gross inattention to the child's safety needs, (c) injuries or medical findings suggesting sexual abuse, (d) signs of severe physical deprivation, (e) extremely dirty and unkempt home, (f) untreated injuries, illnesses, or impairments, (g) unexplained absences from school, (h) apparent caregiver indifference to the child's severe emotional or developmental problems, suggesting emotional abuse, (i) indifference or approval by the caregiver of the child's misbehavior, and (j) abandoned children.

Terminate an Abusive Dating Relationship?

In a study of 82 abused women, Roscoe and Benaske (1985) found that 49 percent of the abused wives had been abused in their dating relationships and 30 percent of the victims eventually married the perpetrator. If you are in a dating relationship in which you have experienced violence, be aware that a pattern of violence is likely to continue. A longitudinal study by O'Leary et al. (1989) found that abuse in courtship tends to continue in marriage.

Terminate an Abusive Marriage Relationship?

Students in the authors' classes were asked if they would end a marriage if the spouse hit or kicked them. Although some said that they would seek a divorce, most felt they would try to work it out.

Seek a Divorce
Those opting for divorce felt they couldn't live with someone who had or would abuse them.

> I abhor violence of any kind, and since a marriage should be based on love, kicking is certainly out of the norm. I would lose all respect for my mate and I could never trust him again. It would be over.

Continue Marriage Relationship
Most felt that marriage was too strong a commitment to end if the abuse could be stopped.

> I would not divorce my spouse if she hit or kicked me. I'm sure that there's always room for improvement

in my behavior although I don't think it's necessary to assault me. I recognize that under certain circumstances, it's the quickest way to draw my attention to the problems at hand. I would try to work through our difficulties with my spouse.

> The physical contact would lead to a separation. During that time, I would expect him to feel sorry for what he had done and to seek psychiatric help. My anger would be so great, it's quite hard to know exactly what I would do.

> I wouldn't leave him right off. I would try to get him to counseling. If we could not work through the problem, I would leave him. If there was no way we could live together, I guess divorce would be the answer.

> I would not divorce my husband because I don't believe in breaking the sacred vows of marriage. But I would separate from him and let him suffer!

> I would tell her I was leaving but that she could keep me if she would agree for us to see a counselor to ensure that the abuse never happened again.

Some therapists emphasize that a pattern of abuse develops if such behavior is not addressed immediately. Some recommend that the first time abuse occurs, the couple should seek therapy. The second time it occurs, they should separate. The third time, they might consider a divorce.

☙ Summary

Violence in relationships refers to the intentional use of physical force designed to hurt or injure another person. Other forms of abuse are verbal or psychological abuse (denigrating the partner), neglect (withholding medical treatment or food from elderly parents), or sexual abuse (rape or fondling a child). One of the most frightening and unexpected aspects of violence and abuse is date rape. The perpetrator is usually a boyfriend or lover who does not plan the rape and often feels he has done nothing wrong after the rape.

Cultural values (might makes right), gender roles (men are superior to and should control women), a family history of violence, alcohol or drug use, and personality characteristics (dependency, jealousy, need to control), are factors that contribute to abuse in relationships.

It is not unusual for couples to continue their relationship after violence has occurred. For some individuals, violence is viewed as part of a love relationship. Others have no alternative to the primary relationship. Still others feel they deserve the abuse or would feel guilty if they left the relationship.

Child, sibling, and elder abuse are other forms of abuse in relationships. Granny dumping is a new form of abuse that involves children or grandchildren, who feel burdened with the care of their elderly parents or grandparents, driving them to the emergency entrance of a hospital and dumping them. If the relatives of the elderly patient cannot be identified, the hospital will put the patient in a nursing home at state expense.

Cross-culturally, family abuse patterns vary. The most common form of family violence is wife beating. In some societies, family violence is rare or nonexistent.

Trends in violent and abusive relationships include greater visibility of the subject, more shelters for abused wives, more weight given to the preference of children who want to escape from abusive parents, and mandatory arrest policies for abusers.

Questions for Reflection

1. To what degree have you been exposed to violence and abuse in relationships?
2. At what point would you be willing to terminate an abusive dating or marital relationship?
3. Under what circumstances do you feel children should be allowed to "divorce" parents who abuse them?

References

American Council on Education and University of California. The American freshman: National norms for fall, 1992. Los Angeles, Calif.: Los Angeles Higher Education Research Institute, 1992.

Asbury, Jo-Ellen. Violence in families of color in the United States. *Family Violence: Prevention and Treatment.* Hampton, R. L., T. P. Gullotta, G. R. Adams, E. H. Potter III, and R. P. Weissberg (eds.) Newbury Park, California: Sage Publications, 1993, 113–141.

Barker, R. and D. Branson. Forensic social work: Legal aspects of professional practice. New York: Hallworth Press, 1993.

Bass, E. and L. Davis. *The courage to heal.* New York: Harper and Row, 1988.

Bechhofer, L. and A. Parrot. What is acquaintance rape? *Acquaintance Rape: The Hidden Crime,* A. Parrot and L. Bechhofer, eds. New York: John Wiley and Sons, 1991, 9–25.

Beitchman, J. H., K. J. Zuker, J. E. Hood, G. A. daCosta, D. Akman, and E. Cassavia. A review of the long-term effects of child sexual abuse. *Child Abuse and Neglect,* 1992, *16,* 101–119.

Bethke, T. M. and D. M. DeJoy. An experimental study of factors influencing the acceptability of dating violence. *Journal of Interpersonal Violence,* 1993, *8,* 36–51.

Blau, G. M., M. B. Dall, & L. M. Anderson. The assessment and treatment of violent families. *Family Violence: Prevention and Treatment.* Hampton, R. L., T. P. Gullotta, G. R. Adams, E. H. Potter III, and R. P. Weissberg (eds.) Newbury Park, California: Sage Publications, 1993, 198–229.

Boudreau, F. A. Elder abuse. *Family Violence: Prevention and Treatment.* Hampton, R. L., T. P. Gullotta, G. R. Adams, E. H. Potter III, and R. P. Weissberg (eds.) Newbury Park, California: Sage Publications, 1993, 142–158.

Bowman, M. L. Measuring marital coping and its correlates. *Journal of Marriage and the Family,* 1990, *52,* 463–474.

Boye-Beaman, J., K. E. Leonard, and M. Senchak. Male premarital aggresssion and gender identity among black and white newlywed couples. *Journal of Marriage and the Family,* 1993, *55,* 303–313.

Boyer, D., D. Fine and S. Killpack. Sexual abuse and teen pregnancy. *The Network,* 1991, Summer, 1–2.

Browne, A and D. Finkelhor. Initial and long-term effects: A review of the research. *A Sourcebook on Child Sexual Abuse,* D. Finkelhor, ed., Newbury Park, CA: Sage, 1986, 143–179.

Burt, M. R. Rape myths and acquaintance rape. *Acquaintance Rape: The Hidden Crime,* A. Parrot and L. Bechhofer, eds. New York: John Wiley & Sons, 1991, 26–40.

Busby, Dean M. Violence in the family. *Family Research: A Sixty-Year Review, vol. I,* S. J. Bahr, ed. New York: Lexington Books, 1991, 335–385.

Cazenave, N. A. and M. A. Zahn. Women, murder, and male domination: Police reports of domestic violence in Chicago and Philadelphia. *Intimate Violence: Interdisciplinary Perspectives,* E. C. Viano, ed. Washington, D.C.: Hemisphere Publishing Co, 1992, 83–97.

Conte, J. R. Sexual abuse of children. *Family Violence: Prevention and Treatment.* Hampton, R. L., T. P. Gullotta, G. R. Adams, E. H. Potter III, and R. P. Weissberg (eds.) Newbury Park, California: Sage Publications, 1993, 56–85

Copenhaver, S. and E. Grauerholz. Sexual victimization among sorority women: Exploring the link between sexual violence and institutional practices. *Sex Roles,* 1991, *24,* 31–41.

Daly, M. and M. Wilson. Child abuse and other risks of not living with both parents. *Ethology and Sociobiology,* 1985, *6,* 197–210.

DeMaris, Alfred. Male versus female initiation of aggression: The case of courtship violence. *Intimate Violence: Interdisciplinary Perspectives,* E. C. Viano, ed. Washington, D.C.: Hemisphere Publishing Co, 1992, 111–135.

DeSouza, E. R., T. Pierce, J. C. Zanelli, and C. Hutz. Perceived sexual intent in the U.S. and Brazil as a function of nature of encounter, subjects' nationality, and gender. *The Journal of Sex Research,* 1992, *29,* 251–260.

Dickinson, D. and S. van der Merwe. D.C. pioneers mandatory arrest in domestic disputes. *Nation's Cities Weekly,* March 2, 1992, *15,* 3.

Ellis, Desmond. Woman abuse among separated and divorced women: The relevance of social support. *Intimate Violence: Interdisciplinary Perspectives,* E. C. Viano, ed. Washington, D.C.: Hemisphere Publishing Co., 1992, 177–189.

Elliott, D. M. and J. Briere. The sexually abused boy: Problems in manhood. *Medical Aspects of Human Sexuality,* 1992, *26,* 68–71.

Finkelhor, D., G. Hotaling, I. A. Lewis, and C. Smith. Sexual abuse in a national survey of adult men and women: Prevalence, characteristics, and risk factors. *Child Abuse and Neglect,* 1990, *14,* 19–28.

Finkelhor, D. and K. Yllo. Rape in marriage. *Abuse and Victimization Across the Life Span,* M. B. Straus, ed. Baltimore, Md.: The Johns Hopkins University Press, 1988, 140–152.

Flynn, C. P. Relationship violence by women: Issues and implications. *Family Relations,* 1990, *39,* 194–198.

Frank, J. G. Risk factors for rape: Empirical confirmation and preventive implications. Poster session presented at the 99th annual convention of the American Psychological Association, San Francisco, August 16, 1991.

Gelles, R. J. Family violence. *Family Violence: Prevention and Treatment.* Hampton, R. L., T. P. Gullotta, G. R. Adams, E. H. Potter III, and R. P. Weissberg (eds.) Newbury Park, California: Sage Publications, 1993, 1–24.

Gelles, R. J. and J. R. Conte. Domestic violence and sexual abuse of children: A review of research in the eighties. *Contemporary Families: Looking Forward, Looking Back,* A. Booth, ed. National Council on Family Relations, 1991, 327–340.

Gelles, R. and M. Straus. *Intimate violence.* New York: Simon and Schuster, 1988.

Gibbs, N. 'Till death do us part. *Time,* January 18, 1993, 38–45.

Goetting, Ann. Patterns of marital homicide: A comparison of husbands and wives. *Journal of Comparative Family Studies,* 1989, *20,* no. 3, 16–32.

Hampton, R. L. and A. F. Washington Coner-Edwards. Physical and sexual violence in marriage. *Family Violence: Prevention and Treatment.* Hampton, R. L., T. P. Gullotta, G. R. Adams, E. H. Potter III, and R. P. Weissberg (eds.) Newbury Park, California: Sage Publications, 1993, 113–141.

Harrington, D. and H. Dubowitz. What can be done to prevent child maltreatment? *Family Violence: Prevention and Treatment.* Hampton, R. L., T. P. Gullotta, G. R. Adams, E. H. Potter III, and R. P. Weissberg (eds.) Newbury Park, California: Sage Publications, 1993, 258–280.

Heide, K. M. *Why kids kill parents: Child abuse and adolescent homicide.* Columbus, Ohio: Ohio State University Press, 1992.

Herbert, T. B., R. C. Silver, and J. H. Ellard. Coping with an abusive relationship: I. How and why do women stay? *Journal of Marriage and the Family,* 1991, *53,* 311–325.

Holcomb, D. R., L. C. Holcomb, K. A. Sondag, and N. Williams. Attitudes about date rape: Gender differences among college students. *College Student Journal,* 1991, *25,* 434–439.

Jaffe, N. *Spouse abuse.* New York Public Affairs Committee, 1990.

Johnson, I. M., J. Crowley, and R. T. Sigler. Agency response to domestic violence: Services provided to battered women. *Intimate Violence: Interdisciplinary Perspectives,* E. C. Viano, ed. Washington, D.C.: Hemisphere Publishing Co., 1992, 191–202.

Johnson, T. F. *Elder mistreatment: Deciding who is at risk.* New York: Greenwood Press, 1991.

Kasian, M. and S. L. Painter. Frequency and severity of psychological abuse in a dating population. *Journal of Interpersonal Violence,* 1992, *7,* 350–364.

Knudsen, Dean. Duplicate reports of child maltreatment: A research note. *Child Abuse and Neglect,* 1989, *13,* 41–43.

Koss, M. P. Defending date rape. *Journal of Interpersonal Violence* 1992, *7,* 122–126.

Koss, M. P., T. E. Dinero, C. A. Seibel, and S. L. Cox. Stranger and acquaintance rape. *Psychology of Women Quarterly,* 1988, *12,* 1–24.

Koss, M. P. and J. A. Gaines. The prediction of sexual aggression by alcohol use, athletic participation, and fraternity affiliation. *Journal of Interpersonal Violence,* 1993, *8,* 94–108.

Krug, Ronald S. Adult male report of childhood sexual abuse by mothers: Case description, motivations, and long-term consequences. *Child Abuse and Neglect,* 1989, *13,* 111–119.

Krugman, R. D., M. Lenherr, B. A. Betz, and G. E. Fryer. The relationship between unemployment and physical abuse of children. *Child Abuse and Neglect,* 1986, *10,* 415–418.

Leonard, K. E. and H. T. Blane. Alcohol and marital aggression in a national sample of young men. *Journal of Interpersonal Violence,* 1992, *7,* 19–30.

Levinson, D. *Family violence in cross-cultural perspective.* Newbury Park, Calif.: Sage, 1989.

Lew, M. *Victims no longer: Men recovering from incest and other sexual child abuse.* New York: Harper and Row, 1990.

Lloyd, S. A. and B. C. Emery. Abuse in the family: An ecological, life-cycle perspective. *Family Relations: Challenges for the Future,* T. H. Brubaker, ed. Newbury Park, Calif.: Sage Publications, 1993, 129–152.

Loseke, D. R. *The battered woman and shelters: The social construction of wife abuse.* Albany, N.Y.: State University of New York Press, 1992.

MacAndrew, C. and R. Edgerton. *Drunken comportment: A social explanation.* Chicago: Aldine, 1969.

Majority Staff of the Senate Judiciary Committee. *Violence against women: A week in the life of America.* Washington, D.C., October 1992.

Makepeace, James. Dating, living together, and courtship violence. *Violence in Dating Relationships,* M. S. Pirog-Good and J. E. Stets, eds. New York: Greenwood Press, 1989, 94–107.

Malone, J., A. Tyree, and K. D. O'Leary. Generalization and containment: Different effects of past aggression for wives and husbands. *Journal of Marriage and the Family,* 1989, *51,* 687–697.

Martin, M. J. and J. C. Walters. Child neglect: Developing strategies for prevention. *Family Perspective,* 1992, *26,* 305–314.

Morrow, R. B. and G. T. Sorrell. Factors affecting self-esteem, depression, and negative behaviors in sexually abused female adolescents. *Journal of Marriage and the Family,* 1989, *51,* 677–686.

Murty, K. S. and J. B. Roebuck. An analysis of crisis calls by battered women in the city of Atlanta. *Intimate Violence: Interdisciplinary Perspectives,* E. C. Viano, ed. Washington, D.C.: Hemisphere Publishing Co., 1992, 61–70.

National Clearinghouse for the Defense of Battered Women. July 1990. (125 S. 9th St., Suite 302, Philadelphia, PA 19107, 215/351–0010).

National Clearinghouse on Marital and Date Rape. 1993. Berkeley, California.

Ney, P. G. Transgenerational triangles of abuse: A model of family violence. *Intimate Violence: Interdisciplinary Perspectives,* E. C. Viano, ed. Washington, D.C.: Hemisphere Publishing Co., 1992, 15–25.

NiCarthy, Ginny. *Getting free: A handbook for women in abusive relationships,* 2d ed. Seattle, Wash.: The Seal Press, 1986.

North Carolina Coalition Against Domestic Violence. Domestic violence fact sheet. Spring 1991, P.O. Box 51875, Durham, NC 27717–1875, 919/490–1467.

Novello, A. The domestic violence issue: Hear our voices. *American Medical News,* March 23, 1992, *35,* no. 12, 41–42.

Oates, R. K., A. A. Davis, and M. G. Ryan. Predictive factors for child abuse. *International Perspectives on Family Violence,* R. J. Gelles and C. P. Cornell, eds. Lexington, Mass: Lexington Books 1983, 97–106.

Okun, Lewis. *Woman abuse: Facts replacing myths.* Albany, N.Y.: State University of New York Press, 1986.

O'Leary, K. D., J. Barling, I. Arias, A. Rosenbaum, J. Malone, and A. Tyree. Prevalence and stability of physical aggression between spouses: A longitudinal analysis. *Journal of Consulting and Clinical Psychology,* 1989, *57,* 263–268.

Pagelow, M. D. Adult victims of domestic violence: Battered women. *Journal of Interpersonal Violence,* 1992, *7,* 87–120.

Parrot, A. Recommendations for college policies and procedures to deal with acquaintance rape. *Acquaintance Rape: The Hidden Crime,* A. Parrot and L Bechhofer, eds. New York: John Wiley and Sons, 1991, 368–380.

Pillemer, K. The dangers of dependency: New findings on domestic violence against the elderly. *Social Problems,* 1985, 33, 146–158.

Pillemer, K. A. and D. Finkelhor. The prevalence of elder abuse; A random sample survey. Paper presented at the annual meetings of the Gerontological Society of America, Chicago, November 1986. Reported in R. J. Gelles and M. A. Straus, *Intimate Violence.* New York: Simon and Schuster, 1988, 63.

Pinkney, D. S. Sparing the rod: Activist physicians argue that school punishments reinforce our nation's culture of violence. *American Medical News,* 1992, 35, 45–50.

Pirog-Good, Maureen A. Sexual abuse in dating relationships. *Intimate Violence: Interdisciplinary Perspectives,* E. C. Viano, ed. Washington, D.C.: Hemisphere Publishing Co., 1992, 101–110.

Renzetti, C. M. Building a second closet: Third party responses to victims of lesbian partner abuse. *Family Relations,* 1989, 38, 157–163.

Riggs, D. S. Relationship problems and dating aggression. *Journal of Interpersonal Violence,* 1993, 8, 18–35.

Riza, W. R., R. N. Singh, and V. T. Davis. Differences among males and females in their perception of spousal abuse. *Free Inquiry in Creative Sociology,* 1992, 20, 19–24.

Roscoe, B. and N. Benaske. Courtship violence experienced by abused wives: Similarities in patterns of abuse. *Family Relations,* 1985, 34, 419–424.

Rosen, K. H. and S. M. Stith. The process of leaving abusive dating relationships. Paper, 54th Annual Conference of the National Council on Family Relations, Orlando, Florida, 1992. Used by permission.

Russell, D. E. *Rape in marriage.* Bloomington, Ind.: Indiana University Press, 1990.

Russell, D. E. H. Wife rape. *Acquaintance Rape: The Hidden Crime,* A. Parrot and L. Bechhofer, eds. New York: John Wiley and Sons, 1991, 129–139.

Sharp, D. Tales of drugs, abuse open boy's "divorce" trial. *USA Today,* September 26, 1992, 3A.

Shepard, M. F. and J. A. Campbell. The Abusive Behavior Inventory: A measure of psychological and physical abuse. *Journal of Interpersonal Violence,* 1992, 7, no. 3, 291–305.

Shupe, A., W. A. Stacey, and L. R. Hazlewood. *Violent men, violent couples.* Lexington, Mass.: D.C. Heath and Co., 1987.

Solomon, J. C. Child sexual abuse by family members: A radical feminist perspective. *Sex Roles,* 1992, 27, 473–485.

Statistical Abstract of the United States: 1993, 113th ed. Washington, D.C.: U.S. Government Printing Press.

Steinmetz, S. K. Family violence, *Handbook of Marriage and the Family,* M. B. Sussman and S. K. Steinmetz, eds. New York: Plenum, 1987.

Steinmetz, S. K., and J. S. Lucca. Husband battering. *Handbook of Family Violence,* V. B. Van Hasselt, R. L. Morrison, A. S. Bellack, and M. Herson, eds. New York: Plenum Press, 1988, 233–246.

Stets, J. E. Interactive processes in dating aggression: A national study. *Journal of Marriage and the Family,* 1992, 54, 165–177.

Stets, J. E. Verbal and physical aggression in marriage. *Journal of Marriage and the Family,* 1990, 52, 501–514.

Stets, J. E. and D. A. Henderson. Contextual factors surrounding conflict resolution while dating: Results from a national study. *Family Relations,* 1991, 40, 29–36.

Stets, J. E. and M. A. Straus. The marriage as a hitting license: A comparison of assaults in dating, cohabiting, and married couples. *Violence in Dating Relationships,* M. A. Pirog-Good and J. E. Stets, eds. New York: Greenwood Press, 1989, 33–52.

Straus, M. A. A sociological perspective on the prevention of wife-beating. *The Social Causes of Husband-Wife Violence,* M. A. Straus and G. T. Hotaling, eds. Minneapolis, Minn.: University of Minnesota Press, 1980, 211–232.

Straus, M. A. and S. Sweet. Verbal/symbolic aggression in couples: Incidence rates and relationships to personal characteristics. *Journal of Marriage and the Family,* 1992, *54,* 346–357.

Toufexis, A. Our violent kids. *Time,* June 12, 1989, 52–58.

U.S. House of Representatives, Select Committee on Aging, (May 1991, May 15). *Elder Abuse: What can be done?* (Hearing). Washington, DC: Government Printing Office.

Vaselle-Augenstein, R. and A. Ehrlich. Male batterers: Evidence for psychopathology. *Intimate Violence: Interdisciplinary Perspectives,* E. C. Viano, ed. Washington, D.C.: Hemisphere Publishing Co., 1992, 139–154.

Viano, C. E. Violence among intimates: Major issues and approaches. *Intimate Violence: Interdisciplinary Perspectives,* C. E. Viano, ed. Washington, D.C.: Hemisphere Publishing Co., 1992, 3–12.

Washburne, C. K. A feminist analysis of child abuse and neglect. *The Dark Side of Families: Current Family Violence Research,* D. Finkelhor, R. J. Gelles, G. T. Hotaling, and M. A. Straus, eds. Beverly Hills, Calif.: Sage, 1983, 289–292.

Waterman, C. K., L. J. Dawson, and M. J. Bologna. Sexual coercion in gay male and lesbian relationships: Predictors and implications for support services. *The Journal of Sex Research,* 1989, *1,* 118–124.

White, Melvin. Elder abuse. *Aging and the Family,* S. J. Bahr and E. T. Peterson, eds. Lexington, Mass.: Lexington Books, 1988, 261–271.

Wolf-Smith, J. H. and R. LaRossa. After he hits her. *Family Relations,* 1992, *41,* 324–329.

Contents

13
CHAPTER

Planning Children and Birth Control

Is It True?

1. The degree to which parents are satisfied with their role as parents is related to whether it is their first or subsequent marriage.

2. Whites are more likely to be interested in a childfree marriage than African Americans, Asians, and Hispanics.

3. Based on the number of side effects, women should consider not using the IUD.

4. Teens in the United States have a much lower pregnancy and birth rate than teens in European countries.

5. Only 25 percent of the world's population live in countries where abortion is legally permitted.

1 = T; 2 = T; 3 = T; 4 = F; 5 = F

The most effective contraception for parents is to spend an hour with their children before going to bed.

ROSEANNE BARR ARNOLD

For most people, family size can now be decided by choice, not chance.

NAFIS SADIKK

$\mathcal{R}$ichard Gere said in an interview that he and his wife Cindy Crawford vascilated about whether and when to have children. They were both pro and con on the idea at different times. Although Richard and Cindy may have disagreed about whether and when to have children, they did agree it was important to plan any children they might have.

Parenthood should begin with planning. Before each academic term as a student, you decide how many courses you want to take and when you want to take them. You probably try to avoid overloading your schedule and feel pleased when you get the sequence of courses you want. Successful family planning means having the number of children you want when you want to have them. Although this seems to be a sensible and practical approach to parenthood, many couples leave the number and spacing of their children to chance.

Family planning has benefits for the mother and the child. Having several children at short intervals increases the chances of premature birth, infectious disease, and death for the mother or the baby (Travis, 1988). Parents can minimize such risks by planning fewer children at longer intervals.

Both parents may also benefit from family planning by pacing the financial demands of parenthood. "We spaced our three children every four years," said one father, "so we would have only one child in college at a time."

Conscientious family planning may also reduce the number of children born to parents who do not want them. A child born to rejecting parents is a tragic situation—but a preventable one.

NATIONAL DATA ✄ Ten percent of all U.S. births are not wanted at conception (Williams, 1991).

Some parents are happy with an unintended pregnancy. While an unintended pregnancy may turn out to be a positive experience, it may also lead to an abortion (which may be emotionally and financially stressful) or result in children who are unwanted, resented, and poorly cared for by their parents.

CONSIDERATION

Unintended pregnancies may lead to relationship conflicts in that the pregnant woman, her partner, and their respective families may want different outcomes. For example, the partner may want to continue the pregnancy while the woman may not. In addition, the pregnant woman's parents may want their daughter to place the baby for adoption, while the partner's parents may want their son to marry his pregnant girlfriend and have the baby.

Family planning also benefits society by enabling people to avoid having children they cannot feed and clothe adequately—children whose rearing may have to be subsidized by the taxpayer. Finally, family planning is essential to halting the continuing expansion of the world population and the consequent drain on limited environmental resources.

INTERNATIONAL DATA ❦ The world's population has exceeded 5.25 billion. Every day, an additional 220,000 people are added to the world's population. By the year 2025, it is estimated that the planet will be inhabited by 8.5 billion people (Urzua, 1992).

Without control of population growth, the world faces increased food shortages, unchecked urban growth, environmental damage (including water, soil, and air pollution), depletion of our planet's natural resources, and destruction of the ozone layer. Sadik (1992) suggested that "population may be the key to all the issues that will shape the future: economic growth; environmental security; and the health and well-being of countries, communities, and families" (p. 134).

In this chapter, you are encouraged to consider four basic questions: Do you want to have children? How many? When? What form of birth control will you use to ensure the family size that you want?

❦ Do You Want to Have Children?

In a study of 7,000 undergraduate students, 95 percent reported they wanted to have children (Rubinson & DeRubertis, 1991).

NATIONAL DATA ❦ Seventy percent of college freshmen throughout the United States regard "raising a family" as "essential or very important" (American Council on Education and University of California, 1992).

In this section, we examine the social influences that affect our decision and motivations to have children. We also discuss difficulties and stresses associated with parenthood.

NATIONAL DATA ❦ Over 90 percent of women ages 18–34 expect to have children (*Statistical Abstract of the United States: 1993*, Table 108).

Social Influences on Deciding to Have Children

We live in a pronatalistic, or prochild society. Unless the members of a society have children, the society will cease to exist. The Shakers, also called the United Society of Believers, provide an example of the consequences of a social deemphasis on procreation. Founded in New York in 1787, the Shakers were a religious community that grew to more than 5,000 members by winning others to their faith. Their doctrine included an emphasis on celibacy, which resulted in no marriage, no sexual intercourse, and no children. The effect of

> Increasingly, governmental and societal consensus is emerging in regard to the right of all individuals to seek to improve the quality of their lives for themselves and their children through family planning.
>
> UNITED NATIONS POPULATION FUND

> Families with babies and families without babies are sorry for each other.
>
> E. C. MCKENZIE

Most couples want children in response to both societal influences and personal motivations.

Call it a clan, call it a network, call it a tribe, call it a family. Whatever you call it, whoever your are, you need one.

JANE HOWARD

prohibiting reproduction was to ensure that the Shaker community would eventually cease to exist. Today, only a few members remain who were recruited into the community.

Aware of the importance of reproduction for its continued existence, our society tends to encourage childbearing, an attitude known as *pronatalism*. Our family, friends, religion, government, and schools help to develop positive attitudes toward parenthood. Cultural observances also function to reinforce these attitudes.

Family   Our experience of being reared in families encourages us to have families of our own. Our parents are our models. They married; we marry. They had children; we have children. Some parents exert a much more active influence. "I'm 73 and don't have much time. Will I ever see a grandchild?" asked the mother of an only child. Other remarks parents have made include, "If you don't hurry up, your younger sister is going to have a baby before you do," "We're setting up a trust fund for your brother's child, and we'll do the same for yours," "Did you know that Nash and Marilyn (the child's contemporaries) just had a daughter?" "I think you'll regret not having children when you're old," and "Don't you want a son to carry on your name?"

Friends   Our friends who have children influence us to do likewise. After sharing an enjoyable weekend with friends who had a little girl, one husband wrote to the host and hostess, "Lucy and I are always affected by Karen—she is such a good child to have around. We haven't made up our minds yet, but our desire to have a child of our own always increases after we leave your home." This couple became parents 16 months later.

Religion   Religion may be a powerful influence on the decision to have children. Catholics are taught that having children is the basic purpose of marriage and gives meaning to the union. Although many Catholics use contraception and reject their church's emphasis on procreation, some internalize the church's message. One Catholic woman said, "My body was made by God, and I should use it to produce children for Him. Other people may not understand it, but that's how I feel." Judaism also has a strong family orientation. Couples who choose to be childfree are less likely than couples with children to adhere to any set of religious beliefs.

Government   The tax structures imposed by our federal and state governments support parenthood. Married couples without children pay higher taxes than couples with children, although the reduction in taxes is not sufficient to offset the cost of rearing a child and is not large enough to be a primary inducement to have children.

Governments in other countries have encouraged or discouraged childbearing in different ways. In the 1930s, as a mark of status for women contributing to the so-called Aryan race, Adolf Hitler bestowed the German Mother's Cross on Nazi Germany's most fertile mothers—a gold cross for eight or more children, a silver cross for six or seven, and a bronze cross for four or five.

China has a set of incentives to encourage families to have a maximum of one child. Couples who have only one child are given a "one-child glory certificate," which entitles them to special priority housing, better salaries, a five-percent supplementary pension, free medical care for the child, and an assured place for the child in school. If the couple has more than one child, they may lose their jobs, be assigned to less desirable housing, and be required to pay the government back for the benefits they have received.

ACROSS CULTURES ❧

Special Observances   Our society reaffirms its approval of parents every year by allocating special days for mom and dad. Each year on Mother's Day and Father's Day, parenthood is celebrated across the nation with gifts and embraces. There is no counterpart, such as a Childfree Day.

CONSIDERATION

Despite the tradition of pronatalism in the United States, contemporary values that discourage childbearing and support birth control are also evident. Michaels (1988) suggested that the U.S. tradition of pronatalism has weakened. "The decline in pronatalist values has led to a situation in which those who do not want to have children can make this choice without the fear of extreme social criticism or ostracism" (p. 23).

Individual Motivations for Having Children

Individual motivations, as well as social influences, play an important role in our decisions regarding whether to have children.

Love and Companionship   In a study of 610 married couples, researchers found that children are viewed as important sources of love and affection (Neal, Groat, & Wicks, 1989). Some people feel that having children is one way to avoid loneliness in old age. However, Cohen (1985) suggested that "the loneliest people are those who presumed that their children would forestall a lonely future and who have been disappointed in that hope" (p. 93).

Family Relationships   Many young married couples view children as necessary for "having a real family life" (Neal et al., 1989). Parents may value the relationships that form between their child and other family members, such as the child's grandparents, aunts, uncles, and cousins. Children are also sometimes viewed as a way to strengthen the bond between a couple (Michaels, 1988). Some women may want to become pregnant as a means of pressuring their partner to get married. In a sample of 242 first-time mothers ages 15–42 who were interviewed one year after giving birth, 12% reported that marriage had resulted as a consequence of the baby's birth (Mercer, 1986). When a couple are experiencing relationship problems, they may feel that having a child will bind them more together and save their marriage (Dorman & Klein, 1984).

Attainment of Adult Status   Having a child is one way of attaining adult status and identity.

> The responsibility for new life is expected to elicit mature and conscientious behavior. A new identity emerges; one is now Mother, which is more than just a name. This identity implies a whole new and lasting set of duties, commitments, and values, not the least of which is a new sense of being important, of being truly necessary to another person. (Williams, 1987, p. 307)

Personal Fulfillment   Some adults view having children as "part of being a man or a woman" (Michaels, 1988, p. 47) and thus necessary for the fulfillment of the feminine or masculine role. Parents report feelings of creativity, accomplishment, and competence from the experience of parenthood. Parents also derive a sense of accomplishment from the accomplishments of their children. Parenthood provides mothers and fathers with an important identity, as well as a sense of power. "Children are also seen as a chance to have an effect on the world, particularly by persons who are otherwise powerless" (Williams, 1987, p. 308).

Children may also provide parents with a sense of immortality or expansion of the self. Children represent "a bridge to the future by which one's physical and psychological characteristics can continue beyond the evanescent self" (Williams, 1987, p. 307). Some parents derive gratification from the idea that they will be remembered by their children after the parent dies (Michaels, 1988).

Recapturing Youth   Another motivation for wanting children is that they may provide a mechanism for parents to recapture their own childhood and youth. This may be especially true for men and women who have positive childhood memories (Williams, 1987). One way in which having children helps adults to capture their youth is through play. Children may provide an excuse for adults to play and express the child in themselves that society assumes they have outgrown.

Unconscious Motivations   Reasons for wanting to have a child may exist outside an individual's awareness. For example, Michaels (1988) cited two examples from his clinical experience:

- A woman in her twenties wanted a baby chiefly to compete with her sister, who was pregnant.
- A woman in her thirties wanted a baby in order to gain acceptance by her parents, who had rejected her during her adolescence and college years.

The Self-Assessment on the following page allows you to assess your motivations for parenthood.

Difficulties and Stresses Associated with Parenthood

Every parent knows that parenthood involves difficulties as well as joys. Some of the difficulties and stresses associated with parenthood include the following.

Life-style Changes   Becoming a parent often involves changes in life-style (Neal et al., 1989). Daily living routines often become focused around the needs of the children. Living arrangements may change to provide space for another person in the household. Some parents change their work schedules to allow them to be home more. Food shopping and menus change to accommodate the appetites of children. A major life-style change is the loss of freedom of activity and flexibility in one's personal schedule that comes with parenting. When Hoffman asked a sample of U.S. married couples "What are the disadvantages or bad things about having children . . . ?," the most frequent answer was "loss of freedom." The second most frequent answer was "financial costs" (cited in Michaels, 1988, pp. 34–35).

Financial Cost   Meeting the financial obligations of parenthood is difficult for many parents. Demographers note that high-income families spend more money on rearing their children than low-income families and that the costs of

> You start to recognize the child in yourself, the child in everybody.
>
> ANNIE LENNOX
> (SPEAKING OF HER MOTHERHOOD EXPERIENCE)

> A decision about parenthood can never be entirely rational—even with all the facts in the world . . . the process of reviewing factual information will not necessarily recognize or deal with the powerful but unrecognized feelings that can influence such a personal choice.
>
> JUDITH BLACKFIELD COHEN

> If your vision of parenthood includes only the rosiest images, the life you plan may have little relation to the life you will live.
>
> JUDITH BLACKFIELD COHEN

> Children, from a strictly economically rational viewpoint, are unalloyed economic liabilities for an entire lifetime.
>
> ROBERT JOHN

Child Study Inventory: An Instrument to Assess Motivation for Parenthood

Indicate the answer you feel is the best by placing a one (1) in front of it. Rank the remaining answers (2, 3, and 4) to show your order of preference.

1. Parents expect their children . . .
   F ( )   to fulfill the purpose of life.
   I ( )   to strengthen the family.
   A ( )   to be healthy and happy.
   N ( )   to follow their footsteps.
2. Men want children because . . .
   N ( )   they would like to prove their sexual adequacy.
   F ( )   it is a natural instinct.
   I ( )   they need them to enhance their social status.
   A ( )   they like children.
3. A mother expects her daughter . . .
   I ( )   to give her companionship and affection.
   F ( )   to take the place in the world for which she is destined.
   N ( )   to be like herself.
   A ( )   to be happy and well.
4. Men want children because . . .
   I ( )   children hold the marriage together.
   A ( )   they like to care and provide for children.
   F ( )   it is a function of the mature adult.
   N ( )   they want to perpetuate themselves.
5. A father expects his son . . .
   A ( )   to be happy and well.
   F ( )   to take the place in the world for which he is destined.

   I ( )   to give him companionship and affection.
   N ( )   to be like himself.
6. Women want children because . . .
   A ( )   they like children.
   I ( )   they need them to enhance their social status.
   N ( )   they would like to prove their sexual adequacy.
   F ( )   it is a natural instinct.
7. Generally, people want children because . . .
   F ( )   they are destined to reproduce.
   A ( )   they desire to help someone grow and develop.
   N ( )   they can create someone in their own image.
   I ( )   they provide companionship.
8. A father expects his daughter . . .
   N ( )   to believe in him.
   A ( )   to be happy and well.
   F ( )   to take her place in the world.
   I ( )   to give him companionship and affection.
9. Women want children because . . .
   I ( )   Children hold the marriage together.
   F ( )   it is a function of the mature adult.
   A ( )   they like to care and provide for children.
   N ( )   they want to perpetuate themselves.
10. Women want children because . . .
   F ( )   they are destined to reproduce.
   A ( )   they desire to help someone grow and develop.
   I ( )   they provide companionship.
   N ( )   they create someone in their own image.

(continued on next page)

---

rearing children increase with age. Low-income couples spend $4,330 during their children's first year of life compared to $6,140 for middle-income couples and $8,770 for high-income couples. The cumulative costs of rearing a child who will be 17 years of age in 2007 has been estimated to be $151,170 for low-income families, $210,070 for middle-income families, and $293,400 for high-income families (Exter, 1991). College expenses increase the cost significantly. A four-year education in the years 2007 through 2010 at a public

Child Study Inventory: An Instrument to Assess Motivation for Parenthood

11. Generally, people want children because . . .
   A ( )   they like to care and provide for children.
   N ( )   they want to perpetuate themselves.
   I ( )   children hold the marriage together.
   F ( )   it is a function of the mature adult.

12. A mother expects her son . . .
   F ( )   to take his place in the world.
   I ( )   to give her companionship and affection.
   A ( )   to be happy and well.
   N ( )   to believe in her.

13. Men want children because . . .
   I ( )   they provide companionship.
   N ( )   they create someone in their own image.
   A ( )   they are destined to reproduce.
   F ( )   they desire to help someone grow and develop.

14. Generally, people want children because . . .
   F ( )   it is a natural instinct.
   A ( )   they like children.
   I ( )   they need them to enhance their social status.
   N ( )   they would like to prove their sexual adequacy.

SOURCE: A. I. Rabin (Professor Emeritus) and Robert J. Greene. Department of Psychology, Michigan State University, East Lansing, MI 48824. Reprinted by permission.

Scoring: The Child Study Inventory is composed of item stems related to motivations for parenthood. Each sentence stem is followed by four completion choices. Each choice following the relevant sentence stems can be categorized into one of the basic CSI motivational categories: Altruistic (ALT), Narcissistic (NAR), Fatalistic (FAT), Instrumental (INS).

Scoring is accomplished for each of the four categories by summing the rankings of all completion choices in that category (e.g., all rankings of altruistic choices to obtain an altruistic motivation score). A low score indicates high preference for a given category.

For a more detailed subdivision of scores, the user may score "motivational" items (#2, 4, 6, 7, 9, 10, 11, 13, 14) and "expectancy" items (#1, 3, 5, 8) separately.

REFERENCES:

Counte, M. A. et al. Factor structure of Rabin's Child Study Inventory. *Journal of Personality Assessment,* 1979, *43,* 59–63.

Gordon, R. S. Assessing motivation for parenthood of adult adoptees and adoptive parents. The Wright Institute Studies of Psychiatry. Berkeley, California, 1988.

Rabin, A. I. Motivation for parenthood. *Journal of Projective Techniques & Personality Assessment,* 1965, *29,* 405–411.

Rabin, A. I. amd R. J. Green. Assessing motivation for parenthood. *Journal of Psychology,* 1968, *69,* 39–46.

college will cost $72,000; more than $149,000 at a private college; and $231,000 at an Ivy League school (Farmer & Ling, 1990).

CONSIDERATION

The economic value of children varies greatly across societies and historical time periods. In rural, developing countries (as in early U.S. history), children are viewed as economic assets because they provide valuable work to help sustain their families. However, the role of children has changed in the United States and in other countries with child labor laws and compulsory education. In these countries, children generally represent an economic liability, rather than an economic asset.

Increased Role Demands Another aspect of parenthood involves increased role demands for both parents, but especially for the parent who takes primary responsibility for child care. Some parents enjoy the work involved in the parental role, as reflected in the comments of one mother:

> There is nothing I would rather do than have a baby to take care of. Now that my children are in school, they need me less. I miss breast-feeding, rocking them to sleep, and giving them baths. To me, it wasn't work, it was joy. (Author's files)

Many parents, however, feel burdened by parenting, at least some of the time. One mother, a college student, remarked:

> I don't know how I got through those first three years of parenthood. Every night I was awakened by a crying baby who needed to be fed or changed or rocked back to sleep. During the day, the only time I had to myself was when my daughter was taking a nap; I used that time to study. In the evening, I worked part-time at a restaurant. I was always exhausted. I don't regret it, but once is enough for me. (Author's files)

Worry and Grief Parenthood involves worry or concern about the well-being of one's children (Mercer, 1986., Williams, 1987). Even before the birth of a child, parents worry about whether or not the child will be born "normal" and healthy (Affonso & Mayberry, 1989). Concern over the health and well-being of children continues even when the children are grown and living independently.

Parenthood may also involve grief. Having a child with congenital or acquired defects, illness, or injury may be extremely difficult for the parents to deal with emotionally. (Children with special needs also involve increased role demands on parents and increased financial cost.) Parents whose child dies often continue to grieve to some degree throughout their lives. Even when parents are spared such tragic events, they may experience grief or disappointment regarding their child's grades in school, behavior toward others, involvement in illegal activities, and life-style values and choices in regard to religion, occupation, and sexuality.

Negative Behaviors of Children One study found that the most frequently reported type of stress experienced by mothers of young children was due to their child's negative behavior (Brailey, 1989). Such behaviors included disobeying instructions or refusing to comply with the mother's wishes, demanding excessive attention, fighting or arguing with siblings, and causing damage to household property.

CONSIDERATION

Despite the difficulties and stresses associated with parenthood, most parents are very satisfied with their role as parents. In a national survey, 85 percent of

---

Children are a great comfort in your old age—and they help you reach it faster, too.

LIONEL KAUFFMAN

My mother loved children—she would have given anything if I had been one.

GROUCHO MARX

How sharper than a serpent's tooth it is to have a thankless child.

SHAKESPEARE

parents with children over the age of 16 reported very high levels of satisfaction with their role as parent. Over 80 percent were satisfied with the way their children turned out. Only three percent were not very satisfied with their role as parent (Umberson, 1992). Two researchers compared parental satisfaction of a national sample of American parents and found that greater satisfaction was reported by first-married biological parents than remarried biological parents or stepparents (Ishii-Kuntz & Ihinger-Tallman, 1991).

℘ The Childfree Alternative

NATIONAL DATA ℘ Of all women in the United States between the ages of 18 and 34, almost 10 percent report that they do not expect to have a child (*Statistical Abstract of the United States: 1993*, Table 108).

Women who want to remain childfree tend to cite their age and the stress and worry associated with rearing children. Men are more likely to emphasize the financial demands (Seccombe, 1991). Both spouses may place a greater emphasis on adult goals and activities (Arcus, 1992). They also tend to be politically liberal and pro-choice (Barnes, 1992).

> I would have made a terrible parent.
>
> KATHERINE HEPBURN

Wanting to remain childfree is also related to racial and ethnic background. Whites are most likely to consider marriage without children. African Americans, Native Americans, Mexican Americans and Asian Americans are more likely to be family oriented and to consider children an important part of family life (O'Hare et al., 1991; O'Hare & Felt, 1991; Ahlburg & De Vita, 1992). However, upwardly mobile achievement may sometimes override ethnic influence. African Americans who are striving to achieve social mobility are more likely to be voluntarily childless (Boyd, 1989).

Some couples who do not have children are not childfree by choice. Between 15 percent and 20 percent of U.S. couples are unable to have children and feel relegated to a life of involuntary childlessness. A smaller percentage of couples do not initially decide to be childfree. They put off having children ("We'll wait till we're out of school . . . until we get a house . . . until our careers are established . . . until we have more money") and become satisfied with the childfree lifestyle and decide to continue it. However, those who never have children voluntarily are in the minority.

How happy are the marriages of couples who elect to remain childfree compared to the marriages of couples who opt for having children. While marital satisfaction declines across time for all couples whether or not they have children (MacDermid et al., 1990), children tend to lessen marital satisfaction by decreasing spousal time together, interaction and agreement over finances. In addition, couples who have children report greater satisfaction before their children are born and after they leave home. The greatest drop in marital satisfaction is during the time children are teenagers. Childfree couples do not experience this roller coaster ride (Glenn, 1991).

CONSIDERATION

Is the childfree lifestyle for you? If you get your primary satisfactions from interacting with adults and from your career and if you require an atmosphere of freedom and privacy, perhaps the answer is yes. But if your desire for a child is at least equal to your desire for a satisfying adult relationship, career, and freedom, the answer may be no. The childfree alternative is particularly valuable to persons who would find the demands of parenthood an unnecessary burden and strain.

❧ How Many Children Do You Want?

If you decide to have children, how many do you want? Increasingly, couples (particularly in dual careers) are electing to have one child.

One Child?

Bill and Hillary Clinton and their daughter, Chelsea, have given national visibility to the one-child family.

The one child family is receiving increased media attention.

I think one of the things that has made Chelsea's life bearable as an only child is that we have done so many things together. I have driven her to school every day since kindergarten, unless I was away. The morning is our time.

HILLARY CLINTON

I should have had more children.

MARY TYLER MOORE
(MOTHER OF ONE CHILD)

NATIONAL DATA ❧ Twenty-three percent of married women have one child (*Statistical Abstract of the United States: 1993*, Table 106).

The number of children a couple choose to have is influenced by the society in which the couple lives. In the United States, the two-child norm exerts enormous social pressure on parents of one child to have a second child. In China, the one-child family is actively encouraged and has resulted in a drop in the country's birth rate. Although most only children are stereotyped as being spoiled, selfish, and lonely, data suggest that they are happy, bright, and socially skilled. Toman (1993) said of only children:

> More than other children their age, only children look and act like little adults themselves. This is not only because they have usually spent more time with their parents than other children who have siblings, but also because they can learn how to behave toward a parent as the other parent would and not as another child does. There are no other children to identify with. An only child behaves toward his father they way his mother does, and vice versa. He can also make his parents help and protect him and do things for him more readily than other children can make their parents. Only children are the focus of their [parents'] attention anyway. They don't have to share their parents with other children. Cousins and other children may come to their house, to be sure, but they don't stay for long, and the only child clearly recognizes that he does not have to compete with these other children for his parents' favor (p. 26).

Two Children?

NATIONAL DATA ❧ Fifty-eight percent of all married women have had two or more children (*Statistical Abstract of the United States: 1993*, Table 106).

The most preferred family size in the United States is the two-child family. Couples may choose to have two children for several reasons (Dreyfous, 1991; Knox & Wilson, 1978). Some couples feel that a family isn't complete without two children, and they want their first-born child to have a sibling and companion. Parents may have two children with the hope of having a child of each sex. Many mothers want a second child because they enjoyed their first child and wanted to repeat the experience. Others want to avoid having an only child because of the negative stereotypes associated with only children. Or, parents may not want to "put all their eggs in one basket." For example, some parents fear that if they only have one child and that child dies or turns out to be disappointing, they will not have another opportunity to enjoy parenting.

How does having two children differ from having one? One of the major differences between first-time and second-time parenthood is that second-time parents are not taking on a whole new role, and to this extent the psychological impact may be less dramatic (Goldberg & Michaels, 1988). In addition, couples with one child have already experienced the shift from being a couple to being a family.

Some mothers who had two children reported that having a second child increased their level of stress and exhaustion (Knox & Wilson, 1978). Having a second child means not only meeting the needs of an additional child but also dealing with the sometimes conflictual interactions between the two siblings. Mothers in this study also reported that their marriages were more negatively affected by their second child than by their first.

> **Motherhood is even sweeter the second time around.**
>
> MEL HARRIS

Three Children?

NATIONAL DATA ❧ Seven percent of families in the United States have three children (*Statistical Abstract of the United States: 1993*, Table 73).

Some individuals may want three children because they enjoy children and feel that "three is better than two." In some instances, a couple who have two children of the same sex want to try one more time to have a child of the other sex.

Having a third child creates a "middle child." This child is sometimes neglected, because parents of three children may focus more on the "baby" and the firstborn than on the child in between (Toman, 1993). However, an advantage to being a middle child is the chance to experience both a younger and an older sibling.

> **Children are the parents' riches.**
>
> THOMAS DRAXE

Four or More Children?

NATIONAL DATA ❧ Three percent of families in the United States have four or more children (*Statistical Abstract of the United States: 1993*, Table 73).

Men are more likely to want four or more children than women. Blacks and Mexican Americans are more likely to want larger families than whites (Mindel et al., 1988). Larger families have complex interactional patterns and different values. The addition of each subsequent child dramatically increases the possible relationships in the family. For example, in the one-child family, four interpersonal relationships are possible: mother-father, mother-child, father-child, and father-mother-child. In a family of four, 11 relationships are possible; in a family of five, 26; and in a family of six, 57.

In addition to relationships, values change as families get larger. Whereas members of a small family tend to value independence and personal development, large-family members necessarily value cooperation, harmony, and sharing. A parent of nine children said, "Meals around our house are a cooperative endeavor. One child prepares the drinks, another the bread, and still another sets the table. You have to develop cooperation, or nobody gets fed."

> *The more children you have, the more griefs you have.*
>
> AESOP

CONSIDERATION

When people think about and plan for the size family they want, they rarely take into consideration the possibility of divorce. In deciding how many children you want (if you want any at all), ask yourself the following question: How would you care for the child(ren) if you became divorced and either had primary custody of the child(ren) or had to make child support payments?

Another possibility that affects family size is remarriage. When divorced people with children remarry, they often find themselves in families that are larger than what they had originally planned. For example, a woman with two children who marries a man with 3 children suddenly has five children in her family unit. Given the high rate of divorce (50 percent) and remarriage (80 percent), it is not unrealistic to consider these issues when thinking about the number of children you want to have.

❧ Timing the Birth of Your Children

If you want one or more children, when is the best time to have them? Three of the more significant issues to decide in regard to planning the timing of the first birth include the mother's age, the father's age, and the number of years the couple has been married.

Mother's Age

The age of the mother is related to the baby's birth weight. Birth weight is the greatest single predictor of the baby's current and future health. The more weight the woman gains during pregnancy (up to 35 pounds), the lower the risk of a low-weight baby.

> Life's golden age is when the children are too old to need babysitters and too young to borrow the family car.
>
> E. C. MCKENZIE

NATIONAL DATA 🐾 Mothers aged 25–34 tend to have the lowest risk (about 6 percent) of having a low birth weight baby (defined as a baby weighing less than 5 pounds, 8 ounces). The median weight of all babies at birth is 7 pounds, 7 ounces. The median weight for white babies is 7 pounds, 9 ounces; for black babies, 7 pounds exactly (National Center for Health Statistics, 1989).

Risks to the baby's life also increase with the mother's age. The chance of a chromosomal abnormality is 1 percent if the woman is in her early twenties, 2 percent at ages 35–39, 3 percent at 40, and 10 percent at 45 (Seashore, 1980). A higher proportion of babies born to older mothers die or have Down's syndrome (sometimes improperly called mongolism), a genetic defect caused by an extra chromosome. A Down's syndrome baby is physically deformed, mentally retarded, and has a shorter life span. Having a Down's syndrome baby is a particular concern of women who become pregnant after age 40. Many physicians recommend amniocentesis for these women to determine the presence of this and other chromosomal abnormalities.

Amniocentesis is not without risks. In rare cases (about 2 percent of the time), the fetus may be damaged by the needle even though an ultrasound scan (sound waves beamed at the fetus which produce a detailed image) has been used to identify its position. Congenital orthopedic defects, such as clubfoot, and premature birth have been associated with amniocentesis. Also, if no specific abnormality is detected (as is the case 97.5 percent of the time), this does not guarantee that the baby will be normal and healthy otherwise (Hogge et al., 1986).

An alternative to amniocentesis is chorion villus sampling. Also risky, the procedure involves placing a tube through the vagina into the uterus. Chorionic tissue, which surrounds the developing embryo, is removed and analyzed in the laboratory to assess the presence of genetic defects. The procedure can be performed in a physician's office as early as the eighth week of pregnancy, and results are available in two to three weeks. (Amniocentesis is not performed until the sixteenth week, and results are not known for three or four weeks.)

CONSIDERATION

An increasing number of women are waiting until their thirties and forties (examples include Connie Chung, Farrah Fawcett, Bette Midler, and Meryl

(continued on next page)

Streep) to have their children. For these women, the risks taken by delaying conception may be insignificant compared with the joy derived from motherhood. Michelle Strada had her first child just before her 42nd birthday. She said of her daughter, "She's been so wonderful that we're even thinking about squeezing in another one, believe it or not" (Painter, 1990, D1).

Reasons for the trend toward giving birth at older ages include wider availability of contraception/abortion, which makes such choices possible; improved health care technology, which has raised the age at which a woman may safely have a baby; and increased interest in women pursuing careers first and having their children later (Sapiro, 1990; Travis, 1988).

In addition, Cohen (1985) suggested that

> For many people in their thirties, what they call delaying parenthood is really delaying making a clear personal decision about parenthood. . . . More and more people in their twenties and thirties who have no children are unwilling either to declare themselves permanently childless or to make a decision to go ahead and have children. They may be evasive, uncertain, or ambivalent about the choice, but, in any case, delay is easier for them than decision. (pp. 7, 16)

It's a sign of age if you feel like the morning after the night before, and haven't been anywhere.

E. C. MCKENZIE

Father's Age

The father's age is also a consideration in deciding when to have the first child. Down's syndrome is associated with increased paternal as well as maternal age. Other abnormalities that may be related to the age of the father include achondroplasia (a type of dwarfism), Marfan syndrome (height, vision, and heart abnormalities), Apert syndrome (facial and limb deformities), and fibro-dysplasia ossificans progressiva (bony growths). Such congenital defects are not common (2 percent of all births).

To help reduce birth defects of genetic origin, older couples and those whose family histories show evidence of hereditary defect or disease should consider genetic counseling. Such counseling helps the potential parents to be aware of the chance of having a defective child.

Cooney et al. (1993) studied 307 first-time fathers who had a biological child under age five to determine the best age for the man to become a father. Those becoming a father before age 23 were regarded as "early;" those ages 24–29 were regarded as "on time;" and those age 30 or older were regarded as "late." Being actively engaged in the role of father and enjoying it was most likely to be true of the "late" fathers. The researchers suggested this may be due to greater maturity with age as well as less self-induced career pressure to succeed.

Number of Years Married

Although most spouses are confident about their decision to have children when they are in their twenties or early thirties, they may be ambivalent about how long it is best to be married before having a baby.

One viewpoint suggests that newlyweds need time to adjust to each other as spouses before becoming parents. If the marriage is dissolved, at least there will not be problems of child custody, child-support payments, and single-parent status.

But if couples wait several years to have a baby, they may become so content with their childfree lifestyle that parenthood is an unwelcome change. "We were married for seven wonderful years before Helen was born," recalls one mother. "The adjustment hasn't been easy. We resented her intrusion into our relationship."

CONSIDERATION

Your degree of commitment to your career is also an issue to consider in timing your first child. Although couples have different agreements about childcare, many couples prefer that the wife be primarily responsible for the child on a daily basis. Such allocation of responsibility will be a major barrier to the woman who wants to pursue a full-time career with its demands of training, commitment, mobility, and continuity. Career-oriented women often decide to get their career going before beginning their family or to have their children first and then launch a career. Unless the partners opt to truly coparent, having a child while pursuing a career will be difficult.

Increasingly, couples are deciding to have children in their late thirties and forties. In addition to having their careers established, they experience parenthood at a time when they no longer wonder what the childfree lifestyle would be like. Many have traveled extensively and feel that they now prefer to stay home to rear a family.

Some pregnancies and births occur before the couple get married.

NATIONAL DATA ⚬ Twenty-seven percent of all births to U.S. women are to unmarried mothers (*Statistical Abstract of the United States: 1993*, Table 98).

As noted in Chapter 5, spouses who are premaritally pregnant have a higher risk of marital unhappiness and divorce than those who do not conceive children before marriage (Kraus, 1977).

Timing Subsequent Births

Assuming you decide to have more than one child, what is the best interval between children? Most couples space their children within three years of each other with younger women tending to have longer intervals between births than older women. This interval allows parents to avoid being overwhelmed with the care of two infants, but is short enough so that the children can be companions. In general, small age differences tend to bind siblings more strongly to each other.

> In some families it would be better If the children were properly spaced—about one hundred yards apart.
>
> E. C. MCKENZIE

Children born close together in age are likely to be companions to each other and to form a close emotional bond.

ॐ Contraception

Prior to 1870 (when condoms were first mass-marketed), abstinence was the only way a couple could ensure that the woman would not get pregnant. Today, couples can separate their lovemaking from their babymaking with a variety of birth control procedures. After reviewing the available array of contraceptives, we will examine sterilization and abortion as ways of controlling family size. Most women have no problem getting pregnant. But many get pregnant when they do not want to because they do not use contraception. "I was a freshman and unmarried. The last thing I wanted at that time in my life was a baby," recalls one woman. *Contraception,* the prevention of pregnancy by one of several methods, is an alternative to pregnancy.

All contraceptive practices have one of two common purposes—to prevent the male sperm from fertilizing the female egg or to keep the fertilized egg from implanting itself in the uterus. In performing these functions, contraception permits couples to make love without making babies.

Oral Contraceptives

The birth control pill is the most commonly used method of all the nonsurgical forms of contraception.

NATIONAL DATA ॐ Twenty-five percent of never married women, 15 percent of currently married women, and 15 percent of formerly married women ages 15 to 44 use the pill as their method of contraception (*Statistical Abstract of the United States: 1993,* Table 111).

Although there are more than 40 brands available in North America, there are basically two types of birth control pills—the combination pill and the minipill.

The combination pill contains the hormones estrogen and progesterone (also known as progestin), which act to prevent ovulation and implantation. The estrogen inhibits the release of the follicle-stimulating hormone (FSH) from the pituitary gland, so that no follicle will develop. In effect, an egg will not mature. In other words, A (estrogen) blocks B (FSH), which would have produced C (egg).

The progesterone inhibits the release of luteinizing hormone (LH) from the pituitary gland, which during a normal cycle would cause the mature ovum to move to the periphery of the follicle and the follicle to rupture (ovulation). Hence, there is no ovulation. In this case, A (progestin) blocks B (LH), which would have caused C (ovulation).

The progesterone serves as a secondary protection by causing the composition of the cervical mucus to become thick and acidic, thereby creating a hostile environment for the sperm. So even if an egg were to mature and ovulation were to occur, the progesterone would ward off or destroy the sperm. Another function of progesterone is to make the lining of the uterus unsuitable for implantation.

The combination pill is taken for 21 days, beginning on the fifth day after the start of the menstrual flow. Three or four days after the last pill is taken, menstruation occurs, and the 28-day cycle begins again. To eliminate the problem of remembering when to begin taking the pill every month, some physicians prescribe a low-dose combination pill for the first 21 days and a placebo (sugar pill) or an iron pill for the next seven days. In this way, the woman takes a pill every day.

The second type of oral contraceptive, the minipill, contains the same progesterone found in the combination pill, but in much lower doses. The minipill contains no estrogen. Like the progesterone in the combination pill, the progesterone in the minipill provides a hostile environment for sperm and inhibits implantation of a fertilized egg in the uterus. In general, the minipill is somewhat less effective than other types of birth control pills and has been associated with a higher incidence of irregular bleeding.

Either the combination pill or the minipill should be taken only when prescribed by a physician who has detailed information about the woman's previous medical history. Contraindications—reasons for not prescribing birth control pills—include hypertension, impaired liver function, known or suspected tumors that are estrogen-dependent, undiagnosed abnormal genital bleeding, pregnancy at the time of the examination, and a history of poor blood circulation. The major complications associated with taking oral contraceptives are blood clots and high blood pressure. Also, the risk of heart attack is increased in women over age 30, particularly those who smoke or have other risk factors. Women over 40 should generally use other forms of contraception, because the side effects of contraceptive pills increase with the age of the user. Infertility problems have also been noted in women who have used the combination pill for several years without the breaks in pill use recommended by most physicians.

Although the long-term negative consequences of taking birth control pills are still the subject of research, short-term negative effects are experienced by 25 percent of all women who use them. These side effects include increased susceptibility to vaginal infections, nausea, slight weight gain, vaginal bleeding between periods, breast tenderness, headaches, and mood changes (some women become depressed and experience a loss of sexual desire).

Finally, women should be aware that pill use is associated with an increased incidence of chlamydia and gonorrhea. One reason for the association of pill use and a higher incidence of STDs is that sexually active women who use the pill sometimes erroneously feel that because they are protected from getting pregnant, they are also protected from contracting STDs. The pill provides no protection against STDs; a condom must be worn.

Norplant

In the early 90s, the FDA approved the use of Norplant, a long-acting reversible hormonal contraceptive consisting of six thin flexible silicone capsules (36mm in length) implanted under the skin of the upper arm (see Figure 13.1). Tested in more than 55,000 women in 46 countries, Norplant provides a continuous low dosage of levonorgestrel resulting in protection against pregnancy for up to five years. A newer system, Norplant-2, consists of only two capsules (44 mm in length) and is effective for about three years (Shoupe & Mishell, 1989).

Once implanted, the woman need no longer remember to "take her pill." With an effectiveness rate of more than 99 percent, Norplant is one of the most effective contraceptives available. Other advantages of the Norplant include: (1) it is easily reversible with implant removal; (2) it contains no estrogen, so it does not produce estrogen-related side effects, (3) it may decrease menstrual discomfort and ovulatory pain; and (4) it may reduce risk of endometrial cancer (Hatcher et al., 1990).

Disadvantages of Norplant include: (1) the implants are slightly visible; (2) the initial expense is higher than for short-term methods (the surgical procedure costs about $500; (3) discontinuation of the method requires minor surgery; and (4) users may experience changes in menstruation (e.g., prolonged bleeding, spotting between periods, or no bleeding at all).

Some women are advised not to use hormonal contraceptive implants. Contraindications for Norplant use include acute liver disease, jaundice, unexplained vaginal bleeding, and a history of blood clots, heart attack, heart disease, or stroke (Hatcher et al., 1990).

FIGURE 13.1

Norplant injectables

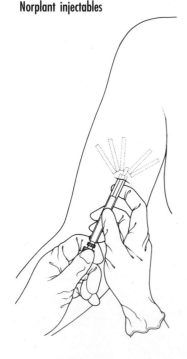

> **CONSIDERATION**
>
> Although the availability of hormonal contraceptive implants, such as Norplant, allows women to make a semi-permanent but reversible choice, critics argue that Norplant may be used as a mechanism to prohibit some women from having children, or used as an incentive to prevent poor women from having children. Robert Blank (1990) observed:
>
> > Given the current negative attitudes of the public toward those on welfare, the increased emphasis on the population problem, the scarcity of public funds for welfare programs, and the emerging focus on the competency of parents, it would not be surprising if the availability of reversible sterilization [such as Norplant] gave impetus to pressures for widespread use of incentives (or coercion) to encourage (or force) sterilization of the poor, retarded, and those otherwise deemed "unfit" (p. 130).

Depo-Provera

A new FDA-approved alternative to Norplant is Depo-Provera. It is a synthetic compound similar to progesterone injected into the woman's arm or buttock. It protects her against pregnancy for three months by preventing ovulation. Depo-Provera has been used by 30 million women worldwide since it was introduced in the late 60s. For women who get their shot every three months, the failure rate is less than one percent.

Side effects of Depo-Provera include menstrual spotting, irregular bleeding, and some heavy bleeding the first few months of use. Mood changes, headaches, dizziness, and fatigue have also been observed. Some women report a weight gain of three to five pounds. Also, after stopping the injections, it takes an average of 18 months before the woman will become pregnant at the same rate as women who have not used Depo-Provera.

Oral contraceptives and other hormonal contraceptives, such as Norplant and Depo-Provera are designed for use by women. In recent years, researchers have developed hormonal contraceptives for use by men (see In Focus 13.1).

Condom

The condom is currently the only form of male contraception. The condom is a thin sheath and has traditionally been made of latex or lamb intestine. But available in 1994 is a new condom made of polyurethane (the same material as the female condom—In Focus 13.2). Unlike the latex condom, the polyurethane condom can be used with petroleum jelly, avoids the latex allergy some people experience, blocks the HIV virus and other sexually transmitted diseases and allows greater sensitivity.

The condom works by rolling it over and down the shaft of the erect penis before intercourse. When the man ejaculates, sperm are caught inside the

If you're going to be responsible for birth control, be *really* responsible. Never use a condom alone—always use a condom in conjunction with a sponge, diaphragm, or pill.

BARBARA WEST, COUNSELOR PLANNED PARENTHOOD OF ALABAMA.

IN FOCUS 13.1

Male Hormonal Contraceptives

Presently, hormonal contraceptives, including the birth control pill, Norplant, and Depo-Provera are used by women; no viable chemical alternatives are currently commercially available for men. However, some research on a male hormonal contraceptive has begun at the University of Washington. Known as testosterone enanthate or TE, a 200mg shot is administered once a week with the effect of lowering sperm production. However, there are drawbacks. It takes months of taking TE before the man becomes infertile (some never do) and months after the injections stop for fertility to be restored. Some men complain of the need to take a weekly shot and report weight gain and acne.

Other hormonal male contraceptives being considered and their drawbacks as shown in the table at the right (Bromwich & Parsons, 1990).

Given the unreliability, loss of libido, and uncertain irreversibility of these male contraceptive drugs, it is unlikely that men will be interested in taking them. In addition, men are unlikely to be willing to take a "pill a day" (too identified with the female pill) or a shot a week (too much trouble and discomfort) for contraceptive purposes. Rather, they would prefer a no-hassle, long-lasting chemical contraceptive that is either injected or implanted and that is reversible. However, drug companies driven by profit have little motivation to make a long-lasting male contraceptive that does not generate a significant return on their research investment as does the female pill (taken daily). In addition, if a man were to have a heart attack that was blamed on the male pill, the product would be feared and demand would cease. All of these factors suggest a long wait (at least ten years) before a male hormonal contraceptive is available to the American public (Prendergast, 1990).

CONTRACEPTIVE DRUG	EFFECT	DRAWBACK
Depo-Provera	Decreases sperm production	Loss of libido; Some sperm still viable
Danazol	Decreases sperm production	Loss of libido
Cyproterone	Decreases sperm production	Loss of libido
Gossypol	Decreases sperm production	Effects not always reversible; Affects potassium levels

---

condom. When used in combination with a spermicidal lubricant that is placed on the inside of the reservoir tip of the condom (to reduce the chance of breaking) as well as a spermicidal or sperm-killing agent that the woman inserts in her vagina, the condom is a highly effective contraceptive.

NATIONAL DATA ❦ Eight percent of the never married women, 11 percent of currently married women, and 3 percent of formerly married women ages 15 to 44 use the condom as their method of contraception (*Statistical Abstract of the United States: 1993*, Table 111).

CONSIDERATION

A latex or polyurethane condom with nonoxynol 9 (spermicide effective in killing the AIDS virus) is the contraceptive that best protects against HIV and other sexually transmitted diseases. Yet, forty percent of sexually active college students reported not practicing safe sex (Morris & Schneider, 1992).Although denial ("I won't get an STD") is a major factor in not using a condom, some men say that it decreases sensation. However, others say having the partner put the condom on their penis during foreplay is an erotic experience, and the condom actually enhances pleasurable feelings during intercourse.

Like any contraceptive, the condom is effective only when used properly. It should be placed on the penis early enough to avoid any seminal leakage into the vagina. In addition, polyurethane or latex condoms with a reservoir tip are preferable, as they are less likely to break. Finally, the penis should be withdrawn from the vagina immediately after ejaculation, before the man's penis returns to its flaccid state. If the penis is not withdrawn and the erection subsides, semen may leak from the base of the condom into the vaginal lips. Alternatively, when the erection subsides, the condom will come off when the man withdraws his penis if he does not hold on to the condom. Either way, the sperm will begin to travel up the vagina to the uterus and fertilize the egg.

In addition to furnishing extra protection, spermicides also provide lubrication, which permits easy entrance of the condom-covered penis into the vagina. If no spermicide is used and the condom is not of the prelubricated variety, K-Y jelly, a sterile lubricant, may be needed. Vaseline or other kinds of petroleum jelly may be used with polyurethane condoms but not with latex condoms (vaginal infections and/or condom breakage may result).

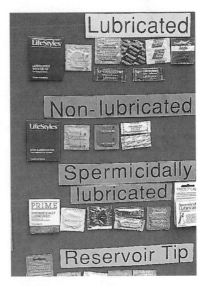

Regardless of the condom used, a lubricant/spermicide should be placed on the inside of the reservoir tip as well as the outside. This helps prevent the condom from breaking.

The female condom is huge—now you can carry your wallet in your condom.

JAY LENO

CONSIDERATION

Condoms are promoted as offering the best protection against transmission of sexually transmitted diseases. However, later in this chapter (in Table 13.1) you may note that the effectiveness of condoms in preventing STD transmission has been estimated to be only 30 percent–60 percent. One reason for this low rate of effectiveness is that some people who use condoms do not use them consistently. In order to be effective in preventing STD transmission (and pregnancy), condoms must be worn during each act of intercourse or oral sex.

In addition, condoms must be used correctly if they are to be effective. In one study, 8 percent of 405 condoms either broke during intercourse or withdrawal, or slipped off during intercourse (Trussell et al., 1992). Of the remaining condoms, 7 percent slipped off during withdrawal. When condoms slipped off during withdrawal it was often related to the use of petroleum jelly or massage oil, which some couples used despite warnings that oil causes deterioration of rubber! The researchers concluded that condom slippage and breakage rates are due largely to incorrect use of the condom and that better education about condom use is needed.

⌇ IN FOCUS 13.2 ⌇

The Female Condom

The *female condom* resembles a man's condom except that it fits in the woman's vagina (see Figure 13.2) to protect her from pregnancy, HIV infection, and other STDs (Wolinsky, 1988). The vaginal condom is a large, lubricated, polyurethane adaptation of the male version. It is about 7 inches long and has flexible rings at both ends. It is inserted like a diaphragm with the inner ring fitting behind the pubic bone against the cervix; the outer ring remains outside the body and encircles the labial area. Like the male version, the condom is not reusable. Female condoms have been approved by the FDA and are being marketed under the brand names "Femidom" and "Reality." The one-size-fits-all device will be available without a prescription and will sell for about $2.25 each.

The vaginal condom is durable and does not tear like latex male condoms, but it is trickier to use. The actual effectiveness rate (against STDs) of the vaginal condom has not been sufficiently studied; it's contraceptive effectiveness is 85 percent (Rosenberg & Gollub, 1992). A major advantage of the female condom is that, like the male counterpart, it protects against transmission of the HIV virus and other STDs. Women and men who have used the vaginal condom are generally satisfied with the device (Gregersen & Gregersen, 1990).

Another type of female condom, which is being tested by International Prophylactic, Inc., consists of a latex condom that may be worn as a G-string by the woman (Hatcher et al., 1990). The crotch of the G-string contains a condom pouch, which is rolled up compactly. When the penis enters the vagina, it pushes the condom pouch up into the vagina.

F I G U R E 13.2:

Female condom

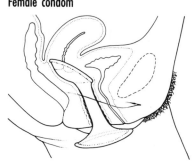

While the term *condom* usually refers to a male contraceptive, a female condom has been developed (see In Focus 13.2).

Intrauterine Device (IUD)

NATIONAL DATA ✺ Less than one percent (.6) of never married women, two percent of currently married women, and two percent of formerly married women ages 15 to 44 use the IUD as their method of contraception (*Statistical Abstract of the United States: 1993,* Table 111).

The intrauterine device, or IUD, is a small object that is inserted by a physician into the woman's uterus through the vagina and cervix. Although 60 million women use the IUD worldwide (40 million in China alone), use of the IUD in the United States is minimal. Due to problems (infertility, miscarriage) associated with IUDs and subsequent lawsuits against manufacturers by persons reporting they were damaged by the device, only two types remain on the U.S. market. The Progestasert releases progesterone directly into the uterus and must be replaced every year by the physician. The Progestasert has the effect of reducing menstrual flow, which reduces the risk of anemia.

The newer Copper T (T-380A) is thought to alter the functioning of the enzymes involved in implantation. It was introduced in the late 80s and preliminary studies show it has a failure rate as low as the pill (Thomas, 1988).

It is thought that the IUD works by preventing implantation of the fertilized egg in the uterine wall. The exact chemistry is unknown, but one theory suggests that the IUD stimulates the entry of white blood cells into the uterus, which attack and destroy "invading" cells—in this case, the fertilized egg. Implantation may also be prevented by the IUD mechanically dislodging the egg from the uterine wall. Side effects of the IUD include cramps, excessive menstrual bleeding, and irregular bleeding, or spotting, between menstrual periods. These effects may disappear after the first two months of use. Infection and perforation are more serious side effects. Users of the IUD have a higher incidence of pelvic inflammatory disease, which infects the uterus and Fallopian tubes and may lead to sterility. In addition, the IUD may cut or perforate the uterine walls or cervix, resulting in bleeding and pain.

FIGURE 13.3:

A T-shaped Intrauterine Device (IUD)

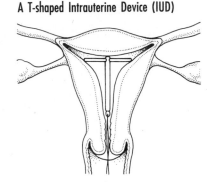

CONSIDERATION

Due to these potential side effects, women should consider using a method of contraception other than the IUD. Some physicians will not fit a woman for an IUD if she has not had a child to avoid any potential future damage to the uterus by the IUD.

Some women are unable to retain the IUD; it irritates the muscles of the uterus, causing them to contract and expel the device. To make sure that the IUD remains in place, a woman should check it at least once a month just after her period. The Progestasert is particularly vulnerable to expulsion.

The fact that the IUD does not prevent fertilization is its greatest advantage and disadvantage. The advantage is that the IUD does not interfere with the body's normal hormonal and physiological responses. The disadvantage is that it permits fertilization and then destroys the fertilized egg, which is morally repugnant to some people. "It's the same as abortion," said one devout Catholic. Also, women who do get pregnant (tubal pregnancies with the Progestasert do occur) while using the IUD must make a decision about whether to leave it in or remove it.

Researchers continue to develop new types of IUDs in an attempt to reduce negative side effects. For example, an IUD currently undergoing clinical trials is the Flexigard Intrauterine Copper Contraceptive (ICC) (Wildermeersch, 1992). Advantages of the ICC include better toleration by the uterus (spontaneous expulsions are virtually nonexistent) and effectiveness for more than five years of use.

Diaphragm

NATIONAL DATA ❧ Two percent of never married women, five percent of currently married women, and three percent of formerly married women ages 15 to 44 use the diaphragm as their method of contraception (*Statistical Abstract of the United States: 1993*, Table 111).

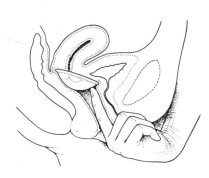

The diaphragm is a shallow rubber dome attached to a flexible, circular steel spring. Varying in diameter from 2 to 4 inches, the diaphragm covers the cervix and prevents sperm from moving beyond the vagina into the uterus. This device should always be used with a spermicidal jelly or cream.

To obtain a diaphragm, a woman must have an internal pelvic examination by a physician or nurse practitioner who will select the appropriate size of diaphragm and instruct the woman how to insert it. She will be told to apply one teaspoonful of spermicidal cream or jelly on the inside of the diaphragm and around the rim and to insert it into the vagina no more than two hours before intercourse. The diaphragm must also be left in place for 6 to 8 hours after intercourse to permit any lingering sperm to be killed by the spermicidal agent.

After the birth of a child, a miscarriage, abdominal surgery, or the gain or loss of 10 pounds, a woman who uses a diaphragm should consult her physician or health practitioner to ensure a continued good fit. In any case, the diaphragm should be checked every two years for fit.

A major advantage of the diaphragm is that it does not interfere with the woman's hormonal system and has few, if any, side effects. Also, for those couples who feel that menstruation diminishes their capacity to enjoy intercourse, the diaphragm may be used to catch the menstrual flow for a brief time.

On the negative side, some women feel that use of the diaphragm with the spermicidal gel is messy and a nuisance. For some, the use of the gel may produce an allergic reaction. Furthermore, some partners feel that the gel makes oral genital contact less enjoyable. Finally, if the diaphragm does not fit properly or is left in place too long, pregnancy and toxic shock syndrome (respectively) can result.

Cervical Cap

The cervical cap is a thimble-shaped contraceptive device made of rubber or polyethelene that fits tightly over the cervix and is held in place by suction. Like the diaphragm, the cervical cap, which is used in conjunction with spermicidal cream or jelly, prevents sperm from entering the uterus. Cervical caps have been widely available in Europe for some time and were approved for marketing in the United States in 1988. The cervical cap cannot be used during menstruation since the suction cannot be maintained. The effectiveness, problems, risks, and advantages are similar to those of the diaphragm.

Vaginal Spermicides

A spermicide is a chemical that kills sperm. Vaginal spermicides come in several forms, including foam, cream, jelly, and suppository. In the United States, the active agent in most spermicides is nonoxynol-9, which has also been shown to kill many organisms that cause sexually transmissible diseases (including HIV). Creams and gels are intended for use with a diaphragm. Suppositories are intended for use alone or with a condom. Foam is marketed for use alone but can also be used with a diaphragm or condom.

NATIONAL DATA ✄ Less than one percent (.2) of never married women, one percent of currently married women, and less than one percent (.5) of formerly married women ages 15 to 44 use foam as their method of contraception (*Statistical Abstract of the United States: 1993*, Table 111).

Spermicides must be applied before the penis penetrates the vagina (appropriate applicators are included when the product is purchased) no more than 20 minutes before intercourse. While foam is effective immediately, suppositories, creams, or jellies require a few minutes to allow the product to melt and spread inside the vagina (package instructions describe the exact time required). Each time intercourse is repeated, more spermicide must be applied. Spermicide must be left in place for at least 6 to 8 hours after intercourse; douching or rinsing the vagina should not be done during this period.

One advantage of using spermicides is that they are available without a prescription or medical examination. They also do not manipulate the woman's hormonal system and have few side effects. A major noncontraceptive benefit of some spermicides is that they offer some protection against the transmission of sexually transmitted diseases, including HIV. However, spermicides should never be depended upon alone to be effective in preventing STD transmission.

The most common problem associated with spermicides is temporary skin irritation of the vulva or penis caused by sensitivity or allergy to the spermicide. (Spermicides should not be used if either partner has an allergic reaction.) Some people regard using spermicides as messy. Lastly, the unpleasant taste of spermicides may interfere with the enjoyment of oral-genital contact.

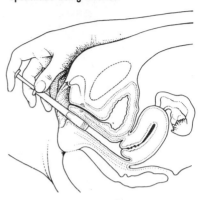

F I G U R E 13.5:
Spermicide being inserted

CONSIDERATION

Contraceptive foams, such as Delfen and Emko, should not be confused with vaginal deodorants, such as Summer's Eve. Vaginal deodorants have no contraceptive value. Spermicidal foams should also not be confused with spermicidal gels that are used in conjunction with a diaphragm. These gels should never be used alone because they do not stick to the cervix as well as foam. In selecting a vaginal spermicide, look for the presence of nonoxynol-9. This has been shown to kill the AIDS virus in laboratory animals.

Vaginal Sponge

The vaginal sponge is two inches in diameter and one and a quarter inches thick and contains spermicide that is activated when the sponge is immersed in water before insertion into the vagina. The woman must wait at least six hours after intercourse before removing the sponge, after which it is discarded. To

FIGURE 13.6:

Contraceptive sponge

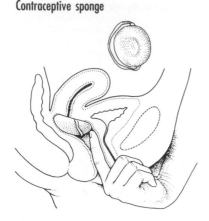

remove the sponge, the woman reaches into her vagina, grabs a small loop that is attached to the sponge and pulls it out. Like condoms and spermicides, the sponge is available in drugstores without a prescription.

A major advantage of the sponge is that it allows for spontaneity in lovemaking. It can be inserted early in the day, may be worn for up to 24 hours, and may be used for more than one act of intercourse without requiring additional applications of spermicide. Disadvantages of the sponge are similar to those discussed earlier for the diaphragm and include allergic reaction, foul odor and discharge if left in the vagina too long, and increased risk for urinary tract infection and toxic shock syndrome (the sponge should never be used during the menstrual period). Vaginal yeast infections, vaginal dryness, and difficulty removing the sponge have also been problems.

Periodic Abstinence

Also referred to as natural family planning, rhythm method, and fertility awareness, *periodic abstinence* involves refraining from sexual intercourse during the period of time each month that the woman is thought to be fertile.

NATIONAL DATA ❦ Less than one percent (.06) of never married women, 2.1 percent of currently married women, and 1.1 percent of formerly married women ages 15 to 44 use periodic abstinence or natural family planning as their method of contraception (*Statistical Abstract of the United States: 1993*, Table 111).

Women who use periodic abstinence must know their time of ovulation and avoid intercourse just before, during, and immediately after that time. Calculating the fertile period involves three assumptions: (1) ovulation occurs on day 14 (plus or minus two days) *before the onset of the next menstrual period;* (2) sperm remain viable for 2–3 days; and (3) the ovum survives for 24 hours (Hatcher et al., 1990).

There are four ways of predicting the time period during which the woman is fertile: the calendar method, the basal body temperature method, the cervical mucus method, and the hormone-in-urine method. These methods may not only be used to avoid pregnancy, they may also be used to facilitate conception if the woman wants to become pregnant. We provide only basic instructions here for using periodic abstinence as a method of contraception. Individuals considering this method should consult with a trained health practitioner for more detailed instruction.

Calendar Method The calendar method is the oldest and most widely practiced method of avoiding pregnancy through periodic abstinence. The calendar method allows women to calculate the onset and duration of their fertile period. When using the calendar method to predict when the egg is ready to be fertilized, the woman keeps a record of the length of her menstrual cycles for eight months. The menstrual cycle is counted from day one of the menstrual period through the last day before the onset of the next period. She then calculates her fertile period by subtracting 18 days from the length of her shortest cycle and 11 days from the length of her longest cycle. The resulting figures indicate the range of her fertility period (Hatcher et al., 1990). It is during this time that the woman must abstain from intercourse if pregnancy is not desired.

For example, suppose that during an eight-month period, a woman had cycle lengths of 26, 32, 27, 30, 28, 27, 28, and 29 days. Subtracting 18 from her shortest cycle (26) and 11 from her longest cycle (32) she knows the days that the egg is likely to be in the Fallopian tubes. To avoid getting pregnant, she must avoid intercourse on days 8 through 21 of her cycle.

CONSIDERATION

The calendar method of predicting the "safe" period may be unreliable for two reasons. First, the next month the woman may ovulate at a different time from any of the previous eight months. Second, sperm life varies; they may live long enough to meet the next egg in the Fallopian tubes.

Basal Body Temperature (BBT) Method   This method is based on determining the time of ovulation by measuring temperature changes that occur in the woman's body shortly after ovulation. The basal body temperature is the temperature of the body at rest on waking in the morning. To establish her BBT, the woman must take her temperature before she gets out of bed for three months. Shortly before, during, or right after ovulation, the woman's BBT usually rises about 0.4–0.8 degrees F (Hatcher et al., 1990). Some women notice a temperature drop about 12 to 24 hours before it begins to rise after ovulation. Intercourse must be avoided from the time the woman's temperature drops until her temperature has remained elevated for three consecutive days. Intercourse may be resumed on the night of the third day after the BBT has risen and remained elevated for three consecutive days.

Cervical Mucus Method   The cervical mucus method, also known as the Billings method of natural family planning, is based on observations of changes in the cervical mucus during the woman's monthly cycle. The woman may observe her cervical mucus by wiping herself with toilet paper.

The woman should abstain from intercourse during her menstrual period, as the mucus is obscured by menstrual blood and cannot be observed and ovulation can occur during menstruation. After menstruation ceases, intercourse is permitted on days during the time no mucus is present or thick mucus is present in small amounts. Intercourse should be avoided just prior to, during, and immediately after ovulation if pregnancy is not desired. Before ovulation, mucus is cloudy, yellow or white, and sticky. During ovulation, cervical mucus is thin, clear, slippery, and stretchy and resembles raw egg white. This phase is known as the "peak symptom." During ovulation, some women experience ovulatory pain referred to as *mittelschmerz*. Such pain may include feelings of heaviness, abdominal swelling, rectal pain or discomfort, and lower abdominal pain or discomfort on either side. Mittelschmerz is useful for identifying ovulation, but not for predicting it. Intercourse may resume 4 days after the disappearance of the "peak symptom" and continue until the next menses. During this time, cervical mucus may be either clear and watery, or cloudy and sticky. There may be no mucus noticed at all during this period (Hatcher et al., 1990).

Advantages of the cervical mucus method include (1) it requires the woman to become familiar with her reproductive system; and (2) it can give early warning about some STDs (which can affect cervical mucus). However, the cervical mucus method requires the woman to distinguish between mucus and semen, spermicidal agents, lubrication, and infectious discharges. Also, the woman must not douche because she will wash away what she is trying to observe.

Hormone-in-Urine Method   A hormone is released into the bloodstream of the ovulating female 12 to 24 hours prior to ovulation. Women can purchase over-the-counter tests such as First Response and Ovutime that are designed to ascertain if they have ovulated.

CONSIDERATION

While natural family planning methods are not as effective as other available methods of contraception, they can be combined with other methods. For example, during a woman's "safe" time of the month, she may have intercourse using a condom.

Withdrawal

Also known as *coitus interruptus,* withdrawal is the practice of the man withdrawing his penis from the vagina before he ejaculates. The actual effectiveness rate of withdrawal in preventing pregnancy is estimated to be about 85 percent. In other words, about 15 percent of women who use withdrawal as their method of contraception become pregnant in the first year (Kost, Forrest, & Harlap, 1991). While withdrawal is not generally advised as a method of effective contraception, some regard it as "a considerably better method than no method at all" (Hatcher et al., 1990, 353).

The advantages of coitus interruptus are (1) it requires no devices or chemicals, and (2) it is always available. The disadvantages of withdrawal include (1) it does not provide protection from STDs, (2) it may interrupt the sexual response cycle and diminish the pleasure for the couple, and (3) it is less effective than some other methods.

There are two reasons why withdrawal is not a reliable form of contraception. First, a man can unknowingly emit a small amount of preejaculatory fluid (which is stored in the prostate or penile urethra or in the Cowper's glands), which may contain sperm. This fluid contains more sperm after the man has recently ejaculated; one drop may contain millions of sperm (Hatcher et al., 1990). In addition, the man may lack the self-control to withdraw his penis before ejaculation or he may delay his withdrawal too long and inadvertently ejaculate some semen near the vaginal opening of his partner. Sperm deposited here can live in the moist vaginal lips and make their way up the vagina.

Douching

While some women believe that douching is an effective form of contraception, it is not. Douching refers to rinsing or cleansing the vaginal canal. After intercourse, the woman fills a syringe with water or a spermicidal agent and flushes (so she assumes) the sperm from her vagina. But in some cases, the fluid will actually force sperm up through the cervix. In other cases, a large number of sperm may already have passed through the cervix to the uterus, so that the douche may do little good.

In effect, douching does little to deter conception and may even encourage it. In addition, douching is associated with an increased risk for pelvic inflammatory disease and ectopic pregnancy (Hatcher et al., 1990).

Postcoital Contraception

Postcoital contraception refers to various types of "morning-after" pills that may be used when the woman has unprotected intercourse during her fertile time of the month. Hatcher et al. (1990) suggested that postcoital methods of contraception "should be reserved for emergency situations only . . . when unprotected intercourse occurred and when medication can be given within 72 hours of exposure" (p. 423).

Ovral   While various types of morning-after pills have been developed, the treatment of choice is a combined birth control pill, which is marketed as Ovral. When used as postcoital contraception, two Ovral pills are taken within 72 hours (preferably between 12 and 24 hours) of coitus, and two more pills are taken 12 hours later. Estimates of the effectiveness of Ovral in preventing continued pregnancy range between 90 and 99 percent (Hatcher et al., 1990). An older treatment of high-dose oral estrogens, known as DES (diethylstibestrol), is no longer recommended due to the high rate of birth defects in women whose pregnancy continued despite treatment with DES.

RU-486   RU-486 is a synthetic steroid that effectively terminates pregnancies within the first nine weeks of gestation. RU-486 is considered to be a method of abortion as well as a form of postcoital contraception. By blocking the normal action of progesterone in the uterus, RU-486 prevents the implantation of a fertilized egg and induces menstruation if implantation has already occurred. When taken with prostaglandin up to eight weeks after conception,

RU-486 is 95–96 percent effective in inducing abortion (Kovacs, 1990; Klitsch, 1991). Hence, some pregnancies continue even if RU-486 is used on day 0 to induce a first trimester abortion. RU-486 has been used in France by over 80,000 women and is also available in Great Britain and China.

CONSIDERATION

Although it is assumed that RU–486 is readily available in France, it remains a highly supervised procedure. Four mandatory visits to government licensed clinics are required. One visit is to decide whether to take the drug; the second visit is a week later to receive the full dose; the third is after two days for prostaglandin; the fourth, after a week or so, is the final checkup (Gooding & Williams, 1991).

Shortly after President Clinton took office in 1993, he increased the availability of RU-486 in the United States. Full FDA approval must be obtained before it will be marketed nationwide.

CONSIDERATION

Postcoital methods of contraception are a controversial issue; some people regard them as a form of abortion, while others regard them as a means of reducing the need for abortion. Advocates of RU-486 point to the fact that worldwide, 200,000 women die annually because of botched illegal abortions and that RU-486 would actually save lives (Baulieu & Rosenblum, 1991).

Effectiveness of Various Contraceptive Choices

In Table 13.1 we present data on the effectiveness of various contraceptive methods in preventing pregnancy and in protecting against sexually transmitted disease. Table 13.1 also describes the benefits, disadvantages, and cost of various methods of contraception.

❧ Sterilization

Unlike the temporary and reversible methods of contraception just discussed, sterilization is a permanent surgical procedure that prevents reproducing. Sterilization may be a contraceptive method of choice when the woman should not have more children for health reasons or when individuals are certain about their desire to have no more children or to remain childfree. Most couples complete their intended childbearing in their late twenties or early thirties, leaving more than 15 years of continued risk of unwanted pregnancy. Due to the risk of pill use at older ages and the lower reliability of alternative

TABLE 13.1

Methods of Sexually Transmitted Disease Protection, from Women's Perspective

METHOD	ESTIMATED EFFECTIVENESS AGAINST SEXUALLY TRANSMITTED DISEASE	CONTRACEPTIVE EFFECTIVENESS		BENEFITS	DISADVANTAGES	COST[b]
		High[a]	Average[a]			
Condom	30–60%	98%	88%	Entails male responsibility; offers high level of protection; is inexpensive	Difficult to negotiate; entails lack of control for woman; may be seen as interrupting sex; may imply unfaithfulness	$0.50
Female condom	Insufficiently studied	Insufficiently studied	85%[c]	Offers high level protection against sexually transmitted disease/HIV	Is visible; expensive; requires negotiation	$2.00
Film[d]	50%	99%	79%	Is easy to use; requires no negotiation	Requires 15 minutes' waiting time; must be applied within 1 hour of intercourse	$1.00
Suppository	50%	99%	79%	Is easy to use; is inexpensive; requires no negotiation	Requires 15 minutes' waiting time; must be applied within 1 hour of intercourse	$0.50
Foam	50%	99%	79%	Is available OTC[e]; requires no waiting time after insertion; requires no negotiation	Requires applicator	$0.50
Jelly/ cream	50%	99%	79%	Is available OTC; inexpensive; requires no negotiation	Requires applicator; must be applied within 1 hour of intercourse	$5.00 per tube

Continued

birth control methods, sterilization has become the most popular method of contraception among married women who have completed their families.

Slightly more than half of all sterilizations are performed on women. Although male sterilization is easier and safer than female sterilization, women feel more certain they will not get pregnant if they are sterilized. "I'm the one that ends up being pregnant and having the baby," said one woman. "So I want to make sure that I never get pregnant again."

TABLE 13.1

Methods of Sexually Transmitted Disease Protection, from Women's Perspective (*continued*)

METHOD	ESTIMATED EFFECTIVENESS AGAINST SEXUALLY TRANSMITTED DISEASE	CONTRACEPTIVE EFFECTIVENESS		BENEFITS	DISADVANTAGES	COST[b]
		High[a]	Average[a]			
Cervical cap	50–75% for cervical pathogens, 0% for others	98%	82%	Is comfortable; can be used repeatedly over 2+ days; is cheaper over reproductive life; requires no waiting time after insertion; no UTIs; rarely requires refitting; may require no negotiation (if not felt by partner); offers excellent cervical protection with low nonoxynol-9 use	Must be fitted; 20–40% women not able to be fitted[f]; requires initial outlay of $100–150; requires vaginal spermicide for best protection against sexually transmitted disease	$0.10
Diaphragm	50–75% for cervical pathogens; trace (10%?) for others due to vaginal dispersion of spermicide	99%	82%	Requires no waiting time after insertion; fits nearly all women; may require no negotiation (if not felt by partner); is cheaper over reproductive life	Must be removed after 10–12 hours; may need to be refitted; carries increased risk of UTIs[g] for some women; requires initial outlay of $50–75	$0.10
Sponge	50%	99%	79%	Is convenient; is available OTC; requires no negotiation; can be used continuously over 24 hours	Can cause irritation, especially with chronic use; brings risk of yeast infection if used continually; requires water to activate spermicide	$1.25
Norplant	None	99%	Insufficiently studied	Is convenient; is removed from sex act	Offers no protection against sexually transmitted disease/HIV; may cause bleeding in some women which may raise risk; carries high initial cost	$300–$500 per insertion; $5–$8 per month

T A B L E 13.1

Methods of Sexually Transmitted Disease Protection, from Women's Perspective (*continued*)

METHOD	ESTIMATED EFFECTIVENESS AGAINST SEXUALLY TRANSMITTED DISEASE	CONTRACEPTIVE EFFECTIVENESS		BENEFITS	DISADVANTAGES	COST[b]
		High[a]	Average[a]			
Withdrawal	Insufficiently studied	96%	82%	Requires no purchases	Is not controlled by woman; is highly user dependent	. . .
Pill	None	99%	96%	Is convenient; is removed from sex act; affords high contraceptive efficacy	Offers no protection against sexually transmitted disease/HIV; may raise risk; is expensive	$12–24/ month
Intrauterine device	None	99%	96%	Is not user dependent	Carries high initial cost; entails risk of PID associated with insertion	$150– 300 per insertion

[a]Highest observed effectiveness; "typical" user effectiveness.

[b]Per act of intercourse, based on average cost to consumer.

[c]Use-effectiveness rate presented at Food and Drug Administration hearings on Reality, January 31, 1992.

[d]Marketed as "VCF" (Vaginal contraceptive film) in the United States and as "C-film" in United Kingdom.

[e]Over-the-counter.

[f]Rate depends on criteria for a good fit, and practitioner criteria have varied widely.

[g]UTI = urinary tract infection.

Source: M. J. Rosenberg and E. L. Gollub. Commentary: Methods women can use that may prevent sexually transmitted diseases, including HIV. *American Journal of Public Health,* 1992, 82, #11, 1473–1478. Copyright 1992 American Public Health Association. Reprinted with permission.

Female Sterilization

NATIONAL DATA ❧ Four percent of never married women, 42.4 percent of currently married women, and 43 percent of formerly married women ages 15 to 44 use surgical sterilization as their method of contraception (*Statistical Abstract of the United States: 1993,* Table 111).

Although a woman may be sterilized by removal of her ovaries (oophorectomy) or uterus (hysterectomy), these operations are not normally undertaken for the sole purpose of sterilization because the ovaries produce important hormones as well as eggs and because both procedures carry the risks of major surgery. But sometimes there is another medical problem requiring hysterectomy.

FIGURE 13.7:

Tubal ligation

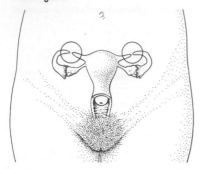

The usual procedures of female sterilization are the salpingectomy, or tubal ligation, and a variant of it, the laparoscopy. Salpingectomy, also known as "tubal ligation" or "tying the tubes," is often performed under a general anesthetic while the woman is in the hospital just after she has delivered a baby. An incision is made in the lower abdomen, just above the pubic line, and the Fallopian tubes are brought into view one at a time. A part of each tube is cut out, and the ends are tied, clamped, or cauterized (burned). The operation takes about 30 minutes. About 700,000 such procedures are performed annually. The cost is around $1,500.

A less expensive and quicker (about 15 minutes) form of salpingectomy, which is performed on an outpatient basis, is the laparoscopy. Often using local anesthesia, the surgeon inserts a small, lighted viewing instrument (laparoscope) through the woman's abdominal wall just below the navel through which the uterus and the Fallopian tubes can be seen. The surgeon then makes another small incision in the lower abdomen and inserts a special pair of forceps that carry electricity to cauterize the tubes. The laparoscope and forceps are then withdrawn, the small wounds are closed with a single stitch, and small bandages are placed over the closed incisions. (Laparoscopy is also known as "the band-aid operation.")

As an alternative to reaching the Fallopian tubes through an opening below the navel, the surgeon may make a small incision in the back of the vaginal barrel (vaginal tubal ligation).

These procedures for female sterilization are highly effective, but sometimes there are complications. In rare cases, a blood vessel in the abdomen is torn open during the sterilization and bleeds into the abdominal cavity. When this happens, another operation is necessary to find the bleeding vessel and tie it closed. Occasionally, there is injury to the small or large intestine, which may cause nausea, vomiting, and loss of appetite. The fact that death may result, if only rarely, is a reminder that female sterilization is surgery and, like all surgery, involves some risks.

Male Sterilization

NATIONAL DATA ❧ About 300,000 men have vasectomies every year (Keen, 1988).

Vasectomies are the most frequent form of male sterilization. They are usually performed in the physician's office under a local anesthetic. Vasectomy involves the physician making two small incisions one on each side of the scrotum so that a small portion of each vas deferens (the sperm-carrying ducts) can be cut out and tied closed. Sperm are still produced in the testicles, but since there is no tube to the penis, they remain in the epididymis and eventually dissolve. The procedure takes about 15 minutes and costs about $350; the man can leave the physician's office within a short time.

Since sperm do not disappear from the ejaculate immediately after a vasectomy (some remain in the vas deferens above the severed portion), another method of contraception should be used until the man has had about 20 ejaculations. He is then asked to bring a sample of his ejaculate to the physicians' office so that it can be examined under a microscope for a sperm count. In about one percent of the cases, the vas deferens grows back and the man becomes fertile again. In other cases, the man may have more than two tubes, which the physician was not aware of.

A vasectomy does not affect the man's desire for sex, ability to have an erection, orgasm, amount of ejaculate (sperm comprise only a minute portion of the seminal fluid), or health. Although in some instances a vasectomy may be reversed, a man should get a vasectomy only if he never wants to have a biological child.

While over a quarter of a million men have vasectomies annually, the number of vasectomies has dropped to less than half of the number of a decade ago. Possible reasons include: (1) men still view sterilization as primarily an option for women; (2) they are aware that reversal of a vasectomy is successful less than half the time; (3) men fear a negative impact of sterilization on their desire for sex.

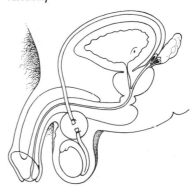

F I G U R E 13.8:

Vasectomy

❧ Avoiding Sexually Transmitted Diseases and Pregnancy

A condom that is put on before the penis touches the other person's body will make it difficult for sexually transmitted diseases or STDs (including genital herpes and HIV) to pass from one person to another (see the Special Topics section on HIV and Other STDs).

It isn't very romantic to talk about STDs with a partner you are about to have sex with, but to ignore STDs one minute is to risk contracting one the next. Contraception should also be discussed before sexual intercourse. Not to do so involves the risk of unwanted pregnancy.

What might a person say about the issues of sexually transmitted diseases and protection from pregnancy before having sexual intercourse or oral sex with a new partner? Maggie Hayes at the University of Oklahoma asked her students how they would handle the situation if they were on an isolated moonlit beach with a person they wanted to have sex with. Some of their responses follow:

> In a situation like this, you have to be open and discuss the consequences. If this "messes up the mood," maybe that's the best thing—better than ending up diseased or pregnant. You can't let your feelings and your hormones [urges] control this situation.

> Even in the heat of passion, one still has to be concerned about HIV and pregnancy. I would first ask if he was going to share something with me that he knew I wouldn't want him to share. I would definitely clarify if necessary. I would also state that I am not ready to be a mother and that some sort of birth control is necessary to continue.

The discussion of protection against pregnancy could be entwined into the romance of the evening, perhaps even made part of verbiage in sexual play. The discussion would probably not be purely sensual—rather one in which feelings of care and love are conveyed.

The discussion of STD would not be nearly as simple. It would be next to impossible to keep this subject within the mood of the evening. One of the parties will probably be offended. Nonetheless, this topic is of vital importance to discuss—mind you, lightly, but it must be done. Perhaps after putting it into perspective for "our future," not to hurt each other, the ground lost can be recovered later in the evening.

I would just have to come right out and question my partner point blank about the subjects. If she had no protection, I'd make a quick trip to the convenience store to buy a condom if possible or abstain if not. If she had an STD, I would take her back to her place and ride off into the sunset as quickly as possible, never to return.

Bringing up a subject like herpes or contraception would seem to detract from the mood more than would abstinence. This fact, along with the guilt feelings I would have to deal with after the experience, with or without protection, has been enough incentive in this situation in the past to get me to stop short of intercourse, so that the beauty of the memory is as great as the beauty of the moment. I'll keep it that way.

"Since this is a new experience for us, we would probably both be more comfortable if we completely leveled with each other about protection. This includes birth control as well as sexually transmitted disease. Is this agreeable with you?" If the partner doesn't want to discuss it, I'd be wary of the partner. I'd also be aware that complete honesty is not always forthcoming in such situations. Open communication enhances any relationship—sexual or otherwise.

People most likely to discuss condoms and contraception with a sexual partner are involved in an ongoing relationship with the partner and have established a pattern of open communication with the partner (Fullilove et al., 1990). In addition, they are also comfortable with and accepting of their own bodies and sexuality.

Persons most likely to use condoms or some other form of contraception have partners who actively support their use (Whitley, 1990) and have relationships in which alcohol or other drugs are not used (Leigh, 1990).

ॐ Teenage Pregnancy

Teenage pregnancy is associated with dropping out of high school, poverty, and low birth weight for the baby. The latter is associated with poor health for the baby.

No human experience is at once so transiently private and lastingly public as an unintended pregnancy.

DANIEL FEDERMAN

NATIONAL DATA ॐ Over one million American teenagers (15–19) become pregnant annually and over half of these give birth to their baby (Ahlburg & De Vita, 1992).

Teenagers have the largest number of unplanned pregnancies of any age group—only about 16 percent of teenage pregnancies are intentional (Hatcher et al, 1990). Teenage girls, both white and black, become pregnant for a number of reasons:

1. Low educational/occupational achievement and goals.
2. High fertility values and desiring a pregnancy.
3. Attitudes of risk-taking.
4. Poor communication skills about sex and contraception.
5. Lack of partner cooperation.
6. Lack of information about contraception.
7. Seeking independence, attaching themselves to a safe partner, or fleeing from an unhappy home situation.
8. Being a member of a society that does not adequately encourage the use of contraception.

Black teenagers are much more likely to be premaritally pregnant and to give birth to their baby. Knight, Dunn, and Vann (1992) noted several reasons for the prevalence of black teenage pregnancy and births. These include higher levels (in contrast to whites) of teenage sexual activity at earlier ages, less interest in having an abortion, less stigma for an out of wedlock pregnancy/birth, greater willingness to have a child while single, greater chance that one's parent had become a parent prior to age 18 with an out of wedlock pregnancy and birth, and less use of effective contraception. Based on their study of 50 black adolescents between the ages of 14 and 17, they recommended:

> Given the generally early initiation of sexual intercourse among African American youth reflected in this and other studies, messages regarding abstinence must be coupled with information about other prevention strategies. Comprehensive, sequential K–12 sexuality education is needed as is community-wide sexuality programs for parents, clergy, and community leaders. Access to community services, including family planning clinics, must be facilitated. African American youth should be aware of the risk for adolescent pregnancy and the factors that impact on that risk. In addition, support and encouragement must be offered to students who remain abstinent and/or want to wait until marriage to have a sexual relationship (p. 11).

The current birth rate to teens (all races combined) in the United States is five times higher than in many European countries. While teen births account for 13 percent of all births in the United States, they account for three percent in France, Germany, and Denmark. Teenagers in these countries are as sexually active as U.S. teenagers but grow up in a context more approving of sex education and availability of contraception (Ahlburg & DeVita, 1992).

The high teenage pregnancy rate and the increasing incidence of HIV infection and other STDs has resulted in the need to reexamine the sex education programs (or lack of them) in the public school system. In addition, some public schools now have school-based clinics, which make condoms available to students.

Most teenage pregnancies are unplanned.

A baby costs $474 a month. How much do you have in your pocket?

POSTER

ACROSS CULTURES ∼

⚕ Abortion

What if an unwanted pregnancy occurs? Seven hundred and four college students were asked by two researchers (Ryan & Dunn, 1988) to order their preference of five possible options for handling an out-of-wedlock, unintended pregnancy. The preferences follow:

Get married and keep child	37.5%
Have an abortion	30.5%
Keep child as single parent	13.9%
Place child for adoption	12.7%
Have grandparents rear child	5.4%

An abortion is defined as the removal of an embryo or fetus from the woman's uterus early in pregnancy before it can survive on its own. Most (89 percent) of all abortions are obtained within the first 12 weeks of gestation (*Facts in Brief,* 1992).

NATIONAL DATA ⚕ Of the 1.6 million abortions performed annually in the United States, 50 percent are obtained by women who are young (age 15 or younger), white (65 percent), and unmarried or never married (83 percent) (*Statistical Abstract of the United States: 1993,* Table 110).

Reasons for seeking an induced abortion reported by 92 pregnant women were fear that the child would cause difficulties with their training and in their work (46 percent), the partner was pressing for an abortion (29 percent), or the woman felt the relationship with her partner was too young to warrant a commitment (20 percent) (Barnett et al., 1992).

Effects of Abortion on Women

A woman with an unwanted pregnancy may be beset by a number of strong feelings: fear ("What will I do now?"); self-anger ("How could I let this happen?"); guilt ("What would my parents think if they knew I was pregnant?"); ambivalence ("Will I be sorry if I have an abortion? Will I be sorry if I don't?"); and sometimes desperation ("Is suicide a way out?").

Legal abortions performed by competent professionals are statistically safer than childbirth, using an IUD, or taking oral contraceptives. Physical complications can occur and include perforation (an instrument punctures the uterine wall), hemorrhage (heavy bleeding), or infection. According to the Alan Guttmacher Institute, less than 1 percent of abortion patients experience a major complication (*Facts in Brief,* 1992).

The American Psychological Association suggested that psychological effects of abortion "are mild and temporary" (Wilmoth, 1989, 7). In a review of studies on the psychological effects of abortion, Adler et al. (1990) concluded

Abortion, for many women, is more than an experience of suffering beyond anything most men will ever know; it is an act of mercy, and an act of self-defense.

ALICE WALKER

that U.S. women who obtained legal abortions experienced the greatest degree of distress *before* the abortion, during the time the decision-making process was occurring. Adler and her colleagues also found a low incidence (5% to 10%) of women who reported severe negative reactions to abortion. For most women, positive reactions (relief) outweighed negative reactions (guilt).

Effect of Abortion on Relationship with Partner

What is the effect of deciding to have an induced abortion on the relationship with one's partner? A team of researchers studied the social and psychological consequences of induced abortion on the relationship between 92 pregnant women and their partners and compared these with a control group of 92 women of similar age, marital status, duration of relationship, number of children, and educational background (Barnett et al., 1992). Just prior to the abortion, the researchers noted more shouting, arguments, and conflict in the couples who experienced the abortion. However, one year later, there were no differences in the number of couples who had separated nor in any remaining qualitative variables (affection, trust, mutual interests).

Abortion Legislation in the United States

In 1973, the U.S. Supreme Court ruled in the famous *Roe v. Wade* case that any restriction on abortions during the first trimester of pregnancy was unconstitutional. During the first three months of pregnancy, the decision to have an abortion was between the pregnant woman and her physician. In the second trimester (fourth through sixth month of pregnancy), the state may regulate the abortion procedure (e.g., require that the abortion be performed in a hospital) so as to protect the woman's health. During the last trimester, the state has an interest in protecting the viable fetus, so the state may restrict or prohibit abortion. In effect, the Supreme Court ruled that the fetus is a potential life and not a "person" until the third trimester. The *Roe v. Wade* decision was based on the right to privacy; government intrusion into the doctor-patient relationship and into a woman's reproductive decisions were seen as violations of that right.

> Abortion is like poverty: no one likes it but it will always be with us.
>
> ROGER SHORT

Since the landmark *Roe v. Wade* decision, a series of rulings regarding abortion have been made. Some of these more recent rulings are described below (Fried, 1990):

1. 1989: *Webster v. Reproductive Health Services*. The Court declared that a state may prohibit "public facilities" and "public employees" from being used to perform or assist abortions not necessary to save the life of the pregnant woman.

2. 1990: *Hodgson v. Minnesota* and *Ohio v. Akron Center for Reproductive Health*. In the Minnesota case, the Court declared that a state could require a pregnant minor to inform both her parents before having an abortion, so long as the law provides the minor to bypass the parents by obtaining a

judicial bypass. A minor may seek this judicial bypass from a judge, who will determine if the minor is "mature" enough to make the abortion decision herself and whether abortion is in the minor's best interest. Reasons why some minors seek a court bypass include fear of parental disapproval, one parent is absent from the home, and the desire to avoid contributing to stress in the family. In the Ohio case, the Court ruled that the state may require a minor to notify one parent, while allowing the judicial bypass alternative. The Court also upheld the constitutionality of requiring waiting periods before the abortion can be performed.

CONSIDERATION

Parental notification laws have been fiercely opposed on the grounds that they increase the likelihood that a pregnant minor will seek an illegal (and often unsafe) abortion to avoid disclosure of the pregnancy to her parent(s). Such was the case for Becky Bell, a 17-year-old from Indianapolis, Indiana, who obtained an illegal abortion in 1988 and died from an abortion-related infection. According to her friends, Becky was unwilling to hurt her parents with news of her pregnancy, so she obtained an illegal abortion. Becky's mother said of the incident, "She died because of a law I didn't know existed" (Sharpe, 1990, 80).

---

3. 1991: In May of 1991, the Supreme Court by a vote of 5 to 4 ruled that federally funded family planning clinics (there are about 4,000 in the United States) are prohibited from giving a woman any information about abortion. This prohibition (labeled by pro-choice advocates as the "gag rule") had the greatest effect on low-income women. When pregnant women asked specifically for abortion information they were told that the family planning clinic "does not consider abortion an appropriate method of family planning" (Marcus, 1991, 2).
4. 1993: Shortly after taking office, President Clinton signed an order repealing the "gag rule."

NATIONAL DATA 🦢 Sixty-four percent of all college and university freshmen throughout the United States "somewhat or strongly agree" that abortion should be legal (American Council on Education and University of California, 1992).

Placing the baby for adoption is an alternative to abortion. About 13 percent of the 704 students in the Ryan and Dunn (1988) study reported that they would give their child up for adoption. Donnelly and Voydanoff (1991) interviewed 24 pregnant or newly postpartum adolescents (ages 12 to 19) who had decided to give their baby to adoptive parents. The background characteristics of these adolescents included being from a small family, feeling that keeping the baby would be a decision she would regret, and wanting to continue in school. They are also "less likely to believe that being a mother will make her feel more like a grown-up, that mothering will be fun, and that not raising the child would be selfish" (p. 407).

CONSIDERATION

Three researchers compared the short-term consequences of 311 young unmarried women who kept their babies with 216 who relinquished them to adoptive parents. The researchers concluded that "young women who place their babies for adoption tend to fare as well or better than those who keep and parent their babies" (Kalmuss, Namerow, & Bauer, 1992, 88).

Abortion from a Cross-Cultural Perspective

ACROSS CULTURES ❧

Abortion "is an option to which people at all times and places have resorted, with or without religious consent, legal approval, or medical supervision" (Tribe, 1990, 52). In this section we look at abortion in other times and places so as to understand the wide range of cultural responses to the abortion issue. On one end of the continuum is the Kafir tribe in Central Asia where an abortion is strictly the choice of the woman. In this preliterate society, there is no taboo or restriction in regard to abortion and the woman is free to exercise her decision to terminate her pregnancy. One reason for the Kafir's approval of abortion is that childbirth in their tribe is associated with high rates of maternal mortality. Since birthing children may threaten the life of significant numbers of adult women in the community, women may be encouraged to abort. Such encouragement is particularly strong in the case of women who are viewed as too young, too sick, too old, or too small to bear children.

Abortion may also be encouraged by a tribe or society for a number of other reasons including practicality, economics, lineage, and honor. Abortion is practical for women in migratory societies. They must control their pregnancies since they are limited in the number of children they can nurse and transport. Economic motivations become apparent when resources (e.g., food) are scarce—the number of children born to a group must be controlled. Abortion for reasons of lineage or honor involves encouragement of an abortion in those cases in which a woman becomes impregnated in an adulterous relationship. To protect the lineage and honor of her family, she may have an abortion.

From a worldwide perspective, about 76 percent of the world's population live in countries where induced abortion is legally permitted (39 percent abortion on request; 24 percent for socioeconomic reasons such as inadequate housing; 13 percent on health grounds). The other 24 percent of the world's population live in countries where abortion is either prohibited or permitted only on grounds of saving the life of the mother (United Nations Population Fund, 1991).

In China and other nations, infanticide is sometimes used to ensure that only male children are reared in a family. A 1990 census in China revealed that 5 percent of infant girls were "missing"—it is suspected that they were killed by midwives on the orders from parents who were intent on having sons (Kristof, 1991).

☙ Trends

One trend in family planning is less social obligation to have children. Childfree couples are being given more social approval and are regarded as "real families" just as are couples with children. In addition, one-child couples have become more common in response to women becoming more involved in their careers.

Increasing numbers of women are also delaying childbearing until their thirties. This is due to a later age at marriage, a desire to pursue careers, and the use of prenatal testing such as amniocentesis and chorion biopsy to diagnose genetic abnormalities. In essence, the age at which a woman may safely have a baby has been increased by technological advancements.

Compared to previous generations, women who reach their thirties without being married are more willing to have a baby and rear the child as a single parent. Not only has the stigma of single-parent motherhood (no longer called "having a child out of wedlock") lessened, the biological clock dictates that in the absence of a husband, parenthood should still be pursued and enjoyed.

Increasingly, unmarried men as well as women are choosing to have and rear a child alone. According to the Census Bureau, there has been a dramatic increase in homes headed by single, never married men, from 22,000 in 1970 to 380,000 in 1991. *People Magazine* identified three single dads including Christensen, a 40-year-old unmarried man in Michigan who paid a surrogate mother to bear his child; Sherman, a 48-year-old Denver man who had a child from a casual relationship and adopted two others; and Brad a 31-year-old gay man who has an adopted daughter. Each of these men were not married but wanted the experience of having a family (Arias et al., 1992).

The immediate future of abortion legislation is likely to protect the *Roe v. Wade* decision. With the election of President Bill Clinton, new Supreme Court nominees are likely to be pro-choice. Already, he has lifted the "gag rule," which prohibited healthcare workers in federally funded clinics from providing information about abortion.

Finally, the abortion debate will continue. Referring to the abortion issue, Rosenblatt (1992) observed, "We have been at war for the past twenty-five years, and the war we have waged on this issue is greater than that of any other nation in history" (p. 98).

It is better to debate a question without settling it than to settle a question without debating it.

JOSEPH JOUBERT (1754–1824)

❧ CHOICES ❧

*T*he decision about one's method of contraception is an important decision for most people.

Which Method of Contraception to Use?

The following series of questions, which are adapted from the Contraceptive Comfort and Confidence Scale (Hatcher et al., 1990) are designed to help you assess whether the method of contraception you are currently using or may be considering using in the future is or will be effective for you.

Contraceptive Comfort and Confidence Scale

Method of birth control you are currently using or are considering using:

_____

Answer YES or NO to the following questions:

1. Have you had problems using this method before?
2. Are you afraid of using this method?
3. Would you really rather not use this method?
4. Will you have trouble remembering to use this method?
5. Have you ever become pregnant using this method? (Or has your partner ever become pregnant using this method?)
6. Will you have trouble using this method correctly?
7. Do you still have unanswered questions about this method?
8. Does this method make menstrual periods longer or more painful?
9. Does this method cost more than you can afford?
10. Could this method cause you or your partner to have serious complications?
11. Are you opposed to this method because of religious beliefs?
12. Is your partner opposed to this method?
13. Are you using this method without your partner's knowledge?
14. Will using this method embarrass your partner?
15. Will using this method embarrass you?
16. Will you enjoy intercourse less because of this method?
17. Will your partner enjoy intercourse less because of this method?
18. If this method interrupts lovemaking, will you avoid using it?
19. Has a nurse or doctor ever told you (or your partner) NOT to use this method?
20. Is there anything about your personality that could lead you to use this method incorrectly?
21. Does this method leave you at risk of being exposed to HIV or other sexually transmitted infections?

Total number of YES answers: _____

Most individuals will have a few "yes" answers. "Yes" answers predict potential problems. If you have more than a few "yes" responses, you may want to talk to your physician, healthcare worker, partner, or friend. Talking it over can help you decide whether to use this method, or how to use it so it will really be effective for you. In general, the more "yes" answers you have, the less likely you are to use this method consistently and correctly.

SOURCE: Adapted from Hatcher et al. *Contraceptive Technology: 1990–1992, 15th rev. ed.* New York: Irvington Publishers, 1990, 150. Address: 195 McGregor St. Manchester, NH 03102. Used by permission.

In choosing a method of contraception, you might want to keep in mind that, if you want a highly effective method of contraception *and* a method that is highly effective in preventing transmission of HIV and other STDs, you may have to use *two* methods (Cates & Stone, 1992). Hence, any method of contraception (except abstinence, of course) should be combined with condom use for maximum protection against HIV and other STDs.

Whether to Have an Abortion? Some Guidelines

Abortion continues to be a complex decision. Of 74 women who waited-
(continued)

⌁ CHOICES ⌁

---

until the 16th week of gestation (or later) to get an abortion, 78 percent said that they waited so long because of the difficulty in making a decision (Torres & Forrest, 1988). Women who are faced with the question of whether to have an abortion may benefit by considering the following guidelines:

1. Consider all the alternatives available to you, realizing that no alternative may be all good or all bad. As you consider each alternative, think about both the short-term and the long-term consequences of each course of action.
2. Obtain information about each alternative course of action. Inform yourself about the medical and financial aspects of abortion and childbearing.
3. Talk with trusted family members, friends, or unbiased counselors. Consider talking with the man who participated in the pregnancy. If possible, also talk with women who have had abortions, as well as women who have kept and reared their baby or placed their baby for adoption. If you feel that someone is pressuring you in your decision making, look for help elsewhere.
4. Consider your own personal and moral commitments in life. Understand your own feelings, values, and beliefs concerning the fetus and weigh those against the circumstances surrounding your pregnancy.

℘ Summary

The decision whether to become a parent is one of the most important decisions you will ever make. Unlike marriage, parenthood is a role from which there is no easy withdrawal. Individuals may try out marriage by living together, but there is no such trial run for would-be parents.

Spouses, children, and society all benefit from family planning. These benefits include less health risk to mother and child, fewer unwanted children, decreased economic burden for the parents and society, and population control.

The decision to become a parent is encouraged (sometimes unconsciously) by family, peers, religion, government, education, and cultural observances. The reasons people give for having children include social expectations, influence of spouse, accident, a sense of immortality, personal fulfillment and identity, and the desire for a close affiliative relationship.

Some couples opt for the childfree lifestyle. Reasons wives give for wanting to be childfree are more personal freedom, greater time and intimacy with their spouses, and career demands. Husbands also are motivated by the desire for more personal freedom. They mention disinterest in being a parent and the desire to avoid the responsibilities of parenthood as reasons for choosing a childfree lifestyle.

The most preferred family size in the United States is the two-child family. Some of the factors in a couple's decision to have more than one child are the desire to repeat a good experience, the feeling that two children provide companionship for each other, and the desire to have a child of each sex.

The primary methods of birth control are contraception, sterilization, and abortion. With contraception, the risk of becoming pregnant can be reduced to practically zero, depending on the method selected and how systematically it is used. Contraception includes birth control pills, which prevent ovulation; the IUD, which prevents implantation of the fertilized egg; condoms and diaphragms, which are barrier methods; as well as vaginal spermicides and sponge, and the rhythm method. These methods vary in effectiveness and safety.

Sterilization is a surgical procedure that prevents fertilization, usually by blocking the passage of eggs or sperm through the Fallopian tubes or vas deferens, respectively. The procedure for female sterilization is called salpingectomy, or tubal ligation. Laparoscopy is another method of tubal ligation. The most frequent form of male sterilization is vasectomy.

Teenage pregnancies in the United States are usually unintended pregnancies. One option for women faced with an unintended and unwanted pregnancy is abortion.

Trends in family planning include more childfree marriages, more one-child families, and women being older at the time of their first birth. In addition, an increasing number of unmarried women and men in their thirties are opting to have and rear a child without a spouse. Finally, under the Clinton administration, restrictions on abortions are likely to lessen.

Questions for Reflection

1. What impact have your experiences in the family in which you were reared had on your desire for children? If you want children, how does the number of siblings you have influence the number of children you want?
2. To what degree do the only children you know fit the stereotype of being lonely and spoiled?
3. To what degree are you pro-choice or pro-life regarding abortion?

References

Adler, N. E., H. P. David, B. N. Major, S. H. Roth, N. F. Russo, and G. E. Wyatt. Psychological responses after abortion. *Science,* 1990, 248, 41–44.

Affonso, D. D., & L. J. Mayberry. Common stressors reported by a group of childbearing American women. *Pregnancy and Parenting,* P. N. Stern, ed. New York: Hemisphere, 1989, 41–55.

Ahlburg, D. A. and C. J. De Vita. New realities of the American family. *Population Bulletin,* 1992, *47,* 1–44.

American Council on Education and University of California. The American freshman: National norms for fall, 1992. Los Angeles, Calif.: Los Angeles Higher Education Research Institute, 1992.

Arcus, M. E. Family life education: Toward the 21st century. *Family Relations,* 1992, *41,* 390–393.

Arias, R., P. Lambert, J. Grenwalt, V. Bane, J. Grandolfo, L. McNeil, and R. Beach. Singular dads. *People Magazine,* August 31, 1992, 35–39.

Barnes, F. The family gap. *Reader's Digest,* July 1992, 48–54.

Barnett, W., N. Freudenberg, and R. Willie. Partnership after induced abortion: A prospective controlled study. *Archives of Sexual Behavior,* 1992, *21,* 443–455.

Baulieu, Etienne-Emile and M. Rosenblum. *The abortion pill.* New York: Simon & Schuster, 1991.

Blank, Robert H. *Regulating reproduction.* New York: Columbia University Press, 1990.

Bomwich, P. and T. Parsons. *Contraception: The facts.* Oxford: Oxford University Press, 1990.

Boyd, R. L. Minority status and childlessness. *Sociological Inquiry,* 1989, *59,* 331–342.

Brailey, L. J. Stress experienced by mothers of young children. *Pregnancy and Parenting,* P. N. Stern, ed. New York: Hemisphere, 1989, 157–168.

Cates, W., Jr. and K. M. Stone. Family planning, sexually transmitted diseases and contraceptive choice: A literature update 1. *Family Planning Perspectives,* 1992, *24,* 75–82.

Cohen, J. B. *Parenthood after 30? A guide to personal choice.* Lexington, Mass.: Lexington Books, 1985.

Cooney, T. M., F. A. Pedersen, S. Indelicato, and R. Palkovitz. Timing of fatherhood: Is "on time" optimal? *Journal of Marriage and the Family,* 1993, *55,* 205–215.

Donnelly, B. W. and P. Voydanoff. Factors associated with releasing for adoption among adolescent mothers. *Family Relations,* 1991, *40,* 404–410.

Dorman, M., & D. Klein. *How to stay 2 when baby makes 3.* New York: Prometheus Books, 1984.

Dreyfous, L. In lean times, more couples opt for having only one child. *The Daily Reflector,* Greenville, NC, 1991 (Oct. 13), p. 2G.

Exter, T. The costs of growing up. *American Demographics,* 1991, *13,* 59–60.

Facts in Brief: Abortion in the United States. New York: Alan Guttmacher Institute, 1992.

Farmer, R. and R. Ling. *The baby's budget book.* Dallas, Tex.: Shadetree Publications, 1990.

Fried, Marlene Gerber. Key United States Supreme Court abortion and privacy cases. *From Abortion to Reproductive Freedom: Transforming a Movement,* M. G. Fried, ed. Boston, Mass.: South End Press, 1990, 45–48.

Fullilove, M. T., R. E. Fullilove, K. Haynes, and S. Gross. Black women and AIDS prevention: A view towards understanding the gender rules. *The Journal of Sex Research,* 1990, *27,* 47–64.

Glenn, N. D. Quantitative research on marital quality in the 1980s: A critical review. *Contemporary Families,* Alan Booth, ed. Minneapolis, Minn.: National Council on Family Relations, 1991, 28–41.

Goldberg, W. A., & G. Y. Michaels. Conclusion. The transition to parenthood: Synthesis and future directions. *The Transition to Parenthood: Current Theory and Research,* G. Y. Michaels & W. A. Goldberg, eds. New York: Cambridge University Press, 1988, 342–360.

Gooding, J., and R. Williams. RU486 (the French Abortion pill). *American Health,* 1991, December, 65–69.

Gregersen E. and B. Gregersen. The female condom: A pilot study of the acceptability of a new female barrier method. *Acta Obstetricia et Gynecologica Scandinavica,* 1990, *69,* 73.

Hatcher, R. A., F. Stewart, J. Trussell, D. Kowal, F. Guest, G. K. Stewart, and W. Cates. *Contraceptive technology: 1990–1992,* 15th rev. ed. New York: Irvington, 1990.

Hogge, W. A., S. A. Schonberg, and M. S. Golbus. Chronic villus sampling: The experiences of 1,000 cases. *American Journal of Obstetrics and Gynecology,* 1986, *154,* 1249–1252.

Ishii-Kuntz, M. and M. Ihinger-Tallman. The subjective well-being of parents. *Journal of FamilyIssues,* 1991, *12,* 58–68.

Jones, E. F. and J. D. Forrest. Contraceptive failure rates based on the 1988 NSFG. *Family Planning Perspectives,* 1992, *24,* 12–19.

Kalmuss, D., P. B. Namerow, and U. Bauer. Short-term consequences of parenting versus adoption among young unmarried women. *Journal of Marriage and the Family,* 1992, *54,* 80–90.

Keen, H. A decline in vasectomies. *Maclean's,* May 2, 1988, 10.

Klitsch, M. Antiprogestins and the abortion controversy: A progress report. *Family Planning Perspectives,* 1991, *23,* 275–282.

Knight, S., P. Dunn, and S. Vann. A pilot study of parenthood and sexuality: The perceptions of black adolescents. Paper, American Public Health Convention, Washington, D.C. November 10, 1992. Used by permission.

Knox, D. and K. Wilson. The differences between having one and two children. *Family Coordinator,* 1978, *27,* 23–25.

Koop, C. Everett. A measured response: Koop on abortion. *Family Planning Perspectives,* 1989, *21,* 31–32.

Kost, K., J. D. Forrest, and S. Harlap. Comparing the health risks and benefits of contraceptive choices. *Family Planning Perspectives,* 1991, *23,* 54–61.

Kovacs, L. Future direction of abortion technology. *Baillieres Clinical Obstetrics and Gynecology,* 1990, *4,* 407–414.

Kraus, J. Shotgun weddings: Trends in the sociopathology of marriage. *Australian and New Zealand Journal of Psychiatry* 1977, *11,* 259–264.

Kristof, N. D. A mystery from China's census: where have young girls gone? *The New York Times,* 1991, June 17, pp. A1, A8.

Leigh, B. C. The relationship of substance use during sex to high-risk sexual behavior. *The Journal of Sex Research,* 1990, *27,* 199–213.

MacDermind, S. M., T. L. Huston, and S. M. McHale. Changes in marriage associated with the transition to parenthood: Individual differences as a function of sex-role attitudes and changes in the division of household labor. *Journal of Marriage and the Family,* 1990, *52,* 475–486.

Marcus, R. Court upholds ban on abortion advice. *News and Observer,* Raleigh, N.C., May 24, 1991, 1–2.

Mercer, R. T. *First-time motherhood: Experiences from teens to forties.* New York: Springer Publishing Co., 1986.

Michaels, G. Y. Motivational factors in the decision and timing of pregnancy. *The Transition to Parenthood: Current Theory and Research,* G. Y. Michaels and W. A. Goldberg, eds. New York: Cambridge University Press, 1988, 23–61.

Mindel, C. H., R. W. Habenstein, and R. Wright, Jr., eds. *Ethnic families in America: Patterns and variations,* 3d ed. New York: Elsevier, 1988.

Morris, J. and D. Schneider. Health risk behavior: A comparison of five campuses. *College Student Journal,* 1992, *26,* 390–398.

National Center for Health Statistics. Advance report of final natality statistics, 1987. Monthly Vital Statistics Report, *38,* no. 3, suppl. Hyattsville, Md.: Public Health Service, 1989.

Neal, A. G., H. T. Groat, and J. W. Wicks. Attitudes about having children: A study of 600 couples in the early years of marriage. *Journal of Marriage and the Family,* 1989, *51,* 313–328.

Newman, S. *Parenting an only child.* New York: Doubleday, 1990.

O'Hare, W. P. and J. C. Felt. Asian Americans: America's fastest growing minority group. *Population Trends and Public Policy,* February 1991. Population Reference Bureau.

O'Hare, W. P., K. M. Pollard, T. L. Mann, and M. M. Kent. African Americans in the 1900s. *Population Bulletin,* 1991, *46,* 1–40.

Painter, K. Joys override obstacles for late bloomers. *USA Today,* May 11, 1990, D1, D2.

Prendergast, A. Beyond the pill. *American Health,* October 1990, 37–44.

Rosenberg, M. J. and E. L. Gollub. Commentary: Methods women can use that may prevent sexually transmitted disease, including HIV. *American Journal of Public Health*, 1992, *82*, 1473–1483.

Rosenblatt, R. *Life itself: Abortion in the American mind.* New York: Random House, 1992.

Rubinson, L. and L. DeRubertis. Trends in sexual attitudes and behaviors of a college population over a 15-year period. *Journal of Sex Education and Therapy*, 1991, *17*, 32–40.

Ryan, I. J. and P. C. Dunn. Association of race, sex, religion, family size, and desired number of children on college students preferred methods of dealing with unplanned pregnancy. *Family Practice Research Journal*, 1988, *7*, 153–161.

Sadik, N. Public policy and private decisions: World population and world health in the 21st century. *Journal of Public Health Policy*, 1992, *13*, 133–139.

Sapiro, V. *Women in American society*, 2d ed. Mountain View, Calif.: Mayfield, 1990.

Seashore, M. R. Counseling prospective parents about possible genetic disorders in offspring. *Medical Aspects of Human Sexuality*, 1980, *14*, no. 11, 97–98.

Seccombe, K. Assessing the costs and benefits of children: Gender comparisons among childfree husbands and wives. *Journal of Marriage and the Family*, 1991, *53*, 191–202.

Sharpe, Rochells. She died because of a law. *Ms.*, July/August 1990, 80–81.

Shoupe, Donna and Daniel Mishell. Norplant: Subdermal implant system for long-term contraception. *American Journal of Obstetrics and Gynecology*, 1989, *160*, 1286–1292.

Statistical Abstract of the United States: 1993, 113th ed. Washington, D.C.: U.S. Bureau of the Census, 1993.

Teachman, Jay D. and Paul T. Schollaert. Economic conditions, marital status, and the timing of first births: Results for whites and blacks. *Sociological Forum*, 1989, *4*, 27–46.

Thomas, P. Contraceptives: Break due after decade of drought. *Medical World News*, March 14, 1988, 49–68.

Toman, W. Family constellation: Its effects on personality and social behavior. New York: Springer Publishing Co., 1993.

Torres, A., and J. D. Forrest. Why do women have abortions? *Family Planning Perspectives*, 1988, *20*, 169–176.

Travis, C. B. *Women and health psychology: Biomedical issues.* Hillsdale, N.J.: Lawrence Erlbaum Associates, 1988.

Tribe, L. H. *The clash of absolutes.* New York: W. W. Norton, 1990.

Trussell, J., D. L. Warner, and R. A. Hatcher. Condom slippage and breakage rates. *Family Planning Perspectives*, 1992, *24*, 20–23.

Umberson, D. Relationships between adult children and their parents: Psychological consequences for both generations. *Journal of Marriage and the Family*, 1992, *54*, 664–674.

United Nations Population Fund. *Population policies and programmes: Lessons learned from two decades of experience.* Nafis Sadik, ed. New York: New York University Press, 1991.

Urzua, R. The demographic dimension. *UNESCO Courier*, January 1992, 14.

Whitley, B. E. College student contraceptive use: A multivariate analysis. *Journal of Sex Research*, 1990, *27*, 305–313.

Wildemeersch, D. A. New IUDs. In a new look at IUDs—Advancing contraceptive choices: Abstract of oral papers. *Contraception: An International Journal*, 1992, *45*, 273–298.

Williams, J. H. *Psychology of women: Behavior in a biosocial context* (3rd ed.). New York: W. W. Norton, 1987.

Williams, L. B. Determinants of unintended childbearing among never-married women in the United States: 1973–1988. *Family Planning Perspectives*, 1991, *23*, 212–221.

Wilmoth, G. APA challenges Koop's abortion report. Advancing the Public Interest, 1989 (Winter), 7.

Wolinsky, H. A woman's condom? *American Health Magazine*, June 1988, 10.

Contents

❧ 14 ❧
CHAPTER

Becoming a Parent

Is It True?

1. Only fresh semen should be used for artificial insemination.

2. Over half of all adoptions are by relatives.

3. The pregnant woman is advised to eat the same number of servings of a balanced diet as a nonpregnant woman.

4. Both husbands and wives experience an upswing in sexual interest during the third trimester of pregnancy.

5. Only 10 percent of infertile couples who try in-vitro fertilization in one of the 300 clinics available in the United States end up with a baby.

1 = F; 2 = T; 3 = F; 4 = F; 5 = T

It is just the biggest honor of all—to be pregnant, to be waiting for your child to come. It's an amazing thing. It's like no other feeling of joy in the world that I can compare.

WHITNEY HOUSTON

Learning to scuba dive involves learning to adapt to a radically different environment. Training involves becoming familiar with how water pressure affects the body's physiology and determining how deep one can go and for how long without getting "the bends" on ascent. Failure to adequately prepare for the transition from land to sea can be fatal. On the other hand, mastering the skills of scuba diving can result in an incredible array of beautiful and wonderful underwater experiences.

Although federal regulations require certification training to ensure a safe transition from land to water, no such training is required in the transition to parenthood. Our society seems to assume that parenthood is natural and that the transition is easy. We suggest that like all other major changes in one's environment, the transition to parenthood represents a challenge, which may benefit from some awareness before the plunge. In this chapter we review the transition to parenthood from fertilization through birth to the early months of adjustment for the new mother, father, and family. We begin with a review of fertilization and conception.

Fertilization and Conception

Fertilization takes place when a woman's egg, or ovum, unites with a man's sperm. This may occur through sexual intercourse or artificial insemination, or more recently, through the method of "test-tube" or *in-vitro* fertilization.

At orgasm, the man ejaculates a thick white substance called semen, which contains about 300 million sperm. Once the semen is deposited in or near the vagina, the sperm begin to travel up the vagina, through the opening of the cervix, up the uterus, and into the Fallopian tubes. If the woman has ovulated (released a mature egg from an ovary into a Fallopian tube) within eight hours, or if she ovulates during the two or three days the sperm typically remain alive, a sperm may penetrate and fertilize the egg.

CONSIDERATION

Although popular usage does not differentiate between the terms *fertilization* and *conception,* fertilization refers to the union of the egg and sperm while conception refers to the fertilized egg that survives through implantation on the uterine wall.

> Hence, not all fertilizations result in conception. Pregnancy refers to the state of having conceived with emphasis on the developing fetus.

Since a woman is fertile for only about 48 hours each month, when is the best time to have intercourse to maximize the chance of pregnancy? In general, 24 hours before ovulation is the best time. There are several ways to predict ovulation including breast tenderness, a "pinging" sensation in the woman's abdomen at the time of ovulation, keeping a record of the woman's basal body temperature, and examining the cervical mucus.

The position during intercourse may also be important for fertilization. In order to maximize the chance of fertilization, during intercourse, the woman should be on her back and a pillow should be placed under her buttocks after receiving the sperm so a pool of semen will collect near her cervix. She should remain in this position for about 30 minutes to allow the sperm to reach the Fallopian tubes.

Infertility

Infertility is defined as the inability to become pregnant after at least one year of regular sexual relations without birth control, or the inability to carry a pregnancy to live birth.

NATIONAL DATA Infertility affects between 15 and 20 percent of married couples in the United States (Higgins, 1990).

Causes of Infertility   Forty percent of infertility problems are attributed to the woman, 40 percent to the man, and 20 percent to both partners (Derwinski-Robinson, 1990). Some of the more common causes of infertility in men include low sperm production, poor semen motility, effects of sexually transmitted diseases such as chlamydia, gonorrhea, and syphilis, and interference with the passage of sperm through the genital ducts due to an enlarged prostate. The causes of infertility in women include blocked Fallopian tubes, endocrine imbalances that prevent ovulation, dysfunctional ovaries, chemically hostile cervical mucus that may kill sperm, and effects of sexually transmitted diseases.

Psychological Reactions to Infertility   Infertility is a major negative life event for those who experience it. Both marital and sexual satisfaction decline as the couple become involved in treatment for their infertility (Pepe & Byrne, 1991). A team of researchers studied 185 married infertile couples and concluded the following (Abbey et al., 1992):

> As hypothesized, the stress associated with infertility had deleterious effects on women's and men's global and intimacy life quality. . . . The greater the fertility

I didn't have children because I can't have children.

VICTORIA PRINCIPAL

Infertility is truly a bio-psycho-social condition.

CONSTANCE SHAPIRO

Women who are influenced by narrow gender role definitions . . . experience infertility as an unbearable defect.

P. C. DAVIS

problem stress, the lower men's and women's self-esteem and internal control and the greater their interpersonal conflict. Even though infertility may seem to be especially relevant for sexual and marriage issues, its strongest impact was on global well-being (p. 415).

RESOLVE is a national advocacy and support group for infertile couples. Based in Somerville, Massachusetts, RESOLVE has 57 chapters in 38 states. The phone number is 617-623-1156.

While some infertile couples choose to remain childfree, others choose to adopt a child. Other infertile couples choose to undergo some form of treatment in an attempt to achieve a pregnancy.

Pepe and Byrne (1991) analyzed completed questionnaires from 40 infertile women who identified the various treatments they sought in their attempt to affect fertility over a 14-month period:

Fertility drugs	60%
Artificial insemination by husband	40%
In vitro fertilization	30%
Surgery	32%
Artificial insemination by donor	13%

We now explore some of these alternatives.

Fertility Drugs

> All these hormones make you edgy and depressed. It's really hard to keep even.
>
> ROSEANNE ARNOLD ON HER INFERTILITY TREATMENTS

Fertility drugs may be used to treat hormonal imbalances, induce ovulation, and correct problems of the menstrual cycle. Frequently used drugs include Clomid and Pergonal (both are trade names). Fertility drugs are associated with an increased risk of multiple births.

NATIONAL DATA ❧ Between 1982 and 1989 the rate of higher-order multiple births among U.S. women increased from 40 to 78 per 100,000 live births. This increase is largely attributed to the rise in use of ovulation-inducing drugs for treating infertility (Kiely, Kleinman, & Kiely, 1992).

Artificial Insemination

When the sperm of the husband is low in count or motility, the sperm from several ejaculations may be pooled and placed directly into the cervix. This procedure is known as *artificial insemination* of the wife by the husband (AIH). Out of more than 700 university students, 76 percent said artificial insemination of the wife with the husband's sperm was acceptable (Dunn, Ryan, & O'Brien, 1988).

When sperm from someone other than the husband is used to fertilize a woman, the technique is referred to as artificial insemination by donor (AID). There is less acceptance for AID than for AIH. Out of more than 700 university students, only 20 percent said artificial insemination of the wife by donor was acceptable (Dunn et al., 1988).

NATIONAL DATA   In the United States, about 30,000 infants are conceived each year through the use of artificial insemination (Foreman, 1990, 7A).

In the procedure of artificial insemination, a physician or the woman's partner who has been trained by the physician deposits the sperm through a syringe in the woman's cervix and places a cervical cap over her cervix, which remains in place for 24 hours. On the average, it takes about three inseminations before fertilization occurs.

CONSIDERATION

Due to concerns about HIV infection, the American Fertility Society has issued a set of guidelines for donor insemination clinics and physicians. These include:

1. The donor's sperm should be screened for genetic abnormalities and sexually transmitted diseases.
2. All semen should be quarantined for 180 days and retested for HIV.
3. Fresh semen should never be used.
4. The donor should be under age 50 in order to diminish hazards related to aging (Foreman, 1990, 7A).

In reality, only about half of physicians who regularly perform artificial inseminations test sperm donors for genetic defects or HIV status. Only 27–28 percent require donors to be tested for syphilis or gonorrhea (Office of Technology Assessment, 1988). The most blatant misuse of donor sperm was that of Cecil Jacobson, a fertility physician, age 55, who used his own sperm (without the knowledge of his patients) to father up to 75 children (Stone, 1992). (He was sentenced to five years in prison and ordered to pay over $100,000 in damages).

Sometimes the donor's and the husband's sperm are mixed, so that the couple has the psychological benefit of knowing that the husband may be the biological father. One situation in which the husband's sperm is not mixed with the donor's sperm is when the husband is the carrier of a genetic disease, such as Tay-Sachs disease.

There are about 85 sperm banks in the United States, including the Repository for Germinal Choice. This controversial sperm bank in Escondido, California, specializes in providing sperm from men of known intellectual achievement. Among their donors have been three Nobel prize winners in science. No donor to the sperm bank has an IQ under 140. Critics charge that such a sperm bank resembles Hitler's attempts to build a master race.

Artificial Insemination of Surrogate Mother

Sometimes artificial insemination does not help a woman to get pregnant (for example, her Fallopian tubes may be blocked or her cervical mucus may be hostile to sperm). The couple who still want a child but decided against adoption may consider parenthood through a *surrogate mother.* There are two types of surrogate mothers. One is the contracted surrogate mother who supplies the egg, is impregnated with the husband's sperm, carries the child to term, and gives the baby to the man and his partner. A second type is the surrogate mother who carries the baby, to whom she is not genetically related, to term. This surrogate mother does not supply the egg; rather, she is implanted with the fertilized egg of another woman who cannot carry a baby to term but wishes to have a child.

Legally, there are few guidelines to protect involuntary childless couples who engage a surrogate mother for procreative services. The surrogate can change her mind and decide to keep the child. Such a case occurred in 1991 when surrogate mother Elvie Jordon changed her mind when she discovered that the couple she gave her baby to were getting divorced. Jordon filed suit to get custody of 17-month-old Marissa who was living with Bob Moschetta (the biological father and ex-husband of Cindy Moschetta). The Superior Court Santa Anna, California, Judge Weiben-Stock ruled that Elvie Jordon and Bob Moschetta (the biological mother and father) would share joint legal and physical custody of Marissa (Cindy Moschetta was ruled as having no legal rights and was given no visitation privileges).

CONSIDERATION

Previously, the courts have been reluctant to regard the surrogate mother as having parental rights to her biological child. The Jordon case illustrates that the biological mother may be given legal rights to the child she bore. However, surrogates who change their mind and want to keep their baby are rare.

There is limited acceptance of surrogate motherhood by university students. Only 15 percent of over 700 university students said that having a baby by means of a surrogate mother was acceptable (Dunn et al., 1988).

Ovum Transfer

Another alternative for the infertile couple is ovum transfer. The sperm of the male partner is placed by a physician in a surrogate woman. After about five days, her uterus is flushed out (endometrial lavage) and the contents are analyzed under a microscope to identify the presence of a fertilized ovum, which is inserted into the uterus of the otherwise infertile partner. Although the embryo can also be frozen and implanted at a later time, fresh embryos are more likely to result in successful implantation (24 percent if fresh versus eight percent if frozen) (Levran et al., 1990).

Infertile couples who opt for ovum transfer, also called embryo transfer, do so because the baby will be biologically related to at least one of them (the father) and the partner will have the experience of pregnancy and childbirth.

Out of more than 700 university students, 26 percent said that having a baby via ovum transfer was acceptable (Dunn et al., 1988).

In-Vitro Fertilization

About 2 million couples cannot have a baby because the woman's Fallopian tubes are blocked or damaged, preventing the passage of the eggs to the uterus. In some cases, blocked tubes can be opened via laser-beam surgery or inflating a tiny balloon within the clogged passage. When these procedures are not successful (or when the physician decides to avoid invasive tests and exploratory surgery), in-vitro (meaning "in glass"), also known as test-tube fertilization, is an alternative.

Over 20,000 live births to date began with fertilization in a culture or Petri dish.

Using a *laparoscope* (a narrow, telescope-like instrument inserted through an incision just below the woman's navel to view the tubes and ovaries), the physician is able to see a mature egg as it is released from the woman's ovary. The time of release can be predicted accurately within two hours. When the egg emerges, the physician uses an aspirator to remove the egg, placing it in a small tube containing a stabilizing fluid. The egg is taken to the laboratory, put in a culture or Petri dish, kept at a certain temperature-acidity level, and surrounded by sperm from the woman's partner (or donor). After one of these sperm fertilizes the egg, it divides and is implanted by the physician in the wall of the woman's uterus. Usually, several fertilized eggs are implanted in the hope that one will survive.

Occasionally, some fertilized eggs are frozen and implanted at a later time. This procedure is known as *cryopreservation*. In the meantime, any number of things could occur; for instance, the couple may get divorced and disagree over who owns the frozen embryos. Such was the case of Mary Sue Davis and Junior Davis who took their disagreement to court. The court awarded the embryos to Ms. Davis (Fitzgerald, 1989). On appeal, the decision was overturned.

Student acceptance of in-vitro or test-tube fertilization is much greater than student acceptance of surrogate motherhood. Out of more than 700 university students, 55 percent said that having a baby via in-vitro or test-tube fertilization was acceptable (Dunn et al., 1988).

Louise Brown of Oldham, England, was the first baby to be born by in-vitro fertilization. Since her birth in 1978, over 300 clinics in the United States have emerged to duplicate this procedure resulting in about 20,000 live births.

NATIONAL DATA   Between 6 and 15 percent of couples who use in-vitro fertilization subsequently give birth to a baby (Consumer Protection Issues Involving In-Vitro Fertilization Clinics, 1989).

Other Reproductive Technologies

A number of new procedures have emerged to increase the chance of successful fertilization and conception.

Infertility has become an industry with revenues of $2 billion a year.

PAULA DEWITT

Gamete Intra-Fallopian Transfer (GIFT) A major problem with in-vitro fertilization is that the embryo may not implant on the wall of the uterus. Only about 15 or 20 percent of the fertilized eggs will implant. To improve this implant percentage (to between 40–50 percent), physicians place the egg and sperm directly into the Fallopian tube where they meet, fertilize, drift down into the uterus and implant. Since the term for sperm and egg together is gamete, the procedure is called *gamete intra-Fallopian transfer* or GIFT.

Zygote Intra-Fallopian Transfer (ZIFT) This procedure involves fertilizing the egg in a lab dish and placing the zygote or embryo directly into the Fallopian tube. ZIFT has a success rate similar to gamete intra-fallopian transfer.

Microinjection Some infertility cases are the result of sperm that lack motility. In those cases, a physician may inject sperm directly into the egg by means of microinjection.

Partial Zona Drilling (PZD) Eggs most likely to implant on the uterine wall are those whose shells have been poked open. To enhance the implantation process, physicians isolate an egg and drill a tiny hole in its protective shell. This procedure is known as *partial zona drilling* (or PZD).

CONSIDERATION

Although the infertile couple have an array of alternatives from which to choose, there is a considerable economic cost for such choices. Pamela and Johnathan Loew of Los Angeles, an infertile couple, gave bith to Alexandra. The cost of the pregnancy which Pamela carried to term follows (Elmer-Dewitt, 1991):

Two GIFT procedures	$18,000
Eight artificial inseminations	8,000
One frozen embryo transfer	1,000
Miscellaneous tests	3,000
	$30,000

Infertile couples seeking to get pregnant through one of the over 300 IVF (in-vitro fertilization) clinics should make informed choices by asking questions including the following:

What is the center's pregnancy rate and how is pregnancy defined? The rate should include only pregnancies verified by ultrasound, not so-called chemical pregnancies.

What is the pregnancy rate for other women with similar diagnosis?

How many cycles are attempted per patient? How many couples who use IVF end up with a baby? About 10 percent is the norm.

ᔆ <u>Adoption</u>

There are over 200,000 women seeking to adopt a child annually with over two million reporting that they have ever sought to adopt a child (Bachrach et al., 1991). Michelle Pfeiffer is one of them; she adopted a baby girl in 1993.

NATIONAL DATA ᔆ Over 100,000 adoptions take place in the United States annually. One-half of these are by relatives and half by nonrelatives. Of the 51,157 adoptions by nonrelatives in 1991, 39 percent were through a public agency, 31 percent were through independent channels, and 29 percent were through a private agency (*Statistical Abstract of the United States: 1992*, Table 599).

Among the five million adopted individuals in the United States today are Gerald Ford, NBC-TV celebrity Faith Daniels, and Dave Thomas of Wendy's Hamburgers. Terms used for adoption today are "place for adoption" and "make an adoption plan" rather than "give away" and "put up for adoption."

If the parents are white, the child they would like to adopt is usually a white healthy infant. Less often are they interested in adopting a retarded, handicapped, or older child, so there is an abundance of these children available for adoption. Over 36,000 "special needs" children (handicapped, teenagers) are in foster care homes waiting to be adopted (Gibbs, 1989).

Couples or individuals wanting to adopt a child have three options: state-agency adoption, private-agency adoption, and direct adoption. State-agency adoptions are less expensive (only legal fees are involved) but they take longer (from nine months to forever) and have more stringent requirements about who can adopt. Spouses over 50 are usually considered too old; some agencies say that 25 is too young. Although unmarried heterosexual women and men are allowed to adopt, in most cases, homosexual individuals are prohibited from doing so.

Private-agency adoptions are more expensive, but there is a shorter waiting period for anxious would-be parents. Golden Cradle is a nonprofit adoption agency that connects mothers who want to give up their babies with couples who want to adopt babies. The program provides free room and board for a mother-to-be at the home of an adoptive couple (who will later adopt from some other mother), free hospitalization, and free medical care. In exchange, the couple wanting a baby pays $10,000. The phone is 215/289-BABY.

Other private agencies may specialize in adoptions of babies from Korea, Colombia, India, and the Philippines. These are legal adoptions, and the couples are provided with either babies or young children.

Direct adoptions occur when a physician connects a couple who wants a baby with a pregnant woman who wants to give up her baby. Eighty percent of the adoptions in California are direct adoptions. In most cases, the pregnant teenager recognizes that she doesn't have the resources to take care of her baby so the mother gives up her baby. In direct adoptions, the mother knows the

> Put another man's child in your bosom, and he'll creep out at your elbow. That is, cherish or love him, he'll be naturally affected toward you.
>
> JOHN RAY

Couples sometimes adopt a child with a different racial heritage.

spouses who adopt her baby; in agency adoptions, the mother does not know them. There are also two differences between state- and private-agency adoptions. In state-agency adoptions, the biological mother can change her mind within 30 days and get her baby back; this is usually not the case in private adoptions. Also, parents who adopt a child from a state agency can take the child back if they are not satisfied; they usually cannot do so if the adoption is through a private agency.

Adoptions are expensive. Infant adoptions through a private agency or attorney can cost up to $30,000 (Adoption Works for Everyone, 1992). Adoptions of older children, those with special needs, and those with mixed racial backgrounds are generally less expensive. Care should be taken not to give money directly to a pregnant woman who is considering adoption or to the father of the baby or other relatives. Such an act can be construed as baby buying and is a felony in some states. Involving an attorney as an intermediary may avoid legal problems. The National Adoption Center, 1218 Chestnut St., Philadelphia, PA 19107 (1–800–TO–ADOPT) may be contacted for information.

CONSIDERATION

It is assumed that most adoptions involve a couple adopting one child. However, Dr. Howard Barnes (Chair of the Department of Child Development and Family Relations at East Carolina University) and his wife adopted 5 siblings. They already had two biological children.

In this section, we have reviewed various alternatives for responding to the knowledge that one is infertile. The following Self-Assessment is designed to help you examine your preferences for various alternatives.

℘ Pregnancy

Immediately after the egg is fertilized by the sperm in the Fallopian tube, the egg begins to divide and is pushed by hairlike cilia down the Fallopian tube into the uterus, where it attaches. The developing organism is called an embryo for the first three months and a fetus thereafter.

Detecting pregnancy as early as possible is important. Not only does doing so enable the woman to begin prenatal precautions and medical care during the most vulnerable stage of fetal development, early diagnosis may permit early detection of an ectopic pregnancy. In an ectopic pregnancy, the embryo begins to develop outside the uterus. Most ectopic pregnancies occur in the Fallopian tube; however, they may also occur in the cervix, abdominal area, or ovary.

NATIONAL DATA ℘ About 70,000 ectopic pregnancies or one percent of all pregnancies occur each year (Siller & Azziz, 1991).

A ship under sail and a big-bellied woman are the handsomest two things that can be seen common.

BEN FRANKLIN

SELF-ASSESSMENT ∾

Acceptance of Adoption and Five Alternative Fertilization Techniques

The purpose of this survey is to obtain your opinion about the methods used to treat infertility. Medical and social sciences have developed several ways to enable infertile couples to have children. Listed below are six such ways. Using the scale below, please indicate the degree to which you would find the following acceptable for married couples. Circle the corresponding number in the space provided that best represents the degree of YOUR acceptance of each method of treatment for infertility:

5 Extremely unacceptable to me
4 Unacceptable to me
3 Undecided
2 Acceptable to me
1 Extremely acceptable to me

1. Artificial insemination with husband   1 2 3 4 5
   (placing sperm in the woman's body by
   a medical technique, rather than
   through sexual intercourse, in which
   sperm from the husband is used to
   fertilize the wife's egg in her body)
2. Artificial insemination with donor   1 2 3 4 5
   (placing sperm in the woman's body by
   a medical technique, rather than
   through sexual intercourse, in which
   donor sperm from a man other than her
   husband is used to fertilize the wife's egg
   in her body)
3. In-vitro fertilization (egg is surgically   1 2 3 4 5
   removed from woman's body and
   fertilized with husband's sperm in a lab
   dish in a laboratory, then placed back in
   the wife's uterus)
4. Surrogate (substitute) motherhood (wife   1 2 3 4 5
   is unable to conceive so another woman
   is fertilized with husband's sperm by
   artificial insemination and carries the
   child to term, then gives it to the wife
   and her husband immediately at birth)

5. Embryo transfer (the wife is unable to   1 2 3 4 5
   produce an egg to be fertilized but is
   able to carry a child during pregnancy.
   Another woman's egg is fertilized with
   the husband's sperm by artificial
   insemination. The fertilized egg is then
   removed and transferred to the uterus of
   the wife, who carries and delivers the
   baby at term)
6. Adoption (the couple adopts a child   1 2 3 4 5
   born to another mother and father)

Scoring In designing the survey, the authors did not compute a total score for students' attitudes. They presented mean acceptance levels for each method.

Interpreting Your Score Undergraduate students in health courses at two southeastern universities completed the survey. In the university with a predominantly black student population, all sections of personal health classes were asked to participate ($n = 182$). In the other university, with a predominantly white student population, students enrolled in half of the sections of the personal health course were randomly selected to participate ($n = 573$). Attitudes of black students from the predominantly white university were not statistically different from those of the predominantly black university. There were so few white students from the predominantly black university and so few students at either school who were neither white nor black that their data were not included in the analyses. In Table 1 (from Dunn, Ryan, & O'Brien, 1988), the data for white and black respondents are summarized, including analyses of differences by race. Overall, black students were less accepting of the infertility options surveyed.

SOURCE: Survey items were obtained from Patricia Dunn, East Carolina University, Department of Health, Physical Education, Recreation and Safety, Greenville, NC 27858. Used by permission.

(continued on next page)

SELF-ASSESSMENT ~

Acceptance of Adoption and Five Alternative Fertilization Techniques *continued*

TABLE 1

Percent Distribution for Level of Acceptability of Methods Dealing with Infertility by Race

| Method | Race | LEVEL OF ACCEPTANCE[a] | | | | | |
		VA	A	U	UA	VUA	X^{2b}
Adoption	Black	44.9	33.4	11.0	3.2	7.3	18.0
	White	58.1	31.7	4.9	1.6	3.5	$p<.002$
AI-Husband	Black	23.9	42.9	15.7	10.3	7.2	29.5
	White	42.2	38.2	11.9	4.6	2.9	$p<.002$
In-Vitro fertilization	Black	8.6	42.1	23.9	12.8	12.4	14.7
	White	18.5	38.4	28.8	8.3	5.8	$p<.002$
AI-Donor	Black	2.0	12.4	19.0	33.6	32.7	18.0
	White	4.5	18.5	28.8	24.4	23.5	$p<.002$
Surrogate mother	Black	2.0	11.4	22.8	26.9	36.7	8.1
	White	2.0	14.1	29.6	29.4	24.6	$p>.002$
Embryo transfer	Black	2.8	17.5	34.2	24.0	21.2	6.7
	White	3.0	25.3	33.6	23.0	14.8	$p>.002$.

[a] VA = Very Acceptable; A = Acceptable; U = Undecided; UA = Unacceptable; VUA= Very Unacceptable.

[b] approximation for the Kruskal-Wallis Test, here with one degree of freedom.

Source: Published by permission of the *Journal of Sex Research*, a publication of the Society for the Scientific Study of Sex.

Analyses of differences by sex revealed a statistically significant difference only for adoption, with women more accepting of adoption. Religious preference was related to a difference in acceptability of artificial insemination by donor. Catholics and Protestants were less accepting of this option than were students who indicated their religious preference as "other" or "none."

As you completed this survey, you may have noticed that the wording of the items calls for your opinion of married couples' (husband and wife) use of these technologies. It would be interesting to assess attitudes toward their use by single people or unmarried couples. This study was published in 1988. Do you think the acceptability of the use of these technologies by married or by unmarried people would be different now, in the 1990s?

REFERENCE

Dunn, P. C., I. J. Ryan, & K. O'Brien. College students' acceptance of adoption and five alternative fertilization techniques. *Journal of Sex Research*, 1988, *24*, 282–287. Published by permission of the *Journal of Sex Research*, a publication of the Society for the Scientific Study of Sex.

An ectopic pregnancy is potentially dangerous and signs of such a pregnancy should be taken seriously. These include sudden intense pain in the lower abdomen, irregular bleeding, or dizziness that persists more than a few seconds.

Prenatal Care During Pregnancy

Ensuring a healthy baby depends on adequate nutrition, moderate weight gain, and avoidance of substances like alcohol, nicotine, cocaine, and other drugs that are harmful to the fetus. Some women do not receive prenatal care which results in an increased risk of a premature infant.

> **CONSIDERATION**
>
> Ideally, women should attend to their nutrition before becoming pregnant. Not only should they eat a balanced diet of protein, vegetables, fruits, grains and calcium, they should have more servings per day than the nonpregnant woman. Pregnant women should also avoid foods high in sugar and fat. Ideally, underweight women should gain weight and overweight women should lose weight *before* becoming pregnant (Travis, 1988).

Pregnant women who select a balanced diet help to ensure a healthy baby carried to term. Eating fresh vegetables is particularly helpful in avoiding folate deficiency.

Pregnant women should also eliminate their alcohol intake to avoid *Fetal Alcohol Syndrome* (FAS), which refers to the negative consequences for the fetus and infant of the mother who drinks alcohol at or above the level of a social drinker. A heavy drinker is defined as "anyone who regularly has one drink a day (say a glass of wine before dinner) and additionally may have two or three drinks in an occasional evening (perhaps at a party or dining out)" (Travis, 1988, 119). A social drinker would drink even less. Negative consequences for the developing infant include increased risk of low birthweight, growth retardation, facial malformations, intellectual retardation (IQs range from 50 to 75), and emotional instability. Avoiding alcohol intake during the early weeks of pregnancy is particularly critical; however alcohol consumed in the later months may impede organ growth. "Professional advice to pregnant women is consistent: If you're pregnant, don't drink" (Travis, 1988, 121). And, since you usually do not know if you are pregnant for 1–2 months after fertilization, don't drink alcohol if you are trying to get pregnant or are not using a reliable method of contraceptive.

NATIONAL DATA ❧ It is estimated that 20 percent of mothers consume alcohol during pregnancy (National Center for Health Statistics, 1993).

Smoking cigarettes during pregnancy is also associated with harm to the developing fetus.

NATIONAL DATA ❧ Almost 20 percent of white mothers and almost 16 percent of black mothers smoked during their most recent pregnancy (National Center for Health Statistics, 1993).

Smoking is often associated with lower birthweight babies, small-for-date babies, premature babies, spontaneous abortions, lower Apgar scores (Apgar measures infant vitality at birth) and higher fetal/infant deaths. In addition, when 223 children with cancer were compared with 196 controls, children whose mothers smoked during pregnancy had a 90 percent higher risk of acute lymphocytic leukemia. If the fathers smoked, there was a 40 percent increased risk of the children contracting leukemia and a 60 percent increased risk of lymphoma and brain cancer (John et al., 1991).

Concerned about the health of their babies, some pregnant women avoid not only alcohol and nicotine but also caffeine and over-the-counter drugs like aspirin and antihistamines. Although there is no conclusive evidence that caffeine has a serious detrimental effect on the developing baby, a physician should be consulted in regard to continuing medications before and during pregnancy. "Ideally, consumption of nonprescription drugs should stop completely *prior* to conception" (Chez, 1991, 56).

Illegal drugs (also nonprescription drugs) such as marijuana and cocaine should be avoided. The latter has been associated with lower birth weight babies, lower IQ, and oversensitiveness to stimulation.

Psychological Changes During Pregnancy

Affonso and Mayberry (1989) assessed the stresses of 221 women during and after pregnancy (81 in the first trimester, 80 in the third trimester, and 60 in the postpartum period). Stress related to physical issues was the most frequently reported problem. "The total group identified fatigue, disturbed sleep, feeling physically restricted, and nausea or vomiting as the most common physical distresses" (p. 46). The second most frequently experienced stressor was associated "with 'weight gain' and feelings of being 'fat,' 'unattractive,' and 'distorted.' " (p. 48).

The third most frequently reported concern during pregnancy was for the "baby's welfare and dealing with changes relative to household arrangement and restrictions in physical activities, especially as the woman nears childbirth" (p. 49). Some of the women reported they were plagued by thoughts such as "Something might happen to my baby;" "Am I doing the right thing to protect my baby;" and "I shouldn't have done this because now I'm worried about how it affected my baby" (p. 49).

As women near the end of their pregnancy, fears of pain, complications, the threat of a cesarean delivery are high intensity stressors. Throughout pregnancy, some women feel trapped; they feel that they have begun a course of action from which they cannot easily withdraw (Engel, 1990).

The man experiences his own set of feelings during the time of pregnancy. Shapiro (1987) interviewed 227 expectant and recent fathers and noted several concerns:

She's in a hopeful way.

ETHEREGE

1. *Queasiness.* Respondents in Shapiro's study reported that their greatest fear before birth was coping with the actual birth process. They were queasy about being in the midst of blood and bodily fluids and felt they would faint or get sick. Most did neither.

2. *Worry over Increased Responsibility.* Over 80 percent reported feeling that they were now the sole support for three people. Many took second jobs or worked longer hours.

3. *Uncertain Paternity.* Half of the men feared that the child their partner was carrying was not their own. "For most of them, such fears were based less on any real concern that the wife had been unfaithful than on a general insecurity brought on by being part of something as monumental as the creation of life" (p. 39).

4. *Fear of the Loss of Spouse and/or Child.* Some men feared that both the wife and baby might die during childbirth and that they would be alone. They also feared that their baby would be brain damaged or defective in some way.

5. *Fear of Being Replaced.* The words of one respondent reflect a common feeling among expectant fathers—that of being replaced:

> The one thing that really scares me is that the best of our lives together will be gone as soon as the baby is born . . . in some ways, I'm feeling displaced . . ." (42).

> The trend is clear: the boys who got fathered want to be fathers, and the boys who didn't fear it.
>
> **FRANK PITTMAN**

℅ Miscarriage and Perinatal Death

A miscarriage is the spontaneous abortion of an embryo too young to live outside the womb—usually due to a chromosomal abnormality (Wilcox et al., 1988).

> He that begins to live begins to die.
>
> **FRANCIS QUARLES**

NATIONAL DATA ℅ Between 10 and 20 percent of all known pregnancies end in a miscarriage (Friedman & Gath, 1989).

Until recently, there was little recognition that the woman (and her partner) may experience profound grief for the loss of the fetus. Remarks such as "Don't worry, you'll try again soon," or "It's only Nature's way," are intended to minimize the impact of the miscarriage. In a study of 65 women who had miscarried anywhere from 2 to 21 weeks after conception, a sense of sadness was universal; 30 percent of the women reported feelings of frustration, disappointment, or anger (Cole, 1987). Many women blamed themselves for the miscarriage; some felt that they were being punished for something they had done in the past.

> Death surprises us in the midst of our hopes.
>
> **THOMAS FULLER**

> **CONSIDERATION**
>
> Miscarriage may produce marital stress caused by the different ways that men and women react to the event. Men tend to be action-oriented, to seek distraction in movies or vacation while women tend to relive the miscarriage over and over again. "In this dynamic, the wife may perceive her husband's suggestions to go out as unhelpful or uncaring, while the husband may see his wife's desire to talk about the event as obsessive. The two withdraw from each other, and other unresolved strains in the marriage may surface" (Cole, 1988, 65).

Individuals may seek assistance in adjusting to a miscarriage through SHARE (St. Elizabeth's Hospital, National Share Office, Belleville, Ill. 62222, 618/234–2415), which is a nationwide organization with 200 chapters. SHARE gives validity to the woman's grief, encourages her to give her miscarried fetus a name, to get footprints, and to have a ceremony recognizing the death of the fetus. Rather than try and minimize the event, SHARE encourages the woman to process all of her grief. Doing so is regarded as a very natural and healthy way to cope with a profound sadness.

Perhaps even more devastating than miscarriage is perinatal death, which is the death of an infant near the time of birth. A fetal death occurs when an infant is born dead. Early infant death refers to the death of an infant within seven days of birth. Like a miscarriage, fetal and infant deaths result in the parents experiencing shock, denial, anger, and intense grief.

₭ Choosing a Childbirth Method

Couples who give birth to a child have several methods from which to choose, including Lamaze, Dick-Read, Bradley, and LeBoyer.

NATIONAL DATA ₭ Between 50 and 80 percent of U.S. women participate in a childbirth preparation course prior to a hospital delivery (Duncan & Markman, 1988).

Lamaze Method

I took Lamaze classes; I wasn't having a baby—I was having trouble breathing.

STEVEN WRIGHT

Preferred by an increasing number of couples, the Lamaze method of childbirth, often called "natural" or "prepared" childbirth, was developed by French obstetrician Fernand Lamaze. The method is essentially a preparation for childbirth, in which the woman and her partner take six one-and-a-half-hour classes during the last trimester of pregnancy, usually with several other couples. The goal of these sessions is to reduce the anxiety and pain of childbirth by viewing it as a natural process, by educating the couple about labor and delivery, and by giving them specific instructions to aid in the birth of their baby.

There are several aspects of the Lamaze method:

1. *Education about childbirth.* The instructor explains the physiology of pregnancy, stages of labor, and delivery.
2. *Timed breathing exercises.* Specific breathing exercises are recommended for each stage of labor to help with the contractions by refocusing the laboring woman's attention and keeping the pressure of the diaphragm off the uterus. These exercises are practiced between sessions, so that the couples will know when and how to use them when labor actually begins.
3. *Pain control exercises.* The woman is taught to selectively tense and relax various muscle groups of her body (for example, her arm muscles). She then learns how to tense these muscle groups while relaxing the rest of her body, so that during labor she can relax the rest of her body while her uterus is contracting involuntarily.
4. *Husband's involvement.* A major advantage of the Lamaze method is the active involvement of the husband in the birthing event. His role (or that of a coach substitute if the father is not available) is to tell his wife when to start and stop the various breathing exercises, give her psychological support throughout labor, and take care of her in general (get ice, keep her warm, and so on).

Most couples report that the sharing of the labor and delivery is one of the most significant and memorable events of their lives. Many husbands who are with their wives during labor and delivery take photographs or videotape the event.

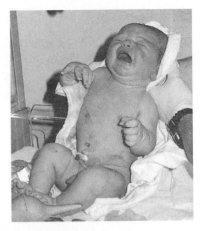

A goal of all childbirth methods is a healthy baby.

Dick-Read Method

Grantly Dick-Read introduced his concept of prepared childbirth in the 1930s, about a decade before Lamaze. He believed it was a woman's fear of childbirth that produced the physical pain during delivery and the pain could be avoided by teaching the woman to relax. Similar to the Lamaze method, Dick-Read classes emphasize breathing and relaxation exercises, basic information about the birth event, and the husband's support. In addition, they focus on preparation for parenthood.

Bradley Method

Another lesser known method of childbirth was developed by a Denver obstetrician, Robert Bradley. Also known as "husband-coached childbirth," the Bradley method focuses on the couple—their marital communication, sexual relationship, and parental roles—as well as on relaxation exercises and proper nutrition during pregnancy. An important aspect of the Bradley method is the couple's relationship with their physician. They are encouraged to deal with issues such as the kind of delivery they want (hospital or home birth) and breast feeding well in advance of the birth. The Bradley method emphasizes a couple's freedom to choose the type of birth experience desired. If the physician is reluctant to cooperate, the couple is encouraged to seek another physician.

LeBoyer Method

The LeBoyer method of childbirth is named after its French founder, Frederick LeBoyer, who has delivered more than 10,000 babies using his own method. The goal of a LeBoyer birth experience is to make the infant's transition to the outer world as nontraumatic as possible. The delivery room into which the baby is born is quiet and dimly lit. After emerging from its mother, the baby is placed on the mother's abdomen, where she gently strokes and rubs her child. The umbilical cord is cut only after it stops throbbing in the belief that this will help the newborn's respiratory system adjust to its new environment.

After a few moments, the baby is immersed in water that is the approximate temperature of the amniotic sac which has housed the baby for the past nine months. The infant is allowed to relax and enjoy the bath. Then the baby is wrapped in layers of cotton and wool and placed next to the mother. Placing babies on their backs is avoided because it is felt the spine should not be stressed this soon after birth.

Medication-Centered Childbirth Methods

The preceding methods emphasize drug-free deliveries. But some women, even those who prepare for a drug-free childbirth experience, find it difficult to tolerate the pain associated with childbirth and choose to be medicated during labor. Two commonly used procedures for administering anesthesia are the caudal and epidural. Both involve introducing drugs into the spinal column, which eliminates the pain typically involved in childbirth. The caudal involves placing a needle at the base of the tailbone; the epidural involves placing the needle further up the backbone. The result—a pain-free delivery—is the same.

Other women prefer medications, which are usually administered intravenously, to alleviate labor pain at the onset of three to five contractions. These analgesics reduce the pain but allow the woman to be aware of the childbirth process. A woman should not view herself as a "failure" if she feels the need for medication.

❧ Transition to Parenthood

Although the transition to parenthood typically refers to the period of time from the beginning of pregnancy through the first few months after the birth of

❧ IN FOCUS 14.1 ❧

Cesarean Births

Most pregnant women anticipate that their baby will be born by passing through the vaginal canal. As a result, pregnant women may receive little or no information about Cesarean births until the physician decides it is necessary. In Cesarean section, an incision is made in the woman's abdomen and uterus and the baby is removed. The term does not derive from the Roman emperor Caesar being delivered this way but from a law passed during Caesar's reign that made it mandatory for woman dying in the advanced stages of pregnancy to have their babies removed by surgical means.

Twenty-three percent of births in the United States in 1990 were by cesarean section (National Center for Health Statistics, 1993). Cesarean deliveries are most often performed when there would be risk to the mother or baby through normal delivery; as examples, the fetus may be positioned abnormally, the head may be too large for the mother's pelvis, or the woman may have diabetes or develop toxemia during pregnancy. The woman is put to sleep with general anesthesia or given a spinal injection, enabling her to remain awake and aware of the delivery.

Although Cesareans are major surgery, the risk of death to the mother is less than two percent. When death occurs, it is usually the result of a preexisting condition, such as severe toxemia or heart disease—not a result of the surgery itself. The Cesarean section is regarded as one of the safest of all abdominal surgeries and holds the record for the fewest postoperative problems.

Some women who undergo childbirth through Cesarean section experience negative psychological consequences. Travis (1988) noted,

Mothers often feel a sense of failure because their role in delivery was peripheral rather than central. Additionally there may be feelings of anger or frustration directed toward the physician, husband, or infant (p. 156).

Behavioral consequences of Cesarean section may also be negative. Travis (1988) found that, compared to women who delivered vaginally, women who delivered by cesarean section tend to discuss motherhood (one year after the birth) in more negative terms. Women who have had a C-section were also found to delay longer in responding to their infants crying.

Until recently, a woman who had a C-section had to have all subsequent births by C-section, and physicians were accused of creating a market for Cesarean surgery. But due to advances in surgical techniques, the American College of Obstetricians and Gynecologists reversed its 75-year-old policy and said that some women who have a Cesarean delivery for their first child can have subsequent vaginal deliveries. These are referred to as VBACs (vaginal births after Cesarean delivery). In 1990, of 100 births to women with previous cesarean delivery, 19.9 were vaginal births (National Center for Health Statistics, 1993).

Not all physicians are willing to perform a vaginal delivery if the woman has had a previous Cesarean. However, VBACs are slowly increasing. Organizations that can help locate a supportive physician include The Cesarean Prevention Movement (P. O. Box 152, Syracuse, New York 13210) and Informed Homebirth/Informed Birth and Parenting (P. O. Box 3675, Ann Arbor, Michigan 48106).

---

the baby, the transition actually begins before conception. Goldberg and Michaels (1988) synthesized the body of research on the transition to parenthood and identified several factors and interventions that influence this transition (see Table 14.1). These factors and interventions "explain why some individuals and relationships adapt smoothly to the transition whereas others face numerous difficulties that may even reach crisis proportions (p. 351).

TABLE 14.1

Factors and Interventions Influencing the Transition to Parenthood

	PRECONCEPTION	PREGNANCY	POSTNATAL
Factors associated with a smooth transition to parenthood	Well-functioning marriage Adequate social support network Good relationship with own parents Adequate socioeconomic status History of psychological health History of physical health Strong motivation to become a parent Social climate supportive of children and families	Supportive spousal relationship Adequate social support network (emotional, tangible, and cognitive support from family and friends) Adequate socioeconomic status Adequate prenatal care Good relationship with obstetrician Psychological health (low anxiety, low depression, high self-esteem, good self-concept, high autonomy, high affiliation) Medically and psychologically satisfactory birth experience	Well-functioning marriage; satisfaction with division of labor Psychological health Satisfaction with work and family roles Positive change and growth in self-concept Successful adaptation to parenthood (synchronous parent-infant interaction, development of secure attachment, sensitivity to child's developmental needs) Closer intergenerational ties Well-functioning social support network Adequate socioeconomic status Adequate well-baby care
Factors associated with a difficult transition to parenthood	History of psychiatric problems Low motivation to become a parent Psychological conflicts over femininity, masculinity History of physical health problems Economic hardship Marital distress Stress and deficits in support from family, friends, and community	Maternal anxiety and depression Psychological problems Economic problems Teenager; teenage head of household Advanced maternal or parental age Maternal or fetal medical complications during pregnancy Birth problems (maternal medical complications; birth of an ill, premature, or handicapped infant) Marital distress; lack of spousal support Stress and deficits in social support network	Poor adjustment to parenthood Reactivation of unresolved psychological needs Role conflict, strain, overload Extended postpartum depression Negative change in self-concept Guilt, ambivalence, grief, and mourning if infant ill, premature, or handicapped Separation from infant due to maternal or infant health problems Financial problems Marital distress Stress and deficits in social support network
Interventions (strategies to assist prospective and active parents at each phase of the transition to parenthood)	Learn decision-making skills to assist decisions about whether and when to have a baby Learn to use social support network effectively Couple (marital) therapy to resolve conflicts; work on communication skills	Childbirth preparation to impart educational information, promote spousal support, alleviate maternal experience of pain and need for medication during labor Preparation for parenthood—anticipatory guidance (what to expect from baby, changes to expect in lifestyle, marital and employment roles) Communication skills for couples Prenatal care Medical, educational, and social-psychological care for pregnant teenagers Government subsidies for economically disadvantaged women (e.g., the WIC Program)	Informal support programs, e.g., drop-in center, peer support group, resource and referral Formal support programs, e.g., parent education, home visitors, counseling, group therapy Learn special caregiving for ill or handicapped infant Pediatric well-baby care Good quality childcare Emotional, tangible, and cognitive support from family and friends

Source: Adapted from Goldberg, W. A. & G. Y. Michaels. Conclusion. The transition to parenthood: Synthesis and future directions Table 1 (pp. 352–353). *The Transition to Parenthood: Current Theory and Research,* G. Y. Michaels & W. A. Goldberg, eds. New York: Cambridge University Press, 1988, 342–360. Used by permission.

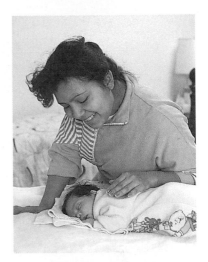

Some sociologists theorize that there is a biological basis for the emotional attachment between a mother and her infant.

CONSIDERATION

Goldberg (1988) noted:

> The transition to parenthood is important not only because it represents a milestone in the new parent's development, but because it marks the beginning of the new child's development. The new parent's capacity to make a successful adjustment at this time may set a future course of effective, competent parenting, whereas serious difficulties in adjustment may lead to, or exacerbate, marital discord and promote difficulties in providing for the child's needs (p. 2).

Transition to Motherhood

In general, the birth of a baby results in a more profound change for the mother than for the father (Wilkie & Ames, 1986). What is the nature of these changes and how do women adjust to their new role as mothers?

Reaction To Childbirth   Although childbirth and the labor preceding it are sometimes thought of as a painful ordeal, some women describe the birthing experience as "fantastic," "joyful," and "unsurpassed." A strong emotional bond between the mother and her baby usually develops early, so that mother and infant resist separation. Sociobiologists suggest that there is a biological basis for the attachment between a mother and her offspring. The mother alone carries the fetus in her body for nine months, lactates to provide milk, and produces oxytocin—a hormone excreted by the pituitary gland during the expulsive stage of labor that has been associated with the onset of maternal behavior in lower animals.

Not all mothers feel joyous after childbirth. Emotional bonding may be temporarily impeded by a mild depression, characterized by irritability, crying, loss of appetite, and difficulty in sleeping. From 50 to 70 percent of all new mothers experience "baby blues"—transitory symptoms of depression 24–48 hours after the baby is born. About 10 percent experience *postpartum depression*—a more severe reaction than "baby blues" (Kraus & Redman, 1986).

Postpartum depression is believed to be a result of the numerous physiological and psychological changes occurring during pregnancy, labor, and delivery. Although the woman may become depressed in the hospital, she more often experiences these feelings within the first month after returning home with her baby. Most women recover within a short time; some (about five percent) seek therapy to speed their recovery. To minimize "baby blues" and postpartum depression, one must recognize that having misgivings about the new infant is normal and appropriate. In addition, the woman who has negative feelings about her new role as mother should elicit help with the baby from her family so that she can continue to keep up her social contacts with friends.

Choosing Priorities   For some women, motherhood is the ultimate fulfillment; for others, the ultimate frustration. Priorities must be established. When forced to choose between her job and family responsibilities (the babysitter does not show up, the child is sick or hurt, etc.), the employed woman and mother (unlike the man and father) generally responds to the latter role first. (Grant et al., 1990; LaRossa, 1988; Mischel & Fuhr, 1988).

Women who make the smoothest adjustment to the birth of a new child tend to be those who have sufficient social support so they are not overwhelmed by the experience, and who do not try to be selfless and perfect. One midwife who had just had a baby herself observed:

> People need to be told what the realities are. When you have a new baby, life does not just go on like it did before. You're not going to get the house cleaned as often, or you might have pancakes for dinner three nights in a row (Massenda, quoted in Michaelson, 1988, 254).

Transition to Fatherhood

I can see doing this Dad thing with Cindy.

RICHARD GERE

The role of father varies by society and ranges from playmate to disciplinarian to full-time caregiver (Harkness & Super, 1992). While, historically, the father's role in the United States has been to protect and provide for his family, this role is expanding to include more active participation in childcare. In a random sample of 190 male college students who one day intended to become fathers, 57 percent perceived their own father figures to be involved fathers; 93 percent intended to be the "new" involved father (Penland & Darling, 1992).

Fathering is the most masculine thing a man can do.

FRANK PITTMAN

To become a father is not hard, to be a father is, however.

WILHELM BUSCH

Fathers with Newborns and Older Children   Fathers who participate in the delivery of their infants and have contact with them the first hour after birth experience an early context of communicating and active care of their offspring (Briesemeister & Haines, 1988). However, the image of the father as an active and equal participant in childcare is largely true of only a portion of middle class professionals such as educators, artists, physicians, and social workers. Mothers continue to perform over 90 percent of the active childcare (LaRossa, 1988) and often feel overburdened (Biller, 1993).

I love being a Dad. My only problem is that, when I'm working so much, I don't get to see as much of the parenting process as I'd like.

TOM SELLECK

As infants grow into children, interaction of the father with his children tends to increase, particularly if the children are boys. National data on the interaction fathers have with their adolescents show that fathers spend more time with their sons than their daughters. Sons in single-child families are particularly advantaged in terms of paternal attention and time. Daughters who have brothers also benefit in that "the presence of sons draws the father into more active parenting" (Harris & Morgan, 1991).

CONSIDERATION

Just as there is the myth of the absentee father in African-American families, there is the myth of noninvolvement with caregiving by African-American fathers. In a study of 45 African American fathers of preschool children, two researchers observed that although the fathers spent less time taking care of their preschoolers than did the mothers (2.8 hours versus 6.7 hours per day), they "were accessible and involved with their children" (Ahmeduzzaman & Roopnarine, 1992, 705). Factors associated with greater involvement of the fathers included higher income, education, and stability of the marriage. In another study, 48 percent of black fathers reported spending three or more hours a day feeding, dressing, bathing, and putting a preschooler to bed in contrast to 32 percent of Hispanic fathers and 23 percent of non-Hispanic white fathers (Jacobsen & Edmondson, 1993).

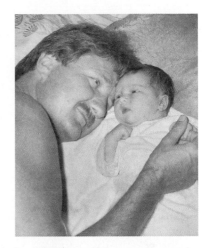

Some fathers establish a close emotional bond with their infant.

Increased Sense of Financial Responsibility   Given our society's expectation that fathers bear primary financial responsibility for their families, the birth of a baby sometimes "arouses anxieties in men about their capacity to provide" (Fedele et al., 1988, 97). "Some fathers, fearing responsibility, run from it, leaving their families to fend for themselves without emotional or financial support" (Greenberg, 1986, 71). However, "many begin to put in more hours at work in order to bring home more money or to be a better father-provider" (Fedele et al., 1988, 97). Some wives regard this increased time away from home to earn more money as a "retreat from involvement with the baby and the whole family enterprise" (Cowan & Cowan, 1988, 136). Indeed, fathers are not likely to dramatically increase their involvement with children "as long as achievement in market work continues to grab a hunk of their attention" (LaRossa & Reitzes, 1993, 466).

New fathers talk about making time for their children whereas experienced fathers talk about putting in time with their children.

KERRY DALY

Jealousy of the Baby   Some men are jealous of the baby and the attention that is diverted from them to the baby. One new father said:

> My wife and I were really close. We would spend a lot of time together. We would walk together, hold each other, play cards, fish, or we would stay home and watch TV, lie on the couch together. Now whatever spare time we have together, the baby is there—and its going to be that way for a long time. I couldn't accept that that's the way it has to be (quoted in Greenberg, 1986, 88).

It is far easier for a father to have children than for children to have a real father.

POPE JOHN XXIII

Resolving this jealousy may require that the couple get help with childcare so that they can spend more recreational and leisure time together. In addition, fathers may increase their involvement in childcare so that child-centered activities become activities shared by the couple.

We have been discussing the adjustment of parents to babies who are healthy and normal. But about 1 percent or more of all births are babies with heart malformations, urogenital anomalies, cleft lip or palate, and various musculoskeletal anomalies (National Center for Health Statistics, 1992), which may make adjustment to parenthood more difficult. In addition, babies who cry a great deal and have irregular sleep patterns make adjustment on the part of the parents more difficult (Belsky & Rovine, 1990).

Don't measure fatherhood by clock time; measure it by memories time.

KEN LEWIS

❦ Transition from Being a Couple to Being a Family

How does pregnancy affect a couple's relationship and sexual interaction, and what happens to their relationship after the baby is born?

The Couple's Relationship During Pregnancy

Saunders and Robbins (1989) studied the nature of changes in couples' relationships during their first pregnancy by comparing 48 couples in the first trimester with 52 couples in the third trimester. In general, pregnancy was associated with positive changes such as increased communication (about their relationship) and increased feelings of love for each other. In addition, the partners spent as much time together later in pregnancy as they did during the early months and reported greater marital satisfaction as the pregnancy progressed. However, in spite of these positive changes, couples also reported more conflict in the third trimester of pregnancy as compared to the first trimester.

CONSIDERATION

Although these data are generally a favorable commentary on positive associations of pregnancy, the researchers were careful to point out that the sample was very biased. Not only were these couples enrolled in prenatal classes, they volunteered to participate in the study. It is possible that couples who do not agree on whether to take prenatal classes together and who do not volunteer to let a researcher study their relationship may have a different relationship experience during pregnancy than the couples who were studied.

The Couple's Sexual Relationship During Pregnancy

Sexual desire, behavior, and satisfaction change during pregnancy. Eighty-one couples provided information the 13th and 14th week of pregnancy and again within one week after the birth of the baby. In regard to sexual desire, 40 percent of the women reported diminished sexual desire during the first and second trimester. Seventy-four percent reported decreased sexual desire during the third trimester. For their husbands, 9 and 17 percent reported decreased sexual desire the first and second trimester respectively and 64 percent during the third trimester (Bogren, 1991).

CONSIDERATION

Even if the desire for intercourse decreases during a woman's pregnancy, "there is still a great need for close physical contact. Hugging, holding, caressing, and cuddling may be extremely satisfying forms of sexual expression . . ." (Wilkerson & Bing, 1988, 381).

In regard to sexual frequency, 41 percent of the women reported decreased sexual frequency during the first trimester, 40 percent during the second trimester, and 90 percent during the third trimester. The percentages of husbands reporting decreased frequencies for the first, second, and third trimester were 30, 40 and 83 respectively (Bogren, 1991).

Some couples do not have intercourse during pregnancy because the health care provider tells them not to do so. In a study of 52 pregnant women, 17 percent reported being told to abstain totally from intercourse during pregnancy (Gauna-Trujillo & Higgins, 1989).

CONSIDERATION

Does having intercourse during pregnancy involve a risk to the baby? Generally not. Women who have had a previous miscarriage or who are experiencing vaginal bleeding, ruptured membranes, or threatened premature labor should consult their physician about intercourse during pregnancy. In the absence of these complications, most couples can continue intercourse as late in pregnancy as they desire.

In regard to sexual satisfaction, 35 percent of the women in the Bogren (1991) study reported decreased sexual satisfaction during the first trimester, 30 percent during the second trimester, and 55 percent during the third trimester. The percentages reporting decreased sexual satisfaction for the first, second, and third trimesters for the husbands were 22, 26, and 76 respectively (Bogren, 1991).

However, some couples experience increased sexual satisfaction during pregnancy. For both partners, freedom from worry about contraception may add to relaxation and enjoyment of sexual activities. In addition,

> Increased vascularity and engorgement of breasts, labia, and vagina enhance sexual response during pregnancy. . . . Women often experience heightened sexual tension, more intense orgasms, and more enjoyment of sexual activities (Wilkerson & Bing, 1988, 381).

The Couple's Relationship After the Birth of the Baby

After the birth and return home from the hospital, how does the baby's presence affect the marital happiness of the spouses, who are now mother and father? The answer is unclear (Belsky & Rovine, 1990). Some studies suggest that children increase marital happiness; others suggest the opposite.

Children Increase Marital Happiness   Some studies report that having a baby is associated with improving the marital relationship. Out of a total of 30,000 parents, 43 percent said they felt closer to their spouses after they had children (Greer, 1986). In another study of 75 fathers and 115 mothers, one researcher observed that couples who reported a high degree of marital satisfaction prior

What most children learn by doing is how to drive their parents almost crazy.

E. C. MCKENZIE

to the birth of their baby were more likely to experience positive changes as a result of the baby than spouses who reported a low degree of marital satisfaction prior to the birth (Harriman, 1986).

Children Decrease Marital Happiness   Other parents feel that their marital satisfaction decreases after the birth of their baby. Cowan and Cowan (1992) followed 72 expectant couples and 24 childfree couples for 10 years and noted a decrease in relationship satisfaction among parents due to unfulfilled expectations, different patterns of engagement into the role of parent, and different perceptions of their role as lovers/partners. Both partners were surprised that the baby did not bring them closer together. The husbands viewed themselves less in the role of the parent than did the wives, and the wives viewed themselves less in the role of lover than did the husbands. The greater the discrepancies, the greater the unhappiness.

> **CONSIDERATION**
>
> Cowan and Cowan (1992) have developed a program designed to assist couples in preparing for the changes that occur in the transition from spouse to parent. Some of the suggestions include:
>
> 1. Share expectations. Discuss private notions about one's ideal family. Also share any anxieties about the new role and its impact on self, the relationship, and work.
> 2. Make time for talk, sex, and togetherness. Since the demands of the new baby will take time away from the couple, it is important that they make time for communication, sex, and doing things together "even if the laundry or dinner dishes have to wait" (p. 78).
> 3. Don't be afraid of conflict. "Regard a fight as information that something is wrong in the relationship. The trick is not to worry that you are having a struggle, or to avoid a fight" (p. 78).
> 4. Talk with a friend or co-worker. Talking with others who have experienced the transition from spouses to parents helps break one's feelings of aloneness and isolation. However, be careful not to divulge information that may result in the spouse feeling betrayed. Some mental health centers offer parenting groups to discuss such changes.

Regardless of how children affect the feelings spouses have about their marriage, spouses report more commitment to their relationship once they have children (Stanley & Markman, 1992). Figure 14.1 illustrates that the more children a couple have, the more likely they are to stay married. A primary reason for this increased commitment is the desire on the part of both parents to provide a stable family context for their children. In addition, parents of dependent children may keep their marriage together in order to maintain continued access to their children and to maintain a higher standard of living for their children. Finally, people with small children (especially

---

The transition to parenthood holds the potential for drawing parents into more separate worlds at a time when they dreamed of making a world together.

PHILIP A. COWAN
CAROLYN PAPE COWAN

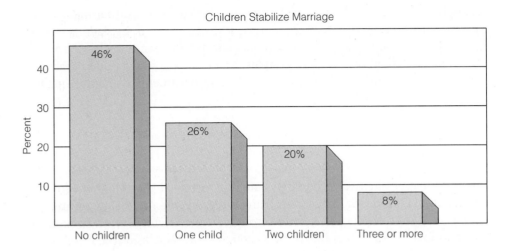

Children Stabilize Marriage

F I G U R E 14.1
Percent of couples getting divorced by number of children

mothers) feel more pressure to stay married regardless of how unhappy they may be. Hence, while children may decrease happiness, they increase stability since there is pressure to avoid divorce.

CONSIDERATION

Most of the research on the effects of children on a couple's relationship has been conducted on heterosexual couples. However, Koepke et al. (1992) noted that a third of lesbians have children, which represents over 1.5 million lesbian mothers and conducted a study to assess the effects of children on their relationships. Koepke and her colleagues compared 19 lesbian couples who had children with 28 lesbian couples who were childfree. While solid and happy relationships existed for both sets of couples, those with children scored significantly higher on relationship and sexual satisfaction. The researchers interpreted these findings as possibly reflecting higher levels of dissatisfactions in the women's previous heterosexual marriages, which when contrasted with their current relationships created a stark contrast. For example, one of the lesbian mothers commented:

> I am very pleased with my relationship. After 19 years of marriage, I didn't know one could have such an intimate and fulfilling relationship. I'm so glad to be lesbian. I would never again be in any relationship except a lesbian relationship. Even given all the problems, it beats by 100 percent being in a relationship with a man (p. 227).

Children Do Not Affect Marital Happiness Some research suggests that children neither increase nor decrease marital happiness. In a study comparing married couples who had children with those who did not have children, the

We are convinced that the seeds of new parents' individual and marital problems are sown long before the baby arrives.

CAROLYN PAPE COWAN
PHILIP A. COWAN

researchers (MacDermid, Huston, & McHale, 1990) observed that the spouses in both groups reported declines in love feelings, marital satisfaction, doing things together, and positive interactions. The parents were no less happy in their marriages than the childfree couples. The researchers concluded that "The transition to parenthood is not an inescapable detriment to marital quality" (p. 485).

☙ Trends

The use of reproductive technologies such as artificial insemination, in-vitro fertilization, and ovum transfer is being used by an increasing number of people who cannot conceive a child through sexual intercourse. In spite of the cost and low rate of actual births, most couples are socialized to have children and will explore all options before giving up the goal.

The legal issues raised by these developments are numerous. Does a surrogate mother have a right to her baby if she changes her mind after delivery? If a deformed child results from an artificial insemination in a surrogate mother, do the parents who paid for the child have a right to reject it? What are the responsibilities of a sperm bank to provide sperm that is free of defects? Do frozen embryos have inheritance rights from the people who produced them?

Genetic engineering (also called biotechnology)—manipulating an organism's genes so that the "good" genes are passed on and the "bad" genes disappear—is not likely to be used on humans in the near future. Genetic engineering has been used to create plants that are resistant to frost, disease, and herbicides, leaner pigs, and cows that produce 25 percent more milk, but altering human genes is illegal.

In response to the feeling of being "medically managed," expectant parents have begun to question some of the medical procedures and policies involved in hospital births. Due to consumer demand, practices such as excluding the father or support person from labor and delivery, perineal shave, enema, episiotomy, and long separation of the newborn infant from the parent(s) have been dropped from standard orders by many physicians.

Lastly, more fathers are actively participating in the birth of their children, in taking care of their children and in taking off work to be with their children. "That they are important to the nurturance and education of children is apparent" (Walters & Chapman, 1991, 107). However, increased involvement of fathers is dependent on a reevaluation of what we believe about gender roles (Biller, 1993). For example, it is often assumed that women are "naturally" better caregivers than men.

❧ CHOICES ❧

Among the choices involved in becoming a parent are whether to have the birth in a hospital, in one's home, or in a birthing center, and what reproductive technologies may be used to achieve what goals. The latter set of choices have implications not only for parents, but also for their children and for society.

Home, Hospital, or Birthing Center for Birth of Baby?

Travis (1988) suggested that the choice of whether to give birth at home or in a hospital is related to one's perspective on childbirth:

> Should childbirth be viewed as a natural process, usually resulting in spontaneous delivery of healthy alert infants to healthy attentive mothers? Or is it more appropriate to perceive the process as a medical event with relatively high risk of disease or death to both women and infants?"
> (p. 150).

The American College of Obstetricians and Gynecologists view childbirth as a medical event that should take place in a hospital. Part of the reason why the medical profession does not advocate home births is the fear of being sued if something goes wrong during a home birth.

Although over 95 percent of all U.S.. births occur in the hospital, some expectant parents are concerned that traditional childbirth procedures are too impersonal, costly, and potentially dangerous. Those who opt for home birth are primarily concerned about avoiding separation from the new infant, maintaining control over who can be present at the delivery, and avoiding what they view as unnecessary medical management.

The nurse-midwife is most often asked to assist in home births. Some nurse-midwives are certified members of the American College of Nurse-Midwives and have successfully completed a masters degree in nurse-midwifery offered at various universities, including Georgetown, Emory, St. Louis, and Columbia.

What is the relative safety of home versus hospital births? A study designed to answer this question revealed that except in special cases, home births involve no extra risks than births in hospitals. However, the researchers warned that in cases of delayed labor, breech birth, or fetal distress, a hospital is the safer environment (Holmes, 1988).

Rather than choose between having their baby in a hospital or at home, some women prefer a birthing center, which is more likely to be available in larger metropolitan areas. Birthing centers provide special rooms for the woman to experience labor and the staff is more likely to consist of certified nurse-midwives than obstetricians.

National data suggest that low-risk mothers who choose to have their babies in birthing centers are no more likely to have poor birth outcomes or to require a cesarean section than are low-risk women who give birth in the hospital (Rooks et al., 1989). When complications do arise, birthing centers transfer the mother and baby to the hospital.

Choices Resulting from New Reproductive Technologies

The various ways in which physicians can manipulate the fertilization process (in-vitro fertilization, surrogacy, ovum transfers, prenatal testing) have created a new range of choices in regard to pregnancy. Examples of such choices are given in the following paragraphs:

Example One   A young woman who wants to delay pregnancy and child-rearing until after she has established herself professionally in a career may have her "healthy eggs" in her youth extracted, frozen and later artificially inseminated when she is in her forties or fifties. Doing so would reduce some of the risks associated with birth defects in women who elect to have children during middle age. Alternatively, a middle-age woman may want to use an egg from a younger woman that has been artificially inseminated with her partner's sperm.

What are the disadvantages of delaying pregnancy through the use of reproductive technologies? Risk to the fetus and risk to the mother are the

(continued)

---

predominant problems. While some of the risks to the fetus can be avoided by using a "young egg" ("old eggs" are much more likely to be defective), the middle-aged pregnant woman is much more likely to be diabetic, overweight, and have high blood pressure, which may also impact the fetus negatively. In addition, what are the implications for the child who will have two elderly parents who may die before her or his graduation from high school? Joni Mitchell decided to have a baby at age 52 and was implanted with a fertilized egg from a young woman (her husband was the sperm donor). She said of the implications for her age and its effect on her child, "If I can raise him or her until age 30, then he should be able to make it on his own" (quoted in Gorman, 1991, 62).

Example Two Couples who have genetic histories including sickle-cell anemia or cystic fibrosis may have such defects tested for in several embryos and implant only those without the defects. But if embryos are destroyed because of a genetic defect, can sex of the embryo also be used as a basis for discarding the embryo?

❦ Summary

Pregnancy begins with fertilization and conception (implantation of the fertilized egg on the uterine wall). Various means of achieving pregnancy/conception include artificial insemination of a woman by her husband and/or donor, artificial insemination of a surrogate mother, ovum transfer, and in-vitro fertilization. Some of these procedures are used by the 15–20 percent of U.S. married couples who are infertile (unable to conceive after one year of regular intercourse without birth control).

Prenatal care helps to ensure a healthy baby and mother. Pregnant women should receive adequate nutrition and avoid substances that are or may be harmful to the fetus (e.g., alcohol, nicotine, cocaine). Moderate exercise may be beneficial during pregnancy when exercise is not contraindicated by the presence of risk factors. Prescription and nonprescription medications should only be taken with the approval of a competent physician.

Pregnancy sometimes involves stress, concern over body image, worry over increased responsibility and changes in lifestyle, worry over the health of the baby and the mother, and fear of pain during childbirth. Expectant fathers report some worry over increased financial responsibility and fear of being replaced by the child.

Some expectant parents, who are dissatisfied with traditional, hospital-managed deliveries, are choosing alternative childbirth methods, including the Lamaze, Dick-Read, Bradley, and LeBoyer methods. When vaginal delivery presents a risk to the mother or baby, a Cesarean section may be performed.

The transition to parenthood is usually more profound for the mother whose hormonal system is altered, who may experience postpartum depression, and who is confronted with ordering her priorities. Most women tend to place family considerations above career considerations.

Fathers who interact with their newborns soon after birth experience a context that may lend itself to increased childcare. Fathers tend to become more involved in childrearing as their children age. When fathers are involved with their children, it is more often their sons.

While pregnancy is likely to involve greater communication, it may also increase conflict. In addition, sexual desire, frequency and satisfaction often decrease throughout pregnancy. Research findings regarding how children affect marital happiness are inconsistent. However, having children is associated with greater commitment and marital stability.

Trends in parenthood involve increased use of technological means to achieve pregnancy/conception, increased use of genetic engineering, and more fathers involved in parenting. More birthing centers have also emerged, giving increased control of the birthing event to parents.

Questions for Reflection

1. To what degree are artificial insemination, surrogate mothers, in-vitro fertilization, and ovum transfers options you would consider if you and your partner were having difficulty becoming pregnant and wanted a baby?
2. As a woman, to what degree would you expect your husband to share the work of parenting if you had a baby?
3. As a man, to what degree would you want to share the work of parenting with your wife if you decided to have a baby?

References

Abbey, A., F. M. Andrews, and L. J. Halman. Infertility and subjective well-being: The mediating roles of self-esteem, internal control, and interpersonal conflict. *Journal of Marriage and the Family,* 1992, *54,* 408–417.

Adoption works for everyone: A beginner's guide to adoption. 1992. (No author listed.) Available from Wendy's International, Inc., P. O. Box 256, 4288 West Dublin-Granville Road, Dublin, Ohio 43017.

Affonso, D. D. and L. J. Mayberry. Common stressors reported by a group of childbearing American women. *Pregnancy and Parenting,* Phyllis Stern, ed. New York: Hemisphere, 1989, 41–55.

Ahmeduzzaman, M. and J. L. Roopnarine. Sociodemographic factors, functioning style, social support, and fathers' involvement with preschoolers in African American families. *Journal of Marriage and the Family,* 1992, *54,* 699–707.

Bachrach, C. A., K. A. London, and P. L. Maza. On the path to adoption: Adoption seeking in the United States, 1988. *Journal of Marriage and the Family,* 1991, *53,* 705–718.

Belsky, J. and M. Rovine. Patterns of marital change across the transition to parenthood: Pregnancy to three years postpartum. *Journal of Marriage and the Family,* 1990, *52,* 5–19.

Biller, H. B. *Fathers and families.* Westport, Conn.: Auburn House, 1993.

Bogren, Lennart Y. Changes in sexuality in women and men during pregnancy. *Archives of Sexual Behavior,* 1991, *20,* 35–45.

Briesemeister, L. H. and B. A. Haines. The interactions of fathers and newborns. *Childbirth in America: Anthropological Perspectives,* K. L. Michaelson, ed. South Hadley, Mass.: Bergin and Garvey, 1988, 228–238.

Chez, Ronald A. Identifying maternal/fetal risks before pregnancy. *Medical Aspects of Human Sexuality,* April 1991, 54–58.

Cole, D. It might have been: Mourning the unborn. *Psychology Today,* 1987, *21* (7), 64–65.

Consumer protection issues involving in-vitro fertilization clinics. Hearing before subcommittee on Regulation, Business Opportunities, and Energy of the Committee on Small Business. House of Representatives, 101st Congress, Washington, D. C., March 9, 1989.

Cowan, C. P. and P. A. Cowan. Is there love after baby? *Psychology Today,* July/August 1992, *25,* 58–63.

Cowan, P. A. and C. P. Cowan. Changes in marriage during the transition to parenthood: Must we blame the baby? *The Transition to Parenthood: Current Theory and Research,* G. Y. Michaels and W. A. Goldberg, eds. New York: Cambridge University Press, 1988, 114–154.

Derwinski-Robinson, B. Infertility and sexuality. *Sexual Health Promotion,* C. I. Fogel and D. Lauver, eds. Philadelphia: W. B. Saunders, 1990, 291–304.

Dewitt, P. M. In pursuit of pregnancy. *American Demographics* May, 1993, 48–55.

Duncan, S. W. and H. J. Markman. Intervention programs for the transition to parenthood: Current status from a prevention perspective. *The Transition to Parenthood: Current Theory and Research,* G. Y. Michaels and W. A. Goldberg, Eds. New York: Cambridge University Press, 1988, 270–310.

Dunn, P. C., I. J. Ryan, and K. O'Brien. College students' level of acceptability of the new medical science of conception and problems of infertility. *Journal of Sex Research,* 1988, *24,* 282–287.

Elmer-Dewitt, P. Making babies. *Time,* September 30, 1991, 56–63.

Engel, Nancy Sharts. The maternity cycle and sexuality. *Sexual Health Promotion,* Catherine I. Fogel and Diane Lauver, eds. Philadelphia: W. B. Saunders Company, 1990, 179–205.

Fedele, N. M., E. R. Golding, F. K. Grossman, and W. S. Pollack. Psychological issues in adjustment to first parenthood. *The Transition to Parenthood: Current Theory and Research,* G. Y. Michaels and W. A. Goldberg, eds. New York: Cambridge University Press, 1988, 85–113.

Fitzgerald, M. Couples fawn over frozen embryos, expert says. *USA Today,* August 9, 1989, 3A.

Foreman, S. Risk is small in hiding the identity of donor. *USA Today,* March 26, 1990, 7A.

Friedman, T., and D. Gath. The psychiatric consequences of spontaneous abortion. *British Journal of Psychiatry,* 1989, *155,* 810–813.

Gauna-Trujillo, B. and P. G. Higgins. Sexual intercourse and pregnancy. *Pregnancy and Parenting,* Phyllis N. Stern, ed. New York: Hemisphere Publishing Corp., 1989, 31–40.

Gibbs, Nancy. The baby chase. *Time,* October 9, 1989, 86–89.

Goldberg, W. A. Introduction: Perspectives on the transition to parenthood. *The Transition to Parenthood: Current Theory and Research,* G. Y. Michaels and W. A. Goldberg, eds. New York: Cambridge University Press, 1988, 1–20.

Goldberg, W. A. and G. Y Michaels. Conclusion. The transition to parenthood: systhesis and future directions. *The Transition to Parenthood: Current Theory and Research,* G. Y. Michaels and W. A. Goldberg, eds. New York: Cambridge University Press, 1988, 342–360.

Gorman, C. How old is too old? *Time,* September 30, 1991, 62.

Grant, L., L. A. Simpson, Z. L. Rong, and H. Peters-Golden. Gender, parenthood, and work hours of physicians. *Journal of Marriage and the Family,* 1990, *52,* 39–49.

Greenberg, M. *The birth of a father.* New York: Continuum Publishing Co., 1986.

Greer, K. Today's parents: How well are they doing? *Better Homes and Gardens,* October 1986, 36–46.

Harkness, S. and C. M. Super. The cultural foundations of fathers' roles: Evidence from Kenya and the United States. *Father-Child Relations: Cultural and Biosocial Contexts,* Barry S. Hewlett, ed. New York: Aldine de Gruyter, 1992, 191–211.

Harriman, L. C. Marital adjustment as related to personal and marital changes accompanying parenthood. *Family Relations,* 1986, *35,* 233–239.

Harris, K. M. and S. P. Morgan. Fathers, sons, and daughters: Differential paternal involvement in parenting. *Journal of Marriage and the Family,* 1991, *53,* 531–544.

Higgins, B. S. Couple infertility: From the perspective of the close-relationship model. *Family Relations,* 1990, *39,* 81–86.

Holmes, P. Squeeze on alternatives to hospital births. *New Statesman,* 1988, *116,* 6.

Jacobsen, L. and B. Edmondson. Father figures. *American Demographics,* 1993, August, 22 et passim.

John, E. M., D. Savitz, and D. P. Sandler. Prenatal exposure to parents' smoking and childhood cancer. *American Journal of Epidemiology,* 1991, *133,* 123.

Kiely, J. L., J. C. Kleinman, and M. Kiely. Triplets and higher-order multiple births: Time trends and infant mortality. *American Journal of Diseases in Children,* 1992, *146,* 862–868.

Koepke, L., J. Hare, and P. B. Moran. Relationship quality in a sample of lesbian couples with children and childfree lesbian couples. *Family Relations,* 1992, *41,* 224–229.

Kraus, M. A. and E. S. Redman. Postpartum depression: An interactional view. *Journal of Marital and Family Therapy,* 1986, *12,* 63–74.

LaRossa, R. Fatherhood and social change. *Family Relations,* 1988, *37,* 451–457.

La Rossa, R. and D. C. Reitzes. Continuity and change in middle class fatherhood, 1925–1939: The Culture-conduct connection. *Journal of Marriage and the Family,* 1993, *55,* 455–468.

Levran, D., J. Dor, E. Rudak, L. Nebel, I. Ben-Shlomo, Z. Ben-Rafael, and S. Mashiach. Pregnancy potential of human oocytes: The effect of cryopreservation. *New England Journal of Medicine,* 1990, *323,* 1153–1156.

MacDermid, S. M., T. L. Huston, and S. M. McHale. Changes in marriage associated with the transition to parenthood: Individual differences as a function of sex-role attitudes and changes in the division of household labor. *Journal of Marriage and the Family,* 1990, *52,* 475–486.

Michaelson, K. L. Childbirth in America: A brief history and contemporary issues. *Childbirth in America: Anthropological Perspectives,* K. L. Michaelson, ed. South Hadley, Mass.: Bergin and Garvey, 1988, 1–32.

Mischel, H. N. and R. Fuhr. Maternal employment: Its psychological effects on children and their families. *Feminism, Children and the New Families,* S. M. Dornbusch and M. H. Strober, eds. New York: Guilford Press, 1988, 194–195.

National Center for Health Statistics. 1992. *Advance report of new data from the 1989 birth certificate.* (Monthly Vital Statistics Report, vol. 40, no. 8, supp. 2). Hyattsville, Md.: U. S. Public Health Service.

National Center for Health Statistics. Advance report of maternal and infant health data from the birth certificate, 1990. Monthly vital statistics report, Vol. 42, No. 2, suppl. Hyattsville, Maryland; Public Health Service, 1993.

Office of Technology Assessment. *Artificial insemination: Practice in the United States, summary of a 1987 survey—Background paper.* Washington, D.C.: U. S. Government Printing Office, 1988.

Penland, M. R. & C. A. Darling. Predicting fathering styles: Traditional vs "new" fathers. Paper, 54th Annual Conference, National Council on Family Relations, Orlando, Florida, 1992. Used by permission.

Pepe, M. V. and T. J. Byrne. Women's perceptions of immediate and long-term effects of failed infertility treatment on marital and sexual satisfaction. *Family Relations,* 1991, *40,* 303–309.

Rooks, J. P., N. L. Weatherby, E. K. Ernst, S. Stapleton, D. Rosen, and A. Rosenfield. Outcomes of care in birth centers. *New England Journal of Medicine,* 1989, *321,* 1804–1811.

Saunders, R. B. and E. Robbins. Changes in the marital relationship during the first pregnancy. *Pregnancy and Parenting,* Phyllis N. Stern, ed. New York: Hemisphere Publishing Corp., 1989, 13–29.

Shapiro, J. L. The expectant father. *Psychology Today,* January 1987, 36–42.

Siller, Barry and Ricardo Azziz. New ways of managing ectopic pregnancy. *Medical Aspects of Human Sexuality,* March 1991, 30–39.

Stanley, S. M. and H. J. Markman. Assessing commitment in personal relationships. *Journal of Marriage and the Family,* 1992, *54,* 595–608.

Statistical Abstract of the United States: 1992, 112th ed. Washington, D.C.: U. S. Bureau of the Census, 1992.

Stone, A. Virginia "babymaker" on trial. *USA Today,* February 10, 1992, 3A.

Travis, C. B. *Women and health psychology: Biomedical issues.* Hillside, N.J.: Erlbaun Assoc., 1988.

Walters, L. H. and S. F. Chapman. Changes in legal views of parenthood: Implications for fathers in minority cultures. *Fatherhood and Families in Cultural Context,* F. W. Bozett and S. M. H. Hanson, eds. 1991, 83–113.

Wilcox, Allen J., C. R. Weinberg, J. F. O'Connor, D. D. Baird, J. P. Schlatterer, R. E. Canfield, E. G. Armstrong, and R. C. Nisula. Incidence of early loss of pregnancy. *The New England Journal of Medicine,* 1988, *319,* 189–194.

Wilkerson, N. N. and E. Bing. Sexuality. *Childbirth Education: Practice, Research, and Theory,* F. H. Nichols and S. S. Humenick, Eds. Philadelphia: W. B. Saunders Company, 1988, 376–393.

Wilkie, C. F. and E. W. Ames. The relationship of infant crying to parental stress in the transition to parenthood. *Journal of Marriage and the Family,* 1986, *48,* 545–550.

Contents

❧ 15 ❧
CHAPTER
Rearing Children

Is It True?

1. Research consistently finds that conflicts between parents and their children inevitably increase during the period of adolescence.

2. The most preferred day care arrangement by parents of children two and under is to have the child taken care of by the grandmother.

3. U.S. government funded day care centers are likely to begin by the mid-nineties.

4. In Sweden, it is against the law for parents to spank their children.

5. Requiring an adolescent to be drug tested is one alternative in helping an adolescent stop abusing drugs.

1 = F; 2 = F; 3 = F; 4 = T; 5 = T

If there is anything that we wish to change in the child, we should first examine it and see whether it is not something that could better be changed in ourselves.

CARL JUNG

John Wilmot, the Earl of Rochester in the seventeenth century, noted that before he got married, he had six theories about bringing up children. Later in his life he commented that he had six children but no theories. His observation rings a bellof truth for parents. Yet most adults, with or without children, have some notion about what constitutes "good" and "bad" parenting practices. In this chapter we review some of the various approaches to childrearing as well as some of the more salient issues with which parents are confronted. We begin by discussing some of the realities of parenthood.

Realities of Parenthood

Although each parent's experience of parenthood is unique, some of the realities of parenthood are universal. In this section, we will make some generalizations about the realities of parenthood.

Parenthood Is Only One Stage in Life

Parents of newly adult children often lament, "Before you know it, your children are grown and gone." Although parents of infants sometimes feel that the sleepless nights will never end, they do end. Unlike the marriage relationship, the parent-child relationship inevitably moves toward separation. Just as the marital partners were alone before their children came, they will be alone again after their children leave. Except for occasional visits with their children and possibly with grandchildren, the couple will return to the childfree lifestyle.

Typical parents are in their early fifties when their last child leaves home. Since the average woman and man can expect to live to 79 and 72 respectively (National Center for Health Statistics, 1993b), spouses in a continuous marriage will have a minimum of over 20 years together after their children leave home. Hence, parenthood might best be described as only one stage in marriage and in life. Indeed, assuming individuals marry at age 24, have two children at three-year intervals, and die at age 77, they will have children living with them about 30 percent of their lifetime and 40 percent of their marriage.

Rearing children, and so handing on life like a torch from one generation to another

PLATO

I know how to do anything. I'm a mom.

ROSEANNE ARNOLD

One parent said:

> We had three kids, and I loved taking care of all of them. I think the happiest time in my life was when my husband and I would wake up in the morning and they would all be there. But that's changed now. They are married and have moved several states away. I know they still love me and they call to stay in touch, but I rarely see them anymore (Author's files).

Parents Are Only One Influence

Although parents often take the credit—and the blame—for the way their children turn out, they are only one among many influences on child development. Peers, siblings, teachers, and the mass media are also influential. Although parents are the first significant influence, peer influence becomes increasingly important and remains so into the college years. During this time, children are likely to mirror the values and behaviors of their friends and agemates.

> It is not strange that he who has no children brings them up so well.
>
> CONFUCIUS

CONSIDERATION

Teenagers often become enthralled with their peer groups and may distance themselves from their parents. But this is more likely to occur among whites than blacks. Based on interviews with a sample of 942 black and white adolescents, the researchers found that the black youths "described their friendship relations as somewhat less intimate, perceived less peer pressure, and reported a lower need for approval from peers than did white youths" (Giordano et al., 1993, 285).

Siblings also have an important and sometimes lasting effect on each other's development.

Television is another influence on children. Television is a major means of exhibiting language, values, and lifestyles to children that may be different from those of the parents. One father had Home Box Office and Showtime disconnected because he did not want his children seeing the movies and specials on those channels. Another parent went through the television guide each week and marked the programs he would not allow his children to watch. The guide was left on top of the television, and the children were to look at what programs had been approved before they turned it on.

NATIONAL DATA 🕉 Between the ages of 2 and 17, children watch an average of 23 hours of television per week (Stipp, 1993).

Children are also influenced by different environmental situations. An only daughter adopted into an urban, Catholic, upper-class family will be

Television is a frequent and pervasive influence in the lives of children. Parents are often opposed to the values (violence, casual sex, unprotected sex) transmitted through television.

exposed to a different environment than a girl born into a rural, Southern Baptist, working-class family with three male children. Some of the potentially important environmental variables include geographic location, family size, the family's social class, religion, and racial or ethnic background.

Internal physiological happenings in the developing child will also influence the child's behavior. Particularly during pubertal development, hormones that may influence social behavior are released into the bloodstream of both sexes.

CONSIDERATION

Because parents are only one of many influences on their children, they should be careful about taking the credit or the blame for the way they turn out. "It's not in the books," said a professor of psychology. "My wife and I have modeled a relatively conservative but ambitious life for our children and had hoped that they would want to become professionals. But they met a group in college and decided to drop out and join this commune. That was 10 years ago. It's not what we wanted for them, but they're happy."

Parenthood Demands Change as Children Grow Up

The most common mistake parents make is that they don't allow their children to make their own choices.

HERB SCHACHT

The demands of parenthood change as the children move through various developmental stages. Infants, toddlers, preschoolers, pre-adolescents (8–11), new adolescents (12–15), middle adolescents (15–18), and young adults (18–22) all exhibit different behaviors and require different emotional, social, and psychological resources from parents. Over time the child is growing from a state of total dependence to one of total independence. Knowing how much freedom to give at what age for what events is a challenge for most parents. During adolescence, effective childrearing has been likened to flying a kite— the string must be let out to give the kite height; if the string is kept too tight, it will snap and the kite will plummet.

Each Child Is Different

No two children are alike—particularly if one is yours and the other isn't.

E.C. MCKENZIE

Children differ in their tolerance for stress, in their capacity to learn, in their comfort in social situations, in their interests, and in innumerable other ways. Parents soon become aware of the specialness of each child—of her or his difference from every other child they know and from children they have read about. Parents of two or more children are often amazed at how children who have the same parents can be so different. Some differences between children may be due to differences in sex and differential gender role socialization. Parents who have only male children report more conflict in the family than parents who have only female children (Falconer et al., 1990).

Children also differ in their mental and physical health. Over 250,000 babies are born each year with birth defects including 20,000 severely retarded, 16,000 with a profound hearing loss, and 8,000 with cerebral palsy. Since most parents expect the perfect baby, these defects create unforseen financial worries and present special emotional challenges to the parents.

Parenting Styles Differ

Parents in different social classes rear their children differently. In general, middle-class parents tend to be concerned about their children being independent and creative while working-class parents tend to emphasize the importance of conformity. Middle-class parents who value self-direction function in a supportive parental role. Working-class parents who value conformity adopt a parental role that emphasizes imposing constraints on their children (Luster, Roades, & Haas, 1989). Specific parenting styles are presented in the Choices section at the end of the chapter.

Parenting styles also differ across societies. For example, Polynesian children learn to view not only their mother and father but also their grandparents and all relatives of equivalent age as parents. In practice, multiple parenting in Polynesia means that a number of people will be involved in the life-transition ceremonies, that the children will have a number of houses they regard as home, and that they will have an array of adults who nurture them, love them, and protect them.

Among the Chinese, "mother-child relations tend to be close and affectionate, in contrast to father-child relations marked by greater affectional distance, perhaps even tension and antagonism" (Ho, 1989, 160). The In Focus 15.1 insert provides more information about childrearing among the Chinese.

ACROSS CULTURES ∿

❧ Folklore About Childrearing

To encourage adults to have and rear children, certain folklore romanticizing the experience has emerged. Such folklore is necessary since the experience of childrearing is often more difficult than parents report thinking it would be (Kalmuss et al., 1992). Some of the folklore (widely held beliefs not supported by facts) surrounding parenting is discussed in the following sections (LeMasters & DeFrain, 1989):

Parents of young children should realize that few people, and maybe no one, will find their children as enchanting as they do.

BARBARA WALTERS

Myth 1: Rearing Children Is Always Fun

Would-be parents see television commercials of young parents and children and are led to believe that playing in the park with their 4-year-old is what childrearing is all about. Parenthood is portrayed as being a lot of fun. The truth is somewhat different than the folklore:

Rearing a family is probably the most difficult job in the world.

VIRGINIA SATIR

> The idea of something being fun implies that you can take it or leave it, whereas parents do not have this choice. Fathers and mothers must stay with the

---

❧ IN FOCUS 15.1 ❧

Chinese Childrearing Patterns

Even though Chinese Americans are the largest of the Asian American groups in the United States (over one million) they represent less than one half of one percent of the total U.S. population (O'Hare & Felt, 1992). Although not all Chinese American families are alike, some of the patterns of childrearing characteristic of Chinese American families include the following:

1. *Father Dominance.* Chinese families have traditionally been patriarchal whereby males, particularly the father and eldest son have had dominant roles. Chinese American children are taught that the source of authority in their family is the father. The father maintains his authority and respect in the family by means of emotional distance. Chinese children do not question their father's authority.

2. *Punishment.* Physical punishment is generally not used for children in Chinese American families (Wong, 1988a). Rather, the mechanism of social control in Chinese families involves creating a sense of shame. Children who disobey are taught to feel that they bring disgrace not only to themselves but to their family and whole collective group. This pattern may account for the low level of juvenile delinquency among Chinese Americans.

3. *Sibling Modeling.* Older siblings are expected to care for younger siblings and to be good role models. Children are not allowed to be aggressive with other siblings. Children spend most of their time around adults and older children and are expected to behave as adults.

4. *Value for Education.* Chinese children learn early that education is important. The source of this value is from the Confucian respect for learning, the parents' belief that education is the way to security and a better life, and the desire of parents to receive social status from the Chinese community for having a college educated or professional child (Wong, 1988a).

5. *Care for the Elderly.* Chinese children are also socialized to respect and take care of their elderly. This norm is embedded in the tradition of male dominance—in exchange for being given a dominant role in the family, eldest sons were to ensure the care of their parents. Today, "studies suggest that family members are the primary source of assistance for the elderly Chinese and that assistance from social service agencies and professional persons is almost nonexistent" (Wong, 1988a, 250).

6. *Intermarriage.* While two-thirds of Chinese Americans marry other Chinese, increasingly they are crossing racial lines to marry whites (Wong, 1988b). A major reason for such a trend is the dissatisfaction of acculturated (Americanized) Chinese females who want a more egalitarian partner than the traditional Chinese male is prepared to be.

You don't know what trouble is until your kids reach the age of consent, dissent, and resent—all at the same time.

E.C. MCKENZIE

child and keep trying, whether it is fun, or whether they are enjoying it or not. . . . Rearing children is hard work; it is often nerve-racking work; it involves tremendous responsibility; it takes all the ability one has (and more); and once you have begun, you cannot quit when you feel like it (pp. 22, 23).

Myth 2: Good Parents Inevitably Produce Good Kids

It is assumed that children who turn out "wrong"—who abuse drugs, steal, and the like—have parents who really did not do their job. We tend to blame parents when children fail. But good parents have given both their emotional and material resources to their children and the children have not turned out well. One mother said:

> We live in one of the finer suburbs of our city, our children went to the best schools, and we spent a lot of time with them as a family (camping, going to the beach, skiing). But our son is now in prison. He held up a local grocery store one night and got shot in the leg. We've stopped asking ourselves what we did wrong. He was 23 and drifted into friendships with a group of guys who just decided they would pull a job one night (Author's files).

A corollary to the belief that good parents will produce goods kids is the idea that parents know what kind of kids they are producing. But a study comparing what parents thought their children's attitudes and values were on religion, drugs, and sex with what their children's beliefs actually were showed that parents had inaccurate perceptions (Thompson et al., 1985).

Myth 3: Love Is the Essential Key to Effective Childrearing

Parents are taught that if they love their children enough, they will turn out okay. Love is seen as the primary ingredient, which if present in sufficient quantities, will ensure a successful child. But most parents love their children dearly and want only the best for them. Love is not enough and does not guarantee desirable behavior. One parent said:

> We planned our children in courtship, loved them before they got here, and have never stopped loving them. But they are rude, irresponsible, and hardly speak to us. We are frustrated beyond description. We've done everything we know how to do in providing a loving home for them, but it hasn't worked (Author's files).

Myth 4: Children Are Always Appreciative

Most parents think of childrearing in terms of love, care, and nurturing—and also in terms of giving their children things. Parents may assume their children will appreciate their tender loving care and the material benefits, like clothes, computers, and cars they bestow. That assumption may be wrong. Children often think parents are supposed to love them and give them things. They view material benefits as their birthright.

Good parenting does not ensure that one's children will never get into trouble with the law.

Q. What's the toughest thing about being a father?

A. You're afraid to lose something so much, you're afraid to be that much in love.

BRUCE SPRINGSTEEN (*ROLLING STONES INTERVIEW*)

Better that the young wife should bring forth a serpent than bear an ungrateful child.

SADI

CONSIDERATION

It is a mistake for would-be parents to embark on the adventure of having children with the expectation that they will always be appreciated. For the most part, parenting involves a lot of selfless giving with no thought of a return. One parent said, "The best part about being a parent is loving your children. If they love you back or appreciate what you are doing, you get a bonus. But don't expect it" (Author's files).

New parents quickly learn that raising
children is a kind of desperate
improvisation.

BILL COSBY

Myth 5: Parenting Comes Naturally

The lack of attention given to systematic parent education in our society (there are more driver education than parent education courses) reflects a belief that when one has a child, what the parent needs to know to take care of the child and rear the child will come naturally. Cooke (1991) challenged this belief by interviewing both novice and expert mothers of six- to ten-month-old infants. The novice mothers had no previous children, no previous experience with children, and no formal education related to child development, childrearing, or related areas. The expert mothers had at least one older child, extensive experience with other children, and formal education in child development and child rearing.

Cooke (1991) observed clear differences between the respective thinking, knowledge, and behaviors of novice and expert mothers. In general, novices were less able to identify the cues provided by the child in regard to the child's goals and needs and were less knowledgeable about child development. For example, the novices did not know what behaviors it was appropriate to expect of a child at what age. Cooke (1991) recommended that new parents be exposed to parent education learning experiences, which provide skills in focusing on children's needs and goals and to become familiar with child development literature. An example of a parent education program was described by Thompson et al. (1993). Significant improvements were noted in the parents who completed the program. Without such training, we tend to duplicate the parenting patterns we experienced as children (Simons et al., 1993).

Myth 6: Family Values Are Easy to Instill

"Family values" is a concept most parents want to instill in their children. Cox (1992) identified what this term typically means:

1. Strong respect for other people; an appreciation for the differences that others bring.
2. The ability to discuss differences and find peaceful and cooperative means to resolve differences.
3. Sticking with something even when it becomes tough; working through difficult areas to build character, loyalty, and respect.
4. Making and keeping commitments.
5. Maintaining one's personal integrity at all times.
6. Being thoughtful toward others and providing a helping hand whenever possible.
7. Being aware of community needs and one's ability to provide some service to that community.

It is what we value, not what we have,
that makes us rich.

E.C. MCKENZIE

Other values that help to strengthen families are good communication, togetherness, and a strong spiritual dimension (Schvaneveldt & Young, 1992).

Instilling these values is difficult because the larger society, in contrast to parents, may encourage individualistic rather than familistic values. And since the youth in families are exposed to influences beyond the family, family values are likely to be diluted.

❦ Approaches to Childrearing

There are several theoretical approaches to rearing children (see Table 15.1). In examining these approaches, it is important to keep in mind that no single approach is absolutely superior to another. What works for one child may not work for another. Any given approach may not even work with the same child at two different times.

Developmental-Maturational Approach

For the past 60 years, Arnold Gesell and his colleagues at the Yale Clinic of Child Development have been known for their ages-and-stages approach to childrearing. Their *developmental-maturational approach* has been widely used in the United States. Let's examine the basic perspective of this approach, some considerations for childrearing, and some criticisms of the approach.

Basic Perspective Gesell views what children do, think, and feel as being influenced by their genetic inheritance. Although genes dictate the gradual unfolding of a unique person, every individual passes through the same basic pattern of growth. This pattern includes four aspects of development: motor behavior (sitting, crawling, walking), adaptive behavior (picking up objects and walking around objects), language behavior (words and gestures), and personal-social behavior (cooperativeness and helpfulness). Through the observation of hundreds of normal infants and children, Gesell and his co-workers have identified norms of development. Although there may be large variations, these norms suggest the ages at which an average child displays various behaviors. For example, on the average, children begin to walk alone (although awkwardly) at age 13 months and use simple sentences between ages 2 and 3.

Considerations for Childrearing Gesell suggested that if parents are aware of their children's developmental clock, they will avoid unreasonable expectations. For example, a child cannot walk or talk until the neurological structures necessary for those behaviors have matured. "Parents who provide special educational lessons for their babies are wasting their time," because the infants are not developmentally ready to profit from the exposure (Scarr, 1984, 60). Also, the hunger of a 4-week-old must be immediately appeased by food, but at 16 to 28 weeks, the child has some capacity to wait because the hunger

Parents love their children as soon as they are born but children love their parents only after time has elapsed and they have acquired understanding.

ARISTOTLE

T A B L E 15.1

Theories of Childrearing

THEORY	MAJOR CONTRIBUTOR	BASIC PERSPECTIVE	FOCAL CONCERNS	CRITICISMS
Developmental Maturational	Arnold Gesell	Genetic basis for each child passing through predictable stages	Motor behavior Adaptive behavior Language behavior Social behavior	Overemphasis on biological clock Inadequate sample to develop norms Demand schedule questionable Upper-middle class bias
Behavioral	B. F. Skinner	Behavior is learned through operant and classical conditioning	Positive reinforcement Negative reinforcement Punishment Extinction Stimulus response	Deemphasis on cognitions of child Theory too complex to be accurately/appropriately applied by parent Too manipulative/controlling Difficult to know reinforcers and punishers in advance
Parent Effectiveness Training	Thomas Gordon	The child's world view is the key to understanding the child	Change the environment before attempting to change the child's behavior Avoid hurting the child's self-esteem Avoid win-lose solutions	Parents must sometimes impose their will on the child's How to achieve win-win solutions is not specified
Socioteleological	Alfred Adler	Behavior is seen as attempt of child to secure a place in the family	Insecurity Compensation Power Revenge Social striving Natural consequences	Limited empirical support Impractical Child may be harmed taking "natural consequences"
Reality	William Glasser	Behavioral problems children develop result from inability to cope with stress	Irrational narcissism Emotional precociousness Vicarious living	Parental love not sole determinant of outcome Children are exposed to many socialization agents Child may be endangered if approach is followed

pains are less intense. In view of this and other developmental patterns, Gesell suggested that the infant's needs be cared for on a demand schedule; instead of having to submit to a schedule imposed by parents, infants are fed, changed, put to bed, and allowed to play when they want. Children are likely to be resistant to a hard and fast schedule because they may be developmentally unable to cope with it.

In addition, Gesell emphasized that parents should be aware of the importance of the first years of a child's life. In Gesell's view, these early years assume the greatest significance because the child's first learning experiences occur during this period.

Criticisms of the Developmental-Maturational Approach Gesell's work has been criticized because of (1) its overemphasis on the idea of a biological clock, (2) the deficiencies of the sample he used to develop maturational norms, (3) his insistence on the merits of a demand schedule, and (4) the idea that environmental influences are weak.

Most of the children who were studied to establish the developmental norms were from the upper-middle class. Children in other social classes are exposed to different environments, which influence their development. So norms established on upper-middle class children may not adequately reflect the norms of children from other social classes.

Gesell's suggestion that parents do everything for the infant when the infant wants it has also been criticized. Rearing an infant on the demand schedule can drastically interfere with the parents' personal and marital interests. As a result, most U.S. parents feed their infants on a demand schedule but put them to bed to accommodate the parents' schedule (Shea, 1984).

Behavioral Approach

The *behavioral approach* to childrearing, also known as the *social learning approach,* is based on the work of B. F. Skinner. We will now review the basic perspective, considerations, and criticisms of this approach to childrearing.

Basic Perspective Behavior is learned through classical and operant conditioning. *Classical conditioning* involves presenting a stimulus with a reinforcer. For example, infants come to associate the faces of their parents with food, warmth, and comfort. Although initially only the food and feeling warm will satisfy the infant, later just the approach of the parent will soothe the infant. This may be observed when a father hands his infant to a stranger. The infant may cry because the stranger is not associated with pleasant events. But when the stranger hands the infant back to the parent, the crying may subside because the parent represents positive events and the stimulus of the parent's face is associated with pleasurable feelings.

Find out what a child will work for, and what a child will work to avoid; then systematically manipulate these contingencies and you can change behavior.

JACK TURNER

Other behaviors are learned through *operant conditioning,* which focuses on the consequences of behavior. Two principles of learning are basic to the operant explanation of behavior—reward and punishment. According to the reward principle, behaviors that are followed by a positive consequence will increase. If the goal is to teach the child to say "please," doing something the child likes after he or she says "please" will increase the use of "please" by the child. Rewards may be in the form of attention, praise, desired activities, or privileges. Whatever consequence increases the frequency of something happening is, by definition, a reward. If a particular reward doesn't change the behavior in the desired way, a different reinforcer needs to be tried.

The punishment principle is the opposite of the reward principle. A negative consequence following a behavior will decrease the frequency of that behavior; for example, the child could be isolated for five or ten minutes following an undesirable behavior. The most effective way to change behavior is to use the reward and punishment principles together to influence a specific behavior. British psychiatrist Michael Rutter (1984) commented:

> Not just stopping children from doing things—that doesn't seem to me to be the way, and in any case it doesn't work in the long run. You have to provide children with alternatives, to teach them what they should be doing, rather than what they should not be doing (p. 64).

Considerations for Childrearing Parents often ask, "Why does my child act this way, and what can I do to change it?" The behavioral approach to childrearing suggests the answer to both questions. The child's behavior has been learned through being rewarded for the behavior; the child's behavior can be changed by eliminating the reward for or punishing the undesirable behavior and rewarding the desirable behavior.

The child who cries when the parents are about to leave home to go to dinner or see a movie is often reinforced for crying by the parents' staying home longer. To teach the child not to cry when the parents leave, the parents should reward the child for not crying when they are gone for progressively longer periods of time. For example, they might initially tell the child they are going outside to walk around the house and they will give the child a treat when they get back if he or she plays until they return. The parents might then walk around the house and reward the child for not crying. If the child cries, they should be out of sight for only a few seconds and gradually increase the amount of time they are away. The essential point is that children learn to cry or not to cry depending on the consequences of crying. Because children learn what they are taught, parents might systematically structure learning experiences to achieve specific behavioral goals.

Criticisms of the Behavioral Approach Professionals and parents have attacked the behavioral approach to childrearing on the basis that it is deceptively simple and does not take cognitive issues into account. Although the behavioral approach is often presented as an easy-to-use set of procedures for child management, many parents do not have the background or skill to implement the procedures effectively. What constitutes an effective reward or punishment, presented in what way, in what situation, with what child, to influence what behavior are all decisions that need to be made before attempting to increase or decrease the frequency of a behavior. Parents often do not know the questions to ask or lack the training to make appropriate decisions in the use of behavioral procedures. One parent locked her son in the closet for an hour to punish him for lying to her a week earlier—a gross misuse of learning principles.

Behavioral childrearing has also been said to be manipulative and controlling, thereby devaluing human dignity and individuality. Some professionals feel that humans should not be manipulated to behave in certain ways through the use of rewards and punishments.

Finally, the behavioral approach has been criticized because it de-emphasizes the influence of thought processes on behavior. Too much attention, say the critics, has been given to rewarding and punishing behavior and not enough attention has been given to how the child perceives a situation. For example, parents might think they are rewarding a child by giving her or him a bicycle for good behavior. But the child may prefer to upset the parents by rejecting the bicycle and may be more rewarded by their anger than by the gift.

Parents who must cope with severe behavior problems may find practical help in Toughlove (see In Focus 15.2).

> The reward of a thing well done is to have done it.
>
> EMERSON

Parent Effectiveness Training Approach

Thomas Gordon developed a model of childrearing based on parent effectiveness training (PET).

Basic Perspective   Parent effectiveness training focuses on what children feel and experience in the here and now—how they see the world. The method of trying to understand what the child is experiencing is active listening, in which the parent reflects the child's feelings. For example, the parent who is told by the child, "I want to quit taking piano lessons because I don't like to practice" would reflect, "You're really bored with practicing the piano and would rather have fun doing something else."

PET also focuses on the development of the child's positive self-concept. To foster a positive self-concept in their child, parents should reflect positive images to the child—letting the child know he or she is liked, admired, and approved of.

> Children aren't happy unless they have something to ignore—that's what parents are for.
>
> OGDEN NASH

Considerations for Childrearing   To assist in the development of a child's positive self-concept and in the self-actualization of both children and parents, Gordon recommended managing the environment rather than the child,

> You can learn many things from children. How much patience you have, for instance.
>
> FRANKLIN P. JONES

Toughlove

Although not based on a specific childrearing theory, TOUGHLOVE is a self-help organization of parents (none of whom profess to have "professional qualifications" other than experience) who have difficulty controlling severe problem behaviors of their teenage children, including drug abuse, physical abuse of parents, staying away from home without explanation, using obscene language to parents, and stealing from other family members. These parents feel overwhelmed with the magnitude of their child's unacceptable behavior and helpless to cope with it. They may have had "good kids" up until the teen years but are now experiencing behaviors in their children that they never imagined could occur.

TOUGHLOVE parents meet weekly with other parents in groups of about 10 to discuss their children and potential solutions to their behavior problems. The typical format is for each parent to tell what problems she or he is experiencing. Other group members will comment on having had a similar problem, what they did, and how it worked out. Although there is no pressure to talk about one's problems or to take action, once a parent decides to discuss a problem and becomes committed to a course of action, the group members will ask at the next meeting if the parent followed through and what the consequences were. TOUGHLOVE parents are very supportive of each other.

The group setting eliminates the parents' feeling that they are the only parent whose children have gotten out of control, that they are embarrassed at their inability to cope with the situation, and that they have some reason to be ashamed. TOUGHLOVE parents take the position that they are people too and that they have a right to expect their children to behave appropriately. The TOUGH part becomes operative in the withdrawal of family resources when children consistently disregard parental requests (York & York, 1989). For example, a child who says, "I am going to smoke dope whether you like it or not," may, as a last resort, be asked to find somewhere else to live. The child who is arrested for drunk driving for the third time is left in jail for three days even though his parents could bail him out.

The larger community consisting of teachers, probation officers, social workers, therapists, and citizens may also be involved in helping parents in TOUGHLOVE. For example, a child who takes drugs and has a history of lying about doing so may be taken to school by the parents, watched carefully at school by the teacher, have weekly meetings with a caseworker, and be taken home by another member of the TOUGHLOVE group. The community pulls together to try to help the parents control their child's negative behavior. The emphasis is not on blaming anyone but on correcting the behavior problem. There are more than 1500 chapters of TOUGHLOVE in the United States and other countries. Information about a chapter in your community can be obtained from the co-founders of TOUGHLOVE, David and Phyllis York, (P.O. Box 1069; Doylestown, PA 18901; 215/348–7090.

---

engaging in active listening, using "I messages," and resolving conflicts through mutual negotiation. An example of environmental management is putting breakables out of reach of young children. Rather than worry about how to teach children not to touch breakable nik-naks, it may be easier to simply move them out of their reach.

The use of active listening becomes increasingly important as the child gets older. When Joanna is upset with her teacher, it is better for the parent to reflect the child's thoughts than to take sides with her. Saying "You're angry that Mrs. Jones made the whole class miss play period because Becky was chewing gum," rather than saying "Mrs. Jones was unfair and should not have made the whole class miss play period," shows empathy with the child without blaming the teacher.

Gordon also suggested using "I" rather than "you" messages. Parents are encouraged to say "I get upset when you're late and don't call," rather than "You're an insensitive, irresponsible kid for not calling me when you said you would." The former avoids damaging the child's self-concept but still encourages the desired behavior.

Gordon's fourth suggestion for parenting is the no-lose method of resolving conflicts. He rejects the use of power by parent or child. In the authoritarian home, the parent dictates what the child is to do and the child is expected to obey. In such a system, the parent wins and the child loses. At the other extreme is the permissive home, in which the child wins and the parent loses. The alternative, recommended by Gordon, is for the parent and the child to seek a solution that is acceptable to both and to keep trying until they find one. In this way, neither parent nor child loses and both win.

Criticisms of the Parent Effectiveness Training Approach   Although much is commendable about PET, parents may have problems with two of Gordon's suggestions. First, he recommended that because older children have a right to their own values, parents should not interfere with their dress, career plans, and sexual behavior. Some parents may feel they do have a right (and an obligation) to "interfere."

Second, the no-lose method of resolving conflict is sometimes unrealistic. Suppose a 16-year-old wants to spend the weekend at the beach with her boyfriend and her parents do not want her to do so. Gordon says to negotiate until a decision is reached that is acceptable to both. But what if neither the parents nor the daughter can suggest a compromise or shift their position? The specifics of how to resolve a particular situation are not always clear.

Socioteleological Approach

Alfred Adler, a physician and former student of Sigmund Freud, saw a parallel between psychological and physiological development. When a person loses her or his sight, the other senses (hearing, touch, taste) become more sensitive—they compensate for the loss. According to Adler, the same phenomenon occurs in the psychological realm. When individuals feel inferior in one area, they will strive to compensate and become superior in another. Rudolph Dreikurs, a student of Adler, has developed an approach to childrearing that alerts parents as to how their children might be trying to compensate for feelings of inferiority. Dreikurs's suggestions are based on Adler's theory.

Basic Perspective   According to Adler, it is understandable that most children feel they are inferior and weak. From the child's point of view, the world is filled with strong giants who tower above him or her. Because children feel powerless in the face of adult superiority, they try to compensate by gaining attention (making noise, becoming disruptive), exerting power (becoming

> If you have never been hated by your child, you have never been a parent.
>
> BETTE DAVIS

aggressive, hostile), seeking revenge (becoming violent, hurting others), and acting inadequate (giving up, not trying). Adler suggested that such misbehavior is evidence that the child is discouraged or feels insecure about her or his place in the family. The term *socioteleological* refers to social striving or seeking a social goal—in the child's case, the goal of a secure place within the family.

Considerations for Childrearing   When parents observe misbehavior in their children, they should recognize it as an attempt to find security. According to Dreikurs, parents should not fall into playing the child's game by, say, responding to a child's disruptiveness with anger, but should encourage the child, hold regular family meetings, and let natural consequences occur. To encourage the child, the parents should be willing to let the child make mistakes. If John wants to help Dad carry logs to the fireplace, rather than Dad saying "You're too small to carry the logs," John should be allowed to try and encouraged to carry the size limb or stick that he can manage. Furthermore, Dad should praise John for his helpfulness.

Along with constant encouragement, the child should be included in a weekly family meeting. During this meeting, such family issues as bedtimes, the appropriateness of between-meal snacks, assignment of chores, and family fun are discussed. The meeting is democratic; each family member has a vote. Such participation in family decision making is designed to enhance the self-concept of each child.

Finally, Dreikurs suggested that the parents let natural consequences occur for their child's behavior. If a daughter misses the school bus, she walks or is charged "taxi fare" out of her allowance. If she won't wear a coat and boots, she gets cold and wet. Of course, parents are to arrange suitable consequences when natural consequences will not occur or would be dangerous if they did. For example, if a child leaves the video games on the living room floor, they could be taken away for a week.

Criticisms of the Socioteleological Approach   The socioteleological approach to childrearing has been criticized because it lacks supportive empirical research and is occasionally impractical. It is fair to say that some of the other childrearing approaches already discussed also lack solid empirical support.

The impracticality of the socioteleological approach is sometimes illustrated by letting children take the natural consequences of their action. This may be an effective childrearing procedure for most behaviors, but it can backfire. Letting children develop sore throats in the hope that it will teach them the importance of wearing a raincoat in the rain is questionable.

Reality Therapy Approach

Based on the work of William Glasser and his parent involvement program (PIP), the *reality therapy* approach to childrearing focuses on the developing child and teenager.

> Children are more likely to live up to what you believe of them.
>
> LADY BIRD JOHNSON

Basic Perspective Glasser suggested that the young child is irrationally narcissistic, emotionally precocious, and incapable of coping with frustration and stress. These qualities cause the behavioral problems children exhibit—from not cleaning their rooms to taking drugs. By irrational narcissism, Glasser means the child is completely self-centered and views everything in terms of "what's in it for me." Emotional precociousness means that the child is insensitive to the needs of others and seeks to manipulate others' emotions to serve the child's own ends. According to Glasser, the child's greatest character flaw is not being able to cope with stress and quitting rather than working through a problem. Children do not have the confidence in themselves to figure out what to do when something goes wrong or the perseverance to make a bad situation better.

Television is the villain behind these flaws. The hours children spend in front of this "mindless tube," according to Glasser, are destructive—not because the content of television is so awful, but because children are not using this time to interact with others, to develop social skills, and to learn about life by experiencing it. They are living vicariously.

Considerations for Childrearing Glasser suggested that nothing parents can do for their children is more valuable than spending time with them. This communicates to children that they are loved and valued, which is a prerequisite for developing their confidence to persevere in spite of setbacks. Spending time with children also helps them to learn social skills, to learn another person's point of view, and to learn to share with others. Participation in family rituals, such as religious holidays, birthdays, vacations, and Sunday dinner, may help to bond family members to each other.

The reality therapy approach to childrearing emphasizes the right of children to make their own choices. Parents are urged to give children responsibility for their choices and to let them take the consequences. This principle is similar to the Adlerian principle of natural consequences. "My child has a right to fail in school," said one parent. This viewpoint acknowledges that only the child can decide what course of action to take (for example, whether to study or not) and that accepting the consequences for decisions is an effective way of learning how to make decisions.

Criticisms of the Reality Therapy Approach Like most childrearing approaches, the reality therapy approach looks good on paper. Spending time with children, giving children the right to make their own decisions, and letting natural consequences follow are suggestions with which parents might find it easy to agree. However, the basic premise of the reality therapy approach is that the love relationship between the parent and the child is the critical variable that determines the way the child turns out. This premise is suspect. One parent said:

> I've spent half my life with my son, including regular fishing trips when he was a small boy and working with him in Scouts when he was older. His teacher

> In bringing up children, spend on them half as much money and twice as much time.
>
> LAURENCE PETER

told me the reason he is doing poorly in school is because I haven't spent enough time with him to show my love for him. Baloney! (Author's files)

Children are subject to a wide variety of influences, and parent behavior—regardless of how loving or stable it is—is only one aspect of the child's socialization.

In addition, as with the socioteleological approach, some parents may have a difficult time standing by waiting for children to learn from their own decisions. For example, does a parent allow a 15-year-old to buy a motorcycle and learn through experience that turning curves too fast can cost a leg? Does a parent permit his or her child to be unconcerned about grades to the point of not being able to graduate?

Although you may not adhere to any one particular approach to childrearing, you probably do have a perspective on the permissiveness or strictness of child discipline. The Child Discipline Scale in the Self-Assessment is designed to help you identify this perspective.

❧ Principles of Effective Parenting

Most people have an awareness of what constitutes effective parenting. Most undergraduate students are aware that clear communication and active listening with one's child are important parenting skills (Dickson & Dukes, 1992). Other principles of effective parenting include providing praise, discipline, security, and encouraging responsibility.

Provide Praise

Since children first depend on their parents for the development of their self-concept, it is important that parents regularly praise them. "Catch your children doing good" is a favorite phrase of child development experts. The effect is to create good feelings that the child has about himself or herself. Renowned family therapist Virginia Satir (1972) noted over twenty years ago the importance of having a positive sense of self-worth or self-esteem.

> . . . the crucial factor in what happens both inside people and between people is the picture of individual worth that people have of themselves. . . . Integrity, honesty, responsibility, compassion, love—all flow easily from the person who has high self-esteem or self-worth (p. 22).

Feelings of worth can only flourish in an atmosphere where individual differences are appreciated, mistakes are tolerated, communication is open, and the rules are flexible—the kind of atmosphere that is found in a nurturing family.

VIRGINIA SATIR

A child is fed with milk and praise.

MARY LAMB

CONSIDERATION

Two researchers emphasized a potential hazard of having a high sense of self-esteem. Unless one's positive self-feelings are based on "emotional connec

(continued on page 586)

SELF-ASSESSMENT ∿
Child Discipline Scale

This scale is designed to measure the degree to which you have a strict or a permissive view of disciplining children. There are no right or wrong answers. After reading each sentence carefully, circle the number that best represents your feelings.

1 Strongly disagree   4 Mildly agree
2 Mildly disagree   5 Strongly agree
3 Undecided

	SD	MD	U	MA	SA
1. Parents should not insist that their children be obedient.	1	2	3	4	5
2. The idea that children should be seen but not heard is archaic.	1	2	3	4	5
3. Children develop best when you let them do what they want.	1	2	3	4	5
4. If you are too strict with your children, you hamper their development.	1	2	3	4	5
5. A whipping is never acceptable.	1	2	3	4	5
6. Children usually respond better (change their behavior) to talking than to physical punishment.	1	2	3	4	5
7. If you love your children you will avoid physical punishment.	1	2	3	4	5
8. It is not important that a child's room be clean.	1	2	3	4	5
9. Parents should relax and let children use the house to enjoy themselves.	1	2	3	4	5
10. A parent can be successful even though his or her children are not particularly obedient.	1	2	3	4	5
11. "Spare the rod and spoil the child" is not a particularly effective way to rear children.	1	2	3	4	5
12. It is better for your children to view you as a friend than as an authority.	1	2	3	4	5

	SD	MD	U	MA	SA
13. It is better to be permissive than strict with children.	1	2	3	4	5
14. To be creative and free are more important qualities than to be obedient.	1	2	3	4	5
15. It is good for children to ask their parents why rather than to be blindly obedient.	1	2	3	4	5
16. It is not necessary to be strict with your children in order for them to respect you.	1	2	3	4	5
17. It is better to place a child in "time out" than to spank him/her for misbehavior.	1	2	3	4	5
18. Parents should always talk with their children about misbehavior before punishing them.	1	2	3	4	5
19. It is worse for children if their parents have strict requirements for their behavior than if the parents are easygoing about their expectations.	1	2	3	4	5
20. Children should not be required to perform chores.	1	2	3	4	5

Score: _____

Scoring: Add the numbers you circled. The response that suggests a permissive view of discipline is 5 (strongly agree), and the response that suggests a strict view of discipline is 1 (strongly disagree). Therefore, the higher your total score (100 is the highest possible score), the more permissive you are in your beliefs about childrearing and the lower your total score (20 is the lowest possible score), the more strict you are in your childrearing beliefs. A score of 60 places you at the midpoint between the extremes. *Note: This Self-Assessment is designed to be thought provoking; it is not intended as a clinical evaluation device.*

One of the most important principles of effective parenting is for parents to spend time with their children.

tions" to others in one's family, self-esteem may be expressed as "greater selfishness and excessive individualism" (Burr & Christensen, 1992, 464, 462). They suggested that high positive self-esteem, which develops from strong emotional connections with others, is the most healthy variety of self-esteem. From this perspective, praising children to make them feel good about themselves is valuable only in the sense that it endears them to family members who encourage them.

Discipline Inappropriate Behavior

Nurturing parents see themselves as leaders, not bosses.

VIRGINIA SATIR

Better a little chiding than a great deal of heartbreak.

SHAKESPEARE

While selectively looking for opportunities to praise children with the goal of engendering positive feelings of self-worth, parents also must provide limits to children's behavior. This sometimes involves punishing negative behavior. Unless parents provide negative consequences for lying, stealing, and hitting, children can grow up to be dishonest, to steal, and to be inappropriately aggressive. Time out, or removing the child from being with others to a place of isolation for one minute for each year old the child is, has been shown to be an effective means of consequating inappropriate behavior. Withdrawal of privileges (watching television, playing with friends) is also effective. (Physical punishment is less effective in reducing the negative behavior, teaches the child to be aggressive, and encourages negative emotional feelings toward the parents. This issue is further examined in the Choices section at the end of this chapter.) When using time out or the withdrawal of privileges, parents should make it clear that they disapprove of the child's behavior, not the child.

CONSIDERATION

Although providing negative consequences for inappropriate behavior is important, it is more important to notice and give attention to the prosocial behavior. Rather than looking for and punishing lying, stealing, and aggressiveness, it is often more effective to look for and comment on telling the truth, being honest, and negotiating rather than becoming aggressive.

Provide Security

In the "Peanuts" comic strip, Linus and his blanket have come to symbolize the need for security, order, and stability. Predictable responses from parents, a familiar bedroom or playroom, and an established routine help to encourage a feeling of security in children. Such a feeling provides them with the needed self-assurance to venture beyond the family. If the outside world becomes too frightening or difficult, a child can return to the safety of the family for support. Knowing it is always possible to return to an accepting environment enables a child to become more involved gradually with the world beyond the family.

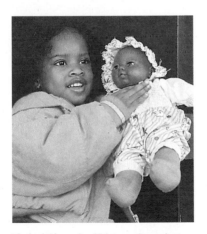

Black children should be taught pride in their color and in their racial heritage.

CONSIDERATION

Black parents sometimes encounter unique issues in providing a feeling of security for their children. Growing up in a racist society may engender feelings of insecurity if black children are not taught to view black as beautiful, to confront racism appropriately, and to be proud of their racial heritage. These and other concerns are addressed in the new book *Raising Black Children* (Comer & Poussaint, 1993).

Encourage Responsibility

Giving children increased responsibility encourages the autonomy and independence necessary to be assertive and independent. Giving children more responsibility as they grow older can take the form of encouraging them to choose healthy snacks, what to wear, and when to return from playing with a friend (of course, the parents should praise appropriate choices). Children not given more control and responsibility for their own lives remain dependent on others. Successful parents may be defined in terms of their ability to rear children who can function as independent adults. One way to ensure such success is to give children increasing responsibility that is age appropriate as they get older.

I want my children to make their own choices.

MICHAEL JORDAN

&ptitle; Conflicts Between Parents and Teenagers

All grown-ups were once children, although few of them remember it.

ANTOINE DE SAINT–EXUPERY

Conflicts between parents and children may increase during adolescence as teenagers spend more money and strive for independence. In regard to money, 15 to 17 year olds spend $43 per week in contrast to 9 to 11 year olds who spend $4.80 per week (Stipp, 1993). However, an increase in parent-child conflict is not inevitable during the teenage years. Based on a study of mothers, fathers, and adolescents in 80 families, the researchers observed no increase in conflict during early adolescence (Galambos & Almeida, 1992). Below are several suggestions for keeping conflicts with teenagers at a low level.

Treat people as if they were what they ought to be and you help them become what they are capable of being.

GOETHE

1. Catch them doing what you like rather than criticizing them for what you don't like. Adolescents are like everyone else—they don't like to be criticized but do like to be noticed for what they do that is good.
2. Ignore some things. One adult said that when he was 13, he stayed up late, stole one of his father's cigarettes, and smoked it while watching television. Although he thought that his father was asleep, he was surprised by his father who walked into the room where he was smoking. When his father saw his teenager smoking, he said nothing, turned around, and went back to bed. The father never spoke of the incident. The effect on the adolescent was to feel the tolerance for experimentation from his father that he wanted. After finishing the cigarette, he never smoked again.
3. Provide information rather than answers. When teens are confronted with a problem try to avoid making a decision for them. Rather, it is helpful to provide information on which they may base a decision. What courses to take in high school and what college to apply for are decisions that should be made primarily by the adolescent. The role of the parent might best be that of providing information or helping the teenager obtain information.
4. Be tolerant of high activity levels. Some teenagers are constantly listening to loud music, going to each other's homes, and talking on the telephone for long periods of time. Parents often want to sit in their easy chair and be quiet. Recognizing that it is not realistic to expect teenagers to be quiet and sedentary may be helpful in tolerating their disruptions.
5. Engage in some activity with your teenagers. Whether it is renting a video, eating a pizza, or taking a camping trip, it is important to structure enjoyable activities with your teenagers. Such activities permit a context in which to communicate with them. One parent goes on a three-day hiking/camping trip with each of his three children every summer. "It gives us an opportunity to connect," he noted.

Responding to Teenage Drug Abuse

One of the fears of today's parents is that their teenager will abuse drugs.

NATIONAL DATA ❧ Forty-six, 13, and 2 percent of individuals age 12 to 17 reported that they have used alcohol, marijuana, and cocaine respectively in the past. Twenty, 4, and less than .4 percent reported that they currently use alcohol, marijuana, and cocaine (*Statistical Abstract of the United States: 1993*, Table 208).

In a study of 169 resident students at a northeastern university, 88 percent, 25 percent, and 5 percent reported that it was acceptable to use alcohol, marijuana, and cocaine respectively when attending a party with friends (McCormack et. al., 1993).

Various factors associated with the use of drugs include peers who use drugs, low self esteem, alcoholic parents, poor relations with parents, poor school performance, low IQ, inadequate moral development, and being male (Carpenter et al., 1988; McCormack et al., 1993). For the drug abuser, the use of drugs or alcohol ultimately causes a problem in all areas of life—health, school, work, home, and social relationships. Parents *can* help to prevent their son or daughter from abusing drugs. If their prevention efforts fail, however, they should be ready to respond.

One of the greatest fears of parents is that their teenagers will drink and drive.

Drug Prevention: The Best Medicine

It is easier to do everything possible to ensure that your teenager does not begin to use drugs than it is to try to stop the drug use once it has begun. Some specific things parents can do to discourage drug abuse in their teenagers have been recommended by Louis Meador, a drug therapist and educator who has worked with teenagers and their families.

Be a Good Example   Parents who come home from their jobs and drink liquor until bedtime are teaching their children that alcohol is used to relieve stress—the more alcohol, the better. Regardless of what you say, your children will attend to what you do.

Just as getting drunk models abuse of alcohol, moderate use of alcohol models drinking control. Children who are reared in homes in which their parents drink alcohol in moderation are most likely to avoid becoming alcoholics. On the other hand, children who are reared in homes in which one or both parents abuse alcohol or in homes in which alcohol is forbidden are most likely to become alcoholics. An alcoholic from a nondrinking home said, "My folks made a big thing out of never drinking alcohol and told me I was never to do it. I rebelled against them, starting drinking at 17, and haven't quit" (Author's files).

Parents who use marijuana, cocaine, or other illegal drugs serve as role models for teenagers to use these same drugs. If your goal is for your child not to use any of these drugs, you should not use them yourself. To do so is to teach your child that drug use is acceptable behavior. And your saying "I'm older and know what I'm doing" won't mean much to your teenager.

Misuse of prescription drugs carries the same caveat. Although your physician may have prescribed tranquilizers to relieve stress, taking more than

The main problem with teenagers is that they're just like their parents were at their age.

E.C. MCKENZIE

the recommended dosage is similar to drinking more than a couple of cocktails or beers. If your children see you taking aspirin for a headache, valium for your nerves, and Dalmane to sleep, the message is clear—drugs are the answer to pain, stress, and insomnia.

There may also be a genetic link to the potential to abuse drugs. Individuals whose parents, grandparents, or siblings have a history of substance abuse or major depression are much more likely to abuse drugs themselves.

CONSIDERATION

Some parents who once abused drugs but no longer do so wonder if they should tell their teenager of their earlier drug use. Two issues are at stake in such a situation. One, is it appropriate to lie to your teenager under any conditions? And two, what impact will the knowledge of your drug use have on your teenager's drug use? In regard to the first issue, one parent said that she "would never lie to her child because she would lose faith in me." But another parent said, "Everybody lies about something, and there may be some good reasons to lie to your kids about drugs." One of these "good" reasons follows:

> If you tell your children that you use or have used drugs, they may use the fact that you did to justify their doing so. And while you may be able to handle marijuana or cocaine or whatever, your teenager may not be able to do so. People have different biochemical makeups, and the drug a parent may not get addicted to the child might. So think carefully before you tell your children that you use or have used drugs. The drug may have an entirely different (and possibly addictive) effect on them.

An alternate perspective is to tell the truth. If you have used drugs, say so but explain the context of your doing so, the hazards, and the reasons you feel it is unwise to take drugs.

Consult a Professional Drug Abuse Counselor   Drug abuse can be a difficult family problem, and there are no quick and easy solutions. Family therapy, in which the whole family is involved, is the treatment of choice when drug abuse surfaces. In addition, individual therapy for the abuser is indicated and should focus on teaching the adolescent to cope with the stress of life without drugs as well as how to say no to friends who offer drugs. Improving the adolescent's self-esteem should also be a focus of therapy (Rosenberg et al., 1989). Both family and individual treatment are available through local mental health centers.

Keep Communication Channels Open   Teenagers who are troubled about school, work, and social relationships are more vulnerable to drug use than teenagers who make good grades, enjoy their after-school jobs, and have

The most difficult thing of all, to keep quiet and listen.

AULUS GELLIUS

meaningful social relationships. The best way for parents to recognize that their teenager is becoming despondent is to keep the channels of communication open.

Open communication translates into less drug use. Children who enjoy their parents' approval are less likely to do something (drink, take drugs) if they know their parents will disapprove of the action. Good communication does not eliminate the possibility that children will drink or take drugs, but it does reduce the chance that they will. Parents can learn how to listen reflectively, respond empathetically, and help their children make wise decisions (Tebes et al., 1989). Training seminars designed to teach parents these skills are sometimes offered in local mental health centers.

When Drug Abuse Is Already Happening

A parent who becomes aware that a son or daughter is already involved in drugs should assess the situation. Drinking a beer at a party is not the same as getting drunk before school; taking a draw on a marijuana cigarette is not the same as having a bag of dope in a sock drawer. The parent should be careful not to overrespond to the smell of alcohol or something different from cigarette smoke in a child's room, for example. It is appropriate to ask, "What do I smell?" rather than accuse a son or daughter of drinking alcohol or smoking marijuana.

Assuming that the teenager admits to having had a beer or smoked some "dope," the parents' response will differ depending on their values. Some parents absolutely abhor the use of any alcohol or dugs; in these cases, they may tell the teenager this is completely unacceptable behavior, withdraw privileges ("you can't have the car for a month"), and encourage the teenager to recognize that alcohol and marijuana are drugs that should be left alone.

Some parents are more liberal and feel that controlled drug use is acceptable. "I've been using drugs since I was 18," said one 50-year-old parent. "And I've never missed a day at work. Nor has my efficiency dropped one iota. I am just very careful in terms of what drugs I take, how much, how often, and in what context. I think these are the more important issues."

If, however, a teenager has gone overboard and becomes a drug abuser (drugs are affecting his or her health, grades, and social relationships), the following steps, directed toward the parent, are indicated.

Confront Your Teenager Armed with evidence (the teenager is drunk or in possession of a bag of dope, a container of cocaine, pills, or some other drug), make your teenager aware that you know of the drug use. Cutting through your teenager's denial that he or she uses drugs is difficult but important for both teenager and parent.

Ask for Your Teenagers' Point of View   Be careful not to criticize or belittle your teenager, but ask for an explanation of why he or she drinks, smokes, snorts, or whatever. It is not unusual for teenagers to feel very guilty about what they are doing; once confronted by their parents, some teenagers are anxious to stop. "I drifted in over my head," said one teenager to her parents, "and I really am sick of it and want to stop."

No matter how much kids resent authority, they resent even more being left with none at all.

ART LINKLETTER

Make an Agreement   One alternative is to make it clear to your child that you will not tolerate drug use. One parent told her 16-year-old:

> Your father and I know that you get tired of us butting into your life. But we feel that drugs can harm you, and we ask that you stop as long as you are living with us. To ensure that you are not using drugs, we want you to have your urine analyzed weekly. If Steve Howe, the two-million dollar pitcher for the New York Yankees, can have his urine tested every other day to help him remain clear of drugs, this may also be helpful for you. If we discover that you are still using drugs, we will send you to an in-patient drug rehabilitation center.

CONSIDERATION

Parents who monitor where their adolescents are and what they are doing have fewer problems with adolescent drinking and delinquency. Such monitoring in conjunction with making it clear to the adolescents that they are loved, valued, and accepted is particularly predictive of fewer such problems (Barnes & Farrell, 1992).

Single employed parents often have more difficulty monitoring their children; thus, children of single employed parents are more likely to use marijuana and participate in serious illegal activity (Haurin, 1992). Such parents might consider forming a network with other families to help monitor their children.

Support Groups   Former drug abusers meet weekly in local chapters of Narcotics Anonymous (NA), patterned after Alcoholics Anonymous, to help each other continue to be drug-free. The premise of NA is that the best person to help someone who is abusing drugs is someone who once abused drugs. NA members of all ages, social classes, and educational levels provide a sense of support for each other to remain drug-free.

If the substance-abuse problem is alcohol, Alcoholics Anonymous (AA), is an appropriate support group (national headquarters mailing address: AA General Service Office, P.O. Box 459, Grand Central Station, New York, NY 10017). There are over 15,000 AA chapters nationwide; the one in your community can be contacted by looking in the Yellow Pages of your local telephone directory. Al-Anon is an organization that provides support for family members of drug abusers. Such support is often helpful to parents coping with a teenage drug abuser.

Other Issues Concerning Parents

Getting children to avoid abusing drugs is only one of many issues that concern most parents. Other issues include death of a child, teenage suicide, day care, teenage sexuality, and children leaving home.

Death of a Child

The number of infant deaths is shocking and the event is devastating.

NATIONAL DATA Over 38,000 infants under one year of age die annually (National Center for Health Statistics, 1993).

The four leading causes of infant death are congenital anomalies, sudden infant death syndrome, disorders relating to short gestation and unspecified low birthweight, and respiratory distress syndrome.

Of the death of her baby, one mother wrote:

> When Thomas died at the age of seven months, he died a baby—a very lovable, cuddly baby. The crisis of his death stripped away our coping skills. . . . In a heartbeat, we had become a bereaved family. Once again, our emotions took roller-coaster rides. . . . In the aftermath of intense grief, new values emerged. No, I would never have chosen this way, but I want to survive. Desire to survive is the necessary ingredient for healing to begin (Farnsworth, 1988, 1).

Adjusting to the death of one's child involves a similar pattern to adjusting to the death of any person we love. The typical sequence involves denial, intense grief, followed by anger, numbness and mourning, followed by recognition that life must go on, followed by a new level of functioning. Waves of grief may still return on the anniversary of the death, on the birthday, and on other special occasions. Over time, the wounds may heal but are never forgotten.

> Somewhere in my journey, I became aware of my choices. I could spend the rest of my days bitter and angry over my plight. Or I could choose to forgive life, to remember that I am not the only one who has had pain. In forgiving, I opened the door to life and love and new possibilities. I feel rich again (Farnsworth, 1988, 60).

In the grieving process, men may heal more quickly than women. Based on a study of 33 couples who had experienced the death of a child, the researcher (Bohannon, 1990) observed that husbands generally experienced lower levels of grief intensity than did their wives and that these levels were consistently lower across time.

Death surprises us in the midst of our Hopes.

THOMAS FULLER

The life of the dead is placed in the memory of the living.

CICERO

Teenage Suicide

While death of an infant or young child is devastating (among other reasons because the infant or child is viewed as being helpless), death by suicide (equally as devastating) involves choice and ensuing guilt feelings on the part of the parents of "what did we do wrong?"

NATIONAL DATA ◊ Among U.S. teenagers, white males between the ages of 15 and 19 are the most vulnerable to suicide with 19.4 per 100,000 population committing suicide. In contrast, 10.3 black males per 100,000 commit suicide. The corresponding figures for white and black females are 4.5 and 2.3 per 100,000. The highest suicide rates are among those over 85 years of age—71.9 white males per 100,000 population. (*Statistical Abstract of the United States, 1992*, Table 125).

Since adolescence is a particularly turbulent time, parents might be aware of the danger signs that suggest the adolescent is becoming suicidal. These signs include:

- Adolescent is withdrawn for long periods of time and shows no interest in social interaction. The adolescent has few or no friends.
- Adolescent abuses alcohol or drugs. He or she frequently gets "high."
- Adolescent has no respect for authority—parents, teachers, or police.
- Adolescent engages in indiscriminate sex with numerous sexual partners. No emotional bonds are established with sexual partners.

These signs suggest the need for communication from the parents to the child about his or her behavior, thoughts, and emotional state. This may be done directly or in the context of family therapy. In those cases where the adolescent has the potential to harm him or herself, the adolescent may need to be hospitalized.

But life, being weary of these worldy bars, Never lacks power to dismiss itself.

SHAKESPEARE

Day Care

Many parents are concerned about who will take care of their children when both parents are earning an income. Day care is defined as any of the many different types of arrangements that are used to provide supervision and care to children when the parents are unable to do so. For the employed mother, the care of her child in her absence is of critical and primary concern. Over half (54.1 percent) of new mothers in one study reported, "I worry about using day care for my baby" (Shuster, 1993). Fathers are also concerned about the day care their children receive. A study of 37 first time fathers with a working spouse and an infant 4–5 months who had been in day care at least a month revealed that 22 percent were worried that their baby was not safe in day care. Over half (55 percent) were not satisfied with their opportunities to work part time and about one third (32 percent) were dissatisfied with their parental leave time (Shuster, 1992).

NATIONAL DATA ❧ Of the more than 9 million U.S. children under the age of 5 whose mothers are employed outside the home, 31 percent are cared for in a home other than their own, 30 percent are cared for by relatives in their own home, and 30 percent are taken care of by an organized day care facility (*Statistical Abstract of the United States: 1993*, Table 610).

When the child is age two and under, the preferred day care arrangements are (in order of preference) the parent takes care of the child in the home (68 percent), the child is taken to someone else's home other than a family member (13 percent), the child is taken care of by a member of the extended family, usually a grandmother (9 percent), and the child is taken care of by a sitter, friend, or neighbor (5 percent). Only five percent at this age are taken to a day care center (Caruso, 1992). These data are based on responses from 476 parents of two-year-olds who live in four Connecticut communities.

Employed parents are concerned that their children get good quality care. Friends are most often consulted to recommend a day care facility. Priorities in day care selection include health and safety issues, caregiver quality, and child's social and educational development (Bradbard et. al., 1992).

State licensing regulations of day care centers are supposed to provide a "floor of quality" for day care programs. However, these regulations often fall short of recommended standards (Teleki, Snow, & Reguero de Atiles, 1992).

CONSIDERATION

Before enrolling their child in a daycare facility, parents might ask: What are the licensing requirements in the state in which the facility is located and is the license current? Are the caregivers educated in child psychology and development and/or early childhood education? Is there 35 square feet of space per child indoors and 75 square feet per child in outside areas? Does the center take care of sick children? Is a pediatric nurse practitioner or pediatrician on call at all times? What is the ratio of children to staff for the respective age groups? The ratio *recommended* by the National Association of Pediatric Nurse Associates and Practitioners follows (McGuire, 1989):

Infants to 18 months	4:1
18 months to 2 years	5:1
2–3 years	8:1
3–4 years	10:1
5–6 years	15:1
7 years and older	20:1

These recommended ratios are usually not followed. For example, in Louisiana the ratio of infants to 18 months and staff is 8:1.

What are the effects of day care on children? While the data are inconsistent, it seems that day care does not necessarily adversely affect the infant-mother bond and tends to facilitate positive preschool social behavior (Field et al., 1988). The risks are highest for infants in day care for more than 20 hours a week during their first year. Parents are advised to be very selective about the day care they provide for their child during the first year (Belsky, 1988).

Some parents tire of traditional day care and hire an *au pair.* These are usually European women (age 18 to 25) who help with childcare duties 5½ days a week for one year in exchange for room and board and the right to attend classes in their spare time. About 1,000 *au pairs* enter the United States annually. *Au pair* means "on par," or "equal"—the hosts must be willing to treat them as part of the family. The popularity of *au pairs* has also resulted in the training and hiring of American-born nannies. Families with children under the age of 3 are particularly interested in hiring an *au pair* or a nanny. (See Childcare, Special Topic 4, in Resources and Organizations for more information.)

For parents who cannot afford day care, an *au pair,* or a nanny, help from the government is needed. The National Research Council of the National Academy of Sciences has recommended that the federal government and the states should expand subsidies to help make quality childcare available to low-income families. In addition, the Council recommended that the federal government should require employers to provide unpaid, job-protected leave for parents of infants under age one.

Teenage Sexuality

Since pregnancy and contracting HIV or other STDs are realistic possibilities for anyone who is sexually active, parents are concerned about the sexuality of their teenagers.

NATIONAL DATA   Based on data from the National Research Council (1987), by age 20, 83 percent of males and 74 percent of females report that they are "sexually active."

In a sample of 883 adolescents, Thornton (1990) found that at age 16, 37 percent of males and 19 percent of females had experienced sexual intercourse. At age 17, the percentage of males and females who had experienced intercourse were 54 and 38, respectively.

Parents cope with their anxiety by denial ("My teenager doesn't have sex"), by passivity ("My teenager may be having sex but knows what to do"), or by education. The latter involves talking with their teenager about HIV and other STDs, providing condoms and contraception, or making an appointment (for the teenager) with a health care provider who will provide the information.

Children Leaving Home: The Empty Nest Syndrome

While researchers disagree on the definition of the *empty nest,* this term typically refers to the period when the children have left home (for college, marriage, or work) and the spouses are alone as they were before the children were born. The children's leaving is usually a gradual process and is associated with their emotional and economic independence (Barber, 1989).

While marital happiness increases when children leave home (White & Edwards, 1990), most parents have mixed emotions about their children leaving home. Having an "empty nest" means relief from the relentless responsibility of caring for children, more privacy, and freedom to do as one wishes. But to many parents, an empty nest also creates feelings of sadness over not having spent enough time with their children, loneliness, and worry about how the children are doing.

The degree to which parents have negative feelings about their children leaving home is related to the degree of investment in the parental role. Women who have been full-time mothers with no external career may experience the greatest impact. But fathers who are emotionally close to their children may also experience a deep sense of loss. Barber (1989) noted, "There is little support for the notion that the empty nest syndrome is widespread or pertains solely to women" (p. 20).

There may be ethnic differences in the empty nest syndrome. Blacks and Mexican American women in traditional families may experience the syndrome to a lesser degree because they usually have economic roles outside the family. In addition, their large extended family system results in an overlap between the rearing of their own children and the rearing of grandchildren.

I'm going to clean this dump—just as soon as the kids are grown.
ERMA BOMBECK

Being a mother is what I think has made me the person I am.
JACQUELINE KENNEDY ONASSIS

❧ Trends

New parents will continue to enter their childrearing role more or less naively; most couples wait until they have a child to begin talking about their concerns about the childrearing role. Of course, no one book, lecture, or course can adequately prepare a person for what it means to rear a child. Those who have had a great deal of responsibility for the care of younger siblings probably have a better idea than most.

Although some European countries (Sweden) have day care centers operated by the state, such a government funded day care program in the United States is not likely. Not only are owners of private day care centers against the government becoming a competitor for low-cost day care, conservative right wing individuals feel that mothers should stay in the home and rear their children. Some contend that day care centers would encourage more women to work outside the home, which would further weaken the American family.

❧ CHOICES ❧

---

*P*arents are faced with innumerable choices in rearing their children. These include which type of punishment to use, whether to reward positive behavior, how much freedom to give how soon, and how long to allow children to continue to live at home.

Which Type of Punishment Is Best?

Parents who adopt the behavioral approach to childrearing believe that to learn appropriate behavior, children must be rewarded for certain behaviors and punished for others. Although parents may agree that praise and privileges are ways of rewarding children for positive behavior, they may choose different forms of punishment.

Some parents have the "spare the rod, and spoil the child" philosophy and inflict physical pain on their children as punishment (Greer, 1986). Examples of such punishment include being beaten on the buttocks with a belt or leather strap, being whipped on the legs, buttocks, and back with a switch, and being slapped or knocked down. One parent said, "If you don't give them a good beating now and then, they forget who's boss and they don't mind you."

Other parents feel that corporal punishment is unnecessary or wrong and elect to put their children in "time out" (removing the child to a place of isolation) or to withhold privileges for inappropriate behavior:

> When my 6-year-old says 'Nah' rather than polite 'No' or 'No ma'am,' I tell her to go to the bathroom. She knows that means she is being punished for being disrespectful. For her brother who didn't get home until 1:30 a.m., when he was supposed to be in at midnight, I took the car away from him for two weeks.

The decision to choose a corporal or noncorporal method of punishment should be based on the consequences of use. In general, the use of "time out" and withholding of privileges seem to be as effective in stopping undesirable behavior as corporal punishment.

Beatings and whippings will also temporarily decrease the negative verbal and nonverbal behaviors, but there are major side effects. First, punishing children by inflicting violence teaches them that it is okay to physically hurt someone you love. Hence, parents may be inadvertently teaching their child to use violence in the family. Second, parents who beat their children should be aware that they are teaching their children to fear and to avoid them (the parents). Third, children who grow up in homes in which corporal punishment is used are more likely to be aggressive and disobedient (Kandel, 1990). Aware of the negative consequences of corporal punishment of children, it is against the law in Sweden for parents to spank their children.

Increasingly, parents are becoming aware of the positive benefits of the use of noncorporal methods of punishment. Both parents who had abused their children and a control group who had not abused their children reported that the use of "time out" was more acceptable than spanking (Kelley et al., 1990).

To Reward or Not Reward Positive Behavior?

Most parents agree that some form of punishment is necessary to curb a child's inappropriate behavior, but there is disagreement over whether positive behavior (taking out the trash, cleaning up one's room, making good grades) should be rewarded by praise, extra privileges, or money. Some parents feel that a child should do the right things anyway and that to reward them is to bribe them. One parent said, "My kid is going to do what I say because I say so, not because I am going to give him something for doing it."

Other parents feel that both the child and the parent benefit when the parents reward the child for good behavior. Rewarding a child for a behavior will likely result in the child engaging in that behavior more often, so that the child develops a set of positive behaviors. The parents, in turn, feel good about the child.

❧ CHOICES ❧

Which Parenting Style?

There are several styles from which parents may choose in rearing their children:

Authoritarian. Parents demand obedience from their children and severely punish disobedience. Unless tempered with love and affection, children tend to resent this style of parenting.

Permissive-Indulgent. Parents allow their children to do as they please and give them things to make them happy. There is very little conflict because the children usually get their way. Some children lose respect for parents who allowed too much freedom.

Permissive-Neglecting. Unlike permissive-indulgent parents who know where their children are and what they are doing, permissive-neglecting parents are often unaware of the child's whereabouts or behavior. The parents are preoccupied with their own lives. Children growing up under this style often feel that they are not wanted.

Permissive-Firm. Parents give children the freedom to experience their world but put firm restrictions on the children. Children learn that they can explore their world, but within parentally prescribed limits. They experience both the trust of being allowed to explore and the affection of their parent's firmness.

How Long Should Children Live with Their Parents?

Over 30 percent of college freshmen in the United States live with their parents the first semester they are in college (American Council on Education and University of California, 1992). Their motivations are to save money, continue living in a stable environment, and avoid the psychological risk of going out on their own. In general, children live with their parents because they need to rather than because the parents need for them to (Ward & Spitze, 1992).

Given the choice, both parents and adult children prefer to live independently. However, when circumstances dictate that they live together, doing so does not generally have negative effects on parent-child relations. Such was the conclusion of Ward and Spitze (1992), who studied the co-residence patterns of 811 parents and their 2,358 children (aged 22+).

In another study, 609 middle-aged parents (mean age 51) who had children in their homes reported their satisfaction with the arrangement depended on the level of conflict (Aquilino & Supple, 1991). Those with high interpersonal conflict and low positive interaction (sometimes influenced by the unemployment and financial dependency of the offspring) reported the most negative feelings about the presence of adult children in their home. In addition, parents whose children returned home because of divorce or separation and those who brought grandchildren with them reported lower levels of parental satisfaction. In summarizing their findings, Aquilino and Supple (1991) noted:

> Co-residence does not lead inevitably to parental dissatisfaction with the living arrangement or to troubles in the parent-child relationship. A solid majority of parents in this sample indicated high levels of satisfaction with the adult child's presence in the home. Frequency of shared leisure time and enjoyable time was far greater than the frequency of open disagreements and arguing, especially among mothers and daughters (p. 25).

This study emphasizes the importance of parents and returning offspring making expectations clear about employment, financial arrangements, and parenting responsibilities prior to the return of the offspring into the familial unit. Since most parents report satisfaction, the return of children can be a life enriching challenge.

℘ Summary

Rearing children is one of the most demanding tasks an individual ever undertakes, and it requires that parents keep their role in perspective. Parenthood is only one stage in the person's marriage and life. In addition, parents are only one influence in the lives of their children; the joys and problems of childrearing change as the children mature; each child is different; and the goals of childrearing may differ. Some parents want obedient children; others want children who are independent and self-reliant.

Extensive folklore has arisen to make the role of parent more palatable to adults to encourage a commitment to childrearing. Would-be parents are led to believe that childrearing is fun, that good parents will produce good children, that love is enough for successful parenting, children will appreciate the sacrifices parents make for them, parenting comes naturally, and family values are easy to instill. These beliefs do not reflect the realities of parenthood.

There are a number of childrearing approaches to help parents with the problems of parenting. The developmental-maturational approach focuses on what the child will be able to do when and suggests that parents should not demand of children what they are developmentally unable to deliver. The behavioral approach assumes that behavior is learned and that parents can get their children to engage in the behavior they want by rewarding desirable behavior and punishing undesirable behavior. Parent effectiveness training focuses on the communication between parent and child and encourages the parents to negotiate with their children when conflicts occur. The socioteleological approach views the negative behavior of children as a result of feelings of inferiority and suggests regular family council meetings to give children a voice in what happens in the family. The reality therapy approach focuses on the necessity of letting children make their own choices and learning from them.

In addition to drug abuse, parents are also concerned about infant and childhood death, teenage suicide, quality day care, teenage sexuality and children leaving home.

New parents will continue to enter the parenting role naively. Since most parents work outside the home, they will become increasingly concerned about the government's role in national day care. The chance of a nationally funded day care program is low.

Questions for Reflection

1. Which childrearing approach appeals to you? Why?
2. How do you feel about putting your child in day care?
3. How do you feel about "spare the rod, and spoil the child" as a method of disciplining children?
4. As a parent, how would you respond to your teenager abusing drugs?

References

American Council on Education and University of California. The American freshman: National norms for fall, 1992. Los Angeles, Calif.: Los Angeles Higher Education Research Institute, 1992.

Aquilino, W. S. and K. R. Supple. Parent-child relations and parent's satisfaction with living arrangements when adult children live at home. *Journal of Marriage and the Family*, 1991, *53*, 13–27.

Barber, Clifton E. Transition to the empty nest. *Aging and the Family*, Stephen J. Bahr and Evan T. Peterson, eds. 1989, 15–32. New York: Free Press

Barnes, G. M. and M. P. Farrell. Parental support and control as predictors of adolescent drinking, delinquency, and related problem behaviors. *Journal of Marriage and the Family*, 1992, *54*, 763–776.

Belsky, Jay. The effect of infant day care reconsidered. *Early Childhood Research Quarterly*, 1988, *3*, 235–272.

Bohannon, Judy R. Grief responses of marital dyads following the death of a child: A longitudinal study. *Omega: The Journal of Death and Dying*, 1990, *22*, 111–123.

Bradbard, M. R., C. A. Readdick, R. C. Endsley, and E. G. Brown. How and why parents select day care for their school age children: A study of three communities. Paper presented at 54th Annual Conference of the National Council on Family Relations, Orlando, Florida, November 1992. Used by permission.

Burr, W. R. and C. Christensen. Undesirable side effects of enhancing self-esteem. *Family Relations*, 1992, *41*, 460–464.

Carpenter, C., B. Glassner, B. D. Johnson, and J. Loughlin. *Kids, drugs, and crime*. Lexington, Mass.: D.C. Heath and Company, 1988.

Caruso, G. L. Patterns of maternal employment and childcare for a sample of two-year-olds. *Journal of Family Issues*, 1992, *13*, 297–311.

Comer, J. P. and A. F. Poussaint. *Raising black children*. New York: NAL-Dutton, 1993.

Cooke, B. Thinking and knowledge underlying expertise in parenting: Comparisons between expert and novice mothers. *Family Relations*, 1991, *40*, 3–13.

Cox, E. Strengthening our values. *CalFam*, Fall 1992, 1–19.

Cutler, B. Roack-a-buy baby. *American Demographics*, 1990, *12*, 21–34.

Dickson, L. F. and R. L. Dukes. The effects of gender and role context on perceptions of parental effectiveness. *Free Inquiry in Creative Sociology*, 1992, *20*, 11–24.

Falconer, Clark W., K. G. Wilson, and J. Falconer. A psychometric investigation of gender-tilted families: Implications for family therapy. *Family Therapy*, 1990, *39*, 8–13.

Farnsworth, Elizabeth B. *Journey through grief*. Atlanta, Ga.: Susan Hunter, 1988.

Field, Tiffany, W. Masi, S. Goldstein, S. Perry, and S. Parl. Infant day care facilitates preschool social behavior. *Early Childhood Research Quarterly*, 1988, *3*, 341–359.

Galambos, N. L. and D. M. Almeida. Does parent-adolescent conflict increase in early adolescence? *Journal of Marriage and the Family*, 1992, *54*, 737–747.

Giordano, P. C., S. A. Cernkovich, and A. DeMaris. The family and peer relations of black adolescents, *Journal of Marriage and the Family*, 1993, *55*, 277–287.

Greer, K. Today's parents: How well are they doing? *Better Homes and Gardens*, October 1986, 34–36.

Haurin, R. J. Patterns of childhood residence and the relationship to young children outcomes. *Journal of Marriage and the Family*, 1992, *54*, 846–860.

Ho, David Y. F. Continuity and variation in Chinese patterns of socialization. *Journal of Marriage and the Family*, 1989, *51*, 149–163.

Kalmuss, D., A. Davidson, and L. Cushman. Parenting expectations, experiences, and adjustment to parenthood: A test of the violated expectations of framework. *Journal of Marriage and the Family*, 1992, *54*, 516–526.

Kandel, D. B. Parenting styles, drug use, and children's adjustment in families of young adults. *Journal of Marriage and the Family,* 1990, *52,* 183–196.

Kelly, M. L., N. Grace, and S. N. Elliott. Acceptability of positive and punitive discipline methods: Comparisons among abusive, potentially abusive, and non-abusive parents. *Child Abuse and Neglect,* 1990, *14,* 219–226.

LeMasters, E. E. and J. DeFrain. *Parents in comtemporary America: A sympathetic view,* 5th ed. Belmont, Calif.: Wadsworth Publishing Co., 1989.

Luster, K., Roades, and B. Haas. The relation between parental values and parenting behavior: A test of the Kohn hypothesis. *Journal of Marriage and the Family,* 1989, *51,* 139–147.

McCormack, A. S., A. M. Laybold, and C. F. Budd. Stress, and substance use: Student attitudes toward alcohol, marijuana, and cocaine. *College Student Journal,* 1993, *27,* 715–730.

McGuire, M. *Parent's guide to choosing quality child care.* Compiled by National Association of Pediatric Nurse Associates and Practitioners, 1989.

National Center for Health Statistics. Advance report of final mortality statistics, 1990. Monthly vital statistics report, vol. 41 no. 7, suppl. Hyattsville, MD.: Public Health Service, 1993.

National Center for Health Statistics. Advance report of final mortality statistics, 1991. Monthly vital statistics report, vol. 42 no. 2, suppl. Hyattsville, MD: Public Health Service, 1993b.

National Research Council. *Risking the future: Adolescent sexuality, pregnancy, and childbearing* (Table 2–6). Washington, DC: National Academy Press, 1987.

O'Hare, W. P. and J. C. Felt. Asian Americans: America's fastest growing minority group. Population Trends and Public Policy, February 1991, no. 19, by Population Reference Bureau, Inc.

Rosenberg, M., C. Schooler, and C. Schoenbach. Self-esteem and adolescent problems: Modeling reciprocal effects. *American Sociological Review,* 1989, *54,* 1004–1019.

Rutter, M. Resilient children. *Psychology Today,* March 1984, 57–65.

Satir, V. *Peoplemaking.* Palo Alto, Calif.: Science and Behavior Books, Inc., 1972.

Scarr, S. What's a parent to do? *Psychology Today,* May 1984, 58–63.

Schvaneveldt, J. D. and M. H. Young. Strengthening families: New horizons in family life education. *Family Relations,* 1992, *41,* 385–389.

Shea, J. Department of Child Development and Family Relations, East Carolina University, Greenville, N.C. Personal communication, 1984. Used by permission.

Shuster, C. A typology of maternal responses to integrating parenting and employment. *Family Relations,* 1993, *42,* 13–20.

Shuster, C. First-time fathers' experiences using infant day care and combining parenting and employment. Paper presented at NCFR Annual Conference, 1992. Dr. Claudia Shuster, Associate professor, School of Education, Central Connecticut State University. Used by permission.

Simons, R. L., J. Beaman, R. D. Conger, and W. Chao. Childhood experience, conceptions of parenting, and attitudes of spouse as determinants of parental behavior. *Journal of Marriage and the Family,* 1993, *55,* 91–106.

Statistical Abstract of the United States: 1992, 112th ed. Washington, D.C.: U.S. Bureau of the Census.

Statistical Abstract of the United States: 1993, 113th ed. Washington, D.C.: U.S. Bureau of the Census.

Stipp, Horst. New ways to reach children. *American Demographics,* 1993, August, 50–56.

Tebes, J. K., K. Grady, and D. L. Snow. Parent-training in decision-making facilitation: Skill acquisition and relationship to gender. *Family Relations,* 1989, *38,* 243–247.

Teleki, J. K., C. W. Snow, and J. Reguero de Atiles. A comparative study of 1981 and 1991 childcare center licensing regulations in the United States. Paper, Annual Conference of the National Association for the Education of Young Children, New Orleans, La., November 1992. Used by permission.

Thompson, L., A. C. Acock, and K. Clark. Do parents know their children? The ability of mothers and fathers to gauge the attitudes of their young adult children. *Family Relations,* 1985, *34,* 315–320.

Thompson, R. W., C. R. Grow, P. R. Ruma, D. L. Daly, and R. V. Burke. Parent education: Evaluation of a practical parenting program with middle- and low-income families. *Family Relations,* 1993, *42,* 21–25.

Thornton, A. The courtship process of adolescent sexuality. *Journal of Family Issues,* 1990, *11,* 239–273.

Ward, R., J. Logan, and G. Spitze. The influence of parent and child needs on co-residence in middle and later life. *Journal of Marriage and the Family,* 1992, *54,* 209–221.

Ward, R. A. and G. Spitze. Consequences of parent-adult child co-residence. *Journal of Family Issues,* 1992, *13,* 553–576.

White, L. and J. N. Edwards. Emptying the nest and parental well-being: An analysis of national panel data. *American Sociological Review,* 1990, *55,* 235–242.

Wong, M. G. The Chinese American family. *Ethnic Families in America: Patterns and Variations,* eds. C. H. Mindel, R. W. Habenstein, and R. Wright, Jr., eds. New York: Elsevier, 1988a, 230–257.

Wong, M. G. A look at intermarriage among the Chinese in the United States in 1980. Paper presented at the Conference on Racial and Ethnic Relations in the 1990s, Texas A&M University, 1988b.

York, Phyllis and David York. *Toughlove: Beyond the last straw.* Audio/workbook. Doylestown, PA: Toughlove Inc. 1989.

Contents

16
CHAPTER

Divorce and Widowhood

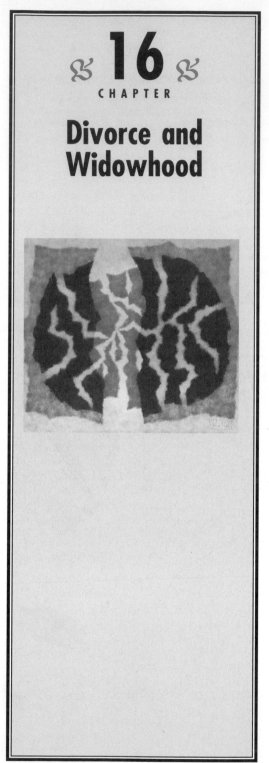

Is It True?

1. Spouses in their first marriage are quicker to divorce than spouses in their second marriage.

2. In a study of 109 people who divorced, the most common advice they would give to others contemplating divorce is to "work it out."

3. Most divorced parents have joint custody of their children.

4. Having a spouse who converts to another religion is grounds for divorce among the Hindu in India.

5. Most women age 75 and older are widows.

1 = F; 2 = T; 3 = F; 4 = T; 5 = T

Divorce may be a painful wound that cannot heal, a living and continuing memorial to an idealized past, a rationale for a persistent "victim career" or, conversely, an opportunity for constructive change, a turning point in life toward the fulfillment and expansion of one's potential.

MORDECAI KAFFMAN

*S*hortly before her death, Margaret Mead was interviewed about her long and fascinating life. At one point in the interview, the interviewer asked Mead to comment on her "failed" marriages. Mead replied, "I didn't have any failed marriages. I've been married three times—and each marriage was successful" (Dychtwald, 1990, 212). Thus, the meanings individuals attach to divorce may range from failure to success.

In this chapter we examine the termination of a marriage by divorce as well as by death. Both are accompanied by a range of emotions such as frustration, grief, relief, hope, and sometimes growth. First, we examine divorce.

For the first time in our history, two people entering marriage are just as likely to be parted by divorce as by death.

LENORE WEITZMAN

℘ Divorce

NATIONAL DATA ℘ More than one million divorces (1,194,000) take place in the United States annually (National Center for Health Statistics, 1993). Of couples who divorced, those in their first, second, and third marriages were married an average of 11, 7, and 5 years (National Center for Health Statistics, 1990). The average number of years from marriage to divorce of all marriages is 7.1 (*Statistical Abstract of the United States: 1993*, Table 144).

It has been estimated that two-thirds of all first marriages in the United States will end in divorce (Martin & Bumpass, 1989). Does the high rate of divorce in our society mean that the family institution is weak? Not necessarily. Table 16.1 describes strengths of family life in the United States identified by 30 marriage and family specialists. The strengths are presented in order of greatest agreement by the panelists. In addition, it should also be noted that most divorced people remarry which emphasizes the high value individuals place on marriage.

Causes of Divorce

Determining the causes of divorce is not easy. The reasons are embedded in the individuals, their interaction, and the society in which they live. First, let's look at societal factors that contribute to divorce.

TABLE 16.1

Current Strengths of Family Life in the United States

At their best, families allow for developing one's personhood while maintaining connection and intimacy.

At their best, families can offer support and safety and a way of passing values to our children.

Increased awareness of effects of drug and alcohol problems in a family context.

Some increased awareness of child physical and sexual abuse and battering.

Although fathers have not increased their involvement in the home dramatically, there have been small improvements in this area, which are leading in the right direction.

More openness to discussion of previously taboo subjects.

Increased awareness of effects of alcoholism and abuse on later generations, hence more attention given to dealing with these issues.

U.S. citizens (middle and upper class) experience a wide variety of choices and opportunities.

Recent attempts to counter sexist imbalances in parenting and other areas of family life.

Increased awareness of gender issues by men and women.

Movement (slow) toward more egalitarian marriages and parenting.

Increased awareness of significance of parent-child relationships and the impact of the family system on children.

Source: Adapted from Fish, L. S. and J. L. Osborn. Therapists' views of family life: A Delphi study. *Family Relations,* 1992, 41, 409–416. Table 1 on page 410. Copyright 1992 by the National Council on Family Relations, 3989 Central Avenue, NE, Suite 550, Minneapolis, Mn 55421. Reprinted by permission.

Societal Factors   Divorce is a product of the society in which it occurs.

> The rising divorce rate does not mean that people are losing faith in marriage, but that they believe marriage can be better than it often is. Giving up on *a* marriage is very different from giving up on *marriage.*
>
> GARY LEE

CONSIDERATION

That divorce is responsive to conditions created by society is illustrated by the Puritans during the colonial period; they did not approve of divorce just because spouses were unhappy. In Massachusetts, there was an average of one divorce per year from 1639 to 1760 (Morgan, 1944). However, restricting divorce does not always mean that couples stay together. "With divorce hard to obtain in prerevolutionary times, colonial newspapers were filled with offers of rewards for runaway wives and social announcements that couples had parted" (Schrof, 1992, 63).

A number of factors have combined to make divorce increasingly common in America. They include the following.

DECREASED EXPECTATION THAT MARRIAGE IS A PERMANENT RELATIONSHIP.   The high divorce rate in the United States means that most people know several individuals or couples who are divorced. One consequence of such knowledge is to open the possibility that one's own marriage may end in divorce. In Focus 16.1 suggests it may no longer be realistic to expect two people to stay married until one of them dies.

CHANGING FAMILY FUNCTIONS.   Many of the protective, religious, educational, and recreational functions of the family have largely been taken over by outside agencies. Family members may now look to the police, the church or synagogue, the school, and commercial recreational facilities rather than to each other for fulfilling these needs. The result is that although meeting emotional needs remains a primary function of the family, there are fewer reasons to keep the family together.

DECREASED ECONOMIC DEPENDENCE OF WIFE.   In the past, the unemployed wife was dependent on her husband for food and shelter. No matter how unhappy her marriage was, she stayed married because she was economically dependent on her husband. Her husband literally represented her lifeline.

Finding gainful employment outside the home made it possible for the wife to afford to leave her husband if she wanted to. Now that almost 70 percent of all wives are employed (and this number is increasing), fewer and fewer wives are economically trapped in an unhappy marriage relationship. Wives who earn an income may feel able to survive financially on their own; thus employed wives are more likely to leave an unhappy marital relationship. In addition, unhappy husbands may be more likely to divorce if their wives are employed and able to be financially independent.

FEWER MORAL AND RELIGIOUS SANCTIONS.   The Catholic church no longer excommunicates divorced Catholics who remarry. Many priests and clergy recognize that divorce may be the best alternative in a particular marital relationship and attempt to minimize the guilt members of their congregation may feel at the failure of their marriage. Increasingly, marriage is more often viewed in secular rather than religious terms. Schultz (1990) studied divorce patterns in 19th century New England and noted that ideological changes are important influences in divorce rates.

> *Divorce may be seen as an adaptive response to the changing nature of marriage and the family, which now strongly emphasizes companionship, nurturant socialization, and the meeting of emotional needs.*
>
> DOUGLAS SPRENKLE
> FRED PIERCY

> *Divorces are made in heaven.*
>
> OSCAR WILDE

> *Divorce, the public brand of a shameful life.*
>
> THOMAS FARNELL

CONSIDERATION

Some consideration has been given to bringing the stigma of divorce back. In response to the alarming incidence of divorce and the devastation to spouses and children that follows, a conservative movement has suggested hiring court appointed lawyers who would argue in defense of every marriage involving children, bringing back the stigma of divorce by shunning divorced women and men, and voicing disapproval of divorce at local forums like PTA meetings (Schrof, 1992).

"Till Death Do Us Part": Are We Expecting too Much?

The expectation that marriages be permanent persists in spite of the high divorce rate in our country. After looking at the social pressures which perpetuate the norm of "till death do us part," we suggest some possible reasons why this norm is not well achieved and suggest that expecting marriages to be permanent may be expecting too much.

SOCIAL PRESSURES TOWARD PERMANENT MARRIAGE RELATIONSHIPS

There are many pressures in our society which support the institution of marriage and the idea that marriages should be permanent. These pressures stem from our cultural norms and our religious and economic institutions.

Cultural Norms

Our culture socializes us to believe that the appropriate role for an adult in our society is that of spouse. We are socialized by our parents, peers, and media to seek marriage. Although alternatives to marriage such as singlehood and living together have become more acceptable in our society, the cultural norm is still in favor of marriage.

Social pressures to stay married are less obvious but, nonetheless, just as strong. We often assume that divorce happens to other people and that our marriage will be permanent—at least we are taught that it *should* be.

Married people want their married friends to stay married to buttress their own lifestyle and needs. When friends get divorced, they often move away, change friends, and are no longer available as a couple.

Religious Institution

In addition to widespread socialization for a permanent marriage relationship, most religious organizations convey a clear message about the permanence of marriage relationships. The traditional religious wedding vows carry the dictim "Until death do us part" making it clear that the union is a spiritual one ordained by God who expects us to make good on our promise.

Economic Institution

While the divorced represent a new market with expanding needs, businesses prefer to sell in units. The more family units, the greater the sales volume and subsequent profit.

Many divorced individuals have less discretionary income to spend. Weitzman (1985) observed that women report a 73 percent decrease in their standard of living the first year after divorce.

MOST U.S. MARRIAGE RELATIONSHIPS ARE NOT PERMANENT

Two researchers project that two-thirds of all first marriages in the United States will end in divorce (Martin & Bumpass 1989). While divorce is a visible index of the frequency with which marriage relationships terminate, unaccounted for is the percentage of nonmarital relationships (living together relationship, friendships, other premarital love relationships) which do not continue until the death of one partner. One might assume that in the absence of cultural, religious and economic pressures to maintain these relationships that their rate of dissolution would be even higher than the divorce figures we can document.

NEGATIVE CONSEQUENCES FOR REQUIRING THAT MARRIAGES BE PERMANENT

There are two primary negative consequences which stem from the norm that marriage relationships be permanent: spouses who are unhappy/abused are more likely to stay married and spouses who divorce are severely punished.

Evidence that unhappy spouses stay married is found in the data on marriage happiness across time, the percentage of spouses who have extramarital affairs, and the percentage of marriages in which there is spouse abuse. Studies on marital happiness and duration of marriage have reached similar conclusions—in general, the longer spouses are married, the less happy they report their marriages as being (Lee, 1988).

Regarding extramarital intercourse, one-half of husbands and a similar percentage of wives report having engaged in intercourse with someone other than their spouse during the marriage (Thompson, 1983). In one British study, 73 percent of the respondents reported sexual intercourse outside of marriage (Lawson, 1988). Regardless of the percentage, extramarital sex has been associated with poor quality marriage relationships (Thompson, 1983).

As for spouse abuse, about one-fourth of all spouses

IN FOCUS 16.1

have experienced violence in their relationships. In about half of these relationships, both the husband and the wife were violent (Flynn, 1990).

For spouses who do end their marriage, the price is high. Foremost is guilt about not having lived up to the cultural ideal to stay married. "I am a failure" is a frequent thought by the recently divorced. Some evidence suggests that divorced women feel more guilty than divorced men about their divorce (Farnsworth et al., 1989). Women are traditionally more conforming and may feel more victimized by the expectation of permanence than men.

The emotional pain following divorce is also devastating. Since custody is awarded to the woman in 90 percent of the cases, men are separated from their children and children are separated from their fathers. All parties to the divorce—spouses and children—are socialized to regard these separations in negative rather than in positive terms.

When married spouses are compared with the divorced, the latter report a much lower level of personal happiness. In a national sample of respondents age 18 and older, about 38 percent of those married reported that they were "very happy" in contrast to about 18 percent of the divorced (Glenn & Weaver, 1988). Other researchers have also observed that the psychological positive feelings of the divorced are "markedly poorer than that of the married" (Cove & Shin, 1989, 140).

CONCLUSION

Is the expectation that spouses stay married until death do them part unrealistic? Maybe. While there may be positive individual, couple, and societal reasons for wanting to maintain stable, committed, emotionally satisfying marriage relationships, the cultural norm and the attendant negative sanctions may do more harm than good. What is needed is an all out search for the relationship technology to maintain positive long-term relationships. Until such knowledge and application are available, we might consider the effects of unbridled bludgeoning of individuals who do not conform to the cultural norm of permanent marriage relationships.

Alternatively, we might give equal attention to the social reality that many relationships are not permanent and learn how to view these in more positive ways.

Whether you call them temporary, transitory or short-term, relationships of this nature are here to stay. You are undoubtedly having them now whether you realize it or not. And short-term relationships are neither inherently superior nor inferior to long-term ones. It's just that they are a fact of life in this rapidly changing world and that to feel emotionally fulfilled—or perhaps even to survive—all of us need to develop a different goal for relationships than duration (Coleman & Edwards, 1979, 5).

REFERENCES

Coleman, E., B. Edwards, *Brief Encounters*. New York: Double-day & Company, 1979.

Cove, W.R., H. Shin. The psychological well-being of divorced and widowed men and women. *Journal of Family Issues,* 1989, *10,* 122-144.

Ember, M. Warfare, sex ratio, and polygyny, *Ethnology,* 1974, *13,* 197-206.

Glenn, N.D., C.N. Weaver, The changing relationship of marital status to reported happiness. *Journal of Marriage and the Family,* 1988 *50,* 317-24.

Farnsworth, J., M.A. Pett, and D.A. Lund, Predictors of loss management and well-being in later life widowhood and divorce. *Journal of Family Issues,* 1989, *10,* 102-121.

Flynn, C.P. Relationship violence by women: issues and implications. *Family Relations,* 1990, *39,* 194-198.

Lawson, A. *Adultery: An Analysis of Love and Betrayal,* New York: Basic Books, 1988.

Lee, G.R. Marital satisfaction in later life: the effects of nonmarital roles. *Journal of Marriage and the Family,* 1988, *50.* 775-783.

Martin, T.C., and L.L. Bumpass, Recent trends in marital disruption. *Demography,* 1989, *26,* 37-52.

Mills, C.W. The professional ideology of social pathologists. *American Journal of Sociology,* 1942, *49,* 165-180.

Thompson, A.P. Extramarital sex: a review of the research literature. *Journal of Sex Research,* 1983, *19,* 1-22.

Weitzman, L.J. *The Divorce Revolution.* Riverside, NJ: Free Press, 1985.

SOURCE   Adapted from J. Turner, D. Knox, and C. Schacht. "Till death do us part": A deviant norm? Reprinted with permission. *Free Inquiry in Creative Sociology,* 1991, *19,* no. 1, 189–192.

DIVORCE MODELS.   As the number of divorced individuals in our society increases, the probability increases that a person's friends, parents, siblings, or children will be divorced. The more divorced people a person knows, the more normal divorce will seem to that person. The less deviant the person perceives divorce to be, the greater the probability the person will divorce if that person's own marriage becomes strained.

NATIONAL DATA ℘ Almost one-fourth (24.2%) of all freshman college students in the United States have parents who are divorced or separated (American Council on Education and University of California, 1992).

LESS PARENTAL CONTROL OVER MATE SELECTION.   In the past, American parents have had more control over whom their son or daughter married; such factors as family background, social class, and property were given priority. The result of such parentally controlled mate selection was that the partners had more in common than love feelings. Today, however, love is usually the primary consideration in the decision to marry, and feelings of love are sometimes not enough to weather 50 years together.

Until death do us part meant we died and I parted.

A DIVORCÉE

SOCIETAL GOAL OF HAPPINESS.   The goal of happiness is viewed by our society as a major reason to marry. When spouses stop having fun, they often feel there is no reason to stay married.

> ### CONSIDERATION
>
> The reason you stay married may not be the same reason you get married. Most people marry for love, fun, and happiness. However, marriage sometimes blunts these emotions and focuses the spouses' attentions on work and childrearing. Asian Americans and Mexican Americans have lower divorce rates than whites or blacks because they consider the family unit to be of greater value than their individual interests. To be unhappy is less likely to result in movement toward divorce for these groups (Mindel et al., 1988).

LIBERAL DIVORCE LAWS.   All states now recognize some form of no-fault divorce. Although the legal terms are "irreconcilable differences" and "incompatibility," the reality is that spouses can get a divorce if they want to without having to prove that one of the partners is at fault (for example, adultery). In most states, separation for a period of six months to a year (with no intention of returning) constitutes grounds for divorce. When such a ground is used, neither partner is legally regarded as being "at fault."

> ### CONSIDERATION
>
> One consequence of "no fault" divorces has been an increased number of divorced women plunging into poverty. When blame could be assigned to the

husband, who often had superior economic resources, the ex-wife was compensated in property settlement and alimony. With neither partner at fault, the ex-wife is not entitled to any extra economic benefits.

Although legal grounds for divorce in the United States have moved away from finding one partner at fault, divorce laws in some other societies still target a "guilty party." Grounds for divorce among the Hindus in India include adultery, conversion to another religion, and having an STD in a communicable form. A spouse guilty of any of these can be divorced (Pothern, 1989).

CONSIDERATION

As we shall see in the section on consequences of divorce, legal detachment is often the easiest part of getting divorced. The emotional, financial, social, and parental issues are much more difficult and felt for years to come (Hammond, 1992).

Individual and Relationship Factors   Although various societal factors may make divorce a viable alternative to marital unhappiness, they are not sufficient to "cause" a divorce. One spouse must actually initiate divorce proceedings. Reasons why a spouse might seek a divorce include the following.

NEGATIVE BEHAVIOR.   People marry because they anticipate greater rewards from being married than from being single. During courtship, each partner engages in a high frequency of positive verbal and nonverbal behavior (compliments, eye contact, physical affection) toward each other. The good feelings the partners share as a result of this high frequency of positive behaviors encourage them to get married to ensure that each will be able to share the same experiences tomorrow.

Just as love feelings are based on positive behavior from the partner, hostile feelings are created when the partner engages in a high frequency of negative behavior. Negative behaviors that wives typically complain about in marriage therapy sessions include "doesn't show an interest in what I say, think or feel, criticizes me, drinks too much, and doesn't help with the childcare/housework." Husbands typically complain that their wife "doesn't want sex, criticizes too much, gets upset when I want a few beers with my friends, and nags me about doing stuff."

When a spouse's negative behavior continues to the point of creating more costs than rewards in the relationship, either partner may begin to seek a more reinforcing situation. Divorce (being single again) or remarriage may appear to be a more attractive alternative than being married to the present spouse.

If I were the man that you wanted, I would not be the man that I am.

LYLE LOVETT

Courtship is a surf and turf dinner overlooking the ocean; marriage is a peanut butter and jelly sandwich.

MARTY ZUSMAN

Now there is somebody new, These dreams I been dreaming have all fallen through.

BONNIE RAITT

LACK OF CONFLICT RESOLUTION SKILLS.   While every marriage relationship experiences conflict, not every couple has the skills to effectively resolve conflict. Some partners respond to conflict by withdrawing emotionally from the relationship; others respond by attacking, blaming, and failing to listen to their partner's point of view. Without skills to resolve conflict in their relationships, partners drift into patterns of communication that may escalate rather than resolve conflict. (Communication and conflict are discussed in Chapter 9).

RADICAL CHANGES.   "He's not the same man I married" is not an uncommon cry. People may undergo radical changes (philosophical or physical) after marriage. One minister married and decided seven years later that he did not like being a minister. He left the ministry, got a Ph.D. in psychology, and began to drink and have affairs. His wife, who had married him in the role of minister, now found herself married to a psychologist who spent his evenings at bars with other women. They divorced.

Because people change throughout their life, the person he or she selects at one point in life may not be the same partner he or she would select at another. Margaret Mead, referred to at the beginning of this chapter, noted that her first marriage was a student marriage, her second a professional partnership, and her third, an intellectual marriage to her soul mate with whom she had her only child. At each of several stages in her life, she experienced a different set of needs and selected a mate who fulfilled those needs.

Spouses may also experience severe physical changes. One wife was in an automobile accident that broke her neck and put her in a wheelchair. "The car and my neck were not the only things that were wrecked," she said of the accident. "It changed our marriage. I was no longer the worker, companion, and lover I had been. We divorced."

BOREDOM.   A 26-year-old woman who had been married for four years said, "It's not that my husband is terrible. I'm just tired of the same thing all the time. I dated a lot before I was married, and I miss the excitement of new people." "Satiated" best describes her feelings. She was bored, as though she had been watching the third rerun of a TV movie. She viewed divorce as a means of freeing herself from a stale relationship.

EXTRAMARITAL RELATIONSHIP.   While most spouses are monogamous most of the time, about 50 percent of all husbands and wives have intercourse with someone other than their spouse at least once during their marriages (Thompson, 1983). Spouses who feel mistreated by their partners or bored and trapped sometimes consider the alternative of a relationship with someone who is good to them, exciting, new, and who offers an escape from the role of spouse to the role of lover.

Extramarital involvements sometimes hurry a decaying marriage toward divorce because the partner begins to contrast the new lover with the spouse. The spouse is often associated with negatives (bills, screaming children, nagging); the lover, almost exclusively with positives (clandestine candlelight dinners, new sex, emotional closeness). The choice is stacked in favor of the lover. Although most spouses do not leave their mate for a lover, the existence of an extramarital relationship may weaken the emotional tie between the spouses so that they are less inclined to stay married.

Negative behavior, lack of negotiation skills, radical changes, boredom, and extramarital relationships are only five of the reasons people say that they want to get divorced. Others include "can't hold a job," "too much drinking," "too authoritarian," "doesn't understand me," "lousy lover," "physical abuse," and "no longer in love." Regardless of the reason, the motivation is to get away from the spouse in order to live alone or with someone new.

Movement Toward Divorce

Relationships go through certain stages when they are winding down. Socio-biologists suggest that the "winding down" from the romantic love phase begins within three years, which is the requisite amount of time to rear the offspring to the point where the mother can take care of both herself and her baby without the constant help of a partner. Couples who have a second child tend to delay their vulnerability to divorce until the second child is around three or four (Fisher, 1992). Hence, couples rarely divorce when there is a new infant.

Figure 16.1 reflects the various stages partners go through as they disengage. Having lost some of the romance that helped to ensure a high frequency of positive verbal and nonverbal behavior, the first stage involves decreasing the frequency of positive behavior and increasing the frequency of negative behavior toward each other. This behavior usually translates into fewer compliments, less affection, and more criticism and hostility. Gottman (1991) noted that couples on the path to divorce disengage and become emotionally withdrawn from each other.

> I probably stayed in the marriage longer than I should have because I knew what people would say. Other people get divorced, but my marriage wasn't supposed to fail.
>
> JOAN LUNDEN

CONSIDERATION

It is not unusual for married individuals to contemplate divorce. Of 181 spouses in the United States, 20 percent reported they had thought about separation during the previous year (Bugaighis et al., 1985–1986). Among 2,000 spouses in Bangkok, Thailand, 13 percent of the men and 28 percent of the women reported having thought about divorce or separating sometime in the last three years (Edwards et al., 1992).

The degree of marital unhappiness necessary to keep a couple moving toward divorce is influenced by length of marriage, barriers, and alternatives. If a couple has been married for a relatively short time and have no children they are more likely to get divorced (have a low tolerance for marital unhappiness)

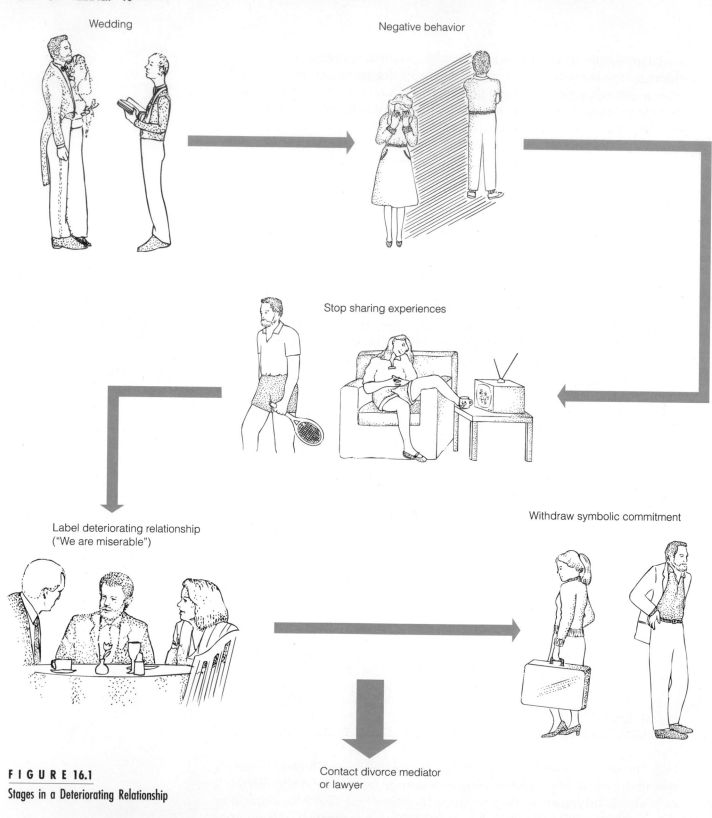

FIGURE 16.1

Stages in a Deteriorating Relationship

than couples who have been married a long time, have children, and have few alternative partner possibilities. These latter couples have a high tolerance for marital unhappiness (White & Booth, 1991).

Once the partners become emotionally withdrawn, they often stop spending time together. Some live apart, increasing the chance they will divorce. Failure to spend time together makes it impossible for spouses to recreate the positive feelings necessary to motivate them to stay married.

As thoughts of divorce continue and feelings between the marital partners grow more distant, the deteriorating relationship may be negatively labeled. One partner, more often the wife, eventually says, "I think we should get a divorce." At this point one or both partners may seek legal advice or the couple may decide to consult with a divorce mediator.

Then comes a public demonstration that the marriage is ending. The spouses take off their rings, go alone (or with someone new) to events they would normally attend together, and tell family, friends, children, and co-workers of the impending separation. Once the symbols of the marriage are withdrawn, one spouse often moves out. Once spouses separate, the chance that they will eventually get divorced dramatically increases.

> Love is the quest, marriage the conquest, divorce the inquest.
>
> E.C. MCKENZIE

CONSIDERATION

The progression toward divorce can be stopped at any point, but the earlier the better. The best place to stop it is in the beginning when either partner becomes upset at the behavior of the other. Talking about what is upsetting and negotiating a change in the behavior will take the source of negative feelings out of the relationship. Otherwise, the negative feelings move the spouses toward the next stage of divorce, and the difficulty of reversing the pattern increases.

Some people who have divorced recommend extreme caution before deciding to end a marriage and encourage an all out effort to salvage the relationship. Rigdon and Pett (1992) asked 109 persons who were divorced what advice they would offer to others who are contemplating divorce:

> Although none of the participants had "saved their marriages," the most common advice given was that other people at least try to do so. The participants advised that persons try to save the marriage by seeking marital and individual counseling. Redoubling efforts to communicate and to share feelings and thoughts with one's spouse were identified ways of trying to save the marriage (p. 88).

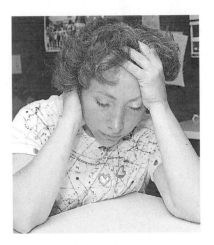

Spouses contemplating divorce sometimes become sad, withdrawn, and despondent.

A divorce becomes final when a judge issues a judgment declaring that the marriage has ended under the laws of a particular state. If the couple has children, the divorce decree will specify custody of the children, the visitation rights of the noncustodial parent, and the amount of child support due to the custodial parent. Some spouses can decide these issues themselves and have their decisions written into the divorce agreement. Other spouses are so hostile they hire an attorney who may criticize the partner in court as punishment and

> I knew all about divorce except what it felt like.
>
> MEL KRANZLER

an attempt to get more money. Some attorneys encourage this hostility so that they can spend more time on the case, increasing the fees they charge. An alternative to litigation is mediation (see In Focus 16.2).

Characteristics of Divorced People

Spouses who get divorced tend to have different characteristics than those who stay married (Bumpass, Martin, & Sweet, 1991; Heaton, 1991; Canabal, 1990). Some of these include:

1. Marrying in teens
2. Premarital pregnancy
3. Low income
4. Having divorced parents
5. No high school education
6. Having little in common
7. Not spending time together
8. Urban residence
9. Having no children
10. Having only female children
11. Having another partner available
12. Living in the western, south central, mountain, or Pacific region
13. Interreligious marriage
14. Interracial marriage
15. Low-status occupation
16. Courtship of less than one year
17. Being in a second marriage
18. Married less than five years
19. Having a seriously ill child
20. Having an alcoholic spouse
21. Not religiously devout
22. Having no preschool children
23. Thinking seriously about divorce
24. Talking about divorce with the spouse
25. Being a combat veteran
26. Being black or Hispanic
27. Male unemployment
28. A cohabitation history
29. Education heterogamy

CONSIDERATION

The above list of divorce characteristics should be viewed cautiously. Although unlikely, it is possible that someone with many of the above characteristics could be happily married, just as someone with none of these characteristics could get divorced. Each of us is a potential candidate for divorce (even Ann Landers divorced after 36 years).

Completing the Divorce Proneness Scale in the Self-Assessment section provides one index of the probability of getting divorced. It is only suggestive and should be considered as such.

Consequences of Divorce

Based on a national sample of over 6,000 individuals, divorced people report more unhappiness, more depression, and being less healthy than married people. And each subsequent time a person divorces, the greater the negative

Divorce Mediation

DEFINITION OF DIVORCE MEDIATION

Mediation involves spouses who have decided to separate or divorce meeting with a neutral third party (mediator) to negotiate the issues of (1) child custody and visitation, (2) child support, (3) property settlement, and (4) spousal support. Mediation is not for everyone. Mediation does not work where there is a history of spouse abuse, where the parties do not disclose their financial information, where one party is controlled by someone else (e.g., a parent), where there is the desire for revenge, or where the mediator is biased. The latter can be mitigated by selecting a mediator who is a member of national professional organizations (Kramer, 1992).

BENEFITS OF MEDIATION

1. *Relationship.* Spouses who choose to mediate their divorce have a better chance for a more civil relationship because they cooperate in specifying the conditions of their separation or divorce. Mediation emphasizes negotiation and cooperation between the divorcing partners. Such cooperation is particularly important if the couple has children in that it provides a positive basis for discussing issues in reference to children across time.
2. *Economic.* Mediation is less expensive than litigation. The cost of hiring an attorney and going to court over issues of custody and division of property is around $12,000. A mediated divorce costs about $1,000 (Neumann, 1989). What the couple spend in legal fees they cannot keep as assets to later divide.
3. *Less Time Consuming.* A mediated divorce takes two to three months versus two to three years if the case is litigated.
4. *Avoid Public Exposure.* Some spouses do not want to discuss their private lives and finances in open court. Mediation occurs in a private and confidential setting.
5. *Greater Overall Satisfaction.* Mediation results in an agreement developed by the spouses, not one imposed by a judge or the court system. A comparison of couples who chose mediation with couples who chose litigation found that those who mediated their own settlement were much more satisfied with the conditions of their agreement. In addition, children of mediated divorces adjust better to the divorce of their parents than children of litigated divorces (Marlow & Sauber, 1990).

BASIC MEDIATION GUIDELINES

1. *Children.* What is best for a couples' children is a primary concern of the mediator. Children of divorced parents adjust best under three conditions: (a) the noncustodial parent is allowed regular and frequent access; (b) the children see the parents relating in a polite and positive way; and (c) both parents talk positively about the other parent and neither parent talks negatively about the other to the children.
2. *Fairness.* It is important that the spouses display a sense of justice. Each partner must feel the agreement is fair with neither party being exploited or punished. It is "fair" for both parents to contribute financially to the children. It is "fair" for the noncustodial parent to have regular access to his or her children.
3. *Open disclosure.* The spouses will be asked to disclose all facts, records, and documents to ensure an informed and fair agreement regarding property, assets, and debts.
4. *Other Professionals.* During mediation the spouses may be asked to consult an accountant regarding tax laws. In addition, spouses are encouraged to consult an attorney throughout the mediation and to have the attorney review the written agreements, which result from the mediation. However, during the mediation sessions, all forms of legal action against each other (the spouses) should be stopped.
5. *Confidentiality.* The mediator will not divulge anything the spouses say during the mediation sessions without the permission of the spouses. The spouses are asked to sign a document stating that should they not complete mediation, they agree not to empower any attorney to subpoena the mediator or any records resulting from the mediation for use in any legal action. Such an agreement is necessary for the spouses to feel free to talk about all aspects of their relationship without fear of legal action against them for such disclosures.

SOURCES: Kramer, V. Mediation: Perils, pitfalls, and benefits. *Mothering,* Fall 1992, 101–107.

Marlow, L. and S. R. Sauber. *The handbook of divorce mediation.* New York: Plenum Publishing Co., 1990.

Neumann, D. *Divorce mediation: How to cut the cost and stress of divorce.* New York: Holt, Henry, and Company, 1989.

effects (Kurdek, 1991). Some reasons for the devastating emotional experiences some divorced people encounter include the following.

Emotional and Psychological Consequences   In spite of the prevalence of divorce and the suggestion that it may be a path to greater self-actualization or fulfillment, most divorced people report some amount of personal disorganization, anxiety, unhappiness, and loneliness (Song, 1991). Feelings of depression and despair occur in response to three basic changes in the divorced person's life: termination of a major source of intimacy, disruption of the daily routine, and awareness of a new status—divorced person. Going through a divorce can also lead to feelings of failure or defeat, especially if the other partner initiated the divorce. But the partner who initiates the divorce also undergoes considerable stress and guilt in making the decision to separate. One study found that the partner who initiated the divorce experienced more trauma than the noninitiator (Buehler, 1987).

If you are married, you probably did so because you were in love and wanted to share your life with another. Like most people, you needed to experience feelings of intimacy in a world of secondary relationships. One reason divorce hurts is that you lose one of the few people who knew you and who, at least at one time, did care about you. Heim and Snyder (1991) reported that feeling alienated and detached from one's marital partner is a strong predictor of depression for both men and women.

Divorce also shatters your daily routine and emphasizes your aloneness. Eating alone, sleeping alone, and driving alone to a friend's house for companionship are role adaptations made necessary by the destruction of your marital patterns. Depression and suicide, for both whites and blacks, are much more frequent among divorced persons than married persons (Stack, 1989; Broman, 1988).

Although we tend to think of divorce as an intrinsically stressful event, one researcher suggested that the amount of stress involved in a divorce is determined by how stressful the marriage was (Wheaton, 1990). In marriages that are very stressful, a divorce may be beneficial in allowing unhappy spouses to escape from a chronically stressful situation. In very stressful marriages then, going through a divorce may actually reduce more stress than it creates.

CONSIDERATION

Diedrick (1991) noted that women fare better emotionally after separation and divorce than men. She explained that not only are women more likely to have a stronger network of supportive relationships than men but that they are likely to profit from divorce by developing a new sense of self-esteem and confidence since they are thrust into a more independent role.

SELF-ASSESSMENT ∽

The Divorce Proneness Scale

This scale is designed to measure the degree to which you may be prone to get a divorce. There are no right or wrong answers. After reading each sentence carefully, circle the number that best represents your feelings.

1 Strongly disagree	4 Mildly agree
2 Mildly disagree	5 Strongly agree
3 Undecided	

		SD	MD	U	MA	SA
1.	My parents have (or had) an unhappy marriage.	1	2	3	4	5
2.	My closest friends are divorced.	1	2	3	4	5
3.	Marriage is not necessarily a lifetime commitment. It is okay to get divorced under certain conditions.	1	2	3	4	5
4.	I am not a religious person.	1	2	3	4	5
5.	My partner and I have a roller coaster relationship—we alternate between very good and very bad times together.	1	2	3	4	5
6.	I don't think it is easy to be monogamous.	1	2	3	4	5
7.	When love is gone, it is better to divorce than stay in a loveless marriage till you die.	1	2	3	4	5
8.	My parents do not approve of the person I married or want to marry.	1	2	3	4	5
9.	My partner and I have been separated because we were angry at each other.	1	2	3	4	5
10.	My partner and I have different interests—we don't really like to do the same things.	1	2	3	4	5
11.	My partner and I have different values.	1	2	3	4	5

		SD	MD	U	MA	SA
12.	My partner and I spend very little of our free time together.	1	2	3	4	5
13.	My partner and I show very little physical affection to each other.	1	2	3	4	5
14.	My partner and I don't really like each other's friends.	1	2	3	4	5
15.	I believe that divorce is an acceptable way out of a bad marriage.	1	2	3	4	5
16.	My partner and I have considered divorce.	1	2	3	4	5
17.	I don't really love my partner anymore.	1	2	3	4	5
18.	My partner and I do not communicate well with each other.	1	2	3	4	5
19.	I can't tell my partner how I really feel about a lot of things.	1	2	3	4	5
20.	My partner and I get along best when other people are around.	1	2	3	4	5

Scoring: Add the numbers you circled. The response that suggests the greatest proneness toward divorce (strongly agree) is 5, and the response that suggests the least proneness toward divorce is 1 (strongly disagree). Therefore, the higher your total score (100 is the highest possible score), the greater your chance of divorce and the lower your total score (20 is the lowest possible score), the lower your chance of divorce. A score of 60 places you at the midpoint between the extremes.

NOTE: This Self-Assessment is designed to be thought provoking; it is not intended as a clinical evaluation device.

Divorce is an emotional and financial disaster.

JACK WRIGHT

Financial Consequences   Divorce has been referred to as a financial disaster. While wealthy spouses may split their estates, pay alimony, and still experience little to no lifestyle change, the rest of us would be more likely to move from houses to apartments, to drive cars longer before trading them, and to eat out less often.

Divorce has a more detrimental economic effect on women and children because women typically earn less income than men, and divorce means they no longer have access to the higher salary of the husband. Alimony sometimes helps but being awarded alimony is rare.

NATIONAL DATA ❧   Of 20,610,000 divorced women, 16 percent were awarded alimony payments *(Statistical Abstract of the United States: 1993,* Table 612).

Child support (rather than alimony) is more often awarded to the mother with custody. However, it is often not enough.

NATIONAL DATA ❧   Although 77 percent of divorced women with children were awarded child support, it averaged less than $3,500 per year *(Statistical Abstract of the United States: 1993,* Table 612).

The economic status of families is on the decline and, unfortunately, the future appears ominous. Young families with children, and especially those headed by females alone, are considered to be the most vulnerable.

STEVEN WISENSALE

The percent of divorced women receiving child support should increase with the implementation of the Family Support Act in 1994. The provisions of this act call for child support orders to be automatically withheld from the noncustodial parent's paycheck. The only exceptions are if the courts find good cause not to withhold or parents draw up an alternative written agreement.

CONSIDERATION

Court-ordered child support payments from fathers are a relatively recent phenomenon. Before the 1920s, a divorced father was not legally obligated to pay child support. Rather, children were considered assets of the family head; his duty to support them ended if he wasn't in the home to receive the wages the children could earn through their own labor (Coontz, 1992).

A father may not pay child support for several reasons—he may be attempting to get back at an ex-wife who will not allow access to his children; he may have a new wife with new financial obligations; or he may be unemployed (the courts do not recognize the first two reasons as legitimate).

In a study of divorced women, 71 percent said that financial difficulties were their major problem (Amato & Partridge, 1987). Financial problems are most severe for women who have never worked, who have limited employment histories, and who have little education (Choi, 1992).

One researcher observed the economic consequences of divorce for women and suggested the following:

Young women must be encouraged to stay in school and invest in their own future. They must be made to realize that they may have to support their family without the help of a spouse should divorce occur (Mauldin, 1990, 145).

> **CONSIDERATION**
>
> One of the keys in changing the economic consequences of divorce for women is to change societal values and attitudes. Maudlin (1990) suggested that if societal attitudes encourage women to prepare for a traditional family life and discourage them from preparing to work outside the home, women will continue to suffer economic consequences following divorce. In additional, unless women are encouraged to prioritize their employment above their family they will suffer greater economic hardships if divorce occur.

Separation from Children: A Phenomenon for Fathers

One consequence of divorce for many men is that they will usually have less contact with their children. In the typical case, the father will move out of the home and be allowed "visitation" privileges. Although these can vary depending on the respective parents, a common scenario is every other weekend, splitting holidays, and four weeks in the summer. This translates into approximately 82 of 365 (or 22.4 percent) occasions in which the children sleep overnight with the father. Dudley (1991) noted that one of the most pervasive problems experienced by noncustodial fathers is:

> suffering caused by the feeling that they have lost their children. This occurs because they may no longer see their children on a regular basis or they must "visit" in a way that is quite different than they were used to when they lived with their children (p. 279).

Dudley (1991) identified 84 divorced fathers (mean of 6 years) who reported infrequent contact with their children. Forty percent of the fathers who saw their children infrequently reported the primary reason was interference on the part of the former spouse who reportedly refused to provide access to the children or who talked negatively to the children about their father. Two-thirds of these fathers reported they had to return to court over visitation issues.

I hate divorce. After 10 years, it hurts as much as it ever did.

PETER FELDNER
(DIVORCED FATHER)

Quality time happens in the middle of quantity time.

ANONYMOUS

> **CONSIDERATION**
>
> Custodial mothers who are angry at their ex-husbands may attempt to turn their children against the father. Noncustodial fathers are victims of this assault and feel helpless. Robert Bly (1990), who emphasized the importance of fathers in the lives of their children, particularly sons, wrote:
>
> > A friend told me that about 35, he began to wonder who his father really was. He hadn't seen his father in about ten years. He flew out to Seattle, where his father was living, knocked on the door, and when his father opened the door, said, "I want you to understand one thing. I don't accept my mother's view of you any longer."
> > What happened? I asked.
> > "My father broke into tears, and said, 'Now I can die.' " Fathers wait. What else can they do? (p. 25).

Not all divorced fathers grieve over the absence of contact with their children, and some voluntarily give them up. Such was the case of one man who said:

> It is my belief that it is better for my son not to be confused by two daddies. I was a child who didn't see his father from 3 to 33 and have NO hard feelings. I have raised two wonderful stepchildren as my own kids for the past 14 years and I have by design given up my right as a father so as not to confuse my son. I believe that his development is more important than my rights (Dudley, 1991, p. 282).

Adjustment After Divorce

You say I'll be fine,
It only takes time,
Someday that may be true,
But, it's too soon to tell.

BONNIE RAITT

Given that divorce is, for most people, an emotionally difficult experience, what are some ways to successfully cope with this experience? The following list contains some suggestions from a clinical psychologist (Turner, 1993) and researchers of divorce adjustment (Hammond, 1992; Goodman, 1992; Rigdon & Pett, 1992).

1. *Consider contacting a divorce mediator rather than an attorney.* Attorneys are trained to channel divorcing spouses into an adversarial pattern of relating. This pattern keeps conflict and hostility high while minimizing the chance to relate amicably. In addition, the money spent on attorneys puts an additional financial stress on the divorcing individuals.

2. *Take some responsibility for the divorce.* Since marriage is an interaction between the spouses, one person is seldom totally to blame for a divorce. Rather, both spouses share in the demise of the relationship.

We're sorting through what's left of you and me. They're paying yard sale prices for each golden memory.

SAMMY KERSHAW

3. *Learn from the divorce.* View the divorce as an opportunity to improve one's self for future relationships. What did you do that you might consider doing differently in the next relationship?

4. *Create positive thoughts.* Divorced people are susceptible to feeling as though they are a failure and are "no good." Improving their self-esteem is important for divorced persons. This can be done by systematically thinking positive thoughts about one's self. One technique is to write down 21 positive statements about one's self ("I am honest," "I am a good cook," "I am a good parent," etc.) and transfer these to seven 3 X 5 cards each containing three statements. Take one of these cards with you each day and read the thoughts to yourself at three regularly spaced intervals (e.g., ten in the morning, four in the afternoon, ten at night). This ensures that you are thinking good things about yourself and are not allowing yourself to drift into a negative set of thoughts.

It's just one of those things that I can't do nothing about . . .
Your love is just one of those things I have to learn to live without.

PAM TILLIS

5. *Avoid alcohol and other drugs.* The stress and despair that some people feel following a divorce makes them particularly vulnerable to the use of alcohol or other drugs; women may be more vulnerable than men (Doherty et al., 1989). Drugs and alcohol should be avoided because they produce an endless negative cycle. For example, stress is relieved by

Here I go again,
Mixing misery and gin.

MERLE HAGGARD

alcohol; alcohol produces a hangover and negative feelings; the negative feelings are relieved by more alcohol, producing more negative feelings, etc.

6. *Relax without drugs.* Deep muscle relaxation can be achieved by systematically tensing and relaxing each of the major muscle groups in the body. Alternatively, Yoga, transcendental meditation, and intense prayer can cause a deep state of relaxation. Whatever the form, it is important to schedule a time each day to get relaxed.

7. *Engage in aerobic exercise.* Exercise not only helps to counteract stress but also to avoid it. Jogging, swimming, riding an exercise bike, or other similar exercise for thirty minutes every other day increases the oxygen to one's brain and helps facilitate clear thinking. In addition, aerobic exercise produces endorphins in the brain, which create a sense of euphoria ("runner's high"). In addition, good health in general is associated with life satisfaction in older divorced individuals (Hammond, 1992).

8. *Engage in fun activities.* Divorced people tend to sit at home and brood over their "failed" relationship. This only compounds their depression. Doing what they have previously found enjoyable—movies, horseback riding, skiing, attending sporting events, etc.—provides an alternative to sitting on the couch alone.

9. *Continue interpersonal connections.* Adjustment to divorce is easier when intimate interaction with friends and family are continued (Bursik, 1991). This is particularly true if the individuals divorce past the age of 45 (Goodman, 1992) and for men. When divorced women and men are compared in regard to life satisfaction, men report more dissatisfaction. One researcher suggested that such lower satisfaction among men isrelated to their lack of skills in maintaining social supports (Hammond, 1992).

10. *Let go of the ex-partner.* Partners who stay negatively attached to the ex by harboring resentment and trying to "get back at the ex" and who do not make themselves available to new relationships limit their ability to adjust to a divorce (Tschann et al., 1989).

11. *Allow time to heal.* Since self-esteem usually drops after divorce, a person is often vulnerable to making commitments before working through feelings about the divorce. The time period most people need to adjust to divorce is between 12 and 16 months (Turner, 1993). Although being available to others may help to repair one's self-esteem, getting remarried during this time should be considered cautiously.

Relationship with Ex-spouse

It is assumed that ex-spouses hate each other and have only hostile interactions with each other following a divorce. Researcher Constance Ahrons, who studied the relationships between 98 pairs of ex-spouses, observed four patterns of ex-spouse relationships (Stark, 1986).

> Whenever you decide to become concerned about what other people say or do to you, you become their victim by letting them control your feelings.
>
> **JAMES WALTERS**

> No one that we have ever loved is totally lost, and it is very hard to lose someone that we have loved a little and hated a lot.
>
> **GEORGE VAILLANT**

Perfect Pals   These ex-spouses (12 percent of the sample) continued to be involved in each other's lives. Neither spouse had remarried or was living with someone else. One such couple shared a duplex apartment, so that their children could come and go freely between the homes.

Cooperative Colleagues   Comprising 38 percent of the sample, these ex-spouses were able to minimize potential conflicts and to have a moderate amount of interaction. Basically, they made an effort to get along because it was in the best interest of the children.

Angry Associates   Unable to contain their anger and hostility, 25 percent of the sample had a moderate amount of interaction but most of it was unpleasant. They were unable to separate their roles of spouse and parent.

Fiery Foes   Another 25 percent of the sample consisted of ex-spouses who had little interaction but always fought when they did. Their feelings toward each other were bitter and acrimonious. Masheter (1991) also examined the post-divorce relationships of 111 men and 154 women and found that 21 percent reported hostile feelings. One writer commented on such hostile relationships:

> . . . [divorce] is becoming an area of unfinished business between husbands and wives who thought they were through with each other. Simmering antipathy between ex-spouses who find themselves yoked to each other because of alimony and child custody arrangements is not unusual. But deliberate harassment, whether physical or psychological, is something else. It is the symptom of a dysfunctional divorce, and it is of increasing concern to the legislature, the courts, the police, and especially the victims (Belson, 1991, 75).

When children are involved, one parent may abduct the child or children from the parent who has custody. It has been estimated that over 163,000 children have been abducted and taken to another state with the intent to keep the child away from the custodial parent (Finkelhor et al., 1991).

> **CONSIDERATION**
>
> In some cases the acrimony extends to abducting the family dog. Such was the case of a woman who left her house and state and moved to another part of the country so that she could continue the relationship with her dog without the interference from her ex-husband. Such abductions are not considered with the same seriousness as child abductions since dogs are considered stolen property as opposed to kidnapping a person (Cauley, 1993).

After divorce, new partners seem to affect men and women differently. Men's psychological adjustment seems to be enhanced by having a new partner. "Women's psychological adjustment, by contrast, apparently is not so

---

To a large degree, the amount of post-divorce harassment is a function of how capable the people themselves are of solving their own problems.

MICHAEL MICHEL

One of the most recognized triggers that can almost instantly transform an amicable divorce into a war zone is the appearance of a third party. They have been replaced, and the blow often results in the loss of emotional control.

EVE BELSON

Don't tell me what to do, you've already said we were through . . .

PAM TILLIS

much promoted by new supportive relations, as it is negatively affected by the presence of conflictual relationships between significant family members. Women appear to be more affected by the residual hostility from the past marriage and problematic relations between partners and children in their new marriages or relationships (Coysh et al., 1989).

Relationship with Former In-Laws Forty-nine separated and divorced spouses shared how their divorce had affected the relationship with their former in-laws. In general, "loss of contact and change in the quality of the relationship occurred rapidly once the separation had become known" (Amert, 1988, 684). Only 11 percent of these ex-spouses maintained good relationships with their former in-laws following the separation.

Sexuality After Divorce

Of the more than 2 million people getting divorced, most will have intercourse within one year of being separated from their spouse. The meanings of intercourse for the separated or divorced vary. For many, intercourse is a way to reestablish—indeed, repair—their crippled self-esteem. Divorce is often a shattering emotional experience. The loss of a lover, the disruption of a daily routine, and the awareness of a new and negative label ("divorced person") all converge on the individual. Questions like "What did I do wrong?" "Am I a failure?" and "Is there anybody out there who will love me again?" loom in the minds of the divorced. One way to feel loved, at least temporarily, is through sex. Being held by another and being told that it feels good gives people some evidence that they are desirable. Because divorced people may be particularly vulnerable, they may reach for sexual encounters as if for a lifeboat. "I felt that as long as someone was having sex with me, I wasn't dead and I did matter," said one recently divorced person.

Whereas some divorced people use sex to mend their self-esteem, others use it to test their sexual adequacy. The divorced person may have been told by the former spouse that he or she was an inept lover. One man said his wife used to make fun of him because he was occasionally impotent. Intercourse with a new partner who did not belittle him reassured him of his sexual adequacy and his impotence ceased to be a problem. A woman described how her husband would sneer at her body and say no man would ever want her because she was so fat. After the divorce, she found men who thought she was attractive and who did not consider her weight to be a problem. Other divorced men and women say that what their spouses did not like, their new partners view as turn-ons. The result is a renewed sense of sexual desirability.

Beyond these motives for sexual interactions, many divorced people simply enjoy the sexual freedom their divorced state offers. Freed from the guilt that spouses who have extramarital intercourse experience, the divorced can have intercourse with whomever they choose.

Before getting remarried, most divorced people seem to go through predictable stages of sexual expression. The initial impact of the separation is followed by a variable period of emotional pain. During this time, the divorced may turn to sex for intimacy to soothe some of the pain, although this is rarely achieved.

This stage of looking for intimacy through intercourse overlaps with the divorced person's feeling of freedom and the desire to explore a wider range of sexual partners and behaviors than marriage provided. "I was a virgin at marriage and was married for 12 years. I've never had sex with anyone but my spouse, so I'm curious to know what other people are like sexually," one divorced person said.

But the divorced person soon tires of casual sex. One man said he had been through 22 partners since his divorce a year ago. He likened his situation to that of a person in a revolving door who is in motion but isn't going anywhere. "I want to get in a relationship with someone who cares about me and vice versa." The pattern is typical. Many divorced people initially use sex to restore their ailing self-esteem and to explore sexual parameters, but they soon drift toward sex within the context of an affectionate love relationship.

CONSIDERATION

It is sometimes believed that the divorced, as a group, have a wide, varied, and frequent sex life. National data on 340 divorced people suggest otherwise. In the past 12 months, 28 percent had no sexual partners; 46 percent had one sexual partner. Women were more likely than men to have had no sexual partners. Regarding age, those over 35 were more likely to have had no sexual partners than those under 35 (35 percent versus 4 percent) (Stack & Gundlach, 1992).

❦ Children and Divorce

NATIONAL DATA ❦ Over one million children experience the divorce of their parents annually (*Statistical Abstract of the United States: 1993*, Table 144).

Effects of Divorce on Children

> We need new terminology. The label "children of divorce" confuses children's lives with adult lives.
>
> KATHERINE R. ALLEN

Table 16.2 reflects the way 115 adult children (73 women, 42 men) perceived the positive and negative consequences of their parents getting divorced. Among the positive consequences were (1) the perception that the parents were happier being apart than together, (2) the decreased tension in the household, and (3) the opportunity to spend some time alone with each parent, which resulted in getting to know them better. Negative outcomes included the loss of feeling part of a family unit, losing ready access to both parents, and finding it more difficult to arrange family gatherings (Lang & Pett, 1992).

	N[a]	Percent
Positive Outcomes		
Parents		
Parents happier apart, not hurting each other anymore	109	23.2
Mother happier, doing things for herself now	54	11.5
Father happier, doing things for himself now	21	4.5
Subtotal	(184)	(39.2)
Adult Child		
Learned something from parents' divorce	74	15.8
Decreased tension at family gatherings	73	15.7
Have gotten to know parents on individual basis	63	13.4
Relief from parental fighting	37	7.8
Work harder at own marriage now	23	4.9
Don't have to see parent(s) as often	15	3.2
Subtotal	(285)	(60.8)
Total	469	100.0
Negative Outcomes		
Family Relationships		
Loss of family unity	130	21.7
Arranging family gatherings harder now	86	14.4
Have to work harder to see parents	61	10.2
Parents' hostility still creates tension in family	59	9.8
Parents' financial problems affects family members	23	3.8
Subtotal	(359)	(59.9)
Parental Relationships		
Poor relationship with parent now	58	9.7
Seeing a parent unhappy	47	7.8
Feel responsible for parent	30	5.0
My children don't get to see their grandparents as often	19	3.2
Have to work at staying neutral with parents	12	2.0
Subtotal	(166)	(27.7)
Adult Child		
Lack of trust in own relationships	37	6.2
Feel angry and confused	17	2.8
Not a part of father's new family	14	2.4
Stress on own marriage	4	0.7
Have to buy individual presents for parents now	2	0.3
Subtotal	(74)	(12.4)
Total	599	100.0

TABLE 16.2

Perceived Positive and Negative Outcomes of Parental Divorce

[a]The *N*s indicate the number of responses for the reasons listed.

Source: Nancy E. Lang and Marjorie A. Pett. Later-life parental divorce: The adult child's experience. *Family Perspective,* 1992, *26,* 121–146, Table 4. Reprinted with permission of Brigham Young University.

Previous research on the effects of divorce on children has produced mixed results. In a broad comprehensive study, two researchers analyzed data from over 81,000 people in 37 studies and concluded that "divorce (or permanent separation) has broad negative consequences for quality of life in adulthood" (Amato & Keith, 1991, 54). These researchers found that adult children of divorced parents experienced lower levels of psychological well-being (depression, low life satisfaction), family well-being (low marital quality, divorce), socioeconomic well-being (low educational attainment, income, and occupational prestige), and physical health. "These results lead to a pessimistic conclusion: the argument that parental divorce presents few problems for children's long-term development is simply inconsistent with the literature on this topic" (p. 54).

Berman (1991) interviewed 40 men and women whose parents had divorced and discovered that some continued to carry wounds from the experience. Low self-esteem, difficulty trusting others, difficulty with intimacy and fear of commitment were some of the problems she observed. Those who reported coping well with their parents' divorce had parents who remarried and were no longer angry at each other.

In spite of the research suggesting negative outcomes for divorced children, Lauer and Lauer (1991) compared 313 adults (mean age of 35) from intact-happy, intact-unhappy, death-disrupted, and divorce-disrupted families and observed "few if any, long-term differences in such things as self-esteem, social competence, dating behavior, and relational attitudes" (p. 289). The researchers concluded:

> Without minimizing the short-term and long-term trauma of experiencing an unhappy or disrupted family during childhood, it may be that most people are not as handicapped in the long run as some professionals have suggested. In spite of their doubts and various self-deprecating statements, most of those from disrupted and intact-unhappy families were able to form meaningful intimate relationships (p. 289).

> The social consequences of family change over the past few decades have been largely negative, especially for children.
>
> DAVID POPENOE

CONSIDERATION

The differences in the findings of these studies may be related to the different perceptions that individuals have of an event (divorce) and not to the event itself. Divorce, by itself doesn't do anything to children. It is how the parents teach their children to regard the event and the children's relationship with the respective parents after the divorce that influences the eventual outcome.

In addition, recent research suggests that the amount of parental conflict children are exposed to is central to the child's adjustment, self-esteem, and psychological well-being. Such conflict exists in intact families and may subside after a divorce. Hence, the processes of interaction and the quality of relationships the child is exposed to may be more important than family structure (Demo, 1992; Demo, 1993).

Minimizing Negative Effects of Divorce on Children

Researchers have identified the conditions under which a divorce has the least negative consequences for children (Amato, 1993; Pett et al., 1992; Isaacs, 1988; Tschann et al., 1989; Guidubaldi, 1988).

1. The parents have a cordial and cooperative relationship throughout the separation, divorce, and post-divorce period. In contrast, putting the child in conflict can be difficult. One daughter of divorced parents said:

   > My father told me, "If you love me, you would come visit me," and my mom told me, "If you love me, you won't visit him."

2. Both the custodial and noncustodial parent continue to spend time with the children and to communicate to them that they love them and are interested in them.
3. Children who usually live with custodial mothers following divorce are encouraged by the mother to maintain a regular and stable visitation schedule with their father.
4. Young, unmarried offspring report more disruption in relationships and family rituals caused by divorce than older married individuals. This finding by Pett et al. (1992) may be the basis of the belief that it is sometimes better for parents to wait until their children are "grown" before divorcing.
5. A temperament on the part of the child which allows her or him to adjust to change easily. Kalter (1989) found that the reaction of a child to divorce is influenced by the child's temperament. Some children are not easily frustrated and readily adapt to change; others have difficulty with even minor changes.

> **What is needed is a new social movement that stresses a lasting, monogamous, heterosexual relationship, which includes the procreation of children.**
>
> DAVID POPENOE

CONSIDERATION

Some children may benefit from support groups for children of divorce as a way to feel less isolated and to know that what they are thinking and feeling is similar to what other children are going through. These groups are often available through local mental health centers. Individual counseling may also help some children cope with and adjust to their parents' divorce.

---

6. In terms of who is granted custody of the child after divorce, matching the sex of the parent with the sex of the child is irrelevant. Based on a national study of almost 4,000 eighth graders, Downey and Powell (1993) concluded, "of the 35 social, psychological and educational outcomes studied, we cannot find even one in which both males and females benefit significantly from living with the same-sex parent" (p. 55).

> **Anger and ego aside, at the core of the differing scenarios are two issues: Cash and custody.**
>
> SUSAN SCHINDENETTE ON THE DIVORCE OF LONI ANDERSON AND BURT REYNOLDS

❧ Alternatives To Divorce

Divorce is not the only means of terminating a marriage. Others include annulment, separation (legal or informal), and desertion.

Annulment

The concept of annulment has its origin in the Roman Catholic church, which takes the position that marriage is indissoluble, except by death. Ten percent of 216 Catholics reported that annulment was the way their first marriage ended (O'Flaherty & Eells, 1988). An annulment states that no valid marriage ever existed and returns both parties to their premarital status. Any property exchanged as part of the marriage arrangement is returned to the original owner. Neither party is obligated to support the other economically.

Common reasons for annulments are fraud, bigamy, under legal age, impotence, and insanity. A university professor became involved in a relationship with one of his colleagues. During courtship he promised her that they would rear a "house full of babies." But after the marriage, she discovered that he had had a vasectomy several years earlier and had no intention of having more children. The marriage was annulled on the basis of fraud—his misrepresentation of himself to her. Most annulments are for fraud.

Bigamy is another basis for annulment. In our society, a person is allowed to be married to only one spouse at a time. If another marriage is contracted at the time a person is already married, the new spouse can have the marriage annulled. All 104 wives of confessed and convicted bigamist Giovanni Vigliotto were entitled to have their marriages to him annulled.

Most states have age requirements for marriage. When individuals are younger than the minimum age and marry without parental consent, the marriage may be annulled if either set of parents does not approve of the union. However, if neither set of parents or guardians disapproves of the marriage, it may be regarded as legal; the marriage is not automatically annulled.

Intercourse is a legal right of marriage. In some states, if a spouse is impotent, refuses to have intercourse, or is unable to do so for physical or psychological reasons, the other spouse can seek and may be granted an annulment.

Insanity and a lack of understanding of the marriage agreement are also reasons for annulment. Someone who is mentally deficient and incapable of understanding the meaning of a marriage ceremony can have a marriage annulled. However, being drunk at the time of the wedding is insufficient grounds for annulment.

Although annulments are granted by civil courts, a Catholic who divorces and wants to remarry in the Church must have the first marriage annulled by the Church. Grounds for Church annulment vary widely; the result is that Catholics seeking to annul their first marriage must find a reason the Church will accept. In some cases, marriages have been annulled even though the couple has been married several years and has children. Julio Iglesias had his marriage of eight years (which included three children) annulled.

Separation

There are two types of separation—formal and informal. In December 1992, Prime Minister John Major announced the official formal separation of the Prince (Charles) and Princess (Diana) of Wales and noted that there were no plans for divorce. Such a separation occurs as infrequently as an annulment and is designed for unhappy couples who (for personal, religious, or social reasons) do not wish to divorce.

Typical items in a formal separation agreement include: (1) the husband and wife live separately; (2) their right to sexual intercourse with each other is ended; (3) the economic responsibilities of the spouses to each other is limited to the separation agreement; and (4) custody of the children is specified in the agreement, with visitation privileges granted to the noncustodial parent. The spouses may have emotional and sexual relationships with others, but neither party has the right to remarry. Although some couples live under this agreement until the death of one spouse, others draw up a separation agreement as a prelude to divorce. In some states, being legally separated for one year is a ground for divorce.

An informal separation (which is much more common) is similar to a legal separation except that no lawyer is involved in the agreement. The husband and wife settle the issues of custody, visitation, alimony, and child support between themselves. Because no legal papers are drawn up, the couple is still married from the state's point of view.

Attorneys advise against an informal separation (unless it is temporary) to avoid subsequent legal problems. For example, after three years of an informal separation, a mother decided that she wanted custody of her son. Although the father would have been willing earlier to sign a separation agreement that would have given her legal custody of her son, he was now unwilling to do so. Each spouse hired a lawyer and had a bitter and expensive court fight.

Desertion

Desertion differs from informal separation in that the deserter walks out and breaks off all contact. Although either spouse may desert, it is usually the husband who does so. A major reason for deserting is to escape the increasing financial demands of a family. Desertion usually results in nonsupport, which is a crime.

The sudden desertion by a husband sometimes has more severe negative consequences for the wife than divorce would. Unlike the divorced woman, the deserted woman is not free to remarry for several years. In addition, she

Desertion is the poor man's method of divorce.

E.C. MCKENZIE

receives no child support or alimony payments, and the children are deprived of a father.

Desertion is not unique to husbands. Although infrequent, wives and mothers also leave their husbands and children. Their primary reason for doing so is to escape from an intolerable marriage and feeling trapped by the role of mother. "I'm tired of having to think about my children and my husband all the time—I want a life for myself," said one woman who deserted her family. "I want to live too." But such desertion is not without its consequences. Most mothers who desert their children feel extremely guilty.

Widowhood

A marriage relationship may also be ended by the death of one spouse.

NATIONAL DATA   About one-fourth of men age 75 and older and two-thirds of women age 75 and older are widowers and widows (*Statistical Abstract of the United States: 1993*, Table 61). There are 2.4 million widowers (2.7 percent of the population) and 11.3 million widows (11.7 percent of the population) (*Statistical Abstract of the United States: 1993*, Table 59). On average, women outlive men by seven years (National Center for Health Statistics, 1993b).

As a society, we tend to avoid acknowledging the reality of death. We speak of people "passing away" and being placed in "memorial gardens" rather than of people dying and being buried in the ground. In our society, "we have a phobia about death" (LaNeave, 1993). To help view death as a normal part of life, courses on death and dying are being offered in some high schools (Moore, 1989), as well as in colleges and universities. The unrealistic attitudes about death that are perpetuated in our society contribute to the fact that the death of a spouse may be one of the most severe social and personal crisis events we experience. One widow described her husband's death as "the most difficult tragedy of my life, which has caused a change in my lifestyle, friends, and finances . . . you never get over it completely. My husband has been dead 27 years, and I still think about him and the life we shared every day."

Although the death of a spouse may be very traumatic, in some cases it may relieve more stress than it creates. For example, caring for a spouse who is chronically ill and in great pain may be incredibly stressful. The level of stress may actually decrease after the death of the chronically ill spouse.

The level of stress experienced by a widowed person also depends on the quality of the marital relationship prior to the spouse's death. Wheaton (1990) found that the distress and grief felt after a spouse's death and may be less intense if the marriage was problematic.

The Bereavement Process

Although every individual reacts somewhat differently, widows and widowers go through similar stages as they adjust to the death of their partner.

One time I was hitchhiking and a hearse stopped. I said, "No thanks . . . I'm not going that far."

STEVEN WRIGHT

Death

Death is black.
It smells like dead roses.
It tastes like burnt cookies.
It sounds like a quiet room.
And it feels like a broken heart.

KIMBERLY JONES
(REPRINTED WITH PERMISSION OF KIMBERLY JONES AND REBECCA BAKER JONES)

These stages usually involve shock, denial, anger, deep grief, disorientation (sometimes), and construction of a new identity as a person without a partner. Sometimes this process begins when the person is alive. Some spouses whose partner has been diagnosed as having cancer report moving away intrapsychically (decreasing their marital commitment) when compared with spouses whose partners are healthy (Swensen & Fuller, 1992).

> ### CONSIDERATION
>
> The initial impact of a spouse's death may be devastating, but most people can adjust to the loss. Time and other relationships seem to help. "It took about two years for me to get over the pain, loneliness, and self-pity I felt after she died," said one widower. "And I still get a wave of sadness at Christmas, the anniversary of her death, her birthday, and our wedding date. I'm remarried now, and that helps a lot to get over thinking about it every day." The widowed spouse might consider that the immediate and intense pain felt at the time of the spouse's death usually decreases over time. Some find that joining a bereavement support group is helpful in adjusting to the death of one's spouse. Such support groups are often available through local mental health centers.

Adjustment for Widows

Although both women and men go through similar stages of bereavement, each person responds differently to particular aspects of the adjustment. Many wives are married to husbands who make more money than they do, and a husband's death often means an end to the much needed regular monthly check. "Aside from missing my husband terribly," recalls one widow, "it means I'll have to move out of this house because we didn't have insurance to pay off the house and my salary won't cover the house payment each month."

Other widows experience difficulties in making decisions. "Paul and I always talked everything over, and I depended on him to make the final decision." Decisions about selling property, moving into smaller living quarters, and buying health insurance may be particularly difficult for the woman who has always depended on her husband to make such decisions.

But there are compensating factors for widows. The widow is more likely than the widower to derive emotional satisfaction from her children and grandchildren. She is also more likely to be welcome in the home of the son or daughter, where she can help with the household responsibilities.

In addition, widows have more people with whom they share a similar role than widowers do. Large churches may have Sunday school classes for widows; community centers offer special programs for them. Between interactions with other widows and with children and grandchildren, the widow is likely to continue her traditional domestic activities, which often give order and stability to her life. Although her husband is gone, what she does each day does not change that much.

You can bless loss because a precondition of loss is having had what you most wanted.

RON HAAK

The death of a spouse is a major life crisis event.

I never let Buddy go. I froze in time. I'm still the same person as the day Buddy died.

MARIA ELENA HOLLY

The traditional widow wore a black dress, sat on the porch and watched the young people go skiing. The modern widow wears a bathing suit and goes skiing herself.

WILLIAM GOODE

While good health is the greatest predictor of positive self-esteem among the elderly widowed, good relationships with grandchildren is also important (Forsyth & Robin, 1992). Having a sense of control in the present and a hope of self-determination in the future are also important (p. 85).

Nonwhites and persons in close-knit ethnic communities are often characterized by more structured roles for widows, less of a couple orientation between husband and wife, and more developed support systems for the widowed. For these reasons, Blacks, Mexican Americans, and Asian Americans tend to have an easier adjustment to the role of widow than whites. For example, nonwhites are more likely to house and care for widows inside the kinship system, whereas whites are more likely to live alone after the death of a spouse (Pitcher & Larson, 1989).

Adjustment for Widowers

The greatest challenge of all in late life comes with the loss of intimates—husbands, wives, and also friends.

PAUL THOMPSON

Whereas most wives expect to be a widow some day (and can have a psychological dress rehearsal), few husbands expect to be widowers. However, men who lose their spouses do not seem to face the economic hardship widows do. In a study of 27 widowers, money was not mentioned as one of the more serious concerns (Clark et al., 1986). The two most frequently cited problems were loneliness and accepting the fact that the mate had died.

Most of the men had found ways to help them cope with their loneliness. Over one-half of them saw their children at least once a week, and 85 percent reported having a "close" relationship with at least one child (see In Focus 16.3). Over 70 percent had close friends they saw each week, and many were members of a social or religious organization.

When asked what they did to help them cope with the death of their spouses, most of these men cited being with their family, reading, and believing in God. Dating someone new also helped; almost one-half of these men had done so.

Another problem that many widowers face is difficulty in coping with domestic tasks. Husbands who have been socialized into rigid gender role patterns of behavior may have relied on their wives to perform most domestic chores. In the event of their spouse's death, these husbands may find themselves unprepared to take care of basic domestic needs, such as cooking, shopping, and laundry.

Sexuality After Being Widowed

The 13 million widowed in the United States differ from the divorced in their sexual behavior. In general, widowed men and women have sexual interactions less frequently than those who are divorced. A major reason is the lack of an available partner, but others feel they are "cheating" on the deceased. "It's a guilty feeling I get," expressed one widower, "that I shouldn't want to get involved with someone else and that I shouldn't enjoy it."

The Sandwich Generation: Caring for Widowed and Elderly Parents

Not all widows are elderly, and not all elderly parents are widowed. Nevertheless, adult children are often challenged with the responsibility of taking care of their elderly parents. They are called the *sandwich generation* because they are caught between caring for their own children and caring for their parents. In 90 percent of the cases these caregivers are women with an average age of 57 (Dychtwald, 1990). Reasons for increasing numbers in the sandwich generation include:

1. *Longevity.* The over-85 age group, the segment of the population most in need of care, is the fastest growing segment of our population.
2. *Chronic disease.* In the past, diseases took the elderly quickly. Today, prevalent diseases such as arthritis and Alzheimer's do not offer "an immediate death sentence, but rather a lifetime imprisonment" (Dychtwald, 1990, 239).
3. *Fewer children to help.* The current generation of elderly had fewer children than the elderly in previous generations. Hence, the number of children to look after them is smaller. Those who are an only child have no one with whom to share the care of elderly parents.
4. *Commitment to parental care.* Contrary to the myth that children in the United States abrogate responsibility for taking care of their parents, children institutionalize their parents only as a last resort.

Caring for a dependent aging parent requires a great deal of effort, sacrifice, and decision making on the part of five million adults in the United States who cope with the situation daily. Some examples:

- An only son drives hundreds of miles every week to the next state to cut his aging mothers grass, pay her bills, and fill her refrigerator with groceries. While there, he must also arrange for the plumber to fix the toilet and talk with the social worker who is suppose to visit.
- A family moves grandmother's daybed into the living room since they cannot afford the cost of a nursing home. The family of four take turns feeding, changing her diapers, and sitting with her. The children have asked, "When is grandmother going to die?"

- A graduate student drops out of school so that she can spend her time with her mother whose husband recently died. The mother has Alzheimer's and sometimes does not recognize her daughter. The daughter's husband feels abandoned and has left her.

The emotional toll is heavy. Guilt, resentment, and anger are the most commonly reported feelings. The guilt comes from having promised the parents that they would be cared for when they became old and frail. Paying off the promise often entails more than the children ever expected. Or the offspring may feel guilty that they resent disrupting their own lives to care for their parents. Or they may feel guilty that they are angry about the frustration their parents are causing them. "I must be an awful person to begrudge taking my mother supper," said one daughter. "But I feel that my life is consumed by the demands she makes on me, and I have no time for myself."

CARING FOR A WIDOWED OR AGING PARENT—SOME SUGGESTIONS

Be Realistic. Responding to the needs of an aging parent is not easy, and there is no magic solution. Don't be unhappy if there isn't a quick answer to every problem. Accept the fact that caring for an aging parent is one of the more difficult challenges you will ever face.

Involve Siblings. More than 85 percent of all adult children have brothers or sisters. Because some offspring live closer to or have closer relationships with one or both parents, they may inadvertently wind up as almost total caregivers for their aging parents. It is a mistake not to involve your brothers and sisters in the care of parents. Tell them that your parents can no longer fend for themselves, and ask them to help you help them. If the siblings cannot offer practical support, they may be responsible enough to send money. Try to arrange it so that they send you a specified amount every month to help pay for the costs of caring for your parents. Whatever the nature of the support, ask for it.

(continued on next page)

·~ IN FOCUS   16.3 ~·

Communicate Openly. It is important to keep communication channels open with your parents. Tell them how you feel, try to engage them in conversation, and don't "spring" anything on them. Some children decide on their own that it is time to put their parent in a nursing home, drive them to the door, and dump them. They avoid bringing up the subject of "nursing home" for fear that their parents will react with hurt and anger. Such fears are realistic. Interviews with the elderly in need of care revealed that the elders fear being a burden, hide their troubles and feelings, and generally feel no sense of contribution to the household (Parsons et al., 1989).

Express Love. Such open discussions with your parents may be difficult and should be tempered with expressions of love. Tell your parents that you love them. Touch them. Hug them. Show them that you care about them and intend to see that their needs are taken care of. Elderly people often spend a lot of time alone and sometimes wonder if anyone cares for them.

Investigate the Meals-on-Wheels Program. For individuals with full-time jobs and children of their own, the need for support in caring for an elderly parent is particularly great. Many communities offer a Meals-on-Wheels program in which the local council on aging will send a well-balanced meal twice a day to persons who are homebound, who can't prepare food for themselves, and who have no one to do it for them.

The Meals-on-Wheels program is particularly helpful to adults whose aging parents live in another town or state. "I called up the local council on aging in the county in which my mother lives," said one daughter, "told them I had a mother who lived there and who needed food and could they help. They took food to her door twice a day, every day. It was a lifesaver for both of us."

Investigate Elderly Day Care. Another way you can get a break from constant attention to the needs of your aging

parent is through a program that provides a place for you to take your parent during the day. Elderly day care, available in some communities, allows employed adults to take their parents to the day care center in the morning and return after work. The parent has shelter, food, and others to interact with throughout the day and can stay with the son or daughter at night. "This is a wonderful program for us," said one daughter. "This way we didn't have to put my mother in a nursing home but had full-time coverage for her."

Investigate Chore-Service Program. Similar to the Meals-on-Wheels and elderly day care programs, the chore-service program sends someone to help the elderly do chores that they cannot do by themselves. If you live in another town or state, you may be able to provide chore services for your aging parent long distance (for example, someone to mop the kitchen floor, clean the gutters, and grocery shop).

Meals-on-Wheels, elderly day care, and chore-service programs are not available in every city. You should contact your county Council on Aging or your local Social Services Department to determine the nearest location to you of self-help facilities for the elderly. Your parents' physician may also be aware of what resources for the elderly are available in your community.

Explore Organizations to Join. A number of organizations have evolved for persons who are caring for an aging parent. Children of Aging Parents (CAPS, 2761 Trenton Road, Levittown, PA 19056) has more than 12,000 members who are experiencing similar concerns. Joining such an organization helps to reduce the feeling that you are facing the problems of caring for an aging parent alone. An additional resource is the National Support Center for Families of the Aging (P.O. Box 245, Swarthmore, PA 19081). A newsletter, "Advice for Adults with Aging Parents," is available from Helpful Publications, Inc. (310 West Durham Street, Philadelphia, PA 19119).

Social expectations also do not support sexual expression among the widowed. Some older widows are considered "too old" for sex. The lack of an available sexual partner, feelings of guilt at the idea of cheating on the deceased, and an unsupportive social context seem to conspire against the widowed. When a group of widows (ages 67–78) were asked how they coped with their sexual feelings when they had no partner, they responded:

> Only by keeping busy. Keep occupied with various activities and friends.
> Do physical exercise. Have many interests, hobbies.
> We just have to accept it and interest ourselves in other things.
> By turning to music or other arts, painting, dancing is excellent . . . using nurturant qualities, loving pets, the elderly, shut-ins. Reading, hiking . . . lots more. My mind controls my sex desires (Starr & Weiner, 1982, 165–167).

Another way that some widows may cope with their sexual needs is through masturbation. However, given the generally negative view our society has of masturbation, some widows may not consider this option.

✍ Preparation for Widowhood

Planning ahead for eventual widowhood may be difficult because it forces us to confront our own and our spouse's mortality. But as one widow said, "It's not as hard as making the arrangements later." There are several key areas to consider in preparing for the death of either spouse. Such preparation includes giving careful, early attention to wills, insurance, titles, and funeral expenses.

Wills

A will ensures that your money and property will be left to the people you want to have them. If you die intestate (without leaving a will), the state in which you lived will decide who gets what and how much. For example, suppose a married man with no children dies intestate. Although he may want his wife to have everything, she may get only half if the state law provides that his parents are entitled to half of his estate.

Rosenfeld (1992) interviewed 315 people aged 65 and older to identify patterns in estate giving. Most (44) were what he called "harmonizers" in that they gave to each child according to his or her need. Another 31 percent he referred to as "equalizers" in that they gave the same amount to each of their offspring. Still another 14 percent gave to the person who would take care of them in their old age, and 11 percent (distancers) gave to an institution, such as a school or religious group.

Under federal law, an estate tax (also known as an inheritance or transfer tax) return must be filed for every estate with gross assets of more than $600,000. And any tax due must be paid at the time the return is filed. Estates valued at less than $600,000 are not taxed.

Although a will is necessary in preparing for the death of a spouse, two additional documents are important when either spouse becomes incapacitated. A Living Will is a document stating that should you become terminally ill, with no hope for recovery, you do not want your life prolonged by artificial

Absence of a regular sexual partner is a continuing effect of widowhood for many spouses.

I have never wanted to live to be old, so old I'd run out of friends or money.

MARGOT FONTEYN

The best time to die is when you are on top and in your prime . . . that way you don't have to experience the slow humiliation and deterioration of coming down.

A MORTICIAN

means. A Living Will can be obtained from the Society for the Right to Die (250 West 57th Street, New York, NY 10107), a nonprofit organization. California, Idaho, and Wisconsin require that the document be re-signed every five years; Georgia has a seven-year re-signing requirement.

The second document, Power of Attorney, allows your spouse or someone whom you designate to sign papers on your behalf in the event that you become incapacitated and are unable to do so. For example, if you were brain dead and your spouse needed income, he or she could sell land that you owned if you had signed a Power of Attorney.

Insurance

Having made a will, check your life insurance policy for amount, type of payment, and ownership of policy. Assuming that the insured feels that the face value of the policy is adequate, check to see if the payments are to be made monthly or in a lump sum. One widow was only allowed to receive monthly payments of $125 instead of the lump sum she needed to pay off her house.

Titles

Valuable things such as houses, cars, and checking accounts may be subject to estate taxes if they are part of the deceased spouse's estate. If these are listed in the wife's name, they are considered her property and consequently not part of the husband's estate. Of course, if the wife dies first, the husband will face the inheritance tax problems she was to have avoided. So some balance of ownership is desirable. Retitling property to achieve a balance is only advisable, however, in a stable relationship. The transfer of ownership of large items followed by a divorce may create havoc.

Funeral Expenses

Currently, the cost of a funeral may range from $1,500 to $15,000. The average cost is around $10,000. The price includes embalming, casket, funeral service, use of the building for visitation, and cars for transportation to the cemetery.

The federal government now requires funeral homes to itemize the cost of their services and materials before an individual agrees to any arrangements. In addition, funeral homes are required to give price information over the telephone to permit customers to shop around. Embalming is often not necessary; it is usually required only if the death was caused by a specific contagious disease such as polio, diphtheria, or tuberculosis.

Alternative ways to avoid traditional funeral expenses include donating the body to medical research, cremation, and joining a memorial society. If you want to consider body donation, contact a medical school near you and ask about the procedure for donating your body for medical research and teaching. This usually involves completing an application specifying your wish that your body be donated to a certain medical school. At the time of your death, your spouse would then contact a local mortician, who would make the necessary arrangements with the medical school. Although you have donated your body to medicine, the traditional funeral service may still be held, with your body being transferred to the medical school rather than to a cemetery afterward; or your body may be removed to the medical school immediately after death, and a memorial service may be held later. In either case, the medical school usually pays the embalming fee and the cost of transporting your body up to 200 miles.

Cremation is another alternative. The cost is usually about $200. As with body donation, a memorial service may be held at a cost of around $1,000.

δ Trends

The number of people seeking a divorce may decrease. The number of divorces in the United States has stabilized since the early 80s. In 1981 the number of divorces per 1,000 population was 5.3. Since then the rate has dropped and for the last few years has been 4.7 (National Center for Health Statistics, 1993; *Statistical Abstract of the United States: 1993,* Table 140). (In Japan, the rate is 1.26 per 1000; in the U.K, the rate is 2.89 per 1000.)

Reasons for the stabilization of divorce rate may be related to the recession (there are fewer divorces in difficult economic times), a return to familism (not all researchers agree), a determination on the part of those from divorced families not to repeat the experience of their parents, and older age at first marriage (Brubaker & Kimberly, 1992).

Those who do divorce will more often be those who are over the age of 45. These older marrieds have begun to divorce more often in recent years (Brubaker & Hennon, 1992). Their doing so may be a function of them having been socialized to be less conservative rather than a function of their age.

Divorce mediation will also become more widespread. Rather than end their relationship in an expensive and hostile court fight, more spouses will negotiate the conditions of their settlement with the aid of a divorce mediator. Mediating the issues of custody, visitation, child support, and spouse support (if there is any), usually saves both time and money. More importantly, mediation facilitates a more cooperative co-parenting relationship between ex-spouses who have children and it sets the stage for negotiating rather than litigating subsequent issues as they come up. An increasing number of jurisdictions have mandatory child custody mediation programs, whereby parents in a custody dispute are required to attempt to resolve their dispute through mediation before their case may be heard in court. At this time, the states of California, Delaware, and Maine have enacted mandatory mediation legislation requiring all parties requesting a custody or visitation hearing first attempt to settle the dispute in mediation (Arditti, 1991). More states will enact similar legislation.

Legal changes will include more granting of custody to the father. Indeed, single-father families is one of the fastest growing family structures in the United States. One percent of all children lived alone with their father in 1970 in contrast to over three percent in 1992 (*Statistical Abstract of the United States: 1993*, Table 80). Such a rise has been influenced by the surge of women into the workforce resulting in a reevaluation of traditional roles assigned to fathers. As fathers have become closer with their children they are more willing to come forward and claim the nontraditional parenting role for themselves.

Another trend in our society is the establishment of mandatory parent education programs for parents who are getting a divorce (Association of Family and Conciliation Courts, 1993, Personal Communication). For example, in Cobb County, Georgia, divorcing parents must participate in a court-mandated four-hour educational program called "Children Coping with Divorce." The program teaches divorcing parents to remain a stable force in their children's lives and addresses age and developmental factors that parents should consider in caring for their children; pitfalls to avoid and skills to help children cope are also emphasized. Over 94 percent of parents who participate in the program evaluate the program as being "helpful" to "extremely helpful." Other similar court-mandated programs include "Sensible Approach to Divorce" (Wyandotte County, Kansas) and "Parenting After Divorce" (Orange County, North Carolina).

⤻ CHOICES ⤳

Since more than one-half of all divorces involve children, a basic decision to be made in a divorce is who gets custody of the children? The options include the mother, the father, or joint custody.

There are two separate custody decisions that divorcing parents must make (or a judge must make for them). These two decisions involve the determination of legal custody and physical custody. Legal custody refers to the legal right to make decisions in reference to a minor child. Such decisions include those relating to medical care and education. Legal custody may be granted to one parent, who would have sole responsibility for making decisions in reference to the child. Alternatively, parents may have joint legal custody, whereby both parents would have legal input into the medical and educational decisions regarding the child.

❦ CHOICES ❦

Physical custody refers to where the child will live. Most custody battles are fought over physical custody, not legal custody. The following sections refer to choices involving physical custody of children.

Who Gets the Children? Custody Criteria of Parents

Nine out of 10 custody decisions after divorce result in one parent (usually the mother) receiving primary physical custody of the children with the other parent (usually the father) receiving visitation rights. This arrangement is usually decided on by the divorcing couple. "That's good," said one attorney, "because if spouses don't make their own decisions, the courts will make their choices for them."

The criteria that parents and judges use to determine who will get physical custody of the children include age of the children, sex of the children, emotional relationship of the parents with the children, time available to spend with the children, living conditions, income, and previous care (physical and emotional) of the children by the respective parents.

Who gets physical custody has implications not only for the child but also for the parents. Research demonstrates that parents who get custody of children will continue to benefit from the children being emotionally attached to them. Conversely, the emotional attachment of the children to

noncustodial parents tends to decrease (White et al., 1985).

Custody to One Parent?

When the parents disagree about who should have physical custody of the children, a judge must decide. In the past, preference has been given to the mother. Awarding custody to the mother, particularly of younger children, is based on the "tender-years doctrine," which holds that young children need their mother and it is in their best interests to live with her.

This doctrine was challenged by Ken Lewis, a divorced father of two daughters, who contended that the "tender-years doctrine" was an insidious example of sex discrimination. He won custody of his children on the grounds that the word *mother* is a verb and that he had demonstrated better mothering skills than the biological mother. Fathers for Equal Rights of Michigan and Canada (P.O. Box 2272, Southfield, MI 48037) is an organization for fathers seeking divorce and custody reform. Dr. Lewis (Child Custody Evaluation, Inc., P.O. Box 202, Glenride, PA 19038) now specializes in interviewing all parties involved in a custody case and making recommendations to the judge. He has evaluated over 600 cases, and the judges have followed his recommendations in over 90 percent of them.

When one spouse gets primary physical custody, the relationship the child has with the noncustodial parent

weakens over time (Hobart, 1988). "As time since the separation passes and as their parents remarry, children's contact with absent parents diminishes further" (Seltzer & Bianchi, 1988).

Joint Custody?

An alternative to sole custody that is increasingly being considered by parents and the courts is joint custody. Over half of the states have enacted legislation authorizing joint custody. Fewer than 15 percent of separated/divorced couples actually have a joint custody arrangement—these are more often higher income, urban couples (Donnelly & Finkelhor, 1993). In a typical joint physical custody arrangement, the parents continue to live in close proximity to each other. The children may spend part of each week with each parent or may spend alternating weeks with each parent.

One potential disadvantage of joint custody is that it tends to put hostile ex-spouses in more frequent contact with each other so that the marital war continues. Children do not profit from being subjected to such bickering and the relationships with parents are not significantly better. In a national study of children whose parents had a joint custody arrangement, the researchers found "no evidence" of less conflict or better relationships with parents than if they lived with one parent and saw the other on a visitation basis (Donnelly & Finkelhor, 1992).

(continued)

But joint custody has a positive side. Ex-spouses may fight less if they have joint custody because there is no inequity in terms of the parents' involvement in the children's lives. Children will benefit from the resultant decrease in hostility between parents who have both "won" them. Unlike the sole-parent custody outcome, in which one parent (usually the mother) wins and the father is banished, children under joint custody may continue to benefit from the love and attention of both parents. Children in homes where joint custody has been awarded might also have greater financial resources available to them than children in sole-custody homes—fathers awarded joint custody are more likely to pay child support (Arditti, 1991).

Joint physical custody may also be advantageous in that the stress of parenting does not fall on one parent, but rather is shared. One mother who has a joint custody arrangement with her ex-husband said, "When Jamie is with her Dad, I get a break from the parenting role, and I have a chance to do things for myself. I love my daughter, but I also love having time for myself." Another joint parenting father said, "When you live with your kids everyday, you're just not always happy to be with them. But after you haven't seen them for 3 days, it feels good to see them again."

Depending on the level of hostility between the ex-partners, their motivations for seeking sole or joint custody, and their relationship with their children, any arrangement could have positive or negative consequences for the spouses and the children. In those cases in which the spouses exhibit minimal hostility toward each other and have strong emotional attachments to their children, as well as the desire to remain an active influence in their children's lives, joint custody may be the best of all possible choices.

Relationship with Ex-Spouse?

Spouses who divorce must make a choice in terms of what kind of relationship they will have with each other. This choice is crucial, in that it not only affects their lives, but also their children's lives.

Traditionally, custody "battles" have been hostile and bitter relationships between spouses. The caustic custody fight between Mia Farrow and Woody Allen in 1993 over their three children reflected the high level of acrimony characteristic of such custody disputes. Everyone loses when this type of relationship is allowed to develop. The parents continue to harbor negative feelings for each other, and the children are caught in the crossfire. They aren't free to develop or express love for either parent out of fear of disapproval from the other parent. Ex-spouses might consider the costs to their children of continuing the hostility and call a truce on their behalf. Everyone will profit from the choice. In the next chapter we emphasize the benefits of co-parenting after divorce.

Summary

Societal factors contributing to divorce include a decreased expectation that marriage is permanent, loss of family functions, increased economic independence of wives, fewer moral/religious sanctions, and liberal divorce laws. Individual factors include a high frequency of negative behavior, a low frequency of positive behavior, lack of conflict resolution skills, and extramarital relationships.

Divorce mediation is becoming an alternative to a litigated divorce. With the help of a mediator, the spouses agree on parenting access, division of property, spousal support, and child support. A document is created and given to an attorney to process it through the court so that it becomes legal. Mediated divorces are less expensive, time consuming, and acrimonious when compared to litigated divorces.

For most, divorce represents a difficult transition. Loss of self-esteem, lack of money, and concern over children are among the potential consequences of divorce. But divorce may also represent a bridge from an unhappy relationship and personal confinement to new relationships and personal growth. For many, divorce is also the beginning of a new life. Conditions predicting a positive divorce adjustment include reducing one's stress through regular exercise and relaxation, avoiding alcohol and drugs, engaging in enjoyable activities with friends, delaying any new marital commitments for 12 to 18 months, and thinking positive thoughts about one's self.

Researchers disagree on the long-term negative effects of divorce on children. Researchers agree that the relationship between the parents is a critical factor in the child's adjustment—greater acrimony equals a more difficult adjustment. Joint custody is most beneficial to the child when the parents have a reasonably cordial relationship after the divorce.

Death terminates marriages that do not end by divorce, annulment, or desertion. Adjusting to the death of one's spouse is one of the most difficult life crises a person experiences. Although the trauma of widowhood cannot be avoided, it can be eased by attending to various concerns, such as wills, insurance, titles, and funeral arrangements. A great deal of money can often be saved by drawing up a will, having adequate life and health insurance, putting property in the wife's name, and donating one's body to a medical school.

Trends in divorce include a stabilization of the divorce rate (and possibly a decline), increased divorce mediation, increased custody to the father, and the establishment of mandatory parent education programs for divorcing parents.

Questions for Reflection

1. How do you feel about the high rate of divorce in the United States? Do you feel it is a sign of a decaying society because it reflects people's lack of commitment to family life? Or is the high divorce rate a sign of family strength because it reflects that people value marriage so much that they are unwilling to remain in unhappy marriages?
2. Do you feel the people you know who have gotten divorced are glad they did so? Why do they feel this way? Do you think they are better off? Why or why not?

3. How comfortable would you be discussing funeral arrangements with your partner? Do you feel the potential money saved is worth the discomfort you might feel?

References

Amato, P. R. Children's adjustment to divorce: Theories, hypotheses, and empirical support. *Journal of Marriage and the Family,* 1993, *55,* 23–28.

Amato, P. R. and B. Keith. Parental divorce and adult well-being: A meta-analysis. *Journal of Marriage and the Family,* 1991, *53,* 43–58.

Amato, P. R. and S. Partridge. Women and divorce with dependent children: Material, personal, family, and social well-being. *Family Relations,* 1987, *36,* 316–320.

American Council on Education and University of California. The American freshman: National norms for fall, 1992. Los Angeles, Calif.: Los Angeles Higher Education Research Institute, 1992.

Amert, Anne-Marie. Relationships with former in-laws after divorce: A research note. *Journal of Marriage and the Family,* 1988, *50,* 679–686.

Arditti, J. A. Child support noncompliance and divorced fathers: Rethinking the role of paternal involvement. *Journal of Divorce and Remarriage,* 1991, *14,* 107–120.

Association of Family and Conciliation Courts. (329 West Wilson St., Madison, Wisconsin 53703–3612). Personal communication. January, 1993.

Belson, E. Unfinished business. *OrangeCoast,* July 1991, 75–89.

Berman, C. *Adult children of divorce speak out.* New York: Simon and Schuster, Inc., 1991.

Bly, Robert. *Iron John.* Reading, Mass.: Addison-Wesley Publishing Company, 1990.

Broman, C. L. Satisfaction among Blacks: The significance of marriage and parenthood. *Journal of Marriage and the Family,* 1988, *50,* 45–51.

Brubaker, T. H. and C. B. Hennon. Late life divorce and its implications for family life education. *Family Perspective,* 1992, *26,* 11–34.

Brubaker, T. H. and J. A. Kimberly. Challenges to the American family. *Family Relations,* T. H. Brubaker, ed. Newbury Park, Calif.: Sage Publications, 1992, 3–16.

Buehler, C. Initiator status and divorce transition. *Family Relations,* 1987, *36,* 82–86.

Bugaighis, M. A., W. R. Schumm, A. P. Jurich, and S. R. Bollman. Factors associated with thoughts of marital separation. *Journal of Divorce,* 1985–1986, *9,* 49–59.

Bumpass, L. L., T. C. Martin, and J. A. Sweet. The impact of family background and early marital factors on marital disruption. *Journal of Family Issues,* 1991, *12,* 22–42.

Bursik, K. Correlates of women's adjustment during the separation and divorce process. *Journal of Divorce and Remarriage,* 1991, *14,* 137–162.

Canabal, M. E. Economic approach to marital dissolution in Puerto Rico. *Journal of Marriage and the Family,* 1990, *52,* 515–530.

Cauley, L. Interview in regard to pets in divorce. "20/20," ABC Television. February 26, 1993.

Choi, N. G. Correlates of the economic status of widowed and divorced elderly women. *Journal of Family Issues,* 1992, *3,* 38–54.

Clark, P. G., R. W. Siviski, and R. Weiner. Coping strategies of widowers in the first year. *Family Relations,* 1986, *35,* 425–430.

Coontz, S. *The way we never were: American families and the nostalgia trap.* New York: Basic Books, 1992.

Coysh, William S., J. R. Johnston, J. M. Tschann, J. S. Wallerstein, and M. Kline. Parental post-divorce adjustment in joint and sole physical custody families. *Journal of Family Issues,* 1989, *10,* 52–71.

Demo, D. H. The relentless search for effects of divorce: Forging new trails or tumbling down the beaten path? *Journal of Marriage and the Family*, 1993, *55*, 42–45.

Demo, D. H. Parent-child relations: Assessing recent changes. *Journal of Marriage and the Family*, 1992, *54*, 104–117.

Diedrick, P. Gender differences in divorce adjustment. *Journal of Divorce and Remarriage*, 1991, *14*, 33–46.

Doherty, William J., S. Su, and R. Needle. Marital disruption and psychological well-being. *Journal of Family Issues*, 1989, *10*, 75–85.

Donnelly, D. and D. Finkelhor. Does equality in custody arrangement improve the parent-child relationship? *Journal of Marriage and the Family*, 1992, *54*, 837–845.

Donnelly, D. and D. Finkelhor. Who has joint custody? Class differences in the determination of custody arrangements. *Family Relations*, 1993, *42*, 57–60.

Downey, D. B. and B. Powell. Do children in single-parent households fare better living with same-sex parents? *Journal of Marriage and the Family*, 1993, *55*, 55–71.

Dudley, J. R. Increasing our understanding of divorced fathers who have infrequent contact with their children. *Family Relations*, 1991, *40*, 279–285.

Dychtwald, Ken. *Age wave*. New York: Bantam Book, 1990.

Edwards, J. N., T. D. Fuller, S. Vorakitphokatorn, and S. Sermsri. Female employment and marital instability: Evidence from Thailand. *Journal of Marriage and the Family*, 1992, *54*, 59–68.

Finkelhor, D., G. Hotaling, and A. Sedlak. Children abducted by family members: A national household survey of incidence and episode characteristics. *Journal of Marriage and the Family*, 1991, *53*, 805–817.

Fisher, H. E. *Anatomy of love: The natural history of monogamy, adultery, and divorce*. New York: W. W. Norton and Co., Inc., 1992.

Forsyth, C. J. and C. A. Robin, Grandparents and self-esteem. *Free Inquiry in Creative Sociology*, 1992, *20*, 83–86.

Goodman, C. C. Social support networks in late life divorce. *Family Perspective*, 1992, *26*, 61–81.

Gottman, J. M. Predicting the longitudinal course of marriages. *Journal of Marital and Family Therapy*, 1991, *17*, 3–7.

Guidubaldi, J. Differences in children's divorce adjustment across grade level and gender: A report from the NASP-Kent State Nationwide Project. *Children of Divorce: Empirical Perspectives on Adjustment*, Sharlene A. Wolchik and P. Karoly, eds. New York: Gardner Press, Inc., 1988, 185–231.

Hammond, R. J. Differences in life satisfaction among late-life divorced and separated males and females: A path analysis. *Family Perspective*, 1992, *26*, 45–59.

Heaton, T. B. Time-related determinants of marital dissolution. *Journal of Marriage and the Family*, 1991, *53*, 285–295.

Heim, S. C. and D. K. Snyder. Predicting depression from marital distress and attributional processes. *Journal of Marital and Family Therapy*, 1991, *17*, 67–72.

Hobart, Charles. The family system in remarriage: An exploratory study. *Journal of Marriage and the Family*, 1988, *50*, 649–661.

Isaacs, M. B. The visitation schedule and child adjustment: A three-year study. *Family Process*, 1988, *27*, 251–256.

Kalter, Neil. *Growing up with divorce*. New York: Free Press/Macmillan, 1989.

Kolata, Gina. Child Splitting. *Psychology Today*, 1988, *22*, 34–37.

Kurdek, L. A. The relations between reported well-being and divorce history, availability of a proximate adult, and gender. *Journal of Marriage and the Family*, 1991, *53*, 71–78.

LaNeave, S. Personal communication. January 28, 1990. Greenville, N.C. 27858.

Lang, N. E. and M. A. Pett. Later-life parental divorce: The adult child's experience. *Family Perspective*, 1992, *26*, 121–146.

Lauer, R. H. and J. C. Lauer. The long-term relational consequences of problematic family backgrounds. *Family Relations,* 1991, *40,* 286–290.

Maccoby, E. E., C. E. Depner, and R. H. Mnookin. Co-parenting in the second year after divorce. *Journal of Marriage and the Family,* 1990, *52,* 141–155.

Martin, T. C. and L. L. Bumpass. Recent trends in marital disruption. *Demography,* 1989, *26,* 37–52.

Masheter, C. Post-divorce relationships between ex-spouses: The roles of attachment and interpersonal conflict. *Journal of Marriage and the Family,* 1991, *53,* 103–110.

Mauldin, Teresa A. Women who remain above the poverty level in divorce: Implications for family policy. *Family Relations,* 1990, *39,* 141–146.

Mindel, C. H., R. W. Habenstein, and R. Wright, Jr. *Ethnic families in America: Patterns and variations.* New York: Elsevier, 1988.

Moore, C. M. Teaching about loss and death to junior high school students. *Family Relations,* 1989, *38,* 3–8.

Morgan, E. S. *The Puritan family.* Boston: Public Library, 1944.

National Center for Health Statistics, Births, marriages, divorces and deaths for February 1993. Monthly Vital Statistics report; vol. 41, no. 9. Hyattsville, Md.: Public-Health Statistics, 6525 Belcrest Road, Hyattsville, Maryland 20782.

National Center for Health Statistics. Advance report of final mortality statistics, 1990. Monthly vital statistics report; vol. 41, no. 7, suppl. Hyattsville, Md.: Public Health Service, 1993b.

National Center for Health Statistics. Advance report, final divorce statistics, 1987. Monthly vital statistics report, vol. 38, no. 12, suppl. 2. Hyattsville, Md.: Public Health Service, 1990.

O'Flaherty, Kathleen M. and Laura W. Eells. Courtship behavior of the remarried. *Journal of Marriage and the Family,* 1988, *50,* 499–506.

Parson, Ruth J., E. O. Cox, and P. J. Kimboko. Satisfaction, communication and affection in caregiving: A view from the elder's perspective. *Journal of Gerontological Social Work,* 1989, *13,* 9–20.

Pett, M. A., N. Lang, and A. Gander. Late-life divorce. *Journal of Family Issues,* 1992, *13,* 526–552.

Pett, M. A. Editor's comments on this special issue: Consequences of later life divorce. *Family Perspective,* 1992, *26,* 1–9.

Pitcher, B. L. and D. C. Larson. Early widowhood. *Aging and the Family,* Stephen J. Bahr and Evan T. Peterson, eds. Lexington, Mass.: Lexington Books, 1989, 59–81.

Pothern, S. Divorce in Hindu society. *Journal of Comparative Family Studies,* 1989, *20,* 377–392.

Rigdon, I. S. and M. A. Pett. Helpfulness for older persons experiencing divorce: Connectedness to oneself and to others. *Family Perspective.* 1992, *26,* 83–95.

Rosenfeld, J. P. Old age, new heirs. *American Demographics,* May 1992, 46–49.

Schrof, J. M. Wedding bands made of steel. *U.S. News and World Report,* April 6, 1992, 62–63.

Schultz, M. Divorce patterns in nineteenth-century New England. *Journal of Family History,* 1990, *15,* 101–115.

Seltzer, J. A. and S. M. Bianchi. Children's contact with absent parents. *Journal of Marriage and the Family,* 1988, *50,* 663–677.

Song, Y. I. Single Asian American women as a result of divorce: Depressive affect and changes in social support. *Journal of Divorce and Remarriage,* 1991, *14,* 219–230.

Stack, Steven. The impact of divorce on suicide in Norway, 1951–1980. *Journal of Marriage and the Family,* 1989, *51,* 229–238.

Stack, S. and J. H. Gundlach. Divorce and sex. *Archives of Sexual Behavior,* 1992, *21,* 359–367.

Stark, E. Friends through it all. *Psychology Today,* May 1986, 54–60.

Starr, B. D. and M. B. Weiner. *The Starr-Weiner report on sex and sexuality in the mature years.* New York: McGraw-Hill, 1982.

Statistical Abstract of the United States: 1993, 113th ed. Washington, D.C.: U.S. Bureau of the Census, 1993.

Swensen, C. H. and S. R. Fuller. Expression of love, marriage problems, commitment, and anticipatory grief in the marriages of cancer patients. *Journal of Marriage and the Family,* 1992, *54,* 191–196.

Tschann, Jeanne M., Janet R. Johnston, Marsha Kline, and Judith S. Wallerstein. Family process and children's functioning during divorce. *Journal of Marriage and the Family,* 1989, *51,* 431–444.

Turner, Jack. When mediation fails. Presented at conference on Mediation in Relationships. East Carolina University, Fall 1989. Revised for the fourth edition of this text in 1993.

Wheaton, Blair. Life transitions, role histories, and mental health. *American Sociological Review,* 1990, *55,* no. 2, 209–223.

White, L. K. and A. Booth. Divorce over the life course: The role of marital happiness. *Journal of Family Issues,* 1991, *12,* 5–21.

White, L. K., D. B. Brinkerhoff, and A. Booth. The effect of marital disruption on child's attachment to parents. *Journal of Family Issues,* 1985, *6,* no. 1, 5–22.

Contents

17
CHAPTER

Remarriage and Stepfamilies

Is It True?

1. Older divorced women are less likely to remarry than older divorced men.

2. It is estimated that by the year 2000, stepfamilies will outnumber all other family types in the United States.

3. Remarriages have a higher divorce rate than first marriages.

4. Couples who have a child of their own in their second marriage are more likely to stay married than couples who do not have a child.

5. Children report more difficulty adjusting to a stepfather than to a stepmother.

1 = T; 2 = T; 3 = T; 4 = T; 5 = F

And if love takes you in,
Take all the love you can find,
And hope it comes again

KIM CARNES AND DAVE ELLINGSON

"C oming Around Again" was a popular song by Carly Simon in the early nineties. It reflected the experience of individuals in more than a million remarriages every year. Indeed, serial marriage, or being married to more than one person in one's lifetime, is becoming more common. In this chapter we examine the realities of remarriage and stepfamilies.

🍃 Remarriage

Various data on remarriage in the United States are available.

NATIONAL DATA 🍃 About 40 percent of marriages are remarriages (Brubaker & Kimberly, 1992). Whites, followed by Hispanics, followed by blacks, are the most likely to remarry (Ahlburg & De Vita, 1992). The median age of the divorced woman getting remarried is 33.6; the divorced man, 37 (*Statistical Abstract of the United States: 1993*, Table 143). The average interval from the end of the first marriage to the beginning of the second marriage is about 3 years (the older the person, the longer the interval) (Brubaker & Kimberly, 1992).

In the United States, some individuals are more likely to remarry than others. Young women remarry more quickly than older women. "Women divorced after age 40 have a low probability of remarriage" (Ahlburg & De Vita, 1992, 17). Age does not appear to be a factor in the remarriage of men.

The absence of children also increases the chance of remarriage for the woman but makes no difference for the man. However, having a high income increases the chance of remarriage for men but not for women (Ahlburg & De Vita, 1992).

> I will marry again. I am looking for a man in my life.
>
> IVANA TRUMP

CONSIDERATION

Most divorced individuals are open to the possibility of becoming involved in another love relationship. Sometimes, rather than try to meet someone new, they try to locate a previous love and rekindle the relationship. Warren Bennis, twice divorced, sent a note which read, "Any chance you can have dinner with me on October 13? Yours, Warren" to Grace Gabe M.D. to whom he was engaged thirty years earlier. She was also "single again" and open to the possibility of seeing her old flame. They met for dinner and eventually remarried.

(continued)

Some of the guidelines in rekindling old flames suggested by Dr. Gabe (1993) include:

1. *Anticipate stages of re-entry.* Rather than plunge headlong into the old love affair, most couples have "periods of moving very close alternate with periods of needing some emotional distance . . . Your old sweetheart may wait longer than you want between communications or might cancel a date because the reconnecting may be too much too soon" (p. 36).

2. *Be aware that the original problems will reactivate.* After the euphoria of the reunion has passed, the old issues will resurface. This is healthy and the partners have the life experience of years to help work through these old issues together.

3. *Review the original breakup and reach consensus.* "Reviewing the reasons for the breakup of the old relationship may be painful or at least difficult. But it must take place between the sweethearts. If you can't do this, don't start anything with an idea of getting back together." (p. 38). Consensus implies that both partners develop a shared view of why the relationship failed and why it would not have worked back then.

4. *Respect the partner's previous love history.* During the years apart, each partner likely had other important love relationships. Validate these rather than minimize them. Recognize that you do not "have a monopoly on the partner's attachments" (p. 63).

ACROSS CULTURES

Although getting remarried is regarded as an option by both women and men in the United States, such is not the case in all societies. In a study of 200 divorced or separated men and women in a major urban area in central India, the majority of the women had no interest in getting remarried. One reason is that they were only allowed to remarry widowers whereas divorced men could marry single women of their choice (Pothern, 1989).

Preparing for Remarriage

A sample of 100 men and 105 women was asked how they prepared for getting remarried. Over half of the sample reported that they prepared for getting remarried by living together (Ganong & Coleman, 1989).

When remarried spouses who had lived together were compared with remarried spouses who had not lived together, those who had cohabited reported fewer marital disagreements and problems. They also reported higher levels of affection in their relationship (Ganong & Coleman, 1989).

Some couples seek help from others in preparation for remarriage. For example, some couples go through counseling, attend support groups or remarriage/stepparent education programs, and/or consult with friends who have had experience in a remarriage situation. In addition, many couples seek advice on remarriage and stepfamily living from books and other written materials.

In preparing for remarriage, couples may also discuss important issues and concerns. Some topics that couples preparing to remarry might discuss include the following:

1. Finances
2. Discipline of children/stepchildren
3. In-laws
4. Housing
5. Careers
6. Relationship with ex-spouse

Kaplan and Hennon (1992) developed a "Remarriage Education: Personal Reflections Program," which emphasizes making explicit each partner's expectations for how family roles should be executed. For example, who is to perform the provider, housekeeper, child rearer, recreational, sexual, therapeutic, and kinship roles in the remarriage? Since expectations are likely to be different because of the different ways in which roles were allocated in the previous relationships of the respective partners, communicating about the expectations early in the new relationship is critical.

Issues Involved in a Remarriage

Individuals considering remarriage must deal with certain issues. These include the following (Roberts & Price, 1985–1986; Goetting, 1982):

Boundary Maintenance   Movement from divorce to remarriage is not a static event that happens in a brief ceremony and is over. Rather, ghosts of the first marriage in terms of the ex-spouse and, possibly, children must be dealt with. The parents must decide how to relate to the ex-spouse in order to maintain a good parenting relationship for the biological children and, at the same time, to keep an emotional distance to prevent problems from developing with the new partner. Some spouses continue to be emotionally attached to the ex-spouse and have difficulty breaking away. However, boundary ambiguity does not appear to be a major problem for remarried spouses (Pasley & Ihinger-Tallman, 1989).

Emotional Remarriage   Remarriage involves beginning to trust and love another person in a new relationship. Such feelings may come slowly as a result of negative experiences in the first marriage.

Psychic Remarriage   Divorced individuals considering remarriage may find it difficult to give up the freedom and autonomy of being single again and develop a mental set conducive to pairing. This transition may be particularly difficult for people who sought a divorce as a means to personal growth and

I've forgotten just how warm a pair of loving arms can be. But every time you hold me now it all comes back to me. It's looking like this heart of mine is finally on the mend . . . am I getting use to being loved again?

GENE WATSON

We all have a picture of a family. It is usually not a stepfamily.

JUDY OSBORNE

autonomy. These individuals may fear that getting remarried will put unwanted constraints on them.

Community Remarriage This stage involves a change in focus from single friends to a new mate and other couples with whom the new pair will interact. The bonds of friendship established during the divorce period may be particularly valuable because they have lent support at a time of personal crisis. Care should be taken not to drop these friendships.

Parental Remarriage Because most remarriages involve children, people must usually work out the nuances of living with someone else's children. Since mothers are usually awarded primary physical custody, this translates into the new stepfather adjusting to her children. If a spouse has children from a previous marriage who do not live primarily with him or her, the new spouse must adjust to these children on weekends, holidays, vacations, or other visitation times.

Economic Remarriage The second marriage may begin with economic responsibilities to the first marriage. Alimony and child support often threaten the harmony and sometimes even the economic survival of second marriages. One wife said that her paycheck was endorsed and mailed to her husband's first wife to cover his alimony and child support payments. "It irritates me beyond description to be working for a woman who lived with my husband for seven years," she added. In another case, a remarried woman who was receiving inadequate child support from her ex-spouse felt too embarrassed to ask her new husband to pay for her son's braces.

Legal Remarriage Partners in a second marriage may have legal responsibilities in the form of alimony and child support payments to the first marriage. These responsibilities cannot be abandoned with the beginning of a new marriage. The individual must take on a new set of responsibilities while maintaining former responsibilities.

Legal documents that may be appropriate include an asset inventory (to establish what each new spouse owns and brings into the marriage), a premarital agreement (to specify what assets owned by whom will go to whom if the marriage ends in divorce or when it ends with the death of one spouse), and a living trust, in which assets from one spouse are transferred to a third party so that the new spouse will not be tempted to ask, "Can we use that money?"

Some spouses feel it is not romantic to draw up legal documents specifying what will happen to the assets and money in a relationship. These spouses take the position that such an action smacks of distrust. But a lawyer and social worker who have dealt with the problems in remarriages said, "Facing possible outcomes does not make them happen" (Bernstein & Collins, 1985, 389).

Remarriage for the Widowed

NATIONAL DATA   There are 11.3 million widowed women and 2.5 million widowed men. The median age of the widow who remarries is 54; the widower, 63 (*Statistical Abstract of the United States, 1993,* Tables 59 and 143).

Remarriage for the widowed is usually very different from remarriage for the divorced. The widowed are usually much older, their children are grown, and they are less likely to remarry.

A widow or widower may marry someone of similar age or someone who is radically older or younger. Marriages in which one spouse is considerably older than the other are referred to as "May-December marriages." Here, we will discuss only "December marriages," in which both spouses are elderly.

In a study of 24 elderly couples, the need to escape loneliness or the need for companionship was the primary motivation for remarriage (Vinick, 1978). The men reported a greater need to remarry than the women. Most of the spouses met through a mutual friend or relative (75 percent) and married less than a year after their partner's death (63 percent).

The children of the couples had mixed reactions to their remarriages. Most of the children were happy that their parents were happy and felt relieved that the companionship needs of their elderly parent would now be met by someone on a more regular basis. But some children also disapproved of the marriage out of concern for their inheritance rights. "If that woman marries dad," said a woman with two children, "she'll get everything when he dies. I love him and hope he lives forever, but when he's gone, I want the farm."

> You would not think they had lost a husband, you would fancy they were looking for one.
>
> ST. JEROME

Happiness in Second Marriages

How happy are second marriages when compared to first marriages? The data from 16 studies comparing first and second marriages suggest that first marriages are happier. However, "the difference appears to be miniscule and certainly not substantial" (Vemer et al., 1989, 721).

Some aspects of remarriages may represent an improvement over first marriages. Couples who remarry point to four major differences between their second and first marriages (Keshet, 1988).

1. *Communication.* Communication in the second marriage was more open with the partners having greater skills in talking about their relationship and issues with which they were confronted.
2. *Less conflict.* The marital conflict that did occur was expected and was more easily tolerated. Unlike in their first marriages, the partners felt that it was acceptable for them to disagree.
3. *More egalitarian.* The power in the second marriage was more balanced. "The women felt more included and respected by their second husbands" (pp. 30–31).

> You can live happily ever after if you're not after too much.
>
> E.C. MCKENZIE

Although second marriages are not necessarily less happy, they are more prone to divorce. Booth and Edwards (1992) compared spouses who were first-time married with those who had been married before. The researchers identified several characteristics of spouses in remarriages that may contribute to their increased risk of divorce. These include the following:

1. Having poor relationships with parents and in-laws (who help to stabilize couples)
2. Having more frequent thoughts about getting divorced
3. Being less tolerant of an unhappy marriage and more willing to get a divorce

❦ Stepfamilies

It is estimated that by the year 2000, stepfamilies will outnumber all other family types in the United States (Darden & Zimmerman, 1992). In this section, we will examine how stepfamilies differ from nuclear families, how they are experienced from the viewpoint of women, men, and children, and the developmental tasks that must be accomplished to make a successful stepfamily.

Definition and Types of Stepfamilies

A stepfamily consists of remarried spouses with at least one of the spouses having a child from a previous relationship. Stepfamilies are also referred to as reconstituted, remarried, binuclear, new extended, or blended families. The term *blended* is used because the new marriage relationship is blended with the children of at least one previous marriage.

Stepfamilies via divorce are a relatively new phenomenon. The sequence of marriage-death-remarriage which was characteristic of the early 20th century has shifted to a new sequence of marriage-divorce-remarriage.

NATIONAL DATA ❦ About 15 percent of all married couples have at least one stepchild (Dainton, 1993).

Types of stepfamilies include the following:

1. Stepfamilies in which children live with their remarried parent and stepparent.
2. Stepfamilies in which the children from a previous marriage visit with their remarried parent and stepparent.
3. An unmarried couple living together in which at least one of the partners has children from a previous relationship who live with or visit them.
4. A remarried couple in which each of the spouses brings children into the new marriage from the previous marriage.

The stepfamily is so much more complicated than a first marriage . . . think of your relatives coming for Thanksgiving and not going home.

EMILY VISHER

Keeping peace in the family requires patience, love, understanding, and at least two television sets.

E.C. MCKENZIE

5. A couple who not only bring children from previous marriages but who, in addition, have a child of their own.

Unique Aspects of Stepfamilies

Stepfamilies are unique compared to nuclear families. Unlike the nuclear family, in which the children are genetically related to both parents (except in cases of adoption or pregnancies resulting from some types of reproductive technology), children in the stepfamily are biologically related to only one parent.

Stepfamilies have also experienced a crisis event. The children may have been removed from one biological parent (whom they often desperately hope will reappear and reunite with the parent), and the spouse has experienced emotional disengagement and physical separation from a once-loved partner due to divorce or death. Jane, who is divorced with two children, said:

> It's been two years since I divorced Bill, and it's been hard for all of us. The children miss their father a great deal, and they still ask sometimes, "When are you and daddy getting back together?" It hurts me to know that they are separated from their father. But it would hurt even more for me to have to live with their father. Yet I miss being a family and look forward to getting remarried. (Author's files)

But when the remarriage comes, the problems aren't over. When stepfamilies are compared to first families, the spouses in stepfamilies tend to report problems due to the different ways the new spouses view the children—"hers," "his," and "theirs" (Hobart, 1988).

Children in a biological family have also been exposed to a relatively consistent set of beliefs, values, and behavior patterns. When children enter a stepfamily, they "inherit" a new parent who brings a new way of living into the family unit.

Likewise, the new parent now lives with children who may have been reared differently from the way in which the stepparent would have reared them if he or she had been their parent all along. One stepfather explained:

> It's been a difficult adjustment for me living with Molly's kids. I was reared to say "Yes sir" and "Yes ma'am" to adults and taught my own kids to do that. But Molly's kids just say "yes" or "no." It rankles me to hear them say that, but I know they mean no wrong with "yes" and "no" as long as it is said politely and that it is just something that I am going to have to live with.

Another uniqueness in stepfamilies is that the relationships between the biological parent and children have existed longer than the relationships between the adults in the remarriage. Jane and her twin children have a nine-year relationship and are emotionally bonded to each other. But Jane has known her new partner only a year, and although her children like their new stepfather, they hardly know him.

It takes a heap of livin' in a house t' make it home.

EDGAR A. GUEST

> **CONSIDERATION**
>
> A parent's emotional bond with children (particularly if they are young and dependent) from a previous marriage may weaken a remarriage from the start. As one parent says, "Nothing and nobody is going to come between me and my kids." However, new spouses may view such bonding differently. One spouse said that such concern for one's own children was a sign of a caring and nurturing person. "I wouldn't want to live with anyone who didn't care about his kids." But another said, "I feel left out and that she cares more about her kids than me. I don't like the feeling of being an outsider."

The short history of the relationship between the child and stepparent is one factor that may contribute to increased conflict between these two during the child's adolescence. Hobart (1988) observed that adolescents may "become aware of their increased power and act more provocatively toward their stepparents" (p. 182).

Another unique feature of stepfamilies is that unlike children in the nuclear family who have one home they regard as theirs, children in stepfamilies have two homes they regard as theirs. In some cases of joint custody, children spend part of each week with one parent and part of each week with the other parent; they live with two sets of adult parents in two separate homes.

Money, or lack of it, from the ex-spouse may be a source of conflict. In some stepfamilies, the ex-spouse is expected to send child support payments to the parent who has custody of the children. Less than one-half of these fathers send any money; those who do may be irregular in their payments.

NATIONAL DATA 🦋 The average amount of child support money paid to mothers who are awarded child support is $249 per month, or $2995 per year (*Statistical Abstract of the United States: 1993*, Table 612).

Fathers who pay regular child support tend to have higher incomes, be remarried, live close to their children, and visit them regularly (Teachman, 1991). They are also more likely to have legal shared or joint custody, which helps to ensure that they will have access to their children (Dudley, 1991).

Fathers who do not voluntarily pay child support and are delinquent by more than one month may have their wages garnished by the state. Some fathers change jobs frequently and move around to make it difficult for the government to keep up with them.

> **CONSIDERATION**
>
> The ex-husband sending money to the biological mother creates the illusion for the stepfather that the ex-husband will take care of the expenses for the children. In reality, child support payments cover only a fraction of what is actually spent

on a child, so that the new stepfather may feel burdened with more financial responsibility for his stepchildren than he bargained for. This may engender negative feelings toward the wife in the new marriage relationship.

New relationships in stepfamilies experience almost constant flux. Each member of a new stepfamily has many adjustments to make. Issues that must be dealt with include how the mate feels about the partner's children from a former marriage, how the children feel about the new stepparent, and how the newly married spouse feels about the spouse sending alimony and child support payments to an ex-spouse. In general, it takes at least two years for newly remarried spouses to feel comfortable together and five to seven years for the whole family to feel comfortable. Some marriages and families feel comfortable much more quickly; some never do.

CONSIDERATION

Adjustments are more difficult in complex than simple stepfamilies (Schultz et al., 1991). The former involves children from both parents whereas the latter involves the children from only one of the new spouses.

> Each set of parent and child or children brings to the relationship a package of expectations, traditions, rules, and roles that must be meshed with those of the other set of parent and children. In addition, relationships with two other biological parents and possible stepparents and assorted relatives with different expectations, rules, and roles are areas of potential conflict between the partners, with former partners, and with the children (p.563).

Stepfamilies are also stigmatized. Stepism, like racism, involves prejudice and discrimination (Darden & Zimmerman, 1992). We are all familiar with the wicked stepmother in *Cinderella*. The fairy tale certainly gives us the impression that to be in a stepfamily with stepparents is a bad thing. Such negative stereotyping has affected stepfamilies to the degree that some remarried couples hide the fact that the children are from a previous marriage (Dainton, 1993).

Nobody's family can hang out the sign, "Nothing the matter here."
CHINESE SAYING

CONSIDERATION

Although stepfamilies are stigmatized, "the vast majority of stepfamilies appear to function rather well. Indeed, there is little to distinguish the overall description of family life, offered by both parents and children, in step- and first-marriage families" (Furstenberg, 1987, 56).

Stepparents also have no childfree period. Unlike the biological family in which the newly married couple typically has their first child about two-and-one-half years after their wedding, the remarried couple begin their marriage with children in the house.

Finally, there are profound legal differences between nuclear families and stepfamilies. While biological parents in nuclear families are required to support their children in all states, only five states require stepparents to provide financial support for their stepchildren. And this support may often stop if there is a divorce (Fine & Fine, 1992). Also, in the event that a stepparent dies without leaving a will, stepchildren generally may not inherit property from stepparents because there are no blood ties. In the case of divorce, stepparents are usually accorded few rights in regard to custody; more rights in regard to visitation.

The differences between nuclear families and stepfamilies are summarized in Table 17.1.

Just as a person must pass through various developmental stages in becoming an adult, a stepfamily goes through a number of stages on its way to becoming a fully functioning family (see In Focus 17.1).

TABLE 17.1
Differences Between Nuclear Families and Stepfamilies

NUCLEAR FAMILIES	STEPFAMILIES
1. Children are (usually) biologically related to both parents.	1. Children may be biologically related to only one parent.
2. Both biological parents live together with children.	2. One biological parent does not live with children as a result of divorce or death. In the case of joint physical custody, the children may live with both parents, alternating between them.
3. Beliefs and values of members tend to be similar.	3. Beliefs and values of members are more likely to be different due to different backgrounds.
4. Relationship between adults has existed longer than relationship between children and parents.	4. Relationship between children and parents has existed longer than relationship between adults.
5. Children have one home they regard as theirs.	5. Children may have two homes they regard as theirs.
6. The family's economic resources come from within the family unit.	6. Some economic resources may come from ex-spouse.
7. All money generated stays in the family.	7. Some money generated may leave the family in the form of alimony or child support.
8. Relationships are relatively stable.	8. Relationships are in flux: new adults adjusting to each other; children adjusting to stepparent; stepparent adjusting to stepchildren; stepchildren adjusting to each other.
9. No stigma is attached to nuclear family.	9. Stepfamilies are stigmatized.
10. Spouses had childfree period.	10. Spouses had no childfree period.
11. Inheritance rights are automatic.	11. Stepchildren do not automatically inherit from stepparents.
12. Rights to custody of children are assumed if divorce occurs.	12. Rights to custody of stepchildren are usually not considered.

❧ IN FOCUS 17.1 ❧

From Outsider to Intimate: Stages in Becoming a Stepfamily

Papernow (1988) identified a seven-stage process of development in stepfamilies which may be collapsed into four:

Stage 1: *Fantasy*. Both spouses and children bring rich fantasies into the new marriage. Spouses fantasize that their new marriage will be better than the last one. If the person they are marrying has adult children, they assume that these children will not be part of the new marriage. Young children have their own fantasy—they hope that their biological parents will somehow get back together—that the stepfamily is temporary.

Stage 2: *Reality*. Instead of realizing their fantasies, new spouses find that stepchildren and ex-spouses interfere with their new life together. Stepparents feel that they are "outsiders" in an already functioning unit. "Jealousy, resentment, and inadequacy are the stepparent's everyday companions in early stepfamily life" (p. 63).

Stage 3: *Doing Something about It*. Initially the stepparent assumes a passive role and accepts the frustrations and tensions of stepfamily life. Eventually, however, the resentment reaches a level where the stepparent is driven to make changes. The stepparent makes the partner aware of the frustrations and suggests that the marital relationship should have priority some of the time. The stepparent may also make specific requests, such as reducing the number of conversations the partner has with the ex-spouse, not allowing the dog on the furniture, or requiring the stepchildren to use better table manners. This stage is successful to the degree that the partner supports the recommendations for change.

Stage 4: *Strengthening Pair Ties*. During this stage the remarried couple prioritize and solidify their relationship. At the same time, the biological parent must back away somewhat from the parent-child relationship so that the new partner can have the opportunity to establish a relationship with the stepchildren. This relationship is the product of small units of interaction and develops slowly across time. Many day-to-day activities such as watching television together, eating meals together, and driving in the car together provide opportunities for the stepparent-stepchild relationship to develop. It is important that the stepparent not attempt to replace the relationship that the stepchildren have with their biological parents.

❧ Strengths of Stepfamilies

Stepfamilies have both strengths and weaknesses. Strengths include children's exposure to a variety of behavior patterns, their observation of a happy remarriage, adaptation to stepsibling relationships inside the family unit, and greater objectivity on the part of the stepparent.

Exposure to a Variety of Behavior Patterns

Children in stepfamilies experience a variety of behaviors, values, and lifestyles. They have had the advantage of living on the inside of two families. One 12-year-old said:

> My real mom didn't like sports and rarely took me anywhere. My stepmother is different. She likes to take me fishing and roller skating. She recently bought me a tent and is going to take me camping this summer.

Variety's the very spice of life, that gives it all its flavour.

WILLIAM COWPER

Happier Parents

Single parenting can be a demanding and exhausting experience. Remarriage can ease the stress of solo parenting and provide a happier context for the parent. Research by Kurdek and Fine (1991) suggests that wives are happier in stepfamilies than husbands and are more optimistic about stepfamily living. One daughter said:

> Looking back on my parents' divorce, I wish they had done it long ago. While I miss my dad and am sorry that I don't see him more often, I was always upset listening to my parents argue. They would yell and scream, and it would end with my mom crying. It was a lot more peaceful (and I know my mom was a lot more happy) after they got divorced. Besides, I like my stepdaddy. Although he isn't my real dad, I know he cares about me.

Opportunity for New Relationship with Stepsiblings

While adjusting to a new stepsibling is sometimes difficult, most of these relationships become positive and continue in adulthood.

While some children reject their new stepsiblings, others are enriched by the opportunity to live with a new person to whom they are now "related." One 14-year-old remarked, "I have never had an older brother to do things with. We both like to do the same things and I couldn't be happier about the new situation." Some stepsibling relationships are maintained throughout adulthood. Two researchers (White & Riedmann, 1992) analyzed national data and assessed the degree to which full and step/halfsiblings keep in touch as adults. They found that while step/halfsiblings see each other less often, "adults report substantial contact with their step/halfsiblings and only 0.5% of stepsiblings were so estranged that they did not at least know where their step/halfsiblings lived" (p. 206). Characteristics of those more likely to maintain contact included being female, black, younger, and geographically closer.

More Objective Stepparents

Due to the emotional tie between a parent and a child, some parents have difficulty discussing certain issues or topics. A stepparent often has the advantage of being less emotionally involved and can relate to the child at a different level. One 13-year-old said of the relationship with her father's new wife:

> She went through her own parents' divorce and knows what it's like for me to be going through my dad's divorce. She is the only one I can really talk to about this issue. Both my dad and mom are too emotional about the subject to be able to talk about it.

According to Papernow (1988), a stepparent may be the ideal person for stepchildren to talk with about sex, their feelings about their parents' divorce, career choices, drugs, and other potentially charged subjects.

℘ Women in Stepfamilies

Some of the concerns women in stepfamilies have include accepting and being accepted by the new partner's children, adjusting to alimony and child support payments to an ex-wife, having the new partner accept her children and having her children accept him, and having another child in the new marriage.

Accepting Partner's Children

"She'd better think a long time before she marries a guy with kids," said one 29-year-old woman who had done so.

This stepmother went on to explain:

> It's really difficult to love someone else's children. Particularly if the kid isn't very likable. A year after we were married, my husband's 9-year-old daughter visited us for a summer. It was a nightmare. She didn't like anything I cooked, was always dragging around making us late when we had to go somewhere, kept her room a mess, and acted like a gum-chewing smart aleck. I hated her, but felt guilty because I wanted to have feelings of love and tenderness. Instead, I was jealous of the relationship she had with her father, and I wanted to get rid of her. I began counting how many days until she would be gone.
>
> You can hide your dislike for awhile, but eventually you must tell your partner how you feel. I was lucky. My husband also thought his daughter was horrible to live with and wasn't turned off by my feelings. He told her if she couldn't act more civil, she couldn't come back. The message to every woman about to marry a guy with kids is to be aware that your man is a package deal and that the kid is in the package.

Partner's Children Accepting Stepmother

NATIONAL DATA ℘ Of all stepparents, 18 percent are stepmothers (Glick, 1989).

Children are much more reluctant to accept a new stepmother than a new stepfather. The role of the child's biological mother is so powerful that the stepmother's role may be viewed either as marginal or nonexistent. In addition, if the stepchild allows a relationship to develop with the stepmother, the biological mother may get upset. A stepchild may need to keep distance in the relationship with the stepmother to avoid conflicted loyalties (Fischman, 1988).

Adjusting to Alimony and Child Support

In addition to the potential problems of not liking the partner's children, there may be problems of alimony and child support. As noted earlier, it is not unusual for a wife to become upset when her husband mails one-quarter or

Be a stepmother kindley as she will, There's in her love some hints of winter's chill.

D'ARCY W. THOMPSON

one-third of his income to a woman with whom he used to live. This amount of money is often equal to the current wife's earnings. Some wives in this position see themselves as working for their husband's ex-wife—a perception that is very likely to create conflict.

Her New Partner and How Her Children Will Accept Him

For some remarried wives, two main concerns are how her new husband will accept her children and how the children will accept him. The ages of the children are important in these adjustments. If the children are young (age 3 or younger), they will usually accept any new adult into the natural parent's life. On the other hand, if the children are in adolescence, they are struggling for independence from their natural parents and do not want any new authority figures in their lives.

Whether the new spouse will accept the children is unpredictable. Some men enjoy children and relate to them easily, as did the man who built a new house "for my new family." Other men find it difficult to enjoy children, particularly those with whom they have no biological link.

Having Another Child

A national study of women in second marriages revealed that about two-thirds have a baby within six years (Wineberg, 1992). Some men delight in the prospect of a child with their new wife. Others feel that they have had enough children and do not want any more. One husband in a second marriage said, "I've got two kids of my own, and I certainly don't want any more. But my new wife wants one, so I guess we'll have one."

Some remarried couples feel that having their own child will help to cement their new bond. Two researchers (Ganong & Coleman, 1988) compared remarried couples who had reproduced together with couples in stepfamilies who had no mutual child. Based on measures of adjustment (Dyadic Adjustment Scale) and affect (Inventory of Family Feelings) there were no differences between the couples.

Having a child in a second marriage is associated with increasing the stability of the relationship and reducing the probability of divorce (Wineberg, 1992). The researcher suggested that "couples with a mutual birth may tolerate more marital stress before considering divorce than couples with no mutual children" (p. 885).

❧ Men in Stepfamilies

Men in stepfamilies may or may not have children from a previous relationship. Three possible stepfamily combinations include a man with children married to a woman without children, a man with children married to a woman with children, and a man without children married to a woman with

> Dating is hard with a child. . . . But I must say I found it a wonderful screening device. If they didn't last through that dinner where you introduce them to your child, they weren't worth having.
>
> KATE KAPSHAW

children. Data from national studies have suggested that the experience for African American stepfathers and white stepfathers is similar (Fine et al., 1992).

NATIONAL DATA ❧ There are over two million households with a stepfather present (Marsiglio, 1992).

Man with Children Married to a Woman without Children

Whether the man's children live with him or visit, there is a cultural expectation that the new wife care for and entertain his children. This "instant mother" phenomenon is problematic because the children may reject her or because she has had limited opportunities to develop a relationship with the children.

Another concern is whether the new wife will want children of her own.

Man with Children Married to a Woman with Children

As more men are awarded custody of their children, an increasing number of stepfamilies will include two sets of children. While the number of relationships to manage increases with each new person added to the family, the role of the stepfather appears to be enhanced when the father has his biological children living in the household. This was the conclusion of a team of researchers who studied the family context of 60 stepfathers (Palisi et al., 1991):

> . . . stepfathers may be drawn closer to their stepchildren, and they may have fewer negative attitudes toward them because of the strategies they adopt in striving to treat both sets of children in an equitable manner. The presence of their biological children in the household may, in effect, force them to parent to a greater extent than if they had merely been absorbed into a pre-existing family. It becomes incumbent upon them to constitute a viable living pattern and take a more active role with regard to all children in the household. This may lead them to minimize negative thoughts and feelings about their stepchildren and also to exaggerate positive attitudes about stepchildren in the interests of fairness (p. 102).

Men who become committed to women with children soon begin to spend time in the context of the children. Over half (56%) of divorced mothers who were dating again reported that they included their children in the activities with their future spouse at least once a week (Montgomery et al., 1992).

Man without Children Married to a Woman with Children

The adjustments of the never married, divorced, or widowed man without children who marries a woman with children are primarily related to her children, their acceptance of him, and his awareness that his wife is emotion-

It is not flesh and blood but the heart which makes us fathers and sons.
SCHILLER

One of the more frequent shocks for new stepparents is the realization that they don't feel the same about all the children.
GINI CUCUEL

ally bonded to her children. Unlike childfree marital partners, who are bonded only to each other, the husband entering a relationship with a woman who has children must accept her attachment with her children from the outset.

Lou Everett (1991) interviewed six stepfathers and identified two primary factors that contribute to a positive stepfather-stepchild relationship: (1) Active involvement in teaching the stepchild something mutually valued. Just spending time with the stepchild (eating meals, watching television) had no positive effect on the relationship. Teaching the stepchild (how to skate, fish, fly a kite) made the stepfather feel as though he was contributing to the development of the stepchild and endeared the stepchild to the stepfather, and (2) An intense love relationship between the stepfather and the biological mother of the stepchild. "Men who love their wives are more tolerant of their stepchildren," observed Dr. Everett.

Marsiglio (1992) analyzed data from 195 men in stepfamilies and observed, that they, like the stepfathers in the Everett study reported more positive relationships with stepchildren to the degree that they were happy with their partners. In addition, 55 percent reported that it was "somewhat true" or "definitely true" that "having stepchildren is just as satisfying as having your own children" (p. 204). And, those who were living together had similar perceptions of their stepfathering role to those who were married.

CONSIDERATION

Here are some questions a man without children might ask a woman who has children:

1. How do you expect me to relate to your children? Am I supposed to be their friend, daddy, or what?
2. How do you feel about having another child? How many additional children are you interested in having?
3. How much money do you get in alimony and child support from your ex-husband? How long will this last?
4. What expenses of the children do you expect me to pay for? Who is going to pay for their college expenses?
5. How often are you in contact with your ex-husband? To what degree are you still emotionally involved with him?

Children in Stepfamilies

President Bill Clinton grew up in a stepfamily. A lot of children are growing up in stepfamilies.

NATIONAL DATA   About six million children currently live in stepfamilies and 35 percent of children born in the 80s can expect to live in a stepfamily (Glick, 1989).

Stepchildren have viewpoints and must make adjustments of their own when their parents remarry. They have experienced the transition from a family in which their biological parents lived together to either living alone with one parent (usually the mother) or alternating between the homes of both parents, to a stepfamily with a new stepparent.

CONSIDERATION

In regard to the adjustment of the children after a divorce, is it better for the custodial parent to wait a long time before beginning a new committed relationship or to move rather quickly into a new relationship? A team of reseachers studied 58 remarried families and 69 divorced but not remarried families in which there was a least one child between the ages of 9 and 13. They found:

> In the first months after remarriage, children whose mothers had moved relatively quickly to a new relationship displayed more social competence and directed less negative behavior toward their residential parents than children whose mothers began a later courtship. Moreover, remarried family relationships appeared less negative when courtship was introduced earlier after separation . . . (Montgomery et al., 1992, 693).

Problems experienced by children in stepfamilies often revolve around feeling abandoned, having divided loyalties, discipline, and stepsiblings.

Some stepchildren feel that they have been abandoned twice—once when their parents got divorced and again when the parents turned their attention to their new marital partners. One adolescent explained:

> It hurt me when my parents got divorced and my dad moved out. I really missed him and felt he really didn't care about my feelings. But we adjusted with just my mom, and when everything was going right again, she gets involved with this new guy and we've got baby sitters all the time. I feel like I've lost both parents in two years.

Some children in stepfamilies feel abandoned not only when their parents divorce but when each parent marries someone new and turns his/her attention to the new partner.

CONSIDERATION

Coping with feelings of abandonment is not easy. It is best if the parents assure the children that the divorce was not their fault and that they are loved a great deal by both parents. In addition, the parents should be careful to find a balance between spending time with new partners and spending time with the children.

Divided loyalties is another issue children must deal with in stepfamilies. Sometimes they develop an attachment for a stepparent that is more positive than the relationship with the natural parent of the same sex. When these feelings develop, the children may feel they are in a bind. One adolescent boy explained:

One of the more difficult adjustments for stepchildren is to accept discipline from a stepparent.

I don't think any parent should be using corporal punishment and certainly not a stepparent.

GINI CUCUEL

The rage between savage beasts is not so great, as the hate and rancour between brothers living in dissention.

STEFANO GUAZZO

My real dad left my mother when I was 6, and my mom remarried. My stepdad has always been good to me, and I really prefer to be with him. When my dad comes to pick me up on weekends, I have to avoid talking about my stepdad because my dad doesn't like him. I guess I love my dad, but I have a better relationship with my stepdad.

For some adolescents, the more they care for the stepparent, the more guilty they feel, so they may try to hide their attachment. The stepparent may be aware of both positive and negative feelings coming from the child.

Stepchildren may also have a less close relationship with their stepparent than children have with their biological parent in two-parent families that have not experienced divorce. Three researchers assessed the activity level and feelings of adults in a variety of family structures and noted that stepparents "engaged in child-related activities and/or expressed positive feelings toward children less frequently than did original parents" (Thomson et al., 1992, 375).

Discipline is another issue for stepchildren. "Adjusting to living with a new set of rules from your stepparent," "accepting discipline from a stepparent," and "dealing with the expectations of your stepparent" are situations 80 percent of more than 100 adolescents in stepfamilies said they had experienced (Lutz, 1983). At least two studies have identified the stepmother as the more difficult stepparent to adjust to from the child's point of view (Fine & Kurdek, 1992; Johnson et al., 1988). This is probably because the woman is more often in the role of the active parent, which increases the potential for conflict with the child.

Siblings may also be a problem for stepchildren. They experience higher levels of stress in stepfamilies if they have stepsiblings than if they do not (Lutz, 1983). The stress seems to be a result of more arguments among the adults when both sets of children are present and the perception that parents are more fair with their own children:

I could bounce the ball in the den and my stepdad would jump all over me. But let my stepsister bounce it and he wouldn't say a word. All I want is to be treated fairly, and that's not what's happening in this family.

Stepsiblings also compete for space, which leads to bitter territorial squabbles. The children who are already in the house may feel imposed upon and threatened. The entering children may feel out of place (Kutner, 1989).

CONSIDERATION

To minimize territorial squabbles, it is important that each child has a private space. When children fight over who gets which bedroom, some resolve the conflict by having the children change bedrooms each year (Bernstein, 1989).

Some evidence supports the belief that children tend to have greater well-being in nuclear families compared to stepfamilies. Data from a nationally representative sample of 17,110 children under age 18 revealed that children living with mothers and stepfathers were more likely than those living with both biological parents to have repeated a grade of school, to have been expelled, to have been treated for emotional or behavioral problems, and to report more health problems (Dawson, 1991).

> **CONSIDERATION**
>
> Academic difficulties of children in stepfamilies may reflect the effects of divorce and instability in the child's past. For example, when the biological parents were going through a divorce, they may not have kept a watchful eye on the school performance of their children.

Stepfamily living is often difficult for everyone involved: remarried spouses, children, even ex-spouses, grandparents, and in-laws. While some of the problems begin to level out after two or three years, many continue for five to seven years or longer (Beer, 1988). Many couples become impatient with the unanticipated problems that are slow to abate, and they divorce. The Stepfamily Success Scale in the Self-Assessment provides a way to predict the degree to which you might have a relatively easy adjustment in a stepfamily.

Are afflictions aught
But blessings in disguise?

DAVID MALLET

❧ Developmental Tasks for Stepfamilies

A developmental task is a skill that, if mastered, allows the family to grow as a cohesive unit. Developmental tasks that are not mastered will bring the family closer to the point of disintegration. Some of the more important developmental tasks for stepfamilies are discussed in this section.

Allow Time for Relationship between Partner and Children to Develop

In an effort to escape single parenthood and to live with one's beloved, some individuals rush into a remarriage without getting to know each other. Not only do they have limited information about each other, their respective children may have spent little to no time with their intended stepparent. One stepdaughter remarked, "I came home one afternoon to find a bunch of plastic bags in the living room with my soon-to-be stepdad's clothes in them. I had no idea he was moving in. It hasn't been easy." Both adults and children should have had meals together and spent some time in the same house before becoming bonded by marriage as a family (Bloomfield, 1993).

New stepparents who spend time with their stepchildren help develop an emotional bond with them.

Nurture the New Marriage Relationship

Because the demands of family interaction can become intense—even excessive—it is important that the new wife and husband allocate time to be alone to nurture their relationship (Beer, 1992). They must take time to communicate, demonstrate affection to each other, share their lives, and have fun together. One remarried couple goes out on a date each Saturday night for dinner and a movie—without the children. "If you don't spend time alone with your partner, you won't have one," says one stepparent.

Have Realistic Expectations

Because of the complexity of meshing the numerous relationships involved in a stepfamily, it is important to be realistic. Dreams of "one big happy family" often set up stepparents for disappointment, bitterness, jealousy, and guilt. "It takes from two to five years for a stepfamily to begin to emerge. Be patient" (Boley, 1989, 4). Just as nuclear and single parent families do not always run smoothly, neither do stepfamilies.

Accept Your Stepchildren

Rather than wishing your stepchildren were different, it is more productive "to accept your stepchild's looks, personality, habits, manners, behavior, style of dress, speech, choice of friends and feelings—all of which you had nothing to do with" (Boley, 1989, 4). All children have positive qualities; find them and make them the focus of your thinking.

Stepparents may communicate acceptance of their stepchildren through verbal praise and positive or affectionate statements and gestures. In addition, stepparents may communicate acceptance by engaging in fun activities with their stepchildren and participating in daily activities such as homework, bedtime preparation, and transportation to after-school activities. Funder (1991) studied 313 parents who had been separated five to eight years and who had become involved with a new partner. In general the new partners were very willing to be involved in the parenting of their new spouse's children (see Table 17.2). Such involvement was highest when the children lived in the household.

Reveal and Understand Emotions

An important task for remarried spouses is to deal with and resolve feelings of loss, pain, anger, and bitterness that often exist after a divorce. If left unresolved, such feelings tend to interfere with current marriage and family relationships.

It is also important to encourage children to express and process their feelings. Children should not be punished for expressing negative emotions

	RESIDENT			NONRESIDENT		
PARENT FUNCTION	STEPMOTHER %	STEPFATHER %	ALL %	STEPMOTHER %	STEPFATHER %	ALL %
GUARDIANSHIP DECISION						
Diet	91	51	59	31	00	28
Education	72	62	64	7	18	8
Religion	38	31	32	4	00	3
Right and wrong	94	93	94	42	27	41
Dress	84	65	69	39	27	38
Music and clubs	69	64	65	14	27	15
Health care	94	69	74	16	9	16
Friends	75	59	62	13	27	14
CUSTODIAL/DAY-TO-DAY						
Discipline	94	92	92	49	55	58
Buy clothes	88	38	48	39	27	37
Pay basics	72	88	85	18	64	28
Pay hobbies	63	75	73	23	45	25
Doctor/dentist	81	57	61	13	9	13
Birthdays	91	93	93	57	55	57
School functions	72	65	66	15	9	14
Go to sports events	75	78	78	26	36	36
Discuss problems	94	91	92	50	45	50
Holidays	91	86	86	55	73	57
Help with housework	84	83	84	20	36	21

Source: Funder, Kate. "New partners as co-parents," *Family Matters,* April 1991, no. 28, p. 45. Used by permission of the Australian Institute for Family Studies, 300 Queen Street, Melbourne, 30000, Victoria, Australia.

toward stepfamily members. However, they should be encouraged to express emotions in productive ways.

Establish Your Own Family Rituals

One of the bonding elements of nuclear families is its rituals. Stepfamilies may integrate the various family members by establishing common rituals. Such rituals may include summer vacations, visits to and from extended kin, and religious celebrations. "Even if one does not wholeheartedly participate, by just being part of the group one is included in its membership and its evolving history" (Whiteside, 1989, 35).

Decide about Money

Lack of money is trouble without equal.
RABELAIS

Money is an issue of potential conflict in stepfamilies because it is a scarce resource and several people want to use it for their respective needs. The father wants a new computer; the mother wants a new car; the mother's children want bunk beds, dance lessons, and a satellite dish; the father's children want a larger room, clothes, and a phone. How do the newly married couple and their children decide how money should be spent?

Some stepfamilies put all their resources into one bank and draw out money as necessary without discriminating whose money it is or for whose child the money is being spent. Others keep their money separate; the parents have separate incomes and spend them on their respective biological children. Neither pattern is superior to the other in terms of marital satisfaction (Lown et al., 1989). However, it is important for remarried spouses to agree on whatever financial arrangements they live by.

In addition to deciding how to allocate resources fairly in a stepfamily, remarried couples may face decisions regarding sending the children/stepchildren to college. Remarried couples may also be concerned about making a will that is fair to all family members.

Give Authority to Your Spouse

How much authority the stepparent will exercise over the children should be discussed by the adults before they get married. Some couples divide the authority—each spouse disciplining his or her own children. But children may test the stepparent in such an arrangement when the biological parent is not around. One stepmother said, "Jim's kids are wild when he isn't here because I'm not supposed to discipline them."

CONSIDERATION

It is often helpful for the adults to tell their respective children that they must respect the wishes of the stepparent. Stepparents can't grab authority. They must become a partner with the natural parent, who then gives authority to the new spouse. Unless children view each parent as an authority figure, they are likely to undermine the relationship between the adults. Visher and Visher (1990) recommended that the stepparent become a friend first before becoming an authoritative and disciplining parent. They noted that this process can only occur slowly and that it is a mistake to force the authoritative role first.

As a practical matter, it is often the biological parent in stepfamilies who does the disciplining. When the biological parent is not present, the stepparent is in charge.

The biological parent should support the new stepparent in front of the children. This helps prevent the children from driving a wedge between the couple and gives the children a reason to accept the new partner.

Support Child's Relationship with Absent Parent

A continued relationship with both biological parents is critical to the emotional well-being of the child. Ex-spouses and stepparents should encourage children to have positive relationships with both biological parents. However, in one study, the researchers found that one-fourth of divorced parents said that they sometimes refused to let the other parent see the children (Maccoby et al., 1990).

Cooperate with the Child's Biological Parents and Co-parent

Visher and Visher (1990) recommended the development of a "parent coalition," which means that the adults from both of the child's households be cooperative and actively involved in the rearing of the children.

> For many adults, unfortunately, it is not possible to work out a cooperative rather than a competitive relationship with an ex-spouse, even on such an important topic as sharing in the care of their mutual children. Nevertheless, there are an increasing number of remarried supra family systems in which the adults have recognized the value of such cooperation, both for themselves as well as for their children (p. 10).

Funder (1991) studied 313 parents who had been separated five to eight years and who had become involved with a new partner. The involvement and cooperation of this new partner with the nonresident biological parent depended on the relationship between the spouse and his or her former spouse. If that relationship was bitter and resentful, there was little co-parenting of the two sets of parents on behalf of the child. Where good relationships existed with the ex-spouse, a parental coalition became a reality.

Children whose parents divorce benefit from continued access to and interaction with their grandparents.

Grandparents are perceived as the kid's buddies, allies, confidants. They are there, in a sense, to buffer the effects of parenthood, offering an ear, a hug, and a perspective.

SONIA TAITZ

CONSIDERATION

Masheter (1991) examined the post-divorce relationships of 111 men and 154 women and found that about half (52 percent) had at least monthly contact and one-fourth (25 percent) had weekly contact with their ex-spouse. This frequency of contact in combination with the fact that 43 percent reported friendly feelings toward the ex-spouse suggest that more families could co-parent than do.

Support Child's Relationship with Grandparents

It is important to support children's continued relationships with their natural grandparents. This is one of the more stable relationships in the stepchild's changing world of adult relationships. Regardless of how ex-spouses feel about their former in-laws, they should encourage their children to have positive feelings for their grandparents. One mother said, "Although I am uncomfortable around my ex-in-laws, I know my children enjoy visiting them, so I encourage their relationship."

Stepfamily Success Scale

This scale is designed to measure the degree to which you and your partner might expect to have a successful stepfamily. There are no right or wrong answers. After reading each sentence carefully, circle the number that best represents your feelings.

1 Strongly disagree

2 Mildly disagree

3 Undecided

4 Mildly agree

5 Strongly agree

	SD	MD	U	MA	SA
1. I am a flexible person.	1	2	3	4	5
2. I am not a jealous person.	1	2	3	4	5
3. I am a patient person.	1	2	3	4	5
4. My partner is a flexible person.	1	2	3	4	5
5. My partner is not a jealous person.	1	2	3	4	5
6. My partner is a patient person.	1	2	3	4	5
7. My partner values our relationship as much as the relationship with his or her children.	1	2	3	4	5
8. My partner understands that it is not easy for me to love someone else's children.	1	2	3	4	5
9. I value the relationship with my partner as much as the relationship with my children.	1	2	3	4	5
10. I understand that it will be difficult for my partner to love my children as much as I do.	1	2	3	4	5
11. My partner and I have amicable relationships with our ex-spouses.	1	2	3	4	5
12. My children and those of my partner will live with the ex-spouse.	1	2	3	4	5

	SD	MD	U	MA	SA
13. We will have plenty of money in our stepfamily.	1	2	3	4	5
14. I feel positively about my partner's children.	1	2	3	4	5
15. My partner feels positively about my children.	1	2	3	4	5
16. My children and those of my partner feel positively about each other.	1	2	3	4	5
17. My partner and I will begin our stepfamily in a place neither of us has lived before.	1	2	3	4	5
18. My partner and I agree on how to discipline our children.	1	2	3	4	5
19. My children feel positively about my new partner.	1	2	3	4	5
20. My partner's children feel positively about me.	1	2	3	4	5

Scoring: Add the numbers you circled. 1 (strongly disagree) is the most negative response you can make, and 5 (strongly agree) is the most positive response you can make. The lower your total score (20 is the lowest possible score), the greater the number of potential problems and the lower the chance of success in a stepfamily with this partner. The higher your total score (100 is the highest possible score), the greater the chance of success in a stepfamily with this partner. A score of 60 places you at the midpoint between the extremes of having a difficult or an easy stepfamily experience.

NOTE: This Self-Assessment is intended to be thought provoking and suggestive, it is not a clinical diagnostic instrument.

𝒮 Trends

Due to an increased number of divorced parents getting remarried, stepfamilies have become increasingly visible in American society. It is estimated that one-third of all children will become stepchildren before age 18 (Glick, 1989). As stepfamilies become more normative in our society, they will probably lose some of the stigma they now carry.

Stepfamilies will continue to reach out for help. Members of stepfamilies have already established national organizations for support. These include the Stepfamily Association of America, Inc. (215 Centennial Mall South, Suite 212, Lincoln, NE 68508, 402/4777-7837) and Stepfamily Foundation (333 West End Avenue, Apt. 11c, New York 10023, 212/877-3244). In addition, a number of self-help books on stepfamily living are available (Coleman & Ganong, 1989; Coleman & Ganong, 1988), as well as skills training programs developed specifically for parents in stepfamilies (Nelson & Levant, 1991).

At the present time, family law does not provide clear and comprehensive rules about the stepparent-stepchild relationship. For example, should stepparents be legally responsible to economically support the stepchildren during the remarriage? If the remarriage terminates should stepparents provide child support for stepchildren? Should stepparents have visitation rights if the remarried couple divorce? Because of the increased number of stepfamilies in our society, laws will be developed that apply to this segment of our population.

⌁ CHOICES ∿

Never married and divorced individuals with children have choices to make about entering a stepfamily. The various issues for each of these individuals to consider follow.

A Never Married Man Marrying a Divorced Woman with Children?

The following diagrams emphasize the positive and negative consequences of a "yes" or "no" decision. They are helpful in making many kinds of decisions. First, we suggest how they may help the single man in deciding whether to marry a divorced woman with children.

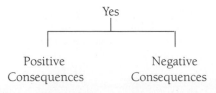

Yes

Positive Consequences — Negative Consequences

Yes The positive consequences of marrying a divorced woman with children include continuing the love relationship with the woman, having a ready-made family, and avoiding the pain of living without the beloved. Because the man making such a decision will be emotionally involved with the woman, a major factor in his decision will be his emotional outlook.

(continued)

~: CHOICES :~

One man said:

> I love her and want to be with her, whether she has kids or not. If you try to add and subtract everything about human relationships as though you are keeping a ledger, you are missing the point. My happiness depends on my being with her, and marriage means that we will continue our lives together, since we don't believe in living together.

In addition to being able to live with the loved person in a marriage relationship, another positive consequence of marrying a divorced person with children is having a ready-made family. "I've always wanted children, and I think her kids are great," said a prospective groom. "We've been camping together as a family, and it was nothing but fun. I don't seen any problem down the road with these kids."

Another positive outcome is avoiding a negative one:

> If I don't marry her, I'm forced to go back to bars and talk to people I'm not interested in. I love her, and deciding not to marry her would mean loneliness and pain.

Every decision has positive and negative consequences. What are the negative consequences of deciding to marry a divorced woman with children? Jealousy over the emotional bond between the woman and her children, the presence of an ex-husband who may be calling and com-

ing by to get the kids, and the costs associated with rearing the children are potential problems. One man who married (and subsequently divorced) a woman with two children said:

> It didn't work out for us. I was jealous of the time she gave to her own kids and knew that I was always second. I also didn't like her ex around, even though it was for a brief time each week. Just to see the guy who had sex with my wife for 15 years unnerved me. And the money was a real problem. Her ex never paid enough child support to cover what the kids cost, and I got tired of paying for kids who weren't really mine. Besides, they both needed braces, and that got us deeply in debt. I'd say marrying a woman with kids isn't worth it, no matter how much you love her.

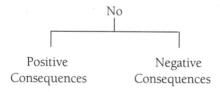

No Suppose the man decides not to marry the divorced woman with children. What are the positive and negative consequences of his decision? On the positive side, he has avoided the potential problems of feeling jealous of the bond between the woman and her children, of having to deal with an ex-spouse, and of feeling financially

responsible for children that are not biologically his. By making a single decision, he has avoided a lot of potential headaches (and maybe a divorce, since 60 percent of remarriages do not last).

On the other hand, there are some losses associated with deciding not to marry her. The primary one is the emotional pain he would feel as a result of terminating the relationship with her. "In these situations," said one man, "I'm a real sucker for romance. I do what I feel every time. And living without this woman is something I can't do."

After listing the positive and negative consequences of a "yes" and "no" decision, a final decision can be made by examining how the consequences look on paper. Assign weights to the different consequences if necessary. For example, on a 10-point scale (10 = tops), how important is it to have a ready-made family, to continue the love relationship, or to avoid going in debt over children who are not biologically yours? Getting the issues on paper and looking at them sometimes helps in making a decision.

How the decision feels is also important. Regardless of how it looks on paper, your feelings will play an important role in determining the final decision. "If the decision doesn't feel right in your heart, it isn't right," said one person.

A Never Married Woman Marrying a Divorced Man with Children?

It is not unusual for a single woman to become emotionally involved with a divorced man who has children. Although the ex-wife frequently has custody of their children, they may visit and he will probably pay child support. The process just described is helpful in examining the issues involved (see earlier diagrams).

Yes The positive consequences for the single woman marrying a divorced man with children would be similar to those of the single man marrying a divorced woman with children: continuing the love relationship, benefiting from a ready-made family, and avoiding the pain of losing the partner.

The negative consequences of a "yes" decision may also include competing with the children for the husband's time. One woman said:

> Since we both worked all week, I wanted the weekend to enjoy by ourselves. But he wanted his kids to visit us on the weekends. I went along with it for awhile, but finally told him I didn't like it. He said, "My kids are coming to this house every Saturday as long as they want to. If you don't like it, leave." I tried to get along with them, but I just ended up cooking and doing the laundry for them. I felt like a maid for his kids, who were interfering in our marriage.

No The positive outcome of a decision not to marry a divorced man with children is avoiding the problems of stepchildren visiting frequently and taking money out of the marriage and giving it to the husband's ex-wife.

The negative consequence of deciding not to marry is the flood of bad feelings—loneliness, depression, and pain—that often follow a decision to walk away from an emotionally important relationship.

It is critical to keep in mind that no decision will have all positive or negative consequences. Every decision will involve trade-offs.

A Divorced Woman with Children and a Divorced Man with Children Marrying?

Divorced people sometimes prefer each other because they know the person has an experiential understanding of the divorced state. "I won't date single people," said one divorced woman. "They have no appreciation for what it is like to be divorced and they certainly don't know anything about the parent-child bond." Marrying someone with children has its own problems. (Refer again to the earlier diagrams.)

Yes Marrying someone who understands divorce and children is perhaps the greatest benefit of deciding to marry a divorced person with children. Because they know how intense the parent-child bond is, they are not as likely to feel jealous of this relationship. In addition, they have ex-spouses too and can empathize with the need and discomfort of interacting with an ex.

Mother and father role models for each other's children are also a benefit for adults and children. "I need a mother for my kids, and she needs a daddy for hers, so it's a good trade-off," said one father. "I wouldn't say I'm getting married for that reason, but it sure is a plus."

The negative consequences of a decision to blend two families together are problems of the wife's children accepting their stepfather, the husband's children accepting their stepmother, and the children accepting each other. These factors will influence the degree to which the new family becomes a cohesive unit. To expect that such a fusion will occur quickly and smoothly is unrealistic.

No The decision against blending two families will result in avoiding the potentially negative consequences just described. On the other hand, such a decision will terminate an emotional relationship with someone who knows what divorce, children, and single parenting are all about.

℅ Summary

About 80 percent of divorced people remarry. The issues encountered by those considering a remarriage involve establishing trust in a new relationship, boundary maintenance with the ex-spouse, meshing finances, and relating to stepchildren.

A stepfamily is a married couple in which at least one of the spouses has had a child in a previous relationship. Stepfamilies have been stigmatized as not being "real" families. However, it is estimated that by the year 2000, stepfamilies will outnumber all other family types. The strengths of stepfamilies include exposure to a variety of behavior patterns, a happier parent, and greater objectivity on the part of the stepparent.

Women, men, and children sometimes experience stepfamily living differently. For women, learning to get along with the husband's children, not being resentful of his relationship with his children, and adapting to the fact that one-quarter to one-third of his income may be sent to his ex-wife as alimony or child support are skills the new wife must develop. She may also want children with her new partner or may bring her own children into the remarriage. In the latter case, she is anxious that her new husband will accept her children.

Men in stepfamilies have similar concerns. Getting along with their wife's children, paying for many of the expenses of their stepchildren, having their new partner accept their own children, and dealing with the issue of having more children are among them.

Children must cope with feeling abandoned and problems of divided loyalties, discipline, and stepsiblings.

Developmental tasks for stepfamilies include allowing time for partners and children to get to know each other, nurturing the new marriage relationship, deciding whose money will be spent on whose children, deciding who will discipline the children and how, revealing and understanding emotions, and supporting the child's relationship with both parents and natural grandparents. In addition, spouses should support the child's relationship with the absent parent. Both sets of parents and stepparents should form a parenting coalition in which they cooperate and actively participate in childrearing.

Trends include the increased visibility of stepfamilies and continued sharing of stepfamily problems and solutions by individuals involved in stepfamily living. In addition, courts will recognize that stepfamilies have issues that are not covered in traditional family law.

Questions for Reflection

1. How capable do you think you are of loving someone else's children?
2. How accepting would you be of a new spouse who could not accept your children?
3. How would you feel if your stepchildren never accepted you as a member of the family? What could you do to try to change their attitude?

References

Ahlburg, D. A. and C. J. De Vita. New realities of the American family. *Population Bulletin,* 1992, *47,* 1–44.

Beer, W. R. *American stepfamilies.* New Brunswick, N.J.: Transaction Publishers, 1992.

Beer, W. R., ed. *Relative strangers.* Lanham, Maryland: Rowman and Littlefield, 1988.

Bernstein, Anne C. *Yours, mine, and ours.* New York: Charles Scribner's Sons, 1989.

Bernstein, B. E. and S. K. Collins. Remarriage counseling: Lawyer and therapist's help with the second time around. *Family Relations,* 1985, *34,* 375–391.

Bloomfield, Harold. *Making peace in your stepfamily.* Westport, Conn.: Hyperion Press Inc., 1993.

Boley, Carol D. When you're mom no. 2. *Focus on the Family,* July 1989, 3–4.

Booth, A. and J. N. Edwards. Starting over: Why remarriages are more unstable. *Journal of Family Issues,* 1992, *13,* 179–194.

Brubaker, T. H. and J. A. Kimberly. Challenges to the American Family. *Family Relations,* T. H. Brubaker, ed. Newbury Park, Calif.: Sage Publications, 1993, 3–16.

Coleman, M. and L. H. Ganong. *Bibliotherapy with stepchildren.* Springfield, Ill.: Charles C. Thomas, 1988.

Dainton, M. Myths and misconceptions of the stepmother identity. *Family Relations,* 1993, *42,* 93–98.

Darden, E. C. and T. S. Zimmerman. Blended families: A decade review, 1979 to 1990. *Family Therapy,* 1992, *19,* 25–31.

Dawson, D. A. Family structure and children's health and well-being: Data from the 1988 national health interview survey on child health. *Journal of Marriage and the Family,* 1991, *53,* 573–584.

Dudley, J. R. Exploring ways to get divorced fathers to comply willingly with child support agreements. *Journal of Divorce and Remarriage,* 1991, *14,* 121–135.

Everett, Lou. Abstract, "Factors that contribute to stepfather-stepchild relationships." *Scientific Sessions Abstracts: Creating Nursing's Future,* Sigma Theta Tau. International Honor Society, Tampa, Florida, 1991.

Fine, M. A., P. C. McKenry, B. W. Donnelly, and P. Voydanoff. Perceived adjustment of parents and children: Variations by family structure, race, and gender. *Journal of Marriage and the Family,* 1992, *54,* 118–127.

Fine, M. A. and David R. Fine. Recent changes in laws affecting stepfamilies. *Family Relations,* 1992, *41,* 334–340.

Fine, M. A. and L. A. Kurdek. The adjustment of adolescents in stepfather and stepmother families. *Journal of Marriage and the Family,* 1992, *54,* 725–736.

Fischman, Joshua. Stepdaughter wars. *Psychology Today,* 1988, *22,* 38–45.

Funder, K. New partners as co-parents. *Family Matters,* April 1991, no. 28, 44–46.

Furstenberg, Frank F. The new extended family: The experience of parents and children after remarriage. *Remarriage and Stepparenting,* Kay Pasley and Marilyn Ihinger-Tallman, eds. New York: Guilford Press, 1987, 42–61.

Gabe, Grace. Rekindling old flames. *Psychology Today,* 1993, *26,* 32–39, 62, 63.

Ganong, L. H. and M. Coleman. Do mutual children cement bonds in stepfamilies? *Journal of Marriage and the Family,* 1988, *50,* 687–698.

Ganong, L. H. and M. Coleman. Preparing for remarriage: Anticipating the issues, seeking solutions. *Family Relations,* 1989, *38,* 28–33.

Glick, P. C. Remarried families, stepfamilies, and stepchildren: A brief demographic profile. *Family Relations,* 1989, *38,* 24–27.

Goetting, A. The six stations of remarriage: Developmental tasks of remarriage after divorce. *Family Coordinator,* 1982, *31,* 213–222.

Gorman, T. *Stepfather.* Boulder, Co.: Gentle Touch Press, 1983.

Hobart, Charles W. Perception of parent-child relationships in first married and remarried families. *Family Relations,* 1988, *37,* 175–182.

Kaplan, L. and C. B. Hennon. Remarriage education: The personal reflections program. *Family Relations,* 1992, *41,* 127–134.

Keshet, J. K. The remarried couple: Stressors and successes. *Relative Strangers,* William R. Beer, ed. Lanham, Maryland: Rowman and Littlefield, 1988.

Kurdek, L. A. and M. A. Fine. Cognitive correlates of satisfaction for mothers and stepfathers in stepfather families. *Journal of Marriage and the Family,* 1991, *53,* 565–572.

Kutner, Lawrence. In blended families, rivalries intensify. *The New York Times,* January 5, 1989. CL et passim.

Lown, J. M., J. R. McFadden, and S. M. Crossman. Family life education for remarriage: Focus on financial management. *Family Relations,* 1989, *38,* 40–45.

Lutz, P. The stepfamily: An adolescent perspective. *Family Relations,* 1983, *32,* 367–375.

Maccoby, E. E., C. E. Depner, and R. H. Mnookin. Co-parenting in the second year after divorce. *Journal of Marriage and the Family,* 1990, *52,* 141–155.

Marsiglio, W. Stepfathers with minor children living at home. *Journal of Family Issues,* 1992, *13,* 195–214.

Masheter, C. Post-divorce relationships between ex-spouses: The roles of attachment and interpersonal conflict. *Journal of Marriage and the Family,* 1991, *53,* 103–110.

Montgomery, M. J., E. R. Anderson, E. M. Hetherington, and W. G. Clingempeel. Patterns of courtship for remarriage: Implications for child adjustment and parent-child relationships. *Journal of Marriage and the Family,* 1992, *54,* 686–698.

Nelson, W. P. and R. F. Levant. An evaluation of skills training program for parents in stepfamilies. *Family Relations,* 1991, *40,* 291–296.

Palisi, B. J., M. Orleans, D. Caddell, and B. Korn. Adjustment to stepfatherhood: The effects of marital history and relations with children. *Journal of Divorce and Remarriage,* 1991, *14,* 89–106.

Papernow, P. L. Stepparent role development: From outsider to intimate. *Relative Strangers,* William R. Beer, ed. Landham, Maryland: Rowman and Littlefield, 1988, 54–82.

Pasley, B. K. and M. Ihinger-Tallman. Boundary ambiguity in remarriage: Does ambiguity differentiate degree of marital adjustment and integration? *Family Relations,* 1989, *38,* 46–52.

Pothern, S. Divorce in Hindu society. *Journal of Comparative Family Studies,* 1989, *20,* 377–392.

Roberts, T. W. and S. J. Price. A systems analysis of the remarriage process: Implications for the clinician. *Journal of Divorce,* 1985–1986, *9,* 1–25.

Schultz, N. C., C. L. Schultz, and D. H. Olson. Couple strengths and stressors in complex and simple stepfamilies in Australia. *Journal of Marriage and the Family,* 1991, *53,* 555–564.

Statistical Abstract of the United States: 1993, 113th ed. Washington, D.C.: U.S. Bureau of the Census, 1993.

Teachman, J. D. Who pays? Receipt of child support in the United States. *Journal of Marriage and the Family,* 1991, *53,* 759–772.

Thomson, E. S. S. McLanahan, and R. B. Curtin. Family structure, gender, and parental socialization. *Journal of Marriage and the Family,* 1992, *54,* 368–378.

Vemer, E., M. Coleman, L. H. Ganong, and H. Cooper. Marital satisfaction in remarriage: A meta-analysis. *Journal of Marriage and the Family,* 1989, *51,* 713–725.

Vinick, B. Remarriage in old age. *The Family Coordinator,* 1978, *27,* 359–363.

Visher, E. B. and J. S. Visher. Dynamics of successful stepfamilies. *Journal of Divorce and Remarriage,* 1990, *14,* 3–12.

Walker, G. *Second wife, second best?* New York: Doubleday, 1984.

White, L. K. and A. Riedmann. When the Brady bunch grows up: Step/half- and fullsibling relationships in adulthood. *Journal of Marriage and the Family,* 1992, *54,* 197–208.

Whiteside, M. F. Family rituals as a key to kinship connections in remarried families. *Family Relations,* 1989, *38,* 34–39.

Wineberg, H. Childbearing and dissolution of the second marriage. *Journal of Marriage and the Family,* 1992, *54,* 879–887.

Wineberg, J. Childbearing in remarriage. *Journal of Marriage and the Family,* 1990, *52,* 31–38.

Contents

℘ 1 ℘

SPECIAL TOPIC

HIV Infection and Other STDs

Is it True?

1. In January of 1994, a cure for AIDS was developed.

2. Throughout the world, most cases of AIDS are attributed to transmission of the AIDS virus through homosexual sex.

3. Chlamydia can be transmitted through contact with a towel or hot tub in which the bacteria are present.

4. There is no cure for herpes.

5. In the 1980s, the incidence of syphilis in the United States decreased significantly.

1 = F; 2 = F; 3 = T; 4 = T; 5 = F

Safer sex involves choice and planning ahead and a reasonable level of sobriety, lovemaking following from a thoughtful and unfuddled choice of a partner—the kind one would still be glad of by daylight.

MARY CATHERINE BATESON
RICHARD GOLDSBY

*I*n spite of the media attention to AIDS and other sexually transmitted diseases (STDs), high risk sexual behaviors continue to occur.

NATIONAL DATA ꝏ In a study of 10,630 adults, researchers found that between 12 and 31 percent of their respondants reported having more than two sexual partners in the last year and in the last five years respectively. Condom use was low with only 17 percent of those with multiple sexual partners reporting condom use all the time (Cantania et al., 1992).

Discussion of "safe sex" practices between partners is also infrequent. Less than one-quarter of all college freshmen throughout the United States reported that they discussed safe sex with a partner in the last year (American Council on Education and University of California, 1992). Multiple sexual partners, infrequent discussion of safer sex practices, and infrequent use of latex condoms make one vulnerable to HIV infection and other sexually transmissible diseases. In this section, we discuss HIV infection and other sexually transmissible diseases. It is not uncommon to believe inaccurate information about HIV (see AIDS Knowledge Scale).

> Some students have a hard time understanding that the consequence of one unprotected sexual encounter may not be reversible.
>
> AMERICAN COLLEGE HEALTH ASSOCIATION

ꝏ Human Immunodeficiency Virus (HIV) Infection

HIV attacks the white blood cells (T-lymphocytes) in human blood, impairing the immune system and a person's ability to fight other diseases. Of all the diseases that may be transmitted sexually, HIV infection is the most life-threatening.

NATIONAL DATA ꝏ HIV Infection is the tenth leading cause of death in the United States. Of the deaths attributed to HIV, 64 percent were for white males, 24 percent for black males, six percent for black females, and five percent for white females (National Center for Health Statistics, 1993).

Categories and Symptoms

The Centers for Disease Control (CDC) (the official U.S. government public health bureau responsible for tracking disease, whose offices are in Atlanta, Georgia) have identified four categories of HIV infection. The fourth category represents people who have AIDS. Relatively few people who are infected with HIV have AIDS.

SELF-ASSESSMENT

AIDS Knowledge Scale

Please answer the following items using a true or false format. Circle *T* if you believe the statement is *True,* and *F* if you believe it is *False.*

1. Hemophiliacs can get AIDS.
2. AIDS is an epidemic.
3. Only homosexuals get AIDS.
4. The virus that causes AIDS is called Human Immuno-deficiency Virus (HIV).
5. The AIDS virus can remain infectious outside the body for up to ten days if it is at room temperature.
6. One can get AIDS by sharing a meal with a person who has AIDS.
7. People who have AIDS do not develop cancer.
8. Today blood supply in hospitals and blood donation centers is screened for AIDS virus.
9. Impaired memory and concentration and motor deficits may occur in some AIDS patients.
10. One can get AIDS by sharing drug needles.
11. AIDS virus may live in the human body for years before symptoms appear.
12. One can get AIDS from receiving blood or sperm from a donor who has AIDS.
13. By using a condom when having sex, one is always safe from contracting AIDS.
14. The HIV test is a blood test which can tell if a person has AIDS.
15. There is a cure for AIDS.
16. AIDS victims may show extreme tiredness, night sweats, fever, weight loss, diarrhea, etc.
17. One can get AIDS by having sexual intercourse with an infected person.
18. AIDS is spread by sneezing, coughing, or touching.
19. AZT is the only drug approved by the U.S. Food and Drug Administration for the treatment of AIDS.
20. One can get AIDS by having sex with someone who uses intravenous drugs.
21. AIDS can be spread by having contact with towels or bed linens used by a person with AIDS.
22. An infected mother can give the AIDS virus to the baby during pregnancy and/or through breast feeding.
23. About 400,000 people in the United States are infected with the HIV virus.
24. Blacks and Hispanics show higher incidence rates of AIDS than other ethnic groups.
25. More women than men have been infected by the AIDS virus.

Scoring: The following items are true: 1, 2, 4, 8, 9, 10, 11, 12, 16, 17, 20, 22, and 24. The following items are false: 3, 5, 6, 7, 13, 14, 15, 18, 19, 21, 23, 25. The scale is scored by totaling the number of items answered correctly. Possible scores range from 0 to 25. The higher the score, the higher the degree of knowledge of HIV/AIDS.

Comparison: The average score of 68 undergraduate men at a large urban public university on the East coast was 17.41; the average score of 98 undergraduate women at the same university was 17.87

SOURCE: David S. Goh. The development and reliability of the Attitudes Toward AIDS Scale. *College Student Journal,* 1993, 27, 208–214. The scale is on p. 214. Permission granted by *College Student Journal.*

Category 1   Category 1 is comprised of people who have been infected with HIV and have developed antibodies against it. Most people in Category 1 either have no symptoms or exhibit flu-like symptoms—fever, muscular aches and pains, and fatigue. These symptoms, if they occur, surface between two and six weeks after infection. Antibodies may appear in the blood in two months, but more often take 7 months before they reach reliable detectable levels. Before the antibodies are detectable, HIV-infected individuals will test negative for HIV, so they are "silent carriers" of HIV. Although persons with Category 1 HIV

Don't say, "It can't happen to me." It can.

GARLIN LANCASTER (DIED OF AIDS, 1993)

do not have AIDS and may never get it, they are infectious and able to transmit the virus to others (through sex, blood donation, sharing needles, gestation, childbirth and breast feeding).

Category 2   Persons in Category 2 show the presence of HIV antibodies in their blood and may also show a slight decrease in T-4 cells. This suggests that the immune system is under attack, although at this stage, the person still does not have any significant clinical symptoms and may not be aware of having the HIV virus.

An AIDS patient is being comforted by his mother

Category 3   Persons in Category 3, formerly considered to have AIDS-related complex **(ARC)**, show signs of illness. The lymph nodes of the body become swollen and can be felt as small lumps in the armpits, neck, and groin, constituting lymphadenopathy syndrome (LAS). Other symptoms in Category 3 HIV include persistent fever, diarrhea, night sweats, weight loss, fatigue, yeast infections of the mouth and vagina, and reactivation of the chicken-pox virus, causing a painful skin condition called "shingles." These symptoms are usually not life-threatening, unless diarrhea and weight loss are severe. However, persons in Category 3 have a serious risk of progressing to Category 4.

Category 4   Persons in Category 4 are considered to have **AIDS (acquired immunodeficiency syndrome)**. Their bodies are vulnerable to **opportunistic infections,** which would be resisted if the immune system were not damaged. The two most common diseases associated with AIDS are a form of cancer called Kaposi's sarcoma (KS) and pneumocystis carinii pneumonia (PCP), a rare form of pneumonia. Seventy percent of all HIV deaths result from PCP. In Category 4, HIV may invade the brain and nervous system, producing symptoms of neurological impairment and/or psychiatric illness.

Transmission of HIV and High-Risk Behaviors

The human immunodeficiency virus may be transmitted one of five ways:

1. *Sexual contact.* HIV is found in several body fluids of infected individuals, including blood, semen, and possibly vaginal secretions. During sexual contact with an infected individual, the virus enters a person's blood stream through their rectum, vagina, penis (uncircumcised penis is at greater risk because of the greater retention of the partner's fluids), and possibly their mouth during oral sex. Saliva, sweat, and tears are not body fluids through which HIV is transmitted. Table ST1.1 illustrates the high- to low-risk behaviors for contracting HIV and other STDs.

NATIONAL DATA  Women are 17.5 times more likely to become HIV infected from an infected male than men are to contract the disease from an infected female (Stine, 1993).

T A B L E   ST1.1

The Spectrum of Risk for HIV Infection

Sexual behaviors have different levels of risk for different STDs. The following chart depicts risk assuming no protection is used for these behaviors. **Using latex condoms lowers the risk of transmitting STDs by anal, oral, or vaginal intercourse.**

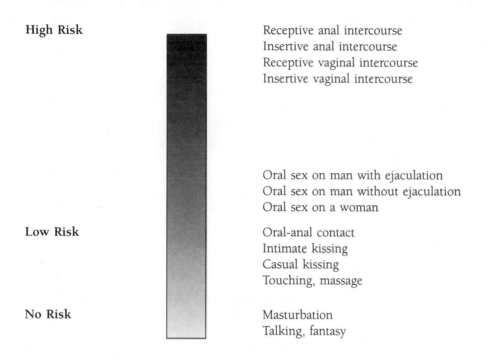

High Risk

Receptive anal intercourse
Insertive anal intercourse
Receptive vaginal intercourse
Insertive vaginal intercourse

Oral sex on man with ejaculation
Oral sex on man without ejaculation
Oral sex on a woman

Low Risk

Oral-anal contact
Intimate kissing
Casual kissing
Touching, massage

No Risk

Masturbation
Talking, fantasy

HARMFUL TO YOUR JUDGMENT

Alcohol	Marijuana
Amphetamines (speed)	Cocaine, Crack
Amyl Nitrite (poppers)	

Source: "Safer Sex," a brochure published by American College Health Association, P.O. Box 28937, Baltimore, MD 21240-8937. Reprinted with permission.

2. *Intravenous drug use.* Drug users who are infected with HIV transmit the virus to other drug users with whom they share needles, syringes, and other drug-related implements.

3. *Blood transfusions.* HIV may be transmitted through receiving HIV-infected blood or blood products. Currently, all blood donors are screened, and blood is not accepted from high-risk individuals. Blood that is accepted from donors is tested for the presence of HIV. However, prior to 1985, donor blood was not tested for HIV. Individuals who received blood or blood products prior to 1985 may have been infected with HIV.

4. *Mother-child transmission of HIV.* There is a 40 percent chance that a pregnant woman infected with HIV will transmit the virus through the placenta to her unborn child. These babies will initially test positive for HIV as a consequence of having the antibodies from the mother's bloodstream. However, not all of these babies will develop AIDS. Although it is rare, HIV transmission through breastfeeding has also been documented (Phair & Chadwick, 1992). It is not the breast milk but the blood which may result from the baby chewing on the nipple of the mother which may transmit HIV.

5. *Organ or tissue transplants and donor semen.* Lastly, receiving transplant organs and tissues, as well as receiving semen for artificial insemination, may involve risk of contracting HIV if the donors were not HIV tested. Such testing is essential and recipients should insist on knowing the HIV status of the organ, tissue, or semen donor.

Sexual Orientation and HIV Infection

In the United States, HIV infection was first seen among homosexual and bisexual men having multiple sex partners. Homosexual transmission is the predominant mode of HIV infection among U.S. males.

NATIONAL DATA ℘ Fifty-seven percent of all U.S. males diagnosed as having AIDS are men who have sex with other men (Centers for Disease Control and Prevention, 1993).

For U.S. women diagnosed with AIDS, the predominant modes of infection are sharing drug injection equipment (46 percent) and heterosexual contact (37 percent) (CDCP, 1993). While homosexual males are at great risk, lesbians are at virtually zero risk from female-to-female contact.

Although only four percent of HIV infection cases in this country have been officially attributed to heterosexual transmission, this rate is increasing (Billy et al., 1993)., In fact, HIV infection cases attributed to heterosexual transmission are growing faster than any other category of HIV cases (Centers for Disease Control and Prevention, 1993).

INTERNATIONAL DATA ℘ According to the World Health Organization, by the year 2000, up to 90% of all HIV infections in the world will have been contracted through heterosexual transmission (Aral & Holmes, 1991).

In third world countries, AIDS is primarily a heterosexual disease.

RICHARD L. RUMLEY, MD

Prevalence of HIV Infection and AIDS

Worldwide at least 12.9 million people were estimated to be HIV infected in 1992 (Goldsmith, 1992). According to the Centers for Disease Control, one in 250 U.S. adults is infected with HIV.

NATIONAL DATA ℘ As of June 1993, 315,390 AIDS cases had been diagnosed in the United States (Centers for Disease Control and Prevention, 1993).

Of those classified (in the United States) as having AIDS, 48 percent are white, 24 percent are black, 14 percent are Hispanic, and .05 percent is Asian/Pacific Islander and American Indian or Alaska Native (Centers for Disease Control, 1993). The chance of heterosexual transmission of HIV is approximately 10 times greater for blacks and four times greater for Hispanics than for whites. Urban minority populations, prostitutes, and those who exchange sex for drugs are regarded as the primary groups among which HIV infection is increasing at epidemic rates (Aral & Holmes, 1991).

CONSIDERATION

Risk group is a term that implies that a certain demographic trait determines who will become infected with HIV. Kerr (1990) noted, however,

> It is not the group one belongs to, but the behaviors one practices that put them at risk for HIV infection. The concept of high-risk groups has led many persons to falsely believe that they are not susceptible to HIV infection since they do not fall into one of these "groups" (p. 431).

Tests for HIV Infection

There are decided benefits from early medical detection of HIV. These include taking medications to reduce the growth of HIV and preventing the development of some life-threatening conditions. An example of the latter is pneumonia, which is more likely to develop when one's immune system has weakened.

HIV counselors recommend that individuals who answer yes to any of the following questions should definitely seek testing:

- If you are a man, have you had sex with other men?
- Have you had sex with someone you know or suspect was infected with HIV?
- Have you had an STD?
- Have you shared needles or syringes to inject drugs or steroids?
- Have you received a blood transfusion or blood products between 1978 and 1985?
- Have you had sex with someone who would answer yes to any of these questions?

Additionally, counselors suggest that if you have had sex with someone whose sexual risk history you do not know or if you have had numerous sexual partners, your risk of HIV infection is increased, and testing should be seriously considered. Finally, if you plan to become pregnant, testing is important.

One test for HIV, *ELISA* (enzyme-linked immunosorbent assay), assesses the presence of antibodies to HIV in the bloodstream of a person who has been exposed to HIV as early as two weeks to three months earlier. The test is relatively inexpensive and serves as a basic screening device. A blood sample is taken from the person's arm and tested in the laboratory. This test does not confirm that the person has or will develop AIDS. Hence, the test is not an "AIDS test" but an HIV antibody test. Because it takes time for antibodies to develop in the body, getting tested more than once increases the accuracy of your information.

Those testing positive after being administered the ELISA test two times will be given a second type of test (*Western Blot*) for more definitive screening. (The Western Blot is considerably more expensive than the ELISA test.) If the result of the Western Blot test is positive, the person has been exposed to HIV and is infected. If the result is negative it is probable that the person does not have HIV. In some cases the result of the Western Blot test is neither positive nor negative, in which case the person may wait a month to have the test repeated (to give time for the antibodies to build up).

Alternatively, instead of repeating the Western Blot test, the person's blood may be tested with the VAL-I.D. PCR (Polymerase Chain Reaction). This is a recently developed test that can detect the HIV virus itself and does not depend on the presence of antibodies to HIV. Hence, it can be used at the earliest stage of HIV and is reliable in as short a time as six weeks after exposure to HIV. It is recommended that newborns be tested with the VAL-I.D. PCR if their mother has been infected with HIV.

A urine test that screens for HIV antibodies has also been developed (Clinical Studies, 1992). While the urine test is easier and less expensive to perform, the researchers cautioned that given the widespread use of urine drug screening in the U.S., it could be used by groups who would discriminate against those who test positive.

Treatment for HIV and Opportunistic Infections.

One drug that is useful (particularly if used early) in treating some people infected with the AIDS virus is azidothymidine (*AZT*). Another drug that has also been given FDA approval is Dideoxyinosine (*DDI*). In limited trials the drug seems to be effective if AZT does not slow the growth of HIV. However, there are side effects such as painful neuritis and pancreatitis. The drug is still considered experimental and is not a cure.

Pentamidine is also helpful in treating PCP (Pneumocystis carinii pneumonia), the pneumonia associated with AIDS. When pentamidine is inhaled directly into the lungs it is dramatically effective in preventing the pneumonia. While pentamidine prevents the PCP parasite from growing, another drug called "566" directly attacks the parasite that causes PCP and kills it.

Given the availability of various drugs, physicians are now beginning to think of AIDS as analogous to diabetes. There is no cure, but it can be managed in some cases. The average cost of treatment per AIDS patient from diagnosis to death is $80,000 (Stine, 1993).

The ultimate medical answer for HIV rests in the identification of a vaccine to eliminate the threat of HIV. Approximately nine HIV vaccines have already been developed, but none have been tested on humans to find out if they will protect against HIV. "At this time, it appears as if it will be 2005 before we know if a vaccine against AIDS will be possible" (Cox, 1992, ix).

In the following sections we consider other sexually transmitted diseases. The relationship of HIV infection to other STDs is being given increased attention by researchers:

> HIV infection leads to altered manifestations of other STDs and thereby probably promotes their spread. Genital and anorectal herpes ulcers normally heal within one to three weeks, but they may persist for months as highly infectious ulcers in persons with HIV infection (Aral & Holmes, 1991, 66).

೮ Chlamydia

Chlamydia trachomatis (CT) is a bacteria that may infect the genitals, eyes, and lungs. Chlamydia (clah-MID-ee-uh) is the most frequently occurring STD on college campuses. Indeed, some health officials believe that chlamydia is the most common sexually transmitted disease.

NATIONAL DATA ೮ Four million cases of chlamydia are detected annually in the United States (Stein, 1991).

Worldwide, it is estimated that 300 million contract sexually transmitted chlamydial infections each year (Sammons, 1991). When the eye infection, chlamydial trachoma, is considered, over 500 million cases are contracted yearly. At least 2 million of the 200 million who contract chlamydia trachoma each year are permanently blinded by the infection; most of these people live in Asia and Africa. The rate of blindness due to chlamydial infections in the United States is much lower, due to climate and the medication readily available to control the infection. Other possible consequences of chlamydia include pelvic inflammatory disease, sterility, a form of infant pneumonia, and premature birth (Aral & Holmes, 1991).

CT is easily transmitted from person to person via sexual contact. The microorganisms are most often found in the urethra of the man, the cervix, uterus, and Fallopian tubes of the woman, and in the rectums of either men or women. In addition to direct contact, CT infections *can* occur indirectly by contact with, as examples, a towel, or a hot tub in which bacteria are present.

Genital-to-eye transmission of the bacteria can also occur. If a person with a genital CT infection rubs his or her eye or the eye of a partner after touching infected genitals, the bacteria can be transferred to the eye, and vice versa. Finally, infants can get CT as they pass through the cervix of their infected mothers during delivery.

CT rarely shows obvious symptoms, which accounts for its being known as "the silent disease." About one in four infected men and at least half of all infected women experience no initial symptoms (Cowley & Hager, 1991). Women and men who are infected with CT usually do not know that they have the disease. The result is that they infect new partners unknowingly, who infect others unknowingly—unendingly.

Although CT often exhibits no symptoms, symptoms do occur in some cases. In men, the symptoms include pus from the penis, a sore on the penis, a sore testis, or a bloody stool. In women, symptoms include low back pain, pelvic pain, a boil on the vaginal lip, or a bloody discharge. Symptoms in either sex include a sore on the tongue, a sore on the finger, pain during urination, or the sensation of needing to urinate frequently. The presence of chlamydia can be determined by a laboratory test. Chlamydia is usually treated with tetracycline, except with pregnant women, who should take a substitute for tetracycline. Although delay in treatment can be devastating, CT is curable if it is diagnosed and treated before the bacteria have had a chance to flourish.

ॐ Genital Herpes

Herpes refers to more than 50 viruses related by size, shape, internal composition, and structure. One such herpes is *genital herpes.* Whereas the disease has been known for at least 2,000 years, media attention to genital herpes is relatively new. Also known as *herpes simplex virus type 2* (HSV–2), genital herpes is a viral infection that is usually transmitted during sexual contact. Symptoms occur in the form of a cluster of small, painful blisters or sores at the point of infection, most often on the penis or around the anus in men. In women, the blisters usually appear around the vagina but may also develop inside the vagina, on the cervix, and sometimes on the anus. Pregnant women may transmit the herpes virus to their newborn infants, causing brain damage or death.

Another type of herpes, *labial* or *lip herpes,* originates in the mouth. *Herpes simplex virus type 1* (HSV–1) is a biologically different virus with which people are more familiar as cold sores on the lips. These sores can be transferred to the genitals by the fingers or by oral-genital contact. In the past, genital and lip herpes had site specificity; HSV–1 was always found on the lips or in the mouth, and HSV–2 was always found on the genitals. But because of the increase in fellatio and cunnilingus, HSV–1 herpes may be found in the genitals and HSV–2 may be found in the lips.

The first symptoms of genital herpes appear a couple of days to three weeks after exposure. At first, these symptoms may include an itching or burning sensation during urination, followed by headache, fever, aches, swollen glands, and—in women—vaginal discharge. The symptoms worsen over about 10 days, during which there is a skin eruption, followed by the appearance of painful sores, which soon break open and become extremely painful during genital contact or when touched. The acute illness may last from three to six weeks. "I've got herpes," said one sufferer, "and it's a very uneven discomfort. Somedays I'm okay, but other days I'm miserable."

As with syphilis, the symptoms of genital herpes subside (the sores dry up, scab over, and disappear) and the person feels good again. But the virus settles in the nerve cells in the spinal column and may cause repeated outbreaks of the symptoms in about one-third of those infected.

Stress, menstruation, sunburn, fatigue, and the presence of other infections seem to be related to the reappearance of herpes symptoms. Although such recurrences are usually milder and of shorter duration than the initial outbreak, the resurfacing of the symptoms may occur throughout the person's life. "It's not knowing when the thing is going to come back that's the bad part about herpes," said one woman.

CONSIDERATION

The herpes virus is usually contagious during the time that a person has visible sores but not when the skin is healed. However, infected people may have a mild recurrence yet be unaware that they are contagious. Aside from visible sores, itching, burning, or tingling sensations at the sore site also suggest that the person is contagious. Using a latex condom reduces the risk of transmitting or acquiring herpes; however the virus may permeate the condom.

At the time of this writing, there is no cure for herpes. Because it is a virus, it does not respond to antibiotics as syphilis and gonorrhea do. A few procedures that help to relieve the symptoms and promote healing of the sores include seeing a physician to look for and treat any other genital infections near the herpes sores, keeping the sores clean and dry, taking hot sitz baths three times a day, and wearing loose-fitting cotton underwear to enhance air circulation. Proper nutrition, adequate sleep and exercise, and avoiding physical or mental stress help people to cope better with recurrences.

Acyclovir, marketed as Zovirax, is an ointment that can be applied directly on the sores, helps to relieve pain, speed healing, and reduce the amount of time that live viruses are present in the sores. A more effective tablet form of acyclovir, which significantly reduces the rate of recurring episodes of genital herpes, is also available. Once acyclovir is stopped, the herpetic recurrences resume. Acyclovir seems to make the symptoms of first-episode genital herpes more manageable, but it is less effective during subsequent outbreaks. Immu Vir—an alternative to acyclovir—is primarily for use by persons who have frequent outbreaks of genital herpes (once a month or more). This ointment is designed to reduce pain, healing time, and number of outbreaks. The drug has no known side effects.

Coping with the psychological and emotional aspects of having genital herpes is often more difficult than coping with the physical aspects of the disease. The In Focus insert discusses common psychological reactions to genital herpes.

∽ IN FOCUS ST1.1 ∽

Psychological Reactions to Genital Herpes

Individuals who become aware they have genital herpes typically go through several psychological stages. Many of these are similar to those experienced in reference to other life crisis events such as the death of a loved one, divorce, or separation. Luby (1981) identified the basic stages and reactions as follows:

1. *Shock, denial, and emotional numbing.* "I never thought it would happen to me" is the overwhelming initial reaction. Such feelings are immediately followed by frantically searching for a cure or for reassurance that the disease can be managed.
2. *Withdrawal.* The person feels unable to cope with the knowledge of having contracted an incurable chronic disease and withdraws from or limits interactions with others.

    "It's hard enough to find someone who is special, who you are attracted to and want to spend time with," said one participant in HELP (a self-help group of individuals who have genital herpes) group discussion. "But when herpes has to be talked about at the beginning of every new relationship, it makes an already difficult situation ten times worse" (Hill, 1987, 1).

    A woman with herpes said:

    I have been very conscientious about not passing the virus on to others. I have gone through months that I would talk to men—but not date them. Or, I would date them, but disappear before things got serious (Silver et al., 1986, 169).

3. *Anger.* Overwhelmed with the flood of emotions, herpes infected individuals feel angry at both the person who infected them and the physician who appears helpless to eliminate the disease.
4. *Fear.* Herpes victims begin to fear how herpes will impact their life in terms of affecting the durability of interpersonal relationships, sexual gratifications, and future children. Questions such as how to tell others of the conta-

gion occur, and fear may reach a level so as to interfere with sexual functioning (e.g., erectile functioning).

5. *Leper effect.* As individuals begin to see themselves as herpes sufferers, they feel ugly, shameful, contaminated, or even dangerous. To combat these feelings some become experts on herpes (known as "herpes graduate students"). Others become "celibate, even religiously moralistically anti-sexual" (Luby, 1981).
6. *Depression.* Continued thoughts of hopelessness and helplessness may occur. Because herpes infected individuals do not know when there will be an outbreak and cannot control the reaction of their partner(s) to such outbreaks, a feeling of "learned helplessness" develops (Silver et al., 1986). In some cases the frustration may reach a level of a deep suicidal depression.
7. *Decomposition.* If the depression continues, the feelings may reactivate underlying psychopathology "and disorganize already inadequate coping strategies" (p. 3).

Individuals' psychological reactions to herpes affect both their resistance to recurrent outbreaks and their level of coping with the disease (Luby, 1981). In their study of 66 subjects who had genital herpes, Silver et al. (1986) noted that those most likely to have repeated outbreaks tend "to view their fate as being beyond their control and who tend to use emotion-focused, avoidant, wishful thinking as a way of attempting to deal with the stress associated with their situation" (p. 170). Hence, coping mechanisms associated with repeated outbreaks were wishful thinking ("If only . . .") and a view that one's life was externally controlled (Silver et al., 1986).

Self-help groups and social support from others are particularly helpful for some herpes sufferers in that they remove the feeling of being isolated and being the only one forced to cope with herpes. The Herpes Resource Center or HELP is a nationwide self-help group for patients with herpes of over 10,000 members. They publish a quarterly newsletter, *The Helper* (P. O. Box 13827, Research Triangle Park, NC 27709, Phone 1-919-361-8488) which features information about the management of herpes.

Human Papilloma Virus (HPV)

There are more than 60 types of **human papilloma virus (HPV).** More than a dozen of these types can cause warts (called **genital warts** or **condyloma**), or more subtle signs of infection in the genital tract. The virus infects the skin's top layers and can remain inactive for months or years before any obvious signs of infection appear. Often warts appear within three to six months. However, some types of HPV produce no visible warts. Any sexual partner(s) of an infected individual should have a prompt medical examination.

HPV can be transmitted through vaginal or rectal intercourse and through fellatio and cunnilingus. In women, genital warts most commonly develop on the vulva, in the vagina, or on the cervix. They may also appear on or near the anus. In men, the warts appear most often on the penis but may appear on the scrotum, anus, or within the rectum.

Because of the different expressions of the virus, it is difficult to obtain an accurate estimate of its prevalence. In a study of 467 women presenting themselves to a university health service for a routine gynecologic exam, 46% had evidence of cervical or vulvar human papillomavirus infections (Bauer et al., 1991). According to Aral and Holmes (1991), "At the moment, genital and anal HPV infections appear to be the most prevalent STDs in the U.S. and a large proportion of sexually active adults seem to be infected" (66).

Currently scientists are studying the factors that increase a person's vulnerability to cancers of the anogenital tract. Vulvar cancer is associated with having a history of HPV (Brinton et al., 1990). While infection with certain types of HPV may be an important factor, many researchers believe that cervical cancer may result from several combined factors. These include smoking, use of oral contraceptives, history of multiple sexual partners, and a dietary deficiency in folic acid (Risk Factors, 1992). There is also evidence that some types of HPV may increase the risk of anal cancer (HPV and Anal Cancer, 1992).

Health care providers disagree regarding the efficacy of treating HPV when there are no detectable warts. However, when the warts can be seen, either by visual inspection or by colposcope, providers do typically advise treatment. There are a number of treatment options. Choosing among them depends upon the number of warts and their location, availability of equipment, training of health care providers, and the preferences of the patient. Most of the treatments are at least moderately effective, but many are quite expensive. They range from topical application of chemicals to laser surgery.

Treatment of warts destroys infected cells, but not all of them, as HPV is present in a wider area of skin than just the precise wart location. "The troublesome news, then, is that with any of these treatments—no matter how good the health care provider—it's possible that the patient will later have one or more recurrences in which new warts develop" (HPV in Perspective, 1991).

❧ Gonorrhea

Also known as "the clap," "the whites," "morning drop," and "the drip," **gonorrhea** is a bacterial infection that is sexually transmissible. Individuals most often contact gonorrhea through having sexual contact with someone who is carrying gonococcus bacteria. Gonococci cannot live long outside the human body. Even though these bacteria can be cultured from a toilet seat, there have not been any documented cases of gonorrhea transmission except through intimate physical contact (Murphy, 1992). These bacteria thrive in warm, moist cavities, including the urinary tract, cervix, rectum, mouth, and throat. A pregnant woman may also transmit gonorrhea to her infant at birth, causing eye infection. Many medical experts recommend gonorrhea testing for all pregnant women and antibiotic eyedrops for all newborns.

Although some infected men show no signs, 80% exhibit symptoms between three and eight days after exposure. They begin to discharge a thick, white pus from the penis and to feel pain or discomfort during urination. They may also have swollen lymph glands in the groin. Women are more likely to show no signs (70% to 80% have no symptoms) of the infection, but when they do, the symptoms are sometimes a discharge from the vagina along with a burning sensation. More often, a woman becomes aware of gonorrhea only after she feels extreme discomfort, which is a result of the untreated infection traveling up into her uterus and Fallopian tubes. Salpingitis (inflammation of the Fallopian tube) occurs in 10–20% of infected women and may cause infertility or ectopic pregnancy (Murphy, 1992).

Undetected and untreated gonorrhea is dangerous. Not only does the infected person pass this disease on to the next partner, but other undesirable consequences may also result. The bacteria may affect the brain, joints, and reproductive systems. Both men and women may develop meningitis (inflammation of the tissues surrounding the brain and spinal column), arthritis, and sterility. In men, the urethra may become blocked, necessitating frequent visits to a physician to clear the passage for urination. Infected women may have spontaneous abortions and premature or stillborn infants.

A physician can detect gonorrhea by analyzing penile or cervical discharge under a microscope. A major problem with new cases of gonorrhea is the emergence of new strains of the bacteria that are resistant to penicillin (Aral & Holmes, 1991). Because of high rates of resistance to penicillins and tetracyclines, the current recommended treatment for gonorrhea is ceftriaxone (Murphy, 1992).

NATIONAL DATA ❧ While rates of gonorrhea have declined among white men and white women to less than 100,000 cases each year, rates among black men near 300,000 cases each year. Among black women, there are about 200,000 cases each year (Schwebke, 1991a).

ଝ Syphilis

Syphilis is caused by bacteria that may be transmitted through sexual contact with an infected individual. Syphilis may also be transmitted from an infected pregnant woman to her unborn baby.

NATIONAL DATA ଝ The incidence of syphilis rose 16% from 1985 to 1989, or 11.4 to 18.4 cases per 100,000. Most of the increase occurred among inner-city ethnic groups of low socioeconomic status. Particularly vulnerable are infants of mothers with syphilis (Schwebke, 1991b).

Although syphilis is less prevalent than gonorrhea, its effects are more devastating and include mental illness, blindness, heart disease—even death. The spirochete bacteria enter the body through mucous membranes that line various body openings. With your tongue, feel the inside of your cheek. This is a layer of mucous membrane—the substance in which spirochetes thrive. Similar membranes are in the vagina and urethra of the penis. If you kiss or have genital contact with someone harboring these bacteria, they can be absorbed into your mucous membranes and cause syphilitic infection. Syphilis progresses through at least three or four stages.

In stage one (primary-stage syphilis), a small sore or chancre will appear at the site of the infection between 10 and 90 days after exposure. The chancre, which shows on the tip of the man's penis, in the labia or cervix of the woman, or in either partner's mouth or rectum, neither hurts nor itches, and, if left untreated, will disappear in three to five weeks. The disappearance leads infected people to believe that they are cured—one of the tricky aspects of syphilis. In reality, the disease is still present and doing great harm, even though there are no visible signs.

During the second stage (secondary-stage syphilis), beginning from two to 12 weeks after the chancre has disappeared, other signs of syphilis appear in the form of a rash all over the body or just on the hands or feet. Welts and sores may also occur, as well as fever, headaches, sore throat, and hair loss. Syphilis has been called "the great imitator" because it mimics so many other diseases (for example, infectious mononucleosis, cancer, and psoriasis). Whatever the symptoms, they too will disappear without treatment. The person may again be tricked into believing that nothing is wrong.

Following the secondary stage is the latency stage, during which there are no symptoms and the person is not infectious. However, the spirochetes are still in the body and can attack any organ at any time.

Tertiary syphilis—the third stage—may cause serious disability or even death. Heart disease, blindness, brain damage, loss of bowel and bladder control, difficulty in walking, and erectile dysfunction may result. Only about half of untreated cases of syphilis reach the final or tertiary stage.

Early detection and treatment is essential. Blood tests and examination of material from the infected site can help to verify the existence of syphilis. But

TABLE ST1.2

HIV and Other Sexually Transmitted Diseases

STD	Symptoms	Treatment	Complications
Acquired immunodeficiency syndrome (AIDS)	Most people who are infected with the human immunodeficiency virus (HIV), show no signs or symptoms until their condition progresses to full blown AIDS. Symptoms of AIDS include: • persistent cough • fever • weight loss • night sweats • skin rashes • diarrhea	There is presently no cure or vaccine to prevent the AIDS virus. Treatments are available to inhibit HIV growth and to fight opportunistic infections.	Opportunistic infections leading to death.
Chlamydia (a unique species of bacteria that causes one of the most widespread STDs in the United States)	Many individuals who are infected show no signs or symptoms of chlamydial infections. Symptoms include: • pain or burning upon urination • discharge from genital area • low-grade fever • lower abdominal pain • frequent need to urinate	Antibiotics	If untreated can cause: • arthritis • sterility • ectopic pregnancy • blindness • pelvic inflammatory disease
Genital herpes (an STD caused by the herpes simplex virus type 2 (HSV-2)	Skin around genital area becomes red and sensitive. Painful blisters and bumps may appear. Other symptoms include: • swollen glands • headaches • muscle aches • fever	There is presently no cure or vaccine to prevent genital herpes. The drug acyclovir has been used to reduce frequency and duration of genital herpes outbreaks.	Women with genital herpes may be at an increased risk for cervical cancer. Pregnant women may transmit the herpes virus to their newborn infants, causing brain damage or death.

such tests are not always accurate. Blood tests reveal the presence of antibodies, not spirochetes, and it sometimes takes three months before the body produces detectable antibodies. Sometimes there is no chancre anywhere on the person's body.

TABLE ST1.2

HIV and Other Sexually Transmitted Diseases (*continued*)

STD	Symptoms	Treatment	Complications
Genital warts (warts or growths that are caused by viruses called human papilloma virus, or HPV, and spread primarily through sexual contact)	Small to large warts or bump-like growths on the genital area. May be pink or red and appear in clusters or alone. There may be no visible warts.	Treatment depends on the size and location of the warts. Podophyllin or surgical methods are commonly used. Recurrences are not unusual.	Women with HPV may be at an increased risk for cervical, vulvar, and anal cancer.
Gonorrhea (an STD caused by a bacterial pathogen and spread through sexual contact)	Many individuals who are infected show no signs or symptoms. Symptoms include: • discharge from the penis or vagina • burning upon urination • urge to urinate frequently • low-grade fever • fatigue	Antibiotics.	If untreated can cause: • permanent damage to the reproductive organs and/or urinary tract • pelvic inflammatory disease • possible sterility • meningitis • arthritis
Syphilis (caused by a bacterium that attacks the nervous and cardiovascular systems and spread through sexual contact)	In the primary stages, a hard, painless chancre or sore will usually appear, then disappear in a few weeks. The secondary stage is characterized by a skin rash and flu-like symptoms. Tertiary syphilis may cause serious disability or even death.	Antibiotics.	If untreated can cause: • damage to the cardiovascular system • damage to the nervous system • blindness • death

Source: Developed for this text by Suzanne Kellerman, M.A., Health Education Manager, Beaufort County Hospital, Washington, N.C. Used by permission of Suzanne Kellerman.

Treatment for syphilis is similar to that for gonorrhea. Penicillin or other antibiotics (for those allergic to penicillin) are effective. Infected persons treated in the early stages can be completely cured with no ill effects. If the syphilis has progressed into the later stages, any damage that has been done cannot be repaired.

ॐ Getting Help for STDs

If you are engaging in unprotected sex or are having symptoms (see Table ST1.2), you should get tested for HIV and other STDs. There are different tests for different STDs. As a woman you must specifically ask for such tests from your gynecologist since they do not routinely perform such tests. If you do not know who to call to get tested, call your local health department or the national STD hotline at 800-227-8922. You will not be asked to identify yourself but will be given the name and number of local STD clinics that offer confidential, free treatment. As noted earlier, the Herpes Resource Center is available for help with herpes. In addition, Duke University in Durham, North Carolina, has opened an AIDS clinic to treat AIDS victims (919/684-2660). For special information about AIDS, call 800-342-2437; in Washington, D.C., call 646-8182.

Prevention of STD Transmission

The best way to avoid getting a sexually transmitted disease is to avoid sexual contact or to have contact only with partners who are not infected. This means restricting your sexual contacts to those who limit their relationships to one person. The person most likely to get a sexually transmitted disease has sexual relations with a number of partners or with a partner who has a variety of partners.

Even if you are in a mutually monogamous relationship, you may be at risk for acquiring or transmitting an STD. This is because health officials suggest that when you have sex with someone, you are having sex (in a sense) with everyone that person has had sexual contact with in the last 10 years.

> **CONSIDERATION**
>
> Partners may believe that they are in a mutually monogamous relationship when they may not be. It is not uncommon for partners in "monogamous" relationships to have extradyadic sexual encounters that are not revealed to the primary partner. Partners may also lie about how many sexual partners they have had and whether or not they have been tested for STDs (Knox, Schacht, Holt, & Turner, 1993).

In addition to restricting sexual contacts, putting on a latex or polyurethane condom (reservoir tip with non-oxynol 9) before the penis touches the partner's body will make it difficult for sexually transmitted diseases to pass from one person to another (See Table ST1.3, on Condom Communication). Natural membrane condoms *do not* block the transmission of STDs. Condoms should be used for vaginal, anal, and oral sex and should never be reused.

After genital or anal contact with a latex or polyurethane condom, it is important to withdraw the penis while it is erect so as to prevent fluid leaking from the base of the condom into the partner's genital area. Condom users should choose brands that have an adhesive strip at the base that prevents the

Anytime you have sex with anyone, use a latex condom with a spermicide. No exceptions.

BETSY RYAN

I'm not comfortable talking about "safe sex," but I always carry a condom with me and put it on as a matter of routine.

A COLLEGE STUDENT

TABLE ST1.3
Condom Communication

IF YOUR PARTNER SAYS ...	YOU CAN SAY ...
I don't have a condom.	Let's get one or satisfy each other in other ways.
I don't have AIDS or any STD.	We can both be infected and not know it.
One time without a condom won't hurt anything.	One time could be enough.
If you insist that I wear a condom it means you think I'm a sleaze.	No it doesn't. It means I care about both of us.
I take the pill; you don't need a condom.	The pill doesn't protect us from getting infections.

condom from slipping off prematurely. If a man is receiving oral sex, he should wear a condom. If a woman is receiving oral sex, she should wear a **"dental dam,"** which is a flat latex device that is held over the vaginal area, preventing direct contact between the woman's genital area and her partner's mouth.

> ### CONSIDERATION
>
> Although using latex condoms with non-oxynol 9 reduces one's risk of STD transmission, it does not eliminate it. For example, HPV may be present on areas not covered by a condom, such as on the scrotum. The herpes virus may penetrate latex condoms. Furthermore, condoms sometimes break or slip off.

Condom slippage and breakage rates were studied at the Emory University Family Planning Program in Atlanta, Georgia (Trussell, Warner & Hatcher, 1992). Seventy heterosexual couples were given standard (Trojan-Enz) and experimental (Pleasure Plus) condoms. Of the 405 condoms which were used 8% either broke during intercourse or withdrawal, or slipped off during intercourse. Of the remaining condoms, 7% slipped off during withdrawal. When condoms slipped off during withdrawal it was often related to the use of additional lubricant, such as petroleum jelly or massage oil, which some couples used despite warnings that oil causes deterioration of rubber! The researchers observed "If they are accurate, these rates indicate a sobering level of exposure to the risks of pregnancy and of infection with HIV or other STDs, even among those who consistently use condoms" (Trussell et al., 1992, p. 22). However, condoms used consistently and correctly are effective (Ryan & Willett, 1993).

Putting a mere balloon between a healthy body and a deadly disease is not safe.

THRESA CRENSHAW

Contents

ಶ **2** ಶ

SPECIAL TOPIC

Sexual Anatomy and Physiology

Is It True?

1. Like the man's penis, the woman's clitoris becomes erect during sexual excitation.

2. Because of the longer length of the male urethra, men are more susceptible than women to cystitis, a bladder inflammation.

3. All adult women should have a pelvic exam, including a Pap test, each year.

4. Fertilization normally occurs in the Fallopian tubes.

5. An average ejaculation contains about 360 million sperm.

1 = T; 2 = F; 3 = T; 4 = T; 5 = T

In the culture in which we live, it is the custom to be least informed upon that subject concerning which every individual should know most—namely, the structure and functions of his/her own body.

ASHLEY MONTAGUE

*T*f we think of the human body as a special type of machine, *anatomy* refers to that machine's part and *physiology* refers to how the parts work. In this topic, we will review the sexual anatomy and physiology of women and men and the reproductive process.

⅋ Female External Anatomy and Physiology

The external female genitalia are collectively known as the *vulva* (VUHL-vuh), a Latin term meaning "covering." The vulva consists of the mons veneris, the labia, the clitoris, and the vaginal and urethral openings (see Figure ST2.1). The female genitalia differ in size, shape, and color, resulting in considerable variability in appearance.

CONSIDERATION

Terms for male genitalia (e.g., penis, testicles) are more commonly known than are terms for female genitalia. Tavris (1992) noted that, in spite of living in a culture that seems sexually obsessed, many women still do not even accurately name their genitals. At best, little girls are taught that they have a vagina, which becomes the word for everything "down there"; they rarely learn they also have a vulva, a clitoris, and labia.

Mons Veneris The soft cushion of fatty tissue overlaying the pubic bone is called the *mons veneris* (mahns-vuh-NAIR-ihs), also known as the *mons pubis*. This area becomes covered with hair at puberty and has numerous nerve endings. The purpose of the mons is to protect the pubic region during sexual intercourse.

Labia In the sexually unstimulated state, the urethral and vaginal openings are protected by the *labia majora* (LAY-bee-uh muh-JOR-uh), or "major lips"—two elongated folds of fatty tissue that extend from the mons to the *perineum*, the area of skin between the opening of the vagina and the anus. Located between the labia majora are two additional hairless folds of skin, called the *labia minora* (muh-NOR-uh), or "minor lips," that cover the urethral and vaginal openings and join at the top to form the hood of the clitoris. Some contend that the clitoral hood provides clitoral stimulation during intercourse.

Women keep trying to degenitalize men's focus and teach them that there are only two erogenous zones—the heart and the skin.

SAM KEEN

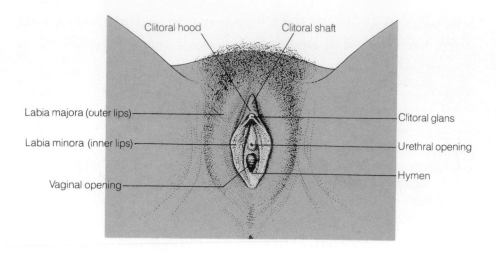

Both sets of labia—particularly the inner labia minora—have a rich supply of nerve endings that are sensitive to sexual stimulation.

Clitoris   At the top of the labia minora is the *clitoris* (KLIHT-uh-ruhs), which also has a rich supply of nerve endings. The clitoris is a very important site of sexual excitement and, like the penis, becomes erect during sexual excitation.

Vaginal Opening   The area between the labia minora is called the *vestibule*. This includes the urethral opening and the vaginal opening, or *introitus* (ihn-TROH-ih-tuhs), neither of which is visible unless the labia minora are parted. Like the anus, the vaginal opening is surrounded by a ring of sphincter muscles. Although the vaginal opening can expand to accommodate the passage of a baby at childbirth, under conditions of tension these muscles can involuntarily contract, making it difficult to insert an object, including a tampon, into the vagina. The vaginal opening may be covered by a *hymen,* a thin membrane.

CONSIDERATION

Probably no other body part has caused as much grief to so many women as the hymen, which has been regarded throughout history as proof of virginity. A newly wed woman who was thought to be without a hymen was often returned to her parents, disgraced by exile, or even tortured and killed. It has been a common practice in many societies to parade a bloody bedsheet after the wedding night as proof of the bride's virginity. The anxieties caused by the absence of a hymen persist even today; in Japan and other countries, sexually experienced women may have a plastic surgeon reconstruct a hymen before marriage. Yet the hymen is really a poor indicator of virtue. Some women are born without a hymen or with incomplete hymens. In others, the hymen is accidentally ruptured by vigorous physical activity or insertion of a tampon. In some women, the hymen may not tear but only stretch during sexual intercourse. Even most doctors cannot easily determine whether a woman is a virgin.

Urethral Opening   Just above the vaginal opening is the urethral opening where urine passes from the body. A short tube, the *urethra*, connects the bladder (where urine collects) with the urethral opening. Because of the shorter length of the female urethra and its close proximity to the anus, women are more susceptible than men to cystitis, a bladder inflammation.

☙ Female Internal Anatomy and Physiology

The internal sex organs of the female include the vagina, pubococcygeus muscle, uterus, and paired Fallopian tubes and ovaries (see Figure ST2.2).

Vagina

CONSIDERATION

Some people erroneously believe that the vagina is a dirty part of the body. In fact, the vagina is a self-cleansing organ. The bacteria that are found naturally in the vagina help to destroy other potentially harmful bacteria. In addition, secretions from the vaginal walls help to maintain its normally acidic environment. The use of feminine hygiene sprays, as well as excessive douching, may cause irritation, allergic reactions, and in some cases, vaginal infection by altering the normal chemical balance of the vagina.

Some researchers have reported that some women experience an extremely sensitive area in the front wall of the vagina one to two inches into the vaginal opening. The spot may swell during stimulation, and although a woman's initial response may be a need to urinate, continued stimulation generally leads to orgasm (Perry & Whipple, 1981). The area was named the *Grafenberg spot* or *G spot,* for gynecologist Ernest Grafenberg who first noticed the erotic sensitivity of this area over forty years ago.

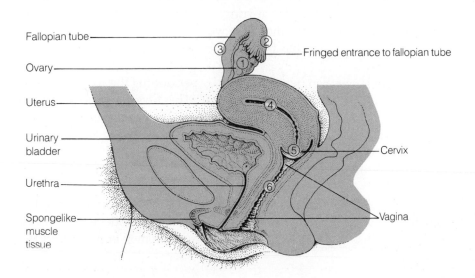

FIGURE ST2.2

Internal Female Sexual and Reproductive Organs

Fallopian tube

Ovary

Fringed entrance to fallopian tube

Uterus

Urinary bladder

Cervix

Urethra

Spongelike muscle tissue

Vagina

F I G U R E ST2.3
Alleged Grafenberg Spot

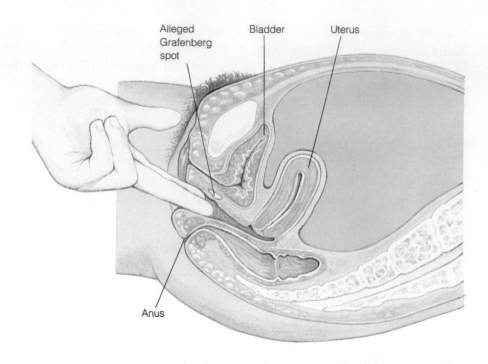

Alleged Grafenberg spot   Bladder   Uterus

Anus

Tavris (1992) criticized the lack of scientific rigor backing the notion of the G spot. Hock (1983) felt that it is a misnomer to refer to the existence of a specific G spot.

> The "G spot" does not exist as such, and the potential professional use of this term would be not only incorrect but also misleading. . . . The entire extent of the anterior wall of the vagina (rather than one specific spot), as well as the more deeply situated tissues, including the urinary bladder and urethral region, are extremely sensitive, being richly endowed with nerve endings (p. 166).

Pubococcygeus Muscle   Also called the PC muscle, the pubococcygeus muscle is one of the pelvic floor muscles that surrounds the vagina, the urethra, and the anus. In order to find her PC muscle, a woman is instructed to voluntarily stop the flow of urine after she has begun to urinate. The muscle that stops the flow is the PC muscle.

A woman can strengthen her PC muscle by performing the *Kegel exercises,* named after the physician who devised them. The Kegel exercises involve contracting the PC muscle several times for several sessions per day. Kegel exercises are often recommended after childbirth to restore muscle tone to the PC muscle, which is stretched during the childbirth process, and help prevent involuntary loss of urine.

Uterus   The *uterus* (YOOT-uh-ruhs), or *womb*, resembles a small, inverted pear, which measures about 3 inches long and 3 inches wide at the top in women who have not given birth. A fertilized egg becomes implanted in the wall of the uterus and continues to grow and develop there until delivery. At the lower end of the uterus is the *cervix,* an opening that leads into the vagina.

CONSIDERATION

All adult women should have a pelvic exam, including a Pap Test, each year. A Pap test is extremely important in the detection of cervical cancer. Cancer of the cervix and uterus is the second most common form of cancer in women. Some women may neglect to get a Pap test because they feel embarrassed or anxious about it or because they think they are too young to worry about getting cancer. For all women over age 20, however, having annual Pap tests may mean the difference between life and death.

FIGURE ST2.4
External Male Organs

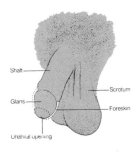

Fallopian Tubes Fallopian (ful-LOH-pee-uhn) *tubes* extend about 4 inches laterally from either side of the uterus to the ovaries. Fertilization normally occurs in the Fallopian tubes. The tubes transport the *ovum,* or egg, by means of *cilia* (hairlike structures) down the tube and into the uterus.

Ovaries The *ovaries* (OH-vuhr-eez) are two almond-shaped structures, one on either side of the uterus. The ovaries produce eggs and the female hormones estrogen and progesterone. At her birth, a woman's ovaries contain about 400,000 immature ova total, each enclosed in a thin capsule forming a follicle. Some of the follicles begin to mature at puberty; only about 400 mature ova will be released in a woman's lifetime.

⅋ Male External Anatomy and Physiology

Although they differ in appearance, many structures of the male (see Figure ST2.4) and female genitals develop from the same embryonic tissue (the penis and the clitoris, for example).

Penis The *penis* (PEE-nihs) is the primary male sexual organ. In the unaroused state, the penis is soft and hangs between the legs. When sexually stimulated, the penis enlarges and becomes erect, enabling penetration of the vagina. The penis functions not only to deposit sperm in the female's vagina but also as a passageway from the male's bladder to eliminate urine. In cross section, the penis can be seen to consist of three parallel cylinders of tissue containing many cavities, two *corpora cavernosa* (cavernous bodies) and a *corpus spongiosum* (spongy body) through which the urethra passes. The penis has numerous blood vessels; when stimulated, the arteries dilate and blood enters faster than it can leave. The cavities of the cavernous and spongy bodies fill with blood, and pressure against the fibrous membranes causes the penis to become erect. The head of the penis is called the *glans.* At birth, the glans is covered by *foreskin.*

Circumcision, the surgical procedure in which the foreskin of the male is pulled forward and cut off has been practiced for at least 6,000 years (Wilkes & Blum, 1990). About 80 percent of men in the United States have been circumcised.

Circumcision was and is an early religious rite for members of the Jewish and Moslem faiths. To Jewish people, circumcision symbolizes the covenant between God and Abraham. In the United States, the procedure is generally done within the first few days after birth. Among non-Jewish people, circumcision first became popular in the United States during the 19th century as a means of preventing masturbation. But research by Masters and Johnson (1966) indicates there is no difference in excitability in men with circumcised and uncircumcised penises.

CONSIDERATION

Should parents choose to have their male infants circumcised? Today the primary reason for performing circumcision is to ensure proper hygiene and to maintain tradition. The smegma that can build up under the foreskin is a potential breeding ground for infection. But circumcision may be a rather drastic procedure merely to ensure proper hygiene which can just as easily be accomplished by pulling back the foreskin and cleaning the glans during normal bathing. However, being circumcised is associated with having a lower risk of contracting the AIDS virus (Bongaarts et al., 1989). Circumcision is a relatively low risk surgical procedure (Lund, 1990). In regard to the actual procedure, the newborn male infant does feel pain; however, such pain can be minimized by administering local anesthesia (Masciello, 1990).

Scrotum　The *scrotum* (SCROH-tuhm) is the sac located below the penis, which contains the *testes*. Beneath the skin covering the scrotum is a thin layer of muscle fibers that contract when it is cold, helping to draw the testes (testicles) closer to the body to keep the temperature of the sperm constant. Sperm can only be produced at a temperature several degrees lower than normal body temperature; any prolonged variation can result in sterility.

ꝋ Male Internal Anatomy and Physiology

The male internal organs, often referred to as the reproductive organs, include the testes, where the sperm is produced, a duct system to transport the sperm out of the body, and some additional structures that produce the seminal fluid in which the sperm is mixed before ejaculation (see Figure ST2.5).

Testes　The male gonads—the paired testes, or testicles—develop from the same embryonic tissue as the female gonads (the ovaries). The two oval-shaped testicles are suspended in the scrotum by the *spermatic cord* and enclosed within a fibrous sheath. The function of the testes is to produce spermatozoa and male hormones, primarily testosterone.

Duct System　Several hundred *seminiferous tubules* come together to form a tube in each testicle called the *epididymis* (ehp-uh-DIHD-uh-muhs), the first part of the duct system that transports sperm. If uncoiled, each tube would be 20 feet long. Sperm spend from two to six weeks traveling through the epididymis as they mature and are reabsorbed by the body if ejaculation does not occur. One ejaculation contains an average of 360 million sperm cells.

The sperm leave the scrotum through the second part of the duct system, the *vas deferens* (vas-DEF-uh-renz). These 14- to 16-inch paired ducts transport the sperm from the epididymis up and over the bladder to the prostate gland. Rhythmic contractions during ejaculation force the sperm into the paired ejaculatory ducts that run through the prostate gland. The entire length of this portion of the duct system is less than 1 inch. It is here that the sperm mix with seminal fluid to form *semen* before being propelled to the outside through the urethra.

Seminal Vesicles and Prostate Gland　The *seminal vesicles* resemble two small sacs, each about 2 inches in length, located behind the bladder. These vesicles secrete their own fluids, which empty into the ejaculatory duct to mix with sperm and fluids from the prostate gland.

Most of the seminal fluid comes from the *prostate gland,* a chestnut-sized structure located below the bladder and in front of the rectum. The fluid is alkaline and serves to protect the sperm in the more acidic environments of the male urethra and female vagina. Males over 45 should have a rectal exam annually to detect the presence of prostate cancer.

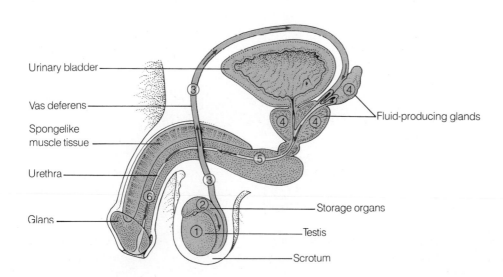

F I G U R E ST2.5

Internal and External Male Sexual Organs

Urinary bladder

Vas deferens

Spongelike muscle tissue

Urethra

Glans

Fluid-producing glands

Storage organs

Testis

Scrotum

A small amount of clear, sticky fluid is also secreted into the urethra before ejaculation by two pea-sized *Cowper's,* or *bulbourethral, glands* located below the prostate gland. This protein rich fluid alkalizes the urethral passage which prolongs sperm life.

CONSIDERATION

The fluid secreted by the Cowper's glands can often be noticed on the tip of the penis during sexual arousal. It may contain stray sperm, so that withdrawal of the penis from the vagina before ejaculation is a risky method of birth control.

Contents

ઝ **3** ઝ

SPECIAL TOPIC

Budgeting, Investing, Life Insurance, and Credit

Is It True?

1. You should set aside a minimum of ten percent of your monthly income for savings.

2. The size of an emergency fund should be about twice your monthly income.

3. Saving and investing should not be considered part of your budget.

4. Unmarried college students should have about $10,000 in life insurance.

5. The three Cs of credit are character, capacity, and capital.

1 = F; 2 = T; 3 = F; 4 = F; 5 = T

Buy it cheap—buy it twice.

LARRY COX

*A*s noted in Chapter 11 on Work and Leisure in Relationships, money is a potentially explosive issue in marriage. How spouses decide about what is "her money," "his money," and "their money," and how many accounts they have in whose names must be negotiated. No one pattern is right for all couples. The most important consideration is that both partners feel comfortable about what they decide.

Other financial issues include developing a budget, investing money for future needs, buying life insurance, and using credit effectively.

Developing a Budget

Developing a budget is a way of planning your spending. Since money spent on X cannot be spent on Y, budgeting requires conscious value choices about which bills should be paid, what items should be bought, and what expenditures should be delayed. Couples need to develop a budget if they are always out of money long before their next paycheck, if they cannot make partial payments or pay off existing bills but keep incurring new debts, or if they cannot save money.

> **CONSIDERATION**
>
> The advantages of developing and following a budget include having money available when you need it, avoiding unnecessary debt, and saving money.

To develop a budget (see Table ST3.1), list and add up all your monthly take-home (after-tax) income from all sources. This figure should represent the amount of money your family will actually have to spend each month. Next, list and add up all of your fixed monthly expenses, such as rents, utilities, telephone, and car payment. Other fixed expenses include such items as life, health, and car insurance. You may not receive a bill for some of these expenses every month, so divide the yearly cost of each item by 12 so that you can budget it on a monthly basis. For example, if your annual life insurance premium is $240, you should budget $20 per month for that expense.

Set aside a minimum of five percent of your monthly income—and more, if possible—for savings, and include this sum in your fixed expenses. By putting a fixed amount in a savings account each month, you will not only have money available for large purchases, such as a car or a major home

A budget is an orderly way of discovering that you can't live on what you're earning.

E. C. MCKENZIE

TABLE ST3.1

Monthly Budget for Two-Earner Couple

BOTH SPOUSES EMPLOYED FULL TIME	
Sources of Income	
Husband's take-home pay	$1,480
Wife's take-home pay	920
Interest earned on savings	17
TOTAL	$2,417
Fixed Expenses	
Rent	$ 450
Utilities	90
Telephone	70
Insurance	85
Car payments and expenses	330
Furniture payments	80
Savings	200
TOTAL	$1,295
DIFFERENCE	$1,122
(Amount available for day-to-day expenses)	
Day-to-Day and Discretionary Expenses	
Food	$ 250
Clothes	170
Personal care	90
Recreation	120
Miscellaneous	110
TOTAL	$ 740

This dual-earner couple should have $382 extra at the end of each month. The reality is that many couples can't or don't live within their income and go into debt each month.

appliance, but you will also have an emergency fund to cover unforeseen expenses like those caused by an extended illness or a long-distance move. The size of an emergency fund should be about twice your monthly income. Although you can personally set aside some of your monthly income for savings, an alternative is to instruct the bank to transfer a certain sum each month from your checking account to your savings account, or you can join a payroll savings plan. Under the latter arrangement, a portion of your monthly salary is automatically deposited in your savings account without ever passing through your hands.

After adding together all your fixed monthly expenses, including savings, subtract this amount from your monthly take-home income. What remains can be used for such day-to-day expenses as food (groceries and restaurant meals),

> Debts are the sour sediment in the lemonade of human existence.
>
> HERMAN SUDERMANN

clothes (including laundry, dry cleaning, alterations, and new clothes), personal care (barber and hairdresser, toilet articles, cosmetics), and recreation (theater, movies, concerts, books, magazines).

CONSIDERATION

If you come out even at the end of the month, you are living within your means. If you have money left over, you are living below your means. If you had to tap your savings or borrow money to pay your bills last month, you are living beyond your means. Knowing whether you are living within, below, or above your means depends on keeping accurate records.

And remember, you must pay taxes on what you earn. The following shows how much tax rates are for 1993. For those earning very high incomes, the Clinton administration is planning to increase their tax rate over the next two years.

Rate for Married Individuals—Joint Return

15% $0 to $36,900

28% $36,900 to $89,150

31% $89,150 and over

Rate for Single Individual

15% $0 to $22,100

28% $22,100 to $53,500

31% $53,500 and over

❧ Investing

Too late is saving at the bottom.

PONTANUS

Saving and investing money should be a part of every budget. By allocating a specific amount of your monthly income to savings or an investment plan, you can accumulate money for both short-term (vacation, down payment on a house) and long-term (college education for children, retirement income) goals.

CONSIDERATION

By investing, you use money to make more money. All investments must be considered in terms of their risk and potential yield. In general, the higher the rate of return on an investment, the greater the financial risk.

There are several ways to invest your money to earn more money. A common method is to put money in a bank or savings and loan institution. Doing so is risk free and your deposit is insured by the federal government.

However, banks pay a relatively low rate of interest compared to other alternatives. Some individuals keep only the amount that they will need quick access to and invest the rest of their funds in alternatives that earn them a greater return.

One alternative to a savings account is to buy blue chip stock in companies such as American Telephone and Telegraph or Eastman Kodak. A complete list is available in the financial section of the newspaper in larger cities. These stocks provide a fairly stable return and are relatively risk free. However, nothing in the stock market is certain. For example, if Nikon Camera invented a new film that offered superior quality at a lower cost, Kodak stock might drop and take your money with it.

There is an even greater risk with speculative stocks—stocks that can radically increase or decrease in value within a short time. Suppose you could afford to lose $500 and were willing to gamble on a high return. You could buy 100 shares of stock at slightly below $5 per share. If the stock is selling for $10 one year later, your original investment would double in value: you would now have $1,000 from your initial investment of $500. But if the stock is selling for $1 per share one year later, you would only realize $100 on your $500 investment. You can lose money as fast as you can gain it. One spouse invested in a company specializing in bananas and looked forward to tripling her investment. But less than a week after she purchased the stock, a hurricane in Puerto Rico wiped out the banana crop, and the value of her stock dropped sharply.

CONSIDERATION

Do not invest in speculative stocks unless you can afford to lose the money. Mutual funds provide a reasonable alternative for small investors.

Fortunately, investment opportunities are not limited to banks and stocks. Table ST3.2 illustrates several investment alternatives and furnishes information on other factors that you should consider in deciding on an investment. In addition to risk and return on investment, the *liquidity,* or the ease with which your investment can be converted into cash, is an important consideration. Stocks and bonds can be sold quickly to provide cash in hand. In contrast, if you have invested in a building or land, you must find a buyer who is willing to pay the price that you are asking for your asset before you can convert it to cash.

The amount of your time required to make your investment grow is also important. A real estate investment can give you a considerable return on your money, but it may also demand a lot of your time—perusing the newspaper, arranging for loans, placing ads, and showing the house, not to mention fixing leaky faucets, mowing grass, and painting rooms.

Also, consider the maturity date of your investment. For example,

> A bank is a place where you can keep the government's money until the IRS asks for it.
>
> E. C. MCKENZIE

suppose you invest in a six-year certificate at a savings bank. Although the bank will pay you, say, 4 percent interest and guarantee your investment, you can't get your principle (the money you deposited) or the interest until the six years is up unless you are willing to pay a substantial penalty. Regular savings accounts have no maturity date. You can withdraw any amount of your money from your savings account at the bank whenever you want it, but you may earn only, say, 3 percent interest on the money while it remains in the account.

A final investment consideration is taxation. Investment decisions should be made on the basis not of how much money you can make but of how much money you can keep. Tax angles should be considered as carefully as risk and yield issues.

Although savings, life insurance, real estate, and stock investments are probably familiar forms of investment to you, the other types of investments listed in Table ST3.2 may need further clarification.

Annuities provide a monthly income after age 65 (or earlier if desired) in exchange for your investment of monthly premiums during your working years. For example, a 65-year-old-man may receive $100 per month as long as he lives (or a lump sum) if he has paid the insurance company $238 annually since age 30.

Bonds are issued by corporations and federal, state, and local governments that need money. In exchange for your money, you get a piece of paper that entitles you to the return of the sum you lend at a specified date (up to 30 years) plus interest on the money. Although bonds are safer than stocks, you could lose all your money if the corporation you lend the money to goes bankrupt. United States Savings Bonds are safe but pay a comparatively low rate of interest.

> Riches are chiefly good because they give us time.
>
> CHARLES LAMB

T A B L E ST3.2

Some Investment Alternatives

TYPE	RISK/YIELD	LIQUIDITY	MANAGEMENT	TAS ASPECTS
Savings Account	Low/3%	Immediate	Self	Interest is taxed.
Treasury bill	Low/4%	3 months to a year	Self	Interest is taxed.
Money market	Low/4%	One week	Broker	Interest is taxed.
Annuity	Low/4%	Retirement	Company	Tax is deferred.
Real estate	Depends/0–25%	Months/years	Self or other	Good tax advantage.
Mutual fund	Moderate/3–30%	One week	Agent	Lower tax if held.
Stocks	Depends/0–100%	One week	Broker	Depends on investment.
Life insurance	Low/3%	Years	Agent	Depends on investment.
Bonds	Depends/8–10%	One week	Broker	Depends on investment.
IRA	Low/3–4%	Retirement	Broker	Tax is deferred.
Certificate of Deposit (CD)	Low/4–5%	Variable	Self	Interest is taxed.

Mutual funds offer a way of investing in a number of common stocks, corporate bonds, or government bonds at the same time. You invest your money in shares of the mutual fund, whose directors invest the fund's capital in various securities. If the securities they select increase in price, so does the value of your shares in the mutual fund.

CONSIDERATION

Because banks and savings and loan institutions pay only a modest return, an increasing number of individuals are buying mutual funds. Morningstar, Inc. and The Mutual Fund Forecaster are publications that recommend specific mutual funds which have earned a relatively respectable return on one's investment in the last several months/years. The respective phone numbers of the publications are 312-427-1985 and 800-442-9000.

Treasury bills (T-bills) are issued by the Federal Reserve Bank. You pay a lower price for the bill than its cash value. For example, you may pay $900 for a T-bill that will be worth $1,000 on maturity. Maturity of the bill occurs at three, six, nine, or 12 months. The longer the wait, the more money paid on the investment.

Money market investments require a payment of $5,000 or more to a stockbroker who uses your money, together with the money others wish to invest, to purchase high interest securities. Your money can be withdrawn in any amount at any time. As with all investments, you pay a fee to the broker or agent for investing your money. In the past several years, increasing numbers of people have put their money in money market funds.

Individual retirement accounts (IRAs) permit you to set aside up to $2,000 each year for your personal retirement fund. The money you put in your IRA is not automatically tax-free. (You must meet certain criteria restrictions.) Each spouse can open his or her own IRA.

> Money is power—power for bread, and power for tinsel.
>
> T. T. LYNCH

CONSIDERATION

A study of 1,245 women between the ages of 40 and 65 revealed that 44 percent had made no plans for where or when they would retire. Furthermore, 85 percent had not engaged in any specific planning behaviors for retirement (assessment of adequate funds, ensuring adequate health protection, etc.) (Turner & Bailey, 1992).

Certificates of deposit (CDs) are insured deposits given to the bank that earn interest at a rate from one day to several years. These high-yield, low-risk investments have become extremely popular. A minimum investment of $500 or more is usually required.

℞ Life Insurance

In addition to saving and investing, it is important to be knowledgeable about life insurance. The major purpose of life insurance is to provide income for dependents when the primary wage earner dies. With dual-earner couples, life insurance is often necessary to prevent having to give up their home when one wage earner dies. Otherwise, the remaining wage earner may not be able to make the necessary mortgage payments.

> **CONSIDERATION**
>
> Unmarried, childfree, college students probably do not need life insurance. No one is dependent on them for economic support. However, the argument used by some insurance agents who sell campus policies is that college students should buy life insurance while they are young when the premiums are low and when insurability is guaranteed. Still, consumer advocates suggest that life insurance for unmarried, childfree college students is not necessary (*Consumer Reports,* 1993).

When considering income protection for dependents, there are two basic types of life insurance policies: (1) term insurance and (2) insurance plus investment. As the name implies, term insurance offers protection for a specific time period (usually one, five, 10, or 20 years). At the end of the time period, the protection stops. Although a term insurance policy offers the greatest amount of protection for the least cost, it does not build up cash value (money the insured would get upon surrendering the policy for cash).

Insurance plus investment policies are sold under various names. The first is straight life, ordinary life, or whole life, in which the individual pays a stated premium (based on age and health) as long as the individual lives. When the insured dies, the beneficiary is paid the face value of the policy (the amount of insurance originally purchased). During the life of the insured, the policy also builds up a cash value (which is tax-free), which permits the insured to borrow money from the insurance company at a low rate of interest. A second type of life insurance is a limited payment policy, in which the premiums are paid up after a certain number of years (usually 20) or when the insured reaches a certain age (usually 60 or 65). As with straight, ordinary life, or whole life policies, limited payment policies build up a cash value, and the face value of the policy is not paid until the insured dies. The third type of life insurance is endowment insurance, in which the premiums are paid up after a stated number of years and can be cashed in at a stated age.

Regardless of how they are sold, insurance plus investment policies divide the premium paid by the insured. Part pays for the actual life insurance, and part is invested for the insured, giving the policy a cash value. Unlike term insurance, insurance plus investment policies are not canceled at age 65.

For decades, insurance companies have pushed whole life policies. They are still a poor buy for most people.

CONSUMER REPORTS

Which type of policy, term or insurance plus investment, should you buy? An insurance agent is likely to suggest the latter and point out the advantages of cash value, continued protection beyond age 65, and level premiums. But the agent has a personal incentive for your buying an insurance plus investment policy. The commission an agent gets on this type of policy is much higher than it is on a term insurance policy.

CONSIDERATION

A strong argument can be made for buying term insurance and investing the additional money that would be needed to pay for the more expensive insurance plus investment policy.

The annual premium for $50,000 worth of renewable term insurance at age 25 is about $175. The same coverage offered in an ordinary life policy—the most common insurance plus investment policy—costs $668 annually, so the difference is $493 per year. If you put this money in the bank at an interest rate of 5 percent, at the end of five years you will have $2,860.32. In contrast, the cash value of an ordinary life policy after five years is $2,350. But to get this money, you have to pay the insurance company interest to borrow it. If you don't want to pay the interest, the company will give you this amount but cancel your policy. In effect, you lose your insurance protection if you receive the cash value of your policy. With term insurance, you have the $2,860.32 in the bank earning interest, and you can withdraw it any time without affecting your insurance program.

It should be clear that for term insurance to be cheaper, you must invest the money you would otherwise be paying for an ordinary life insurance policy. If you can't discipline yourself to save, buy an insurance plus investment policy, which will ensure savings.

Finally, what about the fact that term insurance stops when you are 65, just as you are moving closer to death and needing the protection more? Again, by investing the money that you would otherwise have spent on an insurance plus investment policy, you will have as much or more money for your beneficiary than your insurance plus investment policy would earn.

Whether you buy a term policy, an insurance plus investment policy, or both, there are three options to consider: guaranteed insurability, waiver of premiums, and double or triple indemnity. All are inexpensive and generally should be included in a life insurance policy.

Guaranteed insurability means that the company will sell you more insurance in the future, regardless of your medical condition. For example, suppose you develop cancer after you buy a policy for $10,000. If the guaranteed insurability provision is in your contract, you can buy additional insurance. If not, the company can refuse you more insurance.

> Congress should pass a Truth-in-Insurance law to regulate the sales illustrations that are used to sell life insurance.
>
> CONSUMER REPORTS

Waiver of premiums provides that your premiums will be paid by the company if you become disabled for six months or longer and are unable to earn an income. Such an option ensures that your policy will stay in force because the premiums will be paid. Otherwise, the company will cancel your policy.

Double or triple indemnity means that if you die as the result of an accident, the company will pay your beneficiary twice or three times the face value of your policy.

An additional item you might consider adding to your life insurance policy is a *disability income rider.* If the wage earner becomes disabled and cannot work, the financial consequences for the family are the same as though the wage earner were dead. With disability insurance, the wage earner can continue to provide for the family up to maximum of $3,500 per month or two-thirds of the individual's salary, whichever is smaller. If the wage earner is disabled by accidental injury, payments are made for life. If illness is the cause, payments may be made only to age 65. A 27-year-old spouse and parent who was paralyzed in an automobile accident said, "It was the biggest mistake of my life to think I needed only life insurance to protect my family. Disability insurance turned out to be more important."

CONSIDERATION

In deciding to buy life insurance, it may be helpful to consider the following:

1. *Decide whether you really need insurance.* People with no dependents rarely need it.
2. *Decide how much coverage you need.* The cost of rearing a middle class child from conception through college is approximately $200,000.
3. *Compare prices.* All policies and prices are not the same. In some cases, the higher premiums are for lower coverage.
4. *Select your agent carefully.* Only one in 10 life insurance agents stay in the business. The person you buy life insurance from today may be in the real estate business tomorrow. Choose an agent who has been selling life insurance for at least 10 years.
5. *Select your company carefully.* "John Hancock, Prudential and State Farm are household names but have mediocre or poor life-insurance policies; you can do better buying from a company that may be less well known "(*Consumer Reports,* 1993, 600).
6. *Seek group rates.* Group life insurance is the least expensive coverage. See if your employer offers a group plan.
7. *Proceed slowly.* Don't rush into buying an insurance policy. Consult several agents, read *Consumer Reports,* and talk with friends to find out what they are doing about their insurance needs.

ℛ Credit

You use credit when you take an item home today and pay for it later. The amount you pay later will depend on the arrangement you make with the seller. Suppose you want to buy a color television set that costs $600. Unless you pay cash, the seller will set up one of three types of credit accounts with you: installment, revolving charge, or open charge.

Under the installment plan, you make a down payment and sign a contract to pay the rest of the money in monthly installments. You and the seller negotiate the period of time over which the payments will be spread and the amount you will pay each month. The seller adds a finance charge to the cash price of the television set and remains the legal owner of the set until you have made your last payment. Most department stores, appliance and furniture stores, and automobile dealers offer installment credit. The cost of buying the $600 color television set can be calculated as illustrated in Table ST3.3.

Instead of buying your $600 television on the installment plan, you might want to buy it on the revolving charge plan. Most credit cards, such as MasterCard, and Visa, represent revolving charge accounts that permit you to buy on credit up to a stated amount during each month. At the end of the month, you may pay the total amount you owe, any amount over the stated

If you have cash today, you have credit tomorrow.

CONFUCIUS

Sticking to a budget and paying bills protects a couple's credit.

TABLE ST3.3
Calculating the Cost of Installment Credit

1. The amount to be financed:		
	Cash price	$600.00
	− down payment (if any)	− 50.00
	Amount to be financed	$550.00
2. The amount to be paid:		
	Monthly payments	$ 35.00
	× number of payments	×18
	Total amount repaid	$630.00
3. The cost of the credit:		
	Total amount repaid	$630.00
	− amount financed	−550.00
	Cost of credit	$ 80.00
4. The total cost of the color TV:		
	Total amount repaid	$630.00
	+ down payment (if any)	+ 50.00
	Total cost of TV	$680.00

⤳ **I N   F O C U S   ST3.1** ⤲

The High Cost of Interest Over Time

"What hurts young families so often is the high rate of interest they get saddled with over a 30-year-period when they buy a house," said one father of two children. "House payments in the early years are mostly interest, so it takes forever for the kids to pay off the principal."

The first payment on a $100,000 loan at 7 percent interest for 30 years is $665.25. Only about $50.00 of this amount is applied to the principal. The remainder ($615.25) is interest. Taxes and fire insurance are an additional $50 and $25, respectively, per month. To shorten the total number of years during which a family must pay the bank $665.25 every month, spouses or parents can make separate monthly payments that are applied specifically to the principal. The sooner the principal is paid off, the sooner all payments will stop. Otherwise, the couple will pay $239,490 for the $100,000 house over the 30 year period.

"minimum payment due," or the minimum payment. If you choose to pay less than the full amount, the cost of the credit on the unpaid amount is approximately 1.5 percent per month, or 18 percent per year. For instance, if you pay $100 per month for your television for six months, you will still owe $31.62 to be paid the next month, for a total cost (television plus finance charges) of $631.62.

You can also purchase items on an open charge (30-day) account. Under this system you agree to pay in full within 30 days. Since there is no direct service charge or interest for this type of account, the television set would cost only the purchase price. As examples, Sears and J.C. Penney offer open charge (30-day) accounts. If you do not pay the full amount in 30 days, a finance charge is placed on the remaining balance. Both the use of revolving charge and open charge accounts are wise if you pay off the bill before finance charges begin. In deciding which type of credit account to use, remember that credit usually costs money; the longer you take to pay for an item, the more the item will cost you. In Focus ST3.1 describes the high cost of credit and one way parents of young married couples can help to reduce this burden.

Three Cs of Credit

Whether you can get credit will depend on the rating you receive on the "three Cs": character, capacity, and capital. *Character* refers to your honesty, sense of responsibility, soundness of judgment, and trustworthiness. *Capacity* refers to your ability to pay the bill when it is due. Such issues as the amount of money you earn and the length of time you have held a job will be considered in evaluating your capacity to pay. *Capital* refers to such assets as bank accounts, stocks, bonds, money market funds, real estate, and so on.

If a good face is a letter of recommendation, a good heart is a letter of credit.

LORD LYTTON

CONSIDERATION

It is particularly important that married individuals establish credit ratings in their own name in case they become widowed or divorced. Otherwise, their credit will depend on their spouse; if the spouse dies or divorce occurs, they will have no credit of their own.

It is also important that individuals not depend on credit to pay for necessities such as food, rent, and utilities. Continually spending more than one's income and taking all credit cards to the limit suggests financial trouble and eventual bankruptcy.

SPECIAL TOPIC

Resources and Organizations

Abortion

Pro-Choice

National Abortion Rights Action League
156 15th Street, N. W., Suite 700
Washington, DC 20005

Religious Coalition for Abortion Rights
100 Maryland Ave., N.E. Suite 307
Washington, DC 20002
Phone: 202-543-7032

Pro-Life

National Right to Life Committee
419 Seventh St., N.W., Suite 500
Washington, DC 20045
Phone: 202-626-8800

Feminists for Life of America
81 E. 47th Street
Kansas City, MO 64110

Adoption

National Adoption Center
1500 Walnut Street, Suite 701
Philadelphia, PA 19107
1-800-TO-ADOPT

National Council for Adoption
1930 Seventeenth Street NW
Washington, DC 20009

Child Abuse

National Committee for Prevention of
Child Abuse
332 South Michigan Ave., Suite 1600
Chicago, IL 60604-4357
Phone: 312-663-3520

National Child Abuse Hotline
Phone: 800-422-4453

Child Care

Au Pair in America
102 Greenwich Ave.
Greenwich, CT 06830
Phone: 800-727-AIFS

Contraception

Planned Parenthood Federation of America
810 Seventh Ave.
New York, New York 10019

Communes

Directory of Intentional Communities
c/o Sandhill Farm
Route 1, Box 155
Rutledge, MO 63563

Community Bookshelf, 1993
East Wind Community
Tecumseh, MO 65760

Divorce Mediation

Academy of Family Mediators
355 Tyrol W.
1500 S. Highway 100
Golden Valley, MN 55416
Phone: 612-525-8670

Family Planning

Planned Parenthood Federation of America
810 Seventh Avenue
New York, New York 10019

Fatherhood

Full-Time Dads
P.O. Box 577
Cumberland, ME 04021
Phone: 207-829-5260

Gender Equality

National Organization for Women
1000 16th St., N.W. Suite 700
Washington, DC 20036
Phone: 202-331-0066

American Men's Studies Association
22 East Street
Northampton, MA 01060

Genetic Counseling

>National Foundation for Jewish
>Genetic Disease
>45 Sutton Place South
>New York, NY 10003
>Phone: 212-371-1030

Healthy Baby

>Healthy Mothers-Healthy Babies Coalition
>409 12th Street, SW
>Washington, D.C. 20024-2188
>Phone: 202-863-2458

Homosexual Life Style

>National Gay and Lesbian Task Force
>1734 14th St., N.W.
>Washington, DC 20009-4309
>Phone: 202-332-6483

>National Gay and Lesbian Crisis Line
>800-221-7044

>Parents and Friends of Lesbians and Gays
>(PFLAG)
>P.O. Box 27605
>Washington, DC 20038

Infertility

>Infertility and Reproductive Technology
>American Fertility Society,
>1209 Montgomery Highway
>Birmingham, Alabama 35216-2809

>Eastern Virginia Medical School
>Department of Obstetrics and Gynecology
>Howard and Georgeanna Jones Institute for
>Reproductive Medicine
>601 College Avenue
>Norfolk, VA 23507-1912
>Phone: 804-446-8948

>RESOLVE
>5 Water St.
>Arlington, MA 02174
>Phone: 617-643-2424
>(provides phone counseling and referral for
>persons experiencing infertility)

Marriage Enrichment

>Training in Marriage Enrichment
>American Guidance Service
>4201 Woodland Rd.
>Circle Pines, MN 55014
>Phone: 612-786-4343

Marriage and Family Therapy

>American Association for Marriage and Family
>Therapy
>1100 17th Street, N.W., 10th Floor
>Washington, DC 20036-1906
>Phone: 800-374-2638

Men's Awareness

>American Men's Studies Association
>22 East Street
>Northampton, MA 01060

Pregnancy and Childbirth

>American Society for Psychoprophylaxis in
>Obstetrics
>ASPO/Lamaze
>1840 Wilson Blve., Suite 204
>Arlington, VA 22201

>Healthy Mothers-Healthy Babies Coalition
>Department of Public Affairs
>409 12th St., S.W.
>Washington, DC 20024-2188
>Phone: 202-863-2458

Sex Education

>Sex Information and Education Council of the
>United States (SIECUS)
>New York University
>32 Washington Plaza, 5th Floor
>New York, NY 10003
>Phone: 212-673-3850

Sexual Abuse

>Incest Survivors Anonymous
>P.O. Box 5613
>Long Beach, CA 90805-0613

C. Henry Kempe National Center for the Prevention and Treatment of Child Abuse and Neglect
1205 Oneida St.
Denver, CO 80220

National Center for the Prevention and Control of Rape
5000 Fishers Lane, Room 6C-12
Rockville, MD 20857

National Clearinghouse on Marital and Date Rape
2325 Oak St.
Berkeley, CA 94708

Victims of Incest Can Emerge Survivors (VOICES)
P.O. Box 148309
Chicago, IL 60614
Phone: 800-7-VOICE-8

Sexual Therapy

American Association of Sex Educators, Counselors, and Therapists (AASECT)
435 N. Michigan Avenue
Suite 1717
Chicago, Illinois 60611

Masters and Johnson Institute
24 South Kings Highway
St. Louis, MO 63108
Phone: 314-361-2277

Sexually Transmitted Diseases

American Social Health Association (Herpes Resource Center and HPV Support Program)
P.O. Box 13827
Research Triangle Park, NC 27709

Centers for Disease Control
National Center for Infectious Diseases
Atlanta, GA 30333

Multicultural Inquiry and Research on AIDS (MIRA)
6025 Third St.
San Francisco, CA 94124

National AIDS Hotline
800-342-AIDS
Spanish Speaking 800-344-7432
Hearing Impaired 800-243-7889

National Association for People with AIDS (NAPWA)
1413 K St., N.W., 10th Floor
Washington, DC 20005-3405

National Herpes Hotline
919-361-8488 Monday-Friday 9 A.M. to 7 P.M. Eastern

National STD Hotline
800-227-8922 Monday-Friday 8 A.M. to 11 P.M. Eastern

Single Parenthood

Parents Without Partners International
8807 Colesville Rd.
Silver Springs, MD 20910
Phone: 301-588-9354

Single Mothers by Choice
P.O. Box 1642, Gracie Square Station
New York, NY 10028
Phone: 212-988-0993

Stepfamilies

Stepfamily Association of America, Inc.
215 Centennial Mall South Suite 212
Lincoln, Nebraska, 68508-1834
Phone: 402-477-7837
(For the chapter nearest you, call 1-800-735-0329)

Widowhood

Widowed Person's Service
American Association of Retired Persons
609 E. St. NW
Washington, DC 20049
Phone: 202-872-4700

*These addresses and phone numbers were accurate at the time this section was printed.

References

American Council on Education and University of California. The American freshman: National norms for fall, 1992. Los Angeles, Calif.: Los Angeles Higher Education Research Institute, 1992.

Aral, S. O. and K. K. Holmes. Sexually transmitted diseases in the AIDS era. *Scientific American,* 1991, *264,* 62–69.

Bauer, H. M., Y. Ting, C. E. Greer, J. C. Chambers, C. J. Tashiro, J. Chimera, A. Reingold, and M. M. Manos. Genital human papillomavirus infection in female university students as determined by a PCR-based method. *Journal of the American Medical Association,* 1991, *265,* 472–477.

Billy, J. O. G., K. Tanfer, W. R. Grady, and D. H. Klepinger. The sexual behavior of men in the United States. *Family Planning Perspectives,* 1993, *25,* 52–60.

Bongaarts, J., P. Reining, P. Way, and F. Conant. The relationship between male circumcision and HIV infection in African populations. *AIDS,* 1989, *3,* 373–377.

Brinton, L. A., P. C. Nasca, K. Mallin, M. S. Baptiste, G. D. Wilbanks, and R. M. Richart. Case-control study of cancer of the vulva. *Obstetrics and Gynecology,* 1990, *75,* 859–866.

Cantania, J. A., T. J. Coates, R. Stall, H. Turner, J. Peterson, N. Hearst, M. M. Dolcini, E. Hudes, J. Gagnon, J. Wiley, and R. Groves. Prevalence of AIDS-related risk factors and condom use in the United States. *Science,* 1992, *258,* 1101–1106.

Centers for Disease Control. HIV/AIDS surveillance report. 1992 (July). U.S. Dept. of Health and Human Services.

Center for Disease Control and Prevention. HIV/AIDS surveillance report. Second Quarter Edition U. S. Department of Health and Human Services, Public Health Service, National Center for Infectious Diseases, Division of HIV/AIDS, Atlanta, Georgia 30333, July 1993, 1–19.

Clinical Studies presented at international AIDS meeting. *American Medical News,* 1992 (Aug. 24/31), 33.

Consumer Reports. Life insurance, Part 3: Should you buy a whole-life policy? 1993, September, 595–603.

Cowley, G. and M. Hager. Sleeping with the enemy. *Newsweek,* 1991 (Dec. 9), 58–59.

Cox, F. D. *The AIDS booklet,* 2d ed. Dubuque, Iowa: William C. Brown, 1992.

Eisenberg, Steve. From one lover to another. *Health,* September 1988, 62–65.

Goldsmith, M. F. 'Critical moment' at hand in HIV/AIDS pandemic new global strategy to arrest its spread proposed. *Journal of the American Medical Association,* 1992, *268,* 445–446.

Hearst, N. and S. B. Hulley. Preventing the heterosexual spread of AIDS: Are we giving our patients the best advice? *The Journal of the American Medical Association,* 1988, *259,* 2428–2432.

Hill, T. Herpes and relationships. *The Helper,* Summer 1987, *9,* no. 2, 1, 3–5.

Hock, Z. The G Spot. *Journal of Sex and Marital Therapy,* 1983, *9,* 1166–1167.

HPV and anal cancer. *HPV News,* 1992, 2(2), 11.

HPV in perspective. *HPV News,* 1991, 1(1), 1, 4–7.

Johnson, Robert E., Andre J. Wahmias, Laurence S. Mager, Francis K. Lee, Camilla A. Brooks, and Cecelia B. Snowden. A seroepidemiologic survey of the prevalence of herpes simplex virus type 2 infection in the United States. *The New England Journal of Medicine,* 1989, *321,* 7–12.

Kaplan, H. S. The classification of the female sexual dysfunctions. *Journal of Sex and Marital Therapy,* 1974, *2,* 124–138.

Kerr, D. L. "AIDS SPEAK": Sensitive and accurate communication and the HIV epidemic. *Journal of School Health,* 1990, *60,* 431–432.

Leslie-Harwit, M. and A. Mehus. Sexually transmitted disease in young people: The importance of health education. *Sexually Transmitted Diseases,* January/February 1989, *16,* 15–20.

Knox, D., C. Schacht, J. Holt, and J. Turner. Sexual lies among university students. *College Student Journal,* 1993, 27, 269–272.

Luby, E. Psychological responses to genital herpes. *The Helper,* 1981, 3, 1–3.

Lund, M. M. Perspectives on newborn male circumcision. *Neonatal Network,* 1990, 9, 7–12.

Masciello, A. L. Anesthesia for neonatal circumcision: Local anesthesia is better than dorsal penile nerve block. *Obstetrics and Gynecology,* 1990, 75, 834–838.

Masters, W. H. and V. E. Johnson. *Human sexual response.* Boston, Mass.: Little, Brown, 1966.

Murphy, R. L. Sexually transmitted diseases. *The Biological and Clinical Basis of Infectious Diseases* (4th Ed.), edited by S. T. Shulman, J. P. Phair, and H. M. Sommers. Philadelphia: W. B. Saunders, 1992, 238–268.

National Center for Health Statistics. Advance report of final mortality statistics, 1990. Monthly vital statistics report; vol. 41, no. 7, suppl. Hyattsville, Md.: Public Health Service, 1993.

Perry, J. D., and B. Whipple. Pelvic muscle strength of female ejaculation: Evidence in support of a new theory of orgasm. *Journal of Sex Research,* 1981, 17, 22–39.

Phair, J. P. and E. G. Chadwick. Human immunodeficiency virus infection and AIDS. In *The Biological & Clinical Basis of Infectious Diseases* (4th Ed.) Edited by S. T. Shulman, J. P. Phair, and H. M. Sommers. Philadelphia: W. B. Saunders, 1992, 380–393.

Risk factors for cervical cancer. *HPV News,* 1992, 2(2), 10.

Rosenberg, M. J. and E. L. Gollub. Commentary: Methods women can use that may prevent sexually transmitted disease, including HIV. *American Journal of Public Health,* 1992, 82, 1473–1478.

Ryan, L. L. and K. Willett. Personal communication. Lawrence Memorial Hospital, New London, CT, August, 1993.

Sammons, Robert. Mesa Behavioral Medicine Clinic. Grand Junction, CO. Personal communication, 1991.

Schwebke, J. R. Gonorrhea in the '90s. *Medical Aspects of Human Sexuality,* 1991a, 29, 42–46.

Schwebke, J. R. Syphilis in the '90s. *Medical Aspects of Human Sexuality,* 1991b, 29, 44–49.

Silver, P. S., S. M. Auerbach, N. Vishniavsky, and L. G. Kaplowitz. Psychological factors in recurrent genital herpes infection: Stress, coping style, social support, emotional dysfunction, and symptom recurrence. *Journal of Psychosomatic Research,* 1986, 30, 163–171.

Stein, A. P. The chlamydia epidemic: Teenagers at risk. *Medical Aspects of Human Sexuality,* 1991, 29, 26–33.

Stine, G. J. *Acquired immune deficiency syndrome: Biological, medical, social, and legal issues.* Englewood Cliffs, N.J.: Prentice-Hall, 1993.

Tavris, C. *The Mismeasure of woman.* New York: Simon and Schuster, 1992.

Trussell, J., D. L. Warner, and R. A. Hatcher. Condom slippage and breakage rates. *Family Planning Perspectives,* 1992, 24, 20–23.

Turner, M. J. and W. C. Bailey. Retirement planning among midlife women: Do family characteristics play a role? Paper, National Council on Family Relations 54th Annual Conference, Orlando, Florida, 1992. Used by permission.

Wilkes, M. S. and S. Blum. Current trends in routing newborn male circumcision in New York State. *New York State Journal of Medicine,* 1990, 90, 243–246.

APPENDIX

Relationship Choices Autobiography Outline

Your instructor may ask you to write an interpersonal autobiography as part of the marriage and family course in which you are enrolled. Check with your instructor to ascertain if you may complete an interpersonal autobiography, how much (if any) credit it is worth, and the degree to which your autobiography will be regarded as private and confidential with no one other than your instructor reading your autobiography.

The outline to follow emphasizes the theme of choices in regard to your interpersonal development. Use the outline to develop your paper. Some topics may be too personal and you may choose to avoid writing about them.

I. Choices: Free will versus Determinism

Based on the discussion provided in Chapter 1 of your text, what is your view of the degree to which the interpersonal choices you make are "free" or "determined?" Give examples.

II. Relationship Beginnings

A. *Interpersonal context into which you were born.* How long had your parents been married before you were born? How many other children had been born into your family? How many followed your birth?

B. *Early relationships.* What was your relationship with your mother, father, and siblings when you were growing up? What is your relationship with each of them today? Who took care of you as a baby? If this person was other than your parents or siblings, who was the person (e.g., grandmother) and what is your relationship with that person today? How have these early relationships influenced your sense of trust and comfort in interpersonal relationships?

C. *Early self-concept.* How did you feel about yourself as a child, adolescent, and young adult? What significant experiences helped to shape your self-concept? How do you feel about yourself today?

III. Subsequent Relationships

A. *First love.* When was your first love relationship with someone outside your family? Who initiated the relationship? How long did it last? How did it end? How did it affect you and your subsequent relationships?

B. *Subsequent love relationships.* What other significant love relationships (if any) have you had? How long did they last, how did they end, and how did they affect your life?

C. *Lifestyle preferences.* What are your preferences for never getting married, being married, or living with someone? How would you feel about living in a commune? What do you believe is the ideal lifestyle?

IV. Communication Issues

A. *Parental models.* Describe your parents' relationship and their manner of communicating with each other. How are your interpersonal communication patterns similar and different than theirs?

B. *Relationship communication.* How comfortable do you feel talking about relationship issues with your partner? How comfortable do you feel telling your partner what you like and don't like about his or her behavior?

C. *Sexual communication.* How comfortable do you feel giving your partner feedback about how to please you sexually? How comfortable are you discussing the need to use a condom with a potential sex partner?

V. Sexual Issues

A. *Sex education.* What did you learn about sex from your parents, peers, and teachers (both academic and religious)?

B. *Sexual experiences.* What sexual experiences with others have you had, in what context, with what frequency, and with what effects on you as a child, as an adolescent, and as a young adult?

C. *Sexual values.* To what degree are your sexual values absolutist, legalistic, or relative? How have your sexual values changed since you were an adolescent?

D. *Safer sex.* What is the most "risky choice" you have made in regard to your sexual behavior? What is the safest "choice" you have made in regard to your sexual behavior? How comfortable are you buying and using condoms?

V. Violence and Abuse Issues.

A. *Forced sex.* To what degree have you been pressured or forced to participate in sexual activity against your will as a child, adolescent, or young adult? How did you react to this experience at the time? What is your feeling about the experience now? To what degree have you pressured or forced others to participate in sexual experiences against their will?

VI. Reproductive Issues

A. *Contraception.* What is your preferred form of contraception? How comfortable do you feel discussing the need for contraception with a potential partner?

B. *Children.* How many children (if any) do you want and at what intervals? How important is it to you that your partner wants the same number of children as you do? How do you feel about artificial insemination, sterilization, abortion, and adoption?

APPENDIX

Prenuptial Agreement of a Remarried Couple

Pam and Mark are of sound mind and body, have a clear understanding of the terms of this contract and of the binding nature of the agreements contained herein; they freely and in good faith choose to enter into the PRENUPTIAL AGREEMENT and MARRIAGE CONTRACT and fully intend it to be binding upon themselves.

Now, therefore, in consideration of their love and esteem for each other and in consideration of the mutual promises herein expressed, the sufficiency of which is hereby acknowledged, Pam and Mark agree as follows:

Names

Pam and Mark affirm their individuality and equality in this relationship. The parties believe in and accept the convention of the wife accepting the husband's name, while rejecting any implied ownership.

Therefore, the parties agree that they will be known as husband and wife and will henceforth employ the titles of address: Mr. and Mrs. Mark Stafford, and will use the full names of Pam Hayes Stafford and Mark Robert Stafford.

Relationships with Others

Pam and Mark believe that their commitment to each other is strong enough that no restrictions are necessary with regard to relationships with others.

Therefore, the parties agree to allow each other freedom to choose and define their relationships outside this contract, and the parties further agree to maintain sexual fidelity each to the other.

Religion

Pam and Mark reaffirm their belief in God and recognize He is the source of their love. Each of the parties have their own religious beliefs.

Therefore, the parties agree to respect their individual preferences with respect to religion and to make no demands on each other to change such preferences.

Children

Pam and Mark both have children. Although no minor children will be involved, there are two (2) children still at home and in school and in need of financial and emotional support.

Therefore, the parties agree that they will maintain a home for and support these children as long as is needed and reasonable. They further agree that all children of both parties will be treated as one family unit, and each will be given emotional and financial support to the extent feasible and necessary as determined mutually by both parties.

Careers and Domicile

Pam and Mark value the importance and integrity of their respective careers and acknowledge the demands that their jobs place on them as individuals and on their partnership. Both parties are well established in their respective careers and do not foresee any change or move in the future.

The parties agree, however, that if the need or desire for a move should arise, the decision to move shall be mutual and based on the following factors:

1. The overall advantage gained by one of the parties in pursuing a new opportunity shall be weighed against the disadvantages, economic and otherwise, incurred by the other.
2. The amount of income or other incentive derived from the move shall not be controlling.
3. Short-term separations as a result of such moves may be necessary.

Mark hereby waives whatever right he may have to solely determine the legal domicile of the parties.

Care and Use of Living Spaces

Pam and Mark recognize the need for autonomy and equality within the home in terms of the use of available space and allocation of household tasks. The parties reject the concept that the responsibility for housework rests with the woman in a marriage relationship while the duties of home maintenance and repair rest with the man.

Therefore, the parties agree, to share equally in the performance of all household tasks, taking into consideration individual schedules, preferences, and abilities.

The parties agree that decisions about the use of living space in the home shall be mutually made, regardless of the parties' relative financial interests in the ownership or rental of the home, and the parties further agree to honor all requests for privacy from the other party.

Property; Debts; Living Expenses

Pam and Mark intend that the individual autonomy sought in the partnership shall be reflected in the ownership of existing and future-acquired property, in the characterization and control of income, and in the responsibility for living expenses. Pam and Mark also recognize the right of patrimony of children of their previous marriages.

Therefore, the parties agree that all things of value now held singly and/or acquired singly in the future shall be the property of the party making such acquisition. In the event that one party to this agreement shall predecease the other, property and/or other valuables shall be disposed of in accordance with an existing will or other instrument of disposal that reflects the intent of the deceased party.

Property or valuables acquired jointly shall be the property of the partnership and shall be divided, if necessary, according to the contribution of each party. If one party shall predecease the other, jointly owned property or valuables shall become the property of the surviving spouse.

Pam and Mark feel that each of the parties to this agreement should have access to monies that are not accountable to the partnership.

Therefore, the parties agree that each shall retain a mutually agreeable portion of their total income and the remainder shall be deposited in a mutually agreeable banking institution and shall be used to satisfy all jointly acquired expenses and debts.

The parties agree that beneficiaries of life insurance policies they now own shall remain as named on each policy. Future changes in beneficiaries shall be mutually agreed on after the dependency of the children of each party has been terminated. Any other benefits of any retirement plan or insurance benefits that accrue to a spouse only shall not be affected by the foregoing.

The parties recognize that in the absence of income by one of the parties, resulting from any reason, living expenses may become the sole responsibility of the employed party and in such a situation, the employed party shall assume responsibility for the personal expenses of the other.

Both Pam and Mark intend their marriage to last as long as both shall live.

Therefore the parties agree that should it become necessary, due to the death of either party, the surviving spouse shall assume any last expenses in the event that no insurance exists for that purpose.

Pam hereby waives whatever right she may have to rely on Mark to provide the sole economic support for the family unit.

Evaluation of the Partnership

Pam and Mark recognize the importance of change in their relationship and intend that this CONTRACT shall be a living document and a focus for periodic evaluations of the partnership.

The parties agree that either party can initiate a review of any article of the CONTRACT at any time for amendment to reflect changes in the relationship. The parties agree to honor such requests for review with negotiations and discussions at a mutually convenient time.

The parties agree that, in any event, there shall be an annual reaffirmation of the CONTRACT on or about the anniversary date of the CONTRACT.

The parties agree that, in the case of unresolved conflicts between them over any provisions of the CONTRACT, they will seek mediation, professional or otherwise, by a third party.

Termination of the Contract

Pam and Mark believe in the sanctity of marriage; however, in the unlikely event of a decision to terminate this CONTRACT, the parties agree that neither shall contest the application for a divorce decree or the entry of such decree in the county in which the parties are both residing at the time of such application.

In the event of termination of the CONTRACT and divorce of the parties, the provisions of this and the section on "Property; Debts; Living Expenses" of the CONTRACT as amended shall serve as the final property settlement agreement between the parties. In such event, this CONTRACT is intended to affect a complete settlement of any and all claims that either party may have against the other, and a complete settlement of their respective rights as to property rights, homestead rights, inheritance rights, and all other rights of property otherwise arising out of their partnership. The parties further agree that in the event of termination of this contract and divorce of the parties, neither party shall require the other to pay maintenance costs or alimony.

Decision Making

Pam and Mark share a commitment to a process of negotiations and compromise that will strengthen their equality in the partnership. Decisions will be made with respect for individual needs. The parties hope to maintain such mutual decision making so that the daily decisions affecting their lives will not become a struggle between the parties for power, authority, and dominance. The parties agree that such a process, while sometimes time consuming and fatiguing, is a good investment in the future of their relationship and their continued esteem for each other.

Now, therefore, Pam and Mark make the following declarations:

1. They are responsible adults.
2. They freely adopt the spirit and the material terms of this prenuptial and marriage contract.
3. The marriage contract, entered into in conjunction with a marriage license of the State of Illinois, County of Wayne, on this 12th day of June, 1990, hereby manifests their intent to define the rights and obligations of their marriage relationship as distinct from those rights and obligations defined by the laws of the State of Illinois, and affirms their right to do so.
4. They intend to be bound by this prenuptial and marriage contract and to uphold its provisions before any Court of Law in the Land.

Therefore, comes now, Pam Hayes Carraway, who applauds her development which allows her to enter into this partnership of trust, and she agrees to go forward with this marriage in the spirit of the foregoing PRENUPTIAL and MARRIAGE CONTRACT.

Therefore, comes now, Mark Robert Stafford, who celebrates his growth and independence with the signing of this contract, and he agrees to accept the responsibilities of this marriage, as set forth in the foregoing PRENUPTIAL and MARRIAGE CONTRACT.

This contract and covenant has been received and reviewed by the Reverend Ralph James, officiating.

Finally, comes Karen James and Bill Dunn, who certify that Pam and Mark did freely read and sign this marriage contract in their presence, on the occasion of their entry into a marriage relationship by the signing of a marriage license in the State of Illinois, County of Wayne, at which they acted as official witnesses. Further, they declare that the marriage license of the parties bears the date of the signing of this PRENUPTIAL and MARRIAGE CONTRACT.

~ Index ~

N

O